T0211796

Lecture Notes in Computer Science 11874

Founding Editors

Gerhard Goos
Karlsruhe Institute of Technology, Karlsruhe, Germany
Juris Hartmanis
Cornell University, Ithaca, NY, USA

Editorial Board Members

Elisa Bertino
Purdue University, West Lafayette, IN, USA
Wen Gao
Peking University, Beijing, China
Bernhard Steffen
TU Dortmund University, Dortmund, Germany
Gerhard Woeginger
RWTH Aachen, Aachen, Germany
Moti Yung
Columbia University, New York, NY, USA

More information about this series at http://www.springer.com/series/7409

Raffaele Montella · Angelo Ciaramella ·
Giancarlo Fortino · Antonio Guerrieri ·
Antonio Liotta (Eds.)

Internet and Distributed Computing Systems

12th International Conference, IDCS 2019
Naples, Italy, October 10–12, 2019
Proceedings

 Springer

Editors
Raffaele Montella
Department of Science
and Technology
Parthenope University of Naples
Napoli, Italy

Giancarlo Fortino
University of Calabria
Rende, Italy

Antonio Liotta
Edinburgh Napier University
Edinburgh, UK

Angelo Ciaramella ⓘ
Parthenope University of Naples
Napoli, Italy

Antonio Guerrieri
ICAR
Consiglio Nazionale
delle Ricerche
Rende, Cosenza, Italy

ISSN 0302-9743   ISSN 1611-3349   (electronic)
Lecture Notes in Computer Science
ISBN 978-3-030-34913-4   ISBN 978-3-030-34914-1   (eBook)
https://doi.org/10.1007/978-3-030-34914-1

LNCS Sublibrary: SL3 – Information Systems and Applications, incl. Internet/Web, and HCI

© Springer Nature Switzerland AG 2019
This work is subject to copyright. All rights are reserved by the Publisher, whether the whole or part of the material is concerned, specifically the rights of translation, reprinting, reuse of illustrations, recitation, broadcasting, reproduction on microfilms or in any other physical way, and transmission or information storage and retrieval, electronic adaptation, computer software, or by similar or dissimilar methodology now known or hereafter developed.
The use of general descriptive names, registered names, trademarks, service marks, etc. in this publication does not imply, even in the absence of a specific statement, that such names are exempt from the relevant protective laws and regulations and therefore free for general use.
The publisher, the authors and the editors are safe to assume that the advice and information in this book are believed to be true and accurate at the date of publication. Neither the publisher nor the authors or the editors give a warranty, expressed or implied, with respect to the material contained herein or for any errors or omissions that may have been made. The publisher remains neutral with regard to jurisdictional claims in published maps and institutional affiliations.

This Springer imprint is published by the registered company Springer Nature Switzerland AG
The registered company address is: Gewerbestrasse 11, 6330 Cham, Switzerland

Preface

Following the previous 11 successful editions of the conference – IDCS 2008 in Khulna, Bangladesh; IDCS 2009 in Jeju Island, South Korea; IDCS 2010 and IDCS 2011 in Melbourne, Australia; IDCS 2012 in Wu Yi Shan, China; IDCS 2013 in Hangzhou, China; IDCS 2014 in Calabria, Italy; IDCS 2015 in Windsor, UK; IDCS 2016 in Wuhan, China; IDCS 2017 in Mana Island, Fiji; IDCS 2018 in Tokyo, Japan – IDCS 2019 was the 12th in the series to promote research in diverse fields related to the Internet and Distributed Computing Systems.

Under the influence of the most advanced technologies, human production and life are gradually changing in today's vision of common habits and lifestyles. The impact of Internet-related technologies is fully pervasive, while the evolution of distributed systems, in a wider and semantically consistent meaning, is simply definable as rule-breaking. In this scenario, the non-renounceable features such as complexity management capability, reliable elasticity, dependability, and security are enforced by modern systems such as distributed systems, cloud computing, mobile computing, edge computing, and fog computing in order to provide the best user experience in both human/machine and machine/machine contexts. Strategically, any complex system must be accounted as a cyber-physical system dealing with dynamic events or actions in highly connected environments. For the most part of the novel internet and distributed system based applications leverage diverse and different technologies in order to perform data gathering, processing, and knowledge extraction using machine learning related techniques. In particular, this new class of applications has distinctive running ecosystems where the self-adaptation to unknown situations is not a feature but a design requirement. Although we could state that internet connectivity is *a conditio sine qua non* of any advanced application and/or methodology, the real power still must be unchained. The long-awaited pervasive diffusion of the next generation of cellular networks and, above all, the diffusion of other connection strategies enforce and reinforce the Internet society and related applications to logistics, transportation, food quality control, environmental hazard mitigation, global climate changes, crime fighting, and, in general, any improvement in the quality of life. The academic and industrial worlds are constantly developing and innovating in areas such as machine learning and data science, pushed by enabling technologies such as the Internet of Things and Cloud Computing. In the meantime, accelerators and the computation at the edge, delivering the integration of the digital world with the physical environment, place mankind on the brink of a new scientific, technological, social, and economic revolution.

IDCS 2019 received papers focused on emerging models, paradigms, technologies, and novel applications related to cloud computing, virtualization, distributed systems, Internet of Things, cyber-physical systems, wireless sensor networks, extreme-scale networked systems, and self-adaptive systems.

The audience included researchers and industry practitioners interested in different aspects of the Internet and distributed systems, with a particular focus on practical experiences with the design and implementation of related technologies as well as their theoretical perspectives.

IDCS 2019 received a large number of submissions from which 47 regular papers were accepted after a careful review and selection process. This year's conference also featured four invited talks: (i) "Intelligent Task Scheduling for Distributed Green Cloud Data Centers" by Prof. Mengchu Zhou, New Jersey Institute of Technology, USA; (ii) "Coordinating Distributed Speaking Objects" by Prof. Franco Zambonelli, University of Modena e Reggio Emilia, Italy; (iii) "Scheduling Real-Time Jobs in the Cloud, Research Trends and Challenges" by Prof. Helen Karatza, Aristotle University of Thessaloniki, Greece; and (iv) "Practical Edge-assisted Mobile Computing: The Cases of Augmented Reality and Virtual Reality" by Prof. Ben Hui, University of Helsinki, Finland.

IDCS 2019 was held in the breathtaking Villa Doria d'Angri, University of Naples Parthenope, Italy, on the beautiful hill of Posillipo, located on a cliff by the sea. The conference organization was supported by the Department of Science and Technology of the University of Naples Parthenope and the University of Calabria, Italy.

The successful organization of IDCS 2019 was possible thanks to the dedication and hard work of a number of individuals.

Specifically, we would like to thank our program chairs Sokol Kosta (Aalborg University, Denmark), Sandra Geising (University of Notre Dame, Indiana, USA), Beniamino Di Martino (University of Campania Luigi Vanvitelli, Italy), Min Chen (Huazhong University of Science and Technology, China); our local and program chair Raffaele Montella (University of Naples Parthenope, Italy); our special session co-chairs Sisi Duan (University of Maryland, Baltimore, USA) and Giancarlo Fortino (University of Calabria, Italy); our web chair Claudio Savaglio (University of Calabria, Italy); our finance chair Antonio Guerrieri (ICAR-CNR, Italy); our social media and communication chair Federica Izzo (University of Naples Parthenope, Italy); our publication chair Antonio Liotta (Edinburgh Napier University, UK); our industrial co-chairs Giuseppe Coviello (NEC Laboratories America, USA) and Mukaddim Pathan (Telstra, Australia); our publicity co-chairs Salvatore Venticinque (University of Campania Luigi Vanvitelli, Italy), Jingtao Sun (National Institute of Informatics, Japan), and Fabio Narducci (University of Napoli Parthenope, Italy) for their commendable work with the conference organization. We also express our gratitude to the general chair Ian Foster (University of Chicago, Illinois, USA); the general co-chair Angelo Ciaramella (University of Naples Parthenope, Italy); and the conference co-chairs Raffaele Gravina (University of Calabria, Italy), Giuseppe Di Fatta (University of Reading, UK), and JianhuaMa (Hosei University, Japan) for their support of the conference.

Last but not least, we are grateful for the outstanding work of our secretary and logistics manager Diana Di Luccio (University of Naples Parthenope, Italy) and the volunteer staff members: Juan Armando Barrón Lugo (Cinvestav Tamaulipas, Mexico),

Ciro Giuseppe De Vita, Gennaro Mellone, and Antonio Pilato (University of Naples Parthenope, Italy).

October 2019

Raffaele Montella
Angelo Ciaramella
Giancarlo Fortino
Antonio Guerrieri
Antonio Liotta

Organization

General Chair

Ian Foster — University of Chicago, Illinois, USA

Co-general Chair

Angelo Ciaramella — University of Napoli Parthenope, Italy

Co-chairs

Raffaele Gravina — University of Calabria, Italy
Giuseppe Di Fatta — University of Reading, UK
Jianhua Ma — Hosei University, Japan

Program Chairs

Sokol Kosta — University of Aalborg, Denmark
Sandra Gesing — University of Notre Dame, Indiana, USA
Beniamino Di Martino — University of Campania Luigi Vanvitelli, Italy
Min Chen — Huazhong University of Science and Technology, China

Local/Program Chair

Raffaele Montella — University of Napoli Parthenope, Italy

Special Session Co-chairs

Sisi Duan — University of Maryland, Baltimore, USA
Giancarlo Fortino — University of Calabria, Italy

Web Chair

Claudio Savaglio — University of Calabria, Italy

Finance Chair

Antonio Guerrieri — ICAR-CNR, Italy

Social Media and Communication Chair

Federica Izzo   University of Napoli Parthenope, Italy

Publication Chair

Antonio Liotta   Edinburgh Napier University, UK

Industry Co-chairs

Giuseppe Coviello   NEC Laboratories America, New Jersey, USA
Mukaddim Pathan   Telstra, Australia

Publicity Co-chairs

Salvatore Venticinque   University of Campania Luigi Vanvitelli, Italy
Jingtao Sun   National Institute of Informatics, Japan
Fabio Narducci   University of Napoli Parthenope, Italy

Steering Committee – IDCS Series

Jemal Abawajy   Deakin University, Australia
Rajkumar Buyya   University of Melbourne, Australia
Giancarlo Fortino   University of Calabria, Italy
Dimitrios Georgakopolous   RMIT University, Australia
Mukaddim Pathan   Telstra, Australia
Yang Xiang   Swinburne University, Australia
Giuseppe Di Fatta   University of Reading, UK
Min Chen   Huazhong University of Science and Technology,
                                      China

Program Committee

Mario Cannataro   University of "Magna Græcia" di Catanzaro, Italy
Jesus Carretero   Universidad Carlos III de Madrid, Spain
Kyle Chard   University of Chicago and ANL, USA
Abdelkarim Erradi   Qatar University, Qatar
Rafael Ferreira Da Silva   USC Information Sciences Institute, USA
Xiuwen Fu   Wuhan University of Technology, China
Javier Garcia Blas   Universidad Carlos III de Madrid, Spain
J. L. Gonzalez   Cinvestav-Tamps, Mexico
Ragib Hasan   University of Alabama, USA
Cheol-Hong   Chung-Ang University, South Korea
Pan Hui   University of Helsinki, Finland
Dimitrios Katsaros   University of Thessaly, Greece
Yoonhee Kim   Sookmyung Women's University, South Korea

Giuliano Laccetti	University of Naples Federico II and INFN, Italy
Marco Lapegna	University of Naples Federico II, Italy
Valeria Loscri	Inria, France
Maria-Cristina Marinescu	Barcelona Supercomputing Center, Spain
Carlo Mastroianni	ICAR-CNR, Italy
Jie Mei	Wuhan University of Technology, China
Sergio Ochoa	University of Chile, Chile
Marcin Paprzycki	IBS PAN and WSM, Poland
Riaz Ahmed Shaikh	King Abdul Aziz University, Saudi Arabia
Federico Silla	Universitat Politècnica de València, Spain
Ivor Spence	Queen's University Belfast, UK
Giandomenico Spezzano	University of Calabria, Italy
Ruppa Thulasiram	University of Manitoba, Canada
Xinqing Yan	NCWU, China
NorihikoYoshida	Saitama University, Japan
Mengchu Zhou	New Jersey Institute of Technology, USA

Contents

Table Tennis Stroke Recognition Based on Body Sensor Network

Ruichen Liu$^{(\boxtimes)}$, Zhelong Wang, Xin Shi, Hongyu Zhao, Sen Qiu, Jie Li, and Ning Yang

School of Control Science and Engineering, Dalian University of Technology, Dalian 116024, China
Lrichard@mail.dlut.edu.cn, wangzl@dlut.edu.cn

Abstract. Table tennis stroke recognition is very important for athletes to analyze their sports skills. It can help players to regulate hitting movement and calculate sports consumption. Different players have different stroke motions, which makes stroke recognition more difficult. In order to accurately distinguish the stroke movement, this paper uses body sensor networks (BSN) to collect motion data. Sensors collecting acceleration and angular velocity information are placed on the upper arm, lower arm and back respectively. Principal component analysis (PCA) is employed to reduce the feature dimensions and support vector machine (SVM) is used to recognize strokes. Compared with other classification algorithms, the final experimental results (97.41% accuracy) illustrate that the algorithm proposed in the paper is effective and useful.

Keywords: Motion recognition · Micro-electromechanical systems · Principal component analysis · Support vector machine

1 Introduction

Table tennis is a popular racket sport, it has many benefits to the human health. In table tennis training and competition, the stroke analysis mainly depends on subjective experience and lacks objective evaluation criteria. It is particularly difficult for coaches to find out the players' problems in time because the players' strokes have different styles and the duration of the strokes is extremely short [1]. In order to solve the above problems, we use sensor data to identify the player'stroke motions, which provides a basis for the subsequent evaluation of motion skills [2]. Furthermore, the assessment function based on specific

Supported by National Natural Science Foundation of China under Grant No. 61873044, No. 61803072, No. 61903062 and No. 61473058, Dalian Science and Technology Innovation fund (2018J12SN077), National Defense Pre-Research Foundation under Grant 614250607011708, China Postdoctoral Science Foundation No. 2017M621131 and No. 2017M621132 and Fundamental Research Funds for the Central Universities under Grant DUT18RC(4)036.

© Springer Nature Switzerland AG 2019
R. Montella et al. (Eds.): IDCS 2019, LNCS 11874, pp. 1–10, 2019.
https://doi.org/10.1007/978-3-030-34914-1_1

movements is used to identify the sport characteristics and professional degree of players [3].

Visual technique is a traditional method to investigate the table tennis, but there are still some defects. It is easy to be affected by the scene and the camera installation is inconvenient [4]. With the development of sensors and wireless networks, BSN is widely used in motion analysis, health monitoring and body information collection [5,6]. It can monitor various human body physiological signals (such as heart rate, electromyogram, blood oxygen and motion acceleration) [7]. By collecting the data of players through the BSN, we can recognize the stroke movement, analyze kinematics and calculate the energy consumption of movement [8]. Generally, table tennis stroke recognition can be further extended to many applications, such as VR games, virtual training and table tennis robots. In a word, it is vital to realize the stroke recognition first before the above applications. Therefore, this paper chooses the BSN method for motion recognition.

In previous studies, Blank [9] presents a sensor-based table tennis stroke classification system, it can be used for real-time motion analysis and stroke movement training. Bufton [10] analyzes the table tennis characteristics and investigates the difference between virtual table tennis and realistic table tennis. As a feasible method, it can promote children's sports skills. Wang [11] utilizes a two-layer hidden Markov model(HMM) to identify badminton stroke motion, the system is applied in the real training environment. Pei [12] installs the measurement node inside the racket and uses six-axis sensor data to recognize the stroke actions. Zhang [13] quantifies the stroke motions of table tennis, identifies the differences between experts and novices, and establishes an automatic evaluation model of individual movements. Maeda [14] proposes a table tennis analysis algorithm using image time series, and then uses C4.5 for motion classification. Blank [15] uses piezoelectric sensor to analyze the batting point of table tennis racket, which can be used for practical training and competition to assist table tennis training. Wang [16] proposes a smart badminton actions recognition system comprising of BLE technology, MEMS, cloud technology and machine learning algorithms, and builds the Internet of Things racket sports training framework.

This paper proposes a table tennis stroke classification method based on human inertia data. We use sliding window to segment table tennis stroke data sequence, and then extract time and frequency domain features to reflect player'movement characteristics. PCA is used to reduce dimension of features and SVM is used to classify actions. The method proposed in this paper can be used in real-time applications. The remainder of this paper is organized as follows. Section 2 describes the hardware module and experimental settings. Section 3 introduces the stroke detection, feature extraction and recognition methods of table tennis. Section 4 presents the experimental results and algorithm comparison. Finally, the conclusions are drawn in Sect. 5.

2 Hardware Platform and Experiments Description

2.1 Data Collection System

As shown in Fig. 1, the data collection system includes a computer, a wireless transmission node and several measurement nodes. The measurement node(which is developed by our "LIS" Laboratory) communicates with the personal computer via 2.4 GHz wireless signal. Data is stored offline to avoid data packet loss in wireless network transmission.

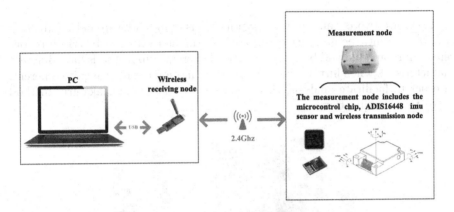

Fig. 1. Data collection system hardware

Each measurement node contains microprocessor, inertial measurement unit (IMU) sensor, lithium battery and SD card. The operational state of the measurement node is controlled by the wireless instructions, and the data is saved on the SD card. In order to avoid the orthogonal error of the sensor and ensure the accuracy of the data, we choose ADIS16448 inertial measurement unit, which contains three-axis acceleration, three-axis acceleration and three-axis magnetometer. The sampling frequency of the sensor is 400 Hz. Table 1 shows the magnetic, angular Rate, and gravity (MARG) specification. The measurement node uses NRF24L01 chip for communication, and the wireless receiving node is connected to the computer through USB interface. The system software is written in C#, and the collected data is processed by MATLAB.

2.2 Experimental Settings and Participants

We recruited nine players and collected their five common table tennis stroke movements. The ages of players range from 22 to 29 years. As shown in Fig. 2, we put the sensors on the player's body because it will affect the stroke weight balance when placing sensor on the racket. Three measurement sensor nodes fitted on suitable nylon bandages were arranged on the surface of player upper arm, lower arm and back.

Table 1. ADIS16448 performances specifications

Unit	Gyroscope	Accelerometer	Magnetometer
Dimensions	3 axis	3 axis	3 axis
Dynamic range	$\pm 1000\,\text{deg/s}$	$\pm 18\,\text{g}$	$\pm 1900\,\mu\text{T}$
Sensitivity (/LSB)	$0.04\,\text{deg/s}$	$0.833\,\text{mg}$	$142.9\,\mu\text{guass}$
Bandwidth (kHz)	330	330	25
Linearity (% of FS)	0.2	0.2	0.1

There are two commonly used grip methods: pen-hold grip and hand-shake grip. At present, the majority of athletes use the hand-shake grip, which is convenient for forehand and backhand strokes. Different grip methods have different characteristics when hitting the ball, and their motion details are quite different. In order to facilitate analysis, this paper chooses the hand-shake grip method for motion classification.

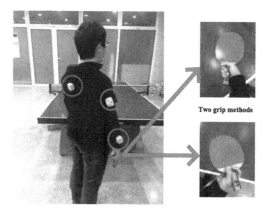

Fig. 2. Placement of measuring node and racket grip methods

3   Methodology

Table tennis stroke recognition process is shown in Fig. 3. The data acquisition part is introduced in the previous chapter. This part mainly introduces stroke detection, feature extraction and recognition method.

3.1   Stroke Detection and Window Segmentation

In the table tennis movement data, the magnetometer data has the smallest range of variation and it has less contribution to motion recognition. This article

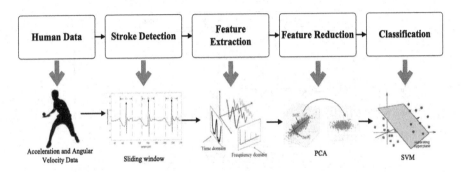

Fig. 3. Diagram of table tennis stroke recognition

uses acceleration and angular velocity data for stroke classification. The raw data shown in Fig. 4 can not be used for motion recognition directly, it needs to be pre-processed and feature extracted first. The sliding window is adopted to segment the stroke action [17].

Sliding window is the most widely used window segmentation technique, it can be expressed as moving a fixed-size window forward in a time series to segment the required data, and finally judge the stroke event according to the threshold. In this paper, we set the acceleration threshold and angular velocity threshold according to multiple tests, if the acceleration and angular velocity amplitude both exceed the threshold, the time series in this window is determined as the stroke sequence. The stroke detection threshold is set to twice the mean of the raw data and the window size is set to 1 s with 50% overlaps between each two adjacent windows.

3.2 Feature Extraction and Reduction

The difference of stroke motion is mainly reflected in the range of amplitude and the angle of rotation. In order to distinguish stroke motion, following features are extracted: mean, variance, kurtosis, covariance, correlation coefficient, skewness, energy and spectral entropy. Energy mainly represents the sum of squares of the basis coefficients obtained after the FFT, which can be defined as follows.

$$Energy = \frac{1}{S_{win}} \sum_{i=1}^{S_{win}} \theta_{xi}^2 \tag{1}$$

here $[\theta_{x1}, \theta_{x2}, ..., \theta_{xSwin}]$ represents signal strength in frequency domain.

Considering not all features affect the classification result and too many features will increase the workload. Reducing feature dimensions can effectively improve the speed of operation and avoid over-fitting. PCA is based on the principle of maximum projection sample interval, which the samples with larger projection interval have better separability. The PCA process is described as follows: calculating the covariance matrix of the normalized samples, then decomposing the covariance matrix and sorting the eigenvalues according to their sizes,

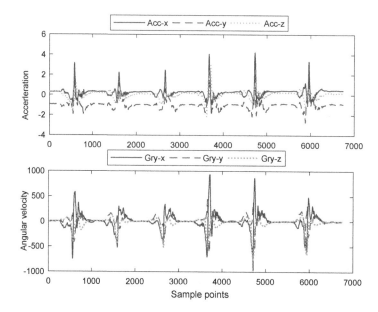

Fig. 4. Acceleration and angular velocity raw data of the table tennis stroke

selecting the eigenvector corresponding to the maximum eigenvalue to form the projection matrix.

3.3   Classification

After preliminary analysis of the features, it can be found that there are obvious differences among the stroke movements. The standard machine learning model has better advantages than the deep learning model and can meet the classification requirements when considering time complexity and training data size.

SVM is a binary classifier algorithm which can achieve multi-classification function by combining multiple binary classifiers. The kernel function is introduced to deal with nonlinear problems [18]. By finding the maximum hyperplane in space, the problem can be transformed into a convex quadratic optimization problem which is equivalent to the minimization of regularized hinge loss function. After introducing lagrange multiplier, the above optimization problem can be transformed into dual problem to solve. The formula is as follows:

$$\min_{\alpha} \quad \frac{1}{2} \sum_{i=1}^{N} \sum_{j=1}^{N} \alpha_i \alpha_j y_i y_j (x_i \cdot x_j) - \sum_{i=1}^{N} \alpha_i \tag{2}$$

$$s.t. \quad \sum_{i=1}^{N} \alpha_i y_i = 0 \tag{3}$$

By solving the problem, we can get the lagrange multiplier $\alpha^* = (\alpha_1^*, \alpha_2^*, ..., \alpha_N^*)^T$. w^* and b^* will be calculated as follows:

$$w^* = \sum_{i=1}^{N} \alpha^* y_i x_i \qquad (4)$$

$$b^* = y_j - \sum_{i=1}^{N} \alpha^* y_i (x_i \cdot x_j) \qquad (5)$$

The decision hyperplane can be obtained by the above parameters. By selecting the kernel function, the optimization problem is transformed as follows:

$$\min_{\alpha} \quad \frac{1}{2} \sum_{i=1}^{N} \sum_{j=1}^{N} \alpha_i \alpha_j y_i y_j K(x_i, x_j) - \sum_{i=1}^{N} \alpha_i \qquad (6)$$

After projecting the point product of data from low-dimensional space to high-dimensional space, the samples in high-dimensional space become linear separable.

4   Experimental Results and Evaluation

This paper identifies five table tennis strokes: forehand drive (FD), block shot (BS), forehand chop (FC), backhand chop (BC) and smash (SH). Players were equipped with three measuring nodes and asked to repeat each stroke motion six times. A total of 270 sample data were collected from nine players for classification. According to the previous analysis, the motion data are segmented by sliding window using acceleration and angular velocity information. After feature extraction, 108-dimensional features are obtained.

According to the table tennis kinematics, forearm is the most active joint in the process of movement, and its measuring nodes provide the most important features for the recognition in the movement process. It can be found from Fig. 5 that the motion recognition result turns out worst when using one node, while it comes out a better result when using three nodes. Increasing measuring nodes can obviously improve the recognition effect.

This paper uses PCA to reduce the feature dimension, the curve in Fig. 5 shows that the recognition accuracy reaches the highest when the dimension is 13. For the SVM algorithm, the parameters are set as follows: C is 10, γ is 1.8. The results were validated by leave-one-out method and the recognition accuracy is 97.41% and the F1 score of the whole system is 0.974. Figure 6 shows that the classification effect of BC and SH is better. But there are too many misclassifications of FD, because its motion characteristics are not obvious. Naive bayes (NB), KNN and C4.5 decision tree are used for classification comparison. The results in Fig. 7 show that the best recognition accuracy is achieved by using SVM method. KNN and SVM are capable of recognizing the motions of FD, BS and FC, but SVM does better than KNN in recognizing the motions of BC and SH.

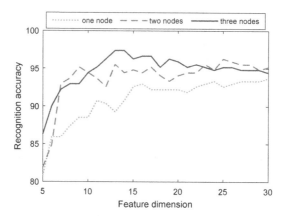

Fig. 5. The recognition accuracy of different feature dimensions

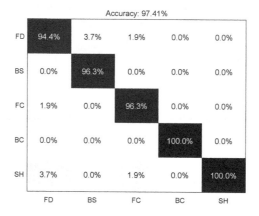

Fig. 6. Confusion matrix of recognition result

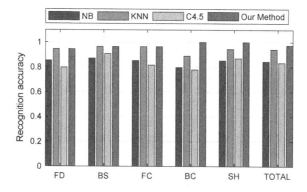

Fig. 7. Comparison of different classification methods

5   Conclusion

In this paper, a recognition method of table tennis stroke motion is proposed. Different from image recognition method, this paper uses BSN to collect human data for analysis. At the stage of data precessing, sliding window is used to detect the stroke and it can segment motion properly. By comparing different feature dimensions, we find the most suitable dimension for our classification system. At the stage of classification, nine athletes were recruited and their five movements were collected to verify the effectiveness of the algorithm. The accuracy of stroke classification is 97.41%. The obtained results show that the SVM provided the best performances compared with the other classification algorithms. By recognizing the players' stroke motions, it can effectively judge whether their movements are standard or not and help them find methods to regulate their movements.

In the future, we plan to apply this method to real-time applications and increase the number of recognizable strokes. Therefore, it is necessary to improve the recognition performance and reduce the calculation time. This paper only identified the stroke motion of hand-shake grip method, we need to distinguish different grip modes in future research.

References

1. Mao, B.-J.: Different techniques comparison in biomechanical analysis of ping pong. Appl. Mech. Mater. **166–169**, 3106–3109 (2012)
2. Muelling, K., Boularias, A., Mohler, B., Scholkopf, B., Peters, J.: Learning strategies in table tennis using inverse reinforcement learning. Biol. Cybern. **108**(5), 603–619 (2014)
3. Wang, Z., et al.: Inertial sensor-based analysis of equestrian sports between beginner and professional riders under different horse gaits. IEEE Trans. Instrum. Meas. **67**, 1–13 (2018)
4. Chen, L., Hoey, J., Nugentt, C.D., Cook, D.J., Yu, Z.: Sensor-based activity recognition. IEEE Trans. Syst. Man Cybern. Part C (Appl. Rev.) **42**(6), 790–808 (2012)
5. Gravina, R., Alessandro, A., Salmeri, A., et al.: Enabling multiple BSN applications using the SPINE framework. In: IEEE 2010 International Conference on Body Sensor Networks (BSN), pp. 228–233. IEEE (2010)
6. Fortino, G., Guerrieri, A., Bellifemine, F.L., Giannantonio, R.: SPINE2: developing BSN applications on heterogeneous sensor nodes. In: IEEE Fourth International Symposium on Industrial Embedded Systems, pp. 128–131. IEEE (2009)
7. Wang, Z., Qiu, S., Cao, Z., Jiang, M.: Quantitative assessment of dual gait analysis based on inertial sensors with body sensor network. Sens. Rev. **33**(1), 48–56 (2013)
8. Mulling, K., Kober, J., Kroemer, O., Peters, J.: Learning to select and generalize striking movements in robot table tennis. Int. J. Robot. Res. **32**(3), 263–279 (2013)
9. Blank, P., HobBach, J., Schuldhaus, D., Eskofier, B.M.: Sensor-based stroke detection and stroke type classification in table tennis. In: Proceedings of the 2015 ACM International Symposium on Wearable Computers, pp. 93–100. ACM (2015)
10. Bufton, A., Campbell, A., Howie, E., Straker, L.: A comparison of the upper limb movement kinematics utilized by children playing virtual and real table tennis. Hum. Mov. Sci. **38**, 84–93 (2014)

11. Wang, Z., Guo, M., Zhao, C.: Badminton stroke recognition based on body sensor networks. IEEE Trans. Hum.-Mach. Syst. **46**(5), 1–7 (2016)
12. Pei, W., Wang, J., Xu, X., Wu, Z., Du, X.: An embedded 6-axis sensor based recognition for tennis stroke. In: IEEE International Conference on Consumer Electronics. IEEE (2017)
13. Zhang, Z.: Biomechanical analysis and model development applied to table tennis forehand strokes. Loughborough University (2017)
14. Maeda, T., Fujii, M., Hayashi, I., Tasaka, T.: Sport skill classification using time series motion picture data. In: Conference of the IEEE Industrial Electronics Society, pp. 5272–5277. IEEE (2015)
15. Blank, P., Kautz, T., Eskofier, B.M.: Ball impact localization on table tennis rackets using piezo-electric sensors. In: ACM International Symposium on Wearable Computers, pp. 72–79. ACM (2016)
16. Wang, Y., Chen, M., Wang, X., Chan, R.H., Li, W.J.: IoT for next-generation racket sports training. IEEE Internet Things J. 1 (2018)
17. Dimitriou, N., Delopoulos, A.: Motion-based segmentation of objects using overlapping temporal windows. Image Vis. Comput. **31**(9), 593–602 (2013)
18. Shi, G., Zou, Y., Li, W.J., Jin, Y., Pei, G.: Towards multi-classification of human motions using micro IMU and SVM training process. In: Advanced Materials Research, vol. 60–61, pp. 189–193 (2009)

The Analysis of the Computation Offloading Scheme with Two-Parameter Offloading Criterion in Fog Computing

Eduard Sopin[1,2](✉) [iD], Konstantin Samouylov[1,2] [iD], and Sergey Shorgin[2] [iD]

[1] Peoples Friendship University of Russia,
Miklukho-Maklaya str. 6, Moscow 117198, Russia
{sopin-es,samuylov-ke}@rudn.ru
[2] Institute of Informatics Problems, FRC CSC RAS,
Vavilova 44-2, Moscow 119333, Russia
sshorgin@ipiran.ru

Abstract. Fog computing provides an efficient solution for mobile computing offloading, keeping tight constraints on the response time for real-time applications. The paper takes into account the variation of tasks by introducing the joint distribution function of the required processing volume and data size to be transmitted. We propose an offloading criterion based on processing and data volumes of tasks and develop an analytical framework for the evaluation of the average response time and average energy consumption of mobile devices. The developed framework is used in the case study.

Keywords: Fog computing · Computing offloading · Response time · Energy efficiency

1 Introduction

Nowadays, continuously increasing numbers of concurrently running applications on mobile devices (MD) increases the computation intensity, which also leads to an increase in energy consumption. However, MDs have limitations on computing performance and power supplies, especially compared to server machines. Fog computing provides an energy-efficient solution for mobile task offloading, bringing the computational infrastructure to the edge of the network.

The capabilities of fog computing attracted considerable attention of researchers. Many works were dedicated to opportunities and challenges of fog, focusing primarily on the networking context of the Internet of Things (IoT) [1,2]. One of the most important issues in mobile computing offloading is the tradeoff between the energy-efficiency and the response time. In [3,4], the

The publication has been prepared with the support of the "RUDN University Program 5100" (mathematical model development) and funded by RFBR according to the research projects No. 18-07-00576 and No. 18-00-01555 (numerical analysis).

© Springer Nature Switzerland AG 2019
R. Montella et al. (Eds.): IDCS 2019, LNCS 11874, pp. 11–20, 2019.
https://doi.org/10.1007/978-3-030-34914-1_2

authors use queuing theory to bring a thorough study on energy consumption, execution delay and payment cost of offloading processes in a fog computing network with three layers: MD, fog and remote cloud. The paper [6] deals with energy-efficient task offloading, focusing on the offloading target decision that takes into account both energy consumption and schedule delay under multiple fog devices. In [5], another decision algorithm is proposed, based on classification and regression tree. The paper [7] compares the effectiveness of cloud-based and edge-based deployments for IoT applications using extensive simulations.

However, despite a number of research papers in the field, there is still a lack of analytical approaches with clear offloading criteria that allows performing optimization in the context of the tradeoff between energy consumption and the response time. In our previous paper [8], we developed an analytical framework for response time analysis that takes into account the variation of tasks in terms of processing volume. In the current work, we propose the offloading criterion based on thresholds on processing volume and data size to be transmitted in case of offloading. The presented analytical framework for response time and energy consumption evaluation takes into account that tasks differ from each other, and they are characterized by joint cumulative distribution function (CDF) of processing volume and data size.

This paper is organized as follows. Section 2 presents the system model, Sect. 3 is devoted to the response time analysis, while Sect. 4 - to the energy consumption analysis. The case study is presented in Sect. 5, and conclusions are drawn in Sect. 6.

2   System Model

We consider a mobile computing offloading scheme, which consists of a fog node and remote cloud computing system. Mobile devices run applications (real-time financial trading applications, gaming applications, virtual reality applications, etc.) that consume a large volume of computing resources and power. According to the offloading criterion, some of the tasks are offloaded to the fog node. The capacity of the fog node is limited, so if too many tasks are offloaded, the fog node becomes congested, and the offloaded tasks are sent to the remote cloud.

Assume there are M MDs connected to a fog node, each of them generates a flow of tasks with intensity λ_i, $i = 1, 2, ..., M$. The distribution of processing volume and data size of tasks from MD i is represented by two-dimensional CDF $F_i(x, y)$, which is the probability that the processing volume w_i (measured in Millions of Instructions, MI) is less than x and the data size s_i (measured in MB) is less than y. Note that we consider a continuous distribution of both processing volume and data size, and the corresponding probability density function (PDF) is denoted by $f_i(x, y)$. We propose the offloading criterion that implies offloading tasks that are "heavy" in terms of processing volume and "light" in terms of data size. Splitting to "heavy" and "light" tasks are done by the threshold W_O on the processing volume and the threshold S_O on the data size. Thus, the offloading probability $\pi_{i,O}$ for the i-th MD may be obtained using PDF $f_i(x,y)$:

$$\pi_{i,O} = \int\limits_{W_O}^{+\infty} \int\limits_{0}^{S_O} f_i(w,s)dwds \tag{1}$$

If a task is processed locally, then the response time consists of processing time on an MD only. If a task is offloaded to the fog node, then the response time obtained is the sum of the transmission delay from MD to the fog node and the processing time on the fog node. Finally, if an offloaded task is sent to the remote cloud, then the response time is the sum of the transmission delay from MD to the fog node, from fog node to the cloud and processing time in the cloud. The energy consumption of an MD is determined by the processing volume of tasks in case of local processing and by the transmitted data volume in case of offloading.

Below we summarize the main assumptions for our model.

1. Each MD produces the Poisson flow of tasks with intensity λ_i (tasks/s).
2. MDs process tasks one by one with the constant serving rate μ_i, $i = 1, 2, ..., M$ (MIPS), thus, the serving process is modeled by means of M/G/1 queue.
3. The transmission delay from the mobile network's access point to the fog node is considered negligibly small. Thus, the transmission delay between an MD and the fog node is the transmission delay in the wireless channel.
4. Total available bitrate R (Mbps) of the wireless network is distributed equally between all simultaneously transmitting MDs. Hence, the transmission process via the wireless network is modeled in terms of M/G/1 PS (Processor Sharing) queue.
5. The fog node allocates computational resources to the tasks using virtual machines (VMs) with the constant serving rate μ_F, the maximum number of VMs in the fog node is N. If a task arriving at the fog node finds all VMs occupied, then it is sent to the remote cloud. The serving process at the fog node is modeled in terms of M/G/N queuing system, where the overloading probability π_F represents the probability that an arriving task is sent to the cloud.
6. The transmission delay between the fog node and the cloud is assumed constant.
7. The cloud also allocates computational resources by means of VMs with the constant serving rate μ_C. We assume that the cloud has an infinite number of VMs and model the serving process in terms of M/G/∞ queuing system.

3   The Response Time Analysis

In this section, we present a mathematical framework that is used for the evaluation of the average response time. Taking into account the notation described above, the mathematical model of the system can be depicted as shown in Fig. 1. First, we analyze the serving latencies on each of serving nodes and transmission delay in the wireless channel separately and then obtain the formula for the total average response time.

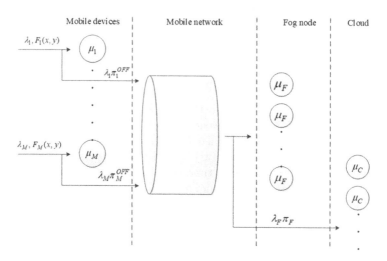

Fig. 1. Mathematical model in terms of queuing network.

3.1   Serving Latency on Mobile Devices

We introduce additional notation for the marginal CDF of processing volume generated by tasks on mobile devices $W_i(x) = \int_0^{+\infty} f_i(x, s)ds$.

The distribution function of the processing volume on a mobile device is determined based on the following assumptions - the task is processed locally if the processing volume is not too large ($w_i \leq W_O$), or the corresponding amount of data exceeds the threshold ($s_i \geq S_O$).

The distribution of processing volume of locally served tasks is determined by conditional CDF $W_{MD,i}(x)$

$$W_{MD,i}(x) = P\left\{ w_i < x | (w_i \leq W_O) \cup (s_i \geq S_O) \right\}. \tag{2}$$

Using conditional probability rules, the CDF $W_{MD,i}(x)$ can be rewritten in the following way:

$$W_{MD,i}(x) = \frac{P\left\{ (w_i < x) \cap ((w_i \leq W_O) \cup (s_i \geq S_O)) \right\}}{P\left\{ (w_i \leq W_O) \cup (s_i \geq S_O) \right\}}. \tag{3}$$

The expression in the denominator of Eq. (3) is simply $1 - \pi_{i,O}$. Then, if $x \leq W_O$, then the probability in the numerator is just $P\{w_i < x\}$. On the other hand, if $x > W_O$, the numerator is given by the probability

$$P\left\{ (w_i \leq W_O) \cup (w_i < x)(s_i \geq S_O) \right\}. \tag{4}$$

The final expression for CDF $W_{MD,i}(x)$ has the following form:

$$W_{MD,i}(x) = \begin{cases} \dfrac{W_i(x)}{1 - \pi_{i,O}}, x \leq W_O, \\ \dfrac{1}{1 - \pi_{i,O}} \left(W_i(W_O) + \int\limits_{W_O}^{x} \int\limits_{S_O}^{+\infty} f_i(w, s)dwds \right), x > W_O. \end{cases} \tag{5}$$

Since the serving rate on the ith MD is constant and equal to μ_i, the CDF $T_{MD,i}(x)$ of the service time is given by

$$T_{MD,i}(x) = W_{MD,i}(\mu_i x) \tag{6}$$

With the serving time distribution, one can easily obtain the average serving time at MD i $t_{MD,i}$, as well as the second moment $t_{MD,i}^{(2)}$. These parameters are used to evaluate the average sojourn time $\tau_{MD,i}$ for locally processed task by means of well-known Pollaczek-Khinchin formula for M/G/1 queue:

$$\tau_{MD,i} = t_{MD,i} + \frac{\lambda_i t_{MD,i}^{(2)}}{2(1 - \lambda_i t_{MD,i})} \tag{7}$$

3.2 Transmission Latency in the Wireless Network

A wireless network is an intermediate node between mobile devices and a fog node. The speed of transmission through a wireless network depends on the number of simultaneously transmitting devices, as well as on the amount of transmitted data. As indicated above, R is the total data rate.

The transmission of tasks via a wireless channel is modeled by M/G/1 queueing system with Processor Sharing (PS) serving policy. Then, according to the processor sharing policy, $\frac{R}{n_t r}$ is the data transfer rate that falls on each of the $n_t r$ currently transmitting devices.

The wireless network transmits only offloaded tasks. The arrivals of tasks to the wireless networks form a Poisson flow since arrivals from each MD represent a sifted Poisson flow, which is still Poisson. Moreover, the sum of Poisson flows is again a Poisson flow. Thus, the arrival intensity λ_F to the wireless network is

$$\lambda_F = \sum_{i=1}^{M} \lambda_i \pi_{i,O} \tag{8}$$

In order to estimate the transmission latency, we obtain the CDF $S_{tr,i}(x)$ of the file size to be transmitted. The CDF is obtained in terms of conditional probabilities:

$$S_{tr,i}(x) = P\left\{s_i < x | (w_i \geq W_O) \cap (s_i \leq S_O)\right\} \tag{9}$$

Using similar technique as for $W_{MD,i}(x)$, one can derive an exact expression for CDF $S_{tr,i}(x)$:

$$S_{tr,i}(x) = \begin{cases} \dfrac{1}{\pi_{i,O}} \displaystyle\int_{W_O}^{+\infty} \int_{0}^{x} f_i(w,s)dwds, x \leq S_O, \\ 1, x > S_O, \end{cases} \tag{10}$$

and the average file size θ is given by the following formula

$$\theta = \sum_{i=1}^{M} \frac{\lambda_i \pi_{i,O}}{\lambda_F} \theta_i, \tag{11}$$

where θ_i is the average file size transmitted by i-th MD, which is easily found using the CDF $S_{tr,i}(x)$.

The average transmission time is obtained by well-known formula for the average sojourn time in the M/G/1 PS queue in case $\frac{\lambda_F \theta}{R} < 1$:

$$\tau_{trF} = \frac{\theta}{R - \lambda_F \theta} \tag{12}$$

3.3 Serving Latency on the Fog Node

The arrival flow to the fog node is the output flow from the wireless network. According to the properties of M/G/1 PS queuing system, the output flow from the wireless network is Poisson flow with the same arrival intensity λ_F. As it was stated in Sect. 2, there are N servers at the fog node, each of them has the service rate μ_F.

The distribution of processing volume of tasks from i-th MD served on the fog node is determined by conditional CDF $W_{F,i}(x)$:

$$W_{F,i}(x) = P\{w_i < x | (w_i > W_O) \cap (s_i < S_O)\} \tag{13}$$

Similarly to previous sections, the CDF $W_{F,i}(x)$ can be rewritten in the following way:

$$W_{F,i}(x) = \begin{cases} 0, x \leq W_O, \\ \dfrac{1}{\pi_{i,O}} \displaystyle\int\limits_{W_O}^{x} \int\limits_0^{S_O} f_i(w,s)dwds, x > W_O \end{cases} \tag{14}$$

The serving time is simply $\frac{w_i}{\mu_F}$, which leads to the following expression for the CDF $T_{F,i}(x)$ of serving time at the fog node:

$$T_{F,i}(x) = W_{F,i}(\mu_F x) \tag{15}$$

The average serving time at the fog node $\tau_{F,i}$ is evaluated using the obtained CDF $T_{F,i}(x)$. If all of N VMs in the fog node are occupied, then arriving tasks are routed to the remote cloud. The overloading probability π_F is evaluated according to the Erlang's formula for M/M/N queuing system, which is valid for M/G/N queue due to the insensitivity property.

$$\pi_{F,i} = \frac{(\lambda_F \tau_{F,i})^N}{N!} \left(\sum_{k=0}^{N} \frac{(\lambda_F \tau_{F,i})^k}{k!} \right)^{-1}. \tag{16}$$

3.4 Serving Latency on the Remote Cloud

The probability of routing to the cloud depends on the state of the fog nodes and does not depend on the processing volume of arriving tasks. Thus, the distribution of required processing volume of tasks arriving at the cloud is equal to the processing volume distribution of offloaded tasks (see formula (14)). The tasks at the remote cloud are served with the constant serving rate μ_C, then the distribution of serving time is

$$T_{C,i}(x) = W_{F,i}(\mu_C x), \tag{17}$$

which allows us to easily evaluate the average serving time at the cloud $\tau_{C,i}$ for tasks from i-th MD.

3.5 The Average Response Time

The total response time is the conditional sum of processing and transmission delays. A task from i-th MD is processed locally with probability $1 - \pi_{i,O}$, on the fog node with probability $\pi_{i,O}(1 - \pi_F)$ and on the cloud with probability $\pi_{i,O}\pi_F$. Thus, the average response time for the tasks from i-th MD is

$$\tau_i = (1-\pi_{i,O})\tau_{MD,i} + \pi_{i,O}(1-\pi_F)(\tau_{trF}+\tau_{F,i}) + \pi_{i,O}\pi_F(\tau_{trF}+\tau_{trC}+\tau_{C,i}), \tag{18}$$

where τ_{trC} is the constant transmission delay between the fog node and the cloud. Finally, the average response time for a task from an arbitrary MD is

$$\tau = \sum_{i=1}^{M} \frac{\lambda_i}{\sum_{j=1}^{M}\lambda_j}\tau_i. \tag{19}$$

Thus, the obtained formulas allow evaluating the average response time using initial two-dimensional CDF $F_i(x,y)$.

4 The Energy Consumption Analysis

In this section, we obtain formulas for the average energy consumption by MDs. An MD consumes energy for local processing of tasks and for transmission of tasks to the access point of the wireless network in case of offloading. The energy consumption for locally executing tasks is proportional to the processing volumes of tasks, then the average energy consumption $E_{pr,i}$ (measured in Joules) during locally executing on i-th MD may be estimated in the following way:

$$E_{pr,i} = P_{pr,i}t_{MD,i}, \tag{20}$$

where $P_{pr,i}$ is the power consumption (W) during the processing of the i-th MD, which is assumed constant for the simplicity.

When it comes to the energy consumption during transmitting, it is also proportional to the transmission time, so the average energy consumption $E_{tr,i}$ of the i-th VD during task transmission is

$$E_{tr,i} = P_{tr,i}\frac{\theta_i}{R}, \tag{21}$$

where $P_{tr,i}$ is the transmission power (W) during processing of the i-th MD. The average energy consumption for any is the weighted sum of processing and transmission energies:

$$E_i = (1 - \pi_{i,O})E_{pr,i} + \pi_{i,O}E_{tr,i}. \tag{22}$$

Finally, the average energy consumption for a task from an arbitrary MD is evaluated similarly to (19).

$$E = \sum_{i=1}^{M} \frac{\lambda_i}{\sum_{j=1}^{M} \lambda_j} E_i. \tag{23}$$

5   Case Study

In this section, we present the results of the conducted case study. Assume that there are $M = 20$ homogeneous MDs with task generating intensity $\lambda_i = 2$ tasks/s and serving rate $\mu_i = 4$ MIPS for all $i = 1, 2, ..., M$. Processing volume and data size of tasks are assumed independent from each other, both having gamma distribution with the following PDF:

$$f(x) = x^{k-1} \frac{e^{-\frac{x}{\delta}}}{\delta^k \Gamma(k)}, \tag{24}$$

where $\delta = 0.75$ for the processing volume and $\delta = 0.25$ for data size distribution, while $k = 2$ for both of them. Note that for the proposed Gamma distribution parameters the average processing volume of a task is 1.5 MIPS and the average data size is 0.5 MB. The wireless network capacity $R = 150$ Mbps and constant transmission time from the fog node to the remote cloud is $\tau_{trC} = 1$ second. The fog nodes can run maximum $N = 8$ VMs, each of them having equal service rate $\mu_F = 6$ MIPS, while the capacity of VMs at the cloud is $\mu_C = 10$ MIPS. To energy consumption parameters, the power consumption during processing is $P_{pr} = 16$ W and the transmission power is 23 dBm, meaning $P_{tr} = 0.2$ W.

Figure 2 depicts the impact of the offloading thresholds on the average response time. The left corner on Fig. 2 corresponds to the highest offloading probability π_O, while at the right corner the offloading probability decreases up to 0. The increase in the average response time in case of large π_O caused by overloading of the fog node and increase in the probability of rerouting to the cloud. On the other hand, when the offloading probability decreases, the load on MDs becomes bigger and causes an increase of waiting time for locally processed tasks. The optimal distribution of tasks is reached in between the extreme points. For the considered case, the minimum average response time is $\tau = 0.41$ s, and it is reached with offloading probability $\pi_O = 0.37$ with offloading thresholds $W_O = 1.6$ and $S_O = 2.5$.

Figure 3 depicts the impact of the offloading thresholds on average energy consumption. One can see that the energy consumption is constantly increasing with the decrease of the offloading probability. Therefore, from the energy-efficiency point of view, the more is offloaded, the better.

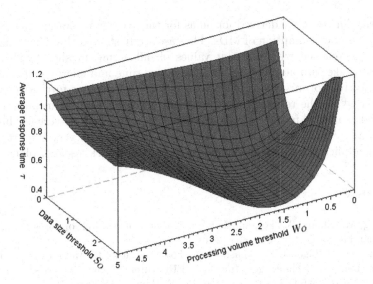

Fig. 2. The impact of the offloading thresholds on the average response time

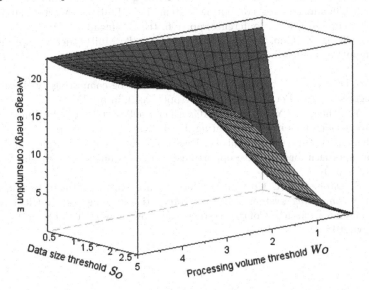

Fig. 3. The impact of the offloading thresholds on the average energy consumption

6   Conclusion

In the paper, we proposed a novel threshold-based offloading criterion for mobile computing offloading. The tasks differ from each other in terms required processing volume and data volume to be transmitted in case of offloading, which is described by two-dimensional CDF $F_i(x, y)$. Using the CDF and its corresponding density function, we derived formulas for the average response time and the average energy consumption of MDs. The case study showed that the minimums of them are reached with different values of offloading thresholds. Therefore, in order to take into account both the response time and energy consumption, multi-objective optimization should be done, which is left for further research.

Note that all the results are obtained in terms of CDFs. It means that the developed analytical framework allows evaluating not only the averages, but also variance and even quantiles of the response time, which is very important for real-time applications. This problem is also in our further research plans.

References

1. Chiang, M., Zhang, T.: Fog and IoT, an overview of research opportunities. IEEE Internet Things J. **3**(6), 854–864 (2016)
2. Puliafito, C., Mingozzi, E., Anastasi, G.: Fog computing for the internet of mobile things: issues and challenges. In: 2017 IEEE International Conference on Smart Computing (SMARTCOMP), pp. 1–6. IEEE, Hong Kong (2017)
3. Chang, Z., Zhou, Z., Ristaniemi, T., Niu, Z.: Energy efficient optimization for computation offloading in fog computing system. In: GLOBECOM 2017–2017 IEEE Global Communications Conference, pp. 1–6. IEEE, Singapore (2017)
4. Liu, L., Chang, Z., Guo, X., Mao, S., Ristaniemi, T.: Multi-objective optimization for computation offloading in fog computing. IEEE Internet Things J. **5**(1), 283–294 (2018)
5. Rahbari, D., Nickray, M.: Task offloading in mobile fog computing by classification and regression tree. Peer-to-Peer Netw. Appl. (2019, in print)
6. Jiang, Y., Chen, Y., Yang, S., Wu, C.: Energy-efficient task offloading for time-sensitive applications in fog computing. IEEE Syst. J. (2019, in print)
7. Casadei, R., Fortino, G., Pianini, D., Russo, W., Savaglio, C., Viroli, M.: A development approach for collective opportunistic edge-of-things services. Inf. Sci. **498**, 154–169 (2019)
8. Sopin, E., Daraseliya, A., Correia, M.: Performance analysis of the offloading scheme in a fog computing system. In: 10th International Congress on Ultra Modern Telecommunications and Control Systems and Workshops (ICUMT), pp. 1–5. IEEE, Moscow (2018)

Protecting Personal Data Using Smart Contracts

Mohsin Ur Rahman[1]([✉]), Fabrizio Baiardi[2], Barbara Guidi[1], and Laura Ricci[1]

[1] Department of Computer Science, University of Pisa, Pisa, Italy
{mohsinur.rahman,guidi,laura.ricci}@di.unipi.it
[2] Department of Philology, Literature, and Linguistics, University of Pisa, Pisa, Italy
fabrizio.baiardi@unipi.it

Abstract. Decentralized Online Social Networks (DOSNs) have been proposed as an alternative solution to the current centralized Online Social Networks (OSNs). Online Social Networks are based on centralized architecture (e.g., Facebook, Twitter, or Google+), while DOSNs do not have a service provider that acts as central authority and users have more control over their information. Several DOSNs have been proposed during the last years. However, the decentralization of the OSN requires efficient solutions for protecting the privacy of users, and to evaluate the trust between users. Blockchain represents a disruptive technology which has been applied to several fields, among these also to Social Networks. In this paper, we propose a manageable, user-driven and auditable access control framework for DOSNs using blockchain technology. In the proposed approach, the blockchain is used as a support for the definition of privacy policies. The resource owner uses the public key of the subject to define flexible role-based access control policies, while the private key associated with the subjects Ethereum account is used to decrypt the private data once access permission is validated on the blockchain. We evaluate our solution by exploiting the Rinkeby Ethereum testnet to deploy the smart contract, and to evaluate its performance. Experimental results show the feasibility of the proposed scheme in achieving auditable and user-driven access control via smart contract deployed on the Blockchain.

Keywords: Blockchain · Access control · RBAC · Social networks

1 Introduction

In today's digital world, online users are generating a large amount of information. Online users are actively engaged on various sites including Facebook, Twitter, Instagram, LinkedIn, etc. In particular, a large amount of personal sensitive information are generated on popular social networking sites. Privacy is the main issue of current Social Network platforms, and several privacy disclosure events have happened, such as Cambridge Analytica[1]. To face the privacy issue,

---

[1] https://www.theguardian.com/technology/2019/mar/17/the-cambridge-analytica-scandal-changed-the-world-but-it-didnt-change-facebook.

© Springer Nature Switzerland AG 2019
R. Montella et al. (Eds.): IDCS 2019, LNCS 11874, pp. 21–32, 2019.
https://doi.org/10.1007/978-3-030-34914-1_3

decentralization has been proposed as a possible solution. A Decentralized Online Social Network (DOSN) is an Online Social Network (OSN) implemented in a distributed environment. During the last years, not only several academic solutions have been proposed [6,12,13], but also online services such as Mastodon[2] and Diaspora[3].

Thanks to the decentralization of data, users have more control over their data. However, decentralization introduces important requirements which have to be met, such as data availability and the information diffusion [14]. As concerns privacy, access control techniques are used to manage the access to data in several fully-decentralized DOSNs [4]. Access control policies are used to express the rights of subjects to access services, and these policies are evaluated at access request time. For instance, in role-based access control system [17], policies are associated with resources in the network and users or groups of users are assigned roles, which determines their applicability to access the protected resources. A DOSN requires that access control policies should be evaluated by users in the network to check if a user can access to a data or not [10]. Considering the dynamism of DOSNs due to the online/offline status of users [9], and the trust problem of choosing users which are not malicious, the validation of privacy policies is a tricky problem, which can be managed by using blockchain technology.

Blockchain technology emerged to the world due to Bitcoin, which was the first global cryptocurrency introduced in 2008 [1]. It is worthy to note that the basic purpose of blockchain was to enable the functionality of a peer-to-peer (P2P) payment system without relying on a third party. In other words, Blockchain is a P2P network for conducting transactions in a secure and transparent manner.

A blockchain is principally a list of records, called blocks. Each block contains the hash of the previous block, and other essential information such as timestamp, and a set of transactions etc. Note that the first block of the chain is called a genesis block, which provides a foundation to create other blocks on top of it.

Ethereum has received significant attention from industry and academia in recent years thank to the introduction of the smart contracts. Because of their resilience to tampering, smart contracts are used in many scenarios such as transfer of money, games etc. [2]. Ethereum supports two types of accounts. Externally Owned Accounts (EOAs) are used to transfer money from one account holder to another one. Furthermore, each EOA is assigned a unique 20 bytes address, which uniquely identifies the account holder in the network. Ethereum also supports contract accounts simply called contracts. Each contract account is associated with a unique code to uniquely identify it in the network. Ethereum accounts are associated with unique public/private key pairs. Transactions can be sent to specific addresses represented by public keys, and only users with the specified destination addresses can access them in the network. The execution

---

[2] https://mastodon.social/about.
[3] https://diasporafoundation.org/.

of transactions in the Ethereum network requires the payment of Ether. Thus, users possessing sufficient Ether can only execute the code of the smart contracts stored on the blockchain. Therefore, Ethereum users are required to purchase gas by paying Ether. The consensus technique used by Ethereum is called Proof-of-Work, which enables miners to solve a cryptographic challenge (i.e., to guess random numbers).

In this paper, we propose a blockchain-based access control for DOSNs. The role-based access control policies are stored on the blockchian, are publicly auditable and permit the verification of the user's rights even when the owner of the data is not logged in the social network. Our decentralized access control management system relies on the DOSN users to grant, revoke or update the access rights by making transactions to execute the respective functions of smart contract. DOSN users are associated with Ethereum accounts in order to uniquely identify themselves in the network. We focus on the Role-based Access Control Model (RBAC) [17] because roles play a vital role in managing the contents of DOSNs. Thus, a DOSN user can send transactions to the access control contract deployed on the blockchian to assign roles to his/her colleagues, to family's and friends' members etc., and to allow only the intended users to access the resources of the resource owner.

The rest of this paper is structured as follows: Sect. 2 is dedicated to the presentation of the background on DOSNs and of the Related Works. In Sect. 3, we discuss the proposed framework. Section 4 presents the results of the performance evaluation. Finally, Sect. 5 concludes the paper.

2   Background and Related Work

Decentralized Online Social Networks (DOSNs) are introduced to overcome privacy issues of current OSNs. DOSNs offer a new revolution for data management, thereby allowing the users to control and manage their own personal information. In other words, DOSNs function as a dynamic peer-to-peer (P2P) network to store the users' profiles without reliance on a single service provider. However, DOSNs introduce many new problems regarding the availability, access control and availability of the shared items [8]. Various architectures for decentralized Online Social Networks have been proposed [5,6,12,13]. Usually encryption operations are used on the stored data such that only clients with the corresponding decryption keys are allowed to decrypt and view the stored contents. Access control is one of the main used technique to manage the access to data in DOSN. Indeed, DOSNs use privacy policies with encryption techniques, in many cases they use the Attribute Based Encryption (ABE) [10].

In detail, LifeSocial.KOM [12], and PeerSoN [5]) are based on encryption. In particular, they combine different encryption schemes in order to protect the privacy of users' contents. Each content generated by a user should be encrypted and replicated on different users' devices. DOSNs, such as My3 [16] and DiDu-SoNet [13], do not rely on encryption techniques, indeed contents remains unencrypted on the devices, and trust is exploited to store data. The privacy solutions adopted by DOSNs must allow user to deny access to unauthorized contacts or to grant access to new contacts, regardless of whether their are based on encryption or not.

One of the main problem in DOSNs is that data are stored on users devices, so they are available as long as users are online. To enhance data availability, users' data are replicated on the devices of different users. It is also worth noticing that the evaluation of privacy policies regarding the data of a user can be evaluated by the user itself if she/he is online, otherwise it must be executed by some trusted node hosting the data replica.

Blockchain technology is a disruptive solution which can be exploited by DOSNs in order to improve privacy systems. During the last years, blockchain has been applied to several scenarios and also to Social Networks. Several social Network platforms [3,15,18] exploiting blockchain have been proposed mainly in order to overcome the privacy problems of current OSNs. In many cases the blockchain is exploited to support techniques for the detection of fake news.

However, to the best of our knowledge, all current Blockchain-based Social Networks do not exploit blockchain as a support to control accesses to the data owned by the users.

3   The Proposed Framework

The basic objective of our proposal is to use the blockchain to store and evaluate role-based access control policies. To achieve this objective, the resource owner can send transactions to the role-based access control smart contract deployed on the Ethereum blockchain in order to assign/evaluate roles to other DOSN users in the network. The access control policies are stored on the blockchain, thereby allowing the resource owner as well as other nodes to check the enforcement of the privacy policies when the contract receives access requests. Our framework is privacy preserving because the real identifies of DOSN users are not disclosed to other users in the network. The main rational behind our approach is motivated from the fact that Ethereum uses a single public address for each account holder. We need to make the following essential configurations to apply the Ethereum platform in our access control system.

– Each DOSN user must be associated with an Ethereum account to uniquely identity itself in the network. Thus, this account allows each peer to claim the deployment of a smart contract, and to assign roles to other DOSN users
– All DOSN users can configure and run the Ethereum client because such devices have sufficient computing capabilities. A DOSN user can use its Ethereum client to directly interact with the blockchain. Indeed, they can also send transactions to execute the main functions of smart contracts.

In our framework, a DOSN user can easily check the blockchain at any time to determine whether he/she is assigned a role from another DOSN user. Furthermore, this approach is intended to achieve distributed auditability, thereby preventing third parties from fraudulently denying the access rights granted by role-based access control policies. It is worthy to note that a subject who wishes to access the resources of the resource owner must assert that it possesses a role that was issued by the resource owner. The architecture of our access control framework is depicted in Fig. 1. The main actors of our framework include the resource owner, a node trusted from the resource owner and subjects (i.e., users who are interested in viewing the resources of the resource owner). The resource owner uses the Ethereum address of the subject in order to define role-based privacy policies using smart contract.

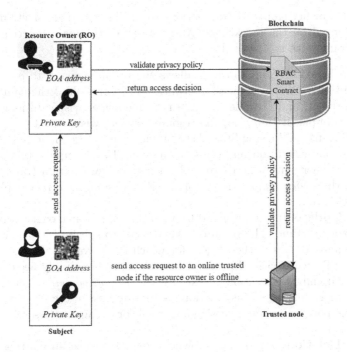

Fig. 1. Architecture of the proposed framework for DOSNs using smart contract

In our approach, the resource owner has a set of trusted nodes where data are stored, as described in [10], in order to guarantee the data availability even when the user is offline. The choice of trusted replica nodes is outside the scope of this article. A generic request is sent to the resource owner when it is online, otherwise it is sent to one trusted node chosen at random. These nodes check the privacy policies to determine the permission associated with roles. Based on the evaluation of access control policies, the subject is either allowed or denied to view or download the private data of the resource owner.

When a new relationship is established between the resource owner and the subject, the later involved in the relationship has to share its public key (i.e., Ethereum address). After verification of the user's identity, the resource owner sends a transaction to the access control contract in order to issue a desired role such as colleague, friend, friend-of-friend or family etc. Finally, after the establishment of a relationship and privacy policy definition using blockchain, the subject can send access requests to the resource owner or to trusted nodes when the former is offline. Finally, after confirming information in the blockchain, the resource owner or trusted node is assured that the asserted role is assigned by the resource owner.

3.1 Main Functions of the Framework

The resource owner can send transactions to invoke the main functions of the RBAC deployed on the blockchain. An overview of the main functions of the proposed framework is given below;

- **Policy Creation:** This function allows the resource owner to issue role to a requesting DOSN user in the network. It requires the Ethereum address of the subject, and the role that the resource owner wishes to assign. As a simple example, if Bob (i.e., the resource owner) wishes to add Alice (i.e., subject) as friend, he simply needs to provide the Ethereum address of Alice, and the role friend and an access permission. To accomplish this goal, the resource owner simply needs to make a new policy creation transaction to execute the *policyAdd()* function of the RBAC smart contract deployed on the blockchain.
- **Policy Update:** In the proposed framework, the resource owner can update a policy at anytime. The resource owner needs to specify the new role, permission and address of the subject for which the privacy policy needs to be updated. To accomplish this goal, the resource owner simply needs to make a policy update transaction to execute the *policyUpdate()* function of the RBAC smart contract. This function requires address of the subject, role and permission as parameters to assign a new role or change the associated access permission.
- **Policy Deletion:** The resource owner can also revoke an existing privacy policy by making a policy revocation transaction to execute the *policyDelete()* function of the RBAC smart contract.
- **Right Transfer:** The resource owner must not only be able to specify who can access the resource, he must also be able to add users who can further delegate that authorization to other users. To accomplish this goal, only users endorsed by the resource owner can send transactions to execute the *roleTransfer()* function of the smart contract. This function requires the link or identification information of the policy and the address of the new user to transfer the access rights. The framework is scalable because the current right holders can further transfer the access rights to new users as well.
- **Access Control:** This function allows the resource owner or trusted nodes to check access permission on the blockchain when an access request is submitted by the subject. To accomplish this goal, the resource owner or trusted nodes perform an access control transaction to execute the *AccessControl()* function of the smart contract.

- **Contract Deletion:** The resource owner can also disable the RBAC smart contract by making a contract deactivation transaction to execute the *deleteRBAC()* function of the RBAC smart contract.

We use two-dimensional mappings from the elements of address (primary key) and role (secondary key) to create, update, revoke and validate these policies in the blockchain.

3.2   Challenge-Response Authentication

The challenge-response protocol is executed when a subject sends an access request to the resource owner or to a trusted node when the former is offline. The basic steps of this protocol are discussed as follows;

- **Declaration:** The aim of this step is to enable the subject to declare that it possesses a unique Ethereum account/address that was used to issue a role, and permission by the resource owner. In our simple example, Alice will assert the role friend to indicate that this role has been issued by Bob in order to access his resources. Thus, the asserted role makes Alice eligible to access the protected resources of Bob.
- **Information Verification:** Given the assertion of the subject, the resource owner or trusted node checks the RBAC policies published on the blockchain to determine weather the corresponding public key was issued a role by the resource owner. Given the data on the blockchain, these nodes will be able to check the information related to the public key of the subject. Finally, the node receiving the request challenges the requesting DOSN user in order to verify his/her real identity (i.e., to determine whether he/she is the true owner of the Ethereum account).
- **Challenge:** The resource owner or trusted node selects a random data d, and asks the subject to sign it.
- **Response:** Response from the subject determines the true owner of the corresponding Ethereum account because the private key is required to sign the message. Therefore, the creation of a correct signature is only possible if the user possesses the corresponding private key. Thus, the message can only be signed by the legitimate owner. To accomplish this goal, we use the following function:

$$S = Sign(pk; address; d) \tag{1}$$

where pk represents the private key of the subject, and d represents the random data sent to sign. Thus, a correct signature is only possible if the subject possesses the corresponding private key which is uniquely defined for each Ethereum account, and it is also unique for each DOSN user. The subject then sends S back to the resource owner or trusted node.
- **Response Confirmation:** The resource owner or trusted nodes will allow the subject to access the protected resources if and only if a correct signature is generated by the subject. To accomplish this goal, the resource owner or trusted node uses the following verification function:

$$confirmResponse(address; d; S). \tag{2}$$

Finally, the resource owner or trusted node will allow access to the resource if and only if the verification process is successful. Please note that the authentication protocol can be executed offline, and the Solidity sha3 [7] function can be used to securely generate the signature. This technique can be used to generate a message signature without disclosing the private key.

4   Performance Evaluation

Every transaction that is used to invoke the function of a smart contract requires the payment of a fee in order to compensate the mining node for the execution of transaction and saving it on the blockchain. Ethereum uses gas to express this fee. Users can purchase gas from the mining nodes by paying Ether. Please note that Gas and Ether are two distinct terms because gas indicates a constant cost of performing an operation on a Blockchain network, whereas Ether is a volatile virtual currency, which is used to pay for the network resources.

4.1   Experiment Setting

We use the solidity [19] programming language to develop a prototype of the proposed RBAC smart contract, and deployed it on the Rinkeby Ethereum testnet. During analysis in the month of April, we observed an average gas value of ≈ 0.000000021 ETH, and 1 Ether ≈ 137.66 USD. Experimental results show that our proposed smart contract requires 1869303 gas for deployment. Therefore, the creation and deployment of our proposed smart contract on the blockchain requires 0.256 USD. However, it is only a single time cost to initialize our proposed RBAC smart contract.

4.2   Results

Table 1 shows the one-time costs of the functions of the proposed smart contract when a subject is assigned a role by the resource owner. It is worthy to note that that a role is assigned to the user together with an additional permission element. As it can be observed from the table, the gas consumption costs are slightly increased. However, the costs of the remaining three functions are always constant because these functions are independent of the main functions of the smart contract (i.e., policy creation and policy updation).

Table 1 also shows that the one-time constant cost of the access control function is 0.0031 USD$. The resource owner can also delete the smart contract from the blockchain by invoking the *deleteRBAC()* function, which performs the suicide or self-destruct operation to remove the code of RBAC from the Ethereum blockchain [11].

We performed an experiment to evaluate the effects of the number of subjects in the RBAC policy on Gas consumption (i.e., when the resource owner assigns role to a group of subjects in a single policy creation transaction). The results of the experiment are presented in Fig. 2(a). Results show that the policy

Table 1. Costs of the different functions of the RBAC smart contract

RBAC function	Gas used	Cost (ether)	USD ($)
policyAdd()	27864	0.000028	0.0038
policyUpdate()	27800	0.000028	0.0038
policyDelete()	22680	0.000023	0.0031
roleTransfer()	51456	0.000051	0.0069
AccessControl()	22808	0.000023	0.0031
deleteRBAC()	13455	0.000027	0.0036

creation and update transaction for 1 Ethereum address require 3,392 gas consumption on the Rinkeby testnet and this cost increases linearly as we increase the number of addresses on these two transactions. We also observed that the contract deployment gas cost also increases linearly as the number of users in the RBAC policy are increased. It is worthy to note that the given results show the applicability of the proposed framework to simultaneously assign the same role to multiple users in a single policy creation transaction.

We performed another experiment to evaluate the effects of the number of bits on gas consumption as shown in Fig. 2(b). Results of the experiment show that each single bit denoting a particular input in the policy creation and updation transactions requires constant amount of gas on the Rinkeby testnet.

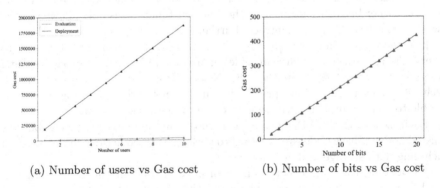

(a) Number of users vs Gas cost   (b) Number of bits vs Gas cost

Fig. 2. Effects of number of users (a) and bits (b) on gas consumption

The privacy policies can be valid if miners have approved all the related transactions to the smart contract deployed on the blockchain, and these transactions are recorded to new blocks. It is worthy to note that the block generation time is directly proportional to the transaction rate (i.e., the more transactions are made, the more time it will take to generate the relevant block). We setup our own private Ethereum network to assess the effects of the number of miners on block generation time. Initially, we configure one miner to mine block. However, as we increased the number of miners, the block generation time decreased and became stable when the number of miners reached to 4 as shown in Fig. 3. Furthermore, we also confirmed the block generation time on Rinkeby testnet.

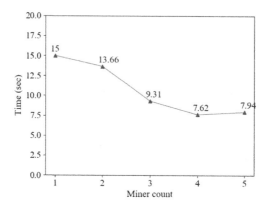

Fig. 3. Block generation time vs. number of miners

4.3 Security Analysis

It is not possible for an adversary to issue role-based policies on behalf of the resource owner because execution of the contract functions is only allowed to the owner of the RBAC smart contract. Furthermore, acting as a subject, the goal of the attacker is to impersonate a role that it does not possess (i.e., it can try to assert false roles to the resource provider or trusted nodes) in order to gain illegal access to the resources of another DOSN user. However, as already discussed, each DOSN user has unique private key in the network, and an adversary is unable to compromise the private keys of the users in the system.

Each user in the DOSN network can chose one or more of its neighbors as trusted nodes. These nodes are selected to perform trusted actions in the network including data storage and access control.

We assume that the cryptographic primitives used in the framework can not be broken by the adversary. Therefore, they are unable to forge the digital signature and to obtain hash collisions. It is worthy to note that the proposed framework is blockchain-oriented, thus, we assume that an adversary can not control a majority of the computing power in the network in order to avoid the 51% attack.

The challenge-response protocol is used to perform a secure verification of the user's identity, role and the associated access permission on the blockchain. The verification steps used in the challenge response protocol can be conducted offline, and latest technologies used in devices such as Near Field Communication (NFC) and Quick Response (QR) codes [20] can be used to effectively transfer the message and signature (Figs. 4 and 5).

"string _eaddress": "0x72bd370ab01ac9cdb1cb24f6408fcd0427e28b46",
"string _role": "friend",
"string _permission": "allow",

Fig. 4. The output of policy creation transaction using Remix IDE [19]

{
    "from": "0xfe0db7907417cb176850e7459599ff4fe1b2175b",
    "topic": "0xff92c090738d04f6256126fa734cbbd01d7fd4e82b501873433f2208134a0860",
    "event": "ReturnAccessResult",
    "args": {
        "0": "0x72BD370AB01AC9CdB1cB24f6408FCD0427e28B46",
        "1": "Access authorized!",
        "2": true,

Fig. 5. The output of privacy policy validation transaction

5   Conclusion and Future Work

In this research, we proposed an auditable and user-driven role-based access control management framework (RBAC) for DOSNs using blockchain technology. DOSN users are associated with Ethereum accounts having unique public, private keys. The public keys serve as addresses of the users while the private keys are used to prove the real identities of DOSN users. Each DOSN user is capable to invoke the assign and revoke functions of the access control contract deployed on the blockchain. Advantages of the proposed scheme include auditability (i.e., the user-role assignment is visible on the blockchain). Thus, any user can easily inspect them at any time. Furthermore, they can include other elements such as expiry time to automatically revoke the role assigned to users. We are planning to extend our work in several directions. We will investigate the possibility of exploiting external storages, such as private clouds, to guarantee data availability for offline users. Furthermore, we are developing a DAPP to interact with a system of different smart contracts on the blockchain including a tool to translate role based access control policies to smart contracts to be deployed on the blockchain.

References

1. Barber, S., Boyen, X., Shi, E., Uzun, E.: Bitter to better—how to make bitcoin a better currency. In: Keromytis, A.D. (ed.) FC 2012. LNCS, vol. 7397, pp. 399–414. Springer, Heidelberg (2012). https://doi.org/10.1007/978-3-642-32946-3_29
2. Bartoletti, M., Pompianu, L.: An empirical analysis of smart contracts: platforms, applications, and design patterns. In: Brenner, M., et al. (eds.) FC 2017. LNCS, vol. 10323, pp. 494–509. Springer, Cham (2017). https://doi.org/10.1007/978-3-319-70278-0_31
3. Bhatia, A., Giometti, R., Nicolas, A.: Sapien: decentralized social news platform (2018)
4. Bodriagov, O., Kreitz, G., Buchegger, S.: Access control in decentralized online social networks: applying a policy-hiding cryptographic scheme and evaluating its performance. In: 2014 IEEE PERCOM WORKSHOPS, pp. 622–628 (2014)

5. Buchegger, S., Schiöberg, D., Vu, L.H., Datta, A.: PeerSoN: P2P social network-ing: early experiences and insights. In: Proceedings of the Second ACM EuroSys Workshop on Social Network Systems, pp. 46–52 (2009)
6. Cutillo, L.A., Molva, R., Strufe, T.: Safebook: a privacy preserving online social network leveraging on real-life trust. IEEE Commun. Mag. **47**, 94–101 (2009)
7. Dannen, C.: Solidity programming. In: Dannen, C. (ed.) Introducing Ethereum and Solidity, pp. 69–88. Apress, Berkeley, CA (2017). https://doi.org/10.1007/978-1-4842-2535-6_4
8. Datta, A., Buchegger, S., Vu, L.H., Strufe, T., Rzadca, K.: Decentralized online social networks. In: Furht, B. (ed.) Handbook of Social Network Technologies and Applications, pp. 349–378. Springer, Boston (2010). https://doi.org/10.1007/978-1-4419-7142-5_17
9. De Salve, A., Dondio, M., Guidi, B., Ricci, L.: The impact of users availability on on-line ego networks: a facebook analysis. Comput. Commun. **73**, 211–218 (2016)
10. De Salve, A., Guidi, B., Mori, P., Ricci, L., Ambriola, V.: Privacy and temporal aware allocation of data in decentralized online social networks. In: Au, M.H.A., Castiglione, A., Choo, K.-K.R., Palmieri, F., Li, K.-C. (eds.) GPC 2017. LNCS, vol. 10232, pp. 237–251. Springer, Cham (2017). https://doi.org/10.1007/978-3-319-57186-7_19
11. Destefanis, G., Marchesi, M., Ortu, M., Tonelli, R., Bracciali, A., Hierons, R.: Smart contracts vulnerabilities: a call for blockchain software engineering? In: 2018 International Workshop on Blockchain Oriented Software Engineering (IWBOSE), pp. 19–25. IEEE (2018)
12. Graffi, K., Gross, C., Mukherjee, P., Kovacevic, A., Steinmetz, R.: LifeSocial.KOM: a P2P-based platform for secure online social networks. In: Peer-to-Peer Comput-ing, pp. 1–2 (2010)
13. Guidi, B., Amft, T., De Salve, A., Graffi, K., Ricci, L.: DiDuSoNet: A P2P archi-tecture for distributed dunbar-based social networks. Peer-to-Peer Netw. Appl. **9**, 1–18 (2015)
14. Guidi, B., Conti, M., Passarella, A., Ricci, L.: Managing social contents in decen-tralized online social networks: a survey. Online Soc. Netw. Media **7**, 12–29 (2018)
15. Konforty, D., Adam, Y., Estrada, D., Meredith, L.G.: Synereo: the decentralized and distributed social network (2015)
16. Narendula, R., Papaioannou, T.G., Aberer, K.: My3: a highly-available P2P-based online social network. In: 2011 IEEE International Conference on Peer-to-Peer Computing, pp. 166–167 (2011)
17. Sandhu, R.S., Coyne, E.J., Feinstein, H.L., Youman, C.E.: Role-based access con-trol models. Computer **29**(2), 38–47 (1996)
18. Scott, N.: Steem. An incentivized, blockchain-based, public content platform. https://steem.com/steem-whitepaper.pdf
19. Tikhomirov, S., Voskresenskaya, E., Ivanitskiy, I., Takhaviev, R., Marchenko, E., Alexandrov, Y.: SmartCheck: static analysis of ethereum smart contracts. In: 2018 IEEE/ACM 1st International Workshop on Emerging Trends in Software Engi-neering for Blockchain (WETSEB), pp. 9–16. IEEE (2018)
20. Want, R.: Near field communication. IEEE Pervasive Comput. **3**, 4–7 (2011)

Towards Environmental Impact Reduction Leveraging IoT Infrastructures: The PIXEL Approach

Ignacio Lacalle[1(✉)], Miguel Ángel Llorente[2], and Carlos E. Palau[1]

[1] Universitat Politècnica de València,
Camino de Vera s/n, 46022 Valencia, Spain
iglaub@upv.es, cpalau@dcom.upv.es
[2] Prodevelop, Plaza Don Juan de Villarrasa 14-5, 46001 Valencia, Spain
mllorente@prodevelop.es

Abstract. Ports are essential nodes in the global supply chain. Usually, the port-cities experience growth and sustainability thanks to the port activities and their related stakeholders. However, it is undeniable that port operations have an impact on the environment, the city and citizens living nearby. To mitigate this impact, the ports of the future will need to count with advanced tools enabling measurement and actuation over the harmful pollution sources. Modelling the footprint and gathering information about the causes are not easy tasks, as ports are complex environments with no standard procedures established yet for these purposes. These challenges are added to another current truth: data about real-time port operations are not optimally gathered neither exploited due to, mainly, a marked lack of interoperability.

PIXEL (Port IoT for environmental leverage) aims at creating the first smart, flexible and scalable solution reducing the environmental impact while enabling optimization of operations in port ecosystems. This approach relies on the most innovative ICT technology for ports building upon an interoperable open IoT platform. PIXEL use-cases are also presented in this paper, aiming to demonstrate, through various analytic services, a valid architecture drawing from heterogeneous data collection, data handling under a common model, data storage and data visualization.

Besides that, PIXEL devotes to decouple port's size and its ability to deploy environmental impact mitigation specifying an innovative methodology and an integrated metric for the assessment of the overall environmental impact of ports.

Keywords: IoT · Small and medium ports · Environmental impact · PIXEL

1 Introduction

Ports are a great example of heterogeneous information hubs. With more than 10 billion tonnes of global goods transported by sea [1], ports are logistics nodes that are essential for the development of each country. Multiple stakeholders operate inside and outside them with different motivations and businesses. Because maritime ports

© Springer Nature Switzerland AG 2019
R. Montella et al. (Eds.): IDCS 2019, LNCS 11874, pp. 33–45, 2019.
https://doi.org/10.1007/978-3-030-34914-1_4

concentrate, in direct link to their transport activities, logistics and industrial activities and interact with urban territories, they need to engage ambitious policies and strategies to become "ports of the future" by lowering the environmental impacts of their activity and by targeting environmental excellency.

During the last few years, several actions help confirming the trend of environmental awareness reclaimed to ports by the administration and the whole society. Besides, there is a consolidated vision arguing that the environmental problem in ports will not be properly addressed and solved until a real market altogether with technological pervasiveness will not be activated. This only will be achieved by measuring. What is not identified, quantified and collected cannot be managed. This vision matches definitions of "Port of the Future" [2] and is aligned with the vision of EcoPorts, which points small ports as a priority for green ports development and sustainable growth [3].

Furthermore, the environmental impact is directly related to the operational activity of the ports [4], such as loading and unloading, berthing, docking, yard management or gate appointments, among others. In this regard, the available operational data in ports, terminals and cities is constantly increasing and technology needed to make more accurate measurements on these assets is getting inexpensive and widely available. This is why the answer to the current status must rely on application of new technologies: data acquisition via modern devices, digitalisation, optimization methods, prediction, data exploitation, monitoring and visualization. Different initiatives have tried to address this challenge, but none of them has undertaken it from an environmental impact mitigation point of view neither integrating all the available and relevant information data sources in a single component (see Sect. 2 of this paper).

Since the 1990s, ports have been equipped with computer tools, programs, sensors and various other technologies to optimize their logistical, industrial, environmental and societal performance ratios. The latter therefore are potentially plenty of information that is, up to now, not exploited to their highest degree. Information interchange is already in place in several port environments through Port Community Systems (PCS) or National Single-Window systems (NSW). However, it is to a large extent limited to official documentation and services of the port authorities [5], meaning a lack of pertinent communication and effective integration of operational data in essential spots such as: port-city engagements, multi-modal transport operations (trains, trucks, etc.), port quality service levels and even port-citizen interaction; redounding in a deteriorate customer, stakeholder and citizen satisfaction. In addition to all this, the digitalization does not reach equally every maritime logistic node (at European and global level). This fact is especially visible on the medium or small ones, where budget is limited and IT services usually depend on external contractors. There has been also proven the lack of guidelines and tools at national level focused on them, turning the compliance with regulations into a stern task to be carried out.

The H2020-funded project PIXEL [6] (Port IoT for Environmental Leverage), denoted as "the project", will address all of those concerns from an optimisation point of view based on new conceptual and technology development relying on information sharing and IoT (Internet of Things). Particularly, PIXEL tackles top environmental and operational concerns potentially improvable by technology. It provides a cloud-based IoT-enabled infrastructure capable to integrate operational data from sensors and devices, legacy port IT systems (PCS or PMS) and open data. With PIXEL, port-city integration and operational information issues will be supported by a common operational ICT (Information and Communications Technology) hub for clustering, harmonising and distributing information to shared management and operation of ports, cities and the hinterland transport network. Finally, the project aims at validating its technological development in for real use-cases. Four European ports (Port of Bordeaux, Port of Monfalcone, Port of Thessaloniki and Port of Piraeus) are participating in the cooperative project as partners of the consortium, therefore the assessment of the solution will be feasible in the short term at a prototype level.

The core of this paper is to describe the original approach of this project. PIXEL components, use cases and methodology are succinctly realised, while the future work and the goals of PIXEL implementation are depicted as well.

2   Related Work

Several projects funded in previous years by the European Commission and other international organizations worldwide have focused on the very topics addressed by this paper: IoT for ports, digitalization and optimization of port operations, environmental impact measuring and mitigation and interoperability in this application domain.

A brief reference of those initiatives is depicted in Table 1 pointing the similarities and differences with the scope of PIXEL.

Table 1. Related works prior to PIXEL project.

Other R&D&I activities	Link to PIXEL
INTER-IoT: H2020 project devoted to achieve interoperability among (at all layers) among IoT platforms	*Similarities*: Interoperability framework for IoT Platforms *Differences:* PIXEL goes further about ports-specific problems while focusing in environment. Therefore it provides data representation for the IoT domain
GreenMarine: Canadian initiative to measure (qualitatively) the environmental impact of US-Canadian ports	*Similarities*: Measuring impact of port divided per type and other considerations *Differences:* Qualitative approach (via surveys) versus (PIXEL) quantitative measurement (through sensors)
PORTOPIA: European initiative for monitoring environmental concerns and indicators in ports	*Similarities:* Environmental indicators identification, sustainability and impact reduction aims. European funding *Differences:* Multi-project, not only based on technology
iCargo aimed at extending the use of ICT towards synchronization of logistics operations to lower CO_2 emissions	*Similarities*: ICT in port field aimed at exploitation with environmental focus *Differences:* not IoT-based, focused on infrastructure. PIXEL relies on modelling, Big Data, and predictions
e-Freight aimed at an optimal and sustainable utilisation of freight transport resources	*Similarities*: optimization, multimodality in transport and sustainability leveraging digital technologies *Differences*: not IoT-based nor environment-focused

3 PIXEL Proposition

The project has worked in four convergent aspects since its very beginning, with the aim of improving port operations and meeting the requirements of the port of the future: *(i)* enabling technologies; *(ii)* use cases for environmental leverage and process optimization; *(iii)* modelling of environmental aspects of port and city operations; and *(iv)* extendibility, benchmarking and application to other ports or transportation hubs (FIg. 1).

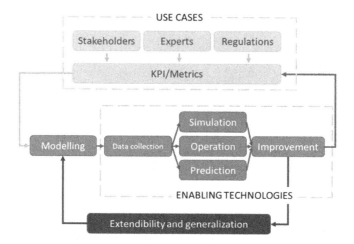

Fig. 1. PIXEL conceptual building blocks

PIXEL uses an ICT-based framework as a basis for the operational data sharing between port agents and advance analytics. Built over state of the art components, it includes new research on this area to satisfy the needs of the project. *(i)* interoperability of document-based management systems with data-centric IoT platforms, *(ii)* pattern recognition from heterogeneous data, *(iii)* prediction algorithms for heterogeneous multi-source data, *(iv)* methodology and software artefacts to allow IoT connectivity to isolated data and *(v)* annotation of environmental and logistic data.

The solution will be validated by applying the developments to improve the energy efficiency of the ports, promote the use of clean energies, improve logistics processes, increase the environmental awareness of all the stakeholders involved and, in general, contribute to reduce the carbon footprint and the environmental impact of the ports and port-related activities. The modelling building block brings simulation capabilities, as well as prediction algorithms implementations. Addressing the environmental part, models enable setting up accurate metrics and what-if cases to represent the different scenarios of the ports, as well as the impact of their operations.

As per theoretical design, the solution explained in this paper is designed to cover every small and medium port scenario. To support this, all the results are designed with the perspective of extendibility, which implies attention to the scalability of resources, architecture allowing third parties participation, excellent communication instructions and use of cutting-edge privacy, authorization and security policies.

4 Technological Baseline

4.1 Reference Architecture

PIXEL achieves the novelties and impacts forecasted by implementing an ICT system capable of gathering every useful data in ports to materialise an automated optimized use of internal and external resources, sustainable economic growth and environmental impact mitigation.

PIXEL challenges such as the establishment of an IoT platform valid for very heterogeneous conditions (different port sizes, different operations, different areas and KPIs (Key Performance Indicator) monitored), makes very appropriate the definition of a reference architecture to keep a common technological and functional blueprint event when the deployments vary and the requirements are in some cases uneven. Furthermore, considering scalability, flexibility and replicability aims, defining a reference architecture for IoT in ports could be fostered if PIXEL is widely adopted after the project. This, in case of achievement, will lay the foundation for a common framework to develop future systems and communications between market players in ports. Finally, the use of a reference architecture provides stability and reliability of the designed solution across multiple scenarios (as is the case in this paper) and throughout the time.

As the genuine disposition for PIXEL architecture is modular, the selection of a reference architecture endears high complexity. With, at least, five different modules to be approached separately (to be later integrated), the number of combinations are more than 1.5 million [7].

There have been a number of proposed architectures, many of them defined in specific contexts and providing solutions to a part of the "world of things". For the construction of PIXEL reference architecture, the study was focused on two of the most relevant current approaches: IIRA [8] and RAMI4.0 [9].

IIRA (Industrial Internet Reference Architecture) is an architecture based on standards designed for IIOT (Industrial-IoT) systems. However, flexibility, scalability and interoperability are not strengths in this approach so after a thorough review it was not selected for the project.

RAMI 4.0 (Referenzarchitekturmodell Industrie 4.0) architecture reference seemed the most appropriate for the project as it defines a service-oriented architecture with high flexibility, in which each of the modules provides services to the other components via a communication protocol across a network. The idea is to divide the architecture into simpler packages easy to realise and focus on their interaction under a SOA (Service Oriented Architecture) schema.

In Fig. 2 there is a relation with the references architectures studied and the modular schema designed for PIXEL. The different modules are explained in Sect. 4.2.

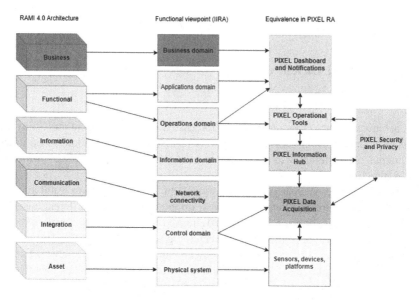

Fig. 2. PIXEL architecture and its equivalents to RAMI and IIRA references.

The following reasons helped determine the choice of RAMI as the reference architecture for PIXEL as well:

- Industrial focus. The applications based on PIXEL are developed in an industrial-like environment (ports). Thus, specific requirements considered in industrial scenarios match better than generic architectures.
- Focus on interoperability: a challenge which is described as a major objective of the project and that will enable the integration of heterogeneous data sources.
- Follows a European initiative that has been implemented in other projects from other domains. This way, the reference architecture of PIXEL will accomplish one of their missions, to make the results more standardized and to be less technology dependent.

4.2 Modules Implementation

After selecting a reference architecture, the project has needed a particular instantiation and design of the different modules. The technical and architectural approach is depicted in Fig. 3.

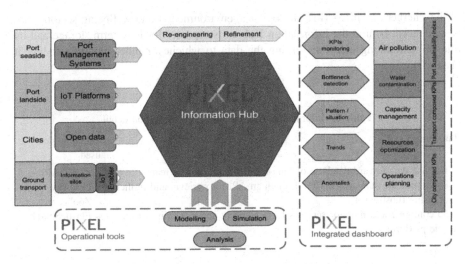

Fig. 3. PIXEL architecture and its modules.

To successfully encompass this system PIXEL leverages some existing technologies in the state of the art and aims at applying them at an innovative field with clear uncertainties. In this section the different modules are analysed: their goal, implementation hints and role within the whole PIXEL solution.

PIXEL Data Acquisition. This module aims at gathering every relevant data of port activities and forwarding it to upper levels of the architecture. The module has been designed and is being developed to collect data from heterogeneous sources: PCS, PMS, SCADA systems, isolated sensors, documentation generators and other different sources. Particularly, for each data source to be included in PIXEL, there is a methodology established that includes the development of an NGSI [10] agent in charge of gathering the data from the source in raw format and upstream it in a formalized data model agreed throughout all the platform. Then, the data is handled by a context broker under a publish-subscribe model. This inner component forms the foundation of data management in PIXEL (Table 2).

Table 2. Data acquisition module implementation detail

Functions	Technologies and concepts used
• To provide a standard way to acquire different data types and protocols • To persist context data • To store short-term historical data	– FIWARE ORION (Context Broker) – Custom data-models inspired on FIWARE data-models – OAuth2 security

PIXEL Information Hub. It is the core element of the architecture, as it constitutes the sink where the different information siloes discharge and store their real-time data. A key innovation potential of this component is underpinned by the fast development of the Internet of Things (IoT) in logistics, environmental and wellbeing sectors. The basic concept behind the Information Hub is its capacity for long-term storage and its role of centralizing element: serving the data to whichever other module needing it (Table 3).

Table 3. Information Hub module implementation detail

Functions	Technologies used
• To push data toward database of long-term storage (downstream) • To prepare the data and serve it through an API for retrieval and further processing (upstream) • To configure and monitor services for scalability and flexibility of the whole platform	– REST API Gateway – Zookeper – ElasticSearch

PIXEL Operational Tools. In PIXEL, several models are elaborated shaping ports' typical processes and applying simulations within the technological infrastructure to be released. To materialise this appliance some Operational Tools are created and executed extracting data from the Information Hub Thus, the role of this module is to bring closer to the user the predictive algorithms and simulation models laying behind the transport-related innovation developed in the project (Table 4).

Table 4. Operational Tools module implementation detail

Functions	Technologies used
• To provide the tools for the UIs associated to each model or predictive algorithm • To execute the models or predictive algorithms • To bring the intelligence to the system To set the analytics capabilities to the user	– Complex Event Processor (CEP) for managing rules, alarms, thresholds – Containerization (Docker) – Custom developments based on microservices and REST APIs

PIXEL Integrated Dashboard. The top modular component of the PIXEL platform contains user-oriented tools. The result of the previous acquisition, modelling, processing and preparation redounds in comprehensible displays for humans to help their decision making. These are composed by monitoring features, KPIs tracking, time evolution of parameters, historic data, reports, forecasting and the rest of capabilities provided by previous layers of the architecture (Table 5).

Table 5. Integrated Dashboard module implementation detail

Functions	Technologies used
• To apply predictive algorithms and models and provide the information to the final user • To calculate a Port Environmental Index • To provide push notifications coming from CEP • Selectable options of visualization for the different agents in the port	– Widget-like interface options – Grafana – Kibana – ElasticSearch – Vue.js

PIXEL Security. Transversally to the other modules, there is a crucial action implemented in the project for ensuring security and sovereignty of the data throughout all the layers. Despite introduced in all components (OAuth), security in PIXEL has its own relevance leveraging top state-of-the art solutions (Table 6).

Table 6. Security module implementation detail

Functions	Technologies used
• Resource access negotiation • Access policies repository • Access policies management	– OAuth 2 – FIWARE KeyRock – FIWARE Vilma

5 Validation Scenarios

The work exposed in this paper is intended to be validated in relevant scenarios with real data. To assess the success of the architecture and its modules and to validate the final product it has to be tested and properly refined. Thus, as it has been mentioned before, the action of the project includes the deployment of several use-cases in four European ports.

The ports selected for this validation fit the required criteria: *(i)* preferred size of ports small-medium (4–15 Mt/year of cargo), *(ii)* ports confronting varying issues related either with data interchange between several agents, city-port questions, environmental impact or any other improvable port operation and *(iii)* providing at least one testbed with greater volume of devices, passengers and operations.

The reader shall realise the need, benefit and assessment traits of every use-case out of the following validation tables created for each scenario that will be undertaken. Besides, respective figures are provided to illustrate the data flow and purpose of the deployments.

5.1 Energy Demand Prediction: Grand Port Maritime de Bordeaux

The Grand Port Maritime de Bordeaux (GPMB) is located on the Atlantic coast, in the city of Bordeaux (France) where the urban-port integration is crucial. It is a focal point of a dense network of communication by river and sea, by air, by rail and by road being a core port of the TEN-T Atlantic Corridor (Table 7).

Table 7. Validation table for Grand Port Maritime de Bordeaux's deployment of PIXEL

Operational and environmental objectives	PIXEL assessment traits targeted
• To adequately dimension the renewable energy networks (especially storage) • To optimize the resources based on the management centered in the self-production • To propose new green policies of energy consumption inside the port • To develop services with over-produced energy • To reduce the carbon footprint impact over the city • To propose innovative strategies for the development of ports through to Big Data analysis	– Development of standard interfaces between PIXEL and PCSs – Interoperability of already existing and new sensors – Implementation of open data exchange mechanisms – Design and execution of predictive algorithms for port traffic evolution – Design and execution of predictive algorithms to estimate the real-time quantity of energy consumed and produced by the port

The Use Case of Grand Port Maritime de Bordeaux shall demonstrate that Port Community Systems are not only regulatory tools: they are communication tools enabling people working in a port to share information and data in order to improve port operations efficiency in a collaborative way (Fig. 4).

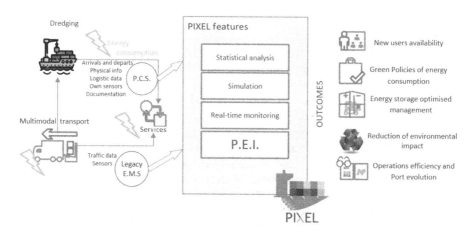

Fig. 4. Grand port maritime de Bordeaux deployment illustration

5.2   Hinterland Intermodal Exchange: Port of Monfalcone

The port of Monfalcone, the authorities of the Friuli Venezia Giulia region, the truck terminal of Gorizia in association with the regional Environment and Health Observatory will use the PIXEL framework to integrate data available in the existing system SILI (Integrated Logistic Information System) in order to share data and cooperate with other stakeholders for operational and planning activities (Table 8 and Fig. 5).

Table 8. Validation table for Port of Monfalcone's deployment of PIXEL

Operational and environmental objectives	PIXEL assessment traits targeted
• Better road planning to reduce urban and extra urban traffic • Providing a better distribution of the waste costs • Monitoring and re-routing of dangerous goods • Reduction of CO_2 emissions and acoustic pollution in port surrounding areas • Disposition of tools to improve the correlation between air pollution and specific diseases • Creating synergies with the other players of the surrounding areas	– Multi-agent inter-modality integration – Integration with SILI system – Algorithms calculating impact and predictive algorithms – Data gathering coming from video-surveillance cameras – Dangerous goods and other environmental hazardous aspects dealt with

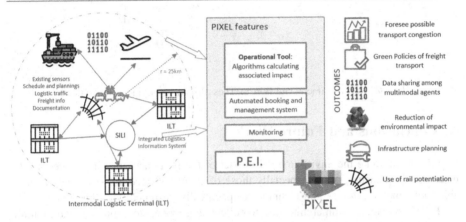

Fig. 5. Port of Monfalcone deployment illustration

5.3 Port-City Integration: The Ports of Piraeus and Thessaloniki

The port city integration validation scenario will be tested in two Greek ports (Thessaloniki and Piraeus), the rationale behind using two ports for the pilots is that in the first the deployment is focused on goods/containers and in the second in passengers. Additionally, Piraeus pilot will be used to evaluate and measure scalability. Both ports are key in the traffic in the area and in the corresponding TEN-T corridors (Table 9).

Table 9. Validation table for Port of Thessaloniki's and Piraeus' deployment of PIXEL

Operational and environmental objectives	PIXEL assessment traits targeted
• Improvement of the access to the seaport Mitigation of traffic-related impacts on the environment • Facilitate transport intramodality in passenger traffic • Incorporate innovative approaches to overcome bottlenecks in the transportation net-work creation of a positive awareness of sustainable transportation methods	– Integration of PCS, PMS, TOS and new installed sensors both environmental and traffic-related – Design and execution of models for air and noise pollution calculation and prediction – Design and execution of predictive algorithms about traffic congestion

To incorporate technological components and harmonise the Greek Ports use-case with the global PIXEL system an effort will be made to homogeneise and integrate data from several software sources (Fig. 6).

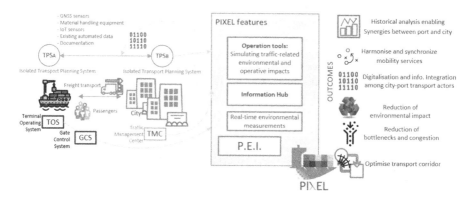

Fig. 6. Port of Piraeus and Port of Thessaloniki deployment illustration

6   Conclusions and Future Work

In order to mitigate the environmental impact of the ports activities it is necessary to measure. To measure, ports (especially those of small and medium size) need action-able tools, methodologies and technology specifically designed with this aim.

PIXEL has realised an architecture to collect, aggregate, store, process and monitor operational and environmental data to provide additional value to port agents.

The project has scheduled the deployment of that architecture in four European ports for the next months. Therefore, the near future work will be focused on evolving the developments from a laboratory prototype into a relevant environment demon-strated product. These actions will allow evaluating the performance and appropri-ateness of the solution.

Furthermore, the ICT solution will be explored to be deployed in new small, medium and big European ports. A robust assessment of its technical and business-related performance is also planned to be conducted in the middle term. The rationale behind the forthcoming actions is to bring innovation and useful ICT equipment to ports aiming at digitalization and environmental impact reduction. With aims of European market validation, a sound strategy will be followed, as well, targeting real impact of PIXEL to the port community. Different entities and experts will be addressed for achieving this validation.

Regarding new research lines drawing from PIXEL, they are diverse. The Con-sortium of the project is conducting a specific task devoted to envisioning how PIXEL developments can be continued and which other technologies and methodologies can be integrated in the future in the solution. For the moment, technologies such as: 5G, advanced cloud processing, edge computing and blockchain for security are thought to be feasibly embeddable. About logistics theory and optimisation purposes, PIXEL might be extended to investigate on mobility management, soil environmental models, synchro-modality and deeper traffic prediction, among others.

Acknowledgements. This work is part of PIXEL project that has received funding from the European Union's Horizon 2020 research and innovation programme under grant agreement No 769355.

References

1. EUROSTAT: European Commission; Maritime Transport of Goods, June 2019
2. Deltares-WWF: Port of the Future Exploratory Study (2017)
3. EcoPorts: Port of the Future Sector. CONFERENCE 2017, Green Energy Ports Conference (2017)
4. Puig, M., Darbra, R.M..: World Seas: An Environmental Evaluation, 2nd edn. Volume III: Ecological Issues and Environmental Impacts, Chapter 31, pp. 593–611 (2019)
5. Celtinkaya, B., Cuthbertson, R., et al.: Sustainable Supply Chain Management, Practical Ideas For Moving Towards Best Practice, p. 264. Springer, Heidelberg (2011). https://doi.org/10.1007/978-3-642-12023-7
6. CORDIS – PIXEL project. https://cordis.europa.eu/project/rcn/214640/factsheet/en
7. Perry, L.: Internet of Things for Architects: IoT Architecture and Core IoT Modules, pp. 26–38. Packt Publishing Ltd, Birmingham (2018)
8. Industrial Internet Consortium, IIRA. https://www.iiconsortium.org/IIRA-1.7.htm
9. Schweichhart, K.: Reference Architectural Model Industrie 4.0 (RAMI 4.0), Leader (act.) (2016)

Adaptive Application Deployment of Priority Services in Virtual Environments

Jesus Carretero$^{(\boxtimes)}$, Mario Vasile-Cabezas, and Victor Sosa

Computer Science and Engineering Department,
University Carlos III of Madrid, Madrid, Spain
jesus.carretero@uc3m.es

Abstract. This paper introduces an adaptive application deployment service for virtualized environments (named DECIDE). This service facilitates the definition of customized cluster/cloud environment and the adaptive integration of scheduling policies for testing and deploying containerized applications. The service-based design of DECIDE and the use of a virtualized environment makes it possible to easily change the cluster/cloud configuration and its scheduling policy. It provides a differentiated service for application deployment based on priorities, according to user requirements. A prototype of this service was implemented using Apache MESOS and Docker. As a proof of concept, a federated application for electronic identification (eIDAS) was deployed using the DECIDE approach, which allows users to evaluate different deployment scenarios and scheduling policies providing useful information for decision making. Experiments were carried out to validate service functionality and the feasibility for testing and deploying applications that require different scheduling policies.

Keywords: Application deployment · Resource management · Application scheduling

1 Introduction

Virtualization technologies provide a way to share resources and to create portable, scalable and elastic applications [1]. Virtual machines facilitate the dynamic building of clusters or clouds. Containers are a lightweight virtualization technique that has demonstrated to be a scalable and high-performance alternative to virtual machines for a more portable and faster deploying of applications [14][?]. Apache Mesos [7] is a resource manager that provides a two-level scheduling mechanism. Mesos slaves (agents) report to master the amount of free resources they can provide and master decides how many resources to offer to the framework, i.e., the system that manages and executes applications. The decisions about which application should receive the next resource offer is based on the Dominant Resource Fairness (DRF) algorithm [3], which is a solution to the problem of fair resource allocation in a system sharing different resources (cpu,

© Springer Nature Switzerland AG 2019
R. Montella et al. (Eds.): IDCS 2019, LNCS 11874, pp. 46–56, 2019.
https://doi.org/10.1007/978-3-030-34914-1_5

memory, storage, etc). However, applications like the federated electronic identification system presented in [2] require a different treatment, where resource fairness is not the main concern. Mesos allows customizing its scheduling module, what motivated us to implement DECIDE. The main contributions of this paper are: (a) design and implementation of a web-based application deployment service (DECIDE) that facilitates the creation of customized cluster or cloud scenarios; (b) implementation of an adaptive deployment service based on user requirements; and (c) prototype of a federated electronic identification system that demonstrates the feasibility of using the DECIDE service and its benefits.

This paper is structured as follows, Sect. 2 presents related work, Sect. 3 introduces the DECIDE architecture and its adaptive deployment algorithm. Section 4 describes our use case. Section 5 depicts experiments and obtained results and Sect. 6 presents conclusions.

2   Related Work

Nowadays, new platforms for resource sharing in virtualized cluster or clouds, such as Mesos, DC/OS (Mesosphere), Kubernetes and Swarm have arisen. Scheduling is a fundamental part that determines quality of service aspects such as response time, availability, service continuity, etc. Mesos [6] is a platform for sharing commodity clusters between multiple diverse cluster computing frameworks, such as Hadoop and MPI. Mesos manages resources, but delegates control over scheduling to the frameworks using a decentralized scheduling model. Mesos resource allocation is called Hierarchical DRF and it is based on online dominant resource fairness (DRF) [7], which provides fairness with dynamic resource partitioning harmonizing the execution of heterogeneous workloads (in terms of resource demand) by maximizing the sharing of resources. The major problem with this policy is that a mistake in the allocation of mandatory resources could leave a high number of tasks pending [5] for an indeterministic duration, which is not possible in prioritized system with some quality of service. DC/OS is a distributed system, cluster manager, container platform, and an operating system [11]. It includes two built-in task schedulers, Marathon (applications) and Metronomo (jobs), and two container runtimes (Docker and Mesos). Docker is a Linux based lightweight container that allows different applications to run isolated from each other but safely share the machine's resources [15]. Docker provides a good basis to run composite applications in the cloud. Therefore, a number of tools emerged that claim to solve the problem. The paper [10] classifies the solutions to deploy a container management solution for multiple hosts and presents they own suite. One possible solution to provide complex environment is to manage dockers using Mesos, as shown in [13]. Kubernetes is an open-source platform created by Google for container deployment operations [4]. It wraps one or more containers into a higher-level structure called a pod, wherein resources are shared. Its scheduler ensures that pods are only placed on nodes that have sufficient free resources. Swarm [9] is an open-source container platform that is the native Docker clustering engine. Swarm turns a pool of Docker hosts into a virtual, single host. Swarm has a single scheduling strategy, called spread, which attempts to schedule a task based on an assessment of the resources available on cluster nodes. Most of the frameworks look for fairness in resource allocation [8], which can be contradictory with a strict priority scheduling policy. Our proposal faces this problem, that we have not seen solved in the literature.

3 Adaptive Deployment of Priority Services in Virtual Environments

This section presents the architecture and algorithm of our proposal of an adaptive application deployment service for virtual environments named DECIDE.

3.1 Architecture and Tools

We have developed a prototype of DECIDE as an upper layer of a Mesos cluster with a virtualized environment supported by Docker. However, our service-based architecture, shown in Fig. 1, allows to use a different cluster environment, for example Kubernetes [1]. The components of DECIDE are: (1) Web-based manager to configure Mesos clusters and to instantiate frameworks in the virtual environment; (2) adaptive deployment service with different scheduling policies which is integrated as framework of Mesos; and (3) application manager to instantiate containers (applications) according to the deployment policies. The most important tools used are: (a) Apache Mesos to manage cluster resources; (b) Dockers as a container platform for deploying applications; (c) Apache Zoo Keeper to provide fault tolerance; (d) HTML5+CSS3+JS (front-end) and Go language (back-end) to develop the deployment services manager and the client simulator.

The 6 main steps (see Fig. 1) to deploy applications are: (1) execution of the web-based interface for user to select the cluster/cloud nodes that comprise the virtualized environment; (2) reading the configuration file that will be sent to MESOS for setting the node roles (MESOS master, agent and Apache Zookeeper); (3) selection of an available scheduling policy; (4) selection of the applications configuration to be sent into MESOS; (5) reading of the previous application configuration profiles to download the container images into the cluster/cloud; and (6) scheduler execution until the whole workload is over.

3.2 Algorithm

The adaptive deployment service includes a generic framework implemented as a decoupled framework of Mesos (Mesos scheduler). The scheduling algorithm determines the order in which applications will be deployed in the containarized infrastructure (Mesos + Docker) according to the scheduling policy configured. The generic framework can be updated to modify the scheduling policy according to the applications requirements. The current prototype of DECIDE includes the

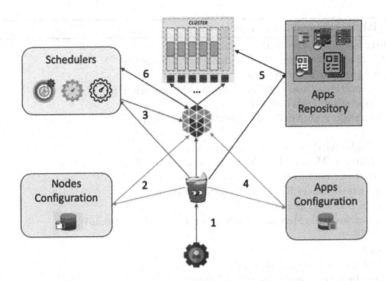

Fig. 1. General architecture of the adaptive deployment service

following scheduling policies: Preemptive Priority and FCFS (First Come First Served). In the current prototype, load balancing strategies were associated to scheduling policies to distribute the workload into the resources offered by Mesos.

For FCFS, Round-Robin load balancing is used and for preemptive priority, resource usage information will be the main indicator, giving always resources first to high priority applications pending.

Algorithm 1 shows the general steps carried out by our deployment service. The external loop in the algorithm verifies that the configured scheduler is a registered Mesos framework. The scheduler waits for the arrival of new application deployment requests or for a signal from Mesos to manage applications. The function $getNextTaskWithHighestPriority()$ returns the next task to be executed depending on the scheduler registered. If it is FCFS, it will return the task in the head of the scheduler queue. If it is using priorities, it will return the task in the head of the highest priority queue that is not empty. This function has an adaptive behavior depending on the scheduling algorithm configured. The internal loop creates a queue of tasks (containerized applications) that will be deployed considering the number of instances required. The deployment service will carry out the load balancing strategy associated to the scheduling policy using the *load-Balancer: RegisterServer* function. The service-based design of DECIDE allows to integrate a component to provide elasticity to the deployed applications. The current prototype of DECIDE does not include this component. However, our use case application implements a manager service that carries out this function. In this way, if all existing servers are saturated, a new server is instantiated, up to the maximum number defined in the application manager is reached. Initially a minimum number of instances defined in the framework are created.

Algorithm 1. Scheduling algorithm

Input: Enqueued applications (tasks)
Output: successful enqueued or deployed applications
1 **while** *SchedulerRegistered* **do**
2   t = waitForaTask() OR availableTaskMesosSignal();
3   enqueueNewTask(tasks,t);
4   nextTask = getNextTaskWithHighestPriority();
5   i = 0;
6   var scheduledTasks = []MesosTasks;
7   **while** *len(Mesos.offeredNodes) < nextTask.Instances AND i < nextTask.Instances* **do**
8   loadBalancer.RegisterServer(nextTask);
9   scheduledTasks [i] = createTask(Mesos.offeredNodes[i],nextTask.Command);
10   i++;
11   **end**
12   deployTasks(scheduledTasks);
13   nextTask.Instances = nextTask.Instances - i;
14   **if** *nextTask.Instances > 0* **then**
15   enqueueTask(tasks,nextTask);
16   **end**
17 **end**

After the internal loop, tasks are deployed. If there are still pending tasks in the request because there were not enough available nodes, they will be enqueued again to be scheduled in the next round. Thus, we can avoid discarding tasks due to a temporary lack of resources.

4   Use Case: European Identity Federation Initiative

The Regulation (EU) 910/2014 [12], the so-called eIDAS Regulation, which is in force in all Member States since the end of 2018, ensures that people and businesses can use their own national electronic identification schemes (eIDs) to access public services in other EU countries where eIDs are available. To implement this system, a federation consisting of a network of eIDAS nodes has been deployed, one per member state, which has the role of Identity Provider for the national electronic identification scheme (eID) from any other country. All Service Providers participating in the network must be subscribed to the eIDAS Node of their country. This is a very ambitious approach, since it enables crossborder authentication of Member States citizens without the need to unify the authentication method (eID Scheme) of the member states participating in the Identity Federation. A detailed description of a previous evaluation of the eIDAS system is shown in [2]. The eIDAS nodes apply FCFS scheduling policy to serve client requests, as it assumes that all requests will have the same priority, which may be not truth in the near future. This is why we have decided to evaluate the eIDAS service applying also a priority-based scheduling as use case.

5   Evaluation

This section presents the evaluation of our deployment service using the eIDAS network use case.

5.1   Experiments Description

To test our proposal, eIDAS Manager, that uses the scheduler to send allocate resources and execute eIDAS nodes in Mesos. We have defined a test scenario as described in Fig. 2. All clients are created in a single node and they send requests to our eIDAS Manager, which uses the deployment framework to allocate and execute eIDAS servers in Mesos.

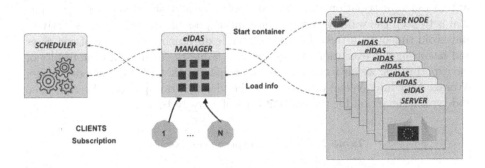

Fig. 2. Architectural view of clients and servers in the experimental scenario

The service has been deployed in the cluster defined in Table 1. The system has been implemented using Dockers on Linux OS. Several dockers are started at the beginning of the system depending on the configuration parameters. The number of dockers evolves with the load following the scheduling policy. Load is distributed among the cluster nodes. Each client requesting for an electronic identification (eID) starts a protocol including 12 messages between the different components of the eIDAS network. Because of consistency and security restrictions, each client request must be managed by the instance of the eIDAS node accepting it, but, in case of preemption, the client can be stopped between two messages. For these experiments, a maximum of 64 simultaneous servers can be instantiated, a parameter that we have defined as a limitation in the MESOS resources. In the case of the scheduling with priorities, we segment users into three groups of priorities, **high, medium, low**. The allocation of priority follows a uniform distribution, so that they subscribe to the server destinations with the same probability.

Table 1. Features of the experimental environment

Feature	Compute 11	Compute 7
Application	eIDAS servers	eIDAS Manager and clients
Nodes	5	1
RAM	128 GB	128 GB
CPU	Xeon E5-2603 v4 12 cores	XeonE7-4807 24 cores
Network	Ethernet 10 Gbps	Ethernet 10 Gbps
HDD	1 TB	1 TB

Two scenarios have been tested (see Table 2), both processing 3750 eID client requests. Every eIDAS client is associated to an eIDAS server that serves its requests. In scenario A, FCFS policy is applied and the eIDAS manager associates a client to an eIDAS server using a Round Robin approach to distribute the load across the servers. In scenario B, priority scheduling is applied and system usage information is used to dynamically allocate server resources. The goal is to keep the waiting time as constant as possible, to enhance interactivity and avoid timeouts in the eID protocol, while optimizing the usage of resources and favouring the execution of high priority requests. To measure the results of the experiments, we have chosen the following metrics: CPU and memory usage; Average time and typical deviation for the identification process; Average time and typical deviation for the waiting time of a ready ID request.

Table 2. Evaluation experiments executed.

Scenario	Scheduler	eIDAS servers	Clients
A	FCFS and Round Robin	up to 64	3750
B	Priorities and node usage	up to 64	3750

5.2 Experiments Results

Scenario A. The scheduler (MESOS framework) has a single queue using FCFS policy. The eIDAS Manager allocates the requests and instantiates resources using Mesos taking the first eID requests in the queue (FCFS) and applying a Round-Robin load balancing policy for all requests, as quality of service is not enforced by the scheduler. Figure 3 shows the CPU and memory usage in every cluster node when executing 3750 clients. eIDAS servers were deployed in Compute 11-2, 11-4, 11-5, 11-6 and 11-7 nodes, while eIDAS manager and clients were deployed in Compute 7-2 node. As may be seen, the distribution of load is mostly uniform across the server nodes, even if two are more loaded. Table 3 shows the time metrics during the experiment. The total execution time for the test is 280 s. In this scenario, eID clients had a low waiting time with a reasonable execution time (Aver. Id time). The maximum number of simultaneous clients processed by the 64 eIDAS servers, before discarding requests, was around 4000. The worst-case execution time (WCET) of a client eID request was 25.17 s for any request.

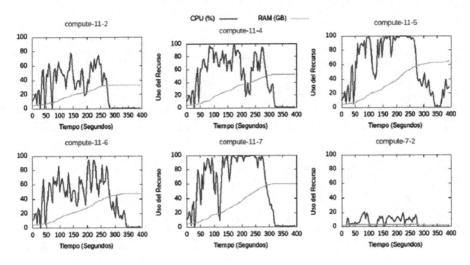

Fig. 3. CPU and memory usage with scenario A

Table 3. Scenario A. Time metrics with FCFS (all time in sec.)

Priority	Aver. wait time	Typical deviation	Aver. Id time	Typical deviation
FCFS	3.21	1.75	18.07	2,14

Scenario B. In this scenario, the scheduler uses priority policy based on one queue per priority (low, medium, high). The eIDAS manager takes the first eID requests in the highest priority queue available and uses resource information provided by Mesos to start dynamically the servers. Figure 4 shows the CPU and memory usage in every node to execute 3750 clients. As may be seen, load distribution changes in the nodes due to the distribution per priority. Again, the node running the eIDAS manager and clients has a negligible load, being able to receive many more client requests. The manager could send the 3750 client requests to the Mesos frameworks, even though the CPU load on some nodes was very high. Memory was not overloaded in any node. The total execution time for the test was 350 s. Table 4 shows how the waiting time is low for high and medium priority clients, as desired, but it is higher for low priority requests. With this policy, the worst-case execution time (WCET) of a high-priority client eID request was 13.73 s. Preemption effect can be appreciated in the execution time, which is higher for lower priority clients, because they are removed from the system when high priority clients arrives and there are not free resources. Obviously, this strict priority policy could lead to starvation of low priority clients, but we are assuming that this fact comes with the policy. To avoid this problem, aging could be applied to clients in low priority queues.

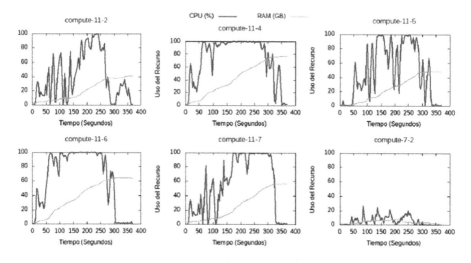

Fig. 4. CPU and memory usage with scenario A

Table 4. Scenario B. Time metrics per priority queue (all time in sec.)

Priority	Aver. wait time	Typical deviation	Aver. Id time	Typical deviation
High	2.83	1.03	8.00	2.87
Medium	3.31	1.72	13.11	2.87
Low	55.15	1.40	20.43	1.2

6   Conclusion

We introduced DECIDE, an adaptive application deployment service for virtualized environments, which provides: (a) a tool to facilitate the setup of customized cluster/cloud environments and the deployment of applications in resource sharing platforms as Mesos; (b) a scheduling and deployment framework for a differentiated services according to user requirements; and (c) a tool for testing different scheduling policies to evaluate their convenience for applications. Setting up a cluster and a framework dedicated to run a distributed application can be a tedious and time consuming work. Mesos is a solution for sharing resources of a cluster where different frameworks can be executed. However, Mesos applies a fairness scheduling policy without considering special needs of applications that require a prioritized access. However, our use case eIDAS might require a different scheduling policy where fairness is not the main requirement. DECIDE is a solution for this type of limitations, providing a polymorphic framework on Mesos to deploy applications using a scheduling policy dynamically selected by users. Experiments demonstrated the DECIDE functionality and its feasibility of use. Future research directions will be to enhance low-priority requests response times and extending the solution to other applications and policies.

Acknowledgments. This work was partially funded by the Spanish Ministry of Economy, Industry and Competitiveness under the grant TIN2016-79637-P "Towards Unification of HPC and Big Data Paradigms".

References

1. Bernstein, D.: Containers and cloud: from LXC to docker to kubernetes. IEEE Cloud Comput. **1**(3), 81–84 (2014)
2. Carretero, J., Izquierdo-Moreno, G., Vasile-Cabezas, M., Garcia-Blas, J.: Federated identity architecture of the european eID system. IEEE Access **6**, 75302–75326 (2018)
3. Ghodsi, A., Zaharia, M., Hindman, B., Konwinski, A., Shenker, S., Stoica, I.: Dominant resource fairness: fair allocation of multiple resource types. In: NSDI, vol. 11, pp. 24–24 (2011)
4. Google: Kubernetes cluster configuration. https://kubernetes.io/docs/user-journeys/users/application-developer/foundational/
5. Greenberg, D.: Building Applications on Mesos: Leveraging Resilient, Scalable, and Distributed Systems. O'Reilly Media, Inc., Newton (2015)
6. Hindman, B., et al.: Mesos: a platform for fine-grained resource sharing in the data center. In: NSDI, vol. 11, p. 22 (2011)
7. Kakadia, D.: Apache Mesos Essentials. Packt Publishing Ltd., Birmingham (2015)
8. Kesidis, G., Shan, Y., Jain, A., Urgaonkar, B., Khamse-Ashari, J., Lambadaris, I.: Scheduling distributed resources in heterogeneous private clouds. In: 2018 IEEE 26th International Symposium on Modeling, Analysis, and Simulation of Computer and Telecommunication Systems (MASCOTS), pp. 102–108. IEEE (2018)
9. Naik, N.: Building a virtual system of systems using Docker Swarm in multiple clouds. In: 2016 IEEE International Symposium on Systems Engineering (ISSE), pp. 1–3. IEEE (2016)
10. Peinl, R., Holzschuher, F., Pfitzer, F.: Docker cluster management for the cloud - survey results and own solution. J. Grid Comput. **14**(2), 265–282 (2016). https://doi.org/10.1007/s10723-016-9366-y
11. Puetm, A.: Mesosphere: DC/OS distributed cloud operating system, June 2019. https://dcos.io/
12. EU Regulation: No 910/2014 of the European Parliament and of the Council of 23 July 2014 on electronic identification and trust services for electronic transactions in the internal market and repealing Directive 1999/93/EC (eIDAS Regulation). European Union, pp. 44–59 (2014)

13. Saha, P., Govindaraju, M., Marru, S., Pierce, M.: Integrating apache airavata with docker, marathon, and mesos. Concurr. Comput.: Pract. Exp. **28**(7), 1952–1959 (2016)
14. Soltesz, S., Potzl, H., Fiuczynski, M., Bavier, A., Peterson, L.: Container-based operating system virtualization: a scalable, high-performance alternative to hypervisors. SIGOPS Oper. Syst. Rev. **43**(3), 275–287 (2007)
15. Turnbull, J.: The Docker Book: Containerization is the New Virtualization (2014)

An Adaptive Restart Mechanism
for Continuous Epidemic Systems

Mosab M. Ayiad and Giuseppe Di Fatta[⊠]

Department of Computer Science, University of Reading,
Whiteknights, Reading, Berkshire RG6 6AY, UK
{mosab.ayiad,g.difatta}@reading.ac.uk

Abstract. Software services based on large-scale distributed systems demand continuous and decentralised solutions for achieving system consistency and providing operational monitoring. Epidemic data aggregation algorithms provide decentralised, scalable and fault-tolerant solutions that can be used for system-wide tasks such as global state determination, monitoring and consensus. Existing continuous epidemic algorithms either periodically restart at fixed epochs or apply changes in the system state instantly producing less accurate approximation. This work introduces an innovative mechanism without fixed epochs that monitors the system state and restarts upon the detection of the system convergence or divergence. The mechanism makes correct aggregation with an approximation error as small as desired. The proposed solution is validated and analysed by means of simulations under static and dynamic network conditions.

Keywords: Distributed computing · Continuous systems ·
Decentralised aggregation · Epidemic protocols · Node churn

1 Introduction

Network services in large-scale distributed systems often require decentralised solutions for monitoring system-wide state and maintaining its consistency. For example, an online service where participants join and leave independently of the service may need to track the number of active participants to successfully complete a specific task [1]. Also, distributed applications for unmanned vehicles may repeatedly attempt to coordinate a universal speed limit to optimise system performance or to avoid catastrophic scenarios [2]. In Wireless Sensor Networks (WSN), devices frequently collect data from their sensors and require to have a view of the network with fresh aggregated information [3]. Recent trends in Edge computing have considered moving Cloud services away from centralised computation and data centres towards the edges of the network: Edge computing can benefit from decentralised monitoring and processing capabilities [4]. Distributed consensus protocols enable decentralisation in Blockchain [5] and ensure that all participants collectively maintain a common transaction ledger

© Springer Nature Switzerland AG 2019
R. Montella et al. (Eds.): IDCS 2019, LNCS 11874, pp. 57–68, 2019.
https://doi.org/10.1007/978-3-030-34914-1_6

without a central authority: these protocols also require a robust and continuous adaptation to changes in the system conditions.

Epidemic protocols are based on a Peer-to-Peer (P2P) paradigm for decentralised communication and computation in large and extreme-scale distributed systems. They adopt randomised communication models inspired by biological systems, which have natural diffusion properties [6]. In general, applications may incorporate one or more epidemic algorithms to implement a desired service and forming a single *epidemic system* for a particular task. Epidemic systems are typically adopted for two main tasks: (1) *information dissemination* and (2) *data aggregation*. In a dissemination task, information that is in the interest of other participants is propagated in the system, e.g., information of updates and failures [7,8]. A data aggregation task uses the epidemic diffusion process to compute a global synopsis of a distributed set of data values. Data aggregation tasks are fundamental for a wide range of services, especially in computing global system properties, e.g., for estimating system size and for resource monitoring [1,3]. Moreover, they can be used as components of more complex applications, such as failure detection [8], distributed data mining [9], system consistency and global consensus [7].

Theoretical and practical analyses have shown stochastic guarantees on the convergence to the desired target of stable epidemic systems [6,7]. Achieving and detecting convergence is critical for many services: for example, it is a prerequisite for actions such as *termination* and *restart* [1,10]. Moreover, real-world systems are generally asynchronous and highly dynamic. Nodes can have arbitrary start times and non-simultaneous processing cycles [7]. Also, nodes usually have access to different clocks, encounter variable communication delays and may lose messages or message order. In dynamic systems, nodes can join and leave arbitrarily (a.k.a 'Node Churn') [10], and may suddenly fail or become unreachable [1].

Node churn and unreliable networks have a detrimental effect on the efficiency and the robustness of epidemic systems [10,11]. In extreme case, the inherent properties of the epidemic systems cannot be guaranteed: tasks may not converge or may converge to incorrect results. Therefore, it is essential to maintain a robust and consistent state at any time for a system to remain operational and predictable. Through constant restarting, an epidemic system can monitor its global state and achieve distributed consistency. Conventional continuous epidemic systems typically use a restart mechanism at fixed time intervals, i.e. *epochs* [1], which may unnecessarily penalise the performance or may not provide sufficient guarantees on the convergence. Some epoch-less techniques provide imprecise approximations and may take a long time for adapting the system to the correct state [3,12,13].

The work in this paper introduces a novel epidemic algorithm with an adaptive restart mechanism. The mechanism restarts an epidemic task upon the detection of convergence or divergence in autonomous and variant epochs. Also, the mechanism ensures correct convergence to the target for all nodes through aggregating nodes decisions and acquiring *consensus* on the restart action. Moreover, the mechanism is lightweight producing small communication overhead, which can be piggybacked on existing protocol messages.

The paper is organised as follows. The model of epidemic systems is described in the next section. In particular, the data aggregation process and the seed selection method are discussed in Sect. 2.1. Section 2.2 describes the intrinsic convergence property of epidemic algorithms and the common methods for detecting local and global convergence. Section 2.3 addresses convergence detection under dynamic network conditions. The proposed algorithm and the restart mechanism are described in Sect. 3. Experimentations and results are presented in Sect. 4. Finally, Sect. 5 lists some related work and Sect. 6 provides conclusive remarks.

2 The Model of Epidemic Systems

An epidemic system consists of a large number of nodes N, connected to a network infrastructure (e.g., the Internet), which cooperate by exchanging messages to provide a system-wide decentralised service. Each node is assigned a unique identifier and communicates with random peers that are selected uniformly from the system (a.k.a *uniform gossip* [6]). The *Node Cache Protocol* (NCP) [14] is a simple peer-sampling service adopted for the purpose of this work, although any other membership protocol with better properties can be used (e.g., [10]).

In this work the epidemic protocols adopt the asynchronous model of '*Symmetric Push-Sum Protocol*' (SPSP) [14]. The model is a non-atomic PUSH-PULL scheme that does not lock waiting for a response after sending a PUSH message. Message order is not guaranteed and message interleaving can be present [10]. Protocols generate a PUSH message in each '*Cycle*'. Cycles are time intervals of fixed length $\mathcal{T}$ that are typically set to be greater of the Round Trip Time (RTT) on the diameter of the network. The parameter $\mathcal{T}$ is sufficient for the delivery of most messages within a cycle [1,7,14]. Moreover, subsequent cycles may overlap among various nodes as global cycle synchronisation is not enforced.

The transport protocol is assumed reliable (e.g., TCP); this limits failure types to node churn. Churn is a collective behaviour in a system where new nodes join and existing nodes depart at arbitrary times. The voluntary or adversary departure of nodes is not specified and both cases are treated as generic node failure. Although new nodes can join the system at any time, they do not participate in the current cycle of the ongoing epidemic task: they start contributing in the following cycle [1]. The fractions of joined and departed nodes in a specific time interval define the churn rates. The distribution of churn rates over time intervals is not assumed constant and there must be a time at which the system is sufficiently stable to allow convergence.

2.1 Data Aggregation and Seed Selection

The proposed restart mechanism and many epidemic systems require global data aggregation and, in particular, the global sum of a distributed set of numeric attributes or measurements. Each node i holds a local data value x_i and for this task it initialises and updates a local tuple τ_i to perform a global aggregation process on the distributed values $\{x_i, 0 < i \leq N\}$. Let τ_i be $\langle \varsigma_i, v_i, w_i \rangle$, where v_i is initialised with x_i, w_i is the weight element of the tuple and ς_i is an identifier further described below. The initialisation of the weights determine the aggregation function. For global summation, the initial weights follows a peak distribution [6,14]. At the start time t_0, it is required to set $w_{\hat{i},t_0} = 1$ at a single node $\hat{i}$ (*seed node*), and $w_{i,t_0} = 0$ at all other nodes. The determination of the seed node $\hat{i}$ in a real-world decentralised system is challenging and requires a leader election step.

To overcome this initialisation issue, we introduce a seed selection method as follows. The tuple identifier ς is used as '*seed*' selector. The seed is a Unique Universal Identifier (UUID) generated by a global function $\mathcal{F}()$. There are two implementations of the function $\mathcal{F}$ used in this work. $\mathcal{F}_\alpha(i,t)$ which computes a UUID given a node identifier i and the current time t. The output of $\mathcal{F}_\alpha(i,t)$ preserves the natural order, such that for any two UUIDs: $U_i = \mathcal{F}_\alpha(i,t_i)$ and $U_j = \mathcal{F}_\alpha(j,t_j)$, $U_i < U_j$, $\iff t_i < t_j \vee t_i = t_j \wedge i < j$. On the other hand, the function $\mathcal{F}_\beta(i)$ generates a random UUID.

Initially, all nodes are seed nodes and the tuple τ_i in each node i is initialised to $\tau_i = \langle \mathcal{F}(), x_i, 1 \rangle$, where each ς_{i,t_0} identifies a unique seed in the system. The initial diffusion process selects only one seed in the system for this epoch. During the diffusion process, seeds propagate in the system following a random-walk fashion and each node performs a selection operation. Apart from the seed initialisation, the data aggregation process is based on SPSP [14].

2.2   Convergence Detection

In epidemic systems for information dissemination or data aggregation, local convergence is achieved when the local states of nodes have reached the desired target within a marginal error. In dissemination tasks, nodes achieve and detect convergence by receiving a copy of a particular information item [7]. In aggregation tasks, each node holds a local value, such as a local attribute or measurement. The data aggregation process aims at computing a numeric target value $\mathcal{V}$ at every node, which corresponds to some global synopsis function (e.g., *average*, *sum*, *max*, *sample*, etc.) over the distributed set of local values. During the epidemic process each node i updates a local estimate $e_{i,t}$ of $\mathcal{V}$ at every cycle t. The convergence process corresponds to a reduction in the variance of the local estimates. Eventually, all nodes converge to the target value when the local estimation error $\varepsilon_{i,t}$ is smaller than a global *tolerance threshold* ϵ [1,6,14].

Methods for local detection of convergence in aggregation processes are heuristic and require application-specific parameters. In a general method [1,14,15], each node i computes the estimation error $\varepsilon_{i,t} = \frac{|e_{i,t} - \mathcal{V}|}{\mathcal{V}}$, and verifies the criterion $\varepsilon_{i,t} < \epsilon$. The method also counts the number of consecutive cycles (Υ) in which the criterion is verified. The parameter Υ is used to avoid a precocious detection of convergence, which may be caused by the fluctuation of $e_{i,t}$. However, this method requires some a priori global knowledge of the target value $\mathcal{V}$. Typically, this information is unavailable or hard to obtain in real-world conditions: it is ultimately the goal of the epidemic process. The method in [7,16] uses a technique based on the moving-average on local and remote estimates in order to approximate the target value and the estimation error. This approach is adopted in this work to compute the Standard Error (SE). SE does not require the correct target and provides less uncertainty in error measurements around the mean in comparison to other statistical measures.

In addition to the local detection of convergence, the detection of *global convergence* may also be required in some epidemic systems [7,15]. Global convergence is needed for acquiring local awareness on the convergence of other nodes, and it is usually achieved through a poll-alike process, in which every node places a vote after the occurrence of a local event (e.g., detection of local convergence). Ultimately, the poll result at each node provides certainty on the occurrence of the event in other nodes. This technique is applied for achieving consensus for global synchronisation in the proposed restart mechanism.

2.3   Convergence Detection Under Churn

Although epidemic processes are intrinsically fault-tolerant thanks to redundancy and the lack of single points of failures, the system dynamics can have a detrimental impact on the data aggregation process due to the violation of the *'mass conservation'* invariant [6,11,14]. The mass refers to the ideal aggregate of the initial values of all nodes in the system, which has to be conserved at all times for the formal correctness of the aggregation process. Previous work [11] has shown that under dynamic conditions, the accuracy of local estimates cannot be guaranteed, leading to an incorrect convergence: results may significantly differ from the true target due to the violation of system mass. Nevertheless, convergence to or divergence from the correct target can still be detected under some moderate churn conditions. In this work, the proposed solution can detect the violation of the system mass invariant to validate or invalidate the aggregation results at convergence.

3   The Adaptive Restart Mechanism

Algorithm 1 is a continuous epidemic process that runs over sequential epochs, where each epoch has an incremental global identifier (ι). The epoch is the restart interval, and two subsequent epoch identifiers may exist in the system for some time after restart. Nodes are enforced to join the epoch with the higher identifier. Epoch length is variant and depends on the detection of convergence or divergence. The algorithm consists of several aggregation processes, sequential and parallel. The process $\mathcal{A}$ corresponds to the intended objective of the epidemic task. The process $\mathcal{C}$ is a subsequent phase for achieving consensus. Nodes join the CONSENSUS phase after they achieve local convergence. Also, the algorithm encompasses a tuple $\mathcal{P}$ of several aggregation processes such that each $p \in \mathcal{P}$ runs in parallel with the process $\mathcal{A}$. Processes in the tuple $\mathcal{P}$ are used for the convergence detection, and their results defines the convergence correctness state (i.e. convergence or divergence).

The intended epidemic task defines the initialisation of the process $\mathcal{A}$. The process $\mathcal{C}$ and processes in $\mathcal{P}$ are all initialised for the aggregate *count*. The process $\mathcal{C}$ counts nodes which have achieved local convergence, and each process p estimates the total number of nodes joined the process $\mathcal{A}$.

Each process $p \in \mathcal{P}$ will initially start with a different random seed identifier at each node in the system. During the aggregation process, seeds of all processes in $\mathcal{P}$ are piggybacked and propagated with the messages from the process $\mathcal{A}$. The seed selection method makes a random selection for each process due to the random seed initialisation. Moreover, a node failure will affect a random seed of each process, and causes each process to achieve different convergence. Convergence state can be verified using local estimates $e_{p,t}$, $\forall p \in \mathcal{P}$. A correct convergence is confirmed when all local estimates in $\mathcal{P}$ converges to the same target, $\forall e_{p,t} \approx \mathcal{V}, p \in \mathcal{P}$. Otherwise, $\exists e_{p,t} \not\approx \mathcal{V}$ indicates a divergence, which implies experiencing dynamical conditions during the aggregation process.

The procedure *DetectConvergence* illustrates convergence detection method. The method calculates the average of estimates in $\mathcal{P}$ every cycle and inserts the average in the queue $\mathcal{Q}$. Eventually, estimates average will converge to an approximation result, and the error among elements of $\mathcal{Q}$ becomes very small. The method verifies the detection of convergence using the SE of $\mathcal{Q}$ and monitoring it approaching the tolerance threshold ϵ_1 for a number of consecutive cycles Υ. Next, the method verifies the state of the convergence using the SE of

---

Algorithm 1. Adaptive Restart Algorithm

Require: ϵ_1, ϵ_2, Υ, $l^{\mathcal{Q}}$, $l^{\mathcal{P}}$.
Initialisation: $\iota = 0$; $\mathcal{Q} = \emptyset$; $\widetilde{\mathcal{P}} = \{\mathcal{A}, \mathcal{C}\} \cup \mathcal{P}$; and $\forall p \in \widetilde{\mathcal{P}}, p \longrightarrow \langle \infty, 0, 0 \rangle$.

---

1 **At start time** t_0 **at node** i:
2 $Restart(1, i, t_0)$
3 $Push(i, t_0)$

---

4 **At each cycle** t **at node** i:
5 $DetectConvergence(i, t)$
6 $Push(i, t)$

---

7 **At event 'receive message** m **from** j**' at node** i:
8 $ResolveEpoch(i, t, m)$
9 **if** $m.reply$ **then**
10   **foreach** $p \in \widetilde{\mathcal{P}}$ **do** $p \longrightarrow \langle p.\varsigma, \frac{p.v}{2}, \frac{p.w}{2} \rangle$
11   Send $\langle \iota, \widetilde{\mathcal{P}}, reply = false \rangle$ to j // PULL to j
12 **if** $m.\iota == \iota$ **then**   // Update local tuples in all processes
13   **foreach** $p \in \widetilde{\mathcal{P}}$ **do**
14   **if** $m.p.\varsigma == p.\varsigma$ **then** $p \longrightarrow \langle p.\varsigma, m.p.v + p.v, m.p.w + p.w \rangle$

```
15  def avg(H = {a₁,...,aₙ}): 1/n Σa                        // Average
16  def se(H = {a₁,...,aₙ}): 1/√n √(1/(n-1) Σ(a − avg(H))²)   // Standard Error
17  procedure Restart(ι,i, t)
18  |   ιᵢ = ι
19  |   phaseᵢ = AGGREGATION
20  |   Aᵢ ⟶ ⟨ℱα(i,t), xᵢ, 1⟩                                // Reset processes
21  |   Cᵢ ⟶ ⟨∞, 0, 0⟩
22  |   foreach p ∈ 𝒫ᵢ do p ⟶ ⟨ℱβ(i), 1, 1⟩
23  procedure Push(i,t)
24  |   foreach p ∈ 𝒫̃ᵢ do              // Divide data elements and copy tuples
25  |   |   p ⟶ ⟨p.ς, p.v/2, p.w/2⟩
26  |   j ⟵ getRandomPeer()                                 // Get random peer
27  |   Send ⟨ιᵢ, 𝒫̃ᵢ, reply = true⟩ to j                    // PUSH to node j
28  procedure DetectConvergence(i,t)
29  |   switch phase do
30  |   |   case AGGREGATION do
31  |   |   |   𝒬ᵢ ∪ avg({p.e : ∀p ∈ 𝒫ᵢ})      // Insert estimates average of 𝒫ᵢ
32  |   |   |   if se(𝒬ᵢ) < ε₁ for Υ cycles then    // Detect local convergence
33  |   |   |   |   if se({p.e : ∀p ∈ 𝒫ᵢ}) > ε₂ then   // Detect divergence
34  |   |   |   |   |   Restart(ιᵢ + 1, i, t)          // Start a new epoch
35  |   |   |   |   else                           // Make transition to CONSENSUS phase
36  |   |   |   |   |   if ℱα(i,t) < Cᵢ.ς then Cᵢ ⟶ ⟨ℱα(i,t), 1, 1⟩
37  |   |   |   |   |   else Cᵢ ⟶ ⟨Cᵢ.ς, Cᵢ.v + 1, Cᵢ.w⟩
38  |   |   |   |   |   phase=CONSENSUS
39  |   |   case CONSENSUS do
40  |   |   |   𝒬ᵢ ∪ Cᵢ.e
41  |   |   |   if se(𝒬ᵢ) < ε₁ for Υ cycles then    // Detect global convergence
42  |   |   |   |   Restart(ιᵢ + 1, i, t)            // Start a new epoch
43  procedure ResolveEpoch(i,t,m)
44  |   if m.ι > ιᵢ then Restart(m.ι, i, t)          // New epoch discovered
45  |   if m.ι == ιᵢ then                            // Resolve seed elements
46  |   |   if m.A.ς < Aᵢ.ς then Aᵢ ⟶ ⟨m.A.ς, xᵢ, 0⟩
47  |   |   if m.C.ς < Cᵢ.ς then
48  |   |   |   Cᵢ ⟶ ⟨m.C.ς, 0, 0⟩ and if phase==CONSENSUS then Cᵢ.v = 1
49  |   |   foreach p ∈ 𝒫ᵢ do
50  |   |   |   if m.p.ς < p.ς then p ⟶ ⟨m.p.ς, 1, 0⟩
```

estimates in $\mathcal{P}$. The criterion validates that the error among local estimates of processes in $\mathcal{P}$ is above a tolerance threshold of ϵ_2. The limits ϵ_1, ϵ_2 and Υ are global application parameters as described in Sect. 2.2.

Upon the detection of divergence in a node i, the node initiates a global restarting process using a new epoch identified $\iota_i + 1$. The restart steps are described in procedure *Restart*. Also, upon the detection of a correct convergence, node i makes a transition to the CONSENSUS phase by starting the process

$\mathcal{C}$. Other nodes may join the phase at the same time or later when they converge. The seed selection process unifies the seed elements, and each node participates in the phase by adding 1 to the total data mass in the process $\mathcal{C}$. In the CON-SENSUS phase, the detection method records the estimate of the process $\mathcal{C}$ in $\mathcal{Q}$ at every cycle. Each node uses the SE of $\mathcal{Q}$ and the thresholds ϵ_1 and Υ to locally detect the convergence of the CONSENSUS phase.

Achieving convergence in the CONSENSUS phase indicates the agreement among nodes to restart the epidemic task as they all have converged to the correct target (i.e. *global convergence*). However, small number of nodes in the CONSENSUS phase are enforced to join the next epoch, although they did not yet detect convergence, which optimises the restart time between epochs. Also, it adapts the epidemic task should it experience any dynamic conditions during the CONSENSUS phase.

Procedure *ResolveEpoch* has two duties: (1) discovering and joining new epochs, and (2) applying the seed selection method to unify seed elements for each process. Each node receives a new epoch identifier starts a new epoch and reinitialise local processes as shown in procedure *Restart*. Also, the procedure updates the local tuples upon the detection of a new seed with smaller identifier. The algorithm in lines 9–11 continue processing the received message and responses to the sender node by a PULL message with the adopted epoch identifier and seed elements. In lines 12–14, the algorithm updates the local tuple for each process.

4   Simulations and Experimental Analysis

The algorithm is validated via simulations using PEERSIM [17]. PEERSIM is a Java-based discrete-event *P2P* simulation tool that is particularly useful to evaluate distributed protocols in large-scale systems. The simulations are event-based and adopt the event-driven engine in PEERSIM. Three events are used in the simulations: (1) *Start Event* occurs only once at the start time of each node. At this event, each node initialises local seed and data elements. (2)*Run Event* is scheduled at every cycle for each node to detect convergence and send PUSH messages. The event at all nodes stops after a predefined number of cycles. (3) *Message Receive Event* is a notification event, in which a receiver node identifies new epochs, applies seed selection method and updates local tuples.

The process $\mathcal{A}$ is initialised for the aggregate *count* targetting system size, and hence, seed elements at all nodes are set using $\mathcal{F}_\alpha(i, t_s)$, where $t_s = [0, t_{off}[$, and t_{off} is a start time synchronisation offset. The settings of threshold parameters follow previous work recommendations in [7,11], and they are set to $\epsilon_1 = 0.5$, $\epsilon_1 = 1$, $\Upsilon = 3$, and $l^\mathcal{Q} = 10$. The protocol NCP is used with k-regular overlay graph initialisation, where $k = 30$.

The cycle length $\mathcal{T}$ is defined as $\mathcal{T} = 2 \times \delta + t_{off}$, where $t_{off} = 250$ ms, δ is the expected maximum propagation delay in Internet. Values of δ are randomly generated using a Weibull distribution with the parameters, $\beta = 4$ that bounds δ to 125 ms, $\eta = 70$ ms is the average delay value, and $\gamma = 25$ ms is the minimum delay. A choice of $\mathcal{T} = 500\,\text{ms}$ is sufficiently large for typical applications and large enough to allow most messages to be delivered within the current cycle.

The results in Fig. 1 illustrate the selection method and restart mechanism performance. In this experiment, node churn is disabled and the result shows the algorithm behaviour under stable conditions. The results for the processes $\mathcal{A}$ and $\mathcal{C}$ are distinguished for clarity. The Fig. 1(a) and (b) show the variation in initial system mass over time. In the figures, data elements approach the correct value as a result of the selection method. Particularly, the Fig. 1(b) presents the decrease in weights mass due to the selection of the correct seed and the discarding of other seeds.

Figures 1(c), (d) and (e) illustrate the correct reach and detection of convergence in each phase. The results validate the algorithm and the restart mechanism efficiency. Each node makes a transition to the CONSENSUS phase after the detection of the convergence. It also restarts the task after achieving convergence in the CONSENSUS phase. The Fig. 1(d) shows the variation in estimation error in all processes, which indicates the reach to a correct convergence, the transition to the CONSENSUS phase, and the voting for the global restarting. Figure 1(e) shows that 100% of nodes achieve and detect convergence in both phases with nodes restarting and joining a new epoch asynchronously.

Figure 1(f) summarises the results of 30 simulation runs for different system sizes. The figure shows logarithmic increase in the restart times (epochs) as the system size increases. It also presents the variation in the epoch length for different sizes.

Results in Figs. 2(a) and (b) illustrate the algorithm behaviour under dynamic conditions. Two experiments are carried out. The first experiment

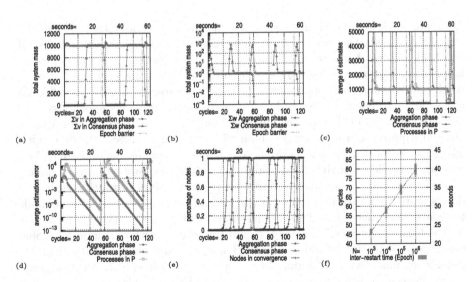

Fig. 1. Algorithm performance under stable conditions, $\mathcal{V} = 10^4$, $\epsilon_1 = 0.5$, $\epsilon_2 = 1$, $\Upsilon = 3$, $l^{\mathcal{P}} = 5$, $l^{\mathcal{Q}} = 10$

examines the algorithm sensitivity to a single node failure and to a modest churn rates. Figure 2(a) shows the results for a single failure injected at cycle 5 followed by the failure of 30% of the system between cycles [60 − 120]. The second experiment tests the algorithm under severe condition when a system loses 75% of its nodes during a task. Figure 2(b) shows the failure of 75% of the system between cycles [15, 195]. In both experiments, results prove the algorithm abilities to validate or invalidate convergence even for a single node failure. The algorithm continues restarting until the system stabilises before it can enter the Consensus phase and return a correct estimation.

The impact of varying the parameter $l^{\mathcal{P}}$ has also been examined; however, results are omitted due to space limitation. The results have shown that the effect was negligible under stable conditions while causing a small increase in overhead to the underlying network. In dynamic conditions, the increase in the number of processes in $\mathcal{P}$ makes validation of convergence more accurate, especially, for the detection of divergence. Although precision is essential for the detection of small amount of churn, e.g. single node failure as shown in Fig. 2(a), the accuracy can also be controlled by the tolerance thresholds, and with low cost. From another perspective, the amount of error that the algorithm can tolerate corresponds to the lost portion of initial system mass. In early cycles of an aggregation process, node failure may cause a major loss in the system mass, however, after convergence the impact of churn fades [11]. Therefore, even large churn rates at late cycles cannot result in divergence detection, the Fig. 2(b) shows the impact of this scenario in the cycles [15, 60].

5   Related Work

A simple restarting mechanism for epidemic protocols was introduced in [1], where global restarting was achieved using fixed length epochs with incremental epoch identifiers. Authors in [12] proposed a technique that restarts two overlapping aggregation processes in epochs of fixed hops. The protocol improves results in dynamic conditions; however, results accuracy can only be validated after the next epoch. The work in [3] introduces a continuous epoch-less data aggregation protocol. The protocol is based on atomic Push-Pull with a timeout and requires prior information about the system to produce accurate results. The *Flow Updating* aggregation protocol [13] operates under dynamic conditions without periodic restarting. Upon failure detection, the protocol uses symmetric exchanges among neighbour nodes and recovers values instantly, and hence delays system convergence. The work in [16] introduces two heuristic methods for convergence detection. The first method uses the moving-average technique for the local detection of convergence, and the second method is used for global convergence detection by utilising parallel aggregation processes. Authors in [15] provide an analysis for local and global convergence, which has shown the need for applications-specific parameters in the detection methods.

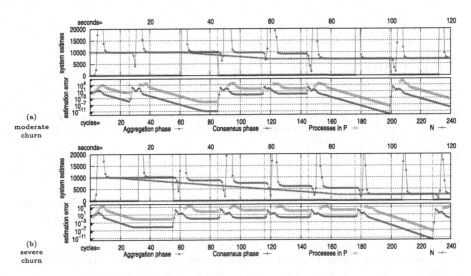

Fig. 2. Algorithm performance under churn, $\mathcal{V} = 10^4$, $\epsilon_1 = 0.5$, $\epsilon_2 = 1$, $\Upsilon = 3$, $l^\mathcal{P} = 5$, $l^\mathcal{Q} = 10$

6 Conclusions

In large and extreme-scale distributed systems, continuous epidemic tasks are useful tools for monitoring and maintaining system consistency. Through periodic restarting, epidemic processes can detect and adapt to new conditions. This work introduces a novel continuous epidemic algorithm with an adaptive restart mechanism. The process restarts either upon acquiring consensus on the global convergence of the epidemic task or upon the detection of divergence. Moreover, the mechanism is lightweight with optimised communication overhead that can be piggybacked with regular message exchange. The detection accuracy of the algorithm can be tuned according to the application preference for any quick approximation or an accurate one that takes longer to compute. Also, the algorithm introduces a decentralised selection method for data aggregation tasks that require single-point initialisation. Simulation results validated the performance of the algorithm under static and dynamic conditions. Further study is required to specify approximation quality through results of multiple aggregation processes, and use results for system-mass restoration under nodes churn.

References

1. Jelasity, M., Montresor, A., Babaoglu, O.: Gossip-based aggregation in large dynamic networks. ACM Trans. Comput. Syst. **23**(3), 219–252 (2005)
2. Cao, Y., et al.: An overview of recent progress in the study of distributed multi-agent coordination. IEEE Trans. Ind. Inf. **9**(1), 427–38 (2013)
3. Rapp, V., Graffi, K.: Continuous gossip-based aggregation through dynamic information aging. In: 2013 22nd International Conference on Computer Communication and Networks (ICCCN), July 2013

4. Costa, P., Leito, J.: Practical continuous aggregation in wireless edge environments. In: 2018 IEEE 37th Symposium on Reliable Distributed Systems (SRDS), October 2018

5. Litke, A., Anagnostopoulos, D., Varvarigou, T.: Blockchains for supply chain management: architectural elements and challenges towards a global scale deployment. Logistics **3**(1), 5 (2019)

6. Kempe, D., Dobra, A., Gehrke, J.: Gossip-based computation of aggregate information. In: Proceedings of the 44th Annual IEEE Symposium on Foundations of Computer Science, 2003 (2003)

7. Ayiad, M.M., Di Fatta, G.: Agreement in epidemic data aggregation. In: 2017 IEEE 23rd International Conference on Parallel and Distributed Systems (ICPADS), December 2017

8. Katti, A., Lilja, D.J.: Efficient and fast approximate consensus with epidemic failure detection at extreme scale. In: 2018 26th Euromicro International Conference on Parallel, Distributed and Network-based Processing (PDP), March 2018

9. Di Fatta, G., et al.: Fault tolerant decentralised K-Means clustering for asynchronous large-scale networks. J. Parallel Distrib. Comput. **73**(3), 317–329 (2013). Models and Algorithms for High-Performance Distributed Data Mining

10. Poonpakdee, P., Di Fatta, G.: Robust and efficient membership management in large-scale dynamic networks. Future Gener. Comput. Syst. **75**, 85–93 (2017)

11. Ayiad, M.M., Di Fatta, G.: Robust epidemic aggregation under churn. In: Fortino, G., Ali, A.B.M.S., Pathan, M., Guerrieri, A., Di Fatta, G. (eds.) IDCS 2017. LNCS, vol. 10794, pp. 173–185. Springer, Cham (2018). https://doi.org/10.1007/978-3-319-97795-9_16

12. Roh, H.-G., Ignat, C.L.: Rapid and Round-free Multi-pair Asynchronous Push-Pull Aggregation. Research report RR-8044. INRIA (2012)

13. Jesus, P., Baquero, C., Almeida, P.S.: Flow updating: fault-tolerant aggregation for dynamic networks. J. Parallel Distrib. Comput. **78**, 53–64 (2015)

14. Blasa, F.,et al.: Symmetric push-sum protocol for decentralised aggregation. In: Proceedings of AP2PS 2011, the Third International Conference on Advances in P2P Systems. IARIA (2011)

15. Bahi, J.M., Contassot-Vivier, S., Couturier, R.: An efficient and robust decentralized algorithm for detecting the global convergence in asynchronous iterative algorithms. In: Palma, J.M.L.M., Amestoy, P.R., Daydé, M., Mattoso, M., Lopes, J.C. (eds.) VECPAR 2008. LNCS, vol. 5336, pp. 240–254. Springer, Heidelberg (2008). https://doi.org/10.1007/978-3-540-92859-1_22

16. Poonpakdee, P., Orhon, N.G., Di Fatta, G.: Convergence detection in epidemic aggregation. In: an Mey, D., et al. (eds.) Euro-Par 2013. LNCS, vol. 8374, pp. 292–300. Springer, Heidelberg (2014). https://doi.org/10.1007/978-3-642-54420-0_29

17. Montresor, A., Jelasity, M.: PeerSim: a scalable P2P simulator. In: 2009 IEEE 9th International Conference on Peer-to-Peer Computing, September 2009

Using Sentiment Analysis and Automated Reasoning to Boost Smart Lighting Systems

Francesco Cauteruccio[1]([✉]) [ID], Luca Cinelli[1] [ID], Giancarlo Fortino[2] [ID],
Claudio Savaglio[2] [ID], and Giorgio Terracina[1] [ID]

[1] DEMACS, University of Calabria, Rende, Italy
{cauteruccio,cinelli,terracina}@mat.unical.it
[2] DIMES, University of Calabria, Rende, Italy
g.fortino@unical.it, csavaglio@dimes.unical.it

Abstract. Smart cities, arising all around the globe, encourage the birth of new and different urban infrastructures, with interesting challenges and opportunities. Within each smart city, a smart community emerges, which integrates technological solutions for the definition of innovative models for the smart management of urban areas. In this paper, we describe the research activities conducted within a smart city project, introducing a novel framework for managing smart lighting systems within a smart community. We start by describing the proposed framework, then we specialize it to the specific use case. One of the main novelties of the proposed approach is the use of automated reasoning and sentiment analysis to boost the smart lighting process.

Keywords: Smart city · Smart lighting · Artificial intelligence · Big data

1 Introduction

A smart city represents the normal evolution of a common city. With different definitions [6], a smart city encompasses its aims in few intelligent features, that are economics, governance, environment, people, mobility and lifestyles. Also, ICT technologies found peculiar spots in the development and building of smart cities [12]. Novel experiences such as Big Data, Data Visualisation, and Internet of Things (IoT) all play an important role in the development of a smart city. Big Data paradigms, tools, and technologies can be used to manage the (possibly) huge amount of data, whereas data visualisation techniques can be exploited to define meaningful and concise representations of data ocean. Finally, IoTs literally become the skin of a smart city: smartphones, computers, sensors and Smart Objects (SOs) in general are the life and soul of a smart city, generating data that can be analysed and exploited to improve citizen quality of life [5].

© Springer Nature Switzerland AG 2019
R. Montella et al. (Eds.): IDCS 2019, LNCS 11874, pp. 69–78, 2019.
https://doi.org/10.1007/978-3-030-34914-1_7

Furthermore, all of the devices installed in urban infrastructures, such as smart lighting systems and traffic management systems, contribute to the ecosystem of a so called *smart community*. A smart community integrates a series of technological solutions for the definition and implementation of innovative models for the smart management of urban areas. One of the main challenges of the next generation of ICT technologies applied to smart communities is the collection, integration, and exploitation of information gathered from heterogeneous data sources, including autonomous smart resources, like SOs, sensors, surveillance systems etc, and human resources, such as posts in social networks. Another key challenge is the application of artificial intelligence tools, such as those based on automated reasoning, to advance state of the art in smart community management.

The present paper is intended to provide a contribution in this setting. Specifically, it introduces a framework for intelligent smart lighting in a smart city environment, which integrates sentiment analysis tools on social posts and automated reasoning on gathered data to improve the quality of service perceived by citizens. To the best of our knowledge, there is no existing proposal in the smart lighting scenario dealing with both such technologies at the same time. Intuitively, posts/tweets in social networks are automatically collected and analyzed via sentiment analysis tools; obtained results are exploited to measure the level of security perceived by the community in specific areas of the city, and even to detect, almost in real time, the occurrence of dangerous events, like accidents. This is carried out by measuring the sentiment of citizens on specific keywords composing an urban taxonomy. Information from social data is then integrated with observations from sensors, and used to pinpoint the specific geographical area of interest. Automated reasoning tools are then activated to identify the actual problems and to compose the best solutions for them. All of these components interact with a Big Data platform storing and managing the vast amount of data collected and handled by the framework.

The framework presented in this paper reflects some of the preliminary research results obtained within the project "Smarter Solutions in the Big Data World", funded within the call "HORIZON2020" PON I&C 2014–2020. The overall project aims at developing a general Big Data platform for analytics and reasoning over Big Data, and three verticalizations are considered: smart cities, which is the main focus of this paper, prognostic, and service desk. In particular, in this paper we present the overall framework first, then we specialize it to the smart lighting use case; finally we provide the formalization for some parts of the use case. Clearly, the framework and the use case include numerous technical aspects that can not be presented in detail in this paper, due to space constraint.

2   Related Work

Different applications contexts have emerged within smart cities. One of the most promising and interesting is that of smart lighting [5]. Smart lighting is important due to a large area of effects: by using smart street lights, different effects can be obtained, such as reduction of energy consumption, intelligent lighting of dangerous zones and interactive feedback about traffic situation and accident signaling. In order to enhance the system, a smart lighting setup should consider two specific parts: collecting and using data. Data collection can be employed on each smart object present in the system; then, it might be used to perform proper actions. Different smart lighting systems have been already presented in the literature [7–9,11,13].

In [11], a control system has been developed for energy efficient lighting. A set of LED lamps, gateway nodes and management software offers real time monitoring and control of the lighting system. The lamps are interconnected under a wireless mesh network implemented by ZigBee technology. Each lamp is provided with a set of sensors and actuators, allowing to observe specific parameters of the lamp itself, thus helping a continuous monitoring in order to detect possible faults.

In [13], a preliminary work towards a complete smart street lighting system is presented. The system takes advantage of a wireless sensor network (WSN) concept, and uses Waspmote as a sensor node. Sensors are used to monitor the amount of energy consumed and dimming time of the street light for logging purposes. Also in [7], a street lighting monitoring and control system based on a WSN is presented. The aim is similar to the previous approach but, in this case, the objective is reached using vehicle detection.

In [9], a smart street lighting system to minimize the energy consumption of a group of street lighting poles has been presented. Outdoor lighting are denoted by different aspects, such as cost, safety and maintenance, which often are controlled by few subjects, such as municipalities or distribution companies. Here, the optimization of electrical energy is achieved by minimizing a cost function involving operational constraints, ambient luminance and traffic flow. The approach bruteforces all the possible scenarios in order to find the one with the least electrical power consumption, while satisfying some required constraints.

An approach related to road lighting has been presented in [8]. Here, the Authors illustrates a dynamic street lighting system installed in Eindhoven, Netherlands, for a long period of time. Different aspects, such as energy saving, commissioning problems and message loss have been considered and analysed. A novel model for describing and simulating dynamic lighting is presented, together with a set of explorative data analysis results.

The smart lighting system proposed in this work differs from these works for two reasons: (i) its focus is not on energy saving but on the provision of the highest levels of perceived security to citizenship and, to this end, a significant contribution is provided by technologies not considered in the past for smart lighting purposes, such as social networks and automated reasoning systems; and (ii) a methodology [4] is exploited to simplify the development of the framework and to foster the interoperability of its building blocks/enabling technologies.

3 Description of the Proposed Framework

This section describes the proposed framework. We first present the overall structure by introducing each component of the framework, and giving the general idea underlying them. Then, we describe the general use case. Finally, we describe the specialization of the framework according to the presented use case.

3.1 Overall Structure of the Framework

The overall aim of the proposed framework focuses on the definition of a data-centric platform capable of supporting knowledge representation and knowledge discovery processes in the context of a smarty community. In particular, the framework aims at providing smart solutions to different problems such as acquisition, integration, management and analysis of data. The framework, and the project it has been developed in, cover a wide variety of contexts related to smart communities. In this paper we focus on the aspects related to the acquisition and interpretation of heterogeneous data in order to improve smart lighting systems, not (only) from the point of view of energy consumption, but mostly from the point of view of security perceived by the community.

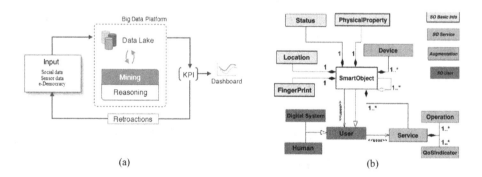

(a)   (b)

Fig. 1. (a) Overall view of the proposed framework and (b) shared meta-data model.

The proposed framework is depicted in Fig. 1(a). It can be divided in four main modules, namely *(i)* Input module, *(ii)* Big Data Platform, *(iii)* KPI analysis and Dashboarding module, and *(iv)* Retroactions module. In the following, we briefly explain at a high level of abstraction each module and related features.

The input module deals with input acquisition from different application contexts. The input module obtains data from different and heterogeneous sources, which in turn might employ different technologies. In the smart city context, heterogeneity of data plays a key role which needs to be considered, thus the input module should be able to combine different technologies and data types under a single framework supporting data acquisition processes. In our context, we focus on data coming from sensors dispersed over a network of smart lighting devices, from existing social networks and from a specifically designed platform supporting an active participation of the community to the activities of the city (an e-Democracy portal).

Data generated from these sources is necessarily overwhelming; as a consequence, a platform for managing Big Data is mandatory. The Big Data platform relies on two main components, namely a data lake and a set of processes for mining and reasoning over data. The data lake component represents the data layer module of the platform; it physically collects the data from the input module, maintaining both raw and elaborated data and enriching them with a set of metadata. Data can be stored in their native format, thus avoiding the requirement of an ETL phase. The Mining & Reasoning component includes different tasks and incorporates both inductive and deductive tools to carry out anomaly detection, data enrichment, sentiment analysis, knowledge representation and reasoning, and so on.

The KPI analysis module focuses on the analysis of collected data in order to define and compute different Key Performance Indicators (KPI). KPIs are used to numerically evaluate different aspects of the context of interest, such as perceived level of security, perceived satisfaction for available services, trends on economical indicators, and so on. Different ways of visualising KPIs and related data, in order to support decision makers, are included in the Dashboarding module. Both time-oriented and geographically-oriented views of available data are provided. Finally, the Rectroactions module strictly depends on the KPI module: it checks for specific KPIs and automatically translates observed data in immediate or scheduled actions. As an example, automatic actions on the smart lighting system can be implemented.

In order to improve the interoperability of these modules and their underlying technologies, a systematic approach along with a shared meta-data model is strongly needed. Indeed, it is well known that the management and the integration in real applications of an IoT system is a challenging and complex task; thus, suitable sets of models, methodologies and techniques are required. Therefore, as previously introduced, the proposed framework takes advantage of ACOSO-Meth [4], a domain-neutral development methodology for analyzing, designing and implementing SOs and IoT systems through a set of metamodels at different levels of abstractions.

In particular, similarly to what has been done in [3], the ACOSO-based SO High-Level meta-data model depicted in Fig. 1(b) has been exploited to support the analysis phase of the proposed system. The model provides an inclusive, but not too complex, high-level SO representation that is shareable among the framework's modules for modeling *(i)* SO's Basic Info, such as SO current Status, Location, and Physical Properties like dimension and weight, and its Fingerprint, namely SO identifier, owner, etc; *(ii)* SO's Augmentation devices, like sensors, actuators, computer units, etc; *(iii)* the services provided by the SO and implemented through a set of basic Operations; and *(iv)* SO's Users, to identify the human users and/or digital systems who benefit from the SO's services.

The instantiation of the ACOSO-based SO High-Level meta-data model on the proposed smart-lamp is reported in Fig. 2 and discussed in Sect. 3.3.

3.2   Specialization of the Framework to the Use Case

The proposed framework is general enough to be exploited in different contexts. The use case we will focus on in this paper refers to a smart lighting system in a smart city. In particular, we are interested in defining a data-centric platform integrated in a smart city environment, in which data coming from sensors and social networks can boost smart lightning, by operating and tuning different smart lighting objects located in the smart city area. The aim of the whole system is to offer citizens with a smart and reliable environment.

Throughout the whole section, we call smart-lamp each of the smart objects belonging to the smart lighting network.

As already indicated in Fig. 1, the input module is devoted to gather data from three different main sources, that are sensors, social networks and e-Democracy systems. Sensors data are gathered from a set of sensors equipped on each smart-lamp and represent different measures, such as temperature, and humidity, but also events, such as presence of a person or presence of rain. Sensors and smart lamps are organized in a Wireless Sensor Area Network (WSAN). Social networks data include geo-localized tweets from Twitter and posts from specific pages on Facebook. Lastly, data from an e-Democracy system represent textual contents produced by citizens and/or municipality operators and posted in an online community; these constitute an immediate interface between citizens and the municipality. All of these data are stored in the data lake, which is directly connected to the Mining & Reasoning module.

The mining part includes a sentiment analysis task and an anomaly detection task. The former focuses on the analysis of the data gathered from social posts: a polarity score, i.e., a degree of positiveness/negativeness, is assigned to each keyword that can be extracted from a post, and is used to intercept crucial information from the citizens. In order to unambiguously single out significant information for the application context, keywords are mapped onto a specific urban taxonomy; this task is carried out with the support of Babelnet [10], one of the most advanced thesauruses currently available. Furthermore, thanks to the geo-localization of posts, information regarding a specific area of the smart city can be analyzed. Anomaly detection works on temporal data gathered from sensors, in order to detect potential anomalies; it exploits the technique for analyzing heterogeneous sensors presented in [2].

The reasoning part focuses on three different aspects:

1. local reasoning on the smart-lamp with actualization on the object itself;
2. local reasoning on the smart-lamp with actualization on the Big Data platform;
3. reasoning on the big data platform with retroaction on the smart-lamp.

Reasoning tasks are carried out with the support of the well known DLV [1] reasoner. Recent improvements to this system allow it to be employed even on

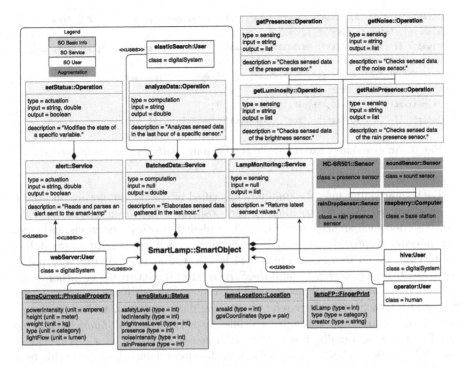

Fig. 2. The ACOSO metamodel of a smart-lamp.

devices with low computational resources and to deal with stream reasoning tasks, directly on the devices. Specifically, local reasoning analyzes local streams coming from sensors in order to detect different situations (such as traffic) and automatically choosing the best illumination intensity based both on the time slot and the perceived level of security in the area. Local reasoning over streams may also trigger alerts for possibly more complex situations that must be checked on the Big Data platform. As an example, patterns of data significantly deviating from the past may activate suspects of anomalous behavior of sensors or of people. This observation may trigger the anomaly detection task on the Big Data platform. Finally, the sentiment analysis on social posts may suggest the presence of particularly dangerous situations in a specific area. Reasoning tasks, applied to the whole set of data can approve or disprove the social observations and, possibly, activate proper alert actions on the smart-lamps.

3.3 Use Case Instantiation

In this section we will focus on the data modeling aspects of the use case formalization. The whole data infrastructure is composed of a set of smart-lamps which are dislocated all over the smart-city zone and modeled according to the instantiated ACOSO-based SO High-Level metamodel reported in Fig. 2.

{ "area": [{ "id": 0, "name": "smart-lamp", "city": "Rende", "province": "CS", "region":
"Calabria", "state": "Italy" }, ...] }
{ "lamp": [{ "id": 0, "lat": 39.3633564, "long": 16.2260241, "area": 0, "prevLamp": null,
"nextLamp": 1, "IP": x.x.x.x, "alertPort": 1, "webPort": 2 }, ...]}
{ "alert": [{ "id": 0, "type": 0, "value": 42, "lamp": 0, "timestamp":
"2019-05-01T18:25:43.511Z" }, ...]}
{ "typeAlert": [{ "id": 0, "type": "light"}, ...]}
{ "user": [{ "id": 0, "user": "foo", "password": "bar" }, ...]}

Fig. 3. An example of saved data in the big data platform in a JSON format.

Each smart-lamp must be uniquely identified in the infrastructure and must be geo-localized in order to identify the position it has been placed at. Furthermore, for each smart-lamp, we need to identify both its previous and next one, in order to provide an order between them. Each smart-lamp offers different services whom users can interact with. Figure 2 shows four different users: *Operator, Hive, ElasticSearch*, and *webServer*. Also, the setup can be either physical or remote, and the operator can check the current state of the smart-lamp. Hive and ElasticSearch users refer to the big data platform, which can interface to the smart-lamp through two different services called *LampMonitoring* and *BatchedData*. Finally, the webServer user can interface to a service called *Alert* which allows to send information to the smart-lamp. Moreover, this user can directly interact with the smart-lamp in order to either check or modify its internal status and she/he can use the LampMonitoring service. More in detail, each service provides a number of features that can be used by the users. The LampMonitoring service returns the latest data sensed from the placed local sensors. Different operations are available and each of them focuses on a specific sensor. As an example, the operation *getLuminosity* retrieves data from the light sensor. Instead, the BatchedData service carries out the analysis of the sensed data in the latest hour. It computes several values and uses the operation *AnalyzeData* together with each specific monitoring operation of each placed sensor. One last important service is Alert: it offers an external interface exploitable from users and automated functions in order to modify the internal status of the smart-lamp through the *setStatus* operation.

The data infrastructure is modeled within the big data platform into a specific portion of the data lake. It consists of five schemata, which are depicted in Fig. 3. In order to provide a clear reading, and without loss of generality, we present an example of the data using a JSON syntax. Each object contained in `area` represents an area within the smart-city, and it is described by an id, a name and geographic attributes. Each object in `lamp` represents a smart-lamp, with its coordinates, the area containing it, its previous and next smart-lamp and various networking parameters, such as IP address and services ports. In the `alert` collection, each object describes an alert and its type. Finally, `user` contains each user of the system, typically human operators who deployed the smart-lamps or who manage them.

```
{"data": [{"id": 0, "timestamp": "2019-05-01T02:03:05.511Z", "type": "humidity", "value":
42},...]}
{"elaboratedData" : [{"type": "noise", "day": 1, "hour": 3, "sample": 3, "value": 42},...]}
{"alert": [{"id": 0, "type": 0, "value": 42, "timestamp": "2019-05-01T14:20:41.511Z",
"recTimestamp": "2019-05-01T14:21:01.511Z", "committed": 0}, ...]}
{"info": {"lamp": 0, "area": 0, "lat:" 39.3633564, "long": 16.2260241, "publicIP": x.x.x.x,
"privateStaticIP": y.y.y.y, "prevLamp": null, "nextLamp": 1}}
```

Fig. 4. An example of local saved data on a smart-lamp in a JSON format.

In order to account for different local computational tasks, each smart-lamp contains a local database which is used to buffer a certain portion of the sensed data. It is worth pointing out that a smart-lamp cannot maintain all of the collected data, thus a local scheduled process is in charge of cleaning old saved data. Figure 4 shows an example of data stored locally on a smart-lamp. Here, the collection `data` contains each sensed data from any sensors on the smart-lamp. Attributes `type` and `value` indicate the type of sensed data, such as presence, light, temperature, rain, etc, and the sensed value respectively. In `elaboratedData`, instead, all of elaborated values are stored. We have a value for a certain type of data, for a specific hour of a specific day of the week, thus having an elaborated value for each combination of type, day of the week and hour. Each object in the array `alert` indicates an alert sent to the smart-lamp. More in detail, the attribute `recTimestamp` represents the time instant in which the alert has been received from the smart-lamp, and `committed` denotes whether an action corresponding to the alert has been successfully performed. Finally, the singleton `info` stores smart-lamp related information, such as id, area and coordinates.

4 Conclusion

In this paper we described some preliminary research activities conducted within a smart city project and, in particular, we focused on the introduction of a novel framework for managing smart lighting systems. The framework combines both social network data and automated reasoning tasks to improve the quality of service. It integrates a Big Data platform for storing and managing the vast amount of collected data. The complexity of the framework has been handled with the help of ACOSO-Meth, a development methodology for SOs and IoT systems providing a meta-data model shared among the framework's modules to foster their interoperability. Finally, we specialized the use case and provided some details on handled data.

Acknowledgement. This work was partially supported by: *(i)* the Italian Ministry for Economic Development (MISE) under the project "Smarter Solutions in the Big Data World", funded within the call "HORIZON2020" PON I&C 2014–2020.

References

1. Alviano, M., Faber, W., Leone, N., Perri, S., Pfeifer, G., Terracina, G.: The disjunctive datalog system DLV. In: de Moor, O., Gottlob, G., Furche, T., Sellers, A. (eds.) Datalog 2.0 2010. LNCS, vol. 6702, pp. 282–301. Springer, Heidelberg (2011). https://doi.org/10.1007/978-3-642-24206-9_17

2. Cauteruccio, F., et al.: Short-long term anomaly detection in wireless sensor networks based on machine learning and multi-parameterized edit distance. Inf. Fus. **52**, 13–30 (2019). https://doi.org/10.1016/j.inffus.2018.11.010

3. Fortino, G., Rovella, A., Russo, W., Savaglio, C.: Towards cyberphysical digital libraries: integrating IoT smart objects into digital libraries. In: Guerrieri, A., Loscri, V., Rovella, A., Fortino, G. (eds.) Management of Cyber Physical Objects in the Future Internet of Things. IT, pp. 135–156. Springer, Cham (2016). https://doi.org/10.1007/978-3-319-26869-9_7

4. Fortino, G., Russo, W., Savaglio, C., Shen, W., Zhou, M.: Agent-oriented cooperative smart objects: from iot system design to implementation. IEEE Trans. Syst. Man Cybern.: Syst. **99**, 1–18 (2017)

5. Gharaibeh, A., et al.: Smart cities: a survey on data management, security, and enabling technologies. IEEE Commun. Surv. Tutor. **19**(4), 2456–2501 (2017)

6. Harrison, C., et al.: Foundations for smarter cities. IBM J. Res. Dev. **54**(4), 1–16 (2010)

7. Lavric, A., Popa, V., Finis, I.: The design of a street lighting monitoring and control system. In: 2012 International Conference and Exposition on Electrical and Power Engineering, pp. 314–317. IEEE, Iasi, Romania (2012)

8. Lukkien, J., Verhoeven, R.: The case of dynamic street lighting an exploration of long-term data collection. In: 2015 IEEE 20th Conference on Emerging Technologies Factory Automation (ETFA), pp. 1–8. IEEE, Luxembourg, Luxembourg (2015)

9. Mahoor, M., Salmasi, F.R., Najafabadi, T.A.: A hierarchical smart street lighting system with brute-force energy optimization. IEEE Sens. J. **17**(9), 2871–2879 (2017)

10. Navigli, R., Ponzetto, S.: BabelNet: the automatic construction, evaluation and application of a wide-coverage multilingual semantic network. Artif. Intell. **193**, 217–250 (2012)

11. Siddiqui, A., Ahmad, A., Yang, H., Lee, C.: ZigBee based energy efficient outdoor lighting control system. In: 2012 14th International Conference on Advanced Communication Technology (ICACT), pp. 916–919. IEEE, PyeongChang, South Korea (2012)

12. Washburn, D., Sindhu, U., Balaouras, S., Dines, R., Hayes, N., Nelson, L.: Helping CIOs understand 'smart city' initiatives. Forrester, Making Leaders Successful Every Day (2010)

13. Yusoff, Y., Rosli, R., Karnaluddin, M.U., Samad, M.: Towards smart street lighting system in Malaysia. In: 2013 IEEE Symposium on Wireless Technology Applications (ISWTA), pp. 301–305. IEEE, Kuching, Malaysia (2013)

In-network Hebbian Plasticity
for Wireless Sensor Networks

Tim van der Lee[✉], Georgios Exarchakos, and Sonia Heemstra de Groot

Eindhoven University of Technology, 5612 AP Eindhoven, The Netherlands
{t.lee,g.exarchakos,sheemstradegroot}@tue.nl

Abstract. In typical Wireless Sensor Networks (WSNs), all sensor data is routed to a more powerful computing entity. In the case of environmental monitoring, this enables data prediction and event detection. When the size of the network increases, processing all the input data outside the network will create a bottleneck at the gateway device. This creates delays and increases the energy consumption of the network. To solve this issue, we propose using Hebbian learning to pre-process the data in the wireless network. This method allows to reduce the dimension of the sensor data, without loosing spatial and temporal correlation. Furthermore, bottlenecks are avoided. By using a recurrent neural network to predict sensor data, we show that pre-processing the data in the network with Hebbian units reduces the computation time and increases the energy efficiency of the network without compromising learning.

Keywords: Recurrent neural network · Wireless Sensor Networks · Hebbian plasticity

1 Introduction

In recent years, the fall of the cost of sensing devices has enabled the deployment of large scale Wireless Sensor Networks (WSNs) to monitor and actuate in different environments. When considering environmental monitoring, it is common to consider hundreds of devices [15]. Environmental monitoring is performed over time on specific geographical regions. Therefore, the data is often correlated spatially and temporally. Indeed, closely located sensors will measure similar data. Depending on the data type, the sensor measurement can also relate to the time of the day and/or the time of the year. It is therefore interesting to study these relations, as they enable data prediction, and thus, outlier detection.

In typical WSN deployments, low-power and low-cost devices are used and the data is processed in the cloud or on a more powerful machine, outside the network. Therefore, a tree topology is usually used to route the sensor data of the network to a gateway, such as enforced by the Routing Protocol for Low-power and Lossy networks (RPL) [24]. A topology example is provided Fig. 1. When scaling up the wireless network, it becomes necessary to increase the number of gateways in order to avoid bottlenecks. However, having too many gateways

© Springer Nature Switzerland AG 2019
R. Montella et al. (Eds.): IDCS 2019, LNCS 11874, pp. 79–88, 2019.
https://doi.org/10.1007/978-3-030-34914-1_8

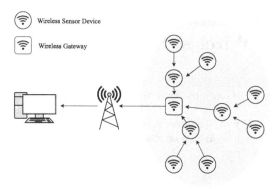

Fig. 1. Typical WSN deployment topology.

will result in creating a bottleneck at the final processing unit. Based on this observation, reducing the data dimension - e.g. at the gateway level- by moving some of the processing to the edge of the network is necessary [19]. Thanks to data correlation, it is reasonable to assume that the gateways will exhibit learning capabilities. Indeed, due to the wireless range of communication, it is likely that -for example- geographical monitoring data of sensors within range of each other is correlated. While powerful data processing techniques such as recurrent neural networks have proven their efficiency in terms of classification, prediction and outlier detection, their use in a WSN context is recent [16,18,22]. In this context, sensors are often battery-powered. Guaranteeing a long lifetime of the network is of greatest importance as it saves on operational costs of the network, such as replacing batteries. In WSNs, data exchanges are contributing the most to the battery depletion of the devices [11].

In this work, we consider a recurrent neural network processing correlated sensor data, and specifically study pre-processing the data within the network using Hebbian plasticity. It is an unsupervised learning mechanism - i.e. it does not generate overhead- and conserves spatial and temporal correlations. We then analyze how performance, energy spent and processing time is affected. Pre-processing the data enables reducing the dimension of the data, reducing the load of the network and avoiding bottlenecks. Bottlenecks are indeed responsible for packet loss, thus, re-transmissions, high energy consumption and delays. These delays may be dangerous if time-critical events have to be detected. While this work highlights the environmental monitoring as a use case, the method can be applied to other predictable time series generated by sensor networks, such as habitat monitoring [21].

In Sect. 2, an overview of the Artificial Intelligence (AI) techniques used in this paper is provided. Section 3 presents our approach, and Sect. 4 validates the approach in terms of performance and wireless energy cost. We conclude this paper in Sect. 5 and explain possible paths for future work.

2   Background

In this section, we describe an overview of the two AI techniques used in this work: Recurrent Neural Networks (RNNs) and Hebbian plasticity. These techniques fall into the scope of Artificial Neural Network (ANNs), which are composed of artificial neurons interconnected together in a structure similar to biological neural networks.

Recurrent Neural Networks

Compared to traditional ANNs, RNNs have their hidden neurons interconnected within the same layer, enabling complex behavior but also memorization of previous data [17,23]. This feature is of particular interest regarding temporally related sensor data. Recent advances in hardware and learning algorithms such as backpropagation have resulted in a popularization of the field, with larger and more complex networks, able to learn faster.

Although theoretically possible, standard RNNs seem to struggle to capture long-term dependencies, due to the vanishing gradient problem [3]. Recently, Long-Short Term Memory (LSTM) neurons [5] have solved this issue. These specific neurons possess a more complex structure with a minor linear interaction with the previous state, enabling more efficient learning of long-term dependencies.

These advances have enabled a variety of application opportunities in WSNs as surveyed in [1]. Diverse problem types are addressed such as localization, security, fault detection or load management. Authors in [16] detail the Dynamic Linear Model (DLM)-LSTM framework composed of a DLM and an LSTM-based neural network. This framework is then used to detect and forecast landslides with low-cost wireless GPS sensors. In [20], the author use a LMS filter and an LSTM network and show that energy can be saved by predicting sensor data, and avoiding packet transmissions. Similarly to environmental monitoring, industrial Internet of Things can benefit from RNNs due to the abundance of spatially and temporally related data [25].

Hebbian Plasticity

RNNs and most neural networks learning algorithms rely on back-propagating the training error to all neurons in order to improve the accuracy. This supervised method is not very costly when running on a CPU or GPU. However, when distributing the learning across machines, this creates significant delays. When it comes to wireless networks, unsupervised learning is of interest as it does not require back-propagating the learning error, hence reducing transmission costs.

Based on biological observations, it is assumed that the synaptic weight between two biological neurons changes according to the interval between their activation. This phenomenon, called Hebbian plasticity, was formalized mathematically by Oja [13] as follows. Let us consider that an output neuron y is triggered by n inputs $\{x_0, ..., x_n\}$ with weights $\{w_0, ..., w_n\}$ according to:

$$y = \sum_{i \in [0,n]} x_i w_i \tag{1}$$

Then, the weight is updated according to:

$$\Delta w_i = y(x_i - yw_i) \times \nu \tag{2}$$

With ν a learning parameter. This specific learning rule has been proven to converge towards the Principal Component Analysis (PCA) of the input data [14]. A variation of this update rule leads to the Independent Component Analysis (ICA) [6]. PCA is a widely used tool for data prediction, as it conserves the main characteristics of correlated input data while being able to reduce the output dimension. Furthermore, it learns in an unsupervised manner and after learning, is able to provide fast online results. Therefore, it makes sense to use it with wireless sensor data and recurrent neural networks.

It has been recently proven that using a combination of both ICA and PCA leads to zero-error blind source separation in a unsupervised manner [7]. In this work, using only PCA is sufficient for the RNN to work on the input data, therefore we will only consider a Hebbian network as presented above.

3   Method

We consider a WSN using a RNN with LSTM cells to actuate on the sensor data. All sensor data must travel through the network toward the RNN processing unit. This congests the network which creates important delays and increases the network's energy consumption. Delays may be decisive if the goal of the RNN is to detect time-critical events. To solve this issue, we investigate the use of pre-processing the data in the wireless network itself using Hebbian plasticity. To do so, we consider that some devices in the network take the role of *aggregator* units. These devices, perform online sensor data fusion to reduce the dimension of the data. An example with A aggregator units is depicted in Fig. 2. N sensors generate data, which are equally fed to A aggregators units. These units learn over time to output m values using Eqs. 1 and 2, which are then given as input to the RNN. As opposed to a deep RNN, a single layer neural network with Oja's learning rule is not computationally costly, and can be run on any low power device.

This method presents the following benefits.

- Hebbian plasticity does not require feedback for learning. Other methods to improve time-series analysis with RNNs such as encoder-decoder networks rely on backpropagation to learn. This exchange between the computing unit and aggregators is costly to do over a wireless medium. Learning in an unsupervised manner does not create additional delays and packet overhead.
- The output of the aggregator units m can be adjusted so that it fits one frame. This allows saving time on the transmissions. Equation eq:learning guarantees learning of the principal components, which allows to reduce the output dimension without loosing meaningful information and correlations.

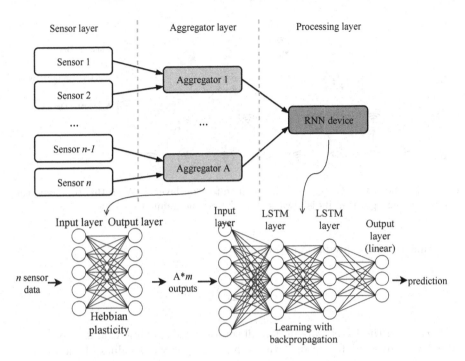

Fig. 2. Functional view of the method with A = 2 aggregator units.

– By clustering the network in this manner, we eliminate the bottleneck at the
RNN processing unit, and create smaller bottlenecks at the aggregator units
which can be processed in parallel.

4   Experimental Validation

We consider a tree topology, as enforced by routing protocols for low-power
devices such as RPL [24]. We assume that the network is a balanced tree $G =
(r, h)$ with $r > 1$ the number of neighbors per devices, and $h > 1$ the depth of the
tree. We consider that only the leaf nodes are sensor devices, i.e. r^h sensors, and
other nodes relay the information to the root of the tree, which then processes
the data with a RNN. We consider replacing some of these relay devices with
aggregator units using Hebbian plasticity as described in Sect. 3. A balanced tree
example is shown in Fig. 3. In this example, the aggregator units are placed on
the second layer of the tree.

In Sect. 4.1, we analyze the impact of these units on the RNN performance.
To do so, the task of the RNN will be to predict the next sensor value. The
RNN is composed of two LSTM layers of the same size as the input layer, and
one linear layer. The Mean Squared Error (MSE) will be used to measure the

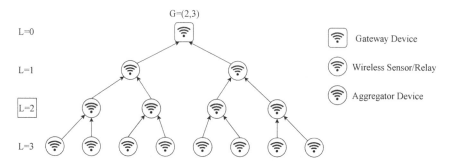

Fig. 3. Balanced tree $G = (2,3)$ with aggregators on layer 2. With this topology, the number of aggregator units is always $A = r^L$ and the number of sensors $N = r^h$.

performance of the prediction. Formally,

$$\text{MSE} = \frac{1}{T} \sum_{t=0}^{T} (Y_t - \hat{Y}_t)^2 \tag{3}$$

with Y_t being the RNN's prediction all sensor values at time t, and $\hat{Y}_t$ being the true value. To emulate sensor data, each sensor generates values of the form

$$f(t) = C_0 + C_1 \sin(\theta_1 t + \phi_1) + C_2 \sin(\theta_2 t + \phi_2) + z \tag{4}$$

with C, θ and ϕ being constant over time but different for each sensor, and z being a Gaussian random variable with mean 0 and standard deviation 0.1 representing noise. This data shape is commonly used to analyze RNN's behavior [4]. The tests are done on 8 CPUs with the neural network framework PyTorch [8].

In Sect. 4.2, we analyze how -and where- adding aggregator units impacts the wireless sensor network in terms of energy efficiency. To do so, we will use the following constants. We consider that a sensor value is a float of size 32 bits. The communication protocol of the network is a low-power wireless protocol such as IEEE 802.15.4 therefore we consider a maximum datarate of 250 kb/s, a packet size of 128 bytes and a payload size of 114 bytes [2]. With these assumptions, we can fine-tune the output of the aggregator units so that their output fits into one frame. The maximum number of floats fitting in one frame is $m = \lfloor \frac{114}{4} \rfloor = 28$. The electrical consumption cost of a packet transmission is estimated to 50 mA [10,12].

4.1 RNN Performance

In a first experiment, we do not consider the topology, but only analyze the performance of the RNN's learning speed with a certain number of aggregator units. The training MSE evolution is presented in Fig. 4. For 20 and 200 devices, we observe that, regardless of the number of aggregator units, training is faster with aggregators. This is due to the fact that one of the characteristics of Hebbian

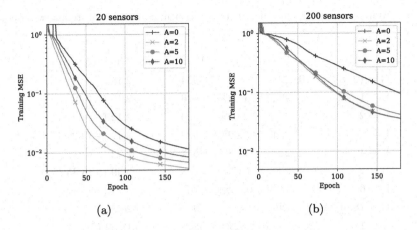

Fig. 4. Training error evolution of the RNN after 180 epochs.

plasticity is to filter out noise. This allows the RNN to detect much faster the sinusoidal patterns, and predict accurately. In Fig. 4a, we observe that learning speed is best with 2 aggregators. Each aggregator unit generates 28 output values. Therefore the more aggregators are added, the more noisy data is generated, which impacts the learning performance. As we see in Fig. 4b, the training speed is not affected with the number of aggregators when the number of devices is large enough.

Table 1. RNN performance metrics for several topologies with 0 aggregators ($A = 0$) and aggregators on different layers L of the balanced tree.

Topology	Data reduction (%)	Test MSE	RNN comp. time (ms)
G = (2, 8) A = 0	0.0	0.452	0.526
L = 1	78.125	0.372 (−17.751%)	0.271 (−48.427%)
L = 2	56.25	0.414 (−8.484%)	0.296 (−43.573%)
L = 3	12.5	0.425 (−5.932%)	0.472 (−10.26%)
G = (2, 9) A = 0	0.0	0.43	1.573
L = 1	89.062	0.383 (−11.005%)	0.269 (−82.862%)
L = 2	78.125	0.403 (−6.396%)	0.299 (−80.955%)
L = 3	56.25	0.411 (−4.49%)	0.486 (−69.061%)
G = (4, 4) A = 0	0.0	0.447	0.548
L = 1	56.25	0.398 (−10.842%)	0.307 (−43.965%)
L = 2	−75.0	0.484 (+8.29%)	1.28 (+133.338%)

In a next step, we compare the testing MSE with and without aggregator units on one of the layers of a balanced tree. All networks have been trained

Table 2. Wireless network efficiency metrics under maximum datarate for two topologies.

Topology	EE (b/J)	Packets sent	Time required (s)
G = (2, 8) A = 0	2285	534	2.18
L = 1	2320 (+1.52%)	526	2.15 (−1.49%)
L = 2	2347 (+2.69%)	520	2.12 (−2.62%)
L = 3	2347 (+2.69%)	520	2.12 (−2.62%)
L = 4	2243 (−1.83%)	544	2.22 (+1.87%)
L = 5	2007 (12.17%)	608	2.49 (+13.85%)
L = 6	1589 (30.46%)	768	3.14 (+43.82%)
G = (8, 4) A = 0	246	4944	20.25
L = 1	253 (+2.82%)	4808	19.69 (2.75%)
L = 2	257 (+4.39%)	4736	19.39 (4.2%)
L = 3	217 (12.09%)	5624	23.03 (+13.75%)

during 390 epochs, and the testing data is separated from the training data. We focus on analyzing the impact of pre-processing the data using Hebbian plasticity. The prediction accuracy can be greatly improved by increasing the number of epochs and fine-tuning the RNN parameters. Results are presented in Table 1. The topology without aggregator units ($A = 0$) is compared with topologies with aggregator units on different layers L of the balanced tree. The data reduction presents the percentage of data filtered out by the aggregators. With aggregator units on the layers closest to the gateway, the data reduction is more important, which also highlights a better performance of the RNN. The computation time is also reduced, due to size of the RNN being proportional to its input data size. However, when the data reduction is negative, i.e. more data is generated by the aggregator units than there is sensor data, an increase in computation time and a lower performance is observed.

4.2   Wireless Energy Efficiency

The Energy Efficiency (EE) metric [9] is commonly given in bits per joule by

$$EE = \frac{\text{datarate}}{\text{energy consumption}} \tag{5}$$

Knowing the topology, we can estimate the energy efficiency of the network in the best case scenario. We assume no interference, no re-transmissions and that the maximum datarate of 250 kb/s is obtained. Results are presented in Table 2. As expected, reducing the sensor data dimension with Hebbian plasticity contributes to sending fewer packets, thus reducing time and energy spent in the network. However, if the aggregator units are not correctly placed, extra data is generated which impacts the wireless network performance. The correct placement appears to depend on the topology. With the balanced tree topologies used, the optimal aggregator placement is in the middle layer as it represents the best trade-off between data reduction and data forwarding. Regarding the RNN's performance, it seems to be always optimal to place the aggregator on the first layer of network. This is indeed where the data reduction is optimal. However, this result depends on the correlation between sensor data. To optimize the wireless network's energy efficiency, the best placement appears to be depending on the topology. Therefore, to optimize the wireless network's energy and/or data reduction, the aggregator placement should be chosen depending on the topology and data of the problem considered.

5 Conclusion

With the density and size of wireless networks increasing, time-critical tasks can be impacted by bottlenecks and network overload. To cope with this issue, moving part of the processing in the network is an appealing solution. To do so, we propose assigning the role of aggregator units to devices in the network which will reduce the size of the data being sent to a processing unit. These Hebbian aggregators use an unsupervised learning mechanism which does not generate packet overhead.

By processing the sensory data with a LSTM-based RNN, we have shown that pre-processing the data in the network allows to both increase the RNN's performance, and reduce its computation time. Furthermore, energy is saved in the network since pre-processing the data reduces the amount of data circulating in the network. The output size of the aggregator units and their placement impact significantly the performance of the RNN and the energy saved in the wireless network. Furthermore, the aggregator units placement highly depends on the data correlation and the physical topology of the network. By fine tuning all these parameters according to an application's requirements, it is possible to find the best trade-off for the network.

Future work will further investigate the link between physical topology, data correlation and aggregator unit placement. Furthermore, a comparison with other unsupervised methods to pre-process the data in the network such as in [20] will be included.

References

1. Ahad, N., Qadir, J., Ahsan, N.: Neural networks in wireless networks: techniques, applications and guidelines. J. Netw. Comput. Appl. **68**, 1–27 (2016)
2. Alves, R.C.A., Margi, C.B.: IEEE 802.15.4e TSCH mode performance analysis. In: 2016 IEEE 13th International Conference on Mobile Ad Hoc and Sensor Systems (MASS), pp. 361–362, October 2016
3. Bengio, Y., Simard, P., Frasconi, P., et al.: Learning long-term dependencies with gradient descent is difficult. IEEE Trans. Neural Netw. **5**(2), 157–166 (1994)
4. Camero, A., Toutouh, J., Alba, E.: Low-cost recurrent neural network expected performance evaluation. arXiv preprint arXiv:1805.07159 (2018)

5. Hochreiter, S., Schmidhuber, J.: Long short-term memory. Neural Comput. **9**(8), 1735–1780 (1997)
6. Hyvärinen, A., Oja, E.: Independent component analysis: algorithms and applications. Neural Netw. **13**(4–5), 411–430 (2000)
7. Isomura, T., Toyoizumi, T.: On the achievability of blind source separation for high-dimensional nonlinear source mixtures. arXiv preprint arXiv:1808.00668 (2018)
8. Ketkar, N.: Introduction to PyTorch. In: Deep Learning with Python, pp. 195–208. Springer, Heidelberg (2017)
9. Kwon, H., Birdsall, T.: Channel capacity in bits per joule. IEEE J. Ocean. Eng. **11**(1), 97–99 (1986)
10. Lee, J.S., Su, Y.W., Shen, C.C., et al.: A comparative study of wireless protocols: Bluetooth, UWB, ZigBee, and Wi-Fi. Ind. Electron. Soc. **5**, 46–51 (2007)
11. Luo, C., Wu, F., Sun, J., Chen, C.W.: Efficient measurement generation and pervasive sparsity for compressive data gathering. IEEE Trans. Wirel. Commun. **9**(12), 3728–3738 (2010)
12. Moridi, M.A., Kawamura, Y., Sharifzadeh, M., Chanda, E.K., Jang, H.: An investigation of underground monitoring and communication system based on radio waves attenuation using ZigBee. Tunn. Undergr. Space Technol. **43**, 362–369 (2014)
13. Oja, E.: Simplified neuron model as a principal component analyzer. J. Math. Biol. **15**(3), 267–273 (1982)
14. Oja, E., Karhunen, J.: An analysis of convergence for a learning version of the subspace method. J. Math. Anal. Appl. **91**(1), 102–111 (1983)
15. Oliveira, L.M., Rodrigues, J.J.: Wireless sensor networks: a survey on environmental monitoring. JCM **6**(2), 143–151 (2011)
16. Pu, F., Xu, Z., Chen, H., Xu, X., Chen, N.: A DLM-LSTM framework for North-South land deformation trend analysis from low-cost GPS sensor time series. J. Sens. **2018**, 11 (2018)
17. Rumelhart, D.E., Hinton, G.E., Williams, R.J.: Learning internal representations by error propagation, Technical report. California University San Diego La Jolla Inst for Cognitive Science (1985)
18. Savaglio, C., Pace, P., Aloi, G., Liotta, A., Fortino, G.: Lightweight reinforcement learning for energy efficient communications in wireless sensor networks. IEEE Access **7**, 29355–29364 (2019)
19. Shi, W., Cao, J., Zhang, Q., Li, Y., Xu, L.: Edge computing: vision and challenges. IEEE Internet Things J. **3**(5), 637–646 (2016)
20. Shu, T., Chen, J., Bhargava, V., de Silva, C.W.: An energy-efficient dual prediction scheme using LMS filter and LSTM in wireless sensor networks for environment monitoring. IEEE Internet Things J. **6**, 6736–6747 (2019)
21. Szewczyk, R., Mainwaring, A., Polastre, J., Anderson, J., Culler, D.: An analysis of a large scale habitat monitoring application. In: Proceedings of the 2nd International Conference on Embedded Networked Sensor Systems, pp. 214–226. ACM (2004)
22. Wang, Y., Zhou, J., Chen, K., Wang, Y., Liu, L.: Water quality prediction method based on LSTM neural network. In: 2017 12th International Conference on Intelligent Systems and Knowledge Engineering (ISKE), pp. 1–5. IEEE (2017)
23. Werbos, P.J., et al.: Backpropagation through time: what it does and how to do it. Proc. IEEE **78**(10), 1550–1560 (1990)
24. Winter, T., et al.: RPL: IPv6 routing protocol for low-power and lossy networks. RFC 6550, RFC Editor, March 2012
25. Zhang, W., et al.: LSTM-based analysis of industrial IoT equipment. IEEE Access **6**, 23551–23560 (2018)

A High Performance Modified K-Means Algorithm for Dynamic Data Clustering in Multi-core CPUs Based Environments

Giuliano Laccetti[1], Marco Lapegna[1(✉)], Valeria Mele[1], and Diego Romano[2]

[1] Department of Mathematics and Applications,
University of Naples Federico II, Naples, Italy
{giuliano.laccetti,marco.lapegna,valeria.mele}@unina.it
[2] Institute for High Performance Computing and Networking (ICAR),
National Research Council (CNR), Naples, Italy
diego.romano@cnr.it

Abstract. K-means algorithm is one of the most widely used methods in data mining and statistical data analysis to partition several objects in K distinct groups, called clusters, on the basis of their similarities. The main problel and distributed clustering algorithms start to be designem of this algorithm is that it requires the number of clusters as an input data, but in the real life it is very difficult to fix in advance such value. In this work we propose a parallel modified K-means algorithm where the number of clusters is increased at run time in a iterative procedure until a given cluster quality metric is satisfied. To improve the performance of the procedure, at each iteration two new clusters are created, splitting only the cluster with the worst value of the quality metric. Furthermore, experiments in a multi-core CPUs based environment are presented.

Keywords: K-Means clustering · Parallel adaptive algorithm · Unsupervised learning · Data mining

1 Introduction

The data clustering problem has been addressed by researchers in many disciplines, and it has several different applications in the scientific world, from biological research, to finance, marketing, logistic, robotics, mathematical and statistical analysis, image processing, identifying patterns, and the classifications of medical tests [2, 30].

Thus, we can say that clustering algorithms are today one of the most important steps in exploratory data analysis and one the most important data mining methodology. They can be seen as unsupervised classification approaches whose main goal is to group similar data with in the same cluster according precise metrics.

When data is so huge that become Big Data, meaning terabytes or petabytes of data with various kinds and quickly increasing, the hottest point is how to get

© Springer Nature Switzerland AG 2019
R. Montella et al. (Eds.): IDCS 2019, LNCS 11874, pp. 89–99, 2019.
https://doi.org/10.1007/978-3-030-34914-1_9

the results in a reasonable time, so parallel and distributed clustering algorithms start to be designed, that essentially fall into one of the following [28]:

- un-automated data distribution algorithms, usually getting better improvements in scaling and speed up, like DBDC [2], PARMETIS [17], Epidemic K-Means [9] and GPU based parallel clustering techniques (for example G-DBSCAN in [3])
- automated data distribution, or MapReduce based [28], algorithms. MapReduce is a framework able to distribute the computation between multiple machines in an automatic fashion. There are MapReduce versions for K-means (PKmeans) [31], for DBSCAN (MR-DBSCAN) [14] and for the GPU based algorithm (GPMR).

There are several surveys, reviews and comparative study about clustering applications and techniques, written in the last twenty years, that one can refer to get an overall picture of the clustering approaches, sequential and parallel, in their evolution to the current state of art (e.g. [16,24,29,30]). Different surveys give often different taxonomies, but all of them name the K-means as one the most popular clustering algorithm, both in the sequential design and in the parallel one. K-means algorithms is the best known Squared Error-based clustering approach [30], because of its simplicity, ability to deal with large number of attributes, and providing good quality clusters with the $N * K * d$ computational complexity where N is the number of elements in data space, K is count of clusters to be identified, and d is the number of attributes/dimensions [12]. Results of K-Means clustering depends on cluster center initialization and it is not able to provide globally optimum results. For different data sets, diverse versions of K-Means clustering must be chosen, and many modified version of the K-means algorithm has been proposed in the last years to decrease the complexity or increase the solution quality [1,15,16,25,27].

The present work joins this research trend. More precisely it describes a parallel K-means algorithm for dynamic clustering where the number of clusters K is defined at run time and it is aimed to realize a trade-off between the algorithm performance and a global quality index for the clusters.

The rest of the paper is organized as follow: in Sect. 2 we introduce our parallel adaptive K-means algorithm, in Sect. 3 we report some implementation details, in Sect. 4 we show the results obtained from experiments we have done to validate the new algorithm, and in Sect. 4 we summarize the work.

2   A Parallel Adaptive K-Means Algorithm

The K-means algorithm is a procedure aimed to define K clusters where each of them contains at least one element and each element belong to one cluster only. A formal description of the procedure follows.

Given a set of N vectors $S = \{\mathbf{s}_n : \mathbf{s}_n \in \mathbf{R}^d \quad n = 1, .., N\}$ in the d-dimensional space, and an integer K, the K-means algorithm collects the items of S in the K subgroups of a partition $\mathcal{P}_K = \{C_k : C_k \subset S \quad k = 1, .., K\}$ of

S, such that $\bigcup C_k = S$ and $C_{k1} \bigcap C_{k2} = \emptyset$ with $k1 \neq k2$, on the basis of their similarity. Usually the similarity between two objects is measured by means the Euclidean norm or some other metric. Its traditional description is then based on the following steps:

Step 1. Assign randomly the N elements $s_n \in S$ to K arbitrary subgroups C_k each of them with N_k items

Step 2. Compute the centers $\mathbf{c}_k$ of the $C^{(k)}$ with the following vector operation:

$$\mathbf{c}_k = \frac{1}{N_k} \sum_{s_n \in C_k} s_n \quad k = 1, .., K \tag{1}$$

Step 3. $\forall \mathbf{s}_n \in S$ find the cluster $C_{\overline{k}}$ minimizing the Euclidean distance from the center of the cluster, that is:

$$\mathbf{s}_n \in C_{\overline{k}} \Leftrightarrow \|\mathbf{s}_n - \mathbf{c}_{\overline{k}}\|_2 = \min_{k=1,..,K} \|\mathbf{s}_n - \mathbf{c}_k\|_2 \tag{2}$$

Step 4. Reassign $\mathbf{s}_n$ to $\in C_{\overline{k}}$
Step 5. Repeat steps 2–4 until there is no change.

One of the major flaws of this algorithm is the need to fix the number of clusters K before the execution. Mainly with large dimensions d and number of elements N is almost impossible to define a suitable K. If it is too large similar items will be put in different clusters. On the other hand, if K is too small, there is the risk that dissimilar items will be grouped in the same cluster.

Furthermore, several studies have shown that the previous algorithm does not produce an analytic solution, and the result strongly depends on the initial assignment of the elements to the clusters [26]. For such reasons the algorithm is executed several times with different vale of K, and some quality index is used to choose a "good solution". To this aim several indices have been introduced in the literature (see for example [12]).

As an example consider the root-mean-square standard deviation (RMSSTD) index:

$$R_{RMSSTD} = \left[\frac{\sum_{k=1}^{K} \sum_{s_n \in C_k} \|\mathbf{s}_n - \mathbf{c}_k\|_2^2}{d(N - K)} \right]^{1/2} \tag{3}$$

that measure the homogeneity of the clusters quality. The RMSSTD quality index decreases when the number of clusters K increases, until a fair homogeneity is reached, so that the optimal number of clusters is then the value of K at which the RMSSTD starts to grow. On the basis of these considerations we can design the following iterative algorithm that increases the number of clusters at each step.

Algorithm 1. iterative K-means algorithm

1) Set the number of clusters $K = 0$

2) **repeat**

      2.1) Increase the number of clusters $K = K + 1$

      2.2) Assign randomly the N elements $s_n \in S$ to arbitrary
           K clusters C_k, each of them with N_k items

      2.3) **repeat**

           2.3.1) Compute the centers $\mathbf{c}_k$ of the C_k as in (1)

           2.3.2) For each $\mathbf{s}_n \in S$ find the cluster $C_{\overline{k}}$ minimizing the
                 Euclidean distance from $\mathbf{c}_k$ as in (2)

           2.3.3) Reassign the elements $\mathbf{s}_n$ to the new clusters

           until (no change in the reassignment)

      2.4) update RMSSTD as in (3)

     until (RMSSTD starts to grow or it is smaller than a given threshold)

This strategy repeatedly tests several partitioning configurations with different values of K and it is possible to implement it only if the Computational Cost (CC) of the kernels is not too large.

The cost of the step 2.3.3 is strongly dependent on how the elements are distributed in the K cluster C_k at the step 2.2. An unsuitable initial assignment can result in a huge number of movement of the elements $\mathbf{s}_n$ among the clusters C_k in order to satisfy the stopping criterion of the iterative structure 2.3.

Our method is then designed to reduce the movements of the elements among the clusters, with the aim of achieving a trade-off between a good initial distribution with a reasonable computational cost.

The main idea of our method is to use the partition $\mathcal{P}_{K-1}$ of the elements already defined in the previous iteration, working only on the clusters with the more dissimilar elements and avoiding to starting over with a random distribution in step 2.2. To this aim, let consider the standard deviation of the elements $\mathbf{s}_k$ in the cluster C_k:

$$\sigma_k = \sqrt{\frac{1}{N_k - 1} \sum_{n=1}^{N_k} (\mathbf{s}_n - \mathbf{c}_k)^2}$$

The value of σ_k can be used to measure the similarity of the elements in C_k. Smaller the value S_k is, closer to the center $\mathbf{c}_k$ are the elements of C_k, and the cluster is composed by similar elements. For a such reason our strategy, in the step 2.2, defines the new partition $\mathcal{P}_K$ by splitting in two subset C_λ and C_μ only the cluster C_{K-1}^* with the largest standard deviation in the previous iteration. When $K = 1$ the partition $\mathcal{P}_1$ is defined by only 1 cluster $C_1 \equiv S$. More precisely:

$$\begin{aligned} K = 1 \quad & \mathcal{P}_1 = \{C_1\} \quad \text{where} \quad C_1 \equiv S \\ K > 1 \quad & \mathcal{P}_K = \mathcal{P}_{K-1} - \{C_{K-1}^*\} \cup \{C_\lambda, C_\mu\} \end{aligned} \tag{4}$$

This strategy is based on the assumption that, at a given iteration K, very similar items have been already grouped in compact clusters with small values for σ_k at the previous iteration $K - 1$, which therefore does not require an assignment to a new cluster. At this regard, it is interesting to note that the idea of reorganizing the elements of a partition, according the value of a given quality index computed at run time, is quite common in many procedures called *adaptive* algorithms. For example, with regard to the iterative algorithms for the numerical integration, many strategies are known for the refinement of the integration domain only where a large discretization error is estimated [8, 18–23].

From what has been said, we propose an adaptive modified K-mean algorithm as follow:

Algorithm 2. adaptive K-means algorithm

1) Set the number of clusters $K = 0$
2) **repeat**
    2.1) Increase the number of clusters $K = K + 1$
    2.2) find the cluster C_{K-1}^* with the largest standard deviation
    2.3) define the new partition of clusters $\mathcal{P}_K$ as in 3
    2.4) **repeat**
        2.4.1) Compute the centers $\mathbf{c}_k$ of the C_k as in (1)
        2.4.2) For each $\mathbf{s}_n \in S$ find the cluster $C_{\overline{k}}$ minimizing the
              Euclidean distance from $\mathbf{c}_k$ as in (2)
        2.4.3) Reassign the elements $\mathbf{s}_n$ to the new clusters
    until (no change in the reassignment)
    2.5) update RMSSTD as in (3)
until (RMSSTD starts to grow or it is smaller than a given threshold)

3   Implementation Details

Following there are some implementation details regarding the proposed parallel adaptive K-means algorithm (see also Fig. 1).

All the elements $\mathbf{s}_n \in S$ are stored, row by row, in a $N \times d$ array. In order to improve the computational cost, our method does not change the order of the rows of the array, when the elements must be moved from a cluster to another one, in the step 2.4.3. In such step, the composition of each cluster is then defined by means of contiguous items in a array PT, pointing to the rows of S representing the elements of the cluster. All the displacements of elements among clusters, required in the step 2.4.3, are then implemented by exchanging only the pointers in the array PT.

In order to identify the contiguous items of the array PT pointing to a given cluster C_k, a suitable data structure is defined: a Cluster Descriptor (CD_k) that contains

- the cluster identifier (k)
- the pointer to the first elements of the cluster in the array PT (F_k)
- the number of elements of the cluster (N_k)
- the center of the cluster ($\mathbf{c}_k$)
- the standard deviation of the elements of the cluster (σ_k).

Finally, the access to these structures CD_k is provided by a Cluster Table (CT), that is a pointers array whose k-th element refers to the cluster descriptor CD_k of the cluster C_k.

This data organization allows quick and efficient access to all clusters information required in Algorithm 2.

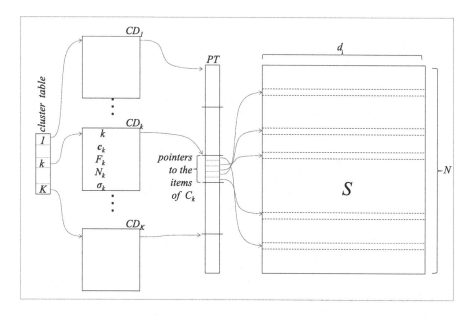

Fig. 1. Data structures organization for the K-means adaptive algorithm

From the analysis of Algorithm 2 and Fig. 1 it is also well evident that the proposed K-means algorithm can benefit from modern parallel architectures. In this work we concentrate the attention on multi-core CPUs with independent processing units (the cores), able to actualize a shared memory programming model on the basis of all High Performance Computing systems. In these CPUs, each core has its own set of processor registers so that the operating system is able to schedule independent threads among them, and a general purposes shared-memory Multiple Program Multiple Data programming model can be used.

From what has been said, in Algorithm 2 we can then introduce parallelism in Algorithm 2 to at least two levels:

Cluster level. With this strategy the degree of parallelism if given by the number of clusters K, so that it is possible to distribute the clusters C_k among the P threads. We use this approach in the step 2.4.1 of Algorithm 2.

Element level. With this strategy the degree of parallelism is given by the number of elements N, so that it is possible to distribute the elements s_n among the P threads. We use this approach in the step 2.4.2 of Algorithm 2.

The only sequential task of Algorithm 2 is the step 2.4.3, where it is required an exclusive access to the array PT, in order to avoid race conditions on the elements of the array. Such a step is then a critical task for the efficiency of the whole algorithm. More precisely, given T_P the elapsed time required to execute Algorithm 2 on P processing units, from the Amdhal law we have:

$$S_P = \frac{T_1}{T_P} = \frac{1}{\alpha + (1-\alpha)/P} \qquad E_P = \frac{T_1}{PT_P} = \frac{1}{\alpha P + (1-\alpha)} \qquad (5)$$

as models for the Speed-up and the Efficiency. From (5), we observe that the *serial fraction* $\alpha = T_s/T_1$, that is the ratio between the time needed to execute the sequential section of the algorithm T_s and the total elapsed time T_1 with $P = 1$ thread, is a severe decay factor for the efficiency.

4 Experimental Results

To test our method, from the accuracy and the efficiency points of view, several experiments have been conducted on a system equipped with a 16-core Intel E7-4850V4 CPU running a 2.1 Ghz and 16 Gbytes of main memory. The algorithms have been implemented in C language under Linux operating system with the POSIX thread library for the thread management.

The experiments have been conducted using the Letter Recognition data set [11] from the UCI Machine Learning Repository [10]. This is a large data set based on $N = 20,000$ unique items, each of them representing the black and withe image of an uppercase letter. The character images are based on 20 different fonts and each letter within these 20 fonts was randomly distorted to produce an item of the data set. Each item was converted into $d = 16$ numerical attributes (statistical moments and edge counts) which were then scaled to fit into a range of integer values from 0 through 15. The classification task for this data set is considered especially challenging because of the wide diversity among the different fonts and because of the primitive nature of the attributes.

The first set of experiment is aimed to compare the performance of our proposed Algorithm 2 with the basic Algorithm 1. In Table 1 we report the number of items s_n displaced in new clusters (*disp*) and the total elapsed time in second (*time*) with 1 core for the generation of $K = 26$ clusters, i.e. one for each letter of the English alphabet.

Table 1. Performance comparison between Algorithms 1 and 2.

Algorithm 1		Algorithm 2	
Disp	*Time*	*Disp*	*Time*
1001349	49.3	130801	21.1

As expected, with the Algorithm 2 we measure a great gain in term of execution time, because it does not displace similar items already grouped in clusters with a small standard deviation σ_k.

Also the multi-threaded execution shows similar performance gains. Table 2 reports the total elapsed time in second (*time*), the Speed-up (S_P) and the Efficiency (E_P) by using $P = 4, 8, 12$ and 16 cores of the CPU.

Table 2. Speed up comparison between Algorithms 1 and 2.

P	Algorithm 1			Algorithm 2		
	Time	S_P	E_P	*Time*	S_P	E_P
4	25.94	1.9	0.48	8.11	2.6	0.65
8	15.40	3.2	0.40	4.58	4.6	0.58
12	11.73	4.2	0.35	3.24	6.5	0.54
16	9.66	5.1	0.32	2.57	8.2	0.51

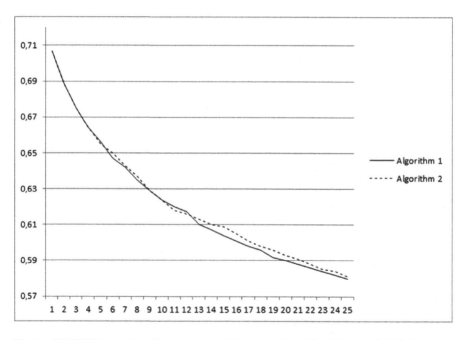

Fig. 2. RMSSTD varying the number of iteration for Algorithm 1 (solid line) and Algorithm 2 (dashed line).

In this case, it is interesting to note that with the Algorithm 2 we have also a significant gain in term of Speed-up and Efficiency. At this regard we remember that the reassignment of the elements $\mathbf{s}_n$ to the new clusters, through a reorganization of the array PT in step 2.4.3, is an inherently sequential task, so that it has a strong impact on the Efficiency. With the reduction of the computational cost of this step, we also reduce the serial fraction of the algorithm, with a significant improvement of the Speed-up and the Efficiency.

A second set of experiments is aimed to measure the accuracy of the solution computed by Algorithm 2. To this aim we use the value of root-mean-square standard deviation RMSSTD, given by (3), as a measure of the global quality index of the generated clusters. Figure 2 shows the value of R_{RMSSTD} versus the number of generated clusters K for both Algorithm 1 and Algorithm 2. These values differ by less 1%, confirming that the Algorithm 2 generates a partition of S very similar to the one computed by the traditional K means algorithm.

5 Conclusions

In this paper we introduced a parallel adaptive approach to improve the performance of dynamic data clustering with the K-means algorithm. The main drawback of this well known algorithm is that the number of clusters K should be fixed as input data, but in several real cases it is very difficult to define such a value in advance. Several algorithms attempts to overcame this problem by finding the optimal value at run time by increasing the number of clusters until some stopping criterion is satisfied, but the computational cost can be very expensive, because the need to reallocate the node of the set at each iteration. Our work addresses this aspect, avoiding the displacement of similar items already grouped into compact clusters, characterized by small values of the standard deviation. The achieved results are very promising, with a clusters quality similar to traditional approaches that redistribute all the items of the set at each step, with a much lower computational cost and a higher performance. Future work can focus on the implementation of Algorithm 2 on other advanced computing environment such as parallel/distributed computers or GPU based systems [6,7,13] with special regard to the issues of fault tolerance and the performance [4,5].

References

1. Abubaker, M., Ashour, W.M.: Efficient data clustering algorithms: improvements over K-means. Int. J. Intell. Syst. Appl. **5**, 37–49 (2013)
2. Aggarwal, C.C., Reddy, C.K.: Data Clustering, Algorithms and Applications. Chapman and Hall/CRC, London (2013)
3. Andrade, G., Ramos, G., Madeira, D., Sachetto, R., Ferreira, R., Rocha, L.: G-DBSCAN: a GPU accelerated algorithm for density-based clustering. Procedia Comput. Sci. **18**, 369–378 (2013)
4. Boccia, V., Carracciuolo, L., Laccetti, G., Lapegna, M., Mele, V.: HADAB: enabling fault tolerance in parallel applications running in distributed environments. In: Wyrzykowski, R., Dongarra, J., Karczewski, K., Waśniewski, J. (eds.) PPAM 2011. LNCS, vol. 7203, pp. 700–709. Springer, Heidelberg (2012). https://doi.org/10.1007/978-3-642-31464-3_71

5. Caruso, P., Laccetti, G., Lapegna, M.: A performance contract system in a grid enabling, component based programming environment. In: Sloot, P.M.A., Hoekstra, A.G., Priol, T., Reinefeld, A., Bubak, M. (eds.) EGC 2005. LNCS, vol. 3470, pp. 982–992. Springer, Heidelberg (2005). https://doi.org/10.1007/11508380_100

6. D'Ambra, P., Danelutto, M., di Serafino, D., Lapegna, M.: Advanced environments for parallel and distributed applications: a view of the current status. Parallel Comput. **28**, 1637–1662 (2002)

7. D'Ambra, P., Danelutto, M., di Serafino, D., Lapegna, M.: Integrating MPI-based numerical software into an advanced parallel computing environment. In: Proceedings of the Eleventh Euromicro Conference on Parallel Distributed and Network-based Procesing, Clematis ed., pp. 283–291. IEEE (2003)

8. D'Apuzzo, M., Lapegna, M., Murli, A.: Scalability and load balancing in adaptive algorithms for multidimensional integration. Parallel Comput. **23**, 1199–1210 (1997)

9. Di Fatta, G., Blasa, F., Cafiero, S., Fortino, G.: Fault tolerant decentralised K-means clustering for asynchronous large-scale networks. J. Parallel Distrib. Comput. **73**(2013), 317–329 (2013)

10. Dua, D., Graff, C.: UCI Machine Learning Repository. University of California, School of Information and Computer Science, Irvine (2017). http://archive.ics.uci.edu/ml

11. Frey, P.W., Slate, D.J.: Letter recognition using Holland-style adaptive classifiers. Mach. Learn. **6**, 161–182 (1991)

12. Gan, D.G., Ma, C., Wu, J.: Data Clustering: Theory, Algorithms, and Applications. ASA-SIAM Series on Statistics and Applied Probability. SIAM, Philadelphia. ASA, Alexandria (2007)

13. Gregoretti, F., Laccetti, G., Murli, A., Oliva, G., Scafuri, U.: MGF: a grid-enabled MPI library. Future Gener. Comput. Syst. **24**, 158–165 (2008)

14. He, Y., Tan, H., Luo, W., Feng, S., Fan, J.: MR-DBSCAN: a scalable MapReduce-based DBSCAN algorithm for heavily skewed data. Front. Comput. Sci. **8**, 83–99 (2014)

15. Huang, Z.X.: Extensions to the K-means algorithm for clustering large datasets with categorical values. Data Min. Knowl. Disc. **2**, 283–304 (1998)

16. Joshi, A., Kaur, R.: A review: comparative study of various clustering techniques in data mining. Int. J. Adv. Res. Comput. Sci. Softw. Eng. **3**, 55–57 (2013)

17. Karypis, G., Kumar, V.: Parallel multilevel K-way partitioning for irregular graphs. SIAM Rev. **41**, 278–300 (1999)

18. Laccetti, G., Lapegna, M.: PAMIHR. a parallel FORTRAN program for multidimensional quadrature on distributed memory architectures. In: Amestoy, P., et al. (eds.) Euro-Par 1999. LNCS, vol. 1685, pp. 1144–1148. Springer, Heidelberg (1999). https://doi.org/10.1007/3-540-48311-X_160

19. Laccetti, G., Lapegna, M., Mele, V., Montella, R.: An adaptive algorithm for high-dimensional integrals on heterogeneous CPUGPU systems. Concurr. Comput. Pract. Exp. **31**, e4945 (2018)

20. Laccetti, G., Lapegna, M., Mele, V., Romano, D., Murli, A.: A double adaptive algorithm for multidimensional integration on multicore based HPC systems. Int. J. Parallel Program. **40**, 397–409 (2012)

21. Laccetti, G., Lapegna, M., Mele, V., Romano, D.: A study on adaptive algorithms for numerical quadrature on heterogeneous GPU and multicore based systems. In: Wyrzykowski, R., Dongarra, J., Karczewski, K., Waśniewski, J. (eds.) PPAM 2013. LNCS, vol. 8384, pp. 704–713. Springer, Heidelberg (2014). https://doi.org/10.1007/978-3-642-55224-3_66

22. Laccetti, G., Lapegna, M., Mele, V.: A loosely coordinated model for heap-based priority queues in multicore environments. Int. J. Parallel Prog. **44**, 901–921 (2016)
23. Lapegna, M.: A global adaptive quadrature for the approximate computation of multidimensional integrals on a distributed memory multiprocessor. Concurr. Pract. Exp. **4**, 413–426 (1992)
24. Patibandla, R.S.M.L., Veeranjaneyulu, N.: Survey on clustering algorithms for unstructured data. In: Bhateja, V., Coello Coello, C.A., Satapathy, S.C., Pattnaik, P.K. (eds.) Intelligent Engineering Informatics. AISC, vol. 695, pp. 421–429. Springer, Singapore (2018). https://doi.org/10.1007/978-981-10-7566-7_41
25. Pelleg, D., Moore, A.W.: X-means: extending k-means with efficient estimation of the number of clusters. In: Proceedings of the 17th International Conference on Machine Learning, pp. 727–734. Morgan Kaufmann (2000)
26. Pena, J.M., Lozano, J.A., Larranaga, P.: An empirical comparison of four initialization methods for the K-means algorithm. Pattern Recogn. Lett. **20**, 1027–1040 (1999)
27. Shindler, M., Wong, A., Meyerson, A.: Fast and accurate k-means for large datasets. In: Shawe-Taylor, J., Zemel, R.S., Bartlett, P.L., Pereira, F.C.N., Weinberger, K.Q. (eds.): Proceedings of 25th Annual Conference on Neural Information Processing Systems, pp. 2375–2383 (2011)
28. Shirkhorshidi, A.S., Aghabozorgi, S., Wah, T.Y., Herawan, T.: Big data clustering: a review. In: Murgante, B., et al. (eds.) ICCSA 2014. LNCS, vol. 8583, pp. 707–720. Springer, Cham (2014). https://doi.org/10.1007/978-3-319-09156-3_49
29. Xu, D., Tian, Y.: A comprehensive survey of clustering algorithms. Ann. Data Sci. **2**, 165–193 (2015)
30. Xu, R., Wunsch, D.: Survey of clustering algorithms. Trans. Neural Netw. **16**, 645–678 (2005)
31. Zhao, W., Ma, H., He, Q.: Parallel K-means clustering based on MapReduce. In: Jaatun, M.G., Zhao, G., Rong, C. (eds.) CloudCom 2009. LNCS, vol. 5931, pp. 674–679. Springer, Heidelberg (2009). https://doi.org/10.1007/978-3-642-10665-1_71

Overcoming GPU Memory Capacity Limitations in Hybrid MPI Implementations of CFD

Jake Choi[1]([✉]), Yoonhee Kim[2], and Heon-young Yeom[1]

[1] Department of Computer Science, Seoul National University, Seoul, South Korea
kidcoder@snu.ac.kr
[2] Department of Computer Science, Sookmyung Women's University,
Seoul, South Korea

Abstract. In this paper, we describe a hybrid MPI implementation of a discontinuous Galerkin scheme in Computational Fluid Dynamics which can utilize all the available processing units (CPU cores or GPU devices) on each computational node. We describe the optimization techniques used in our GPU implementation making it up to 74.88x faster than the single core CPU implementation in our machine environment. We also perform experiments on work partitioning between heterogeneous devices to measure the ideal load balance achieving the optimal performance in a single node consisting of heterogeneous processing units. The key problem is that CFD workloads need to allocate large amounts of both host and GPU device memory in order to compute accurate results. There exists an economic burden, not to mention additional communication overheads of simply scaling out by adding more nodes with high-end scientific GPU devices. In a micro-management perspective, workload size in each single node is also limited by its attached GPU memory capacity. To overcome this, we use ZFP, a floating-point compression algorithm to save at least 25% of data usage in our workloads, with less performance degradation than using NVIDIA UM.

Keywords: CFD · MPI · CUDA · GPU · Compression · Memory

1 Introduction

The rising demand for analyzing more complex aerodynamic applications has led to the development of high-order methods that break through the limitations of conventional 2nd-order finite volume methods (FVM). The high-order methods possess many attractive features: the capability to achieve arbitrary high accuracy with compact stencils, high spectral resolvability fitted to turbulence simulation, and high scalability under large parallel computing systems.

This research was supported by Next-Generation Information Computing Development Program through the National Research Foundation of Korea (NRF) funded by the Ministry of Science, ICT (2015M3C4A7065646).

© Springer Nature Switzerland AG 2019
R. Montella et al. (Eds.): IDCS 2019, LNCS 11874, pp. 100–111, 2019.
https://doi.org/10.1007/978-3-030-34914-1_10

In this paper, the three-dimensional compressible Navier-Stokes equations given by

$$\frac{\partial \mathbf{Q}}{\partial t} + \boldsymbol{\nabla} \cdot \mathbf{F_c}(\mathbf{Q}) = \boldsymbol{\nabla} \cdot \mathbf{F_v}(\mathbf{Q}, \boldsymbol{\nabla}\mathbf{Q}), \tag{1}$$

where $\mathbf{Q}$ are conservative variables and $\mathbf{F_c}(\mathbf{Q}), \mathbf{F_v}(\mathbf{Q}, \boldsymbol{\nabla}\mathbf{Q})$ are convective and viscous fluxes respectively, are considered.

Among various high-order methods, we focus on the discontinuous Galerkin method [21] that is the most widely used in CFD society because of its intuitive form and rigorous mathematical backgrounds. Applying the discontinuous Galerkin method into Eq. (1), we finally get the following weak formulation on each element Ω:

$$\int_\Omega \frac{\partial \mathbf{Q}}{\partial t} \phi dV + \int_{\partial\Omega} \left(\widehat{\mathbf{F_c} \cdot \mathbf{n}} - \widehat{\mathbf{F_v} \cdot \mathbf{n}} \right) \phi dA =$$
$$\int_\Omega \boldsymbol{\nabla}\phi \cdot (\mathbf{F_c} - \mathbf{F_v}) \, dV, \tag{2}$$

where ϕ is the orthogonal basis computed from the modified Gram-Schmidt process [22]. Here, $\widehat{\mathbf{F_c} \cdot \mathbf{n}}$ is a monotone numerical convective flux used in FVM, and $\widehat{\mathbf{F_v} \cdot \mathbf{n}}$ is a numerical viscous flux computed via BR2 method [23].

Both massively multicore GPUs and clusters of CPUs can be used to accelerate such high-order methods of computational fluid dynamics (CFD). CFD workloads are composed of calculation-heavy tasks, where input and output data can be divided into independent portions, with little communication necessary in each iterative step. Therefore, the benefit of performing calculations in parallel outweigh the costs of communication among different independent tasks. In this paper, we initially implement a hybrid MPI implementation to accelerate CFD workloads on both CPUs and GPUs in parallel. We show performance improvements of up to 22% compared to the GPU-only version.

One potential problem that can arise is that data allocated to the GPU could exceed device memory capacity. Workload sizes beyond hundreds of GB cannot be fully contained in even high-end GPU devices like the Tesla P100, which only possess a mere 16 GB of memory capacity. To rectify this, previously unnecessary memory management operations transferring data to and from host memory need to be taken in each iteration step, leading to large overheads. In order to not deal with such nuisances, NVIDIA UM (Unified Memory) [25] can be used to unify the GPU device memory with host memory.

Introduced in CUDA 6, NVIDIA UM is a single memory address space that is accessible from any processor in the system [26]. It allows applications to allocate data that can be written or read to from code running on either CPUs or GPUs. Using UM eliminates the need for explicit memory copies from host memory to GPU device memory. The system will automatically perform page migration on-demand to the memory of the accessing processor. Even though UM provides simplicity in its usage, the system is ignorant of the actual data access patterns of applications using it. In our evaluation, we show that total performance drops significantly if the working set size for the GPU process exceeds its total device memory.

In order to overcome such performance limitations, our GPU implementation utilizes CUDA-based ZFP [31], a floating point compression algorithm, to compress the working set data in the pre-processing step. We achieve lossless compression rates of up to 50%, and perform partial block decompression on the GPU. We evaluate the performance overheads of decompression for various CFD workloads in comparison to the baseline UM performance. We also evaluate the amount of compression we can achieve on the working set without incurring data loss.

To summarize, our paper makes the following contributions:

- We derive GPU kernel implementations of CFD from the CPU version that are optimized to perform better than the cuBLAS library on general consumer commodity GeForce GPUs.
- Our GPU implementation is capable of utilizing NVIDIA UM.
- We utilize MPI to allow parallel execution on both CPUs and GPUs in a heterogeneous environment.
- We use two techniques, ZFP partial block decompression, and GPU memory overwriting to reduce data usage by up to a maximum of 50% with less overhead than simply managing data automatically with UM.

The rest of this paper is structured as follows. We first examine related work in Sect. 2. Subsequently, we describe the implementation of our techniques in three subsections in Sect. 3. We describe our experimental setup and show evaluation results in Sect. 4, and conclude with directions for future work in Sect. 5.

2   Related Work

The field of CFD has an extensive amount of existing literature mainly consisting of GPU implementations that boast magnitude-of-order speedups over sequential single-threaded CPU code. Work using multi-threaded CPU implementations also seem to compete against their GPU counterparts. The common thread of such works is that most advocate using purely homogeneous multi-threaded CPU [19,20] or GPU [8,9,16] implementations, but rarely are hybrid implementations considered. Such works essentially recommend competing implementations with a preference towards one type of architecture. However, our work uses an heterogeneous MPI implementation which can take full advantage of all available processing units. Some GPU implementations are able to utilize multiple devices [11,17,18] for scalability, but these works also do not consider CPU usage in parallel. Albeit there are less common works which suggest efficient methods of using a combination of either MPI or OpenMP to solve CFD problems in heterogeneous systems [28], these works deal with less complex methods that are lower-order. They also do not mention GPU memory capacity issues regarding large workloads at all. Moreover, to the best of our knowledge, we were unable to find any related work that dealt with reducing the data usage of CFD workloads in GPU memory.

3   Implementation

Our GPU implementation has two versions, one using NVIDIA UM, and the other using manual CUDA memory operations. Workload size is limited to GPU device capacity when ordinary `cudaMalloc` is used, but using UM allows the workload size to reach host memory limits. In the latter case we prefetch data from the host to GPU memory by using `cudaMemPrefetchAsync`. Table 1 shows the size of major data arrays along with their access type in our GPU kernels.

When executing our GPU implementation, only one CPU core is responsible for the management of GPU operations. This leaves the other cores idle. By partitioning the workload in the pre-processing stage using ParMETIS [29], we assigned different weights to different MPI processes, allocating a subset of the data to each process. By doing so, we are able to independently execute different processes on either GPU devices or CPU cores, based on the rank of the process. In the following Subsects. 3.1, 3.2, and 3.3, we will explain the GPU optimizations we performed in detail, along with how we used ZFP compression or memory buffer overwriting to save data usage when GPU memory capacity is not sufficient to completely contain the given workload.

3.1   CUDA Optimizations

The CUDA implementation consists of a total of 17 separate kernels. Among these 17 kernels, 9 are used in calculations needed for computing intermediate **rhs** values, 5 are used for updating the **solution** values and the remaining 3 is for calculating the time step after each iteration. A profiling of the kernels using *nvprof* [10] is performed to show which kernels take up the majority of program time in Table 1. Kernels with less execution time are omitted. Among the nine major kernels, three kernels each are responsible for calculating the face, periodic boundary and boundary, and cell values, respectively. We prefix such kernels as *first_loop_#*, *third_loop_#*, and *fourth_loop_#* respectively. Each kernel runs with a different number of spawned threads and blocks. Intermediate data is stored in global memory. If there are no data dependencies among the kernels, we run them in different CUDA streams so that they can run simultaneously when GPU streaming multiprocessors are not fully utilized.

Algorithm 1 shows the CPU and GPU version of *(fourth_loop_3)*. We store spatially close data in shared memory to take advantage of global memory coalescing, exemplified in line 2. We usually set the *blockDim* and *gridDim* of each kernel to match the respective number of cells, points, states or basis values, shown as loop indices in the CPU version, with some exceptions, where the number of spawned threads of the kernel is set to 32 to match the warp thread count, for performance optimization reasons. Using atomic functions for Algorithm 1 shows better performance than shared memory reduction because there

Algorithm 1. Third stage of calculation of cells

Input: 2D vectors **cell_coefficients** as cc, $flux$
Output: 2D vector **rhs** as rhs

CPU Version
1: **for** $i \leftarrow 0$ to num_cells **do**
2:   **for** $j \leftarrow 0$ to num_points **do**
3:     **for** $k \leftarrow 0$ to num_states **do**
4:       **for** $l \leftarrow 0$ to num_basis **do**
5:         **for** $m \leftarrow 0$ to $dimensions$ **do**
6:           $rhs_{i,k,l} \leftarrow rhs_{i,k,l} - (cc_{i,j,l,m} * flux_{i,j,k,m})$
7:         **end for**
8:       **end for**
9:     **end for**
10:   **end for**
11: **end for**

GPU Version
  $i \leftarrow$ blockIdx.x, $j \leftarrow$ blockIdx.y
  $l \leftarrow$ threadIdx.x
1: **procedure** FOURTH_LOOP_3   ▷ Performed in parallel
2:   Declare _ _shared_ _ memory $cc\_$
3:   $cc\_{k,m} \leftarrow cc_{i,j,k,m}$
4:   **for** $k \leftarrow 0$ to num_states **do**
5:     $temp \leftarrow 0$
6:     **for** $m \leftarrow 0$ to $dimensions$ **do**
7:       $temp \leftarrow temp - (cc\_{k,m} * flux_{i,j,k,m})$
8:     **end for**
9:     $atomicAdd\ temp$ to $rhs_{i,k,l}$
10:   **end for**
11: **end procedure**

is little contention amongst the *blockIdx.y* axis blocks for the same memory location, and using reduction will cause poor memory access patterns and lower functional utilization.

3.2 ZFP Compression and Block Decompression

ZFP is a fixed-rate, near-lossless compression scheme that maps small blocks of 4^d values in d dimensions to a fixed, user-specified number of bits per block, thereby allowing read and write random access to compressed floating-point data at block granularity [2]. ZFP shows much higher compression rates for floating-point data compared to other generic lossless compression schemes like Gzip [4], bzip2 [5], or even floating point compression schemes like FPZIP [6]. This is because floating-point values have tailing mantissa bits that are too random to compress effectively [7]. ZFP is also relatively accurate because of its bounded relative error [3]. It supports three modes: fixed-rate, fixed-accuracy, and fixed-

Table 1. List of major data arrays referenced in GPU Kernels and Major Kernels

Array name	RW	% of data usage	Kernel name	Avg. time	% of time
cell_coefficients	R	50.81%	fourth_loop_3	9.74 ms	38.18%
cell_basis_value	R	16.94%	fourth_loop_1	5.93 ms	23.24%
face_owner_basis_value	R	5.77%	third_loop_1	3.95 ms	15.47%
face_neighbor_basis_value	R	5.77%	third_loop_3	2.81 ms	11.01%
face_owner_coefficients	R	5.77%	first_loop_1	1.22 ms	4.79%
face_neighbor_coefficients	R	5.77%	first_loop_3	583.88 μs	2.29%
peribdry_owner_basis_value	R	1.15%	fourth_loop_2	490.32 μs	1.92%
peribdry_neighbor_basis_value	R	1.15%	third_loop_2	334.34 μs	1.31%
peribdry_owner_coefficients	R	1.15%	memcpy HtoD	7.38 μs	1.10%
Flux	RW	3.02%	first_loop_2	125.88 μs	0.49%
solution	RW	0.17%	memcpy DtoD	15.39 μs	0.05%
rhs	W	0.17%			

precision. In fixed-rate mode, each d-dimensional compressed block of 4^d values is stored using a fixed number of bits that we can set as a parameter.

Our scheme uses CUDA ZFP to compress and decompress data in the GPU in parallel. We use fixed-rate mode as the other modes are not supported by CUDA ZFP. The reason for this is because we need random access to the compressed blocks. In fixed-rate mode, the size of all compressed blocks are constant, allowing partial decompression to take place at any order. The number of bits that are used to store each block is input as a parameter to the compression and decompression functions. This parameter needs to exactly be a power of two otherwise the number of actual compressed bits per block will be rounded up to the next largest power of two. Therefore in fixed-rate mode, we can only achieve exact compression ratios of 50%, 75%, 87.5%, and so forth. We directly incorporate the encoding and decoding functions from source, because the GPU API is not exported into the shared library when compiled. Before application modifications are made, we take note of which read-only data buffer would potentially use the greatest amount of space in GPU device memory, and is referenced scarcely. This is because our goal is to minimize decompression overheads and data loss. We encode the largest buffer directly into GPU device memory only once in the pre-processing stages by directly calling the encode launch kernel function for one-dimensional arrays of type *double*.

Decompression is performed directly in the kernels before references to the compressed arrays are made. We modified the device decode functions to work with larger block indices, up to the value limit of type *unsigned long*. Then, we used block decompression in each thread of our calculation kernel which references the data values in the compressed buffer. Because fixed-rate mode requires each block to contains 4^d values, where d = 1, we can obtain 4 decoded 64-bit values from the decode function per CUDA thread. Because the number of threads per CUDA block is equivalent to the **basis value**, some of the threads would have to wait in a synchronization step before the results from the other threads are all stored in shared memory. Once block decompression is finished, the kernel continues with its task. By using block decompression, we can amortize the overhead of decompression in the calculation kernel itself without incurring additional kernel launch overheads, and can discard the decompressed values from shared memory after they are used.

3.3   Overwriting GPU Data Buffers Using Memory Copy

A naive method of saving GPU memory capacity is to keep only the absolute necessary data in GPU device memory. We can perform this by calling `cudaMemcpy` before the kernel referencing the data is launched and calling `cudaFree` immediately after the kernel execution completes before the next kernel is launched. Not only is this method extremely inefficient, it is also impractical to pipeline. Data residing in GPU memory would have to be constantly freed and copied before each calculation step, leading to large data transfer overheads. Additionally, `cudaFree` is a synchronous operation with an internal synchronization call. Therefore we cannot pipeline the kernels with the data transfers.

We use a different technique of avoiding `cudaFree` altogether by sharing buffers across multiple kernels. Like in Sect. 3.2, we select the **cell_coefficients** buffer because it utilizes the largest capacity. Once the kernel using this buffer finishes execution, we simply overwrite its contents using `cudaMemcpy` with the host data that we do not want to store in GPU device memory. We are able to save GPU space because we do not have to `cudaMalloc` distinct buffers for such arrays. Based on Table 1, we are able to theoretically save a maximum of 50% of GPU space if we utilize the largest buffer for all of the required data.

4   Evaluation

4.1   Experimental Setup

We use two experimental environments. The first environment is a single private machine equipped with NVIDIA GeForce GTX 1050 Ti using the Pascal architecture. The CPU we use is an Intel i7-7700 @ 3.6GHz with 4 physical cores. The second environment consists of a single server node equipped with 2 NVIDIA GeForce Titan XP also using the Pascal architecture. The CPU for this node is an Intel Xeon E5-2683 @ 2.1GHz with 2 sockets equipped with 16 cores each.

4.2   Performance Results

Figure 1 shows the performance results of both the CPU and GPU implementation in both environments. The x-axis shows the size of the workload that we used, and the y-axis is the execution time in seconds or the speedup. We notice that the multi-core version utilizing all 8 cores with hyper-threading on shows a maximum speedup of 4.45 times the sequential version. Using the GTX 1050 Ti speeds up performance up to 9.02 times sequential code. Titan XP shows

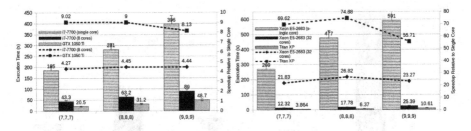

Fig. 1. GeForce GTX 1050 Ti and Titan XP performance results (100 iterations)

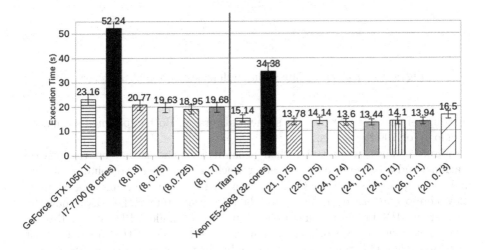

Fig. 2. Hybrid run using MPI on (7, 7, 7) and (10, 10, 10) workloads

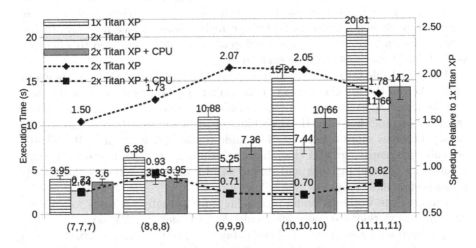

Fig. 3. Hybrid run using MPI on multiple GPU devices

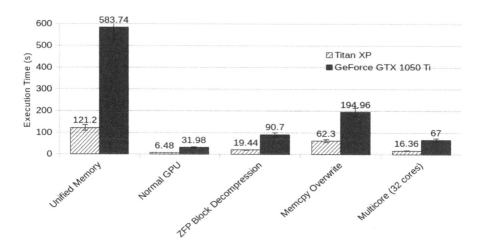

Fig. 4. Comparison of data saving techniques with unified memory

speedups of up to 74.88 times the sequential version. Both experiments ran each workload for 100 iterations.

Figure 2 shows the results when a small workload is run on the private machine, and a bigger one on the server machine. The first two columns of each division denote sole GPU or CPU execution times, and the remaining columns show heterogeneous execution times. The two parameters of the x-axis show the number of MPI processes, and weight given to a single GPU device. Results show that assigning a workload weight of 72% to the GPU causes the most speedup (about 11% compared to GPU-only) for the server machine. We believe the speedup is not completely scalable because of the MPI communication overheads. There are a fewer number of cores co-located near each other in the private machine, causing less communication overheads. Each individual core also has a greater clock frequency, contributing to higher performance per core. In the private machine, we experience a speedup of about 22% compared to when the GTX 1050 Ti executes the code exclusively.

Using multiple GPU devices also further reduce execution time, as shown in Fig. 3. We run the workload in two Titan XPs in parallel using MPI, and assign half the weight to each device. As the workload size becomes larger, performance generally becomes better as the divisibility of the workload from the ParMETIS library becomes more congruent. The middle cases (9, 9, 9) and (10, 10, 10) actually experience a greater than linear speedup, most likely due to the kernels being more optimal in block and thread size to allow the kernel optimizations to work more efficiently.

Running the workload on all processing units actually performs worse than dividing the workload equally into multiple GPU devices. We do not execute the program with too many CPU cores, because partitioning the workload too finely will prevent some MPI processes from receiving any data at all, leading to errors. In order to properly experience program speedup, the GPU device must be assigned the proper ratio of workload depending on its processing power relative to a single CPU core. We use heuristics to find the optimal weight that we have to give each processing unit in the cluster. However, ParMETIS cannot allocate an exactly equal amount of data to each process, which leads to synchronization discrepancies. This could cause CPU cores to lag behind the GPU devices, which would be idle in `MPI_Wait()` while the CPU cores are still busy.

We compare our data usage saving techniques with NVIDIA UM on both GPU devices in Fig. 4. We run a (8, 8, 8) workload for 100 iterations. We performed the experiment by filling up the GPU memory using `cudaMalloc` to guarantee that the UM paging mechanism will be called when the workload executes. When GPU memory is insufficient, resorting to UM slows down program execution more than one order of magnitude because of page faults. We compressed **cell_coefficients** (see Table 1) with a fixed-rate of 50% so that data loss would be minimized. Therefore we were able to save 25% of total data usage and reduced execution time by up to 6.4 times UM. Likewise, we eliminated the **cell_basis_value**, **face_owner_basis_value** and **face_neighbor_basis_value** buffers for our memory copy overwrite technique, saving a total of 28.48% of data usage while achieving a speedup of up to 3 times UM. Memory copy overwrite has more overhead than block decompression, and that is because the time spent in additional `cudaMemcpy` operations exceed the amortized kernel decompression time by more than a factor of two. These operations are repeated five times in each iteration, causing large overheads.

5   Conclusion and Future Work

CFD is a widely researched application relevant to many scientific fields. Implementations of CFD are scalable, as the application running time generally decreases when the number of processing units (GPU or CPU) are increased. However, scarcity of GPU memory compared to host memory limits CFD workloads to GPU device memory capacities.

Our solution, which includes ZFP block decompression and memory copy overwrites allows a minimum of 25% larger CFD workloads to run with adequate performance on different types of commodity GPUs, without resorting to additional money spent on purchasing more GPU devices, or cluster nodes for the need of adding more GPU slots. The effect is for more data to be packed in the GPUs of each cluster node, reducing MPI communication overheads which can potentially hamper the scalability of execution time of the application. Our GPU implementation performs up to 74.88 times faster than the sequential version on cheap, commodity GPUs. Finally, we are able to further increase performance by partitioning the application workload to different MPI processes to utilize all heterogeneous processing units in the cluster.

In future work, we shift our focus to how we can manage multiple CFD applications running simultaneously. We also want to automate the process of finding optimal weights, especially when network nodes are used. Finally, we pursue a generalized compression method in the system layer.

References

1. Lai, J., Li, H., Tian, Z.: CPU/GPU heterogeneous parallel CFD solver and optimizations. In: Proceedings of the 2018 International Conference on Service Robotics Technologies (ICSRT '18), pp. 88–92. ACM, New York (2018). https://doi.org/10.1145/3208833.3208847
2. Lindstrom, P.: Fixed-rate compressed floating-point arrays. IEEE Trans. Vis. Comput. Graph. **20**(12), 2674–2683 (2014). https://doi.org/10.1109/TVCG.2014.2346458
3. Lindstrom, P.: Error distributions of lossy floating-point compressors. Joint Stat. Meet. **2017**, 2574–2589 (2017)
4. Deutsch, P.: GZIP file format specification version 4.3. RFC, vol. 1952, pp. 1–12 (1996). https://doi.org/10.17487/RFC1952
5. Bzip2 (2018). http://www.bzip.org/
6. Lindstrom, P., Isenburg, M.: Fast and efficient compression of floating-point data. IEEE Trans. Vis. Comput. Graph. **12**(5), 1245–1250 (2006)
7. Tao, D., Di, S., Liang, X., Chen, Z., Cappello, F.: Optimizing lossy compression rate-distortion from automatic online selection between SZ and ZFP (2019). https://doi.org/10.1109/TPDS.2019.2894404
8. Niksiar, P., Ashrafizadeh, A., Shams, M., Madani, A.H.: Implementation of a GPU-based CFD Code. In: 2014 International Conference on Computational Science and Computational Intelligence, Las Vegas, NV, pp. 84–89 (2014). https://doi.org/10.1109/CSCI.2014.21
9. Mintu, S.A., Molyneux, D.: Application of GPGPU to accelerate CFD simulation. In: ASME International Conference on Offshore Mechanics and Arctic Engineering, vol. 2: CFD and FSI ():V002T08A001. https://doi.org/10.1115/OMAE2018-77649
10. NVIDIA Corp: Profiler user's guide (2017). https://docs.nvidia.com/cuda/profiler-users-guide/index.html#nvprof-overview. An optional note
11. Griebel, M., Zaspel, P.: Comput. Sci. Res. Dev. **25**, 65 (2010). https://doi.org/10.1007/s00450-010-0111-7
12. Xu, H., et al.: Collaborating CPU and GPU for large-scale high-order CFD simulations with complex grids on the TianHe-1A supercomputer. J. Comput. Phys. **278**(C), 275–297 (2013). https://doi.org/10.1016/j.jcp.2014.08.024
13. Videocardbenchmark.net. PassMark Software - Video Card (GPU) Benchmark Charts (2019). https://www.videocardbenchmark.net/. Accessed 24 May 2019
14. Cpubenchmark.net. PassMark Software - CPU Benchmark Charts (2019). https://www.cpubenchmark.net/. Accessed 24 May 2019
15. Ark.intel.com. Intel product specifications (2019). https://ark.intel.com/content/www/us/en/ark.html. Accessed 24 May 2019
16. Wang, Y., Malkawi, A., Yi, Y.K.: Implementing CFD (computational fluid dynamics) in OpenCL for building simulation (2011)
17. Gorobets, A., Soukov, S., Bogdanov, P.: Multilevel parallelization for simulating compressible turbulent flows on most kinds of hybrid supercomputers. Comput. Fluids **173** (2018). https://doi.org/10.1016/j.compfluid.2018.03.011
18. Oyarzun, G., Borrell, R., Gorobets, A., Mantovani, F., Oliva, A.: Efficient CFD code implementation for the ARM-based mont-blanc architecture. Future Gener. Comput. Syst. **79** (2017). https://doi.org/10.1016/j.future.2017.09.029
19. Wang, Y.X., Zhang, L.L., Liu, W., Cheng, X.H., Zhuang, Y., Chronopoulos, A.: Performance optimizations for scalable CFD applications on hybrid CPU+MIC heterogeneous computing system with millions of cores. Comput. Fluids (2018). https://doi.org/10.1016/j.compfluid.2018.03.005

20. Che, Y., Zhang, L., Xu, C., Wang, Y., Liu, W., Wang, Z.: Optimization of a parallel CFD code and its performance evaluation on Tianhe-1A. Comput. Inf. **33**, 1377–1399 (2014)
21. Cockburn, B., Shu, C.W.: The Runge-Kutta discontinuous Galerkin method for conservation laws V. J. Comput. Phys. **141**, 199–224 (1998)
22. You, H., Kim, C.: High-order multi-dimensional limiting strategy with subcell resolution I. Two-Dimension. Mixed Meshes, J. Comput. Phys. **375**, 1005–1032 (2018)
23. Bassi, F., Crivellini, A., Rebay, S., Savini, M.: Discontinuous Galerkin solution of the Reynolds-averaged Navier-Stokes and k-ω turbulence model equations. Comput. Fluids **34**, 507–540 (2005)
24. Cohen, J., Molemaker, M.J.: A fast double precision CFD code using CUDA. Parallel Computational Fluid Dynamics: Recent Advances and Future Directions (2009)
25. Li, W., Jin, G., Cui, X., See, S.: An evaluation of unified memory technology on NVIDIA GPUs. In: 2015 15th IEEE/ACM International Symposium on Cluster, Cloud and Grid Computing, Shenzhen, pp. 1092-1098 (2015). https://doi.org/10.1109/CCGrid.2015.105
26. Harris, M., Harris, M., Harris, M., Sakharnykh, N., Harris, M.: Unified memory for CUDA beginners—NVIDIA developer blog. NVIDIA Developer Blog (2019). https://devblogs.nvidia.com/unified-memory-cuda-beginners/. Accessed 17 May 2019
27. Harris, M., Perelygin, K., Luitjens, J., Karras, T., Karras, T., Karras, T.: Cooperative groups: flexible CUDA thread programming—NVIDIA developer blog. NVIDIA Developer Blog (2019). https://devblogs.nvidia.com/cooperative-groups/. Accessed 22 May 2019
28. Oteski, L., Colin de Verdiere, G., Contassot-Vivier, S., Vialle, S., Ryan, J.: Towards a unified CPU-GPU code hybridization: a GPU based optimization strategy efficient on other modern architectures (2018)
29. Karypis, G., Kumar, V.: Parallel multilevel k-way partitioning scheme for irregular graphs. In: Proceedings of the 1996 ACM/IEEE Conference on Supercomputing (CDROM), Ser. Supercomputing '96. IEEE Computer Society, Washington, DC, USA (1996). https://doi.org/10.1145/369028.369103
30. NVIDIA: NVIDIA CUBLAS Library (2019). https://developer.nvidia.com/cublas
31. Larsen, M.: mclarsen/cuZFP. GitHub (2019). https://github.com/mclarsen/cuZFP. Accessed 22 May 2019

Using Trust and "Utility" for Group Formation in the Cloud of Things

Giancarlo Fortino[1], Lidia Fotia[2(✉)], Fabrizio Messina[3], Domenico Rosaci[4], and Giuseppe M. L. Sarné[2]

[1] Department DIMES, University of Calabria, Rende, CS, Italy
giancarlo.fortino@unical.it
[2] DICEAM, University Mediterranea of Reggio Calabria, Reggio Calabria, Italy
{lidia.fotia,sarne}@unirc.it
[3] DMI, University of Catania, Catania, Italy
messina@dmi.unict.it
[4] DIIES, University Mediterranea of Reggio Calabria, Reggio Calabria, Italy
domenico.rosaci@unirc.it

Abstract. In this paper we consider a CoT (Cloud of Things) scenario where agents cooperate to perform complex tasks. Agents have to select reliable partners and, in some cases, they don't have enough information about their peers. In order to support agents in their choice and to maximize the benefits during their cooperation, we combined several contributions. First of all, we designed a trust model which exploits the recommendations coming from the ego networks of the agents. Secondly, we propose to partition the agents in groups by exploiting trust relationships to allow agents to interact with the most reliable partners. To this aim, we designed an algorithm named DAGA (Distributed Agent Grouping Algorithm) to form agent groups by exploiting available reliability and reputation and the results obtained in a simulated scenario confirmed its potential advantages.

1 Introduction

Lately, the "Internet of Things" (IoT) and Cloud Computing (CC) converged to achieve the so called Cloud-of-Things [1, 28] (CoT). Also in nomadic contexts [2], CoT supports computational and storing requirements [5] of omnipresent and heterogeneous IoT devices. Furthermore, the association of IoT devices with software agents, working on their behalf on the Cloud [14, 15, 31], allows to take benefit from their social attitudes.

In such a scenario, it is important that an agent, even in the case of unsuitable information, is able to make a good choice about its "partners" (i.e., agents). To this purpose, we propose of supporting agents to form groups of reliable recommenders on the basis of some type of social relationships having place among the group members [6–8, 12]. In particular, we assumed that trust-based processes can potentially support agents in forming groups of reliable recommenders over a CoT context for improving IoT devices activities.

© Springer Nature Switzerland AG 2019
R. Montella et al. (Eds.): IDCS 2019, LNCS 11874, pp. 112–122, 2019.
https://doi.org/10.1007/978-3-030-34914-1_11

We take into account a CoT environment where heterogeneous devices which consume or produce services and/or extract or exchange knowledge are supported by personal software agents running over the CC. Note that each IoT device and its associated agent are considered as the same entity. The agent is able to support the nomadic activities of the devices, i.e. their ability to move from a group to another based on their own convenience [24]. Furthermore, when an agent requires a service (s) to a provider, its choice will be based on its past experience. If the agent has not previous experiences, the agent will rely on the recommendations provided by its community [27]. These opinions/recommendations will be for free if they come from the agents belonging to its group, otherwise a fee has to be paid. For this reason, we have introduced a competitive scenario on which groups (agents) are interested in accepting (belonging to) those agents (groups) denoted by a suitable reliability, helpfulness and utility.

Moreover, we take into account the effectiveness of any agent to recommend any other agent, i.e. to evaluate the helpfulness of any peer, We measure this effectiveness also for a group, as the average of the helpfulness of its members. To maximize the benefits of an agent joining with a group (and vice versa), we designed a distributed algorithm matching devices and groups with the aim of improving individual and global satisfaction [4,6] into the CoT by adopting trust measures for esteeming the agent helpfulness. Compared to the approaches in the literature that consider global reputation, we use the *local reputation* [13] (i.e., the reputation value is only based on the opinions coming from the ego network of the agent). The approach above described gives allows to avoid of performing heavy computational tasks, limiting communication overloads and improving the system reactivity. More, we introduce the utility measure obtained by combining the trust and the utility of the devices (i.e., agent). For utility, we indicate the percentage of skills the agent has compared to the generic group. This measure was introduced because sometimes, to be able to release a service with particular skills, the group might decide to risk by affiliating agents who have a higher percentage of skills regardless of their values of trust. Moreover, like in human societies [21], groups are formed through a voting mechanism that combines reliability and local reputation measures. Finally, we designed a dedicated distributed algorithm for group formation (see Sect. 4).

The rest of the paper is organized as follows. Section 2 illustrates the scenario, while Sect. 3 describes the trust model adopted in our approach, as well as the utility measure and voting mechanism.Section 4 presents the algorithm specifically designed to form groups. In Sect. 5 the related literature is presented. Finally, in Sect. 6 some conclusions are drawn.

2   Scenario

We introduce a CoT environment where devices exchange services and/or extract/exchange knowledge by means of software agents. Each agent has a list of skills needed to deliver a service, denoted by $S = \{k_1, k_2, ..., k_n\}$, where n is the maximum number of skills. More formally, A is the set of software agents living in the Cloud. For convenience, the agents and their trust relationships are represented by means of a directed graph $G = \langle N, L \rangle$ where N represents the set of nodes (i.e., agents) belonging to G, while L is the set of links (i.e., relationships occurring between two agents).

Moreover, we suppose that the agents are free of joining with one or more groups on the basis of their convenience. Each group is managed by an agent administrator that can contact other agents to join with or to remove from the group those agents resulted ineffective. The administrator establishes the number m of skills that its group must possess, where $m <= n$. The main objective is to maximize the effectiveness of individual groups. In other words, this mechanism implies that groups are interested to accept those agents having a high reliability, helpfulness and a number n of skills which coincides with m; at the same time agents are interested to be affiliated with those groups formed by agents with a high reliability and helpfulness. To require a service, an agent can use its past experiences, but if they are not sufficient to perform a good choice it can also require the opinions of other agents. If a_i has not a appropriate direct past experience about a provider agent a_j, it can ask a recommendation $rec \in [0, 1]$ to another agent a_r. This recommendation is free only if a_r is in the same group of a_j. However, the proposed scenario has a competitive nature; in fact, all the services are provided only for payment.

3   The Local Trust Model and the Utility Measure

3.1   The Local Trust Model

In this context, we define the ego-network EN_i of an agent $a_i \in A$ as a sub-graph $EN_i \subseteq G$ including those nodes connected to a_i in a fixed depth (see Fig. 1). For two agents a_i and a_j, the measure of the local trust $T_{i,j}$ that i has about j combines the reliability $rel_{i,j}$ (i.e., a measure of the confidence that a_i has about the capability of a_j of providing good suggestions) and the *local reputation* $rep_{i,j}$ (i.e., a measures of how much, on average, the agents of EN_i estimate the capability of a_j of having good interactions). More in detail, the reliability is an asymmetric measure (i.e., $rel_{i,j} \neq rel_{j,i}$) computed as: $rel_{i,j} = \frac{1}{n} \cdot \sum_{m=1}^{n} f_{i,j}^m$, where $f_{i,j}^m \in [0, 1] \in \mathbb{R}$ is the feedback assigned by a_i to a_j for the m-th interactions carried out with it. To this aim, let $rec_{r,j} \in [0, 1]$ be the recommendation provided by a_r about a_j and let $h_{i,r} \in [0, 1]$ be the (average) helpfulness that a_i perceives about the capability of a_r to give recommendation[1]. In detail, $h_{i,r}$ of a_r perceived by a_i is computed, with respect to the feedback released by a_i for each of the m accepted suggestions provided by a_r to a_i about other agents, as $h_{i,r} = \frac{1}{s} \cdot \sum_{t=1}^{s} |f_t - rec_t|$.

The measure of the relevance of the recommender agents closer in EN_i to a_i, a parameter γ is exploited and computed as $\gamma_{i,r} = 2^{-(\ shortP_{(i,r)} - 1)}$, where

---

[1] If a_r did not provided any suggestion to a_i, then it is assumed that the helpfulness $h_{i,r}$ of a_r perceived by a_i will be set to 0.5.

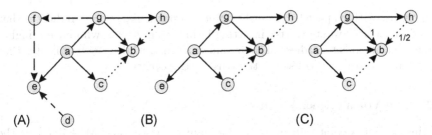

Fig. 1. The EN of agent a including all the nodes of the virtual community for which a direct link (continue line) from a there exists and some other agents indirectly connected to a by a path of length 2 (e.g., all the agents connected to a by dotted line).

$shortP_{(i,r)}$ is the shortest path between a_i and the recommender a_r. By assuming that a_i, in its EN_i, can exploit a number q of recommenders to receive suggestions about a_j, then $rep_{i,j}$ can be calculated as $rep_{i,j} = \frac{1}{q} \cdot \sum_{r=1}^{q} \left(h_{i,r} \cdot \gamma_{i,r} \cdot rec_{r,j} \right)$.

Finally, we calculate the trust measure that an agent a_i has about an agent a_j combining reliability, local reputation and helpfulness as $T_{i,j} = \alpha_i \cdot rel_{i,j} + (1 - \alpha_i) \cdot \beta_{i,j} \cdot rep_{i,j}$, where $\alpha, \beta \in [0,1] \in \mathbb{R}$. In particular, α weights reliability and local reputation for giving more or less relevance to one or other; while $\beta_{i,j} = q/\|EN_i(x)\|$ represents the relevance of the number of recommenders q with respect to the computation of $rep_{i,j}$. The local reputation measure loses of relevance when the number of such nodes is small because a_i has not a suitable amount of information about a_j from its EN_i. Moreover, a "cold start" value of reliability, reputation and helpfulness is assigned to each new agent joining with the system. The "trustworthiness" of a group g perceived by a_i, say $T_{i,g}$, is obtained by averaging all the trust measures computed by a_i for all the agents belonging to g. Similarly, the "trustworthiness" of an agent a_i, as it is perceived by a group g (i.e., $T_{g,i}$), is determined by averaging the trust measures that all the agents belonging to g computed about a_i.

3.2 Utility Measure

The Utility Measure (UM) is represented by a real number obtained by combining the trust $T_{i,g}$ and the utility $u_{i,g}$ of the devices (i.e., agent). $u_{i,g}$ measures how much the agent a_i is useful for the group g. In other words, we can evaluate the percentage of skills the agent a_i has compared to the group g. More formally:

$$u_{i,g} = \frac{NS_i}{NT_g}$$

where NS_i is the number of skills acquired by a_i and NT_g is the number of skills required by g. Now, we calculate the $UM_{g,i}$ that a group g has about an agent a_i as $UM_{g,i} = \zeta_g \cdot u_{g,i} + (1 - \zeta_g) \cdot T_{g,i}$, where ζ_g is a real value, ranging in $[0,1]$, which is set by the administrator of g to weight the relevance he assigns to the trust with respect to the utility of a_i. In particular, $\zeta_g = 1$ indicates that the administrator wants to risk inserting in his group agents who have a higher percentage of skills regardless of their values of trust; while $\zeta_g = 0$ indicates that the administrator only considers the trust of the agents.

3.3 The Voting Mechanism

In this section we introduce voting mechanism based on UM defined in the previous Sect. 3.2. Each time a decision about a new affiliation with a group g has to be taken, it is carried out by a voting of all the agents belonging to g (i.e., each agent gives a vote $v \in \{0, 1\}$ to accept/refuse this agent into g, where $0/1$ means "refuse"/"accept") [22]. The vote depends from (i) the Utility Measure (UM) that the administrator computed about the candidate and (ii) a threshold $\mu_g \in [0, 1]$ that is 0 (i.e., 1) if $UM < \mu_g$ (i.e., $UM \geq \mu_g$). In the following, the voting process of a group g referred to a potential new member

Table 1. Main symbols

Symbol	Description
SA	Set of agents associated with the IoT devices
GT	Graph representing our scenario
EN_i	Set of agents of the ego-network of a_i
G	Set of all the groups
B_i	Set of the groups of a_i
A_g	Set of agents affiliated with a group g
K	Maximum number of new groups an agent can analyze
NG	Maximum number of groups that an agent can join with
NA	Maximum number of agents affiliated with a group
C	Set of candidate groups
$V(\cdot)$	Voting function
R	Set of groups randomly chosen, with $\|R\| \leq NA$
a	Agent
a_g	Agent administrator of the group g
g	Generic group
ta	Time elapsed from the last execution of the procedure for an agent
tg	Time elapsed from the last execution of the procedure for a group
τ	Threshold on the level of trust between an agent and a generic group
τ_g	Time threshold set by the agent administrator of a group
τ_a	Time threshold set by an agent
T	Trust
UM	Utility measure

y will be represented by the voting criterion v previously described, assumed as the output of a function $V(g, v, y)$.

4   The Distributed Agent Grouping Algorithm (DAGA)

In this section, we introduce the Distributed Agent Grouping Algorithm (shortly DAGA). This algorithm is distributed and composed by two different procedures. Algorithm 1 is executed by each agent a_i of the CoT environment to identify, in terms of average value of $T_{i,g}$, the "best" groups to join with, while Algorithm 2, is executed by the group administrator to evaluate if accepting a new member a_i with the group itself on the basis of its UM_i score. The symbols used in the two algorithms are listed in Table 1.

Algorithm 1 is executed by the agent a_i for increasing the overall mutual trust with the related peers in its group configuration. a_i stores the local trust measure $T_{i,g}$ of each group $g \in B_i \subset GT$ contacted in the past and the time t_g elapsed from the last updating. Also, NG is the maximum number of groups that an agent can join with, K is the maximum number of groups an agent is capable to analyze, τ_{a_i} is a time threshold set by the agent a_i and $\tau_i \in [0, 1]$ is a threshold on the trust value between a_i and the generic group $g \in B_i$. Initially, for each group, $T_{i,g}$ is updated if older than τ_{a_i} (lines 1–3). In the following, a set of candidate groups C is built, with $\|C\| < NG$, sorted in decreasing order based on the $T_{i,g}$ values, a set $U = R \bigcup B$ is built, where R is a set of groups randomly chosen. The sets R, U and C might contain both groups already belonging to B_i and new groups randomly selected and inserted into R. By considering the groups in $C \nsubseteq B_i$, a_i could improve the quality of its choices by affiliating itself with those groups. At the end of the two loops (lines 6–16), we obtain $B_i = C$.

Algorithm 2 is executed by the administrator a_g when a_i sends a join request referred to group g. Let $A_g \subset GT$ be the set of the agents affiliated with g, where $\|A_g\| \leq NA$ (with NA the maximum number of agents allowed to be affiliated with g), let the set X be $X = A_g \bigcup a_i$, and let τ_g a time threshold fixed by the administrator a_g. Also, a_g stores the values of the local trust computed by the members of its group for a_i which desires to join with, and the timestamp t_{a_i} of its retrieval. First, a_g asks to the members of its group the updated local trust values about a_i (lines $1 - -5$). Then, two situations might occur:

(a) $\|X\| < R$ (lines 6–11), then all the agents in g give a vote (see Sect. 3.3). The function $V(\cdot)$ provides to combine all the votes to determine if the agent a_i is affiliated with or not in g.
(b) $\|X\| = R$ (lines 12–18), then the agent a_i is affiliated with into the group in place of another agent. To make comparable the agents, a measure is $UM_{g,n}$ of the group vs the agent itself, which is computed as explained in Sect. 3.2 (line 16). In particular, $UM_{g,n}$ denotes the current utility measure between the group g and the agent $b_n \in X \bigcup \{a_i\}$.

Algorithm 1. Algorithm 1 - executed by a CoT agent.

Input: $B_i \subset G, NA, t_g, \tau_{a_i}; R = \{g \in GT\}$ a set of groups randomly selected : $\|R\| = K \leq NG$, $B_i \bigcap R = \{\ \}, U = (B_i \bigcup R)$

1: **for** $g \in U : t_g > \tau_{a_i}$ **do**
2:    Compute $T_{i,g}$ by exploiting the agents belonging to g.
3: **end for**
4: $m \leftarrow 0$
5: Let be $C = \{g \in U : T_{i,g} \geq \tau_i\}$, with $\|C\| = NG$
6: **for all** $g \in C : g \notin B_i$ **do**
7:    send a join request to the agent administrator of g
8:    **if** g accepts the request **then** $m \leftarrow m + 1$
9:    **end if**
10: **end for**
11: **for all** $g \in B_i : g \notin C$ **do**
12:    Sends a leave message to g
13:    $m \leftarrow m - 1$
14:    **if** (m==0) **then break**
15:    **end if**
16: **end for**

Algorithm 2. Algorithm 2 - executed by a_g.

Input: $B_g, NA, a_i, t_g, \tau_g, X = A_g \bigcup \{a_i\};$

1: **for all** $b \in A_g$ **do**
2:    **if** $t_{a_i} \geq \tau_g$ **then** ask to b for updating local trust values of a_i
3:    **end if**
4: **end for**
5: **if** $\|X\| < R$ **then**
6:    **if** $V(g, v, a_i) == 1$ **then** Send an accept message to a_i
7:    **else** Send a reject message to a_i
8:    **end if**
9: **else**
10:    **for all** $b \in X$ **do** compute T_{b,a_i}, $u_{X,b}$
11:    **end for**
12:    Let $X' = \{b_1, b_2, \ldots, b_{\|M_g\|+1}\}$ with $b_i \in X \bigcup \{a_i\}$, ordered by utility measure with $UM_{g,m} \geq UM_{g,n}$ iff $m < n$
13:    **if** $X[\|M_g\| + 1] == a_i$ **then** Send a reject message to a_i
14:    **else**
15:        Send a leave message to the node $X[\|B_g\| + 1]$
16:        Send an accept message to a_i
17:    **end if**
18: **end if**

5   Related Work

The choice of a reliable partner is a critical issue in presence of open and distributed scenarios due to a large variety of potential threats. A Trust system can represent an effective solution, for agents operating in the environments, to avoid unreliable partners [16,32]. A similar approach has been proposed in [9,12,17] for supporting a group/member in accepting/requiring to join with a member/group by proofing that the adoption of trust criteria in such processes allows to create groups more stable over time with respect to other formation strategies. The ratio of the approach is due to the fact that in such groups the members' expectancy of receiving benefits is higher.

In large communities, trust-based groups formation processes often exploit a local trust approach given that their members usually interacts with a limited part of their communities. As two examples, TidalTrust [18] considers the closer neighbors for trust predictions, but if the trust network is too sparse part of them will be neglected; MoleTrust [23] executes on the trust-network a backward search at a fixed maximum depth so that the trust score at depth x only by considering the trust scores at depth $x - 1$. To avoid conflicts and optimize the social utility [33] decisions into a community can be reached by a vote [11], although the risks of a manipulations always exist [10], particularly in software agent communities, where it is easy to verify the effects of each manipulation attempt [30]. A voting mechanism is presented for a wireless device community in [20] where, on the underlying oriented trust-network, the devices propagate (at only one hop distance) and combine their confidence values (considered as trust measures) for admitting/refusing a device on a transmission path based on its trustworthiness (as perceived by the other devices) by means of a local voting scheme. In [34] faulting sensors are identified by trustworthiness measures on a Markov chain of sensors on the basis of a trust-based voting scheme, named *TrustVoting*. Votes are weighted proportionally the distance occurring between voter and target and implicitly reflect how many neighbors referencing the measures coming from of a node.

Some interesting applications of trust systems in IoT and CC scenarios can by find in [3,19,26]. In particular, [3] adopts a *word of mouth* strategy where two IoT devices trust the other devices and propagate their evaluations into the community. In [29] a grid of agent-based sensors acquires and analyzes acoustical signals produced by vehicles in their motion and improves its traffic flow measures by exploiting a distributed trust-system. In [26] a node obtains a trustworthiness measure of each of its friend nodes on the basis of the opinions of the common friends in terms reliability and local reputation measures. In [19], the multidimensional trustworthiness of CC providers is computed by using more sources and trust information, while in [25] a decentralized trust-based model, designed for CC federations, support devices in effectively finding the most suitable providers without the need of exploring their whole space by exploiting trustworthiness information.

6   Conclusions

In this paper, we presented in a CoT scenario a multi-agent context supporting the virtualization of IoT devices over the cloud. For promoting satisfactory agents interactions, we exploited the social attitude of agents to form groups since an agent could be unable to choose a partner if it does not have enough information. As a solution, some suggestions can be asked to those peers perceived as trustworthy. To this aim, we introduce the distributed algorithm DAGA to guide the formation of agent groups in a competitive and cooperative scenario. DAGA provides useful recommendation on the basis of reliability, local reputation, helpfulness and utility measures. Our ongoing research is focused on better analyzing the behavior of this algorithm. In particular, we are theoretically studying the efficiency and the effectiveness of the approach from a statistical viewpoint, and we are performing some experimental campaigns for practically evaluating the advantages introduced by our approach.

Acknowledgment. This work has been developed at the Networks and Complex Systems (NeCS) Laboratory - Department of Engineering Civil, Energy, Environment and Materials (DICEAM) - University Mediterranea of Reggio Calabria.

References

1. Aazam, M., Khan, I., Alsaffar, A.A., Huh, E.-N.: Cloud of things: integrating internet of things and cloud computing and the issues involved. In: 2014 11th International Bhurban Conference on Applied Sciences and Technology, pp. 414–419. IEEE (2014)
2. Aloi, G., et al.: Enabling IoT interoperability through opportunistic smartphone-based mobile gateways. J. Netw. Comput. Appl. **81**, 74–84 (2017)
3. Bao, F., Chen, I.-R.: Dynamic trust management for internet of things applications. In: Proceedings of 2012 International Workshop on Self-aware IoT, pp. 1–6. ACM (2012)
4. Blanchard, A., Horan, T.: Virtual communities and social capital. In: Knowledge and Social Capital, pp. 159–178 (2000)
5. Botta, A., De Donato, W., Persico, V., Pescapé, A.: Integration of cloud computing and internet of things: a survey. Future Gener. Comput. Syst. **56**, 684–700 (2016)
6. Chiu, C.-M., Hsu, M.-H., Wang, E.: Understanding knowledge sharing in virtual communities: an integration of social capital and social cognitive theories. Decis. Support Syst. **42**(3), 1872–1888 (2006)
7. Comi, A., Fotia, L., Messina, F., Pappalardo, G., Rosaci, D., Sarné, G.M.L.: Forming homogeneous classes for e-learning in a social network scenario. In: Novais, P., Camacho, D., Analide, C., El Fallah Seghrouchni, A., Badica, C. (eds.) Intelligent Distributed Computing IX. SCI, vol. 616, pp. 131–141. Springer, Cham (2016). https://doi.org/10.1007/978-3-319-25017-5_13
8. Comi, A., Fotia, L., Messina, F., Pappalardo, G., Rosaci, D., Sarné, G.M.L.: Using semantic negotiation for ontology enrichment in e-learning multi-agent systems. In 2015 9th International Conference on Complex, Intelligent, and Software Intensive Systems, pp. 474–479. IEEE (2015)
9. Comi, A., Fotia, L., Messina, F., Rosaci, D., Sarné, G.M.L.: GroupTrust: finding trust-based group structures in social communities. Intelligent Distributed Computing X. SCI, vol. 678, pp. 143–152. Springer, Cham (2017). https://doi.org/10.1007/978-3-319-48829-5_14
10. Conitzer, V., Sandholm, T.: Universal voting protocol tweaks to make manipulation hard. arXiv preprint cs/0307018 (2003)
11. National Research Council, et al.: Public Participation in Environmental Assessment and Decision Making. National Academies Press (2008)
12. De Meo, P., Ferrara, E., Rosaci, D., Sarnè, G.M.L.: Trust and compactness in social network groups. ACM Trans. Cybern. **45**(2), 205–2016 (2015)
13. De Meo, P., Messina, F., Rosaci, D., Sarné, G.M.L.: Recommending users in social networks by integrating local and global reputation. In: Fortino, G., Di Fatta, G., Li, W., Ochoa, S., Cuzzocrea, A., Pathan, M. (eds.) IDCS 2014. LNCS, vol. 8729, pp. 437–446. Springer, Cham (2014). https://doi.org/10.1007/978-3-319-11692-1_37
14. Fortino, G., Gravina, R., Russo, W., Savaglio, C.: Modeling and simulating internet-of-things systems: a hybrid agent-oriented approach. Comput. Sci. Eng. **19**(5), 68–76 (2017)

15. Fortino, G., Messina, F., Rosaci, D., Sarné, G.M.L.: Using trust and local reputation for group formation in the cloud of things. Future Gener. Comput. Syst. **89**, 804–815 (2018)
16. Fortino, G., Trunfio, P.: Internet of Things Based on Smart Objects: Technology. Middleware and Applications. Springer, Heidelberg (2014). https://doi.org/10.1007/978-3-319-00491-4
17. Fotia, L., Messina, F., Rosaci, D., Sarné, G.M.L.: Using local trust for forming cohesive social structures in virtual communities. Comput. J. **60**(11), 1717–1727 (2017)
18. Golbeck, J.A.: Computing and applying trust in web-based social networks. Ph.D. thesis. University of Maryland, Department of Computer Science (2005)
19. Habib, S., Ries, S., Muhlhauser, M.: Towards a trust management system for cloud computing. In: 2011 IEEE 10th International Conference on Trust, Security and Privacy in Computing and Communications (TrustCom), pp. 933–939. IEEE (2011)
20. Jiang, T., Baras, J.: Trust evaluation in anarchy: a case study on autonomous networks. In: INFOCOM (2006)
21. Marc Kilgour, D., Eden, C.: Handbook of Group Decision and Negotiation, vol. 4. Springer, Heidelberg (2010). https://doi.org/10.1007/978-90-481-9097-3
22. Lai, L.S.L., Turban, E.: Groups formation and. operations in the web 2.0 environment and social networks. Group Decis. Negot. **17**(5), 387–402 (2008)
23. Massa, P., Avesani, P.: Trust-aware recommender systems. In: Proceedings of the 2007 ACM Conference on Recommender Systems, pp. 17–24. ACM (2007)
24. Messina, F., Pappalardo, G., Rosaci, D., Sarné, G.M.L.: A trust-based, multi-agent architecture supporting inter-cloud VM migration in IaaS federations. In: Fortino, G., Di Fatta, G., Li, W., Ochoa, S., Cuzzocrea, A., Pathan, M. (eds.) IDCS 2014. LNCS, vol. 8729, pp. 74–83. Springer, Cham (2014). https://doi.org/10.1007/978-3-319-11692-1_7
25. Messina, F., Pappalardo, G., Rosaci, D., Santoro, C., Sarné, G.M.L.: A trust-aware, self-organizing system for large-scale federations of utility computing infrastructures. Future Gener. Comput. Syst. **56**, 77–94 (2016)
26. Nitti, M., Girau, R., Atzori, L., Iera, A., Morabito, G.: A subjective model for trustworthiness evaluation in the social internet of things. In: 23rd International Symposium on Personal Indoor and Mobile Radio Communications, pp. 18–23. IEEE (2012)
27. Palopoli, L., Rosaci, D., Sarné, G.M.L.: A distributed and multi-tiered software architecture for assessing e-commerce recommendations. Concurr. Computat.: Pract. Exp. **28**(18), 4507–4531 (2016)
28. Parwekar, P.: From internet of things towards cloud of things. In: 2nd International Conference on Computer and Communication Technology, pp. 329–333, September 2011
29. Postorino, M.N., Sarné, G.M.L.: An agent-based sensor grid to monitor urban traffic. In: Proceedings of the 15th Workshop dagli Oggetti agli Agenti, WOA 2014, volume 1260 of CEUR Workshop Proceedings. CEUR-WS.org (2014)
30. Satterthwaite, M.: Strategy-proofness and arrow's conditions: existence and correspondence theorems for voting procedures and social welfare functions. J. Econ. Theory **10**(2), 187–217 (1975)
31. Uckelmann, D., Harrison, M., Michahelles, F.: An architectural approach towards the future internet of things. In: Uckelmann, D., Harrison, M., Michahelles, F. (eds.) Architecting the Internet of Things, pp. 1–24. Springer, Heidelberg (2011). https://doi.org/10.1007/978-3-642-19157-2_1

32. Vamsi, P., Kant, K.: Systematic design of trust management systems for wireless sensor networks: a review. In: 4th International Conference on Advanced Computing & Communication Technologies, pp. 208–215. IEEE (2014)
33. Xia, L.: Computational voting theory: game-theoretic and combinatorial aspects. Ph.D. thesis, Duke University (2011)
34. Xiao, X., Peng, W., Hung, C., Lee, W.: Using sensorranks for in-network detection of faulty readings in wireless sensor networks. In: Proceedings of 6th ACM International Workshop on Data Engineering for Wireless and Mobile Access, pp. 1–8. ACM (2007)

Unsupervised Anomaly Thresholding from Reconstruction Errors

Maryleen U. Ndubuaku[1]([✉]) [ID], Ashiq Anjum[1] [ID], and Antonio Liotta[2] [ID]

[1] University of Derby, Derby, UK
{m.ndubuaku,a.anjum}@derby.ac.uk
[2] Edinburgh Napier University, Edinburgh, UK
a.liotta@napier.ac.uk

Abstract. Internet of Things (IoT) sensors generate massive streaming data which needs to be processed in real-time for many applications. Anomaly detection is one popular way to process such data and discover nuggets of information. Various machine learning techniques for anomaly detection rely on pre-labelled data which is very expensive and not feasible for streaming scenarios. Autoencoders have been found effective for unsupervised outlier removal because of their inherent ability to better reconstruct data with higher density. Our work aims to leverage this principle to investigate approaches through which the optimal threshold for anomaly detection can be obtained in an automated and adaptive fashion for streaming scenarios. Rather than experimentally setting an optimal threshold through trial and error, we obtain the threshold from the reconstruction errors of the training data. Inspired by image processing, we investigate how thresholds set by various statistical approaches can perform in an image dataset.

Keywords: Anomaly detection · Anomaly thresholding · Unsupervised learning

1 Introduction

Ubiquitous Internet of Things (IoT) sensors generate a massive pool of data in continuous streams. By 2020, it is expected that the number of connected devices producing data would be 50 billion which is double the estimate for the year 2015. This demands a radical shift in the way streaming data would be processed. Future stream mining systems would need to have sufficient capacity to handle big data given their velocity, variety, volume, and timeliness [7].

Real-time data mining is relevant in certain applications to capture interesting patterns and changes in the data, often referred to as anomalies. In smart cities, human interactions can be tracked to make informed decisions on interventions [8], while unknown objects can be detected in video surveillance [11,12]. Lightweight systems such as wireless sensor networks can benefit from self-adaptive analytics, like machine learning techniques, to cope with the

© Springer Nature Switzerland AG 2019
R. Montella et al. (Eds.): IDCS 2019, LNCS 11874, pp. 123–129, 2019.
https://doi.org/10.1007/978-3-030-34914-1_12

resource limitations [4]. Sometimes these anomalies can appear as one-off events. At other times, the emerging patterns become the new normal which means the system requires the capacity to detect these changes and adjust to it. Overall, the systems should be able to make decisions quickly on the incoming data streams. The ability to automatically detect the anomalies in sensor data has been a challenging research problem [5].

Deep neural networks have the capability to learn more discriminative representations and have been applied in many recent exploits in computer vision. Autoencoders, a type of deep networks, attempts to reconstruct the input data from its lower dimensional encoded representations in latent space. In anomaly detection, this inherent attribute of autoencoders is exploited. Anomalies are distinguished as the data samples with higher reconstruction errors. In other words, because anomalies are few or not present during training, the decoder is not able to construct it well leading to higher errors. The state-of-the-art approach is to allow the neural network to see only normal data during training and introduce anomalies at the detection phase. As expected, the optimal threshold for capturing anomalies would be easier to obtain in this scenario. By training the network only on normal data, some heuristics have been introduced into the learning process hence the term semi-supervised learning. This approach has limitations in the real-world streaming scenario because 100% of the incoming data streams are not guaranteed to be normal data. Extracting only normal data for training demands a very expensive labelling process to sort it from the massive pool of data [13].

We proposed a method for detecting and filtering anomalies in IoT streaming data in a truly unsupervised fashion. Our method uses an adaptive and automated approach to select an optimal threshold. This addresses the limitation of methods that manually choose a threshold after a laborious trial and error experimentation. Our algorithm is designed for IoT streaming scenarios where training data may contain anomalies in varying proportions. With this, we avoid the costly process of labelling the training data in supervised learning or obtaining only normal data (semi-supervised). This makes it easier to scale to larger datasets and to adapt to changes in patterns over time. Even without adding any additional discriminative components to the deep network like iterative optimisation [9], regularisation [3] or discriminative labelling [10], our method is still able to find thresholds that discriminatively label the data.

2   Related Works

Xia et al. [10] demonstrate that reconstruction errors from autoencoders are discriminative in themselves. They applied an iterative approach that alternates between discriminative labelling and reconstruction learning to compute optimal threshold for anomaly detection. In their case, the normal samples must be from a single class. Chong et al. [6] trained a spatiotemporal autoencoder with video data of normal activities. They experimentally obtained a threshold, through trial and error, that would suitably detect the anomalies during the detection phase. By using only normal data for training, it implies that the labelling or sorting process for streaming data would be expensive and perhaps impracticable for large-scale datasets. In [3], authors designed a discriminative algorithm for multi-class normal and single-class anomaly detection. The computed anomaly threshold is based on cosine similarity. Their approach requires prior knowledge of the structure and density of the normal and anomalous data. The work of [2] focused on novelty detection. They applied an Otsu method to find a threshold based on reconstruction errors. With the threshold, the normal data was filtered and the model was retrained with the filtered dataset to obtain the final and optimal threshold. The retraining process makes the approach computationally expensive. In our work, we would leverage the inherent discriminative property of autoencoders. The reconstruction errors from the training data will be used obtain an optimal threshold.

3   Methodology

Our methodology is based on reconstructing the training data using a trained model and computing the reconstruction errors of each sample. The threshold is then obtained from the errors using a statistical approach.

3.1   Deep Autoencoder

The first phase of the autoencoder training is the encoding. The encoder maps the input $x \in \mathbb{R}^z$ to a code $h \in \mathbb{R}^d$ as $h = f(x)$, where z and d are dimensions of input and latent space respectively. The variable (x) depicts a single layer neural network: $f(x) = s(Wx+b)$. Where $W \in \mathbb{R}^{d \times z}$ and $b \in \mathbb{R}^d$ are the weight and bias of the network respectively while s is a non-linear activation function like the sigmoid. The code, h, for an n-layer network is given as: $h = f_n(f_{n-1}(...f_1(x)))$. At the decoding phase, the decoder reconstructs the input signal by mapping the code h into a reconstruction $\tilde{x} = g(h)$ through a series of computations. The reconstructed input for m-layer decoder is: $\tilde{x} = g_m(g_{m-1}(...g_1(h)))$. Autoencoder parameters are optimised to reduce the reconstruction error (loss) given in (1).

$$L(x, \tilde{x}) = \| x - \tilde{x} \|_2^2 \tag{1}$$

The reconstruction errors for the prediction are computed as a scalar or as a vector. As a vector, it becomes more complex to obtain the optimal threshold for the detection phase which is supposed to be a scalar. Hence, we compute the scalar value of the reconstruction errors using the Eq. (2):

$$L(x, \tilde{x}) = \frac{1}{n} \sum_{i=1}^{n} (y_i - \tilde{y}_i)^2 \qquad (2)$$

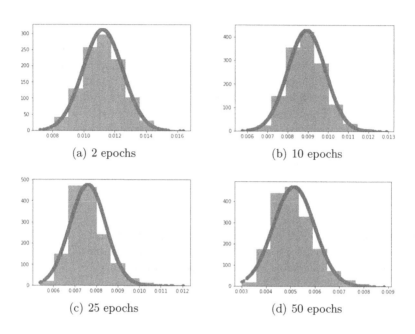

(a) 2 epochs

(b) 10 epochs

(c) 25 epochs

(d) 50 epochs

Fig. 1. Normal distribution of the mean square losses at different epochs

3.2   Anomaly Thresholding

Thresholding is a technique that has been widely applied in image processing [1]. It is useful when an image is to be split into foreground and background. The threshold of an image could be computed to convert a grayscale image to a binary image. For the adaptive thresholding, the threshold values are computed for each sub-image using a statistical method like mean, median or Gaussian. By implementation, the image is usually converted to an array where the operations are performed and then converted back to an image. Algorithm 1 is our proposed algorithm for the anomaly thresholding of the autoencoder network. Where t is a thresholding function applied to automatically compute the optimal threshold. In this case, the threshold is obtained using statistical approaches chosen to be either $t =$ mean, $t =$ median or $t = (\min - \max)/2$.

Algorithm 1. Anomaly thresholding

Require: Training data, xTrain
Ensure: Threshold, t
 1: model = fitAutoencoder(xTrain)
 2: for each Bunch in xTrain do
 3:    reconstructedBunch = modelPredict (Bunch)
 4:    lossTrain = meanSquaredLoss(Bunch, reconstructedBunch)
 5:    lossesTrain = append(lossTrain)
 6:    mean = mean(lossesTrain)
 7: Threshold, t = mean
 8: **for** each Bunch in xTest **do**
 9:    reconstructedBunch = modelPredict (Bunch)
10:    lossTest = meanSquaredLoss(Bunch, reconstructedBunch)
11:   **if** lossTest > t **then**
12:     y = abnormal
13:   **end if**
14: **end for**

---

4   Experimentation

The experiment was done with a convolutional autoencoder network similar to [9]. The dataset used for this task is the MNIST dataset. This dataset consists of handwritten digits from 0 to 9 and their equivalent labels. The labels were only used for the evaluation of the algorithm. To obtain a two-class data, we only used two of the digits where the abnormal data makes up about 1% percent of the data. For the first run, we used digit 2 as the normal dataset and digit 4 as the abnormal. For the second run, we used digit 0 as the normal and digit 4 remains the abnormal. The choice made for the second run was to see how the thresholding performs for classes that are less similar. We observed from the experiment that the sparse data classes produce higher reconstruction errors at the detection phase. This agrees with the assertion about the inherent ability of autoencoders to distinguish data samples using their reconstruction errors [10].

Table 1. Accuracy of various thresholding methods for digits 2 & 4

Thresholding method	2	10	25	50	100
Mean	63.7	61.32	76.70	77.61	78.45
Median	64.0	61.32	75.17	75.67	75.77
Min-max	60.58	63.85	77.76	78.70	84.31

Table 2. Accuracy of various thresholding methods for digits 0 & 4

Thresholding method	2	10	25	50	100
Mean	67.99	74.11	78.13	78.64	79.3
Median	67.94	73.49	74.72	75.03	75.07
Min-max	59.99	77.78	67.94	78.39	71.87

5   Results and Discussion

Tables 1 and 2 shows the accuracy of the anomaly detection for digits 2/4 and digits 0/4 respectively. The accuracy relatively improves with the training time. The mean has the most consistent performance in both scenarios. The mean as a measure of central tendency can be influenced by the presence of outliers. For image processing, this may become problematic during filtering and segmentation. However, in our application this may not be entirely a disadvantage. The mean will be influenced by the higher reconstruction errors of the anomalies to draw towards an optimal threshold value. However, if the anomalies are too few, then the extreme values of reconstruction errors may be dominated by the normality and the threshold may draw towards the normal mean value. Unlike in image processing where median filter works better to suppress outliers, here the median will always tend towards the middle value regardless of the extreme values. Apart from epoch 10 in Table 1 where the mean equals the median, the mean performs better than the median at all other times. Plotting the normal distribution of the mean square losses at varying epochs in Fig. 1 gives us an idea of how the model responds to outliers. We see that the reconstruction losses are minimised with increase in the training data. As the training time increases, the distribution tends to become more skewed to the right showing that there has been more discrimination between the normal and abnormal dataset.

6   Conclusion

In this work, we have proposed an algorithm to automatically and adaptively capture the threshold. We use statistical approaches inspired by image processing to investigate how the detection performs. In future work, we aim to investigate more efficient methods to adaptively capture the threshold. By applying discriminative approaches on the network, like iterative optimisation, we will investigate the influence of other discriminative factors on the detection performance.

References

1. Al-amri, S.S., Kalyankar, N.V., Khamitkar, S.D.: Image segmentation by using threshold techniques. arXiv preprint arXiv:1005.4020
2. Amarbayasgalan, T., Jargalsaikhan, B., Ryu, K.: Unsupervised novelty detection using deep autoencoders with density based clustering. Appl. Sci. **8**(9), 1468 (2018)
3. Aytekin, C., Ni, X., Cricri, F., Aksu, E.: Clustering and unsupervised anomaly detection with l_2 normalized deep auto-encoder representations. In: Proceedings of the IJCNN, vol. 2018-July. IEEE, October 2018
4. Bosman, H.H., Iacca, G., Tejada, A., Wörtche, H.J., Liotta, A.: Spatial anomaly detection in sensor networks using neighborhood information. Inf. Fusion **33**, 41–56 (2017)
5. Cauteruccio, F., et al.: Short-long term anomaly detection in wireless sensor networks based on machine learning and multi-parameterized edit distance. Inf. Fusion **52**, 13–30 (2019)

6. Chong, Y.S., Tay, Y.H.: Abnormal event detection in videos using spatiotemporal autoencoder. In: Cong, F., Leung, A., Wei, Q. (eds.) ISNN 2017. LNCS, vol. 10262, pp. 189–196. Springer, Cham (2017). https://doi.org/10.1007/978-3-319-59081-3_23

7. Erhan, L., et al.: Analyzing objective and subjective data in social sciences: implications for smart cities. IEEE Access **7**, 19890–19906 (2019)

8. Ferrara, E., et al.: A pilot study mapping citizens' interaction with urban nature. In: IEEE DASC/Piom/CyberSciTech, pp. 828–835. IEEE (2018)

9. Guo, X., Liu, X., Zhu, E., Yin, J.: Deep clustering with convolutional autoencoders. In: Liu, D., Xie, S., Li, Y., Zhao, D., El-Alfy, E.S. (eds.) ICONIP 2017. LNCS, vol. 10635, pp. 373–382. Springer, Cham (2017). https://doi.org/10.1007/978-3-319-70096-0_39

10. Xia, Y., Cao, X., Wen, F., Hua, G., Sun, J.: Learning discriminative reconstructions for unsupervised outlier removal. In: Proceedings of the IEEE ICCV, vol. 2015 Inter, pp. 1511–1519 (2015)

11. Yaseen, M.U., Anjum, A., Rana, O., Hill, R.: Cloud-based scalable object detection and classification in video streams. Future Gener. Comput. Syst. **80**, 286–298 (2018)

12. Zamani, A.R., et al.: Deadline constrained video analysis via in-transit computational environments. IEEE Trans. Serv. Comput

13. Zhou, C., Paffenroth, R.C.: Anomaly detection with robust deep autoencoders, pp. 665–674 (2017)

Yet Another Way to Unknowingly Gather People Coordinates and Its Countermeasures

Gabriella Verga, Andrea Fornaia, Salvatore Calcagno,
and Emiliano Tramontana[✉]

Dipartimento di Matematica e Informatica, University of Catania, Catania, Italy
gabriella.verga@unict.it, {fornaia,tramontana}@dmi.unict.it

Abstract. Apps running on a smartphone have the possibility to gather data that can act as a fingerprint for their user. Such data comprise the ids of nearby WiFi networks, features of the device, etc., and they can be a precious asset for offering e.g. customised transportation means, news and ads, etc. Additionally, since WiFi network ids can be easily associated to GPS coordinates, from the users frequent locations it is possible to guess their home address, their shopping preferences, etc. Unfortunately, existing privacy protection mechanisms and permissions on Android OS do not suffice in preventing apps from gathering such data, which can be considered sensitive and not to be disclosed to a third part. This paper shows how an app using only the permission to access WiFi networks could send some private data unknowingly from the user. Moreover, an advanced mechanism is proposed to shield user private data, and to selectively obscure data an app could spy.

Keywords: Android OS · Privacy · Permission · WiFi · Big data

1 Introduction

The widespread adoption of smartphones gives several advantages to both their users and service providers. Generally, apps cater for enhanced services, and can be easily installed on a smartphone. Once installed, apps have access to several *resources* on the smartphone, by resorting to appropriate APIs [10]. Resources are the like of *sensors* for reading GPS user coordinates, amount of light, etc., *file system* for reading and storing data, user *contacts*, *microphone*, etc.

For protecting from apps, several resources of the Android OS are shielded by *permissions*, therefore apps have to declare the needed permissions before accessing the related resource [10]. There are two main permission levels, *normal* and *dangerous*: normal-level permissions are accepted by the user automatically upon installation of the app; dangerous-level permissions are asked to the user, who can grant them by means of a control panel on a per-use basis at runtime. However, normal-level permissions leave the user unaware of which resources the app is accessing and when the app is using them. Such a category comprises

© Springer Nature Switzerland AG 2019
R. Montella et al. (Eds.): IDCS 2019, LNCS 11874, pp. 130–139, 2019.
https://doi.org/10.1007/978-3-030-34914-1_13

Internet, vibration, etc. For dangerous-level permissions, the user is given an alert when the protected resource is going to be used (such an alert can be disabled by the user). Such a category comprises camera, contacts, location, microphone, phone, storage. Then, an app needing location coordinates has to declare dangerous-level permission and the user will be asked to grant it. Unlike other approaches that have focused on data leaks [1], known snippets of malware code [15], or policies granting the use of resources [11], this paper shows how to gain position data without resorting to location APIs.

While operating within the boundaries of the above protection permissions and mechanisms, still an app could compromise the user privacy, that is determine user geo-coordinates even though the user has not granted the use of location resources. For this, an app could silently gather both the id of WiFi networks nearby and that of the smartphone, then an external actor knowing both ids could guess the geo-coordinates. Let us suppose that an app, whose main goal is providing users with a to-do-list, connects to a server to sync data, then it reads the network state, which is a resource guarded by normal permission. Accessing the network could be part of the requirements for the app, since the to-do-list has to be in sync with a server that the user can access from anywhere, e.g. by means of a web app. The network state comprises the id of the WiFi network. Then, by collecting such an id and that of the smartphone, a server can make use of such data to: (i) count the number of people gathering on some places, (ii) tell whether the same person arrives on the same spot at regular intervals, (iii) trace people moving across several spots, (iv) infer the user interests, according to the id of their smartphone. A privacy violation can be identified in that the position of the user, which is determined according to the id of the WiFi network, is known to a third part, without the user being aware. Once the user position is shared to a server, a third part could trace people movements, and collect unique identifiers, such as the phone id.

This paper investigates the above sketched scenario in terms of feasibility (the implementation), the interest that a service provider could have in gathering such data, and means to overcome the weaknesses of the existing protection mechanisms on user devices. In summary, the contributions of this work include: (i) giving a practical example of the problem of gathering user locations, without asking authorisation for the use of location, by means of an apparently harmless app, and then creating targeted ads; (ii) filling in, and constantly updating, a knowledge base using the above data; (iii) a solution to protect the user by analysing and shielding sensitive data at runtime.

2   Related Work

In recent years, smartphone security has matured considerably, and the literature has reported several papers discussing Android security and vulnerabilities [6,7,11,15,17]. The increased importance is due to the possibility to extract plenty of data from devices [7,15,18,22]. Then, such data can be used in many research fields, e.g. the creation of new services for the user [14,16] or for malware detection [5,15]. In [5], authors have proposed a defence mechanism against attacks by means of the analysis of users data traffic (such as WiFi downloaded bytes) and by creating dedicated user profiles.

The extrapolation of data creates new problems in terms of user security and privacy [19]. This is possible given the ability that apps have to interact with sensors and private data managed by the Android OS, and exacerbated by the misunderstanding of security policies by users [9,12]. In Android OS, resources are protected by a mechanism based on permissions, which have been widely discussed in the literature [3,8,11] and constitute a weak point suitable for attacks and data leak.

Several researches have shown the user vulnerability, by acting according to certain available APIs, and the importance of each level of permission (normal, dangerous or otherwise) associated to APIs. Among the techniques available to mitigate risks to user privacy, in [17] the authors have proposed to intercept calls to some APIs that could allow an app to gather private data, and then offer alert messages to the user to make her aware of a possible data leak. The APIs intercepted are regulated by normal or dangerous permissions and the authors explain the importance of analysing both permissions level. In the literature, a well-known example is the use of the ACCESS_WIFI_STATE permission to extrapolate the users physical position without them noticing [13]. While their solution resorts to a more fine-grained permission system, we propose to add some noise on the sensitive WiFi status upon reading it. Additionally, data extracted in our approach are aggregated and can create new knowledge, in order to enhance location estimation, and recommendation for targeted ads [4]. Typically, recommendation systems are generated from locations that users choose to share [20,21].

Our research is based on the indirect identification of the user position through the analysis of the service set identifiers (SSID), for WiFi networks. Unlike others, in our scenario, an app need not access the GPS coordinates and related APIs, while estimating coordinates that are not exact, however suffice for our purposes. Hence, the permission for accessing the GPS coordinates is not needed. Finally, our approach confirms the possibility of monitoring the user when an app declares normal permissions through the implementation of a real use case and offers a real and concrete solution to the problem.

3   Attack Scenario

The identified attack scenario consists of two communicating sub-systems: an app running on an Android OS device and a server-side. The app aims at capturing data available on the device side, i.e. mainly the SSIDs of nearby WiFi, and forward them to the server. The server analyses data to determine the user's current geographical location, and might use it to create targeted ads campaigns.

The identified scenario is a means to highlight the roles that normal permissions have for the user privacy, and to show how to make use of such permissions to find the user's geographical location.

3.1 Creating a Knowledge Base

An app that aims at gathering SSID of nearby WiFis, once installed on the device, would run in the background, and periodically turn on the WiFi (only if turned off), read SSIDs sensed nearby and send collected data to the server-side. If the location of sensed WiFi SSIDs are known to the server, the app determines the user's GPS position based on the SSIDs and their signal strengths. Conversely, if SSIDs are unknown, the app asks the user permission to read the current GPS location, if she accepts, the app will then send the position with the detected SSID. The current position will be used to locate the SSIDs, hence expanding the knowledge base on the server (see Sect. 4). For the APIs reading the GPS position, the app needs a dangerous permission, hence the user has to grant such a permission.

Table 1. For the creation of our knowledge base the following methods of Android OS APIs were used, upon declaration of the related permissions.

Description	Permissions	Class	Method
User Identification	None	Settings.Secure	getString(ContentResolver, String)
User Device Model	None	Build.Model	-
Check WiFi status	ACCESS_WIFI_STATE	WifiManager	isWifiEnabled()
Turn on/off WiFi	ACCESS_WIFI_STATE, CHANGE_WIFI_STATE	WifiManager	enableOrDisableWifi(bool)
Search for known SSID	ACCESS_WIFI_STATE	WifiManager	getScanResults()
Calculate signal level	ACCESS_WIFI_STATE	WifiManager	calculateSignalLevel(String, int)
Describe connection status	ACCESS_NETWORK_STATE, INTERNET	NetworkInfo	isConnected()
Communicate to server	ACCESS_NETWORK_STATE, INTERNET	HttpURL-Connection	writeStream(OutputStream), readStream(InputStream)
Get latitude and longitude in degrees	ACCESS_COARSE_LOCATION or ACCESS_FINE_LOCATION	Location	getLatitude(), getLongitude()

Upon receiving data, the server-side stores, merge, and analyses them. Merging data includes an operation such as the following. SSID values which have been associated with GPS coordinates by an app on a device are shared with apps on other devices whose GPS coordinates are unavailable. Data analysis is performed in order to send targeted ads according to captured SSIDs, using an algorithm that filters ads conforming to geo-locations.

For such an app, the needed permissions and their level are: ACCESS_WIFI_STATE (normal), CHANGE_WIFI_STATE (normal), INTERNET (normal), ACCESS_NETWORK_STATE (normal), ACCESS_COARSE_LOCATION (dangerous), ACCESS_FINE_LOCATION (dangerous). For more details, see Table 1. Permission level is according to Android API level 27.

The following illustrates the relevant code for the app to carry out accesses to SSIDs sensed by an Android device. Figure 1 shows the *getWifiList()* method that returns all the WiFis detected (in the form of a list of strings). In detail, the type of attribute *wifi* is declared as a *WiFiManager*; the *wifiSSIDList()* method calls found in lines 4 and 7 start a scan for the active WiFis and get the SSID attribute of each ScanResult object returned. In line 3, it is checked whether WiFi connectivity is already active; if it is not, it will be activated and then deactivated, in lines 6 and 8, respectively. The implementation of *wifiSSIDList()* method uses *getScanResults()* method to have the SSIDs.

```
1  public List<String> getWifiList() {
2      List<String> toReturn = new ArrayList<>();
3      if(wifi.isWifiEnabled()) {
4          toReturn = wifiSSIDList();
5      } else {
6          wifi.setWifiEnabled(true);
7          toReturn = wifiSSIDList();
8          wifi.setWifiEnabled(false);
9      }
10     return toReturn;
11 }
12
13 private List<String> wifiSSIDList() {
14     List<String> toReturn = new ArrayList<>();
15     List<ScanResult> availNetworks = wifi.getScanResults();
16     if (availNetworks != null && availNetworks.size() > 0)
17         for (ScanResult sr : availNetworks)
18             toReturn.add(sr.SSID);
19     return toReturn;
20 }
```

Fig. 1. The Java code to perform WiFi scan: it enables WiFi (if turned off), looks for available SSIDs and turns off WiFi (if it was off).

4   Architecture of a Leaking Service

Android location APIs can be used by an app to read user position. Considered the related privacy implications, for using such APIs an app has to ask the user to grant a *dangerous*-level permission, i.e. the user has to explicitly allow the app to gather GPS coordinates. The request to access the device position can be motivated by some functionality, such as giving an alert for some goods to buy in a to-do list when the device position is close to a grocery shop. This will allow a server-side to leak this information also for other purposes, such as for ads. In fact, without further policy enforcement [1,2], once the access to the dangerous-level permission has been granted, the user has no control on how extracted data will be used by the app. The only thing that the user can do is to deny the dangerous permission request.

Nevertheless, it is still possible to spot the user position even without asking for a *dangerous*-level permission, i.e. by only leveraging *normal*-level permissions a leak of "partial" data, such as the list of available SSIDs, is viable, without the user knowing about it. By reading a SSIDs list of the nearby WiFi connections, it is then possible to infer the device position, and affect user privacy. A properly designed server-side can collect and fuse leaked data with the ones sensed from other close-by devices, using an underhand crowd approach to complement partial data and improve the spotting precision.

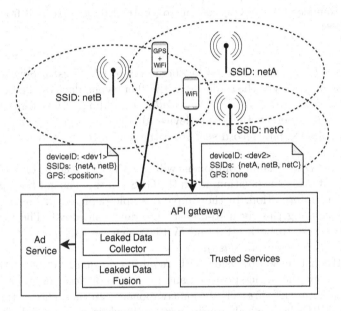

Fig. 2. Server-side architecture: covered by the trusted service behaviour, sensitive device data can be *collected* and *fused* to refine users position. Such data can be then given to third party services (e.g. for advertising), affecting user privacy.

Figure 2 shows the server-side architecture for an Android app disclosing data. In our example, the use case is a simple cloud-based *to-do-list* service accessed through an Android app installed on user devices. This app asks access to several resources (shown in Table 1), such as the *device id*, the *SSIDs list* with the related *signal strength*, and *optionally* the *GPS position*, the only one needing the dangerous permission, whose access can be denied by the user. Other data can be sensed to build a more comprehensive user profile, such as the *device model* which can give some insights about the user income, useful to target ads.

The main components on the server side are: *API gateway*, *Trusted Services*, *Leaked Data Collector*, and *Leaked Data Fusion*. Along with the legitimate behaviour, the app can periodically send the sensed data to the server-side

```
 1  {
 2     androidId : "f05e06f3398c5769",
 3     phoneModel: "Samsung SM-G920F",
 4     timestamp : 10023945,
 5     ssidList: [
 6       "ssid1",
 7       "ssid2",
 8       ... ,
 9       "ssidN"],
10     position:
11     {
12       lat: 111.1111,
13       lng: 22.3334
14     }
15  }
```

```
 1  [
 2     {
 3       ssidName: "ssid1",
 4       position {lat: 11.333, lng: 223.44}
 5     },
 6     {
 7       ssidName: "ssid2",
 8       position {lat: 12.33223, lng: 23.47764}
 9     },
10     ...
11     {
12       ssidName: "ssidN",
13       position {lat: 11.3388,lng: 923.447}
14     }
15  ]
```

Fig. 3. An example of JSON Objects sent to (on the left) and received from (on the right) the server.

through the *API gateway*, covered by the access to the *Trusted Services* of the given app, such as to sync the to-do-list with other owned devices. These data are collected and stored by a *Leaked Data Collector*, adding a timestamped record linked to specific user by the given device id. Figure 3 (on the left) shows an example of a JSON data record sent from the device to the server through the API gateway.

The *Leaked Data Fusion* component will fuse the collected records to build a user profile, inferring the position, when the GPS location has not been provided, by using WiFi information. In the simple example depicted in Fig. 2 there are two devices running the given to-do-list app: `dev1` and `dev2`. The former has granted the access to both GPS and WiFi (which we call *master*), the latter only to WiFi (which we call *slave*).

The SSIDs list sensed by using APIs requiring normal-level permissions can give a clue about the device position, and given two devices the more SSIDs in common the closer they are. The fusion component can then *cluster* the devices with similar SSIDs lists, which are supposed to be close, even though their exact position is unknown (in case of a slave). Information about signal strength can also be used to weight the clustering algorithm and obtain a better clustering precision. Then, the GPS of a master can be used to infer the position of all the other slaves in the same cluster, with a precision proportional to the SSIDs the slave has in common with the master and the related signal strength. Hence, a single close-by device providing GPS coordinates suffices to locate many other devices that have denied GPS use. Furthermore, the server could be provided with the GPS positions of some known SSIDs, further improving the precision of inferred slave positions. This information can be obtained by leveraging external services like *WiGLE*[1], by a manually provided list (mapping known restaurants, parks or public buildings SSIDs), or inferred by the fusion component, in a similar way used to spot slaves. Figure 3 (on the right) shows a list example of known SSIDs coordinates that are used by the server to improve the spotting

---

[1] https://wigle.net.

precision. This can also be sent to the devices for a self *GPS-less* positioning, using signal strength to estimate those SSIDs proximity.

5   User Protection

Given the risk of information leakage, in this section we propose an enhanced defence mechanism that manages to protect user privacy. For the scenario illustrated above, an app can gather the device id and the SSIDs of close-by WiFi networks and pass them to a server. This can be considered a violation of the user's privacy, since the former gives the server a surrogate for the user identity, and the latter a close approximation of her position. To overcome such a privacy violation, the app can be automatically transformed, e.g. by means of the Aspects Oriented Programming (AOP), to intercept all the calls for reading the device id, inspired by the method in [17].

```
1   @Aspect public class TraceAspect {
2       private static final String PCUT =
3           "call (* android.provider.Settings.Secure.*)";
4
5       @Pointcut(PCUT) public void blockedMethods() {}
6
7       @Around("blockedMethods()")
8       public Object weaveJP(ProceedingJoinPoint jp) throws Throwable {
9           Object result = conventionalResult(jp.toString());
10          viewRequestedPermission(jp.toString());
11          return result;
12      }
13  }
```

Fig. 4. An aspect intercepting readings of the device ID. Every call to methods of Secure class is trapped by pointcut PCUT (line 3, 5) and weaveJP() method is executed. Then, the call on line 9 changes the device ID, and the call on line 10 sends an alert to the user.

Therefore, the call pertaining to the *User Identification* request (see Table 1) is intercepted by our provided aspect and the ID is altered using masking techniques, before being sent to the server (see Fig. 4). Moreover, the user can be alerted of such an access. E.g., we could simply apply the Caesar cipher with a value n varying over time. That is, with n = 2, the ID d83c84d1176a3547 becomes f05e06f3398c5769. In this way, even though the server has the SSIDs of close-by WiFi networks, it is unaware of the real user id, hence several data analyses become not meaningful. E.g. the server cannot properly compute the user frequent locations, since the user id varies over time, and cannot profile the user because the real id is hidden by multiple (fake) ids.

Similarly, the read operation of SSIDs can be captured by our provided aspect and the real values changed upon each reading operation, before the app sends them to the server. Making the values of SSIDs vary for each read operation renders the server data base useless, since a device cannot be associated with a list of known nearby WiFis. Additionally, when such altered data need to be used to feed some Android APIs, the aspect can intervene again to reverse the applied masking. On one hand, data leaks can be very difficult to spot among all communications with a server legit from a functional point of view, hence they cannot be blocked. On the other hand, the proposed aspects selectively block private information, and could be automatically made available just before deployment by an agent handling the app market or a certification authority that aims at hardening the app.

6 Conclusions

In recent years, various privacy-related attacks have been performed on mobile devices, due to their widespread use and their multiple functions. The paper presents a possible attack scenario for owners of Android devices consisting in reading a surrogate of the user's position (i.e. sensed SSIDs) without the user's authorisation, and sending such data to a remote actor, hence violating privacy. The information moreon the users' position can be used e.g. for targeted advertising, dependent on the estimated location, or even for more nefarious activities. Furthermore, to overcome such a weakness we present a defence mechanism that protects user privacy, and can change the user id or sensed SSIDs to mask such data. Therefore, information leakage by the app is useless on the server-side.

Acknowledgement. This work has been supported by project CREAMS—Codes Recognising and Eluding Attacks and Meddling on Systems—funded by Università degli Studi di Catania, Piano della Ricerca 2016/2018 Linea di intervento 2.

References

1. Arzt, S., et al.: Flowdroid: precise context, flow, field, object-sensitive and lifecycle-aware taint analysis for Android apps. ACM SIGPLAN Not. **49**(6), 259–269 (2014)
2. Ascia, G., et al.: Making Android apps data-leak-safe by data flow analysis and code injection. In: Proceedings of IEEE International Conference on Enabling Technologies: Infrastructure for Collaborative Enterprises (WETICE), pp. 205–210 (2016)
3. Aung, Z., Zaw, W.: Permission-based Android malware detection. Int. J. Sci. Technol. Res. **2**(3), 228–234 (2013)
4. Cavallaro, C., Verga, G., Tramontana, E., Muscato, O.: Multi-agent architecture for point of interest detection and recommendation. In: Proceedings of XX Workshop From Objects to Agents (WOA) (2019)
5. Di Stefano, A., Fornaia, A., Tramontana, E., Verga, G.: Detecting Android malware according to observations on user activities. In: Proceedings of IEEE International Conference on Enabling Technologies: Infrastructure for Collaborative Enterprises (WETICE), pp. 241–246 (2018)

6. Enck, W.: Defending users against smartphone apps: techniques and future directions. In: Jajodia, S., Mazumdar, C. (eds.) ICISS 2011. LNCS, vol. 7093, pp. 49–70. Springer, Heidelberg (2011). https://doi.org/10.1007/978-3-642-25560-1_3

7. Enck, W., Ongtang, M., McDaniel, P.: Understanding Android security. IEEE Secur. Priv. **7**(1), 50–57 (2009)

8. Felt, A.P., Chin, E., Hanna, S., Song, D., Wagner, D.: Android permissions demystified. In: Proceedings of ACM Conference on Computer and Communications Security, pp. 627–638 (2011)

9. Felt, A.P., Ha, E., Egelman, S., Haney, A., Chin, E., Wagner, D.: Android permissions: user attention, comprehension, and behavior. In: Proceedings of ACM Symposium on Usable Privacy and Security (2012)

10. Google: Android (2019). https://developer.android.com/topic/libraries/support-library

11. Krupp, B., Sridhar, N., Zhao, W.: SPE: security and privacy enhancement framework for mobile devices. IEEE Trans. Dependable Secure Comput. **14**(4), 433–446 (2015)

12. Montealegre, C., Njuguna, C.R., Malik, M.I., Hannay, P., McAteer, I.N.: Security vulnerabilities in Android applications. In: Proceedings of Australian Information Security Management Conference (2018)

13. Nguyen, L., et al.: UnLocIn: unauthorized location inference on smartphones without being caught. In: Proceedings of IEEE International Conference on Privacy and Security in Mobile Systems (PRISMS), pp. 1–8 (2013)

14. Qi, M., Wang, Z., He, Z., Shao, Z.: User identification across asynchronous mobility trajectories. Sensors **19**(9), 2102 (2019)

15. Shabtai, A., Kanonov, U., Elovici, Y., Glezer, C., Weiss, Y.: Andromaly: a behavioral malware detection framework for Android devices. J. Intell. Inf. Syst. **38**(1), 161–190 (2012)

16. Tramontana, E., Verga, G.: Get spatio-temporal flows from GPS data. In: Proceedings of IEEE International Conference on Smart Computing (SMARTCOMP), pp. 282–284 (2018)

17. Tramontana, E., Verga, G.: Mitigating privacy-related risks for Android users. In: Proceedings of IEEE International Conference on Enabling Technologies: Infrastructure for Collaborative Enterprises (WETICE) (2019)

18. Wagner, D.T., Rice, A., Beresford, A.R.: Device analyzer: large-scale mobile data collection. ACM SIGMETRICS Perform. Eval. Rev. **41**(4), 53–56 (2014)

19. Wei, T.E., Jeng, A.B., Lee, H.M., Chen, C.H., Tien, C.W.: Android privacy. In: Proceedings of IEEE International Conference on Machine Learning and Cybernetics, vol. 5, pp. 1830–1837 (2012)

20. Zheng, V.W., Zheng, Y., Xie, X., Yang, Q.: Collaborative location and activity recommendations with GPS history data. In: Proceedings of ACM International Conference on World Wide Web, pp. 1029–1038 (2010)

21. Zheng, V.W., Zheng, Y., Xie, X., Yang, Q.: Towards mobile intelligence: learning from GPS history data for collaborative recommendation. Artif. Intell. **184**, 17–37 (2012)

22. Zheng, Y., Xie, X., Ma, W.Y., et al.: GeoLife: a collaborative social networking service among user, location and trajectory. IEEE Data Eng. Bull. **33**(2), 32–39 (2010)

Computation Offloading with MQTT Protocol on a Fog-Mist Computing Framework

Pietro Battistoni$^{(\boxtimes)}$ ⬢, Monica Sebillo ⬢, and Giuliana Vitiello ⬢

Department of Computer Science, University of Salerno, Fisciano, Salerno, Italy
{pbattistoni,msebillo,gvitiello}@unisa.it
http://www.unisa.it

Abstract. Although computation offloading has been widely discussed into research literature, as an optimisation mechanism that can utilise remote CPU resources on Cloud, it has not been extensively applied in highly constrained devices due to its long latency and the unreliability of the Internet connection. In a previous work, a *Fog-Mist Computing Framework* was proposed, which claims to offer lower latency and remove the need for the persistent Internet connectivity. The *Fog-Mist Computing* underlying architecture is made up of *Fog-Nodes* and *Mist-Node*. The *Mist-Node* are placed directly within the edge fabrics, thus providing the *Mobile Devices* with connectivity services and low latency computational resources. In this paper, the MQTT, a Publisher/Subscriber messaging protocol, is adopted to deploy a Remote Function Invocation among the *Nodes* of such a *Framework*, at the edge of the network.

Keywords: Remote Function Invocation · MQTT · Computation offloading · Fog Computing · Mist Computing · Mobile Device

1 Introduction

The paper "Forecast and Trends" [4] by Cisco estimates that Machine to Machine (M2M) connections, from 6.1 billion in 2017, will reach up to 14.6 billion by 2022. The devices communicating among them will be 1.8 times the global estimated population. Then, the continuously increasing number of connected devices with their amount of data produced requires new concepts and technologies to transform it into useful information.

A *Fog-Mist Computing Framework* [2] was initially proposed to address this challenge. This study deepens the topic and proposes the use of that *Framework* and the deploy of a *Computation Offloading* mechanism among *Mist-Nodes* at the edge of the network, using the MQTT Protocol for *Remote Function Invocation*.

Supported by E3APP project, POR CAMPANIA FESR 2014/2020.

ⓒ Springer Nature Switzerland AG 2019
R. Montella et al. (Eds.): IDCS 2019, LNCS 11874, pp. 140–147, 2019.
https://doi.org/10.1007/978-3-030-34914-1_14

The paper is organized as follows. Section 2 gives a brief description of solution components, while some related works are recalled in Sect. 3. Section 4 describes the proposed method. Some final remarks and future works conclude the paper.

2   The Fog-Mist Computing Architecture

The National Institute of Standard and Technology [8] define a Fog Computing as a layered model facilitating the deployment of distributed applications and services. It enables two fundamental requirements, namely, it improves the latency and removes the necessity for the persistent Internet connectivity.

Fog-Mist Computing architecture is made up of *Fog-Nodes* and *Mist-Nodes*. The *Mist-Nodes* are placed directly within the edge. They feed into the *Fog-Nodes*, placed between the *Mist-Nodes* and centralised *Cloud* services (Fig. 1). The *Mist-Nodes* are a simpler form of *Fog-Nodes*. They offer some computational resources and connectivity services to the end *Mobile-Devices*, sharing the same local network.

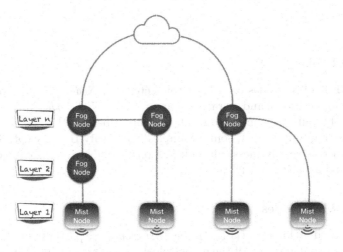

Fig. 1. The Fog-Mist Model

2.1   The MQTT Protocol

MQTT stands for MQ Telemetry Transport [1]. It is a publish/subscribe (*Pub/Sub*) messaging transport protocol, expressly designed to send telemetry data and for the Internet of Things (IoT). It is made up of *Clients* and *Brokers* (Fig. 2). The *Client* code has a tiny footprint, making it suitable for devices with few resources and high constrains. The protocol deals with *Topics* and *Messages*.

The *Pub/Sub* message paradigm provides one-to-many message distribution and decoupling of applications. Three Quality of Service (QoS) for message delivery is offered, namely, "At most once", "At least once" and "Exactly once". The addition of a mechanism to notify interested parties when an abnormal disconnection occurs, makes it resilient and more suitable for conceived purpose.

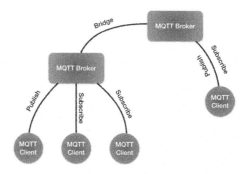

Fig. 2. An example an MQTT components.

2.2 The Broker

The MQTT Broker resides on a local connected *Fog-Node*, which by definition has more computational and storage resources than a *Mist-Node*. An MQTT broker routes the published message to all the subscribers of that message *Topic*. In the following Subsect. 2.4, some examples will clarify the concept. The *Subscribers* can receive any message published on the subscribed *Topic*, almost in real-time and asynchronously.

2.3 The Mist Nodes

In the proposed architecture (Fig. 3), the *Mist-Nodes* are partially meshed, forming a chained configuration of the extensible coverage area of the Wireless Local Network (WLAN). They are co-located with the end devices. Data generated from these devices are processed by the *Mist-Nodes* much faster than by a centralised cloud device. In such a way, they satisfy the requirement of low latency, necessary for devices which have to fast react to stimulus from others physically close connected devices.

2.4 The Client and the Topics

The Client has to reside on each *Mist-Node*. It can *Subscribe* and *Publish* to any *Topics*. A *Topic* has a structure similar to a file path. Each *Broker* has a root '/' *Topic*, and any *Publisher* or *Subscriber* can build a hierarchy on it.

Fig. 3. The proposed architecture

For example: "/Request/*functionA*" and "/Request/*functionB*" are two *Topics*. A *Topic* does not need to be created before. It is created whenever a client *Subscribes* or *Publishes* it the first time.

Any node which subscribes to the Topic "/Request/#" will receive the Message published on both the sub-*Topics* "*functionA*" and "*functionB*". Any Client which subscribes to *Topic* "/Request/*functionA*" will only receive the messages published on this *Topic*.

3   Related Works

Computation offloading refers to the transfer of computational tasks to a remote device or platform. Although computation offloading has been widely discussed into research literature, as an optimization mechanism that can utilize remote CPU resources on Cloud, it has not been extensively applied in highly constrained devices due to its long latency and the unreliability of the Internet connection.

Remote Procedure Call (RPC) architecture, in literature, refers mainly to a client-server model, where the client enquires, and a server provides a service.

A Remote Method Invocation (RMI) still refers to a client-server architecture, but typically involving distributed objects.

Calice et al. in [3] investigate multiple offloading strategies concerning both computation time and energy consumption, related to heterogeneous devices forming mobile-to-mobile opportunistic computing. Le et al. in [7] present a novel distributed execution model that both optimizes mobile application's executions in terms of performance and energy efficiency, and expands mobile device's hardware capability. In [6], Le Minh et al. introduce a new software framework enabling routing Remote Procedure Call (RPC) architecture on multiple groups device-to-device networks, arguing that "the RPC-based or message queue-based techniques are obsolete or unwieldy for mobile platforms".

The cited works, mainly face the challenge of heterogeneous hardware and try to find solution for two of the main issues, inadequate Internet connection and services discovery. By bringing computational power at the edge of the network, the Fog-Mist Architecture does not require a reliable Internet connection. Furthermore, the nature of proposed Fog-Mist Computing Framework, made up of homogeneous firmware *Mist-Nodes*, will avoid the need to know which function is available and by which resources. Then, solutions based on this architecture can benefit from a more straightforward method to Remotely Invoke a Function from another local node, which not necessarily has the same hardware, but that has mainly the same implemented functions.

This work proposes a computation offloading solution, to achieve a Remote Function Invocation (RFI) rather than a Remote Process Call (RPC) or a Remote Method Invocation (RMI), to lower the latency time for the mobile devices, which are connected through Fog-Mist Computing Architecture. Other than from previously cited works, which deal with a higher degree of difficulty, this proposal takes all the advantage of previously mentioned Fog-Mist architecture, mastering many of the issues faced in the related works. Furthermore, the capability to expand mobile device hardware, as mentioned in [7] "Utilizing Nearby Computing Resources for Resource-limited Mobile Devices", is still possible in some cases, achieving a low latency for all sensors and devices on the same layer. Other works care about offloading decisions and resource allocation [5,9]. These topics are out of the scope of this work, which is addressed to leverage resources available from previously proposed Fog-Mist Framework, and it assumes a two-step paradigm based on *Collaboration* and *Competition*, where all node are same.

Finally, it should be pointed out that although the proposed solution has at least one MQTT Broker, which cares about the right routing of messages, it does not have any *Orchestration* or client-server model for the computation offloading.

4   Computation Offloading with MQTT Protocol

In most cases, the *Mist-Nodes* are made up of the same hardware and have the same firmware supplying the same functionalities. What if a *Mist-Node*, whenever needs more computational resources, enquires other sibling nodes for collaboration?

Let the *Demander* be the node which requires the collaboration, and the *Offerer* the node which is available to offer its collaboration. Any node can be a *Demander* or an *Offerer* at any time, without any *Orchestration*.

4.1   The *Demander* and the *Offerer*

The *Demander*. A *Mist-Node* that requires execution of a remote task, or needs some information from other local devices, can *Publish* a message on the local MQTT Broker to demand a *Collaboration* to other siblings, becoming a

Demander. It can wait for an answer while it is too busy to elaborate the task by itself. Once the answer is available to the *Broker*, the *Demander* is notified and can use the results. Instead, if the *Demander* acquires resources to elaborate the answer by itself before it is available from other nodes, then it can proceed with elaboration, ignoring the possible answer.

The *Offerer*. Every local *Mist-Node* subscribes to an earlier defined common *Topic*. In the previous example, the *Topic* could be "/Request/#". Whenever any *Topic* beneath this one, for example "/Request/*functionA*" (Fig. 4), receives a message, it is parsed. If the node has available resources and is in an idle state, it can decide to execute the required elaboration, thus becoming an *Offerer* and will publish the computed answer on the same *Topic*. Indeed, the *Offerer* will know if another *Competitor* node has computed the answer faster because as a *Subscriber* of the *Topic*, in that event, it will be notified by the *Broker*.

4.2   The Messaging

Following the previous examples, the *Message*, when published by a *Demander*, has to be published on a sub-topic of root topic: "/Request/", named as the *Function* required, while the message content has to contain data or parameters that have to be computed by the *Offerer*. For example, a *Demander* which asks for elaboration of *functionA (a,b)*, will publish to the Topic: "/Request/*functionA*" with the message content: "a,b". In such a way, when a new request rises from a *Demander*, all subscribers to the topic "/Request/#", will be notified. The *Offerers* that accept the request, will subscribe to the specific topic "/Request/*functionA*" to be notified in case another *Offerer* answers the request faster, or to publish the answer if it is the fastest. Then, only the *Offerer* that is involved in the *functionA* request, will be notified, keeping free all the other nodes and excluding itself from notification of new requests. The *Offerer* that faster completes the elaboration, will publish the message containing the answer to the *Topic*: "/Request/*functionA*". The *Demander* will be notified together with all the other competing *Offerers*. While the *Demander* can take and use the answer, the other *Offerers* can abort their elaboration, subscribing again to "/Request/#", ready to receive notification of new requests (Fig. 4).

4.3   The Underlying Paradigm

The Collaboration. The *Computation Offloading* starts when a *Demander* *Publishes* a request. A phase of *Collaboration* follows this event, where all the other nodes can spontaneously decide to offer their collaboration. The decision will be based on their busy state, their capacity at the moment of request and no *Orchestration* or *Arbitration* are required.

The Competition. To the Collaboration phase, follows a *Competition* phase, where all the *Offerers* compete. The winner will be the fastest *Node* to *Publish* an answer.

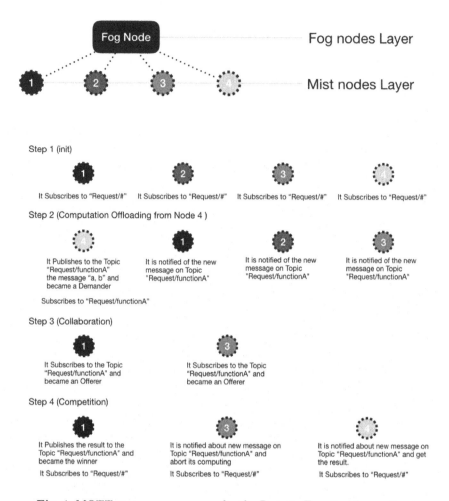

Fig. 4. MQTT messages sequences for the Remote Function Invocation

5   Final Remarks and Future Works

This work describes a basic *Computation Offloading* mechanism among *Mist-Nodes*. It is easily deployed, just leveraging the MQTT protocol, already exploited for other essential tasks in the proposed Fog-Mist Computing Architecture. Being based on a *Collaborative* and *Competitive* paradigm, it implies that an *Orchestration* or a service discovery are not required. The low latency requirement and the unreliability of the Internet connection are featured by proposed Fog-Mist Architecture, while the messaging protocol itself solves QoS issues. The rationale underlying the proposed solution is to exploit the increasing adoption of both the Fog-Computing paradigm and the Pub/Sub protocol, widely used for all solutions where the low latency and the distributed hardware represent strong requirements to be satisfied. Actually, the proposed computation offloading method can be easily deployed on any Fog-Computing Architecture where a *Pub/Sub* messaging solution is already adopted for other tasks. Moreover, even if in the previous example the *Offerer* could be one or more of *Mist Nodes*, in reality this is not limited to it. For example, a *Fog Node*, with a more computational resource, could transparently become an *Offerer*. It could offer, for example, inference for a Deep Learning Model, or in general, a heavy maths computation, to simpler *Mist Nodes*, helping in moving the AI at the Edge.

A test on MQTT protocol performances and the partially meshed network are left as future works.

References

1. Mqtt version 5.0. http://docs.oasis-open.org/mqtt/mqtt/v5.0/mqtt-v5.0.pdf
2. Battistoni, P., Sebillo, M., Vitiello, G.: Experimenting with a fog-computing architecture for indoor navigation. In: 2019 Fourth International Conference on Fog and Mobile Edge Computing (FMEC), pp. 161–165, June 2019. https://doi.org/10.1109/FMEC.2019.8795307
3. Calice, G., Mtibaa, A., Beraldi, R., Alnuweiri, H.: Mobile-to-mobile opportunistic task splitting and offloading. In: 2015 IEEE 11th International Conference on Wireless and Mobile Computing, Networking and Communications (WiMob), pp. 565–572, October 2015. https://doi.org/10.1109/WiMOB.2015.7348012
4. Cisco: Forecast and trends, 2017–2022 white paper
5. Du, J., Zhao, L., Feng, J., Chu, X.: Computation offloading and resource allocation in mixed fog/cloud computing systems with min-max fairness guarantee. IEEE Trans. Commun. **66**(4), 1594–1608 (2018). https://doi.org/10.1109/TCOMM.2017.2787700
6. Le, M., Clyde, S., Kwon, Y.W.: Enabling multi-hop remote method invocation in device-to-device networks. Hum.-Centric Comput. Inf. Sci. **9**(1), 20 (2019). https://doi.org/10.1186/s13673-019-0182-9
7. Le, M., Kwon, Y.W.: Utilizing nearby computing resources for resource-limited mobile devices. In: Proceedings of the Symposium on Applied Computing, SAC 2017, pp. 572–575. ACM, New York (2017). https://doi.org/10.1145/3019612.3019884
8. Iorga, M., Feldman, L., Barton, R., Martin, M.J., Goren, N.S., Mahmoudi, C.: Fog computing conceptual model (2018)
9. Wang, Y., Tao, X., Zhang, X., Zhang, P., Hou, Y.T.: Cooperative task offloading in three-tier mobile computing networks: an ADMM framework. IEEE Trans. Veh. Technol. **68**(3), 2763–2776 (2019). https://doi.org/10.1109/TVT.2019.2892176

Load Balancing in Hybrid Clouds Through Process Mining Monitoring

Kenneth K. Azumah$^{(\boxtimes)}$ ⓘ, Sokol Kostaⓘ, and Lene T. Sørensenⓘ

CMI, Aalborg University, Copenhagen, Denmark
{kka,sok,ls}@cmi.aau.dk

Abstract. An increasing number of organisations are harnessing the benefits of hybrid cloud adoption to support their business goals and achieving privacy and control in a private cloud whilst enjoying the on-demand scalability of the public cloud. However the complexity introduced by the combination of the public and private clouds worsens visibility in cloud monitoring with regards compliance to given business constraints. Load balancing as a technique for evenly distributing workloads can be leveraged together with processing mining to help ease the monitoring challenge. In this paper we propose a load balancing approach to distribute workloads in order to minimise violations to specified business constraints. The scenario of a hospital consultation process is employed as a use case in monitoring and controlling Octavia load balancing-as-a-service in OpenStack. The results show a co-occurrence of constraint violations and Octavia L7 Policy creation, indicating a successful application of process mining monitoring in load balancing.

Keywords: Hybrid cloud · Process mining · Event calculus · OpenStack Octavia

1 Introduction

Lots of data generated in organisations help make decisions about their business. In the healthcare industry the data generally result from processes involving the patient and clinicians, encompassing a wide range of activities such consultations, appointments booking, laboratory and radiological investigations. The collection, processing, and storage of such data present a notable challenge including the extent of IT investment needed, in the form of infrastructure, to ensure that adequate mileage is obtained from the data being generated. Though Cloud Computing eases the IT infrastructure decision-making and risks, the concerns about privacy and security continue to impact on the extent of adoption. Businesses generally protect their sensitive information by storing and processing data in private data centres, where full control offers a high level of assurance of privacy and preservation of business information. It is therefore desirable for companies to keep sensitive data on an internal data centre and process less sensitive, irregular or seasonal workloads in the public cloud. The combination of

© Springer Nature Switzerland AG 2019
R. Montella et al. (Eds.): IDCS 2019, LNCS 11874, pp. 148–157, 2019.
https://doi.org/10.1007/978-3-030-34914-1_15

the public cloud and private data centre is often termed a *hybrid cloud*, with the public cloud providing high scalability potential whilst the private data centre provides privacy for selected data and applications. As a result of the combination of two separate deployment models, a hybrid cloud increases the complexity of managing the overall cloud infrastructure, especially in maintaining privacy and control over data and processes.

Load balancing is one of the major cloud computing strategies [1], designed to help address the challenge of maintaining adequate visibility and control over workload distribution within the cloud. Load balancing is applied in situations requiring high availability of a service—especially in a hybrid cloud where resources are split between one or more private data centres and the public cloud. Basic routing of network packets enables messages to be distributed at the media level (OSI Layer 3) however for more data-aware routing, the host level (OSI Layer 7) is employed in network packet distribution. As a strategy for managing workloads in a hybrid cloud, load balancing employs various algorithms influenced by the industry's business processes or constraints. A business constraint commonly refers to anything that interferes with the profitability of a business endeavour. Among these constraints are company policies on data processing to increase some level of compliance to regulations in the industry. The increasing complexity and dynamic nature of business constraints, however, requires matching sophisticated and more intelligent algorithms to satisfy load balancing objectives. Programming such constraints to provide control and compliance to predefined rules will inherently be procedural. It will be unreasonable to require static verification techniques to define explicitly all possible allowable procedures. This complexity makes regular programming languages virtually unsuitable for monitoring event and process violations as they occur.

Process mining is a rising data-aware technique that has long been used to map out the process model of business activities and provide insight into compliance of the activities to some given process model. The technique employs event data obtained from the log files of the information system generating the activities. Existing solutions however present crucial limitations in a load balancing situation that requires near immediate reactions to service requests [2], [3]. This motivates a study linking process mining and load balancing to achieve near-realtime compliance to given constraints. In this paper, we present a prototype framework that employs layer 7 load balancing as a means of controlling data processing in a hybrid cloud to satisfy as much as possible a given set of business constraints. Our framework extends Octavia, an LBaaS module in OpenStack with a modified implementation of MoBuCon [4], a process mining tool. Our framework is able to dynamically update the load balancer policies based on event data and specified business constraints. The results show how a load balancer can route requests to avoid violating constraints that are dependent on the events occurring within a hybrid cloud.

The remaining sections are organised as follows: We first present background and related work on load balancing and monitoring business constraints via process mining (Sect. 2). Section 3 lays out the architecture and integration of the process mining and load balancing components, and also describes the environment of the experiment. Section 4 presents the preliminary results and Sect. 5 concludes the work.

2   Background and Related Work

A business constraint commonly refers to anything that interferes with the profitability of a business endeavour. This section provides a background on business constraints and how event data can influence load balancing behaviour.

2.1   Business Constraints and Event Calculus

Business constraints are characterised by rules that force an organisation's compliance to certain governing practices. For example, the handling of sensitive data should follow a given sequence within organisations' information systems. The analyses of log files containing event data therefore becomes a crucial aspect of monitoring information systems. Process mining as a data analysis technique relies on three key pieces of event data – **instance identifier, activity name** and **timestamp**. The timestamp provides a chronological order for the capture of activities occurring in information systems. Kowalski formalises the notion of an event in time employing the Horn clause with negation as failure [5]. The resulting event calculus formalisation is executable in a logical manner and therefore presentable as a Prolog program.

Event logs captured from information systems provide a record of activities that occurred in a chronological manner. A group of activities usually culminates in a business process designed to achieve one or more specific goals. By analysing the event logs for the correct order of occurrence of the activities and their duration, deductions can be made about whether the process complies with specified rules. Event Calculus (EC) is characterised by reasoning about change and the effects of an action on conditions that can change over time. EC is thus suitable for monitoring and reporting violations of policies by events occurring in the cloud infrastructure.

Business constraints – hereafter referred to as *constraints* – are expressed graphically using the Declare notation [6]. A constraint specified as **_response(A, B, Cond)_** is a Declare constraint with a data condition *Cond* that states "if event A occurs and Cond holds, event B must occur afterwards". The constraint is said to be *activated* when an event matching a part of the constraint is encountered in the log [7]. Given an event log with traces {A, B, C}, {A, B} and {A, C}, the last trace violates the constraint since B must necessarily follow A for compliance. The traces have the following states: $\{...A\} \rightarrow pend, \{...A, B\} \rightarrow sat, \{...A, B, C\} \rightarrow sat, \{...A, B, C, A\} \rightarrow pend, \{...A, B, C, A, C\} \rightarrow viol$. For each partial trace, the truth-value of the Linear Temporal Logic (LTL) formula [4] generates the state of satisfaction of the constraint, either satisfied *sat*, violated *viol* or pending *pend* [8]. Extending Declare with data-awareness facilitates the monitoring of business constraints [4,6,9].

2.2 Octavia - Load-balancing-as-a-service Overview

OpenStack started in 2010 as a joint project between NASA and Rackspace. Octavia, one of its key projects, provides scalable load-balancing-as-a-service (LBaaS) with layer 7 (L7) content switching capability at layer 2 speeds [10]. When users access services hosted on the cloud, their requests are usually handled by a load balancer. The load balancing algorithm is based on one or more statistics including CPU load, number of connections and affinity settings. Layer 7 Load Balancing is achieved through L7 rules and L7 policies. The **L7 Rule** is a simple, single logical test, which evaluates to either `true` or `false`. An **L7 Policy** is a collection of L7 rules and a defined action when all rules in the policy are matched.

Sharma et al. present a case for evenly spreading workloads across a set of available VMs [11]. In finding an optimal solution, they introduce an algorithm that mimics the way bats locate and identify their prey: bats representing workloads and targeted prey being the virtual machines. Wider issues depending on the content of the workload and data-awareness are not covered.

Rahhali [12] considers and efficient combination of algorithms to optimise energy consumption and response time – both essential QoS parameters in cloud computing. The paper employs well-known heuristics to achieve near-optimal solutions targeting both running time and energy consumption. Their algorithms do not cover data-awareness in the workloads.

Aktas [13] proposes a monitoring software architecture for both preventive maintenance and error detection in a cloud computing environment. The software uses primitive metric data gleaned from logs of the cloud computing operating system and utilises metrics on CPU, memory, and disk usage to trigger reports on measurements that violate preset rules. The paper shows the capacity of the software to handle large volumes of events but the monitoring rules are preset.

Liu and Li [14] present a stratified monitoring model for hybrid clouds and propose key metrics for each monitoring layer putting forth measures to perform as part of data collection for evaluation. The paper employs agent technology towards a monitoring architecture. There are no experiments on implementation and evaluation of the model and its efficiency.

Azumah et al. [15] have proposed a hybrid cloud scheduling with process mining monitoring mechanism that facilitates decision-making of the scheduler. They present their experiments with CloudSim [16], showing an output that employs Event Calculus in determining compliance or otherwise to set a set of given business constraints. The paper shows how process mining monitoring can influence scheduling in the hybrid cloud towards achieving a more desirable and proportionate VM spawning. Their experiment employ synthetic data in a simulated environment.

3   System Specification

3.1   Use Case Scenario

In this work, we employ a hospital scenario where L7 content switching can be of benefit when performing load balancing in a hybrid cloud. Recall one of the benefits of the hybrid cloud is the on-demand availability of public resources when the private datacenter has reached peak capacity. In our hospital scenario, the constraint for processing data in the hybrid cloud is re-routing, as much as possible, highly sensitive data HS to the internal datacenter IDC. The processing of less sensitive data LS can take place in either IDC or public portion of the hybrid cloud EDC. We consider the constraint $conHSCX$ defined as follows: (1) If a patient is provisionally diagnosed with cancer, (2) Laboratory investigations reveal positive markers for cancer (3) The next consultation should be regarded as sensitive data processing and routed accordingly to the internal datacenter.

Table 1. Partial trace involving case IDs during cloud bursting.

#	Case ID	Activity	Timestamp	Route	Activation
L1	PatientA	Diagnose: Cancer	Jan 3, 2019 9:25	EDC	
L2	PatientB	Diagnose: Hypertension	Jan 3, 2019 10:05	EDC	
L3	PatientA	Lab: CA+	Jan 3, 2019 11:01	EDC	
L4	PatientC	Diagnose: Anaemia	Jan 3, 2019 11:02	EDC	
L5	PatientB	Lab: PSA+	Jan 3, 2019 11:30	EDC	
L6	PatientB	Diagnose: Cancer	Jan 4, 2019 10:08	EDC	
L7	PatientA	Consult: GP	Jan 9, 2019 9:02	IDC	conHSCX
L8	PatientA	Lab: FBS	Jan 9, 2019 10:42	IDC	
L9	PatientC	Lab: RBS	Jan 9, 2019 10:50	EDC	
L10	PatientB	Consult: Cancer	Jan 9, 2019 11:21	EDC	
L11	...	...	...	...	...

For instance, the partial trace in Table 1 shows the activation of the conHSCX constraint on account of PatientA having been provisionally diagnosed and then having lab results confirming the diagnosis. The confirmation of the lab results activates conHSCX and classifies subsequent events involving PatientA as highly sensitive as far as the hospital policy is concerned. In the next sections we treat the architectural layout for the evaluation and routing of application server requests based on Octavia L7 policies and rules.

3.2   Architectural Layout and Component Integration

We present the individual components of the architecture together with configuration and extensions that facilitate their integration.

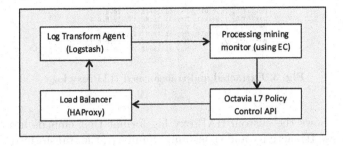

Fig. 1. Highlevel architectural representation with process flow

In the architecture we parse event data generated by the load balancer, *HAProxy* and a simulated application server. To scale the architecture to contain more than one load balancer and application server, a log service *Logstash* is introduced to help aggregate event logs from the various VMs. We filter and transform the Logstash data into our *Process Mining Monitor* (PMM) for further evaluation. Further information is provided by configuring HAProxy to display custom headers using the built-in `http-format`. The application server within the hybrid cloud sends requests with custom headers containing information about activity, timestamp and case ID. By injecting custom headers into each request we enable the load balancer to make more "informed" decisions about routing dynamically. The flow of information between the components is shown in Fig. 1.

We have configured HAProxy to record in its log file each request on the HTTP or application layer that includes the URL requested and the server to which the request was routed alongside the custom headers. Before feeding the information as a message to our implementation of PMM, we extract and analyse the transformed fields: event type, activity name, case id, timestamp, source address and backend server. The source address and the backend machine servicing the request constitute extra resources that we use in the process mining stage. Taking one line in the HAProxy log – `May 31 18:48:14 10.0.0.1:37318 0/0/4/3/16 200 40 - - ---- 0/0/0/0/0 0/0 ''GET /consult HTTP/1.1 caseid:patientA'' –` we extract `patientA`, `/consult`, `May 31 18:48:14`, `10.0.0.1` for input into PMM.

```
May 31 18:48:14 10.0.0.1:37318 0/0/4/3/16 200 40 - - ---- 0/0/0/0/0 0/0 "GET /consult HTTP/1.1 caseid:patientA"
May 31 18:48:15 10.0.0.1:37320 0/0/3/2/16 200 40 - - ---- 0/0/0/0/0 0/0 "GET /consult HTTP/1.1 caseid:patientB"
May 31 18:48:16 10.0.0.1:37322 0/0/14/18/48 200 40 - - ---- 0/0/0/0/0 0/0 "GET /lab HTTP/1.1 caseid:patientA"
May 31 18:48:18 10.0.0.1:37324 0/0/3/2/8 200 40 - - ---- 0/0/0/0/0 0/0 "GET /consult HTTP/1.1 caseid:patientC"
May 31 18:48:19 10.0.0.1:37326 0/0/3/4/18 200 40 - - ---- 0/0/0/0/0 0/0 "GET / HTTP/1.1 caseid:patientA"
May 31 18:48:20 10.0.0.1:37328 0/0/3/2/18 200 40 - - ---- 0/0/0/0/0 0/0 "GET /lab HTTP/1.1 caseid:patientB"
```

Fig. 2. HAProxy logging

```
patientA, /consult, May 31 18:48:14, 10.0.0.1
patientB, /consult, May 31 18:48:15, 10.0.0.1
patientA, /lab,     May 31 18:48:16, 10.0.0.1
patientC, /consult, May 31 18:48:18, 10.0.0.1
patientA, /,        May 31 18:48:19, 10.0.0.1
patientB, /lab,     May 31 18:48:20, 10.0.0.1
```

Fig. 3. Extracted and transformed HAProxy log

Figure 2 shows the custom HAProxy log format that embeds header information on case ID, activity and timestamp. Similarly, the transformed HAProxy log shows event data adapted to the input of PMM – Fig. 3.

3.3   Process Mining Monitor

PMM is a Python extension of the MoBuCon framework [4] that features a Prolog engine for logical evaluation of event traces. Our implementation has two interfaces: `constraint` interface for specification of Declare [17] constraints and `eventdata` interface for feeding events into the Prolog engine; and an output log showing violations that have occurred. We have specified the constraint using an external Declare system[1] and exported the configuration file onto the Octavia host machine to used by the PMM which also reads the event data as it occurs. The constraint specification shown in Fig. 4 represents the use case scenario described in Sect. 3.1 but relates to one case ID. It specifies that all activities after `Results Positive` processing should be confined to the internal datacenter. This means all other activities before such a diagnosis confirmation can be processed in any portion of the hybrid cloud *XDC*. A violation therefore occurs when a trace involving case ID has been processed in EDC after `Result Positive`. We programme PMM to make API calls to the Octavia Worker to create a new policy involving the violated case ID. The next section describes the call to the Octavia Worker API.

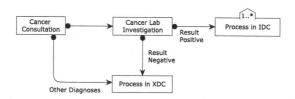

Fig. 4. Constraint specification in declare

3.4   Octavia L7 Policy Control API

We considered all post-*Results Positive* events related to a case ID as highly sensitive (HS) and all others, less sensitive (LS). For HS events all requests are

---

[1] https://www.win.tue.nl/declare/.

to be routed to the *IDC pool* of backend servers whilst all other traffic is routed to any available pool. We focused on creating L7 policies and rules only for the circumstance where HS traffic is routed to EDC. After encountering a violation involving a case ID, PatientA, say, we create a matching L7 policy to redirect further requests to IDC pool as follows: `openstack loadbalancer l7policy create --action REDIRECT_TO_POOL --redirect-pool IDC_pool --name policy01_PatientA listener_hybrid_cloud`. We then add the matching L7 rule to check whether header information contains the involved case ID as follows: `openstack loadbalancer l7rule create --compare-type CONTAINS --type HEADER --key caseid --value patientA policy01_PatientA`. With continued violations occurring for a case ID, `policy02_PatientA` will be the next L7 policy to be created having the same L7 rule as in `policy01_PatientA`. The combination of the two policies has no extra effect on load balancer since their L7 rules are the same. In our setup the listener `listener_hybrid_cloud` on the load balancer is the central port to which all application server requests are sent. It effectively distributes traffic using the ROUND_ROBIN algorithm by default and applies any attached L7 policies.

3.5   Setup and Experimentation

The experiment was ran on a four-core virtual machine with 16 GB memory having Ubuntu 16.04 LTS as operating system (OS). We installed OpenStack using a set of extensible scripts from DevStack[2] (version *train*) to create the hypervisor on top of the Ubuntu OS. The load balancing-as-a-service module, Octavia, was enabled alongside the compute, networking and virtual machine imaging modules. Openstack served as our *hybrid cloud operating system* through which the VMs and load balancer were spawned. Three VMs running the *cirros m1.tiny* flavour of the linux OS each had 512 MB RAM, 1 GB allocated disk space and one VCPU. The load balancer VM running HAProxy had 1 GB RAM, 2 GB disk space and one VCPU. In a live environment, the requests from users hit the load balancer VM and a corresponding event log is kept by the information system showing a record of activities initiated. Because L7 policy impacts the behaviour of the load balancer, API calls to the Octavia Worker for policy changes must be influenced by the process mining monitor.

4   Results and Evaluation

The constraint violations detected by the PMM component trigger L7 policy changes to the load balancer. In our experiment, we measure the correlation of violations and the L7 policies created in the load balancer. This implies comparing the timestamps of occurrence of a violation and L7 policy creation gives an indication of the responsiveness of the overall system. Our experiment recorded 27 occurrences of violations from a synthetic event log. For each of the constraint

---

[2] https://docs.openstack.org/devstack/latest/.

violations, we detected a corresponding creation of an L7 policy and associated L7 rule. The average time for the creation of the policy and rule in our environment is 12.27 s with the quickest time being 7.26 s. The longest time taken to create a L7 policy and rule is measured at 17.95 s. Figure 5 displays the co-occurrence of the constraint violations with the creation of L7 policies. There is a one-to-one correlation between the two factors validating a viable trigger through violation detection from process mining.

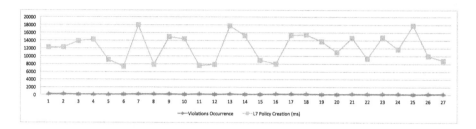

Fig. 5. Co-occurrence of Constraint Violations and L7 Policy Creation

5 Conclusion and Future Work

Decisions for adopting hybrid Cloud Computing generally consider cost, security and privacy as primary factors. The availability of monitoring tools therefore facilitates the decision-making of an organisation towards workload distribution in a hybrid cloud to achieve a high compliance to business constraints. The distribution of the workload is often done via scheduling and load balancing mechanisms. In this paper we have looked at the load balancing-as-a-service mechanism of OpenStack's Octavia project and how it can be controlled through the process mining of event logs generated from the cloud information system. Taking advantage of the filtering mechanism built into Octavia, we triggered the control of the load balancer to re-route application server requests in line with given constraints. We expressed the constraints using the Declare language which enable an event trace to be evaluation either as true (compliance) or false (violation) by the Prolog-embedded MoBuCon process mining tool. Our experiment showed a one-to-one correspondence between violations and the creation of L7 policies of the load balancer to distribute application requests to the appropriate servers. This ultimately increases the compliance of data processing to the given business constraint.

Our setup allowed for one constraint to be programmed into the Octavia project. In the real world however, a business process typically involves multiple constraints to ensure compliance to some given objectives. To apply our setup to such situations therefore invites the control of multiple constraints with the possibility increasing time lags in overall load balancer response. This situation is worth exploring in the future where this work will be expanded to allow the specification of multiple constraints via the Declare [17] tool.

References

1. Azumah, K.K., Sorensen, L.T., Tadayoni, R.: Hybrid cloud service selection strategies: a qualitative meta-analysis. In: 2018 IEEE 7th International Conference on Adaptive Science and Technology (ICAST), pp. 1–8 (2018)
2. Gandhi, R., Hu, Y.C., Zhang, M.: Yoda: a highly available layer-7 load balancer. In: Proceedings of the Eleventh European Conference on Computer Systems - EuroSys 2016, pp. 1–16 (2016)
3. Rathore, N.: Performance of hybrid load balancing algorithm in distributed web server system. Wirel. Pers. Commun. 101(3), 1233–1246 (2018)
4. Montali, M., Maggi, F.M., Chesani, F., Mello, P., van der Aalst, W.M.P.: Monitoring business constraints with the event calculus. ACM Trans. Intell. Syst. Technol. 5(1), 1–30 (2013)
5. Kowalski, R., Sergot, M.: A logic-based calculus of events. New Gener. Comput. 4(1), 67–95 (1986)
6. De Masellis, R., Maggi, F.M., Montali, M.: Monitoring data-aware business constraints with finite state automata. In: Proceedings of the 2014 International Conference on Software and System Process - ICSSP 2014, pp. 134–143 (2014)
7. Maggi, F.M., Dumas, M., García-Bañuelos, L., Montali, M.: Discovering data-aware declarative process models from event logs. In: Daniel, F., Wang, J., Weber, B. (eds.) BPM 2013. LNCS, vol. 8094, pp. 81–96. Springer, Heidelberg (2013). https://doi.org/10.1007/978-3-642-40176-3_8
8. Maggi, F.M., Montali, M., Westergaard, M., van der Aalst, W.M.P.: Monitoring business constraints with linear temporal logic: an approach based on colored automata. In: Rinderle-Ma, S., Toumani, F., Wolf, K. (eds.) BPM 2011. LNCS, vol. 6896, pp. 132–147. Springer, Heidelberg (2011). https://doi.org/10.1007/978-3-642-23059-2_13
9. Maggi, F.M., Di Francescomarino, C., Dumas, M., Ghidini, C.: Predictive monitoring of business processes. In: Jarke, M., et al. (eds.) CAiSE 2014. LNCS, vol. 8484, pp. 457–472. Springer, Cham (2014). https://doi.org/10.1007/978-3-319-07881-6_31
10. Introducing Octavia. https://docs.openstack.org/octavia/latest/reference/introduction.html. Accessed 20 May 2019
11. Sharma, S., Sahil Verma, D., Kiran Jyoti, D., Kavita, D.: Hybrid bat algorithm for balancing load in cloud computing. Int. J. Eng. Technol. 7(4.12), 26–29 (2018)
12. Rahhali, H.: A new conception of load balancing in cloud computing using Hybrid heuristic algorithm. Int. J. Comput. Sci. Issues 15(6), 1–8 (2018)
13. Aktas, M.S.: Hybrid cloud computing monitoring software architecture. Concurr. Comput. Pract. Exp. 30(21), e4694 (2018)
14. Liu, Y.C., Li, C.L.: A stratified monitoring model for hybrid cloud. Appl. Mech. Mater. 719–720, 900–906 (2015). Materials and Engineering Technology
15. Azumah, K.K., Kosta, S., Sørenson, L.T.: Scheduling in the hybrid cloud constrained by process mining. In: Proceedings of the International Conference on Cloud Computing Technology and Science, CloudCom, vol. 2018-Decem, pp. 308–313 (2018)
16. Calheiros, R.N., Ranjan, R., Beloglazov, A., De Rose, C.A.F., Buyya, R.: CloudSim: a toolkit for modeling and simulation of cloud computing environments and evaluation of resource provisioning algorithms. Softw. Pract. Exp. 41(1), 23–50 (2011)
17. Montali, M., Chesani, F., Mello, P., Maggi, F.M.: Towards data-aware constraints in declare. In: Proceedings of the 28th Annual ACM Symposium on Applied Computing - SAC 2013, p. 1391 (2013)

Distributed Processor Load Balancing Based on Multi-objective Extremal Optimization

Ivanoe De Falco[1], Eryk Laskowski[2(✉)], Richard Olejnik[3], Umberto Scafuri[1], Ernesto Tarantino[1], and Marek Tudruj[2,4]

[1] Institute of High Performance Computing and Networking, CNR, Naples, Italy
{ivanoe.defalco,umberto.scafuri,ernesto.tarantino}@icar.cnr.it
[2] Institute of Computer Science, Polish Academy of Sciences, Warsaw, Poland
{laskowsk,tudruj}@ipipan.waw.pl
[3] Université Lille—CRISTAL, CNRS, Lille, France
richard.olejnik@univ-lille1.fr
[4] Polish-Japanese Academy of Information Technology, Warsaw, Poland

Abstract. The paper proposes and discusses distributed processor load balancing algorithms which are based on nature inspired approach of multi-objective Extremal Optimization. Extremal Optimization is used for defining task migration aiming at processor load balancing in execution of graph-represented distributed programs. The analysed multi-objective algorithms are based on three or four criteria selected from the following four choices: the balance of computational loads of processors in the system, the minimal total volume of application data transfers between processors, the number of task migrations during program execution and the influence of task migrations on computational load imbalance and the communication volume. The quality of the resulting load balancing is assessed by simulation of the execution of the distributed program macro data flow graphs, including all steps of the load balancing algorithm. It is done following the event-driven model in a simulator of a message passing multiprocessor system. The experimental comparison of the multi-objective load balancing to the single objective algorithms demonstrated the superiority of the multi-objective approach.

Keywords: Distributed program modelling · Processor load balancing · Multi-objective optimization · Extremal Optimization

1 Introduction

This paper is concerned with advanced optimization methods for distributed program execution control in clusters of processors. It discusses the use of Extremal Optimization (EO) [1,2] in multi-objective algorithms for processor load balancing. EO is a nature inspired optimization method with small computational complexity and low memory requirements. Due to such features the EO approach

© Springer Nature Switzerland AG 2019
R. Montella et al. (Eds.): IDCS 2019, LNCS 11874, pp. 158–168, 2019.
https://doi.org/10.1007/978-3-030-34914-1_16

is an appealing alternative in the design of processor load balancing algorithms. In several our early papers [3,4] we have presented and discussed the use of EO in single objective algorithms for processor load balancing.

Rich with the single objective load balancing experience we have checked if a multi-objective approach could improve the load balancing efficiency by more complex optimization aims and a larger solution space [5]. As demonstrated by the experimental results such an approach has provided better quality of load balancing than the single criterion approach.

The focus of this paper is primarily on comparing the efficiency of the multi-objective EO-based load balancing with different numbers and kinds of considered criteria with different degree of orthogonality. Our multi-objective load balancing algorithms are based on iterative steps executed with dynamically changing objectives (acting as EO global fitness functions). For each objective, an adequate EO local fitness function improves solution elements.

The proposed EO-based solutions are original multi-objective heuristics which are extensions of the known distributed processor load balancing methodology. Good reviews and classifications of classic load balancing methods are presented in [6,7]. Overviews of load balancing methods based on evolutionary algorithms including EO are contained in [4,8,9]. Multi-objective approach applied to EO has already been discussed in several papers [10,11]. However, they are oriented towards general optimization problems and do not cover specific methods for distributed processor load balancing.

When we scan known load balancing methods, we notice that except of our works none include multi-objective EO as the algorithm component. So, the research presented in our papers has clear originality features and shows low computational complexity and limited use of memory space. In the proposed algorithms, a special EO-GS approach (EO with a Guided Search) is applied to provide better convergence guided by knowledge of the problem.

The paper is organized as follows. In Sect. 2 the proposed processor load balancing method is explained, including the applied general multi-objective EO approach and the EO global and local fitness functions. In Sect. 3 the experimental set-up is explained and then the experiment results are given.

2   The Proposed Processor Load Balancing General Method

The processor load balancing method proposed in this paper reduces distributed program execution time by dynamic control of program task assignment $t_k, k \in 1, \ldots, |T|$ to processors (computing nodes) $n, n \in 0, 1, \ldots, |N| - 1$, where T and N are the sets of all the tasks and the computing nodes, respectively. The load balancing method is based on a series of optimization phases in which detection and correction of processor load imbalance is done along the program graphs (Fig. 1). Processors periodically report their current loads to the load balancing control which monitors the current system load imbalance. Load balancing actions (task migrations) for a program are controlled at the level of indivisible tasks which are process threads. When load imbalance is discovered, a multi-objective EO-GS algorithm is executed to identify the necessary task migrations. After migration completion, the control returns to the load imbalance detection.

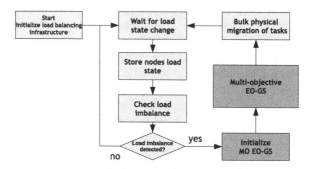

Fig. 1. The general scheme of load balancing based on multi-objective EO with guided search.

The load of the system is evaluated using a CPU availability indicator. It is the percentage of the CPU power available for application threads on the node n: $\text{time}_{\text{CPU}}(n)$. System load imbalance I is defined as a boolean variable based on the difference of the CPU availability between the currently most heavily and the least heavily loaded nodes:

$$I = (\max_{n=0,\ldots,|N|-1}(\text{time}_{\text{CPU}}(n)) - \min_{n=0,\ldots,|N|-1}(\text{time}_{\text{CPU}}(n))) \geq \alpha.$$

The load imbalance equal true requires a load correction. The value of α is determined experimentally (during experiments we set it between 25% and 75%).

An application is characterized by two programmer-supplied parameters, based on the volume of computation and communication tasks: $\text{com}(t_s, t_d)$ is a communication metrics between tasks t_s and t_d, $\text{wp}(t)$ is a load weight metrics introduced by a task t. These metrics can provide exact values, e.g. for well-defined tasks sizes and inter-task communication in regular parallel applications, or only predictions, e.g. when the execution time depends on the processed data. Even when the values are exact, there can be fluctuations of tasks execution or CPU availability, so the dynamic load balancing is required.

A task mapping solution S is represented by a vector $\mu(S) = (\mu_1, \ldots, \mu_{|T|})$ of $|T|$ integers ranging in the interval $\{0, 1, \ldots, |N| - 1\}$. $\mu_i = j$ means that the solution S maps the i–th task t_i onto the computing node j.

2.1   Multi-objective Extremal Optimization

We solve the processor load balancing problem for distributed programs with the use of a multi-objective EO-GS algorithm (MOEO-GS), shown as Algorithm 1. The proposed MOEO-GS algorithm follows the general scheme of EO [1,2] but it

Algorithm 1. Multi-objective EO with Guided Search (MOEO-GS)

1: initialize configuration S at will
2: $S_{\text{best}} \leftarrow S$
3: $D_S \leftarrow \emptyset$ {the set of non-dominated solutions (Pareto-front)}
4: **while** total number of iterations $\mathcal{N}_{\text{iter}}$ not reached **do**
5:     $c \leftarrow$ a criterion for evaluation in the current iteration
6:     evaluate $\phi_{i,c}$ for each variable s_i of the current solution S
7:     rank the variables s_i based on their local fitness $\phi_{i,c}$
8:     choose the rank k according to $k^{-\tau}$ so that the variable s_j with $j = \pi(k)$ is selected
9:     evaluate ω_s for each neighbour $S_v \in Neigh(S, s_j)$, generated by s_j change of the current solution S
10:     rank neighbours $S_v \in Neigh(S, s_j)$ based on the target function ω_s
11:     choose $S' \in Neigh(S, s_j)$ according to the exponential distribution
12:     accept $S \leftarrow S'$ unconditionally
13:     **if** S is non-dominated **then**
14:         include S in D_S, remove dominated solutions from D_S
15:     **end if**
16: **end while**
17: select S_{best} from D_S using $\Phi(S)$
18: **return** S_{best} and $\Phi(S_{\text{best}})$

---

uses a set of EO local and global fitness functions and maintains the Pareto-front of non-dominated solutions.

During an iteration, the selection and solution improvement are performed using a single objective (i.e. a single EO local and a respective single global fitness functions). It is selected in a probabilistic way from the multiple objectives specified for our load balancing problem (the local and global fitness functions used in our MOEO-GS algorithm are defined in the Subsect. 2.2).

The Pareto front is analyzed at the end of the algorithm to deliver the S_{best} solution. To approximate the optimal solution we look for the so-called compromise solution, i.e. that as close as possible to the ideal point. The compromise solution S_{best} is selected from D_S using a given distance measure.

2.2 Global and Local Fitness Functions

We examined MOEO-GS algorithms based on the selective use of up to four objective functions oriented on supporting the load balancing problem: the computational load imbalance in execution of application tasks on processors, the volume of communication between tasks placed on different computing nodes, the task migration number and the influence of migrations on the processor load imbalance expressed as the divergence from a more balanced execution. Our algorithms look for the solutions with lower values of the global fitness (or components with lower values of the local fitness, respectively).

The definitions of fitness functions use two auxiliary formulas:

$$\text{nwp}(S, n) = \sum\nolimits_{t \in T: \mu_t = n} \text{wp}(t)$$

where $\mathrm{nwp}(S, n)$ is the sum of computational loads of program tasks allocated to processor n in the solution S, and

$$W_T = \sum_{t \in T} \mathrm{wp}(t) / \sum_{n=0,\ldots,|N|-1} \mathrm{power}_{\mathrm{CPU}}(n)$$

where $\mathrm{power}_{\mathrm{CPU}}(n)$ is the sum of potential computing powers of all active cores on the node n and W_T is the average computational weight of program tasks attributed to one unit of computational power of processors.

A load imbalance normalization constant is equal to maximal numerical value of the imbalance (i.e. when all tasks are assigned to the slowest processor):

$$D_{\mathrm{norm}} = (|N| - 2) * W_T + \sum_{t \in T} \mathrm{wp}(t) / \min_{n=0,\ldots,|N|-1} \mathrm{power}_{\mathrm{CPU}}(n).$$

The first objective concerns the reduction of the computational load imbalance among executive processors in the system defined by the current MOEO-GS solution S. The global fitness functions $\Phi(S)$ for computational load imbalance represents the numerical load imbalance metrics in the solution S:

$$\Phi_U^1(S) = \begin{cases} 1 & \text{when at least one free node exists} \\ \mathrm{deviation}(S)/D_{\mathrm{norm}} & \text{otherwise} \end{cases}$$

where: $\mathrm{deviation}(S) = \sum_{n=0,\ldots,|N|-1} |\mathrm{nwp}(S, n) / \mathrm{power}_{\mathrm{CPU}}(n) - W_T|$.

The local fitness function for MOEO-GS algorithm for the objective 1 is designed as follows:

$$\phi_U(t) = \gamma * \mathrm{load}(\mu_t) + (1 - \gamma) * (1 - \mathrm{ldev}(t))$$

where the function $\mathrm{load}(n)$ indicates how much the load of node n, which executes t, exceeds the average load of all nodes. It is normalized versus the heaviest load among all the nodes. The function $\mathrm{ldev}(t)$ is defined as the difference between the load metrics of the task t and the average task load on the node μ_t, normalized versus the highest such value for all tasks on the node [4].

The second objective for the MOEO-GS algorithm is the global EO-GS fitness function $\Phi(S)$ for external communication. The function $\Phi_C^1(S) \in [0, 1]$ is a quotient of the sum of external communication volume and the total communication volume in a program:

$$\Phi_C^1(S) = \sum_{s,d \in T : \mu_s \neq \mu_d} \mathrm{com}(s, d) / \sum_{s,d \in T} \mathrm{com}(s, d).$$

The local fitness function for objective 2 is designed as follows:

$$\phi_C(t) = 1 - \mathrm{attr}(t)$$

where the attraction of the task t to its executive computing node $\mathrm{attr}(t)$ is defined as the amount of communication between task t and other tasks on the same node, normalized versus the maximal attraction inside the node [4].

The third objective is concerned with task migrations induced by the current EO-GS solution S. The global fitness function for migration $\Phi_M(S) \in [0, 1]$ is defined as a quotient of migrated tasks, comparing the initial solution:

$$\Phi_M(S) = |\{t \in T : \mu_t^S \neq \mu_t^{S*}\}| / |T|$$

where: μ_t^S is the current node of the task t in the solution S, and μ_t^{S*} is the node of the task t in the initial solution at the start of the algorithm.

The local fitness function $\phi_M(t)$ for migration objective is defined as:

$$\phi_M(t) = \begin{cases} 1 \text{ when the task } t \text{ has migrated} \\ 0 \text{ otherwise.} \end{cases}$$

The $\phi_M(t)$ local fitness function forces the migration of already migrated tasks, thus increasing the probability that finally more tasks will occupy their initial computing nodes.

The fourth objective $\Phi_U^2(S)$ is related to the task migration quality:

$$\Phi_U^2(S) = (\text{totalimpr}(S) + 1)/2$$

where: $\text{totalimpr}(S) = \sum_{n=0,\ldots,|N|-1} \text{improvement}(n)/D_{\text{norm}}$.

We use the function improvement(n) which shows how much the current placement of tasks on a node n improves (i.e. decreases) the total computational load imbalance of the application, comparing the initial task placement:

$$\text{improvement}(n) = |\frac{\text{nwp}(S,n)}{\text{power}_{\text{CPU}}(n)} - W_T| - |\frac{\text{nwp}(S^*,n)}{\text{power}_{\text{CPU}}(n)} - W_T|$$

where S is the currently considered solution and S^* is the initial task placement at the start of the algorithm. The function $\text{totalimpr}(S) \in [-1,1]$ indicates whether there is the improvement (when $\text{totalimpr}(S) < 0$) or deterioration (when > 0) in the total computational load balance in the system comparing the initial placement of tasks of the application. It can be considered as an alternative to $\Phi_U^1(S)$.

Similarly to $\Phi_U^2(S)$, we have designed the fifth optional objective function which relates external communication to the task migration quality. The global function $\Phi_C^2(S)$ can be considered as an alternative to $\Phi_C^1(S)$:

$$\Phi_C^2(S) = (\text{commimpr}(S) + 1)/2$$

where: $\text{commimpr}(S) = \Phi_C^1(S) - \Phi_C^1(S^*)$, S is the currently considered solution and S^* is the initial task placement at the start of the algorithm. The function $\text{commimpr}(S) \in [-1,1]$ indicates whether there is the improvement (when $\text{commimpr}(S) < 0$) or deterioration (when > 0) in the total volume of external communication comparing the initial placement of tasks of the application.

$\Phi_U^2(S)$ and $\Phi_C^2(S)$ variants use the local fitness functions $\phi_U(t)$, $\phi_C(t)$, respectively. To summarize, the following MOEO-GS variants were designed:

MOEO-GS variant name	global fitness functions used
MO-1-GS	$\Phi_U^1(S), \Phi_C^1(S), \Phi_M(S)$
MO-2-GS	$\Phi_U^1(S), \Phi_C^1(S), \Phi_U^2(S)$
MO-3-GS	$\Phi_U^2(S), \Phi_C^1(S), \Phi_M(S)$
MO-4-GS	$\Phi_U^1(S), \Phi_C^1(S), \Phi_U^2(S), \Phi_M(S)$
MO-5-GS	$\Phi_U^2(S), \Phi_C^2(S), \Phi_M(S)$

3   Experimental Assessment of Load Balancing Algorithms

The experiments were done using a simulator built using the adapted DEVS discrete event simulation system (Discrete Event System specification) [12]. The goal of the experiments was to compare the presented variants of multi-criteria MOEO–GS to single criterion EO and EO–GS. Distributed programs were specified as multi-layer macro data flow graphs. The programs were simulatively executed on clusters of processors interconnected by a message passing network.

The simulated model of execution corresponds to parallelization based on the message passing MPI library. The exemplary programs were modelled as Temporal Flow Graphs (TFG), [3], in which a program consists of a set of modules called phases, composed of parallel tasks, Fig. 2. Tasks of the same phase can communicate. At the boundaries between phases there is also a global exchange of data. The experiments were performed using a cluster of Intel i7-based 8–core workstations, under control of the Linux operating system. The DEVS-based simulator and the load balancing algorithms including the EO approach were written in Java, with thread-based parallelization for multi-core machines.

During experiments we used a set of 11 synthetic exemplary programs, which were randomly generated. The number of tasks in an application varied from 64 to 1000. The communication to computation ratio C/E (a quotient of the total communication time to the total execution time) for applications was in the range $[0.05, 0.20]$.

As reference, two single objective load balancing algorithms based on sequential EO were used. The first one, denoted as SO-C, aims in balancing exclusively the computational loads of processor nodes. It is based on a classical sequential EO without guided search. The second one, denoted as SO-WS-GS, is based on a single objective EO with the guided search and is using a global fitness function which is a weighted sum of the three aforementioned criteria (see Subsect. 2.2) according to the equation:

$$\Phi_{\mathrm{WS}}(S) = \Phi_C^1(S)\Delta_1 + \Phi_M(S)\Delta_2 + \Phi_U^1(S)[1 - (\Delta_1 + \Delta_2)]$$

where Δ_1 and Δ_2 are weights from the range $(0,1)$. A comparison of our reference algorithms SO-C, SO-WS-GS to other methods of load balancing like genetic algorithm and deterministic local-search algorithm has been presented in [3].

The parameters used in MOEO-GS, the load balancing control and the single objective SO-WS-GS are similar as these used in experiments presented in [3]. We applied such values of these parameters for which balanced performance between application speedup and migration count was obtained: $\alpha = 0.5$, $\tau = 1.5$, $\lambda = 0.14$, $\beta = 0.5$, $\Delta_1 = 0.13$, $\Delta_2 = 0.17$, $\gamma = 0.75$. We assumed the number of iterations for EO and MOEO $\mathcal{N}_{\mathrm{iter}} = 500$.

Load-balanced execution was studied in systems containing from 2 to 32 homogeneous processors. For experimental purposes we have assumed the cost of migration of a single task to be equal to some percentage of the average

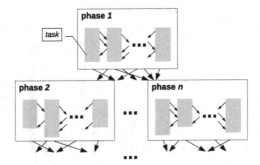

Fig. 2. The general structure of exemplary applications in TFG.

task computational weight: 0%, 20% or 40% of the task weight. The results are averages of 40 runs (i.e. 10 runs, each with 4 different methods of initial task placements: random, round-robin, METIS graph partitioning, packed) [4].

The comparison of the application parallel speedup for both single- and multi-objective EO-based algorithms as a function of the number of executive processors is shown in Fig. 3. The results are averaged over all tested applications and all assumed variants of migration cost. For these applications, the speedup obtained by all multi-objective algorithms except MO-2-GS, is greater than that obtained with single-objective EO reference variants (SO-WS-GS, SO-C).

The migration number statistics are shown in Fig. 4. It gives the average total number of task migrations in application execution with all load balancing algorithms and all migration costs. The MO-3-GS and MO-5-GS variants with top parallel speedup have given the smallest number of task migrations.

Figures 3 and 4 have shown the superiority of multi-objective algorithms over the single-objective ones, especially for a large number of computing nodes (16, 32) on which the application was executed. Here, the multi-objective versions

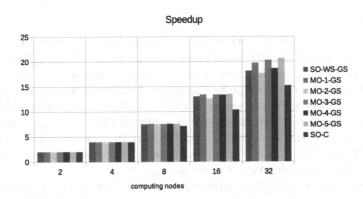

Fig. 3. Application parallel speedup for different numbers of computing nodes for all tested algorithms.

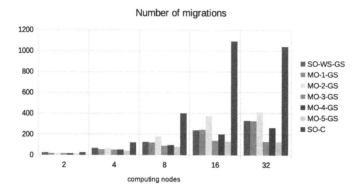

Fig. 4. The number of task migrations per single application execution on different numbers of computing nodes with different load balancing algorithms.

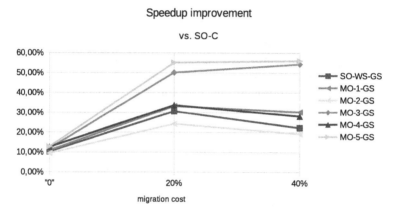

Fig. 5. Relative application speedup improvement for different load balancing algorithms versus SO-C for execution on 32 computing nodes with different migration costs.

MO-1-GS ... MO-5-GS are better than single objective versions SO-C and SO-WS-GS. An exception is MO-2-GS, which does not employ $\Phi_M(S)$ global fitness function, hence it gives a big number of migrations during its run-time.

To better understand the properties of our MOEO-GS algorithms, we have examined the speed-up improvement as a function of migration costs (see Fig. 5). Strong superiority of the multi-objective approach (MO-3-GS and MO-5-GS) over the single objective approach (SO-WS-GS) is clear for larger migration costs (20% and 40% of task computational weight). It confirms that there is a direct inverse relationship in this measure.

The experimental results confirm advantages of the proposed load balancing multi-objective algorithms. For a realistic case with not null migration cost, all multi-objective algorithm variants are much better than the single-objective SO-C algorithm. The conclusions are that out of the proposed MOEO-GS variants,

MO-5-GS is the best suited for systems with the most demanding load balancing requirements (high migrations costs, big number of computing nodes), while MO-3-GS works very well for low or medium migrations costs and the medium number of computing nodes. Our results confirm the advantages of MOEO-GS algorithms which use migration number related global objective functions (i.e. $\Phi_U^2(S), \Phi_C^2(S)$ in MO-3-GS, MO-4-GS, MO-5-GS respectively).

4   Conclusions

Multi-objective approach applied to EO used in processor load balancing in execution of distributed programs has been studied. In the multi-objective EO approach, up to four objectives relevant in distributed processor load balancing are simultaneously controlled: computational load balance, volume of external communication, the number of migrations and the influence of task migrations on processor load balancing. Different global fitness function variants for computational load balancing were designed and verified. The proposed algorithms were assessed by simulation experiments on EO-controlled execution of macro data flow graphs of programs run in distributed systems. The experiments have shown that the multi-objective EO approach included into load balancing algorithms has visibly improved the quality of program execution.

References

1. Boettcher, S., Percus, A.G.: Extremal optimization: methods derived from co-evolution. In: Proceedings of the Genetic and Evolutionary Computation Conference (GECCO 1999), pp. 825–832. Morgan Kaufmann, San Francisco (1999)
2. Lu, Y.Z., Chen, Y.W., Chen, M.R., Chen, P., Zeng, G.Q.: Extremal Optimization: Fundamentals, Algorithms, and Applications, p. 334. CRC Press, Boca Raton (2016)
3. De Falco, I., Laskowski, E., Olejnik, R., Scafuri, U., Tarantino, E., Tudruj, M.: Improving extremal optimization in load balancing by local search. In: Esparcia-Alcázar, A.I., Mora, A.M. (eds.) EvoApplications 2014. LNCS, vol. 8602, pp. 51–62. Springer, Heidelberg (2014). https://doi.org/10.1007/978-3-662-45523-4_5
4. De Falco, I., Laskowski, E., Olejnik, R., Scafuri, U., Tarantino, E., Tudruj, M.: Extremal optimization applied to load balancing in execution of distributed programs. Appl. Soft Comput. **30**, 501–513 (2015)
5. De Falco, I., Scafuri, U., Laskowski, E., Tarantino, E., Olejnik, R., Tudruj, M.: Effective processor load balancing using multi-objective parallel extremal optimization. In: GECCO 2018, Companion Material Proceedings, pp. 1292–1299. ACM (2018)
6. Xu, C., Lau, F.C.M.: Load Balancing in Parallel Computers: Theory and Practice. Kluwer Academic Publishers, Dordrecht (1997)
7. Khan, R.Z., Ali, J.: Classification of task partitioning and load balancing strategies in distributed parallel computing systems. Int. J. Comput. Appl. **60**(17), 48–53 (2012)
8. Mishra, M., Agarwal, S., Mishra, P., Singh, S.: Comparative analysis of various evolutionary techniques of load balancing: a review. Int. J. Comput. Appl. **63**(15), 8–13 (2013)

9. Tanvi, Kaur, K.: A study on extremal optimization based load balancing techniques. Indian J. Comput. Sci. Eng. **8**(2), 95–101 (2017)
10. Ahmed, E., Elettreby, M.F.: On multi-objective evolution model. Int. J. Mod. Phys. C **15**(9), 1189–1195 (2004)
11. Gómez-Meneses, P., Randall, M., Lewis, A.: A hybrid multi-objective extremal optimisation approach for multi-objective combinatorial optimisation problems. Bond University, Griffith University, Australia (2010)
12. Zeigler, B.: Hierarchical, modular discrete-event modelling in an object-oriented environment. Simulation **49**(5), 219–230 (1987)

Argumentation-Based Coordination in IoT: A Speaking Objects Proof-of-Concept

Stefano Mariani[1]([⊠]) [iD], Andrea Bicego[2] [iD], Marco Lippi[1] [iD], Marco Mamei[1] [iD], and Franco Zambonelli[1] [iD]

[1] DISMI – Università di Modena e Reggio Emilia, Reggio Emilia, Italy
{stefano.mariani,marco.lippi,marco.mamei,franco.zambonelli}@unimore.it
[2] Apex Srl, Modena, Italy
abicego@apex.it

Abstract. Coordination of Cyberphysical Systems is an increasingly relevant concern for distributed systems engineering, mostly due to the rise of the Internet of Things vision in many application domains. Against this background, Speaking Objects has been proposed as a vision of future smart objects coordinating their collective perception and action through argumentation. Along this line, in this paper we describe a Proof-of-Concept implementation of the Speaking Objects vision in a smart home deployment.

Keywords: Speaking Objects · Internet of Things · Argumentation-based Coordination

1 Introduction

The *Internet of Things* (IoT) vision is rapidly becoming reality as the possibility of enriching physical objects and places with sensing, actuating, and computing capabilities improves [4], such that everything in our physical and social worlds could participate to coordinated actions to sense and control the world itself [8]—as peer of a large-scale situated network.

Common IoT systems design considers devices as simple providers of services: either sensing services producing *raw data*, or actuating services executing *commands* [4]. Likewise, most designs adopt a *centralised*, cloud-based perspective: raw sensor data is collected at a control point, there analysed to inform decision making algorithms, and finally commands for the actuators are generated and sent. However, recent technological evolution [1,9,19] enables novel scenarios:

- IoT devices are becoming smarter by embedding Artificial Intelligence (AI) algorithms [9]. Hence, on the one hand smart sensors become capable of *understanding* (thus, reporting) situations instead of raw data, while, on the other hand, smart actuators become increasingly *autonomous* and *goal-oriented* [1]. According to [16], such smart objects become, respectively, "speaking objects" and "hearing objects".

© Springer Nature Switzerland AG 2019

R. Montella et al. (Eds.): IDCS 2019, LNCS 11874, pp. 169–180, 2019.
https://doi.org/10.1007/978-3-030-34914-1_17

– IoT systems deployment is increasingly targeting large-scale scenarios where distributed sensing and control approaches are gaining momentum as a complement to cloud-based solutions [19]. Speaking and hearing objects at the Edge of the network will thus have to interact and coordinate with each other in a *distributed* way, to ensure prompt response to *local* situations [21].

As a consequence to such a paradigm shift, *coordination* in IoT is likely to become associated with the capability of *argumenting* about the current and future "state of the affairs" [9], so as to decide how to collectively act towards the system goals. The dimension of *interaction* is the focal point of the Speaking Objects vision, as opposed to, for instance, the smart objects model fostered in [14] and implemented in [10], where the inner structure and functional capabilities of IoT devices are mostly concerned. Indeed, these two ways of interpreting future smart devices are *complementary* rather than in competition, especially if agent-orientation is taken into consideration: the latter mostly deals with the computational dimension of agency, while the former with the interaction dimension. In this context, this paper provides the following contributions:

– we describe a Proof-of-Concept (PoC) realisation of the Speaking Objects vision in a smart home setting
– we discuss PoC feasibility in terms of availability of required hardware and software in the mass market, cost, ease of configuration, deployment
– we discuss how the system architecture outlined in [16] as well as the conversational coordination dialogues described in [17] can be put in practice on the selected hardware and software stack
– we speculate on the benefits the Speaking Objects vision brings along in the target as well as similar scenarios

Accordingly, the remainder of paper is organised as follows: Sect. 2 summarises the core elements of Speaking Objects vision, Sect. 3 describes the smart home application scenario we tailor our Speaking Objects PoC to, Sect. 4 describes the actual implementation and deployment of the PoC in the targeted scenario, Sect. 5 briefly accounts for comparable approaches, and Sect. 6 provides for final remarks and next steps.

2   Speaking Objects

The concept of *smart object* is mostly associated to the opportunity of attaching computational devices to physical objects and places to turn them into remotely controllable *sensors* and *actuators*. However, steady progress in different research areas allows to go beyond these sensing and actuating capabilities.

For instance, advancements in machine learning techniques along with the constant grow of the computational power that can be embedded in everyday sensors is making it possible to perform some degree of data analysis *on-board* Edge devices [5]. To some extent such objects are already becoming "speaking", by evolving from sources of raw data streams to producers of information. As an example, a baby monitor may inform a smart cradle that the baby is trying to stand up (*situation*), rather than simply emitting an alarm sound (*raw data*) when the pressure sensor measures some threshold-breaking value—thus, e.g., the cradle's barriers could raise themselves to prevent the baby from felling off.

Likewise, current actuating appliances are mostly interpreting *commands* and executing them, with no reasoning nor decision making. Hearing objects move from this command-based mode of operation to a *goal-oriented* one: a desirable *state of the affairs* to be achieved is expressed, then the devices autonomously evaluate what to do. For instance one can simply say "I want to sleep" and have the lighting system devise out what to do to satisfy such goal.

A crucial aspect of this setting is that speaking and hearing objects likely need to interact with each other to recognise complex situations or carry out joint deliberation and collective action. Hence, a core element and focal point of the Speaking Objects vision is the requirement of governing *interactions*; in other words, carry out proper *coordination* amongst devices. In fact:

- speaking objects may be in need to exchange information to produce an understanding of the evolving situations
- speaking objects may be consulted by hearing objects about what is happening so as to plan actions
- hearing objects may debate about agreement on a common course of actions whenever a desired state of the affairs requires the cooperation of multiple devices to be achieved

Accordingly, coordination between speaking and hearing objects can be naturally interpreted as a distributed multi-party *conversation*, or *dialogue* [3], where speaking and hearing objects exchange *assertions* about the state of the affairs which can be contradicted or supported by others, in a process akin to *argumentation* [17]. In [20] different dialogue types are described, which are taken as reference in [17] to categorise the kind of conversational coordination sessions that hearing and speaking objects may experience.

Next section depicts the target application scenario we applied our PoC to, by describing the requirements concerning (*i*) the information needed to carry out argumentation, (*ii*) the goal-oriented behaviour of actuators, and (*iii*) the assertion capabilities of sensors. Then, Sect. 4 describes the PoC.

3   Application Scenario

We aim to deal with smart home environments in which different smart functionalities can be provided to inhabitants through a set of hearing and speaking objects scattered throughout the rooms; for instance:

- *Detect home invasion attempts.* Through information seeking, inquiry, persuasion, and deliberation dialogues [20] the hearing and speaking objects cooperate to (*i*) assess whether an home invasion is in place or not, and (*ii*) act accordingly in case it is.

– *Optimise power consumption.* Again through different kinds of conversational coordination instances, the smart devices distributed in the home environment collaborate to *(i)* detect opportunities for power saving, and *(ii)* decide what to do to reduce power consumption.

The details of how such smart capabilities are delivered are covered in next section. Here instead we want to focus on the requirements these functions pose to IoT system engineers. As far as the core elements of the Speaking Objects vision are concerned, they articulate along three dimensions.

Contextual vs. Commonsense Knowledge. There will always be two intrinsically different kinds of information to be managed by smart devices, regardless of the specific application domain the IoT system at hand is deployed to: contextual, and commonsense. The former is the most apparent one, as it includes the data streams produced by sensors while monitoring the environment: it is all the information that regards a specific moment in *time*, portion of *space*, and *facet* of the environment under monitoring (e.g., the temperature in a room at any given moment). The latter is more hideous in nature as it tracks all the knowledge humans usually take for granted as the *basic knowledge*, independent of time and space[1], necessary to correctly interpret other information. For instance, a human being can easily distinguish between an adult and a kid by looking at their height (the contextual knowledge) and considering that kids are usually shorter than adults (commonsense).

Handling both kinds of information poses its own requirements to the system: for instance, as contextual knowledge regards specific facets of the environment at specific time points it will inevitably be generated by Edge devices, at a high pace, possibly also therein stored until transmission to Fog/Cloud nodes for processing, and possibly also consumed by the same devices to frequently argue about the current perceived situation. Commonsense knowledge is instead at the other end of the spectrum, as it is quasi-static information, usually unbound to specific facets of the situation to understand, and also usually implying some heavy processing to make sense of related batches of contextual knowledge— hence unsuitable to be carried out at the Edge.

Summing up, the core requirement for our Speaking Objects PoC that we extract from the above discussion is that we would need Edge devices able to generate, process, and consume contextual knowledge, so as to individually produce simple perceptions and collectively build more complex assertions, and Fog/Cloud computational nodes able to monitor the different perceptions and make sense of the global situation. It is worth noting that commonsense knowledge may actually be exploited to also guide the argumentation process, by deciding for instance what is admissible or not (e.g. an excessively high temperature may indicate failure of a sensor), and which argument is more relevant than another (e.g. a perception agreed upon by many sensors may be deemed as being more relevant than one backed up by a single device).

---

[1] Or, more precisely, commonsense knowledge is affected by time and space on a greater time scale with respect to contextual knowledge.

Without anticipating too much, in Sect. 4 we will describe how Arduino boards have been used as the arbiters of argumentation debates, hence as the owners of the commonsense knowledge needed to make sense of other devices perceptions and decide the winning arguments.

From Perceptions to Assertions. As the Speaking Objects vision fosters increasingly powerful devices able to advance beyond mere raw data generation, towards more complex situation recognition, it raises the requirement for Edge devices to be able to process data locally and transform such data in usable information. Defining precisely what such "usable information" is clearly depends on the application at hand and on the specific goals pursued as well as functionality delivered, hence will be detailed in Sect. 4. Also how such information is generated, that is, which data processing algorithms are executed locally by devices heavily depends on the above aspects. Nevertheless, some anticipations may help clarify.

The sensors we adopted for our PoC are very cheap, off-the-shelf devices with wide availability, hence they are not able to do any processing on-board. The reason for this choice is that we want to speculate on immediate feasibility and widespread adoption of the Speaking Objects approach, hence we cannot assume devices not already in the mass market and cheap enough to be deployed at scale. Nevertheless, to preserve the core Speaking Objects idea of doing processing and argumentation at the Edge, that is in a fully distributed setting, we rely on ESP modules for local processing and on Arduino boards for arbitration.

Goal-Orientation. Likewise for the shift from perceptions to assertions, Speaking Objects fosters goal-oriented devices (mostly, actuator devices) replacing command-based ones: devices should become able to figure out the actions needed to achieve a goal autonomously, rather than being explicitly instructed about what to do. This is possibly the most difficult challenge to deal with as it poses lots of requirements on devices, especially on the software stack there hosted—if a faithful implementation of goal-orientation is sought for. For instance, from a software engineering perspective, goal-orientation naturally calls for agent-based techniques, whose deployment to heavily resource-constrained devices (such as embedded sensors) is yet to be assessed.

Nevertheless, the requirements for such a goal-orientation are clear: devices must be able to represent goals, actions, pre-conditions and post-conditions for both, and perform reasoning to understand, first of all, whether they may play a role with respect to a specific goal, and then, what should they do to achieve it. It is worth noting that this immediately calls for coordination amongst devices, as they will rarely be able to achieve goals individually in real-world scenarios.

As for the previous dimension, the cheap and off-the-shelf nature of the devices we choose for implementing our PoC hinders deployment of a full-fledged agent-based solution in our smart home scenario; nevertheless, ESP modules and Arduino boards deployed at the Edge have been used to implement a very primitive agent notion recognising goals expressions and executing simple "Event

Condition Action" rules [6] to choose the course of actions to be carried out towards each specific goal.

Next section describes the PoC, hence how these requirements have been dealt with in the specific case of our targeted smart home scenario, with the available hardware.

4 Realisation

Based on the Speaking Objects vision summarised in Sect. 2 and the requirements described in Sect. 3, we implemented the Proof-of-Concept IoT system described in the following, which focusses the two functionalities aforementioned: detection of home invasion attempts and optimisation of power consumption. The main contribution we want to deliver here is about how the architecture envisioned in [16] can be actually instantiated on a distributed network of off-the-shelf devices, and how the argumentation-based coordination dialogues sketched in [17] can be implemented. Whereas the latter clearly depends on the specific functionality delivered, hence is described in dedicated sections for home invasion and energy consumption, instantiation of the architecture can be discussed in general and is depicted in Fig. 1.

The bottom layer is populated by sensor and actuator devices scattered throughout the smart home: photoresistors to check illumination levels in each room, sound sensors around windows and doors to perceive suspicious noise levels, accelerometers and avoid sensors, too, to detect windows and doors move-

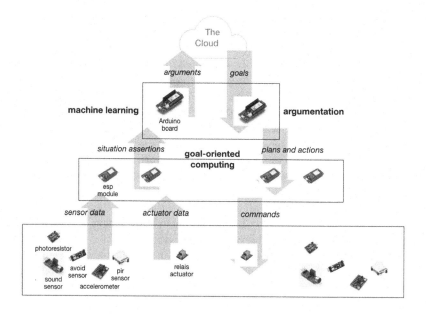

Fig. 1. System architecture of the PoC.

ment, pir sensors in each room to detect the presence of people, and relais actuators to activate electric appliances at will (such as the A/C, electric curtains, etc.). As said, they are extremely cheap and off-the-shelf devices with widespread availability as detailed in Table 1, hence they cannot do computations on their own. Thus we deployed a middle layer of ESP modules, which enable to connect any device to Wi-Fi and do simple computations as they can be programmed similarly to Arduino boards and have a small memory and CPU. Here is were sensor information can be fused together and plans of actions are translated to specific commands for each actuator (the relais). Finally, the top layer is where Arduino boards are networked to carry out most of the rasoning and coordination-related tasks, such as embedding machine learning models to detect complex situations and arbiter argumentation dialogues.

Table 1. Devices exploited for the PoC implementation.

Device	Price	Availability	Store
Arduino MKR 1000 Wi-Fi	30,99	Wide	Official Arduino store
Esp 8266	1,55	Wide	Amazon
Ir sensor (avoid)	3,00	Wide	Amazon
Sound sensor	1,00	Wide	Amazon
MPU6050 (accelerometer)	4,00	Wide	Amazon
Pir sensor	2,90	Wide	Amazon
Relay	3,05	Wide	Amazon

A lesson learnt from this implementation and deployment experience we want to emphasise is that devices such as the Esp modules are crucial as enablers of fully distributed scenarios, as they allow to *(i)* easily connect each embedded sensor to the local network, hence let them communicate with any other device (in our case, the Arduino boards), *(ii)* carry out simple computations powerful enough to undertake basic data processing tasks and rule-based reasoning.

Along this line, although a generally applicable classification of resource-constrained devices w.r.t. their ability to serve as arbitrators for dialogues in Speaking Objects, or more generally as viable executors of machine learning models, is beyond the scope of the paper, some related research work started proposing benchmarks trying to assess where the line between the Edge and the Cloud is [18]. As far we know and experienced, training at the Edge is still problematic, but model application is viable as long as ad-hoc models are exploited [13,15]: in this case, the few MHz of Arduino or ESP modules (80–84) and the few KiB of SRAM available therein (32–96) may suffice.

The following sections describe how the system architecture just commented has been exploited to carry out argumentation-based coordination in IoT.

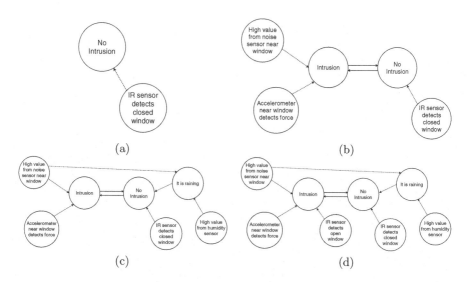

Fig. 2. Temporal evolution of the argumentation graph in the intrusion detection scenario. Nodes and edges are added to the graph as soon as new dialogues occur between the speaking and hearing objects, to reach a final agreement on the state of the affairs.

4.1   Scenario 1: Home Invasion Detection

Figure 2 shows the temporal evolution of the argumentation graph in the intrusion detection scenario. The initial condition (Fig. 2a) is a normal situation at night-time, where the IR window sensor detects that the window is closed. This fact can be modeled with a logic predicate, such as: closed(BedroomWindow).

After a while, a change in the situation occurs as long as the noise sensor detects a value that exceeds some threshold, set a-priori by a *ground common-sense* shared among the devices—as depicted in Table 2. The noise sensor informs the other devices of this fact, with a new logic fact: noise(BedroomWindow). The accelerometer next to the window also detects some force exceeding a fixed threshold (again, fixed in the commonsense) and replies to the other devices: force(BedroomWindow). This is the scenario depicted in Fig. 2b.

Now, the devices ask the humidity sensor for further information, just to investigate whether the noise and force at the window could be due to an ongoing thunderstorm. The answer is positive, thus a new logic fact is shared among

Table 2. Commonsense knowledge formalization in the intrusion detection scenario.

Commonsense knowledge	Logic formalization
High humidity is likely to indicate rain	humidity(X) $\Rightarrow$ rain
In case of rain, there might be some noise	rain $\Rightarrow$ noise(X)
If noise value > ρ, suspicious noise detected	noise(X) > ρ $\Rightarrow$ warning(X)

the devices: `humidity(BedroomWindow)`. From the commonsense knowledge, the devices can infer that such information indicates that it is likely to be raining. Such event could be confirmed also by the information reported by the noise sensor, once again thanks to the commonsense knowledge base. The argument `intrusion(BedroomWindow)` is now currently supported by two premises, namely `noise(BedroomWindow)` and `force(BedroomWindow)`, where the opposing argument `no_intrusion(BedroomWindow)` is supported by `rain`, which in turn is supported by `noise(BedroomWindow)` and `humidity(BedroomWindow)`. This is the scenario of Fig. 2c, where the argument of intrusion detection is likely to be defeated.

Clearly, a major change would come in case, for example, the IR sensor detects an opening of the window: `open(BedroomWindow)`. In this case, in Fig. 2d, the argument of intrusion detection would be likely to win, and an alarm would be triggered.

4.2   Scenario 2: Power Consumption Optimisation

In a second scenario, we exploit speaking and hearing objects to perform smart lighting of an environment. In this case, we avoid the description of the temporal evolution of the argumentation process, and we just refer to the final argumentation graph in Fig. 3, which is obtained after that several dialogues between the devices have come in succession.

In this scenario, the argument that lights should be turned on (or kept turned on) is supported by two facts: *(i)* that a person was observed entering the room, and *(ii)* that we are in a time of the day where there is no sufficient natural light. Conversely, the argument of turning lights off would be supported by the fact that the person is either fallen asleep, or watching TV. These two conditions are known to the smart devices thanks to the learning of user preferences: for example, the devices learnt that the person typically watches TV after dinner, and she likes to do that with the lights turned off.

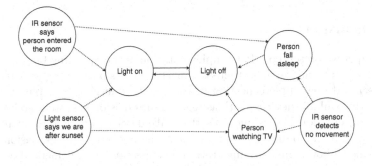

Fig. 3. Argumentation graph describing the scenario of smart lighting.

5   Related Works

Many research efforts aim at dealing with the challenges of IoT systems and applications, in particular as regards building and especially *interconnecting* devices under the smart objects perspective. We here position our PoC with respect to similar efforts. Nevertheless, it is worth pointing out that most of the literature on the subject reveals a limited understanding of the word "coordination", which is often times restricted to device and service discovery, service composition, mere communication, or reactiveness to sensors' perceptions—hence neglecting more complex coordination needs such as negotiation and joint planning.

The work in [7] is one of the few explicitly interested in coordination aspects: it relies on "Event-Condition-Action" rules triggering smart devices functionalities to coordinate their collective operation. Nevertheless, decentralisation appears limited as the rule engine seems centralised. Furthermore, the proposed architecture seems unsuitable for resource constrained devices. Also the agent-oriented middleware proposed in [11] appears to require computational resources beyond Edge devices capabilities, although agent-orientation makes it closer to our interpretation of coordination in IoT—which in the paper is limited to event notification through publish/subscribe brokers.

In [2] instead, whereas coordination is still based on publish/subscribe to support a workflow-like process, mobile devices are explicitly accounted for, hence some degree of limitation in computational resources is considered, nevertheless the coordination challenges mentioned in the paper mostly deal with connectivity issues, not with application level goals. Along this line, the component-based middleware described in [12] specifically targets resource-constrained devices but limits its focus on coordination as connection of input/output "plugs" to trigger devices functionalities.

As anticipated, most of the mentioned approaches and many other in the literature focus on the management and deployment of the smart devices, rather than on the way they can jointly achieve application goals, hence they do not naturally compare to our approach stemming from the Speaking Objects vision.

6   Conclusion

In this paper we presented a PoC implementation of the Speaking Objects vision depicted in [16] and further discussed in [17] in a smart home scenario. We have discussed how implementation of the vision is actually feasible according to currently available devices, both as regards the envisioned system architecture and the conversational coordination setting. We described the requirements that the IoT system has to fullfill so as to support the Speaking Objects vision. Also, we have shown how simple argumentation schemes can be implemented on top of heavily resource-constrained devices. In summary, the Speaking Objects vision can become reality with currently available technology, hence, our ongoing work is devoted to analyse performance of the PoC and scale-up to more complex and large-scale scenarios.

References

1. Agrawal, H., Leigh, S.W., Maes, P.: L'evolved: autonomous and ubiquitous utilities as smart agents. In: ACM International Joint Conference on Pervasive and Ubiquitous Computing, pp. 487–491. ACM, New York (2015)
2. Alcarria, R., Robles, T., Morales, A., Cedeño, E.: Resolving coordination challenges in distributed mobile service executions. Int. J. Web Grid Serv. 10(2/3), 168–191 (2014). https://doi.org/10.1504/IJWGS.2014.060251
3. Amgoud, L., Parsons, S.: Agent dialogues with conflicting preferences. In: Meyer, J.-J.C., Tambe, M. (eds.) ATAL 2001. LNCS (LNAI), vol. 2333, pp. 190–205. Springer, Heidelberg (2002). https://doi.org/10.1007/3-540-45448-9_14
4. Atzori, L., Iera, A., Morabito, G.: The Internet of Things: a survey. Comput. Netw. 54(15), 2787–2805 (2010). https://doi.org/10.1016/j.comnet.2010.05.010
5. Bourzac, K.: Millimeter-scale computers: now with deep-learning neural networks on board, February 2017. https://goo.gl/sciVTC
6. Cano, J., Rutten, E., Delaval, G., Benazzouz, Y., Gurgen, L.: ECA rules for IoT environment: a case study in safe design. In: 2014 IEEE Eighth International Conference on Self-Adaptive and Self-Organizing Systems Workshops, pp. 116–121, September 2014. https://doi.org/10.1109/SASOW.2014.32
7. Cheng, B., Zhu, D., Zhao, S., Chen, J.: Situation-aware IoT service coordination using the event-driven SOA paradigm. IEEE Trans. Netw. Serv. Manag. 13(2), 349–361 (2016). https://doi.org/10.1109/TNSM.2016.2541171
8. Conti, M., et al.: Looking ahead in pervasive computing: challenges and opportunities in the era of cyber-physical convergence. Pervasive Mobile Comput. 8(1), 2–21 (2012)
9. Endler, M., Briot, J.P., Silva, F.S.E., De Almeida, V.P., Haeusler, E.H.: An approach for real-time stream reasoning for the Internet of Things. In: 1st International Workshop on Semantic Multimedia Computing (SMC 2017), Proceedings of the 11th IEEE International Conference on Semantic Computing (ICSC 2017), pp. 348–353. IEEE, San Diego, January 2017
10. Fortino, G., Russo, W., Savaglio, C., Shen, W., Zhou, M.: Agent-oriented cooperative smart objects: from IoT system design to implementation. IEEE Trans. Syst. Man Cybern.: Syst. 48(11), 1939–1956 (2018). https://doi.org/10.1109/TSMC.2017.2780618
11. Fortino, G., Guerrieri, A., Lacopo, M., Lucia, M., Russo, W.: An agent-based middleware for cooperating smart objects. In: Corchado, J.M., et al. (eds.) PAAMS 2013. CCIS, vol. 365, pp. 387–398. Springer, Heidelberg (2013). https://doi.org/10.1007/978-3-642-38061-7_36
12. Goumopoulos, C., Kameas, A.: Smart objects as components of UbiComp applications. Int. J. Multimedia Ubiquitous Eng. 4(3), 1–20 (2009)
13. Gupta, C., et al.: ProtoNN: compressed and accurate kNN for resource-scarce devices. In: Proceedings of the 34th International Conference on Machine Learning (ICML 2017), vol. 70, pp. 1331–1340. JMLR.org (2017). http://dl.acm.org/citation.cfm?id=3305381.3305519
14. Kortuem, G., Kawsar, F., Sundramoorthy, V., Fitton, D.: Smart objects as building blocks for the Internet of Things. IEEE Internet Comput. 14(1), 44–51 (2010)
15. Kumar, A., Goyal, S., Varma, M.: Resource-efficient machine learning in 2 KB RAM for the Internet of Things. In: Proceedings of the 34th International Conference on Machine Learning (ICML 2017), vol. 70, pp. 1935–1944. JMLR.org (2017). http://dl.acm.org/citation.cfm?id=3305381.3305581

16. Lippi, M., Mamei, M., Mariani, S., Zambonelli, F.: Coordinating distributed speaking objects. In: 2017 IEEE 37th International Conference on Distributed Computing Systems (ICDCS), pp. 1949–1960, June 2017. https://doi.org/10.1109/ICDCS.2017.282
17. Lippi, M., Mamei, M., Mariani, S., Zambonelli, F.: An argumentation-based perspective over the social IoT. IEEE IoT J. **5**(4), 2537–2547 (2018). https://doi.org/10.1109/JIOT.2017.2775047
18. Neto, A.R., et al.: Classifying smart IoT devices for running machine learning algorithms. In: Anais do XLV Seminàrio Integrado de Software e Hardware. SBC, Porto Alegre (2018). https://sol.sbc.org.br/index.php/semish/article/view/3429
19. Shi, W., Dustdar, S.: The promise of edge computing. Computer **49**(5), 78–81 (2016). https://doi.org/10.1109/MC.2016.145
20. Walton, D., Krabbe, E.: Commitment in Dialogue: Basic Concept of Interpersonal Reasoning. State University of New York Press, Albany (1995)
21. Yi, S., Li, C., Li, Q.: A survey of fog computing: concepts, applications and issues. In: Proceedings of the 2015 Workshop on Mobile Big Data (Mobidata 2015), pp. 37–42. ACM, New York (2015)

Optimized Analytics Query Allocation at the Edge of the Network

Anna Karanika[1], Madalena Soula[1], Christos Anagnostopoulos[2],
Kostas Kolomvatsos[2(✉)], and George Stamoulis[1]

[1] Department of Electrical and Computer Engineering, University of Thessaly,
37 Glavani Str., 38221 Volos, Greece
{ankaranika,msoula,georges}@uth.gr
[2] School of Computing Science, University of Glasgow,
17 Lilybank Gardens, Glasgow G12 8RZ, UK
{christos.anagnostopoulos,kostas.kolomvatsos}@glasgow.ac.uk

Abstract. The new era of the Internet of Things (IoT) provides the space where novel applications will play a significant role in people's daily lives through the adoption of multiple services that facilitate everyday activities. The huge volumes of data produced by numerous IoT devices make the adoption of analytics imperative to produce knowledge and support efficient decision making. In this setting, one can identify two main problems, i.e., the time required to send the data to Cloud and wait for getting the final response and the distributed nature of data collection. Edge Computing (EC) can offer the necessary basis for storing locally the collected data and provide the required analytics on top of them limiting the response time. In this paper, we envision multiple edge nodes where data are stored being the subject of analytics queries. We propose a methodology for allocating queries, defined by end users or applications, to the appropriate edge nodes in order to save time and resources in the provision of responses. By adopting our scheme, we are able to ask the execution of queries only from a sub-set of the available nodes avoiding to demand processing activities that will lead to an increased response time. Our model envisions the allocation to specific epochs and manages a batch of queries at a time. We present the formulation of our problem and the proposed solution while providing results of an extensive evaluation process that reveals the pros and cons of the proposed model.

Keywords: Internet of Things · Edge Computing · Large scale data · Queries management

1 Introduction

The Internet of Things (IoT) architecture enables the connection and interaction between heterogeneous devices that facilitate the provision of applications via their integration into a common infrastructure. The IoT infrastructure offers the

© Springer Nature Switzerland AG 2019
R. Montella et al. (Eds.): IDCS 2019, LNCS 11874, pp. 181–190, 2019.
https://doi.org/10.1007/978-3-030-34914-1_18

basis where smartphones, wearables etc. can automatically interact and lead to a fully automated world by embedding intelligence into the environment around end users. On top of the IoT, one can envision the Cloud backend infrastructure where data produced by numerous IoT devices are transferred for further processing. The huge volumes of data should be processed to produce knowledge and support intelligent decision making leading to more efficient services. However, the transfer of data to Cloud and the increased waiting time for getting the final response as the outcome of the desired processing activities negatively affects the latency that query requestors enjoy [2]. This problem led to the emergence of Edge Computing (EC) which opposes to the processing power and latency that Cloud offers. Any processing activity is performed locally in a set of EC nodes while being characterized by lower computational power compared to Cloud resources.

Edge nodes can be connected with a number of IoT devices collecting their reported data as observed by their environment. These nodes can serve as 'mediators' for passing the data to Cloud. However, for limiting the latency in the provision of analytics responses, queries processing can be performed locally. When such a setting is the case, the most important research question is to provide an efficient methodology for allocating the incoming queries to the appropriate EC nodes instead of broadcasting them to all the available nodes. The aim is to save resources apart from time and involve only nodes that can return an efficient response as depicted by the data that match with the queries constraints. For instance, it is useless to allocate queries to nodes not having data that match against the defined constraints as the final response will be the empty set. Hence, the resources spent for executing the desired processing are wasted. A model that will build on the distributed nature of the collected data seems to be imperative. We consider abstract entities called Query Controllers (QCs) that are responsible to perform the envisioned allocations of the incoming analytics queries. Such entities can have insights on the EC nodes related to the data they possess as well as their historical performance. We assume that multiple QCs are present at Cloud or at specific locations in the network (e.g., in islands that connect multiple nodes) having interactions with multiple EC nodes, thus, we study the management of the ecosystem QCs-EC nodes.

In this paper, we propose a mechanism that supports the behaviour of QCs, i.e., a QC should efficiently respond in the minimum possible time to further limit the response time. As an allocation, we define the optimal selection of a node for a distinct query determined by the query's characteristics and nodes' current performance. Such a decision-making process is dynamically influenced by the continuously updated data and nodes' performance. We consider that the described problem can be treated as an assignment problem [20] trying to allocate multiple queries to multiple nodes. We propose a cost function for delivering the cost of an allocation for pairs of queries - nodes and implement the solution of our problem adopting the Hungarian Method (adopting the specific algorithm, we enjoy the lowest possible complexity and return the result in the minimum time). We also focus on the 'one-shot' allocation, i.e., the allocation is accepted by the selected node instead of performing an additional reasoning whether the query can be executed locally or be offloaded to peer nodes based on a reward/cost function and the distance in the network (this is the subject of [14]). The efficient allocation of queries to a number of nodes is also the subject of our previous efforts discussed in [15–17] and [18]. The difference of the current model with the aforementioned work is that we deal with queries batch processing and not individual allocations (allocating one query at a time).

The remaining paper is organized as follows. Section 2 discusses the related work while Sect. 3 presents preliminary information and the problem under consideration. Section 4 depicts the proposed solution and in Sect. 5, we provide our experimental evaluation results adopting real and synthetic datasets. Finally, in Sect. 6, we conclude our paper by presenting our future research plans in the domain.

2   Prior Work

EC consists of framework which allows the execution of processing tasks close to the source of data instead of delivering the information to data centers/Cloud [13]. The EC allows edge nodes to respond to service demands locally, reducing bandwidth consumption and network latency [23]. As edge nodes are connected with a number of IoT devices, they can be the host of a virtual or physical data separation process, i.e., they can be part of an ecosystem of distributed datasets. The collected data can be stored in any format that is appropriate for the limited resources of edge nodes and can be retrieved through the execution of the appropriate queries. Practically, queries are requests for information, usually issued by human users, including simple or complex transactions which either read or change the collected data [9]. Queries can be formed through commands in a dedicated language (e.g., SQL) or based on natural language processing. The execution of queries can be performed by specific processors usually adopting query execution plans as mandated by the corresponding management software (e.g., RDBMS). The goal is to increase the performance related to the time required for getting the final response. Outcomes are communicated back to the query requestor while the execution process can be centralized (e.g., in the same machine) or distributed [6].

Data partitioning can be the result of the physical allocation of various nodes connected with reporting devices. Moreover, data partitioning can be adopted to increase the parallelism in the execution of queries, thus, to facilitate manageability and control together with saving time and resources. The interested reader can find a survey on data partitioning algorithms in [22]. The relevant efforts are coming from the database community while gaining increased attention in the community of the management of large scale data. When a 'batch-oriented' processing is adopted, i.e., data are firstly collected and afterwards the separation algorithm is executed, the system has the opportunity to prepare the data and eliminate any heterogeneity. However, this is not the case in EC when the available nodes receive data from IoT devices. The data heterogeneity, at least concerning their format, imposes an additional burden when we want to execute analytics over the incoming streams [4].

Machine learning can be adopted to address not only the increasing amount of data but also the distributed management of the available datasets. In [1], the authors present a comparative analysis of exploratory techniques for large scale data. A framework adopted for the analysis of sensory data targeting to the minimization of data transferred in the network is discussed in [11]. Such an analysis aims at supporting analytics that can be used in decision making in various applications that want to build knowledge on top of the collected data. Analytics refer in various tasks executed over the collected data targeting to reveal knowledge and the hidden aspects of their distribution. An example of analytics is the anomaly detection research domain. An overview of data analytics techniques for anomaly detection is provided in [21]. A 'special' type of analytics are prognostics or predictive analytics [3]. Predictive analytics deal with the identification of the distribution of data and the calculations over specific key performance indicators to reveal their future trends. Hence, decisions can be made not only based on current trends but also on future estimations of the data statistics. In [7], the authors report the effect that the quality of data has on the outcomes of predictive analytics processes and propose a method for improving data quality. The proposed method is aligned with the needs of the maintenance domain when a set of devices and production equipment are those that need to be managed. In [3], the authors propose the SERENA system comprising a number of services, which collectively provide predictive analytics functionalities, enabling predictive maintenance policies to be applied. Other example analytics models are Prism [5], CONTROL [10] and DBO [12] systems. All these systems aim at saving time in the provision of responses adopting sampling or progressive analytics. Usually, the discussed systems are build on top of the MapReduce model (e.g., [8,19]) trying to increase its performance.

3   Preliminaries and Problem Description

We consider a set of N EC nodes (see Fig. 1), i.e., $\mathcal{E} = \{e_1, e_2, \ldots, e_N\}$ owning the corresponding datasets $\mathcal{D} = \{d_1, d_2, \ldots, d_N\}$. In every dataset, the discussed nodes receive and store multivariate data vectors, i.e., $\mathbf{x} = \langle x_1, x_2, \ldots, x_M \rangle$ where M is the number of dimensions. IoT devices observe their environment and send the data to the corresponding nodes feeding through streams the available $\mathcal{D}$. Every EC node can be the host of data coming from multiple IoT devices while each IoT device can report data to multiple EC nodes. We also consider that at every EC node, a processor is devoted to the execution of the incoming queries. Processors adopt specific query execution plans, however, their internal processing activities are beyond the scope of this paper. In front of each node, there is a queue where the incoming queries are placed. The size of the queue and the throughput of the corresponding node affects the current load. When a node is overloaded, it will be characterized by increased latency in the provision of responses. Without loss of generality, we consider that the discussed queue can handle a maximum number of queries and that the size of queues is the same among the available nodes. Formally, for each node, $s_j, j = 1, 2, \ldots, N$ denotes the corresponding processing speed while l_j depicts its load. Specifically, s_j consists of a feature defined by the rate at which data are processed, whereas l_j depicts the amount of queries waiting for execution in the corresponding queue. Without loss of generality, we consider that $s_j, l_j \in [0, 1]$.

At each $t \in \mathbf{T}$ ($\mathbf{T}$ is the discrete time), a query q^t arrives at a QC. q^t has specific characteristics and constraints defined e.g., in the Where clause. Every analytics query target to get the desired data in the minimum time. For this, a deadline could be set. Let c_{q_t} depict the complexity of q_t and τ_{q_t} the corresponding deadline. The former represents the 'magnitude' of calculations required for the conclusion of the transaction, while the latter stands for the time constraint, set by the user or application. Values of these characteristics can vary greatly, all the while resembling those of a real-world functioning system. In [15], we propose a methodology for calculating c_{q_t} adopted in the current work. We focus on c_{q_t} and τ_{q_t} and try to match them against l_j and s_j before we have the corresponding QC deciding for the final allocation. Compared to our previous efforts, the current model incorporates two additional parameters: (a) a cost function indicating the cost that the QC should pay for every allocation it desires to conclude; (b) a batch-oriented approach for the management of a group of queries instead of deciding for each individual query.

The final allocation process adopts a window W that defines the number of queries that will be the subject of our processing mechanism. Actually, the QC adopts a 'sliding window' approach trying to allocate a bunch of queries instead just only one. We consider the function $f(\cdot)$ that takes as inputs W queries and the information for the available nodes and results the final allocations. For every query $q_t^i, i = 1, 2, \ldots, W$, we get the node where it will be allocated, i.e., $f(q_t^i, \mathcal{E}) \rightarrow e_s$ (e_s is the selected node for q_t^i). The appropriateness of the allocations is evaluated based on the aforementioned cost function that takes into consideration the characteristics of both; queries and nodes as already described. There is a high number of combinations between W queries and N nodes, thus, a brute-force model is not the optimal solution to get (near) real-time results. In the following subsection, we present our cost function and the adopted optimization algorithm for concluding the final allocations based on the solution of the known assignment problem, i.e., mapping each of W queries to one of the N available nodes.

4   The Proposed Model

For concluding the final allocations, we propose the use of a simple rewarding mechanism to elaborate on the matching between pairs c_{q_t} - l_j and τ_{q_t} - s_j. Our aim is to 'support' the allocation of complex queries to nodes that exhibit a low load, thus, they can devote resources to the specific query. In addition, when the query deadline is short, we prefer to perform the allocation to a node exhibiting a high speed to conclude the execution as soon as possible. In any case,

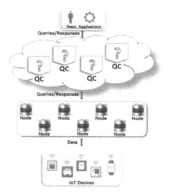

Fig. 1. The envisioned architecture.

both query characteristics should be combined to support an efficient allocation. For each pair, we report on the *Cost of Allocation* (CoA). The CoA consists of two parts; one for each pair. The total CoA equals to the sum of the partial CoAs. The first step is to calculate the rounded ratio ρ of c_{q_t} compared to τ_{q_t}, i.e., $\rho = \frac{c_{q_t}}{\tau_{q_t}}$. It is important to notice that before the conclusion of ρ, c_{q_t} is depicted by the required steps to execute the specific query as indicated by [15]. ρ represents the speed demanded by the query (in execution steps per time unit) to be executed and completed in compliance with τ_{q_t}. Subsequently, s_j is compared to ρ to conclude whether the node is fast enough to serve q_t in the required time interval. Then, l_j is compared to specific thresholds indicating the high and the low ratios, i.e., we aim to support three levels of l_j; low, medium, high. Actually, we propose a fuzzy number to depict the cost for pairing l_j with c_{q_t}. For each level, we define a constant as the corresponding cost. For instance, if the load is over 0.8, we consider a high cost of allocation especially for queries exhibiting a high complexity. For each speed and load combination, an appropriate reward or penalty is attributed to the CoA.

After the calculation of the CoA for each combination between queries and nodes, we conclude a WXN matrix, i.e., $A_{ij} = [CoA_{ij}], i = 1, 2, \ldots, W \& j = 1, 2, \ldots, N$. We treat our problem as an assignment problem and adopt the fastest possible algorithm for solving it. We rely on the Hungarian algorithm as modified by Munkres in [20]. The adopted methodology deals with a combinatorial optimization algorithm which was the first to solve the assignment problem with a 'reasonable' complexity. Without loss of generality, we consider that $W = N$, thus, we target to a one-to-one allocation. Our future work involves many-to-many allocations. The time complexity of the original version of the algorithm is $O(N^4)$, whereas the adopted version yields a complexity of $O(WN^2)$ for orthogonal matrices. Our aim is to perform the envisioned allocations based on the CoAs calculated in the previous step so as to minimize the total allocation cost. If we model the combination between queries and nodes as a graph, we can assign as the total cost, the sum of all the edges participating to the final allocation.

Every vertex (i.e., queries or nodes) in the graph is the endpoint of exactly one edge while the potential value represents the total cost of all edges. Hence, the final cost will be at least as the total potential. The adopted method finds a perfect matching and a potential such that the matching cost equals the potential value. Due to space limitation, we omit a detailed description of the discussed algorithm. In any case, the proposed model results a set of allocations in the form of pairs $\{q_t, e_j\}, \forall t \in \{1, 2, \ldots, W\}, \forall j \in \{1, 2, \ldots, N\}$.

5 Performance Evaluation

We report on the experimental evaluation of our model through a large set of simulations. It should be noted that we developed our simulator in Java and provide a set of classes for the adopted entities (QCs and EC nodes). Our results are related to a set of performance metrics trying to reveal if the envisioned allocations are efficient or not. At first, we focus on the time required to conclude the set of W allocations to check if the proposed method can be adopted to take (near) real time decisions. We define the metric T (in seconds) which represents the time required for concluding an allocation. Our main aim is to reduce the average T value to increase the throughput of QCs. In addition, we focus on the load of the selected node for each concluded allocation. We define the metric Λ depicting the difference of the selected node's load with the lowest load among all nodes. The following equation holds true: $\Lambda = l_{selected} - l_{lowest}$. When $\Lambda \to 0$, the selected node's load is the lowest possible into the group of the available nodes. The opposite stands when $\Lambda \to \infty$. Another metric we adopt is Σ defined as the difference of the highest speed among all nodes with the speed of the selected node. The metric is calculated by: $\Sigma = s_{highest} - s_{selected}$. When $\Sigma \to 0$, the selected node's speed is the highest possible in the group of the available nodes. The opposite stands when $\Sigma \to \infty$. As noted, an optimal allocation is that taking into consideration both nodes' characteristics i.e., speed and load. Hence, we adopt another metric Φ as the linear combination of Λ and Σ. Φ is defined as follows: $\Phi = \alpha \cdot \Lambda + (1 - \alpha) \cdot \Sigma, \alpha \in [0, 1]$. α is adopted to pay more attention in one of the adopted characteristics, however, a value of $\alpha = 0.5$ will give insights on the performance of the system when we pay attention on both s_j and l_j at the same time. Finally, in our simulations, we adopt two real traces, i.e., the Energy efficiency Data Set[1] (we borrow the data related to the heating and cooling load) and the Optical Interconnection Network Data Set[2] (we borrow the data related to the processor and network utilization as well as the channel response time). The adopted values are separated into a number of partitions (i.e., the datasets in the available EC nodes) through sampling and fed into our simulator to depict the l realization while s is randomly selected. We run simulations for 1,000 iterations where queries are set in a QC defining their complexity as described in [15] and taking a random deadline. The characteristics of the available nodes

---

[1] https://archive.ics.uci.edu/ml/datasets/Energy+efficiency.
[2] https://archive.ics.uci.edu/ml/datasets/Optical+Interconnection+Network+.

are retrieved by the aforementioned datasets. Finally, we report on the mean of the adopted performance metrics.

In Fig. 2, we present our results for the T metric. We observe that even for an increased number of nodes, the time required for an allocation is below one second. This makes us to support our view that the proposed mechanism can provide the desired outcomes in (near) real time. This means that the throughput of QCs will increase making them capable of supporting numerous queries with positive impact in the queries requestors.

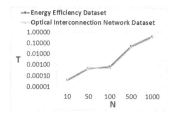

Fig. 2. The performance of our model concerning the T metric.

In Fig. 3, we depict our results concerning Λ and Σ. We observe the stability for both performance metrics no matter the N value. The average difference with lowest possible load is around 0.3–0.4 while the average difference with the highest possible speed is around 0.5. Comparing these results with [15], we observe that the current model exhibits similar performance without the burden of the complex model for delivering the matching process as depicted by [15]. For instance, for Λ, the model presented in [15] results a difference around 0.25–0.35.

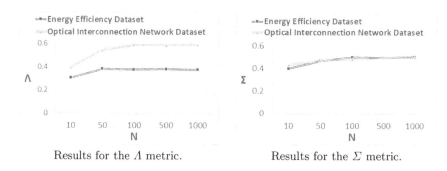

Results for the Λ metric.   Results for the Σ metric.

Fig. 3. Our results related to the lowest load and the highest speed of the selected nodes.

In Fig. 4, we present our results concerning the Φ metric. We observe that, as expected, α affects the final outcome. Based on α, we can focus more on an individual characteristic. For instance, when $\alpha = 0.2$, we get a mode that results a low difference with the optimal node concerning the speed (see Fig. 4). The opposite stands when $\alpha \to 1.0$. In any case, Φ is around 0.35–0.55 (depending on the dataset) which means that the proposed model exhibits a stability while trying to incorporate the optimal decision for both characteristics.

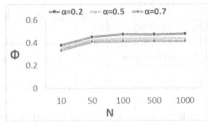

Results for the Φ metric - 1st dataset.

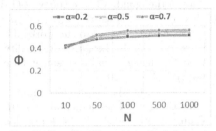

Results for the Φ metric - 2nd dataset.

Fig. 4. Our results related to the lowest load and the highest speed of the selected nodes.

6   Conclusions and Future Work

The distributed nature of data collection and management in the new era of IoT demands for efficient mechanisms that extract knowledge on top of the available datasets. These datasets are usually formulated in edge nodes where IoT devices are connected and report their data. We propose a mechanism that tries to identify the needs of analytics queries and allocate them to edge nodes that can immediately respond and own data that match to their constraints. We present a model for the conclusion of allocations based on the characteristics of both; queries and nodes. The aim is to limit the time for the conclusion and the time for getting the final response. We provide simulation results that reveal the limited time for concluding an allocation leading to the increase of the throughput of the schemes managing the incoming queries. In addition, we provide performance results related to the optimal selection of the available nodes and show the ability of our scheme to select the appropriate nodes. Our future extensions will allow the definition of a scheme that performs allocations in a many-to-many scheme trying to efficiently manage batch of queries arriving in a management entity.

Acknowledgment. This research received funding from the European's Union Horizon 2020 research and innovation programme under the grant agreement No. 745829 & the Greek Secretariat for Research Funding under the project ENFORCE.

References

1. Apiletti, D., et al.: Frequent itemsets mining for big data: a comparative analysis. Big Data Res. **9**, 67–83 (2017)
2. Bangui, H., et al.: Moving to the edge-cloud-of-things: recent advances and future research directions. Electronics **7**, 309 (2018)

3. Bowden, D., et al.: A cloud-to-edge architecture for predictive analytics. In: Workshops of the EDBT/ICDT Conference (2019)
4. Chai, Z., et al.: Towards taming the resource and data heterogeneity in federated learning. In: USENIX Conference on Operational Machine Learning (2019)
5. Chandramouli, B., Goldstein, J., Quamar, A.: Scalable progressive analytics on big data in the cloud. VLDB Endow. **6**(14), 1726–1737 (2013)
6. Chatterjea, S., Havunga, P.: A taxonomy of distributed query management techniques for wireless sensor networks. IJCS **20**(7), 889–908 (2007)
7. Chen, Y., Zhu, F., Lee, J.: Data quality evaluation and improvement for prognostic modeling using visual assessment based data partitioning method. Comput. Ind. **64**(3), 214–225 (2013)
8. Condie, T., et al.: MapReduce online. In: The 7th Conference on Networked Systems Design and Implementation (2010)
9. Cummins, R., et al.: A Polya urn document language model for improved information retrieval. ACM TIS **9**(4), 21 (2010)
10. Hellerstein, J.M., Avnur, R.: Informix under CONTROL: online query processing. Data Min. Knowl. Discovery J. **4**, 281–314 (2000)
11. Huang, Z., Zhong, A., Li, G.: On-demand processing for remote sensing big data analysis. In: IEEE ISPDPA (2017)
12. Jermaine, C., et al.: Scalable approximate query processing with the DBO engine. In: SIGMOD (2007)
13. Khan, W., et al.: Edge computing: a survey. FGCS **97**, 219–235 (2019)
14. Kolomvatsos, K., Anagnostopoulos, C.: Multi-criteria optimal task allocation at the edge. FGCS **93**, 358–372 (2019)
15. Kolomvatsos, K., Anagnostopoulos, C.: An edge-centric ensemble scheme for queries assignment. In: 8th CIMA Workshop (2018)
16. Kolomvatsos, K.: An intelligent scheme for assigning queries. Appl. Intell. **48**, 2730–2745 (2018)
17. Kolomvatsos, K., Anagnostopoulos, C.: Reinforcement machine learning for predictive analytics in smart cities. Informatics **4**, 16 (2017)
18. Kolomvatsos, K., Hadjiefthymiades, S.: Learning the engagement of query processors for intelligent analytics. Appl. Intell. **46**, 96–112 (2017)
19. Logothetis, D., Yocum, K.: Ad-hoc data processing in the cloud. VLDB Endow. **1**(2), 1472–1475 (2008)
20. Munkres, J.: Algorithms for the assignment and transportation problems. JSIAM **5**(1), 32–38 (1957)
21. Murphree, J.: Machine learning anomaly detection in large systems. In: IEEE AUTOTESTCON, pp. 1–9 (2016)
22. Phansalkar, S., Ahirrao, S.: Survey of data partitioning algorithms for big data stores. In: 4th ICPDGC (2016)
23. Yu, W., et al.: A survey on the edge computing for the Internet of Things. IEEE Access **6**, 6900–6919 (2017)

MR-DNS: Multi-resolution Domain Name System

Saidur Rahman[✉] and Mike P. Wittie[✉]

Montana State University, Bozeman, MT 59715, USA
sr.rifat@gmail.com, mike.wittie@montana.edu

Abstract. Users want websites to deliver rich content quickly. However, rich content often comes from separate subdomains and requires additional DNS lookups, which negatively impact web performance metrics such as First Meaningful Paint Time, Page Load Time, and the Speed Index. In this paper we investigate the impact of DNS lookups on web performance and propose Multi-Resolution DNS (MR-DNS) to reduce DNS resolutions through response batching. Our results show that MR-DNS has the potential to improve Page Load Time around 14% on average, Speed Index around 10% on average and reduce DNS traffic around 50%. We also discuss how these gains may be realized in practice through incremental changes to DNS infrastructure.

Keywords: DNS · Web performance

1 Introduction

Modern websites support a broad range of complex and interactive services such as online social networks, e-commerce, streaming video, or gaming. Consumers want websites to deliver full-featured content and to do so seamlessly. However as web developers create richer online experiences, their websites fetch content from a growing number of subdomains, or other URLs embedded in the base HTML, which decreases site responsiveness [10].

To quantify the impact of website responsiveness on user experience the web performance community proposed several web performance metrics, such as First Meaningful Paint (FMP) time, Above The Fold (ATF) time, Page Load Time (PLT) and a composite metric called the Speed Index (SI) among others [7,11,12,18,20]. Subsequently, these metrics have been used as a measuring stick against which to further improve webpage performance. As webpage content grows richer, the number of Domain Name System (DNS) lookups needed to resolve distinctive subdomains increases and negatively impacts web performance metrics and user experience [14].

We propose an experimental method to reduce the number of DNS lookups of page's subdomains. Our method, Multi-Resolution DNS (MR-DNS), reduces the number of DNS request-response round trips through an assumed collaboration between the local DNS (LDNS) and authoritative DNS (ADNS) servers. The two

© Springer Nature Switzerland AG 2019
R. Montella et al. (Eds.): IDCS 2019, LNCS 11874, pp. 191–202, 2019.
https://doi.org/10.1007/978-3-030-34914-1_19

pillars of our approach are the creation of a mapping between a base page and its subdomain by the LDNS and the batching of DNS responses by the ADNS. Although what we propose makes the DNS system more stateful, a significant reimagining of the DNS, the implementation relies on existing DNS extensions and does require new packet formats. The proposed system is also backwards compatible and permits incremental deployment.

We evaluate the impact of MR-DNS on 13 pages from an unmodified Chrome browser (version-75.0.3770.80) on a computer pointed to a custom LDNS server. Our results show that MR-DNS has the potential to reduce PLT by up to 31% and 14.45% on average. We also show reductions in SI of up to 14.67% and 10.15% on average.

The rest of this paper is organized as follows. Section 2 presents the background on DNS and web performance metrics. In Sect. 3 we analyze the structure of subdomains in modern webpages. Section 4 details the design and implementation of MR-DNS. In Sect. 5 we present the results from MR-DNS performance measurement. Section 6 outlines related work in reducing DNS resolution time during webpage loads. Finally, we conclude in Sect. 7.

2   Background

2.1   DNS Resolution Process

Fig. 1 illustrates the process of a DNS resolution [13]. To resolve a new URL such as https://example.com to an IP of its web server, a browser sends a DNS request to a local DNS (LDNS) server operated by the Internet provider (step 1). Assuming the LDNS does not have a valid DNS entry for the requested domain, the LDNS contacts the root DNS server to find the IP of a top-level domain (TLD) server responsible for the `com` portion of the domain (steps 2 and 3). A request to the TLD server returns the IP of the authoritative DNS (ADNS) server, maintained by the organization hosting https://example.com (steps 4 and 5). A subsequent request to the ADNS returns the mapping between the URL and the IP of the server hosting the site (steps 6 and 7). Finally, the

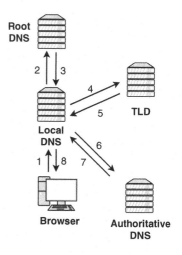

Fig. 1. DNS query path

LDNS returns the resolution to the browser (step 8), which issues an HTTP GET request for site content.

The obtained base page often contains many subdomains that download various assets, such as `img.example.com`. A subdomain may share a portion of the address with a domain already resolved and so may use an ADNS already discovered by the LDNS. Although a subdomain lookup in this case requires only steps 1, 6, 7, 8, the number of subdomain lookups may still be significant. We investigate the number of subdomains in Sect. 3 and the impact of their lookups on web performance metrics in Sect. 5.

2.2 Web Performance Metrics

The web performance community has proposed a number of web performance metrics to objectively measure website responsiveness. The need for multiple metrics comes from the fact that websites provide functionality not only when fully loaded, but also when different aspects of their rendering finish. Figure 2 shows the process of loading and rendering a website along with the labels of the various stages of process completion.

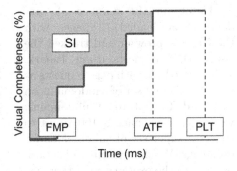

Fig. 2. Web performance metrics

The First Paint is the time when the first pixel is painted onto the screen for instance, a background color of the page and First Meaningful Paint (FMP) time occurs when a page's primary content, such as text, image, or a form field, first appears on the screen [7]. That means the time when the browser paints the content that users are interested in.

Browsers measure FMP from the time of the initial page load request to the rendering of the first visible object above the fold. The metric is useful, because it reflects users' perception of page responsiveness in starting to show content.

Above the Fold (ATF) time occurs when the browser finishes rendering page elements visible in the original browser window, before scrolling down [18]. The metric is useful, because it represents users' perception of then the page finishes to load and is fully visible.

Page Load Time (PLT) occurs at the `window.onLoad` event when the browser finishes receiving data for all the requests issued as part of the page load request [15,22]. PLT may occur after all the page content is visible, for example as data visible below the fold arrives.

Since different users may assign different importance to FMP vs. ATF vs. PLT, the Web performance community developed a composite metric dubbed the Speed Index (SI) that captures them jointly [23]. SI calculates the area above the curve of visual completion to ATF, as illustrated in Fig. 2, based on a series of screenshots of a loading page taken every 100 ms. Several studies have shown a correlation between the SI and the quality of user experience (QoE) [2,12]. To understand the potential of speeding up the resolution of subdomain addresses, in Sect. 5 we will look at the impact on FMP, PLT, and SI.

3   Analysis of Webpage Subdomain Structure

To deliver rich content, modern webpages rely on a large number of subdomains. We wanted to know exactly how many subdomains different webpages contain including 3rd party subdomains and whether browsers use the same ADNS to resolve a large number of these subdomains.

To obtain the number of subdomains we loaded 13 pages with the Chrome browser and tracked the issued DNS requests using Tshark. We observed the each page requests as slightly different set of subdomains on each load. To capture all subdomains, we loaded each page a 100 times to collect a super set of subdomains for each page. We show number of subdomains and the overall size of the page in Fig. 3 on the left and right y-axes, with the address of each page on the x-axis.

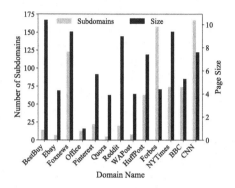

Fig. 3. Subdomain counts.

Based on the figure we observe that web pages have a large number of subdomains. For example, six of the pages have over 100 subdomains each. The number of subdomains is not tightly correlated with page size, which means that even for small pages that the user might expect to load quickly the time of DNS resolution of its subdomains might impact performance.

Next, we wanted to understand how many CDNs support the load of these pages. Since each CDN maintains their own ADNS servers, our goal was to understand the potential of speeding DNS resolutions by modifying a ADNS of one or more CDNs.

Peters and Kayan developed CDN Planet [17], a tool for monitoring performance of DNS and CDNs. One of the CDN Planet tools, CDN Finder, finds the list of subdomains in a website and extracts the Canonical Name Record (CNAME) of each subdomain. CDN Finder then extracts the server portion of the CNAME URL, matches it to a name of known CDNs, and assigns the subdomain to the CDN subdomain count.

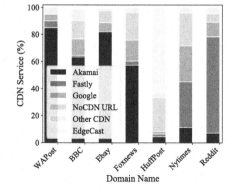

Fig. 4. Subdomain percent by CDN.

In Fig. 4 we show the mapping of subdomains to CDNs for several webpages using CDN Finder. The x-axis shows the different websites, while the y-axis show the percentage of subdomains served by each CDN. The figure shows that most of the subdomains on a given page are served by the CDN that also hosts the base domain. The one exception is bbc.com, where Fastly serves the base page, but most of the subdomains reside on Akamai. We conclude that by improving the DNS lookup process for only one ADNS hosted by one CDN, we might be able to affect a large number of subdomain lookups thereby significantly reducing the impact of DNS resolutions on web performance metrics.

4   Multi-resolution DNS System

To speed up the resolution of subdomains we propose MR-DNS – a DNS extension that enables LDNS to resolve subdomains contained within a webpage in bulk. The system implements a collaboration between the LDNS and ADNS servers that builds a mapping between the base page and the contained subdomains. The ADNS server then uses that mapping to send resolutions for subdomains when it receives a request to resolve the base page.

We illustrate the operations of MR-DNS in Fig. 5. When the browser requests the resolution of a base page domain, the LDNS forwards the DNS request to the ADNS. Instead of sending a single resolution, the ADNS replies with the mapping for the base page domain as well as the mappings for subdomains in the base page known to the ADNS. To form this response, the ADNS needs to know which subdomains belong to a base page – we discuss how to create this mapping momentarily.

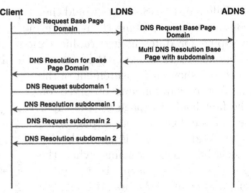

Fig. 5. MR-DNS resolution process.

The ADNS response containing the bulk resolution of subdomains may be to large to fit in a single DNS response message contained within a UDP packet, even when using EDNS0. To communicate multiple resolutions, the ADNS may send multiple DNS responses. The LDNS implementation needs to be modified to, first, cache multiple mappings and, second, accept multiple response packets. Upon receiving ADNS responses the LDNS caches the mappings and responds to the browser with the mapping for the base domain. When the browser requests resolutions for subdomains contained in the base page, the LDNS does not need forward these requests to the ADNS, but simply serves them from its cache. As a result, subdomain resolutions take less time and communications with the ADNS do not hold up web page rendering, which as we show in Sect. 5 speeds up web performance metrics.

To implement MR-DNS the ADNS needs to have a mapping between base page domains and subdomains. Regularly this mapping is not available to the ADNS and is contained within the HTML of pages hosted by a CDN. There are a number of possible approaches to create this mapping. Since most ADNSs are hosted by the same CDN that serves the base page, it is possible for a CDN to conduct a static analysis of page subdomains. That approach, however, might miss subdomains revealed by executing JavaScript, or those hidden under multiple resolutions of CNAMEs [1].

Instead, we propose the approach we take to generate Fig. 3, where the set of page subdomains comes from runtime analysis of DNS requests triggered by a page

TTL	Subdomain	IP List	Last-Use

Fig. 6. Data Structure for ADNS mapping

load. We observe that for a single client the resolution of a base page precedes resolutions for its subdomains. The LDNS may observe DNS requests coming from the same IP for an amount of time to generate a probable mapping between the first request for the base page and the subsequent requests for its subdomains. ADNS stores the mapping information of the domain using a data structure format shown in Fig. 6.

Different LDNS servers would then report that mapping to the ADNS, which could not only combine them into a more accurate mapping, but also create a mapping for different geographic regions based on the similarity of reported subdomain sets and the IP prefix of each LDNS.

Fig. 7 shows a measurement of the number of subdomains observed on the first load of a page vs. the super set of subdomains on a page over many loads. The x-axis shows the different base page domains, while the y-axis shows the normalized number of subdomains. We found that the super set of subdomains can be quite a bit larger than the set of domains observed in any given load. For example only 60% of subdomains on Quora are visible on the first load. As a result the LDNS should repeatedly observe and report page subdomains and let the ADNS comprise the super set of the mapping.

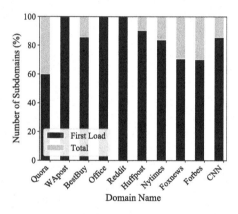

Fig. 7. Subdomain load number.

We explore mapping creation in two modes. In the *CacheCDN* mode the ADNS creates a mapping for all the subdomains hosted by the same CDN as the base page. We obtain the set of subdomains for CacheCDN using the data from Fig. 4. In the *CacheAll* mode the ADNS maintains a mapping of all subdomains contained on a page. There are practical challenges to implementing the CacheAll approach in that the CDN ADNS provides resolutions for domains maintained by other ADNS servers. While there could be cooperative approaches among ADNS servers to implement CacheAll, we do not explore them in this paper. Instead, we consider CacheAll as a theoretical upper limit of the benefit of bulk domain resolution. We observe, however, that as more of page subdomains are hosted by the same CDN, the benefit of the CacheCDN mode will approach the CacheAll mode.

Finally, we need to consider the results of an inaccurate mapping between the base page and its subdomains. In the case where the bulk resolution contains more subdomains then needed, the ADNS will deliver unnecessary mappings to the LDNS. While that may create additional DNS traffic by sending unneeded mappings, we show in Sect. 5 that MR-DNS reduces DNS traffic overall. It may also be possible for the ADNS to deliver mappings that the LDNS already has in its cache, thereby sending unnecessary information. This may be avoided in many cases by setting the time to live (TTL) of subdomains to be the same as the TTL of the base page. The added benefit of synchronized TTLs is that any time a client loads a base page the LDNS will have up-to-date subdomain mappings and make it faster for the ADNS to update LDNS mappings. In the case where the mapping lacks certain subdomains, the LDNS will not be able to satisfy a browser request for these subdomains from its cache and will instead forward the DNS request as it does currently. In either case, the bulk resolution of subdomains does not affect the correctness of the DNS.

5   Evaluation

We demonstrate the effectiveness of MR-DNS to improve web performance metrics by resolving page subdomains in bulk. We also measure MR-DNS resource usage in terms of DNS traffic and LDNS memory usage.

To conduct our measurements we set up customized LDNS and ADNS servers on dedicated Ubuntu 18.04 servers implementing MR-DNS bulk resolution, illustrated in Fig. 8. The first stage in the evaluation process is to create the mapping between

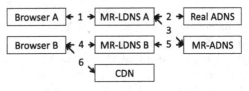

Fig. 8. Experimental setup

the base page and the subdomains for a given page. We load the page using Browser A connected to LDNS A (step 1), which uses the real ADNS servers to resolve all page subdomains (step 2). LDNS A creates the mapping and sends it to MR-ADNS (step 3). In the second stage we collect collect web performance metrics. We load each page on Browser B connected to MR-LDNS B (step 4), which contacts MR-ADNS to obtain the resolution of the base page and the subdomains in bulk (step 5). We configure the network latency between Browser B, MR-LDNS B, and MR-ADNS using netem to reflect the latency between the browser and the real LDNS and ADNS servers for each page. For example, for www.bbc.com, we found the average latency between LDNS and ADNS is 42.113 ms. During the load of a page, Browser B loads each page from the real CDN servers over a network with actual delays and bandwidth limitations from our lab in Bozeman, MT (step 6). For our measurements we used several popular pages from the Alexa list of most popular pages [5]. We load each page 100 times in new Chrome Incognito window each time, to prevent caching, using the Chrome Headless mode. To collect web performance metrics we use Google Lighthouse [8].

5.1   Web Performance Metrics

We show the measurement of web performance metrics in Figs. 9a–c. The x-axis shows the different base page domains, while the y-axis shows FMP, PLT, and SI respectively. The 100% mark of each bar shows the metric value of the page loaded through the unmodified DNS system. The CacheCDN and CacheAll modes show the reduction in each metric value as a percent.

In Fig. 9a we observe that the CacheCDN mode reduces FMP time by as much as 16.76% for WAPost and 4.12% on average. The theoretical improvement of the CacheAll mode reduces FMP time by as much as 31.42% for Reddit and 14.45% on average. In Fig. 9b we observe that the CacheCDN mode reduces PLT by as much as 14.02% for WAPost and 4.89% on average. The theoretical improvement of the CacheAll mode reduces PLT by as much as 31% for Reddit and 16.11% on average. In Fig. 9c we observe that the CacheCDN mode reduces SI by as much as 5.57% for BestBuy and 3.05% on average. The theoretical improvement of the CacheAll mode reduces SI by as much as 14.67% for WAPost and 10.15% on average. Overall, we observe the the CacheCDN mode has a significant potential to reduce both individual and composite web performance metrics thereby improving user QoE. As more of the page content is hosted by a single CDN, the gains of CacheCDN mode approach those of CacheAll mode as for example in the case of Reddit.

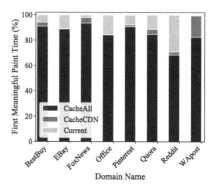

(a) FMP time vs. page domain.

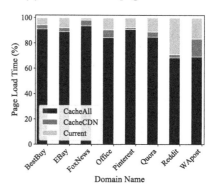

(b) PLT vs. page domain.

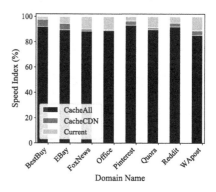

(c) SI vs. page domain.

Fig. 9. Measured web performance.

5.2 Resource Usage

Fig. 10 shows the memory on the LDNS needed to store different numbers of subdomains. The x-axis shows the number of subdomains, while the y-axis shows the cache memory usage, including the domain name, IP address, TTL, and last used time obtained with the `object-sizeof` function on the dictionary data structure. We observe that the memory footprint is highly linear and therefore predictable in the number of subdomains.

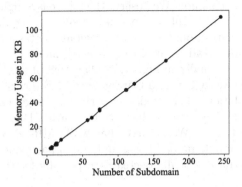

Fig. 10. Subdomain load number.

Table 1. Subdomains in different regions

Domain name	NV	MT	CA	MT ∩ CA	NV ∩ CA	NV ∩ MT	NV ∩ CA ∩ MT
www.bestbuy.com	18	12	19	12	16	12	12
www.ebay.com	12	7	73	7	11	7	7
www.foxnews.com	185	110	181	104	155	104	103
www.office.com	13	10	17	10	11	9	9
www.pinterest.com	18	14	19	13	16	14	13
www.quora.com	4	4	12	3	4	3	3
www.reddit.com	38	20	44	20	38	20	20
www.washingtonpost.com	11	7	14	7	10	6	6
www.forbes.com	198	118	243	105	169	102	102
www.usatoday.com	356	179	329	160	261	159	155
www.weather.com	11	11	13	10	10	8	7
www.walmart.com	76	76	82	59	68	58	58

This information allows us to predict how much memory would be required on the ADNS to store the information reported to LDNS servers in different regions. We measure the number of subdomains observed by LDNS servers in the CacheAll mode in different regions by deploying MR-DNS on AWS servers in N. California (CA), N. Virginia (NV), and on our lab servers in Montana (MT). In Table 1 we show the number of subdomains for each page in the different

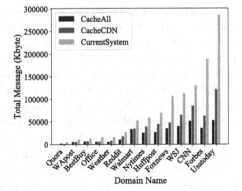

Fig. 11. Subdomain load number.

regions as well as the intersections to show how many domains the regions have in common. We observe that there is a high degree of subdomain overlap between the different regions. As a result the requirement for the ADNS to store subdomains from the different regions creates a relatively low and predictable memory overhead, even in the CacheAll mode.

Finally, in Fig. 11, we show the comparison of three different system CacheAll, CacheCDN, and Current system in terms of total message volume for DNS resolutions. The x-axis shows the base page domain, while the y-axis shows the total DNS traffic in the current, CacheCDN, and CacheAll modes measured using Tshark. We observe that while MR-DNS delivers more domains that may be strictly needed for an individual page load, see Fig. 11, the total volume of DNS traffic actually decreases, especially for the CacheCDN mode.

6 Related Work

Several research projects have proposed solutions to reduce the delay of DNS lookups. Park *et al.* proposed CoDNS to replicate DNS queries to different DNS servers to improve lookup reliability and the latency [16]. A similar tool also replicates DNS queries to different servers to reduce lookup delay by accepting the first response [21]. However, the first responding DNS server might not necessarily offer the best CDN mapping for the client. Goel *et al.* solve this problem by probing the resolved CDN servers before issuing requests for web objects [9].

DNS Pre-Resolve eliminates DNS lookup delay by resolving domain names during page rendering. This pre-resolution, proposed by Google, embedded requests in HTML header which reduces DNS lookup time by giving hints to the browser at the beginning of the HTML and the browser pre-resolve DNS for resources on the page [6]. Shang *et al.* proposed a method to decrease the DNS cache drop rate by utilizing the correlation of requested Web domains to the domains that have a DNS resolution cached [19]. Though these two techniques decrease the impact of DNS on webpage load time, for both cases, the ADNS gets all the requests for all subdomains.

Most similar to our work is the proposal by Almeida *et al.* discuss potential improvement to PLT from reducing DNS lookup delay [1]. They find that for top 10k Alexa websites DNS lookup is responsible for 9.2% of PLT on average, which collaborates an earlier result by Wang *et al.* [22]. Almeida *et al.* also show that pre-resolving webpage sub-domains and pre-staging these resolutions in browser cache, via an oracle, before the page is opened, has the potential to reduce PLT by 8.5%. Their experiment, however, does not pre-resolve all the sub-domains, but only those available through static analysis of page HTML, which does not include domains embedded through JavaScript execution [1].

Chowdaiah has proposed, in an IETF experimental internet draft, for HTTP proxies to intercept base page HTML, parse out web addresses, resolve them proactively, and push the results into client DNS cache [4]. This approach is complimentary to LDNS-ADNS cooperation. The downside of the proxy approach is that the proxy does not know the state of the client DNS cache and so might perform unnecessary resolutions. This problem could be solved by communicating the state of client DNS cache through a shared dictionary approach, but is not considered in the internet draft [3]. Almeida *et al.* found that the speed up of this scheme is limited to 4% reduction in PLT on average [1].

7 Conclusions

DNS lookups affect Web application performance due to the increasing number of webpage subdomains. Although the current DNS may provide fast service, we showed that current techniques could be improved to speed up DNS resolutions. We proposed MR-DNS, a multi-resolution technique that reduce the number of DNS request-response round trips through a collaboration between the LDNS and the ADNS servers. Our measurement study showed that MR-DNS reduces webpage load time by 14% and Speed Index by 10%. MR-DNS also reduces the average traffic of ADNS by 50%. We want to note that we measured these improvements in wired networks. In cellular networks the distance between LDNS and ADNS may be smaller, if the ADNS is hosted by a CDN in the edge network. For those networks, it maybe be practical to implement MR-DNS in the browser between the device and the LDNS to eliminate radio latency in DNS lookups. Overall, we believe that MR-DNS enables a more effective use of existing DNS infrastructure and represents a strategy to improve user experience by reducing DNS lookups for rich content websites.

Acknowledgements. We would like to thank Utkarsh Goel for his helpful insights on the ideas and mechanisms presented in this paper.

References

1. Almeida, M., Finamore, A., Perino, D., Vallina-Rodriguez, N., Varvello, M.: Dissecting DNS stakeholders in mobile networks. In: CoNEXT, December 2017
2. Bocchi, E., De Cicco, L., Rossi, D.: Measuring the quality of experience of web users. SIGCOMM Comput. Commun. Rev. **46**, 8–13 (2016)
3. Butler, J., Lee, W.H., McQuade, B., Mixter, K.: A proposal for shared dictionary compression over HTTP, September 2008
4. Chowdaiah, P.: Method to pre-fetch domain names at HTTP proxy servers, September 2018
5. Developers, A.: The top 500 sites on the web. https://www.alexa.com/topsites
6. Developers, G.: Pre-resolve DNS, December 2016. https://developers.google.com/speed/pagespeed/service/PreResolveDns
7. Developers, G.: First Meaningful Paint, May 2019. https://developers.google.com/web/tools/lighthouse/audits/first-meaningful-paint
8. Developers, G.: Tools for web Developers: Lighthouse, May 2019. https://developers.google.com/web/tools/lighthouse/
9. Goel, U., Wittie, M.P., Steiner, M.: Faster web through client-assisted CDN server selection. In: ICCCN, August 2015
10. Goel, U., Steiner, M., Na, W., Wittie, M.P., Flack, M., Ludin, S.: Are 3rd parties slowing down the mobile web? In: S3@MobiCom (2016)

11. da Hora, D., Rossi, D., Christophides, V., Teixeira, R.: A practical method for measuring web above-the-fold time. In: SIGCOMM, August 2018
12. Hoßfeld, T., Metzger, F., Rossi, D.: Speed index: relating the industrial standard for user perceived web performance to web QoE. In: QoMEX, May 2018
13. Kurose, J.F., Ross, K.W.: Computer Networking: A Top-Down Approach, 6th edn. (2012)
14. Meenan, P.: How fast is your web site? Queue, March 2013
15. Netravali, R.A.: Understanding and improving web page load times on modern networks, February 2015
16. Park, K., Pai, V.S., Peterson, L., Wang, Z.: CoDNS: improving DNS performance and reliability via cooperative lookups. In: OSDI, December 2004
17. Peters, A., Kayan, S.: CDN Finder tool (2019). https://www.cdnplanet.com/tools/cdnfinder/. Accessed 28 April 2019
18. Saverimoutou, A., Mathieu, B., Vaton, S.: Web browsing measurements: an above-the-fold browser-based technique, July 2018
19. Shang, H., Wills, C.E.: Piggybacking related domain names to improve DNS performance. Comput. Netw. **50**, 1733–1748 (2006)
20. Shroff, P.H., Chaudhary, S.R.: Critical rendering path optimizations to reduce the web page loading time. In: I2CT, April 2017
21. Vulimiri, A., Godfrey, P.B., Mittal, R., Sherry, J., Ratnasamy, S., Shenker, S.: Low latency via redundancy. In: CoNEXT, December 2013
22. Wang, X.S., Balasubramanian, A., Krishnamurthy, A., Wetherall, D.: Demystifying page load performance with WProf. In: NSDI, April 2013
23. WebPagetest: WebPagetest Documentation: Speed Index, April 2012. https://sites.google.com/a/webpagetest.org/docs/using-webpagetest/metrics/speed-index

Temporal-Variation-Aware Profit-Maximized and Delay-Bounded Task Scheduling in Green Data Center

Haitao Yuan[1], Jing Bi[2(✉)], and MengChu Zhou[3]

[1] School of Software Engineering, Beijing Jiaotong University,
Beijing 100044, China
htyuan@bjtu.edu.cn
[2] School of Software Engineering in Faculty of Information Technology,
Beijing University of Technology, Beijing 100124, China
bijing@bjut.edu.cn
[3] Department of Electrical and Computer Engineering,
New Jersey Institute of Technology, Newark, NJ 07102, USA
zhou@njit.edu

Abstract. An increasing number of enterprises deploy their business applications in green data centers (GDCs) to address irregular and drastic natures in task arrival of global users. GDCs aim to schedule tasks in the most cost-effective way, and achieve the profit maximization by increasing green energy usage and reducing brown one. However, prices of power grid, revenue, solar and wind energy vary dynamically within tasks' delay constraints, and this brings a high challenge to maximize the profit of GDCs such that their delay constraints are strictly met. Different from existing studies, a Temporal-variation-aware Profit-maximized Task Scheduling (TPTS) algorithm is proposed to consider dynamic differences, and intelligently schedule all tasks to GDCs within their delay constraints. In each interval, TPTS solves a constrained profit maximization problem by a novel Simulated-annealing-based Chaotic Particle swarm optimization (SCP). Compared to several state-of-the-art scheduling algorithms, TPTS significantly increases throughput and profit while strictly meeting tasks' delay constraints.

Keywords: Green computing · Hybrid clouds · Profit maximization · Simulated annealing · Particle swarm optimization · Chaotic search

1 Introduction

A growing number of enterprise applications cost-effectively run in large-scale cloud infrastructure [1]. It is shown that in 2017, the energy consumed by data centers in the U.S. is approximately 78 billion kilowatt-hours. It represents 2.9% of the total energy consumed. It is pointed out that the total energy consumed by data centers would continue to increase by 4% till 2020 [2]. It is also shown that

© Springer Nature Switzerland AG 2019
R. Montella et al. (Eds.): IDCS 2019, LNCS 11874, pp. 203–212, 2019.
https://doi.org/10.1007/978-3-030-34914-1_20

over 57% of the electricity is produced by burning coal in the U.S. Thus, it leads to irreversible and serious damages to our global environment. To decrease the carbon footprint, more and more data centers install green energy facilities and evolve to green data centers (GDCs) with a goal to reach net-zero energy ones. A GDC aims to execute all tasks in the most cost-effective way while tasks' specified delay constraints must be met. Similar to [3], this work is suitable for the scheduling of tasks of delay tolerant applications (e.g., big data processing, scientific computing, and high-performance simulation) with long delay constraints instead of real-time applications such as answering user inquiries. In realistic GDCs, prices of power grid, revenue, wind speed, and solar irradiance all change dynamically with time. Such dynamic variations in these factors bring a high challenge of how to maximize the profit of a GDC while strictly meeting tasks' delay constraints.

Many existing studies are proposed to reduce energy consumption of the GDC by intelligently executing tasks [4,5]. Several studies investigate how to use dynamic differences of prices of power grid to reduce the energy consumption in data centers [4]. Others consider spatial variations of prices of power grid in different sites, to reduce the energy consumption in data centers [5]. Different from these studies, this work aims to maximize the profit of a GDC by jointly utilizing dynamic variations in prices of power grid, revenue, and green energy within tasks' delay constraints. In addition, most studies only meet the average delay constraints of all tasks. However, the long-tail effect of tasks' delay in realistic GDCs means that delay constraints of some tasks are not met [6], which causes adverse impact on a provider's profit. This work aims to meet delay constraints of all tasks by proposing Temporal-variation-aware Profit-maximized Task Scheduling (TPTS) algorithm.

The arrival of tasks is difficult to predict, and therefore it is challenging to execute tasks with constrained resources in a GDC. To avoid GDC overload, an admission control mechanism is typically adopted to selectively reject some tasks [7]. Nevertheless, existing studies fail to provide an explicit relation between the rejection of tasks and service rates of a GDC. This work explicitly gives a mathematical formula of such relation. Then, a constrained profit maximization problem for GDC is formulated, and further solved by a novel algorithm called Simulated-annealing-based Chaotic Particle-swarm-optimization (SCP). In this way, TPTS is proposed to consider dynamic differences of above factors within tasks' delay constraints, and intelligently schedule all tasks to the GDC within tasks' delay constraints. Simulation results with realistic trace data (e.g., Google cluster tasks [8], prices of power grid, solar irradiance and wind speed) are conducted to evaluate TPTS. Extensive simulations demonstrate that TPTS outperforms several state-of-the-art scheduling algorithms with respect to profit and throughput provided that tasks' delay constraints are strictly met.

2   Problem Formulation

Figure 1 illustrates a GDC architecture. Arriving tasks of users are executed with the First-Come-First-Served (FCFS) rule. The information of power grid, solar,

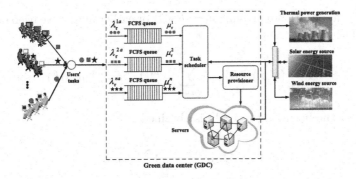

Fig. 1. A GDC architecture.

and wind energy is periodically sent to *Task Scheduler* where TPTS is executed. Based on TPTS, servers in GDC are configured by *Resource Provisioner*.

2.1 Delay Constraint

B_n denotes the delay constraint of tasks of application n. $\mu_{\tau+b}^n$ denotes the task service rate in $\tau+b$ $(0 \leq b \leq B_n)$. Λ_τ^n denotes the number of tasks of application n accumulated during τ intervals. λ_τ^{na} denotes the accumulated task arriving rate of application n in τ. Similarly, D_τ^n denotes the number of tasks executed in τ intervals. L denotes the interval length. Then,

$$\Lambda_\tau^n = \sum_{i=1}^{\tau} \lambda_i^n L \tag{1}$$

$$D_\tau^n = \sum_{i=1}^{\tau} \lambda_i^{na}(1 - \delta(\lambda_i^{na}, \mu_i^n))L \tag{2}$$

Let λ_τ^{nr} denote the remaining task arriving rate of application n in τ. Tasks of application n arriving in $\tau - B_n$ or earlier must be executed in GDC. Then, $\lambda_i^{nr} = 0$ $(i \leq \tau - B_n - 1)$. Thus, λ_τ^{na} is obtained as:

$$\lambda_\tau^{na} = \lambda_\tau^n + \sum_{i=\tau-B_n}^{\tau-1} \lambda_i^{nr} \tag{3}$$

$\delta(\lambda_{\tau+b}^{na}, \mu_{\tau+b}^n)$ denotes the task loss possibility of application n in $\tau+b$. Similar to [9], this work adopts an $M/M/1/C_n/\infty$ queueing system to model servers of application n. C_n denotes task capacity of servers of application n. Then,

$$\delta(\lambda_{\tau+b}^{na}, \mu_{\tau+b}^n) = \begin{cases} \dfrac{1 - \frac{\lambda_{\tau+b}^{na}}{\mu_{\tau+b}^n}}{1 - \left(\frac{\lambda_{\tau+b}^{na}}{\mu_{\tau+b}^n}\right)^{C_n+1}} \left(\dfrac{\lambda_{\tau+b}^{na}}{\mu_{\tau+b}^n}\right)^{C_n} & \mu_{\tau+b}^n > 0, \\[4mm] 1 & \mu_{\tau+b}^n = 0. \end{cases} \tag{4}$$

Tasks of application n arriving in $\tau+b-B_n$ or earlier must have been executed by $\tau+b$. Then,

$$\Lambda^n_{\tau-B_n-1}+\sum_{u=\tau-B_n}^{\tau-B_n+b}(\lambda^n_u L)\leq D^n_{\tau-1}+\sum_{u=\tau}^{\tau+b}(\lambda^{na}_u(1-\delta(\lambda^{na}_u,\mu^n_u))L)\,,0\leq b\leq B_n \quad (5)$$

Then, at the beginning of τ, Λ^n_τ is obtained as:

$$\Lambda^n_\tau=\Lambda^n_{\tau-B_n-1}+\sum_{u=\tau-B_n}^{\tau}(\lambda^n_u L) \quad (6)$$

At the beginning of τ, the expected number of tasks of application n executed in $\tau+b$ $(0\leq b\leq B_n)$ is $\lambda^{na}_{\tau+b}(1-\delta(\lambda^{na}_{\tau+b},\mu^n_{\tau+b}))L$. Then, $D^n_{\tau+B_n}$ is obtained as:

$$D^n_{\tau+B_n}=D^n_{\tau-1}+\sum_{u=\tau}^{\tau+B_n}(\lambda^{na}_u(1-\delta(\lambda^{na}_u,\mu^n_u))L) \quad (7)$$

Due to the task conservation of application n, Λ^n_τ should equal $D^n_{\tau+B_n}$, i.e.,

$$\Lambda^n_{\tau-B_n-1}+\sum_{u=\tau-B_n}^{\tau}(\lambda^n_u L)=D^n_{\tau-1}+\sum_{u=\tau}^{\tau+B_n}(\lambda^{na}_u(1-\delta(\lambda^{na}_u,\mu^n_u))L) \quad (8)$$

2.2   Power Consumption Model

Let σ_n denote the number of tasks of application n executed by each of its powered-on servers per minute. $m^n_{\tau+b}$ denotes the number of powered-on servers of application n in $\tau+b$. Then,

$$\mu^n_{\tau+b}=\sigma_n m^n_{\tau+b} \quad (9)$$

The maximum number of servers for application n is denoted by Ω_n. Let $\daleth=max_{n\in\{1,2,\cdots,N\}}(B_n)$. Therefore, $m^n_{\tau+b}$ must be not greater than Ω_n, i.e.,

$$m^n_{\tau+b}\leq\Omega_n,0\leq b\leq\daleth \quad (10)$$

Let γ denote the power usage effectiveness of GDC. $\bar{P}^n_0$ and $\bar{P}^n_1$ denote the average idle and peak power of each server of application n. $u^n_{\tau+b}$ denotes the CPU utilization of servers of application n in $\tau+b$. $P_{\tau+b}$ denotes the power usage of the GDC in $\tau+b$ [10]. Then,

$$P_{\tau+b}=\sum_{n=1}^{N}\left(m^n_{\tau+b}(\bar{P}^n_0+(\gamma-1)\bar{P}^n_1+(\bar{P}^n_1-\bar{P}^n_0)u^n_{\tau+b})\right) \quad (11)$$

Given the loss possibility $\delta(\lambda^{na}_{\tau+b},\mu^n_{\tau+b})$, the number of tasks of application n that each of its powered-on servers can execute in $\tau+b$ is obtained as

$\frac{L\left(1-\delta(\lambda^{na}_{\tau+b},\mu^n_{\tau+b})\right)\lambda^{na}_{\tau+b}}{m^n_{\tau+b}}$. The busy time of each powered-on server of application n is $\frac{L(1-\delta(\lambda^{na}_{\tau+b},\mu^n_{\tau+b}))\lambda^{na}_{\tau+b}}{\sigma_n m^n_{\tau+b}}$ minutes. Then, $u^n_{\tau+b}$ is obtained as:

$$u^n_{\tau+b} = \frac{(1-\delta(\lambda^{na}_{\tau+b},\mu^n_{\tau+b}))\lambda^{na}_{\tau+b}}{\sigma_n m^n_{\tau+b}} \tag{12}$$

Following (9), (11), and (12), the total energy of GDC in $\tau+b$ is:

$$E_{\tau+b} = \sum_{n=1}^{N}\left(\frac{(\bar{P}^n_0+(\gamma-1)\bar{P}^n_1)\mu^n_{\tau+b}+(\bar{P}^n_1-\bar{P}^n_0)\lambda^{na}_{\tau+b}(1-\delta(\lambda^{na}_{\tau+b},\mu^n_{\tau+b}))}{\sigma_n}L\right) \tag{13}$$

We assume each task is finished in an interval. Let ϖ denote the maximum amount of energy in GDC. Then, $E_{\tau+b}$ must be not greater than ϖ, i.e.,

$$\sum_{n=1}^{N}\left(\frac{g_n\mu^n_{\tau+b}+h_n\lambda^{na}_{\tau+b}(1-\delta(\lambda^{na}_{\tau+b},\mu^n_{\tau+b}))}{\sigma_n}L\right) \leq \varpi, 0\leq b\leq \daleth \tag{14}$$

2.3 Constrained Optimization Problem

Let $\eth^n_{\tau+b}$ denote the revenue of tasks of application n in $\tau+b$. $\theta^n_{\tau+b}$ denotes the payment of each task of application n in $\tau+b$. $\vartheta^n_{\tau+b}$ denotes the penalty of each rejected task of application n in $\tau+b$. Then, $\eth^n_{\tau+b}$ is obtained as:

$$\eth^n_{\tau+b} = \left((1-\delta(\lambda^{na}_{\tau+b},\mu^n_{\tau+b}))\lambda^{na}_{\tau+b}\right)\theta^n_{\tau+b}-\delta(\lambda^{na}_{\tau+b},\mu^n_{\tau+b})\lambda^{na}_{\tau+b}\vartheta^n_{\tau+b} \tag{15}$$

We have the revenue of tasks of all applications from τ to $\tau+b$:

$$f_1 = \sum_{n=1}^{N}\sum_{b=0}^{B_n}\eth^n_{\tau+b} \tag{16}$$

Let $p_{\tau+b}$ denote the price of power grid in $\tau+b$. $E^g_{\tau+b}$ denotes the amount of solar and wind energy in $\tau+b$. The amount of power grid energy consumed in $\tau+b$ is $\mathbf{max}(E_{\tau+b}-E^g_{\tau+b},0)$. Then, we have the power grid energy cost from $\tau+b$ to $\tau+\daleth$:

$$f_2 = \sum_{b=0}^{\daleth}\left(p_{\tau+b}\left(\mathbf{max}(E_{\tau+b}-E^g_{\tau+b},0)\right)\right) \tag{17}$$

Following (1)–(17), the Profit Maximization Problem ($\mathbf{P_1}$) is obtained as:

$$\underset{\mu^n_{\tau+b}}{\mathbf{Max}}\ \{f_1-f_2\}$$

subject to (10), (14), (5), (8), and

$$\mu^n_{\tau+b}>0, 0\leq b\leq B_n \tag{18}$$

$$\mu^n_{\tau+b}=0, B_n<b\leq \daleth \tag{19}$$

Solving $\mathbf{P}_1$ exactly cannot be finished in a require interval, e.g., 5 min. This calls for some intelligent optimization methods. This paper presents a novel one called Simulated-annealing-based Chaotic Particle swarm optimization (SCP). It innovatively combines simulated annealing (helping escape local optima), chaotic local search (refining the solution to a better level), and particle swarm optimization (fast convergence). In SCP, each particle updates its velocity according to positions of particles in the population. Then, the position of each particle is changed by the Metropolis acceptance rule of simulated annealing [11]. In each iteration of SCP, the new position of each particle is further compared with its previous one. The new position of each particle with higher $\hat{f}$ is accepted while that with lower $\hat{f}$ is conditionally chosen according to the Metropolis acceptance rule. In this way, SCP increases the possibility of obtaining global optima to achieve the profit maximization for GDC by escaping from local optima.

Algorithm 1 gives the pseudo code of TPTS. N_I denotes the number of intervals. Line 1 initializes λ_τ^n ($\lceil -B_n \leq \tau \leq \lceil -1 \rceil$) with 0, and initializes λ_τ^{nr} and λ_τ^{na} with λ_τ^n. Line 2 initializes $\Lambda_{\lceil -B_n-1}^n$ and $D_{\lceil -1}^n$ with 0. Line 5 updates λ_τ^{na} based on (3). Line 6 solves $\mathbf{P}_1$ to obtain $\mu_{\tau+b}^n$ via SCP. Line 7 schedules $\lambda_\tau^{na}(1 - \delta(\lambda_\tau^{na}, \mu_\tau^n))L$ tasks to the GDC. Line 8 updates $\lambda_i^{nr}(\tau - B_n \leq i \leq \tau)$. Then, Lines 9–10 update D_τ^n and $\Lambda_{\tau-B_n}^n$, respectively.

Algorithm 1. TPTS

1: $\lambda_\tau^n \leftarrow 0$ ($\lceil -B_n \leq \tau \leq \lceil -1 \rceil$), $\lambda_\tau^{nr} \leftarrow \lambda_\tau^n$ ($\lceil \leq \tau \leq N_I$), $\lambda_\tau^{na} \leftarrow \lambda_\tau^n$ ($\lceil \leq \tau \leq N_I$)
2: $\Lambda_{\lceil -B_n-1}^n \leftarrow 0$, $D_{\lceil -1}^n \leftarrow 0$
3: $\tau \leftarrow \lceil$
4: **while** $\tau \leq N_I$ **do**
5:     Update λ_τ^{na} based on (3)
6:     Solve $\mathbf{P}_1$ to obtain $\mu_{\tau+b}^n$ via SCP
7:     Schedule $(\lambda_\tau^{na}(1 - \delta(\lambda_\tau^{na}, \mu_\tau^n))L)$ tasks to the GDC
8:     Update $\lambda_i^{nr}(\tau - B_n \leq i \leq \tau)$
9:     $D_\tau^n \leftarrow D_{\tau-1}^n + (\lambda_\tau^{na}(1 - \delta(\lambda_\tau^{na}, \mu_\tau^n))L)$
10:    $\Lambda_{\tau-B_n}^n \leftarrow \Lambda_{\tau-B_n-1}^n + \lambda_{\tau-B_n}^n L$
11:    $\tau \leftarrow \tau + 1$
12: **end while**

---

3   Performance Evaluation

TPTS is realized in MATLABand its program is run on a server with a 16-GB DDR4 memory and an Intel Xeon CPU at 2.0 GHz. We adopt real-life tasks, prices of power grid, and green energy to evaluate TPTS. Figure 2 shows task arriving rates of three applications (types 1, 2 and 3) in Google cluster [12] on May 10, 2011. Besides, $L = 5$, $B_1 = 3$, $B_2 = 4$, and $B_3 = 5$. We adopt prices of power grid on May 10, 2011 in New York state. Following [13], $\varpi = 5$ (MWH), $\bar{P}_0^1 = 200$ (W), $\bar{P}_0^2 = 100$ (W), $\bar{P}_0^3 = 50$ (W), $\bar{P}_1^1 = 400$ (W), $\bar{P}_1^2 = 200$

(W), $\bar{P}_1^3 = 100$ (W), $\gamma = 1.2$, $\sigma_1 = 0.05$ tasks/minute, $\sigma_2 = 0.1$ tasks/minute, and $\sigma_3 = 0.2$ tasks/minute. In addition, $C_1 = 12$, $C_2 = 25$, $C_3 = 50$, $\Omega_1 = 3 \times 10^6$, $\Omega_2 = 1.5 \times 10^6$, and $\Omega_3 = 3 \times 10^6$. The execution time of each task is sampled in $(0, L)$. Following [3,14], VM execution prices are sampled in $(0.24, 0.48)$, $(0.16, 0.32)$, and $(0.08, 0.16)$, respectively. In this way, $\theta_{\tau+b}^n$ is obtained.

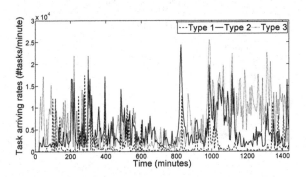

Fig. 2. Real-life tasks of three applications [12].

We further compare TPTS with several state-of-the-art algorithms [15–17] with respect to throughput and profit of the GDC.

1. A1, similar to the cheap-first scheduling algorithm in [15], schedules tasks to GDC according to ranking of prices of power grid within task' delay constraints. Therefore, the most tasks are executed in the interval when the price of power grid is the lowest, while the least tasks are executed in the interval when the price of power grid is the highest.
2. A2 in [16] allocates all delay-constrained tasks to GDC and aims to maximize its profit while meeting tasks' delay constraints. However, it ignores dynamic differences in prices of power grid, and green energy within tasks' delay constraints, and tasks are scheduled immediately in their arriving interval.
3. A3, which is temporal request scheduling algorithm in [17], considers dynamic variations of electricity prices, and green energy. It intelligently schedules tasks to GDC within task' delay constraints. However, it only considers a single application and ignores resource competition among multiple applications, and just aims to minimize the grid energy cost of GDC.

Figure 3 shows the cumulative throughput of TPTS, A1–A3. The cumulative throughput in τ is the sum of tasks scheduled from τ to $\tau+\mathbf{1}$. For example, the cumulative throughput of application 2 in τ is the sum of tasks scheduled from τ to $\tau+B_2$. It is shown the cumulative throughput of TPTS is greater than those of A1–A3 by 77.4%, 64.3% and 81%, respectively. The reason is that A1–A3 all have to selectively execute tasks, and some of them have to be rejected due to the energy limit of the GDC.

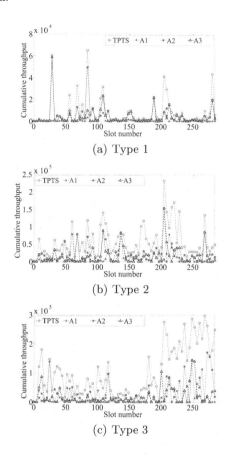

Fig. 3. Cumulative throughput of TPTS, A1–A3.

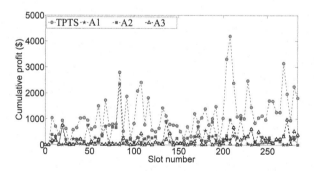

Fig. 4. Cumulative profits of TPTS, A1–A3.

Figure 4 shows cumulative profits of TPTS, A1–A3, respectively. To meet performance requirements of tasks, a service level agreement is specified to define penalty for each rejected task [18]. Therefore, rejected tasks bring the penalty to the GDC provider. Typically, ϑ_τ^n is greater than the maximum profit of each task from τ to $\tau + B_n$. Υ_τ^n denotes the profit brought by each task of application n in τ. Therefore, $\vartheta_\tau^n = max_{i \in \{0,1,...,\daleth\}}(\Upsilon_{\tau+i}^n)$. Similar to Fig. 3, the cumulative profit in τ is the difference between the revenue brought by executed tasks of all applications (f_1), and the power grid energy cost (f_2) from τ to $\tau + \daleth$. Figure 4 shows that compared with A1–A3, the cumulative profit of TPTS is increased dramatically. The reason is that TPTS intelligently executes more tasks in GDC by jointly utilizing dynamic differences in prices of power grid, revenue, and green energy within tasks' delay constraints. Besides, the average execution time of SCP is 3.04 s, which is much less than the length of each interval (5 min), and therefore negligible.

4   Conclusion

The growth of applications deployed in large-scale green data centers (GDCs) significantly increases their energy consumption. GDCs aim to maximize their profit by cost-effectively executing tasks such that their delay constraints are met. The dynamic differences in prices of power grid, revenue, and green energy within tasks' delay constraints make it challenging to maximize the profit of a GDC while strictly meeting delay constraints of tasks. To realize it, a Temporal Scheduling for Profit Maximization (TPTS) algorithm is proposed to consider such dynamic differences, and intelligently schedule tasks to GDCs within their delay constraints. In each interval, a constrained profit maximization problem is formulated and solved by a novel Simulated-annealing-based Chaotic Particle swarm optimization (SCP). Simulation experiments with realistic data are given to prove that compared with several state-of-the-art scheduling algorithms, TPTS significantly improves profit and throughput without violating delay constraints of tasks of all applications.

Acknowledgment. This work was supported in part by the National Natural Science Foundation of China (NSFC) under Grants 61802015 and 61703011, in part by the Major Science and Technology Program for Water Pollution Control and Treatment of China under Grant 2018ZX07111005, and in part by the National Defense Pre-Research Foundation of China under Grants 41401020401 and 41401050102.

References

1. Toosi, A.N., Vanmechelen, K., Ramamohanarao, K., Buyya, R.: Revenue maximization with optimal capacity control in infrastructure as a service cloud markets. IEEE Trans. Cloud Comput. **3**(3), 261–274 (2015)
2. Data Center Energy Use in U.S. http://www.eia.gov/
3. Yuan, H., Bi, J., Tan, W., Zhou, M., Li, B.H., Li, J.: TTSA: an effective scheduling approach for delay bounded tasks in hybrid clouds. IEEE Trans. Cybern. **47**(11), 3658–3668 (2016)
4. Luo, J., Rao, L., Liu, X.: Spatio-temporal load balancing for energy cost optimization in distributed internet data centers. IEEE Trans. Cloud Comput. **3**(3), 387–397 (2015)

5. Rao, L., Liu, X., Xie, L., Pang, Z.: Hedging against uncertainty: a tale of internet data center operations under smart grid environment. IEEE Trans. Smart Grid **2**(3), 555–563 (2011)
6. Zats, D., Das, T., Mohan, P., Borthakur, D., Katz, R.: Detail: reducing the flow completion time tail in datacenter networks. Proc. ACM SIGCOMM **2012**, 139–150 (2012)
7. Krebs, R., Schneider, P., Herbst, N.: Optimization method for request admission control to guarantee performance isolation. In: Proceedings of 2nd International Workshop on Hot Topics in Cloud Service Scalability, pp. 4:1–4:8 (2014)
8. Dabbagh, M., Hamdaoui, B., Guizani, M., Rayes, A.: Energy-efficient resource allocation and provisioning framework for cloud data centers. IEEE Trans. Netw. Serv. Manag. **12**(3), 377–391 (2015)
9. Zhu, Z., Bi, J., Yuan, H., Chen, Y.: SLA based dynamic virtualized resources provisioning for shared cloud data centers. In: Proceedings of 2011 IEEE International Conference on Cloud Computing, pp. 630–637 (2011)
10. Qureshi, A., Weber, R., Balakrishnan, H., Guttag, J., Maggs, B.: Cutting the electric bill for internet-scale systems. SIGCOMM Comput. Commun. Rev. **39**(4), 123–134 (2009)
11. Meer, K.: Simulated annealing versus metropolis for a TSP instance. Inf. Process. Lett. **104**(6), 216–219 (2007)
12. Zhu, X., Yang, L.T., Chen, H., Wang, J., Yin, S., Liu, X.: Real-time tasks oriented energy-aware scheduling in virtualized clouds. IEEE Trans. Cloud Comput. **2**(2), 168–180 (2014)
13. Ghamkhari, M., Mohsenian-Rad, H.: Energy and performance management of green data centers: a profit maximization approach. IEEE Trans. Smart Grid **4**(2), 1017–1025 (2013)
14. Yuan, H., Bi, J., Tan, W., Li, B.H.: Temporal task scheduling with constrained service delay for profit maximization in hybrid clouds. IEEE Trans. Autom. Sci. Eng. **14**(1), 337–348 (2016)
15. Deng, X., Wu, D., Shen, J., He, J.: Eco-aware online power management and load scheduling for green cloud datacenters. IEEE Syst. J. **10**(1), 78–87 (2016)
16. Zuo, X., Zhang, G., Tan, W.: Self-adaptive learning PSO-based deadline constrained task scheduling for hybrid IaaS cloud. IEEE Trans. Autom. Sci. Eng. **11**(2), 564–573 (2014)
17. Bi, J., Yuan, H., Tan, W., Li, B.H.: TRS: temporal request scheduling with bounded delay assurance in a green cloud data center. Inf. Sci. **360**, 57–72 (2016)
18. Ardagna, D., Panicucci, B., Passacantando, M.: Generalized nash equilibria for the service provisioning problem in cloud systems. IEEE Trans. Serv. Comput. **6**(4), 429–442 (2013)

A Lévy Walk and Firefly Based Multi-Robots Foraging Algorithm

Ouarda Zedadra[1]([✉]), Antonio Guerrieri[2], Hamid Seridi[1], and Giancarlo Fortino[2,3]

[1] LabSTIC, Department of Computer Science, 8 May 1945 University, P.O. Box 401, 24000 Guelma, Algeria
{zedadra.ouarda,seridi.hamid}@univ-guelma.dz
[2] CNR - National Research Council of Italy - Institute for High Performance Computing and Networking (ICAR), Via P. Bucci 7-11C, 87036 Rende, CS, Italy
antonio.guerrieri@icar.cnr.it
[3] DIMES, Università della Calabria, Via P. Bucci, cubo 41c, 87036 Rende, Italy
giancarlo.fortino@unical.it

Abstract. Foraging constitutes one of the main benchmarks in robotic problems. It is known as the act of searching for objects/tokens and, when found, transport them to one or multiple locations. Swarm intelligence based algorithms have been widely used in foraging problem. The ambient light sensors technology in nowadays robots makes easy using and implementing luminous swarm intelligence-based algorithms such as the Firefly and the Glow-worm algorithms. In this paper, we propose a swarm intelligence-based foraging algorithm called *Lévy walk and Firefly Foraging Algorithm (LFFA)* which is a hybridizing of the two algorithms Lévy Walk and Firefly Algorithm. Numerical experiments to test the performances are conducted on the ARGoS robotic simulator.

Keywords: Swarm intelligence · Swarm Robotics · Lévy Walk · Firefly algorithm · LFFA algorithm · Central Place Foraging (CPF) · Multi-Robots Foraging (MRF)

1 Introduction

Swarm Robotics is a new approach to the coordination of large numbers of robots inspired by the observation of social insects [12]. It has emerged as the application of swarm intelligence (SI) to Multi-Robots Systems (MRS). Swarm robotics puts emphases on the physical embodiment of individuals and realistic interactions among the individuals and between the individuals and the environment. It is characterized by the emergence of a synchronized behavior at the system level which emerges despite the individuals being relatively incapable, despite the lack of centralized control and despite the simplicity of interactions [13].

In the taxonomy we proposed in [20], we classified Firefly Algorithm (FF) in the *under-exploration category* because this algorithm is matter in theory but it

© Springer Nature Switzerland AG 2019
R. Montella et al. (Eds.): IDCS 2019, LNCS 11874, pp. 213–222, 2019.
https://doi.org/10.1007/978-3-030-34914-1_21

needs to be applied to several applications before its use in real world ones. The FF algorithm is a luminous SI-based algorithm which uses light to coordinate fireflies. Fireflies emit bioluminescent light to attract their mates or prey. The brighter the glow, the more the attraction. The light intensity is proportional to the associated luminescence quantity called luciferin which attracts other glowworms within the variable neighborhood. The standard Firefly algorithm adopts fixed step length which will result in the algorithm easily getting trapped in the local optima and causing low precision. The exploration rate of FF is very limited. FF is useful for MRS but its real application requires Ambient Light Sensors (ALS) technology. It is important to use sensors on each robot, not only in order to help it to get directionally oriented but also to follow light emitted by robot chief or to help to find the goal easier [5].

Lévy Walks (LW) [10] are the most efficient random walk strategies known to efficiently search spaces when targets are sparsely distributed. Such search patterns have a characteristic length scale.

In this work, we consider multi-robot foraging in an unknown environment. The goal is to collect as much as possible targets in a minimum amount of time (foraging time). We propose in this paper a Lévy Walk and Firefly-based foraging algorithm. The two algorithms seem to be complementary since LW allows global search and FF allows local search. With a fine tuning between the two algorithms efficient and reliable foraging strategy could be reached. The proposed algorithm is used to: (1) decrease the super-diffusive behavior of LW by using FF for exploitation (*local exploration* later in the proposed algorithm), (2) increase the exploration rate of FF by using LW (*global exploration* later in the proposed algorithm). Performances were tested numerically using the ARGoS simulator [11]. Some enhancements were already realized on LW algorithm in our previous work [21].

The remainder of this paper is organized as follows: In Sect. 2, we present related works. In Sect. 3 we present the Finite State Machine (FSM) of the proposed LFFA algorithm. In Sect. 4 we present the experimental analysis of LFFA and we compare it to the original FF. Finally, we conclude and present some perspectives in Sect. 5.

2   Related Works

In the literature, Lévy Walk has been used for several robotic search problems. Here, we present some relevant works related to such algorithm. Lenagh and Dasgupta [8] propose a Lévy looped search algorithm to locate mobile targets with a swarm of non-interacting robots. Each searcher returns to its initial position by replacing straight ballistic segments with loops. The length of each loop was sampled from a power-law distribution. Fioriti et al. [2] extend the Levy flight to one moving target positioned according to a radial probability density function, considering also the detection range, i.e. the resolution of an onboard sensor. Numerical simulations confirm the Levy flight superiority compared to the random walk if the search is in the intermediate range of the sensor resolution. Katada et al. [6] propose a three-layered subsumption architecture in order to investigate the effect of the step size of the random walk and the number of robots on a target detection problem. Once a target is detected, robots communicate with a base station via intermediate relay robots due to the multi-hop transmission of wireless communication. A series of real experiments were conducted which confirm that variable step size according to a Lévy probability distribution is useful for an exploration strategy. Further works on Lévy Walk could be found in the mini-review by Krivonosov et al. [7], in which authors survey the state of the field and outline further perspectives.

Firefly has also been used for various robotic search problems and its related works include the papers in the following: Palmieri and Marano proposed in [9] a Discrete Firefly Algorithm (DFA) for mine disarming tasks in an unknown area. The proposed algorithm combines the foraging behavior of colonies of ant [1] and the Firefly algorithm. The first one is used to disperse robots in order to explore regions and the second one is used once a mine is detected to attract other robots in the neighborhood in order to cooperate in disarming the mine itself. Robots use direct communication through broadcast to transmit the location of the detected mine to neighbors in its wireless range. Sutantyo et al. [15] proposed a multi-robot searching algorithm based on a combination of a Lévy walk and an artificial potential field inducing repulsion among robots. Results for up to twenty robots showed that the repulsion increases search efficiency in terms of search time. Sutantyo et al. [14] propose a bio-inspired algorithm for underwater search scenarios. They improve Lévy flight performances through a proposed adaptation strategy based on Firefly Optimization algorithm (FO). Fujisawa and Dobata [3] proposed a group Lévy foraging with an artificial pheromone communication between robots. Each robot had a tank filled with a pheromone (alcohol) which was sprayed around by a micropump. Rovers also carried alcohol and touch sensors and their motion was controlled by a program which took into account the local pheromone concentration.

Both LW and FF algorithms have been hybridized with other meta-heuristics for Numerical Optimization. In [18] Yang and Deb propose a hybrid optimization algorithm called Eagle Strategy which uses the Lévy walk in global search and Firefly in local search for stochastic optimization. Eagle perform the Lévy Walk in the whole domain. Once it finds a prey it changes to local search using the standard Firefly algorithm [17]. Eagle Strategy efficiency is tested on various mathematical functions. Hassanzadeh and Kanan [4] proposed a fuzzy-based FF to increase the exploration and improve the global search of the FF. Yu et al. [19] propose a variable step size Firefly algorithm which adopts a variable step size to standard FF algorithm to solve numerical problems. The proposed algorithm uses a dynamic strategy to adjust the step α in the search process, thus to balance the ability between exploration and exploitation. Experiments were conducted on benchmark functions. FF algorithm uses a full attraction model, which may cause oscillations during the search process and high computational time complexity [16]. To overcome this problem, Wang et al. [16] propose a FF algorithm with neighborhood attraction model inspired by $k - neighborhood$ concept. Each firefly is attracted by brighter fireflies selected from a predefined neighborhood rather than those from the entire population. Experiments were also conducted on benchmark functions.

According to literature works presented in this Section, the only works which use a hybridization of LW and FF algorithms are [14] and [18]. In [14], the random motion element of the FO algorithm is replaced with a random number from the Lévy distribution generator. It was applied to underwater multi-robot exploration problem. In [18], LW is used in global search and FF for local search. Here, it was applied to stochastic optimization.

3   The Proposed Lévy Walk and Firefly Foraging Algorithm (LFFA)

On the basis of algorithms proposed in [14] and [18], we propose here a new foraging algorithm called Lévy Walk and Firefly Foraging Algorithm (LFFA) in which we use walking robots. Some enhancements have been considered in both Lévy Walk and Firefly algorithms in order to increase the performance of the search process. The proposed LFFA algorithm uses: (1) global search using LW, (2) local search using also LW, (3) attraction model using FF each time a target is found. We present in this Section the Finite State Machine (FSM) of the proposed LFFA algorithm (see Fig. 1).

3.1   The Finite State Machine of LFFA Robots and the Pseudo Code of the Different States

According to their sensors input, robots switch between six elementary states: *Global search* (in the composite state *Global exploration*), *Local search* (in the composite state *Local exploration*), *Follow robot light* (in the composite state *Following*), *Follow home light* (in the composite state *Homing*), *Return to Cluster* (in the composite state *Return to cluster*) and *Avoidance* which is accessible from all the states whenever an obstacle or robot are found. The FSM of LFFA robots behavior is given in Fig. 1. Each state is explained as follows:

– **Global search:** each robot explores the search space using random Lévy Walk strategy with long step size. This latter, allows robots to explore the whole search space and to reach new and distant areas. If a target is found, it switches to *Local search* state, else if a light is detected, the robot switches to *Following State follow Robot Light*, else if an obstacle or another robot are located, the robot switches to *Avoidance* state.
– **Local search:** each robot explores the current area using also random Lévy Walk strategy but with small step size. For a fixed time T, the robot executes an intensive search in the current area. When a target is found, the robot picks it and increases its light intensity (*satisfaction parameter*) in order to attract robots in its neighborhood. If the robot reaches its capacity of transport C, it switches to *Follow home light* state. Finally, if $T = 0$ and $satisfaction = 0$ the robot switches to *Global search*.

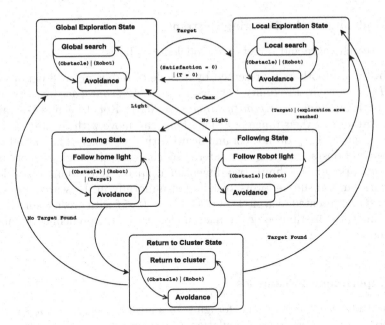

Fig. 1. FSM of LFFA robots

- **Follow home light:** the robot returns home on beacons. It follows the light emitted by home. When the home is reached, it deposits targets and switches to *Return to Cluster* state.
- **Follow robot light:** when a robot with light intensity = 0 detects light in its neighborhood, it turns towards that light source and walks forward until it encounters a target or reaches the light source, it switches then to *Local search* state. If no target light is detected or no target is found, the robot switches to *Global search*.
- **Return to Cluster:** from home, the robot turns with 180° and walks straight forward until a target is found, it switches then to *Local search* state, else it switches to *Avoidance* state if an obstacle or a robot are encountered. If no target is found it switches to *Global search* state.
- **Avoidance:** according to its proximity sensors, the robot turns some degrees in the opposite direction of the encountered obstacle. Then it returns to the last activated state.

4   Experimental Analysis

This Section is divided into three parts: in Sect. 4.1 we present the modeling of the different system components which are robots, search space, and targets; in Sect. 4.2 we propose a set of scenarios to test the performance of the LFFA algorithm; and in Sect. 4.3 we present, compare and discuss the results obtained by LFFA and FF algorithms.

4.1 Modeling of the Foraging System

Robots, search space and targets are modeled as follows:

- **Robots:** are footbots represented by a circle of radius $r_R = 8$ cm, a height of $H_R = 15$ cm, Proximity Sensors $PS_R = 12\,frontal\,sensor$, Proximity Sensor Ring Range $ProximityRange_R = 0.3f$. Robots can sense targets and obstacles in their range of vision. They can move with constant velocity $v = 80$ cm/s. They do not communicate with each other. They avoid other robots and obstacles when encountered by changing the angle of motion.
- **Search space:** is a finite two-dimensional space. It contains obstacles in rectangular and square forms, distributed uniformly in the search space.
- **Target:** represented by a circle of radius $r_t = 0.05f$ with green color. Targets are uniformly distributed or grouped in clusters with a predefined number of targets.

4.2 Experimental Scenarios

In this study, we focus on the foraging of multiple targets by a swarm of nb_Rrobots. The experimental simulation is implemented in the multi-physics robot simulator ARGoS [11] which is able to simulate efficiently large-scale swarms of robots of any kind. We perform several computer simulations to test the performance of the proposed algorithm varying several criteria (number of robots, the capacity of robots). Results of the *LFFA algorithm* are compared with those obtained by *FF* algorithm.

Table 1 illustrates the realized simulation scenarios. Each simulation is run for 480 s and the obstacle density in all simulations is 10%. Data presented here are representative of 50 simulation executions.

Table 1. Parameters of simulation scenarios

Parameter	Value
Scenario 1: *increasing robots number*	
Robots number	80–6400
Target distribution	*clustered*
Targets number	1000
Clusters number	10
Environment size	240 m × 240 m
Scenario 2: *varying capacity of robots*	
Robots number	80
Robot capacity	1–16
Target distribution	*clustered*
Targets number	2000
Clusters number	10
Environment size	120 m × 120 m

Scenario 1 is used to test the influence of increasing the number of robots on the foraging time (in seconds). Thus, we increase robots number from *800 robots to 6400 robots*. While Scenario 2 is used to test the performances of the two algorithms when varying robot capacity. Thus, we vary the capacity from 1 to 16. The capacity is the number of targets transported by a robot in one trip. We used a very simple strategy in the states *Homing* (follow light emitted by the base for homing) and the *Return to Cluster* (follow the direction of the cluster stored before depositing targets).

4.3   Results and Discussion

1. **Results of scenario 1:** The foraging time decreases each time we increase the number of robots (see Table 2 and Fig. 2). With the parameters that have been considered in scenario 1 (see Table 1) over 6400 robots, the foraging time tends to be stable. The proposed algorithm overcomes the original one. Since targets are clustered, it's enough that a robot finds a target, then the attraction process (increasing light intensity) will attract as much as possible neighboring robots. This will increase collected targets, decrease time spent in random walk, and decrease foraging time. In FF algorithm, the foraging time is important in all the simulations. It decreases when increasing the number of robots but it is still important due to the random walk of robots.

Table 2. Foraging time when increasing robots number (scenario 1)

Number of robots	800	1600	3200	6400
Foraging Time in LFFA	*20,71*	*7,51*	*3,48*	*1,62*
Foraging Time in FF	78,91	67,45	52,11	33,5

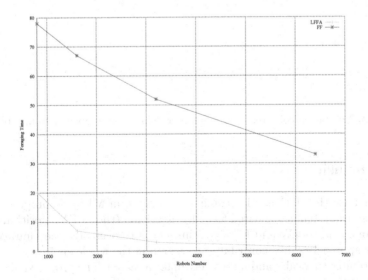

Fig. 2. Foraging time when increasing number of robots from 800 to 6400

2. **Results of scenario 2:** The number of collected targets increases with the increasing of the robot capacity (see Table 3 and Fig. 3). The increase in the number of collected targets is faster in the LFFA algorithm rather than in the FF one. The reason is that the robot benefits of the already found cluster to collect its maximum capacity, which decreases the time spent in homing and returning to cluster when the capacity of the robot is equal to 1. The difference between the two algorithms increases with the increase in capacity and LFFA always gives the best results.

Table 3. Total number of targets when increasing robot capacity (scenario 2)

Robot capcity	1	4	8	16
Total Number of targets in LFFA	*115,4*	*384,3*	*849,7*	*1255,5*
Total Number of targets in FF	15,6	39,6	147,6	234,6

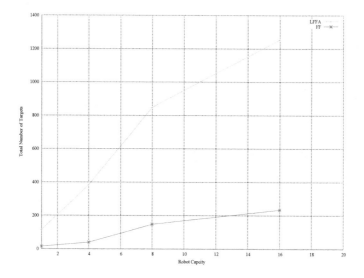

Fig. 3. Number of collected food when increasing robot' capacity from 1 to 16

5 Conclusion

As to enhance the efficiency in search and foraging in MRS, we propose in this paper a swarm intelligence based foraging algorithm (the LFFA algorithm). This algorithm combines LW and FF algorithms so as to overcome the limitations of both the approaches. LW contributes to search in the whole environment, while FF contributes to locally and intensively make a search. The proposed algorithm is simple and effective, and it overcomes in quantitative results the original FF.

In the future, we intend to consider some other scenarios (e.g.: increasing size of the environment, varying density of obstacles) and improve the algorithm with particular energy management behaviors as in [22]. Also, the low-level obstacle avoidance model used can deviate robots from rich areas, and it may influence the correct behavior of the LW algorithm. In this direction, we aim to study its effect and improve it so to maintain the current walk direction of a robot.

References

1. De Rango, F., Palmieri, N.: A swarm-based robot team coordination protocol for mine detection and unknown space discovery. In: 2012 8th International Wireless Communications and Mobile Computing Conference (IWCMC), pp. 703–708. IEEE, August 2012. https://doi.org/10.1109/IWCMC.2012.6314290
2. Fioriti, V., Fratichini, F., Chiesa, S., Moriconi, C.: Levy foraging in a dynamic environment - extending the Levy search. Int. J. Adv. Robot. Syst. 12(7), 98 (2015). https://doi.org/10.5772/60414
3. Fujisawa, R., Dobata, S.: Lévy walk enhances efficiency of group foraging in pheromone-communicating swarm robots. In: Proceedings of the 2013 IEEE/SICE International Symposium on System Integration, pp. 808–813. IEEE, December 2013. https://doi.org/10.1109/SII.2013.6776760
4. Hassanzadeh, T., Kanan, H.R.: Fuzzy FA: a modified firefly algorithm. Appl. Artif. Intell. 28(1), 47–65 (2014). https://doi.org/10.1080/08839514.2014.862773
5. Iureva, R.A., Maslennikov, O.S., Komarov, I.I.: Multiagent robotic systems' ambient light sensor. 10231, 102311J (2017). https://doi.org/10.1117/12.2265042
6. Katada, Y., Nishiguchi, A., Moriwaki, K., Watakabe, R.: Swarm robotic network using Lévy flight in target detection problem. Artif. Life Robot. 21(3), 295–301 (2016). https://doi.org/10.1007/s10015-016-0298-1
7. Krivonosov, M., Denisov, S., Zaburdaev, V.: Lévy robotics, pp. 1–6 (2016). http://arxiv.org/abs/1612.03997
8. Lenagh, W., Dasgupta, P.: Levy distributed search behaviors for mobile target locating and tracking. In: Proceedings of the 19th Annual Conference on Behavior Representation in Modeling and Simulation, pp. 103–109 (2010)
9. Palmieri, N., Marano, S.: Discrete firefly algorithm for recruiting task in a swarm of robots. In: Yang, X.-S. (ed.) Nature-Inspired Computation in Engineering. SCI, vol. 637, pp. 133–150. Springer, Cham (2016). https://doi.org/10.1007/978-3-319-30235-5_7
10. Pina-Garcia, C.A., Gu, D., Hu, H.: A composite random walk for facing environmental uncertainty and reduced perceptual capabilities. In: Jeschke, S., Liu, H., Schilberg, D. (eds.) ICIRA 2011. LNCS (LNAI), vol. 7101, pp. 620–629. Springer, Heidelberg (2011). https://doi.org/10.1007/978-3-642-25486-4_62
11. Pinciroli, C., et al.: ARGoS: a modular, parallel, multi-engine simulator for multi-robot systems. Swarm Intell. 6(4), 271–295 (2012). https://doi.org/10.1007/s11721-012-0072-5
12. Şahin, E., Spears, W.M. (eds.): SR 2004. LNCS, vol. 3342. Springer, Heidelberg (2005). https://doi.org/10.1007/b105069
13. Şahin, E., Girgin, S., Bayindir, L., Turgut, A.E.: Swarm robotics. In: Blum, C., Merkle, D. (eds.) Swarm Intelligence. Natural Computing Series, pp. 87–100. Springer, Heidelberg (2008). https://doi.org/10.1007/978-3-540-74089-6_3

14. Sutantyo, D., Levi, P., Moslinger, C., Read, M.: Collective-adaptive Lévy flight for underwater multi-robot exploration. In: 2013 IEEE International Conference on Mechatronics and Automation, pp. 456–462. IEEE, August 2013. https://doi.org/10.1109/ICMA.2013.6617961

15. Sutantyo, D.K., Kernbach, S., Levi, P., Nepomnyashchikh, V.A.: Multi-robot searching algorithm using Lévy flight and artificial potential field. In: 2010 IEEE Safety Security and Rescue Robotics, pp. 1–6. IEEE, July 2010. https://doi.org/10.1109/SSRR.2010.5981560

16. Wang, H., et al.: Firefly algorithm with neighborhood attraction. Inf. Sci. **382–383**, 374–387 (2017). https://doi.org/10.1016/j.ins.2016.12.024

17. Yang, X.-S.: Firefly algorithms for multimodal optimization. In: Watanabe, O., Zeugmann, T. (eds.) SAGA 2009. LNCS, vol. 5792, pp. 169–178. Springer, Heidelberg (2009). https://doi.org/10.1007/978-3-642-04944-6_14

18. Yang, X.S., Deb, S.: Eagle strategy using Lévy walk and firefly algorithms for stochastic optimization. Stud. Comput. Intell. **284**, 101–111 (2010). https://doi.org/10.1007/978-3-642-12538-6_9

19. Yu, S., Zhu, S., Ma, Y., Mao, D.: A variable step size firefly algorithm for numerical optimization. Appl. Math. Comput. **263**, 214–220 (2015). https://doi.org/10.1016/j.amc.2015.04.065

20. Zedadra, O., Guerrieri, A., Jouandeau, N., Spezzano, G., Seridi, H., Fortino, G.: Swarm intelligence-based algorithms within IoT-based systems: a review. J. Parallel Distrib. Comput. **122**, 173–187 (2018). https://doi.org/10.1016/j.jpdc.2018.08.007

21. Zedadra, O., Idiri, M., Jouandeau, N., Seridi, H., Fortino, G.: Lévy walk-based search strategy: application to destructive foraging. In: Proceedings of the 2018 13th International Symposium on Programming and Systems, ISPS 2018, May 1945, pp. 1–5 (2018). https://doi.org/10.1109/ISPS.2018.8379010

22. Zedadra, O., Seridi, H., Jouandeau, N., Fortino, G.: An energy-aware algorithm for large scale foraging systems. Scalable Comput. **16**(4), 449–466 (2015). https://doi.org/10.12694/scpe.v16i4.1133

An Overview of Wireless Indoor Positioning Systems: Techniques, Security, and Countermeasures

Mouna S. Chebli[(⊠)], Heba Mohammad, and Khalifa Al Amer

Higher Colleges of Technology, Abu Dhabi, UAE
{mshebli,hmohammad,kal-amer}@hct.ac.ae

Abstract. The interest in Indoor position systems (IPSs) had been widely increased recently, due to technological advancement. IPSs provide users with location information of various objects inside big buildings, typically using a mobile device. Different wireless technologies are available to provide location service such RF, Wi-Fi, Bluetooth, Visible Light Communication (VLC), etc. IPSs mainly determine the position by analyzing sensory information which is collected by mobile device continuously on real time, unless the user turned off the service. Various services and security issues had been associated with IPSs. Secure positioning become more important and crucial to the success of the delivered service. Location service network that based on off-air signal measurement is susceptible to numerous attacks (e.g. wormhole, sinkhole and Sybil attacks). This paper aims to provide an integrated view of IPSs, technologies and associated security threats that face such positioning systems. The paper compares different wireless indoor position technologies, explore potential attacks, and evaluate IPS protection mechanism.

Keywords: Indoor positioning · Secure localization · WSN security

1 Introduction

Nowadays, the widespread of mobile devices allowed indoor positioning systems to receive greater attention [1]. IPSs have successfully integrated in different areas including health, assets tracking, child safety [2] and industry [3]. The systems detect the location of objects or humans in closed environment where satellite signals are unavailable or inaccurate. Moreover, GPS cannot be used for indoor positioning due to signal scattering, attenuation, and for the wide marginal error which can be bigger than the space itself. IPSs use two different nodes, the mobile-node and anchor-node. The anchor-nodes give reference points to detect location (e.g. Access Point) [4]. Implementing IPSs using RF can reduce the cost by reusing the existing network infrastructure. If the cost and deployment speed are the main consideration, then it is better to use the existing WLAN infrastructure. However, RFID and Bluetooth IPSs have better precision and accuracy [5]. Hybrid infrastructure can be used to improve the quality of the system [6].

© Springer Nature Switzerland AG 2019
R. Montella et al. (Eds.): IDCS 2019, LNCS 11874, pp. 223–233, 2019.
https://doi.org/10.1007/978-3-030-34914-1_22

Wireless signals weaken while traveling over space, IPSs use different methods to estimate nodes location. Received Signal Strengths (**RSS**) method determines distance between transmitter and receiver by evaluating signal strength at receiving point. RSS based localization is susceptible to localization error caused by low-cost antenna which is used by adversary [7], statistical-test of variance is proposed to overcome this issue. **Proximate** method uses grid of base stations with pre-defined location. When a mobile-node in range of known base-station, then the location will be approximated. If mobile-node is in range of multiple base-stations, then the strongest signal will be considered. **Time of arrival (TOA)** method calculates the propagation time of a radio waves from one transmitter to another receiver, it provides a circle of possible location in two-dimensional space. The center of the circle is the base station, and the radius is the calculated distance [8], as shown in (Fig. 1). This technique requires accurate knowledge of transmission time and confirm that all base stations and mobile nodes are accurately synchronized with precise timing source [9]. **Time Difference of Arrival (TDOA)** method measures the difference time of arrival of the signal emitted by multiple base stations [10] (see Fig. 2). Three base stations create two TDOAs (L1 and L2), the intersection points between L1 and L2 estimates the location of the mobile-node. TDOA needs correct time reference between the measuring units.

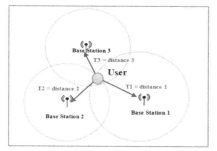

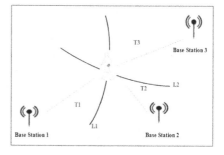

Fig. 1. Time of arrival concept (TOA)   **Fig. 2.** Time difference of arrival concept

Angle of Arrival-AOA method determines the direction of RF signal when emitting from the antenna, this requires at least two angles to detect location. AOA is more complex and needs more expensive hardware. **Fingerprinting** technique determines the location by analyzing scene and compare it with the existing database. It consists of two stages: the first stage, offline stage, survey the area to collect location features and build the matching database. Location features include coordinates, and signals strength from adjacent base station. The second stage, online stage, will compare the current signal features with the database. There are several fingerprinting algorithms including: probabilistic methods, support vector machine (SVM), neural networks, k-nearest-neighbor (kNN), and smallest M-vertex polygon (SMP) [2].

IPS had been discussed by the research community from different perspectives. For instance, some researchers described the IPS in terms of implementation technologies and use, such as research paper [3, 16]. While [11] presented the IPSs from the performance perspective by comparing different performance measurements such as:

accuracy, electricity consumption and coverage range. Visible LED Lighting IPSs have great potential in future due to its low cost, security and high throughput. The research paper [12] surveyed VLC IPSs and discussed systems characteristics, positioning algorithms, and performance. However, few scholars highlighted the security threats and countermeasure aspects in indoor positing systems. Therefore, this paper aims to fill this gap by providing an integrated view of IPS from the security perspective.

2 IPS Network Infrastructure

This section will give a brief introduction of different IPS network infrastructures:

RFID IPS requires micro-circuit, antenna, and RFID reader, system can be passive or active [13]. Passive systems are reflectors. Therefore, it consumes less power than active, and does not require a power source in the mobile node. Active RFID tags are transceiver, it transmits its identification information and signal received from the reader [14]. RFID gives better accuracy and higher precision, it can be 50% precise in the distance of 1 m and accurate for a range less than 2 m. However, it is more complex and requires dense environment of RFID devices.

UWB uses sub-nanosecond radio pulses to send data in a wide range of bandwidth. It can use limited transmission power as restricted by FCC. This technology can be classified as: (1) Impulse Radio (IR-UWB) or (2) carrier-based UWB system. The first system sends narrow pulses with smooth transition (base-band). The second system, carrier based UWB is more complex design, although it is more flexible in selecting frequency [15]. UWB measures the node position using TDOA of the radio frequency signals [16].

Bluetooth IPSs can use two different approaches in defining the position. The first approach is based on proximity and RSS ranging techniques, the second approach is based on applying geometric calculation [5]. Although, geometric calculation is more accurate, it is considered more complex and prone to calculation errors. The low cost of Bluetooth chipset can reduce the price of positioning system implementation.

Visible Light Communication (VLC) is a LED-based IPSs that use visible light signals to transmit data, the installed LED-lamps on the ceiling will act as anchor nodes. VLC uses IEEE 802.15.7 standard and can give highly accurate location with a minimum calculation error [17]. This method found to be the most appropriate one [18]. In the system design, each LED-light will get unique address which represent its coordinate and the unique ID. The receiving nodes will forward the LED-ID to application service to determine location. VLC IPS can use proximate, triangulation or fingerprinting for positioning. The technology has several advantages: it is cost effective due to low energy consumption, longer life expectancy, and reusing the existing lighting system in the building. It does not produce electromagnetic interference, and therefore it is suitable where RF signal is prohibited, VLC is more secure as light cannot penetrate walls, and thus independent systems can be installed in different rooms smoothly. However, the technology is susceptible to different difficulties including: ambient Light, time measurement error, flickering and lens distortion [19]. Moreover, synchronization between LED-lights anchor nodes and mobile devices is very difficult to achieve [20].

WLAN IPSs which reuse the existing network infrastructure will reduce cost, however, WLAN IPS that is based on RSSI localization technique suffer from instability of the signal strength, therefore this system does not have high accuracy and precision. The accuracy of WLAN positioning system that utilizing RSS technique is approximately 1 to 5 m and the precision about 50% in 2 m [5]. Two approaches proposed to reduce errors: mono-objective and multi-objective approaches, both are based on variable neighbor search [6].

ZigBee defines higher level communication protocols that delivers network, security, and application support services operating on top of 802.15.4 standard for personal area network [21]. It is designed for small scale devices that require reliable wireless communication with low data transmission rate and low power consumption. ZigBee network consists of three types of devices coordinator, router, and end nodes [22]. ZigBee positioning systems are simple and operate using low power technology [23].

3 Secure Localization Services

Security is a crucial element when developing any information system, the next section discusses common attacks that would endanger IPSs, available countermeasures and the ability of localization algorithms to defeat the discussed threats.

3.1 Common Attacks

1. **False Node:** the insertion of additional node to the system. It can be used to propagate fake information or to prevent processing of legitimate signals.
2. **Spoofing:** a dishonest node impersonates the identity of legitimate base-station, this would persuade other nodes to believe that it is in a different location. Adversary can spoof management and control frame which can have huge impact on the network [24]. Spoofing can be the first step of DoS or injection attack.
3. **Sinkhole:** is an insider attack where malicious node tries to attract all neighboring node to establish connection with it, then it will attract all traffic from one area [25].
4. **Sybil:** attacker obtains several nodes identities, then use these identities to deceive other nodes. The compromised nodes identities can be replicated to several locations in the network and cause erroneous information [26].
5. **Replay:** involves storing the packets to re-sending then late, this cause the neighboring nodes to believe that the packet is authentic as it is a copy of the original. In this attack, the adversary first will jam the transmission between sender and receiver and will replay the packets in the future and claim that he is the sender [27].
6. **Wormholes:** malicious node records packet at one side of the network and re-transmit and replicate it by another malicious node on the side of the network, this can be done by adding virtual tunnel which has a low latency link [28].
7. **Hello flood:** the malicious node floods the network with hello message with increased power, and that will confuse the routine protocol and the victim node will try to refer to the adversary for localization service [28].

8. **Denial of Service:** DOS attack tries to stop the service by flooding the network with traffics that consume all available resources and deny legitimate nodes from benefit from the service. The attacker can inject bogus broadcast packet and force network nodes to complete expensive signature verification or packet forwarding broadcast authentication [29] which will result denying the service. DOS can occur at any layer of network model as illustrated in Table 1.

Table 1. Denial-of-Service attack at each layer of the network

Layer	Attack
Application	Reprogramming attack
Transport	Desynchronization attacks - Flooding Attacks
Network	Spoofing, routing-control traffic or clustering messages, replaying and homing
Datalink	Collision, exhaustion and unfairness attacks
Physical	Packet jamming and Anchor-Node tempering

3.2 Security Countermeasure

Security Through Cryptography: Malicious nodes can claim the identity of another legitimate entity and then alters the packet contents, this can be eliminated using cryptography and authentication. However, cryptography can only protect from external attacks and cannot defeat dishonest node that sends wrong positioning data. In addition, crypto-system requires additional resources, e.g. better processing speed and larger memory, and most of sensory devices has limited computational power. Therefore, most of secure localization algorithms use non-cryptographic security mechanism [30].

Misbehavior Detection and Blocking: This countermeasure technique involves monitoring nodes behavior over time to decide whether to trust them or not. Any information gathered from untrusted source will be ignored accordingly. To detect malicious node, Liu et al. [31] proposed two different methods. Method 1 compares the estimated distance of the beacon nodes with the average estimated distance of the signal (e.g., AoA, TDoA). If the distance between them is larger than the maximum distance error, then the received beacon is malicious. Method 2 can protect against replay attack and sinkhole, by introducing the idea that malicious beacon will need more time. Mainly, it examines the Round-Trip Time (RTT) between two neighbor nodes and try to detect if it differs significantly from the (RTT) range derived from monitoring network behavior. DRBT [32] proposed blocking untrusted nodes by allowing each base station to monitor the area and contribute in building trust table.

Detecting Location Using Statistical Method: Every anchor node has a specific location in the grid of cells. To determine the location of mobile-node, neighboring anchor-nodes can vote for the location, then the center of the most voted cell can be used as location. If malicious node sends a forgery data, it can be detected by comparing it with the context of the other cells. Another statistical method is using

Minimum Mean Squared Estimation (MMSE) [33]. This will verify if the estimated position is derived from consistent reference. If inconsistent sensor detected it will be revoked, and the node position will be calculated over again. This process will be repeated until all inconsistent nodes revoked. RRB-ScLoc proposed secure localization based on weighted square [34].

Counter Measure Hello-Flood Attack: Anchor nodes at wireless positioning networks are required to broadcast hello message to announce themselves to neighboring nodes. Attacker might inject the network with false hello packets, there are some methods to protect from hello flood attack including multi-path and multi based station data forwarding as described in [35], in this technique each node maintains a number of secret keys which can be used to transmit data to several routes. Another algorithm proposed an enhanced method to protect from Hello flood attack using client puzzle key. This will use a number that constitute a puzzle key, and it will be used to verify the validity of a node. The puzzle key difficulty will be increased when the node sends larger number of hello message (Puzzle difficulty $\propto$ Number of hello messages). Therefore, the node that send a fewer number of hello messages, will be processed first [36].

3.3   Secure Localization Algorithms

This section will discuss different secure localization algorithms.

SeRLoc [37]: Secure range independent localization for wireless sensor networks proposed by Lazos and Poovendran. SeRLoc uses two types of nodes mobile nodes (N) and Locators (L). Locators use omnidirectional antenna and mobile nodes can get location by analyzing signal emitted from locators. Locator propagates its coordinate and the angels of the antenna boundary line. Adversary needs to impersonate multiple beacons to compromise the system. SeRLoc is range-free and distributer mechanism, it is robust against wormhole, impersonate and Sybil attacks. To improve localization accuracy, additional locator nodes must be installed or more directional antenna [38]. SeRLoc assumes that that no jamming of wireless medium will occur, and it cannot protect from attacks that target locator's information [27].

HiRLoc [39]: In this model, node detect its location passively without increasing the number of reference points. The node determines location by intersection beaconframes in the coverage area with multiple reference points. HiRLoc is immune to Sybil attack, wormhole attack, false beaconing and impersonating. HiRLoc utilizes two properties: antenna orientation and communication range. This system uses cryptographic primitives to secure beaconing frames. GSK (Global symmetric key) is used to encrypt beacons frames. HiRLoc has better accuracy than SeRolc, whereas nodes receive multiple beaconing frames from different locators [38]. However, it causes more computation and communication overhead.

SPINE [40]: This system obtains location based on Verifiable Multilateration (VM), the system measures the propagation time of radio signal by examining at least three anchor nodes which provide a robust estimation. SPINE is immune to wormhole, jamming and spoofing attack. It also can prevent dishonest node from distribution fake location. Nodes in SPINE cannot produce wrong distance measurement. Although, SPINE requires a high number of reference points, and it can also cause a bottle-neck in the system [38].

ROPE [41]: This system uses location verification mechanism before the data collection phase which allow the nodes to detect their location without using centralized computation. The system defines two different types of nodes: sensors which equipped with omnidirectional antenna and locators which equipped with M-directional antenna. Every sensory node shares a pairwise key with every locator. To decrease storage size, pairwise keys are derived from master key. ROPE is a robust localization system, it is immune to traffic jamming, spoofing and Sybil attack. It is also resistant to wormhole attack.

DRBTS [32]: Distributed Reputation-based Beacon Trust System aims to exclude malicious beaconing nodes that propagate false location information to the network. The model assumes that every beaconing node monitor its first-hope neighbor to inspect any misbehaving beaconing frame, and then updates the reputation of the neighboring nodes to (NRT) neighbor's reputation table. This table will be used to either trust or reject broadcasted beacon frame based on the voting scheme. The robustness of the DRBTS system enhanced with increasing the number of beacon nodes. The system enables the network to find out which nodes can be trusted when determining the location. DRBTS can protect the network from impersonating, range changing and false beaconing frame.

    The next Tables 2 and 3 will compare all the above localization algorithms using different factors such as behavior, robustness, disadvantages and the immunity to different threats.

Table 2. Secure Localization Algorithms overcoming security threats

System	Defeat region change	Defeat false-beacon	Defeat impersonating	Defeat wormhole	Defeat sybil
SeRLoc [37]	–	No	Yes	Yes	Yes
HiRLoc [39]	–	Yes	Yes	Yes	Yes
SPINE [40]	Yes	–	Yes	Yes	Yes
ROPE [41]	Yes	Yes	Yes	Yes	Yes
DRBTS [32]	Yes	Yes	Yes	No	No
Liu et al. [31]	Yes	Yes	Yes	Yes	No

Table 3. Secure localization systems comparison

System criteria	SeRLoc [37]	HiRLoc [39]	SPINE [40]	ROPE [41]	DRBTS [32]	Liu et al. [31]
Behavior	Prevention	Prevention Filtering	Prevention	Prevention Filtering	Detection	Detection
Cryptography	Encryption and authentication of beacon. Uses Global Symmetric Key	Encryption and authentication of beacon. Uses Global Symmetric key	Symmetric or public key encryption for authenticated distance estimator	Encryption and authentication of the beacon with pairwise keys, able to manage cryptographic primitives.	Encrypt using network wide group key. This allows network observation, and prevents outsiders from eavesdropping.	Beacon frames authenticated using pairwise key establishment
Misbehavior Detection	–	–	–	–	Yes, use reputation and trust base	Compare Distances and examine round trip time (RTT)
Robust	–	–	Verifiable Multination [present probabilistic notion of robust quadrilaterals]	–	Depends on the size of the common neighbor. Higher number of Beacon nodes the more robust DRBTS gets	Robust Statistical Method And voting method
Additional Hardware	Requires Additional Locator with directional antenna to improve accuracy	Requires extra hardware in a beacon node	Needs nanosecond clock, and radio frequency DB devices	Requires directional antenna in beacon nodes	–	Requires redundant beaconing nodes
Disadvantages	Additional locator information must be installed. Assume no jamming happens in wireless medium	Cause more computation and communication overhead	Requires a high number of reference points. Spine might cause a bottleneck in the system	Needs higher hardware requiremens	Dense Network	Needs higher number of anchor nodes
Simple	Yes	Yes	–	Yes	–	–

4 Conclusion

In this research paper, Indoor Positioning Systems had been presented from different security aspects and security countermeasures were discussed. The paper highlighted several security threats that would affect the success of the IPSs significantly.

It had been found that Cryptographic techniques are difficult to implement for real-time systems due to the high computational overhead and hardware requirements such as large primary memory. Therefore, it is important to find alternative methods that would provide secured IPS without relying on cryptography only. The paper compares various secure localization algorithms. The comparison integrated different criteria's such as cryptography, detection behavior, advantages, additional requirements, etc. Each presented threat had been mapped to secure localization algorithm, helping in defining the best algorithm that could be adopted in IPSs. For instance, the security algorithm which could be used to defeat most of the threats is ROPE. Despite the ability of Liu et al. to defeat most of the presented threats, it cannot defeat the Sybil threat.

Although, this paper is considered one of the few papers that described the IPSs in terms of security threats and prevention algorithms, more investigation could be done to evaluate Visible light localization service.

References

1. Li, T., Chen, Y., Zhang, R., Zhang, Y., Hedgpeth, T.: Secure crowdsourced indoor positioning systems. In: IEEE Conference on Computer Communications, Honolulu (2018)
2. Liu, H., Darabi, H., Banerjee, P., Liu, J.: Survey of wireless indoor positioning techniques and systems techniques and systems. IEEE Trans. Syst. Man Cybern. 37(6), 1067–1080 (2007)
3. Mier, J., Jaramillo-Alcázar, A., Freire, J.J.: At a glance: indoor positioning systems technologies and their applications areas. In: Rocha, Á., Ferrás, C., Paredes, M. (eds.) Information Technology and Systems. ICITS 2019. Advances in Intelligent Systems and Computing, vol. 918, pp. 483–493. Springer, Cham (2019). https://doi.org/10.1007/978-3-030-11890-7_47
4. Van Haute, T., et al.: Performance analysis of multiple Indoor Positioning Systems in a healthcare environment. Int. J. Health Geogr. 15(1), 1–15 (2016)
5. Mišić, J., Milovanović, B., Vasić, N., Milovanović, I.: An overview of wireless indoor positioning systems. Infoteh-Jahorina 14, 301–306 (2015)
6. Yassin, A., et al.: Recent advances in indoor localization: a survey on theoretical approaches and applications. IEEE Commun. Surv. Tutorials 19, 1327–1346 (2017)
7. Zafari, F., Kin, L.K.: A survey of indoor localization systems and technologies. IEEE Commun. Surv. Tutorials 21, 2568–2599 (2018)
8. Kim, S., Ha, S., Saad, A., Kim, J.: Indoor positioning system techniques and security. In: IEEE-Forth International Conference on e-Technologies and Networks for Development (ICeND), pp. 1–4 (2015). 10.1109(7328540)
9. Cisco, Wi-Fi Location-Based Services 4.1 Design Guide, Cisco Systems, Inc., San Jose (2008)
10. Disha, A.M.: A comparative analysis on indoor positioning techniques and systems. Int. J. Eng. Res. Appl. (IJERA) 3(2), 1790–1796 (2013)
11. Malik, A., Zulfiqar, T., Javed, M.A., Nafi, N.S., Lodhi, H.: Performance evaluation of Wi-Fi finger printing based indoor positioning system. In: 2018 IEEE Conference on Wireless Sensors (ICWiSe), Langkawi (2018)
12. Zhuang, Y., et al.: A survey of positioning systems using visible LED lights. IEEE Commun. Surv. Tutorials 20(3), 1963–1988 (2018)
13. Bouet, M., Dos Santos, A.L.: RFID tags: positioning principles and localization techniques. In: 1st IFIP Wireless Days, Dubai, pp. 1–5 (2008)
14. Gu, Y., Lo, A., Niemegeers, I.: A survey of indoor positioning systems for wireless personal networks. IEEE Commun. Surv. Tutorials 11(1), 13–32 (2009)

15. García, E., Poudereux, P., Hernández, Á., García, J.J., Ureña, J.: DS-UWB indoor positioning system implementation based on FPGAs. Sens. Actuators A. Phys. **201**, 172–181 (2013)

16. Alarifi, A., et al.: Ultra-wideband indoor positioning technologies: analysis and recent advances. Sensors **16**, 707 (2016)

17. Mousa, F.I.K., Almaadeed, N., Busawon, K., Bouridane, A., Binns, R., Elliot, I.: Indoor visible light communication localization system utilizing received signal strength indication technique and trilateration method. Opt. Eng. Digit. Lib. **57**, 016107 (2018)

18. Brena, R.F.: Evolution of indoor positioning technologies: a survey. J. Sens. **2017**, 21 (2017)

19. Rajagopal, N., Lazik, P., Rowe, A.: Visual light landmarks for mobile devices. In: Proceedings of the 13th International Symposium on Information Processing in Sensor Networks, pp. 249–260. IEEE Press, April 2014

20. Do, T.-H., Yoo, M.: An in-depth survey of visible light communication based positioning systems. Sensors **16**(5), 678 (2016)

21. Hernandez, O., Jain, V., Chakravarty, S., Bhargava, P.: Position Location Monitoring Using IEEE 802.15.4 ZigBee technology. http://www.nxp.com/assets/documents/data/en/brochures/PositionLocationMonitoring.pdf. Accessed 5 Dec 2016

22. Kaushal, K., Kaur, T., Kaur, J.: ZigBee based wireless sensor networks. Int. J. Comput. Sci. Inf. Technol. (IJCSIT) **5**(6), 7752–7755 (2014)

23. Yick, J., Mukherjee, B., Ghosal, D.: Wireless sensor network survey. Comput. Netw. **52**, 2292–2330 (2008)

24. Yang, J., Chen, Y., Trappe, W., Chen, J.: Detection and localization of multiple spoofing attackers in wireless networks. IEEE Trans. Parallel Distrib. Syst. **24**(1), 44–58 (2013)

25. Kibirige, G.W., Sanga, C.: A survey on detection of sinkhole attack in wireless sensor network. arXiv preprint arXiv:1505.01941 (2015)

26. Yuan, Y., Huo, L., Wang, Z., Hogrefe, D.: Secure APIT localization scheme against sybil attacks in distributed wireless sensor networks. IEEE Access **6**(2018), 27629–27636 (2018)

27. Jiang, J., Han, G., Zhu, C., Dong, Y., Zhang, N.: Secure localization in wireless sensor networks: a survey. J. Commun. **6**(6), 460–470 (2011)

28. Singh, V.P., Anand Ukey, A.S., Jain, S.: Signal strength based hello flood attack detection and prevention in wireless sensor networks. Int. J. Comput. Appl. **62**(15), 1–6 (2013)

29. Ning, P., Liu, A.: Mitigating DoS attacks against broadcast authentication in wireless sensor networks. ACM Trans. Sens. Netw. **4**(1), 1–3 (2008)

30. Boukerche, A., Nakamura, E.F., Loureiro, A.A.F.: Secure localization algorithms for wireless sensor networks. IEEE Commun. Mag. **0163–6804**, 96–101 (2008)

31. Liu, D., Ning, P.: Detecting malicious beacon nodes for secure location discovery in wireless sensor network. In: 25th IEEE International Conference on Distributed Computing Systems, pp. 1063–6927 (2005)

32. Srinivasan, A., Teitelbaum, J., Wu, J.: DRBTS: distributed reputation-based beacon trust system. In: 2nd IEEE International Symposium on Dependable, Autonomic and Secure Computing, Indianapolis, pp. 277–283 (2006)

33. Liu, D., Ning, P., Du, W.K.: Attack-resistant location estimation in sensor networks. ACM Trans. Inf. Syst. Secur. (TISSEC) **11**(4), 22 (2008)

34. Mukhopadhyay, B., Srirangarajan, S., Kar, S.: Robust range-based secure localization in wireless sensor networks. In: IEEE Global Communications Conference (GLOBECOM), Abu Dhabi (2018)

35. Hamid, A., Rashid, M., Hong, C.S.: Defense against lap-top class attacker in wireless sensor network. In: 8th International Conference Advanced Communication Technology, pp. 318–323, February 2006

36. Singh, V.P., Jain, S., Singhai, J.: Hello flood attack and its countermeasures in wireless sensor network. IJCSI Int. J. Comput. Sci. Issues **7**(3), 23–26 (2010)
37. Lazos, L., Poovendran, R.: SeRLoc: secure range-independent localization for wireless sensor networks. In: 4th ACM Workshop on Wireless Security, Philadelphia, pp. 21–33, October 2004
38. Srinivasan, A., Wu, J.: A survey on secure localization in wireless sensor networks. In: Wireless and Mobile Communications. CRC Press/Taylor and Francis Group, London (2007)
39. Mohd, W.G., Sharma, S., Saklani, A., Singhal, A.: HiRLoc: high-resolution robust localization for wireless sensor networks. J. Comput. Eng. (IOSR-JCE) **16**(2), 112–115 (2014)
40. Capkun, S., Hubaux, J.-P.: Secure positioning of wireless devices with application to sensor networks. In: Proceedings of IEEE Computer and Communications Societies, vol. 3, pp. 1917–1928 (2005)
41. Lazos, L., Poovendran, R., Capkun, S.: Robust position estimation in wireless sensor networks. In: Proceedings of the 4th International Symposium on Information Processing in Sensor Networks, pp. 324–331 (2005)

Hybrid Software-Defined Network Monitoring

Abdulfatah A. G. Abushagur[1], Tan Saw Chin[1(✉)], Rizaludin Kaspin[2],
Nazaruddin Omar[2], and Ahmad Tajuddin Samsudin[2]

[1] Faculty of Informatics and Computing, Multimedia University,
63100 Cyberjaya, Selangor, Malaysia
sctan1@mmu.edu.my
[2] Telekom Malaysia Research & Development, Cyberjaya, Malaysia

Abstract. Software defined networking (SDN) with OpenFlow-enabled switches operate alongside traditional switches has become a matter of fact in ISP network paradigms which are known as a hybrid SDN (H-SDN) network. When the centralized controller of SDN introduced into an existing network, significant improvement in network use as well as reducing packet losses and delays are expected. However, monitoring such networks is the main concern for better traffic management decision making which can lead to a maximum throughput performance. There is, to our knowledge, only one actual article proposed for H-SDN monitoring scheme so far. Thus, this paper surveys several monitoring methods/techniques for both networks, then propose taxonomy criteria to evaluate the various monitoring methods. The survey includes discussing the design concepts, accuracy and limitations for each, eventually summarize the future research directions for integrated perspective of monitoring in H-SDN networks.

Keywords: Hybrid SDN · Network tomography · Hybrid SDN monitoring

1 Introduction

Software defined networks has recently been emerged (SDN) as a flexible and open source program that enables the administrators to easily monitor the network, it allows them to have a controllable global network view [1, 2]. Although, SDN networks have shown improvement in traffic engineering (TE) implementation, administrations are hesitant to fully deploy SDN due to a variety of reasons the most of which budget constraints and fear of downtime [3, 4]. This gives the birth of incremental devery employment strategy development of SDN networks, only migrating a minimal number of SDN devices in an existing traditional network which leads to what is known a hybrid-SDN (H-SDN) paradigm [5].

H-SDN networks provide an environment for both traditional and SDN devices to coexist and work alongside. However, to gain the benefit of SDN and reach near optimal TE performance with minimal SDN deployment, fine-grained H-SDN monitoring is of interest to ensure QoS. Assuming a few numbers of SDN-R exist in a network with the majority are legacy routers among which share their routing tables using one of the *interior gate protocol* (IGP) standard hop-by-hop routing protocols, e.g. OSPF. In such paradigm the SDN-C controller in H-SDN not only polling SDN-R,

© Springer Nature Switzerland AG 2019
R. Montella et al. (Eds.): IDCS 2019, LNCS 11874, pp. 234–247, 2019.
https://doi.org/10.1007/978-3-030-34914-1_23

rather it needs to peer (P2P) with every legacy router using OSPF-TE protocol in order to collect global link load information [6]. Since legacy routers, however, depends on IGP convergence time to build its routing table, achieving sub-second global link load information timely is not possible. For this reason, *Cheng and Jia* [7] have adopted compressed sensing (CS) based link-load tomography to identify main links for SDN-R placement. SDN-C thus can instantly get the link-load information from those links. To estimate the global link-load information, SDN-C combines both real-time obtained from SDN-R and the historical link-load information which obtained from legacy router relying on temporal correlation. This article, to the best of our knowledge, is the only investigation approach straightforward recently aimed for H-SDN monitoring. Furthermore, unlike the pure SDN networking which has been surveyed extensively [8–10], there is no specific detailed review research and suggestions available so far with regard to the H-SDN monitoring techniques. However, the only surveys related H-SDN were studied by [6, 11, 12], from which *Sandhya et al.* in [11] have comprehensively surveyed different placement strategies transition of possible incremental SDN deployment in a network with legacy devices. *Amin et al.* in [12] have reviewed the researches and developments that carried out recently for H-SDN networks. Although there is no in the survey any mechanism that comprehensively monitoring H-SDN networks related, they have instead focused on works done in a resource management, explaining the importance of the resources and traffic monitoring. And finally, *Huang et al.* [6] in their work's concern, they have focused on how to maximize the traffic-engineering while featuring the existence of centralized control in the legacy networks. The monitoring solutions for H-SDN which have surveyed are more related to the proper migration strategies, e.g. network architecture proposed one strategies of migration in which partially SDN-R deployed and placed in loop-breaking locations to operate as monitor nodes in order for SHEAR controller to detect, locate, and provide bypass routes to the failures. Thus, our paper aims to survey developments in monitoring research for both pure SDN and legacy networks to identify future research directions for H-SDN monitoring by integrating the flexibility and robustness of both respectively.

The paper is structured as follow; monitoring background and monitoring developments in three network paradigms legacy, SDN, and H-SDN will be surveyed in Sect. 2, Sect. 3 discusses the future research direction. Finally, our work conclusion will be presented in the last Sect. 4.

2 Background and Research Developments in Monitoring

In this section we will discuss monitoring background and finally monitoring related developments in both legacy and SDN networking will be reviewed.

2.1 Monitoring Background

Traffic measurement is the main part of monitoring procedure and it is the prerequisite for the decision making of network management (i.e. traffic engineering, QoS, etc.).

Network measurement can be achieved through several phases (see [10]). There are two mechanisms for data measurement namely active and passive mechanisms.

Passive Monitoring Mechanism

In passive mechanism, network components such as switches, and routers are enabled by agents running on them to collect, organize, store and export their collected traffic information data to a collector device or analyzer/controller. The latter dissects the traffic information data allowing by which the management to make the decision. Examples which are among the passive mechanisms that widely accepted monitoring protocols in legacy networks are including; the *Simple Network Management Protocol* (SNMP), NetFlow, and sFlow.

In contrast with legacy agent function, the traffic information data in SDN networks are recorded in OpenFlow enabled devices (switches and routers) for more flexibility. Traffic data then forwarded to the SDN-C either in response to scheduled query messages or pre-planned pushed fashion. The SDN-C then process the data information, organize, and analyze eventually sent back a decision rules to SDN devices where should be maintained and implemented accordingly. Passive method can be used for both packet and flow-based data collections. Although it doesn't add traffic to the normal network traffic, the need for installing agents in every network device (legacy heterogeneous devices) make them less controllable and costly.

Active Monitoring Mechanism

In active measurement, monitoring probe instructions are generated by agents (i.e. certain monitoring nodes or end hosts) and injected into network to acquire responses for network evaluation measurement [13]. Based on the network devices' responses the quality of the network can be assessed and arbitrated accordingly in an instant manner. Unlike the passive method, active method falls only under packet-based data collection and it is more controllable approach and fine-grained monitor.

2.2   Monitoring Developments in Traditional Networks

Network tomography (NT) is one of the approaches which have been studied extensively in legacy network to facilitate monitoring problem in large scale networks, in which the individual link information can be inferred by only monitoring/probing end-to-end paths. However, due to the growth of the *"n"* nodes, probing the entire network paths frequently become impractical due to the large amount of traffic which can add to congestion [14]. Inspiring by the spatial correlation of the network's routing matrix (i.e. paths traverse common links), researchers extensively studied the NT and proposed number of techniques/methods to infer the internal topology/information of the network by only monitoring a few subsets of its entire paths. To this end, the numbers of routers which need to be monitored are only the ones traverses the identified main few paths. Thus, examining the feasibility of techniques that significantly help to decrease the number of sampled paths while keeping acceptable accuracy is of interest. Usually in distributed control network paradigm, monitoring relies on generating probes from one end (source) to another end (destination) to measure path properties such as delay, loss rate, etc. through ping, traceroute. In this section several approaches that have proposed different techniques to address monitoring overhead and latency while maintaining accuracy are reviewed in this section; The key problem of the NT is the proper selection of paths or nodes (monitors) where the end-to-end measurement guarantees the identifiability of all links while care about overhead and computation time as low as possible. Here we consider only active NT which is more accurate and respond more quickly than the passive [15], in which probes need to be generated to collect the monitoring data. *Chen et al.* [16] proposed a path-level tomography-based overlay monitoring system. An algebra method has been leveraged to select linearly independent basis set of active paths. By monitoring only those basis paths, the loss rates of all the rest paths are inferable. Their objective was to reduce the amount of measurements (overhead) trading-off for accuracy. However, the approach only handling the static topology.

Another two approach based on a statistical theory of linear prediction proposed in [17]. The approach aimed at further-reduction paths monitor overhead. The number of paths was significantly reduced while reasonable accuracy has achieved. However, the path selection approach doesn't work if the spatial correlation between links doesn't exist. Bayesian experimental design [18] in which flexible framework called NetQuest has been presented for measurement in large scale networks. The Bayesian experiments design is applied for selecting subset of paths from which the amount of the information gained about the whole network is maximized. The design subjected to given resource constraints. It was actually proposed for choosing properly a subset of paths to probe by which the statistical inference will be improved. Unlike previous studies, Bayesian experiments suggest setting up first the desired subset number of paths (design), then sequentially use a search algorithm to find the optimal paths that maximize a pre-defined utility function to reflect the expected accuracy of an estimator of the properties. By monitoring only 2% of the total paths, authors demonstrated that their inference technique is able to infer the network-wide average delay with only 15% inference error.

For the network that end-to-end metrics performance satisfy the criterion for using the theory of CS, *Coates et al.* presented a scheme based on diffusion wavelets and non-linear estimation function [19]. This is by exploiting the spatial and temporal correlation among the monitored paths of IP networks. Non-linear estimation technique was employed to produce estimates for the non-measured paths using ℓ_1 inimization. The approach does not restrict to the linear relation between path and link metrics. However, results show more variability when compared with the original data as well as a little bias. The framework is good only for small numbers of monitors (small-scale networks) and static routing matrix. *Fan et al. in* [20] adopted the sparse Bayesian learning (SBL) concept to identify congested links. As usual for the case of NT, the inferential function is used to solve the undeterminable linear model. SBL then implemented to solve for link performance metric which assumed to follow zero-mean Gaussian priors. The study approach also concerned about locating the congested links. However, the assumption that the link metrics follows Gaussian with zero-mean priors is unrealistic as link metrics cannot be negative, the estimation error quite high when the link-metrics exhibit less sparse.

Another CS concepts together with *maximum a-posteriori* estimation applied to propose a new loss tomography scheme [21] aimed at improving the most commonly inferential ℓ_1 minimization function. The approach relies on Boolean (for locating link congestion) and linear model (for identifying link congested level). Temporal correlations of link losses were exploited to estimate prior congested probabilities of the links by using the path congested probability based on the Boolean algebra. They learn about the congested path probabilities via multiple snapshots (end-to-end measurement). A weight is then determined to each link according to its congested probability. The two main contributions of this approach are; the weighted ℓ_1 optimization is a linear function which can be solved by any linear programing optimizer, and rather than locating only the congested links, the approach allows also to infer the loss rates of links by which congestion level of each link can be identified.

Li et al. in [22] have proposed a set of algorithms to examine the problem of placing the least amount of monitors while maximizing the number of identifiable links. Authors study the effect of both predictable and unpredictable link-failures on their method. They proved theoretically using proposed algorithms that the arrangement of the determined minimum monitors can estimate all link's performance metrics in time-varying topologies, provided the monitor node can freely choose the measurement paths. However, the number of measurements is not reduced in this scenario rather it is increased, and if concurrent measurements are required, bandwidth-bottleneck of links is highly anticipated. Recently, *Pan et al.* in [23] proposed a monitoring technique based on NT to identify congested links by using end-to-end measurement (e.g. link delay, link loss rate). The approach aimed at considering a non-tree network and source-to-destination involving a multipath routing (single source node to multi destinations). Two greedy algorithms based on Boolean and linear methods (additive) to approximately solve the congested link NP-hard problem. The proposed algorithms demonstrate higher *Detection Rate* and comparably lower *False Positive Rate* when compared with Tomo (see reference in [23]). However, as the number of congested links increase in the network, both algorithms have dropped indicating their limitations. The proposed scheme only deals with a single network user in which only single source was considered, in addition the assumptions that no such two links shared by a set of paths is impractical in non-tree topology.

2.3   Monitoring Developments in SDN Networking

To achieve complete visibility in SDN networking, the SDN-R or OpenFlow switches instructed to forward all traffic to the SDN-C by exchanging messages between them [24]. SDN-C in original OpenFlow calculates for any new flow received by the SDN-R builds a new flow table in which included forwarding rules for the switch to follow, thus aggregation of high number of new flows can lead to a significant overhead at both entities (SDN-C and SDN-R). Furthermore, forwarding or flow tables is a high resource consumption such as TCAM (ternary content addressable memory) since matching fields continuously to include much more header fields, this can have resulted in scalability problem.

Many approaches have been proposed to help tackle aforementioned issues for which we review the following related state-of-the-art literatures. Therefore, rule storage reduction as well as overhead of the packet processing on switches or SDN-R is a very vital in SDN data plane to address scalability problem. To this end, *Yu et al.* in [25] have proposed a model aimed at distributing the monitoring responsibility of any intended flows to the entire network. The system is claimed to be a memory-efficient system and they called it a *distributed and collaborative per-flow monitoring* (DCM) system. Authors by adopting Bloom filters together with the convenience brought by SDN paradigm they designed a customized filter called *two-stage Bloom filters* (TSBF) which can be installed into SDN-R. Meanwhile the CDM component on SDN-C is responsible for monitoring load distribution to all SDN-R (allocation), construct and update the Bloom filter, and false positive detection. The main function of the TSBF firstly is to save the SDN-R process resource by filtering out the packets that are not matching the monitored rules. Secondly, to reduce the false positive probability which is inherently in the Bloom filter. Authors have demonstrated that the DCM was able to provide flow measurement with reasonable accuracy while memory efficiently preserved. However, this approach yet unable to completely eliminate the false positive detection, which means redundancy in processing same flow with more than one switch is possible, furthermore, the requirement of reconstruction the Bloom filters when deleting an entry in the data structure is inflexible.

Su et al. in [26] proposed CeMon, the main objective of CeMon is to design an optimal polling scheme in SDN networks by which minimal monitoring cost can be achieved with high accuracy. Two novel polling schemes have been proposed, one is considered a main namely; *Maximum coverage polling scheme* (MCPS), and the other one is designed to be a complementary for the MCPS which given a name of *Adaptive fine-grained polling scheme* (AFPS). The AFPS were developed to tune or adapt the sampling polling frequency according to the traffic changes. CeMon collects all flows-statistics on selected switches due to which a higher bandwidth cost occurs between the selected switches and the SDN-C. *Hartung and Korner* [27] proposed a flow-level independent monitoring tool in the presentation phase named a SOFTmon. It presents the flow statistics information in a human readable way using charts relying on network nodes (switches), flow tables (flow statistics), and network interconnects (switch ports, interfaces). SOFTmon architecture has three layers; data access layer (the bottom layer), data model, and the graphical user interface (GUI) which comes as a topmost layer allowing interaction by user for data visualization is soft real time. Authors have created an additional time base for counter values duration from which a performance metric can be calculated and achieve a fluent visualization in soft real time. This had led them to some error creation. Mininet with an OpenFlow version 1.3 as well as an SDN research cluster with the typical data centre network topology were used to evaluate the presented application. It was successfully showed its high usability while being easy to operate. However, it only supports a flow-level monitoring application for the network layer. *Varela and Ros* [28] presented a scalable cost-effective flow monitoring methods that can be applied in existing switches-enabled OpenFlow. It is also a flow-level monitoring solution but uses flow sampling-based approach. Their main objective is to address the scalability by helping alleviate the controller overhead and switches' load for which two flow sampling methods are designed. Matches done per-packet arrival in the switch, the counters of packets and bytes then updated only if the packet-arrived failed to match per-flow monitoring entry. However, the system lack security issues that prevent congestion in the controller which my caused by sending high rate malformed messages from malicious attacks. *Queiroz et al.* [29] have utilized several counters that built in SDN network devices helped to develop a new monitoring method called the Big data monitoring method. Using updated counter values of every packet traverses the SDN-R, a fine-grained Big data can be retrieved in streaming manner. As the concern of the authors was about the traffic analysis and characterization, throughput metric of the network that traverses both SDN-C and SDN-R was their interest monitoring parameter. Several resources such as switch ports, flow tables, and flow entries were acquired/collected by probing the SDN-C periodically. The collected data has been categorised into inventory data and streaming data. Authors developed pseudocode algorithm instructed to probe the SDN-C periodically to collect and to keep the populated repository with latest network configuration (network topology). Meanwhile, the streaming data as its name implies, is related to data counters provided by SDN-R and should immediately be forwarded for processing in real time or fine-grained fashion. Nevertheless, the rate of the request must compatible with the updating rate of the parameter in repository otherwise it may yield to intolerable information loss. In addition, the interval between the counter readings was 3 s, which is yet insufficient for high-speed and high-load data networks, which could lead to excessive data loss.

2.4   Summary

This section discusses the comparison between the techniques reviewed in both legacy and SDN networks. We evaluate the performance of surveyed techniques for both legacy and SDN networking based on a number of criteria as in Tables 1 and 2, respectively. Limitations of each technique in both legacy and SDN networks are summarized as well.

3   Future Research Directions

As both SDN and legacy architectures exist in the same network environment, methods developed in both networks which are used for monitoring may be combined to achieve reliable monitoring system in H-SDN. Study proposed by *Cheng and Jia* [7] adopted legacy network-tomography NT method and SDN devices to gather link-load information of only few links instantly and estimate based on temporal-history correlation for the rest. Thus, latency due to IGP convergence time of legacy routers can be addressed and approximate global view obtained. However, the proposal doesn't consider the memory usage of SDN-Rs as they responsible to forward as well all the

Table 1. Monitoring techniques comparison in legacy networks

Research work	Estimator	Network performance					Limitations
		OHC	CT	MAE	ADA	SC	
Statistical method [17, 30]	Linear	R	Poly	0.05	*	*	- It relies on link redundancy characteristic (inconsistence routing matrix) - Restricted to linear relation between Path and link metrics
Algebraic method [31]	Min norm solutions via QR	R	log	0.14	Yes	SN	- Limited to small-scale networks - error will be higher for $\geq$ 1200 paths
NetQuest Bayesian (1) [18]	Linear regressions $\ell_1 - norm$ and $\ell_2 - norm$ minimization and maximum entropy estimation	HR	Poly	0.12	*	LN	- focus on minimizing the number of paths without considering the resources constraints - error is high when paths selected are a few
NetQuest-Bayesian (2) [32]	Bayesian (one of the above)	HR	Poly	0.03	*	LN	- Centralized for inferences analysis (takes time)
CS using Wavelet diffusion basis [19]	ℓ_1 minimization	HR	Poly	0.01	No	*	- Computing the wavelet basis is slow - Estimated data is biased little but more fluctuating - Static routing
Sparse Bayesian learning SBL [20] - delay tomography	Bayesian inference	R	Poly	0.18–0.58	No	*	- Static routing - The link performance vector is assumed to follow zero-mean Gaussian priors (impractical) - For less sparse link metrics (number of

(*continued*)

Table 1. (*continued*)

Research work	Estimator	Network performance					Limitations
		OHC	CT	MAE	ADA	SC	
							congested links large), the estimation error is increased
CS loss tomography [21]	Weighted ℓ_1 minimization	HR	*	0.08-0.32	No	*	- For large-scale network with high degree nodes the estimation error is high - It is not adaptable to the variation of the congested links
Graph Theory (Monitors Placement) [22]	NT (no basis paths)	NR	Poly	*	Yes	LN	- It takes minutes for calculating monitor placement problem - It requires controllable nodes to route their measurement paths - It creates link bandwidth-bottleneck if which is traversed by multiple paths
Boolean and Additive [23]	LP optimization using additive and Boolean statuses	NA	*	NA	No	*	- Only single source network is considered (impractical) - The approach assumed that, no two links shared by a set of paths to have full-rank routing matrix which is impractical in non-tree topology.

- **HEADERS:** OHC: Overhead Cost; CT: Computational Time; MAE: Mean Absolute Error; AD: Adaptability; SC: Scalability, **CONTENTS:** HR: Highly Reduced; R: Reduced; LN: Large Network; SN: Small Network; NA: Not Applicable;

*: corresponding reference does not mention or consider this property, or its support is not sure

Table 2. Monitoring techniques comparison in SDN networks

Research work	System performance						Limitations
	SMC	CMC	ACC	COH	INS	LVL	
DCM [25]	R	NA	Lo	R	√	CG	- False positive exist affecting accuracy - When number of flows increase, the fraction of memory used increase and thus accuracy become worse - Reconstructing the Bloom filter is not flexible
Throughput [33]	NA	Hi	*	R	×	CG	- The approach lacks fine-grained measurement from which traffic engineering can be leveraged - Routing depends on the updating time of the throughput database
CeMon [26]	R	R	Hi	Hi	×	CG	- All flows collected from specified switches results in communication overhead
SOFTmon [27]	NA	*	Hi	*	√	CG	- It doesn't support fine-grained level of monitoring from which TE can be leveraged well
DPI/ML [28]	R	R	M	+	√	CG	- Lack of security issues which may lead to congestion in SDN-C
Big Data [29]	*	Hi	M	+	×	FG	- Update time interval of 3 s between the counter readings yet insufficient for high speed/data networks - An intolerable information loss if the rate of request isn't compatible with the updating rate of repository

- **HEADERS:** SMC: Switch Memory Cost; CMC: Controller Memory Cost; ACC: Accuracy; SC: Scalability; COH: Communication Overhead; INS: Instantaneity; LVL: Details Level
- **CONTENTS:** R: Reduced; NA: Not Applicable; Hi: High; M: Moderate; Lo: Low; CG: Coarse-Grained; FG: Fine-Grained; √/× : It supports the property/Not support; ±: Increased/Decreased
*: Corresponding reference doesn't mention or consider this property

messages of their neighbor legacy-routers to the SDN-C. Besides, latency and packet-loss will be considered as too many monitoring data flows passes one link (SDN-R-to-SDN-C). Several research directions and suggestions for H-SDN monitoring issue based on limitations in

Tables 1 and 2 are given as follow;

1. *Collection data monitoring in legacy part:* reducing latency in legacy network is one of the critical missions when collecting links' metrics, latency scale up with network resources, congestion, and so on. Smart combination between segment routing, allocation of SDN-R, and topology-inference-based NT is needed.

2. *Efficient monitoring:* In large scale H-SDN networks, SDN-R will be responsible for preprocessing the flow statistics of its own link and its neighbor legacy-links' packets, while SDN-C takes the part of analyzing and summarizing the data, thus operation overhead should be reduced in both. For example, concerning traffic matrix of link-load information, adopting OpenTM and DCM approaches [10], while the former reads directly the statistics from each flow accurately, the DCM may employed to filter out the previous flow-entry (old data deleted whenever a change occur or duplicated), such that TCAM memory consumption will be alleviated. Analysis and presenting data which are carried out in SDN-C, thus the new version of data will only be sent to and processed by the SDN-C.

3. *Network overhead:* Transmission of data measurement occur between SDN-R and SDN-C, SDN-R communicate with legacy routers for one scenario, or SDN-C peering with legacy routers. To reduce the network overhead, either an adaptable algorithm for scheduling or efficient querying frequency is needed to tradeoff between accuracy/instantaneity while avoiding network overhead. For example; adopting FlowSense or PayLess approaches [10] where H-SDN network can gain benefit from the former in such that the few number of SDN-R communicate with the SDN-C only whenever a link-load information has changed (passive method), in which matching process will take place in SDN-R, only unmatched data from either legacy-routers or the basis-links will be updated in SDN-R and sent to the SDN-C (see Fig. 1), whereas in the latter the polling time-stamp determined by an adaptive scheduling algorithm.

Figure 1 shows the schematic of suggested monitoring framework in 1, 2, and 3 points of future work. The suggested scheme can be described as follow;

- Segment routing (SR), SDN-R allocation: in each autonomous system or WAN utilizes segment routing wherein the SDN-R become a source router ingress and egress node, but both are controlled logically by the SDN-C which is in turn has SR module-built in. SDN-R source ingress and SDN-R egress nodes represent end-to-end of all possible paths in the network.
- Legacy router (not necessary to be all, in other words selectively using) will peer with SDN-C and provide the topology (IGP-prefix segment, adjacency segment as well as BGP-prefix segment), and that will be updated by peering with SDN-C whenever a change in topology occur.
- When new packet arrived at SDN-R ingress node, SDN-R push the packet and SDN-C map the path to SIDs stack-based with extra traffic load item being pushed into the stack for every adjacency ID (link).

SDN-R will increment the counter and fill-up the flow rate of each link accordingly and update the SDN-C to build its matrix. Whenever traffic into SDN-R then change, SDN-C would be updated immediately by push-based method. Thus link load in SDN-C directly monitored and link utilization for traffic engineering can be accomplished timely, e.g. the flow rate in link 104 exceeds the bandwidth, hence the SDN-C would reroute the traffic through A-C-I-E instead of A-C-D-E, etc.

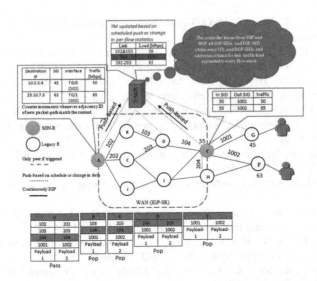

Fig. 1. Schematic depicting monitoring in H-SDN utilizing Segment Routing and Traffic Matrix (SRTM)

4 Conclusion

Whereas H-SDN monitoring is in concern, this work has reviewed the up-to-date monitoring developments in both legacy and SDN networks. In each approach, the survey attempts to include technique's idea, contribution and its limitation. Active network tomography based compressed sensing, Boolean and additive methods for monitoring have been discussed and compared. As for SDN networks, several developed methods to tackle SDN-R and SDN-C memory issues affect accuracy have been discussed and compared. Finally, to suggest research directions for integrated perspective of H-SDN monitoring issues, limitations of the surveyed methods in both legacy and SDN are summarized. Unlike the FlowSense or PayLess, the suggested scheme leveraging the combination of SR and SDN, it can compute the utilization at any point in time passively (almost zero overhead) by updating with every link's load variation. SDN-C can peer any time with intended legacy router (or its neighbor) to confirm load utilization either.

References

1. Isolani, P.H., Wickboldt, J.A., Both, C.B., Rochol, J., Granville, L.Z.: Interactive monitoring, visualization, and configuration of OpenFlow-based SDN. In: Proceedings of the 2015 IFIP/IEEE International Symposium on Integrated Network Management, IM 2015, pp. 207–215 (2015)
2. Rawat, D.B., Reddy, S.R.: Software defined networking architecture, security and energy efficiency: a survey. IEEE Commun. Surv. Tutorials. **19**, 325–346 (2017)

3. Lin, C., Wang, K., Deng, G.: A QoS-aware routing in SDN hybrid networks. In: Procedia Computer Science (2017)
4. Michel, O., Keller, E.: SDN in wide-area networks: a survey. In: 2017 4th International Conference on Software Defined Systems, SDS 2017, pp. 37–42 (2017)
5. Salsano, S., et al.: Hybrid IP/SDN networking: open implementation and experiment management tools. IEEE Trans. Netw. Serv. Manag. **13**, 138–153 (2016)
6. Huang, X., Cheng, S., Cao, K., Cong, P., Wei, T., Hu, S.: A survey of deployment solutions and optimization strategies for hybrid SDN networks. IEEE Commun. Surv. Tutorials **21**(2), 1483–1507 (2019)
7. Cheng, T.Y., Jia, X.: Compressive traffic monitoring in hybrid SDN. IEEE J. Sel. Areas Commun. **36**, 2731–2743 (2018)
8. Cox, J.H., et al.: Advancing software-defined networks: a survey. IEEE Access **5**, 25487–25526 (2017)
9. Rojas, E., et al.: Are we ready to drive software-defined networks? A comprehensive survey on management tools and techniques. ACM Comput. Surv. **51**, 24 (2018)
10. Tsai, P.W., Tsai, C.W., Hsu, C.W., Yang, C.S.: Network monitoring in software-defined networking: a review. IEEE Syst. J. **12**, 3958–3969 (2018)
11. Sandhya, Y.S., Haribabu, K.: A survey: hybrid SDN. J. Netw. Comput. Appl. **100**, 35–55 (2017)
12. Amin, R., Reisslein, M., Shah, N.: Hybrid SDN networks: a survey of existing approaches. IEEE Commun. Surv. Tutorials **20**(4), 3259–3306 (2018)
13. Zhou, D., Yan, Z., Fu, Y., Yao, Z.: A survey on network data collection. J. Netw. Comput. Appl. **116**, 9–23 (2018)
14. Pepe, T., Puleri, M.: Network tomography: a novel algorithm for probing path selection. In: IEEE International Conference on Communications, pp. 5337–5341 (2015)
15. Dusia, A., Sethi, A.S.: Recent advances in fault localization in computer networks. IEEE Commun. Surv. Tutorials **18**(4), 3030–3051 (2016)
16. Chen, Y., Bindel, D., Katz, R.H.: Tomography-based overlay network monitoring. In: Proceedings of the 3rd ACM SIGCOMM Conference on Internet Measurement (IMC 2003), pp. 216–231. ACM, New York (2004)
17. Chua, D.B., Kolaczyk, E.D., Crovella, M.: Efficient monitoring of end-to-end network properties. In: Proceedings - IEEE INFOCOM (2005)
18. Song, L.Q., Zhang, Y.: NetQuest: a flexible framework for large-scale network measurement. IEEE/ACM Trans. Netw. **17**, 106–119 (2009)
19. Coates, M., Pointurier, Y., Rabbat, M.: Compressed network monitoring for IP and all-optical networks (2007)
20. Fan, X., Li, X.: Network tomography via sparse Bayesian learning. IEEE Commun. Lett. **21**(4), 781–784 (2017)
21. Fan, X., Li, X., Zhang, J.: Compressed sensing based loss tomography using weighted $\ell 1$ minimization. Comput. Commun. **127**, 122–130 (2018)
22. Li, H., Gao, Y., Dong, W., Chen, C.: Taming both predictable and unpredictable link failures for network tomography. IEEE/ACM Trans. Netw. **26**(3), 1460–1473 (2018)
23. Pan, S., Zhou, Y., Zhang, Z., Yang, S., Qian, F., Hu, G.: Identify congested links with network tomography under multipath routing. J. Netw. Syst. Manag. **27**(2), 409–429 (2019)
24. Cui, L., Yu, F.R., Yan, Q.: When big data meets software-defined networking: SDN for big data and big data for SDN. IEEE Netw. **30**(1), 58–65 (2016)
25. Yu, Y., Qian, C., Li, X.: Distributed and collaborative traffic monitoring in software defined networks. In: Proceedings of the Third Workshop on Hot Topics in Software Defined Networking, pp. 85–90 (2014)

26. Su, Z., Wang, T., Xia, Y., Hamdi, M.: CeMon: a cost-effective flow monitoring system in software defined networks. Comput. Netw. **92**, 101–115 (2015)
27. Hartung, M., Körner, M.: SOFTmon - traffic monitoring for SDN. Proc. Comput. Sci. **110**, 516–523 (2017)
28. Suárez-Varela, J., Barlet-Ros, P.: Flow monitoring in software-defined networks: finding the accuracy/performance tradeoffs. Comput. Netw. **135**, 289–301 (2018)
29. Queiroz, W., Capretz, M.A.M., Dantas, M.: An approach for SDN traffic monitoring based on big data techniques. J. Netw. Comput. Appl. **131**, 28–39 (2019)
30. Chua, D.B., Kolaczyk, E.D., Crovella, M.: A statistical framework for efficient monitoring of end-to-end network properties. In: Proceedings of ACM SIGMETRICS (Poster Paper), no. Poster Paper, pp. 1–20 (2004). https://arxiv.org/abs/cs/0412037v2
31. Chen, Y., Bindel, D., Song, H.H., Katz, R.H.: Algebra-based scalable overlay network monitoring: algorithms, evaluation, and applications. IEEE/ACM Trans. Netw. **15**, 1084–1097 (2007)
32. Song, H.H., Yalagandula, P.: Real-time end-to-end network monitoring in large distributed systems. In: 2007 2nd International Conference on Communication Systems Software and Middleware, pp. 1–10 (2007)
33. Luong, D.-H., Outtagarts, A., Hebbar, A.: Traffic monitoring in software defined networks using opendaylight controller. In: Boumerdassi, S., Renault, É., Bouzefrane, S. (eds.) MSPN 2016. LNCS, vol. 10026, pp. 38–48. Springer, Cham (2016). https://doi.org/10.1007/978-3-319-50463-6_4

Time-Sensitive-Aware Scheduling Traffic (TSA-ST) Algorithm in Software-Defined Networking

Ng Kean Haur and Tan Saw Chin[✉]

Multimedia University, 63310 Cyberjaya, Selangor, Malaysia
Sctan1@mmu.edu.my

Abstract. Time-sensitive-aware scheduling traffic system is capable to eliminate the queuing delay in the network that resulting hard real-time guarantees. Hence, this article aims to develop a time-sensitive-aware scheduling traffic system which is able to avoid multiple time-sensitive flows from conducting in the same path simultaneously so that the queueing delay can be eliminated. Under this prologue, an algorithm Time-Sensitive-Aware Scheduling Traffic (TSA-ST) is proposed to reduce the time complexity in the transmission schedule while maintaining the quality of the scheduling system. In the end, the transmission schedule will be computed in different network topologies to evaluate the performance and accuracy.

Keywords: Cyber Physical System · Time-Sensitive Software-Defined Networking · Algorithm

1 Introduction

In Cyber Physical System(CPS), deterministic networking and Time-Sensitive Networking (TSN) is used to provide real-time guarantees by which the software and hardware can be operated within the deadline. These networks have their own features example time synchronization and traffic scheduling to maintain the stability of services in CPS. However, CPS is suffered from queuing delay which affects the efficiency to provide hard real-time guarantees strictly. In the research community, there is an idea to solve the real-time problems by using Time-Sensitive Software-Defined Networking (TSSDN). TSSDN [1] is an architecture to combine the traffic scheduling system in Time-Sensitive Networking (TSN) and Software-Defined Networking (SDN). SDN has a centralized network controller (SDN controller) which is connected to all the switches to view the network topology globally. TSSDN utilize the advantage of SDN to facilitate the transmission schedule in the network.

Most of the approaches in traffic scheduling system such as Scheduling with Unconstrained Routing (S/UR), Scheduling with Pathsets Routing (S/PR) and Scheduling with Fixed-path Routing (S/FR) [1] will ensure no multiple time-sensitive flows are conducted in the same path at the same time so that the queueing delay can be eliminated. However, those approach resulting in heavy computation. Hence, an algorithm is proposed under these premises to reduce the time complexity in

© Springer Nature Switzerland AG 2019
R. Montella et al. (Eds.): IDCS 2019, LNCS 11874, pp. 248–259, 2019.
https://doi.org/10.1007/978-3-030-34914-1_24

transmission schedule while maintaining the quality of scheduling system. Finally, the proposed algorithm is evaluated for the effectiveness, accuracy and performance in different network topology.

Section 2 describes the related work of cyber physical system and software-defined networking. Section 3 depicts the proposed algorithm, Time-Sensitive-Aware Scheduling Traffic (TSA-ST) algorithm. The simulation and results will be presented in Sect. 4 and finally conclusion remark in Sect. 5.

2   Related Work

In this section, the related work from the top of the Cyber Physical System (CPS) to down of the Software-Defined Networking (SDN) will all be conducted. Besides, different scheduling approaches will also be further discussed to determine the suitable one for traffic scheduling system.

2.1   Cyber Physical System

There are certain fields which related in the Industry 4.0 example cyber-physical systems, cloud computing and big data [3]. In the field of industrial automation, fieldbus use to be the most important communication systems to provide real-time guarantees [1, 2]. Ethernet is currently replacing traditional fieldbus systems in industry to provide deterministic and real-time control [4, 5]. Industrial Ethernet has a better maximum transmission speed compare with fieldbus. This allows Ethernet to provide a better real-time guarantee for the cyber physical system (CPS) in industry.

2.2   Time-Sensitive Software-Defined Networking (TSSDN)

Time-sensitive networking (TSN) can be considered in deterministic networking to provide real-time guarantees for CPS [1]. To apply Time-sensitive networking (TSN) in a deterministic network, three components in its standards are required. For time synchronization (1st component), IEEE 1588 Precision Time Protocol is used in each of the clocks in the host to ensure the precision of communication. However, an excellent performing scheduling system to route all the time-sensitive flows is still needed to arrange the traffic schedule (2nd component) and select the paths (3rd component). Hence, Software-Defined Networking (SDN) comes in the way. SDN is a network architecture which functions to manage and facilitate the network performance [7]. Switches in the traditional IP network are connected to the controllers while the switches and controllers in the SDN are separated. The reason is that switches in SDN has only data forwarding function while the controller is uplifted as SDN controller to control them. This global view allows the administrator to change the traffic network from centralization controller with the implementation of MAPE loop (Nayak, Dürr and Rothermel 2015). Besides, topology change, flow control, deployment of new application and modifications of the existing application can also be done centrally.

This is exactly what the time-sensitive-aware scheduling traffic system needed. By computing the transmission schedule in the SDN controller, time-sensitive flows can be visualized clearly. Hence, the queueing delay in the time-sensitive traffic can be eliminated since no multiple time-sensitive flows are allowed to allocate in the same path at the same time. This architecture is known as Time-Sensitive Software-Defined Networks (TSSDN) [1].

2.3 Time-Sensitive-Aware Scheduling Traffic System

There are few approaches which provide excellent scheduling in Time-Sensitive Networking. One approach named Resource Constrained Project Scheduling with Temporal Constraints uses Resource Constrained Project Scheduling (RCPS) [8] to minimize the schedule length and temporal constraints. Another approach named tt-scehdule uses Satisfiability Moduolo Theories (SMT) [9] to minimize the contention of frames. However, not all of the approaches capable to provide hard real-time guarantee which is required in TSSDN. Real-time normally means the response can be done within a short time before the deadlines. Hard real-time means that the response must absolutely be done every time and not allowed any attempt to fail. For the scheduling approaches above, they are capable to apply only for static schedules. The reason is that the approaches require long execution time which is not suitable to provide hard real-time guarantees for online scheduling example TSSDN [10]. Besides, the time-sensitive flows are not routed in these approaches but directly be given. The ignorance of the possible influence of time-sensitive flows may lead to the bottleneck of the routes. In contrast, there are few approaches such as Scheduling with Unconstrained Routing (S/UR), Scheduling with Pathsets Routing (S/PR) and Scheduling with Fixed-path Routing (S/FR) which shows excellent time-sensitive scheduling results during the execution [1]. These approaches route the time-sensitive flows to all the possible paths in order to maximize the number of time-sensitive flows in the network.

3 Time-Sensitive-Aware Scheduling Traffic (TSA-ST) Algorithm

The proposed algorithm, Time-Sensitive-Aware Scheduling Traffic (TSA-ST) will modify S/FR approach which had the lowest execution time compared with S/PR and S/UR. The aim is to reduce the time complexity of network scheduling compared with all approaches while maintaining the maximum number of flows approximately.

Figure 1 represents the pseudocode of the proposed algorithm, TSA-ST. In this pseudocode, there are three major parts which are weighing swapping and allocation. First of all, declare the input i, time-sensitive flows, input j, number of links, input k, time-slots and input $f_{i, j}$, links with respective time-sensitive flow. Input $f_{i, j}$ indicated as "1" when the time-sensitive flows require specific link while "0" when no required. Next, initialize the output $c_{k, j}$, links with respective time-slot and output $c_{k, j}$, flows with respective time-slot. Output $c_{k, j}$ indicated as "1" when link in the specific time-slot was allocated while "0" when link is available. On the other side, output $t_{i, k}$ indicated as "1" when time-sensitive flow is allocated to specific time-slot while "0" when no allocation. Then, initialize objective function, maxFlow as "0".

Algorithm:	Time-Sensitive-Aware Scheduling Traffic (TSA-ST) Algorithm
Input:	TS: time-sensitive flows, i ∈ TS; E: number of links, j ∈ E; T: number of time-slots, k ∈ T; LF: links with respective flow, $f_{i,j}$ = LF
Output:	FT: flows with respective time-slot, $t_{i,k}$ = FT; maxflow

1. For all time-sensitive flows, sum up the number of links as weight, w[i]
2. Swap time-sensitive flows and their links according weight, w_i in ascending order
3. Initialize the availability of flows, check[i] = 1
4. For all time-sensitive flows, if the flow is available, check[i] = 1
5.   Initialize the availability of links, counter = 1
6.   For all links, if the links is available, counter = 1
7.   Allocated the flow into the time-slot, $t_{i,k}$ = 1
8.   Allocated the links into the time-slot, $c_{k,j}$ = 1
9.   Maximum number of flows increment by 1, maxflow += 1
10.   Flow is not available, check[i] = 0
11. Return maxflow, flow with respective time-slot, $t_{i,k}$

Fig. 1. Time-Sensitive-Aware Scheduling Traffic (TSA-ST) algorithm

After providing the input, we will proceed with the first major step which is weighing. For each time-sensitive flow, the number of the links are required to sum up and calculated as the weight of the flow, w[i]. After that, the weight of each flow, w[i] will be passed to the second major step, swapping. In the swapping process, time-sensitive flows and their respective links, $f_{i,j}$ will be arranged according to the sequence of the weight of the flow, w[i] in ascending order. In this case, time-sensitive flow with lesser links required will be given a higher priority to allocate in the time-slots. Finally, followed with the last step which is allocation. During the allocation process, variable check[i] and variable counter are initialized as "1". Check acts as a constraint to determine the availability of time-sensitive flow to allocate into time-slot while counter acts as a constraint to determine the availability of links to allocate into time-slot. If both check and counter are indicated as "1", the flow and all its links are available to allocate in the time-slot by which flows with respective time-slot, $t_{i,k}$ and links with respective time-slot, $c_{k,j}$ will be indicated as "1". Hence, the maximum number of flows, maxflow will be increment by 1 and the status of certain flow, check [i] will be indicated as "0" which is not available. This allocation process will be repeated until all the time-sensitive flows are executed. In the end, TSA-ST algorithm will return the flows with respective time-slot, $t_{i,k}$ and the maximum number of flows, maxflow.

4   Simulation Result and Discussion

The simulation testing for S/UR approach, S/PR approach, S/FR approach and the proposed algorithm, TSA-ST algorithm will initially focus on the scheduling runtime versus time-slots, time-sensitive flows and in 8-nodes, 11-nodes and 31-nodes extended star topologies as shown in Fig. 2.

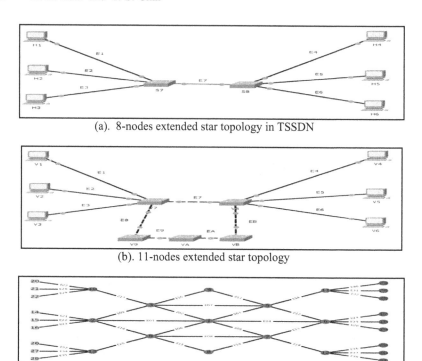

(a). 8-nodes extended star topology in TSSDN

(b). 11-nodes extended star topology

(c). 31-nodes extended star topology

Fig. 2. Extended Star topologies in TSSDN

Figure 3 are the results of simulation testing. In the following, 31-nodes extended start topologies and 100 time-sensitive flows are fixed to test the scheduling runtime for all the approaches against the number of time-slots. The number of time-slots will be increased accordingly in the sequence of 3, 30 and 100.

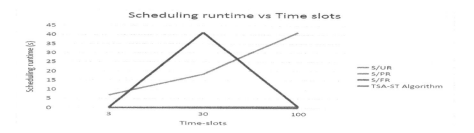

Fig. 3. Scheduling runtime vs time-slots

Figure 4 are the results of simulation testing. In this following, 100 time-slots and 100 time-sensitive flows are fixed to test the scheduling runtime for all the approaches against the topology size. The size of topologies will be increased according to the number of nodes in the sequence of 8-nodes, 11-nodes and 31-nodes extended star topology.

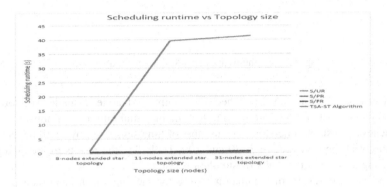

Fig. 4. Scheduling runtime vs topology size

Figure 5 are the results of simulation testing. In this following, 31-nodes extended star topology and 100 time-slots are fixed to test the scheduling runtime for all the approaches against the time-sensitive flows. The number of time-sensitive flows will be increased accordingly in the sequence of 3, 30 and 100.

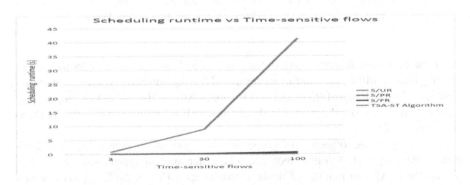

Fig. 5. Scheduling runtime vs time-sensitive flows

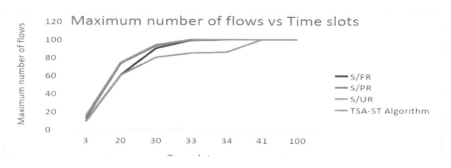

Fig. 6. Maximum number of flows versus time-slots

After the simulation testing of scheduling runtime, 31-nodes extended star topology and 100 time-sensitive flows are fixed to test the maximum number of flows for all the approaches against the time-slots. The number of time-sensitive flows will be increased accordingly in the sequence of 3, 30 and 100. Table 5 is the results of the simulation testing. Figure 6 are the results of simulation testing

In overall, the results of simulation testing for each approach have their pros and cons. The proposed algorithm has the fastest runtime while S/UR has the highest maximum number of flows. Table 1 represents the conclusion of each approach.

Table 1. Summary of S/UR, S/PR, S/FR, proposed algorithm

Performance	S/UR	S/PR	S/FR	TSA-ST
Complexity of scheduling	High	Moderate	Low	Low
Quality of the schedules	High	Moderate	Low	Low
Runtime	Slow	Moderate	Fast	Very Fast

In the next part, different network topologies which are created by famous random graph generator will be used to further compared the ILP formulation and the proposed algorithm. Erdős–Rényi (ER) model and Barabási–Albert (BA) model topologies [11] will be used to compare the proposed algorithm with ILP formulation in S/FR approach as shown in Fig. 7.

According to the objective of proposing an algorithm to reduce the time complexity, the proposed algorithm requires to be faster than all approaches while maintaining the maximum number of flows approximately. Hence, S/FR approach which has the fastest runtime is more suitable to compare with the proposed algorithm. The topologies which used as the comparison are Barabasi-10-nodes topology, Barabasi-20-nodes topology, Erdos-10-nodes topology and Erdos-20nodes-topology shown in Fig. 4. Table 2 provides the value of attributes in different topologies such as sum of the nodes and sum of the links.

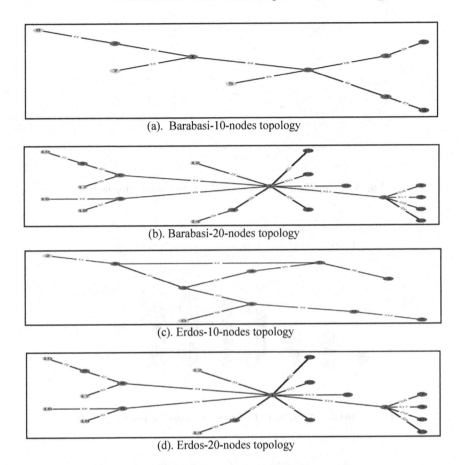

(a). Barabasi-10-nodes topology

(b). Barabasi-20-nodes topology

(c). Erdos-10-nodes topology

(d). Erdos-20-nodes topology

Fig. 7. Barabasi and Erdos topology

Table 2. Value of attributes in different topologies

Row labels	Sum of number of nodes	Sum of number of links
Barabasi-10-nodes topology	10	9
Barabasi-20-nodes topology	20	19
Erdos-10-nodes topology	10	10
Erdos-20-nodes topology	20	26

In the next simulation, 100 time-sensitive flows is used to test the runtime and the maximum number of flows of S/FR and the proposed algorithm in Barabasi-10-nodes topology. The time-slots are increasing from 10 slots by 10 until all the 100 time-sensitive flows are executed. The simulation in S/FR and proposed algorithm are presented in Figs. 8 and 9. In this simulation, the proposed algorithm has a faster runtime compared with S/FR approach while the maximum number of flows for both proposed algorithm and S/FR approach remain the same. The simulation of S/FR and

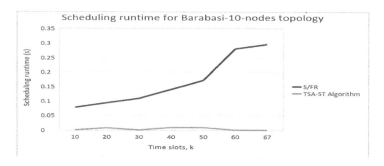

Fig. 8. Comparison of runtime in Barabasi-10-nodes topology

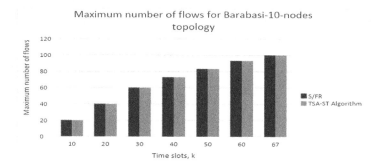

Fig. 9. Maximum number of flows in Barabasi-10-nodes topology

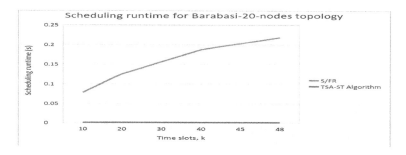

Fig. 10. Comparison of runtime in Barabasi-20-nodes topology

proposed algorithm in Barabasi-20-nodes topology are presented in Figs. 10 and 11 of 100 time-sensitive flows to test the runtime and maximum number of flows. The time-slots are increasing from 10 slots by 10 until all the 100 time-sensitive flows are executed. In this simulation, the proposed algorithm has a faster runtime compared with S/FR approach. However, the maximum number of flows for proposed algorithm is lesser than S/FR approach for 8 time-sensitive flows during the 48 time-slots.

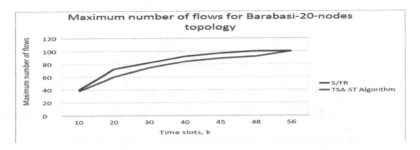

Fig. 11. Maximum number of flows in Barabasi-20-nodes topology

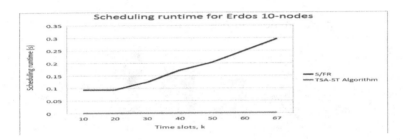

Fig. 12. Comparison of runtime in Erdos-10-nodes topology

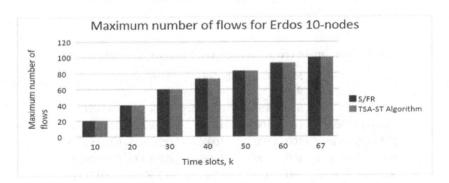

Fig. 13. Maximum number of flows in Erdos-10-nodes topology

The simulation of S/FR and the proposed algorithm in Erdos-10-nodes topology are presented in Fig. 12 and Fig. 13 using 100 time-sensitive flows to test the runtime and maximum number of flows. The time-slots are increasing from 10 slots by 10 until all the 100 time-sensitive flows are executed. In this simulation, the proposed algorithm has a faster runtime compared with S/FR approach while the maximum number of flows for both proposed algorithm and S/FR approach remain the same.

Finally, the simulation of S/FR and proposed algorithm in Erdos-20-nodes are presented Figs. 14 and 15 using 100 time-sensitive flows to test the runtime and maximum number of flows. The time-slots are increasing from 10 slots by 10 until all

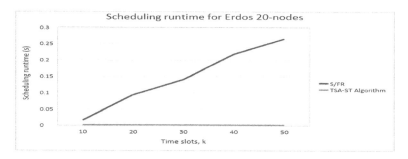

Fig. 14. Comparison of runtime in Erdos-20-nodes topology

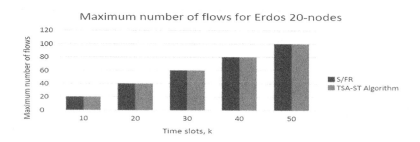

Fig. 15. Maximum number of flows in Erdos-20-nodes topology

Table 3. Summary of comparison between Proposed Algorithm and S/FR

Topology	Maximum number of flows			Runtime (s)	
	S/FR	TSA-ST	Accuracy	S/FR	TSA-ST
Erdos-10-nodes	100	100	100%	0.296875	0.00109318
Erdos-20-nodes	100	100	100%	0.265625	0.00187438
Barabasi-10-nodes	100	100	100%	0.296875	0.00109323
Barabasi-20-nodes	100	92	92%	0.218750	0.00171813

the 100 time-sensitive flows are executed. In this simulation, the proposed algorithm has a faster runtime compared with S/FR approach while the maximum number of flows for both proposed algorithm and S/FR approach remain the same. Table 3 represents the overall summary of the comparison between the proposed algorithm and S/FR approach in different topologies which are built in Erdős–Rényi (ER) model and Barabási–Albert (BA) model. Overall, the results of simulation testing by comparing the proposed algorithm, TSA-ST with S/FR approach proves the reduction of time complexity in the proposed algorithm. Besides that, most of the maximum number of flows for the proposed algorithm in different topologies are approximate to the S/FR approach except the Barabasi-20-nodes topology which has a minor difference.

5 Conclusion

This article proposed a new complexity-aware algorithm, TSA-ST for Time-Sensitive-aware Software Defined Networking Scheduling Traffic system (TSSDN-ST) on minimizing the queueing delay in Cyber Physical System (CPS) in automation industry for supporting Industrial 4.0. TSA-ST is proposed to reduce the time complexity of scheduling traffic system while retaining the quality approximately. The proposed TSA-ST algorithm is performance evaluated compared with Scheduling with Unconstrained Routing (S/UR), Scheduling with Pathsets Routing (S/PR) and Scheduling with Fixed-path Routing (S/FR) in different large size topologies. The proposed TSA-ST algorithm has successfully reduced the time complexity of the transmission schedule, attained 100 times faster performance in the transmission schedule while maintaining the quality of scheduling.

References

1. Nayak, N.G., Dürr, F., Rothermel, K.: Time-sensitive software-defined networks for real-time applications. In: Proceedings of the 24th International Conference on Real-Time Networks and Systems, pp. 193–202. ACM (2016)
2. Wang, S., Wan, J., Zhang, D., Li, D., Zhang, C.: Towards smart factory for industry 4.0: a self-organized multi-agent system with big data based feedback and coordination. Comput. Netw. **101**, 158–168 (2016)
3. Sreedharan, V.R., Unnikrishnan, A.: Moving towards industry 4.0: a systematic review. Int. J. Pure Appl. Math. **117** (2017).http://acadpubl.eu/jsi/2017-117-20-22/articles/20/84.pdf
4. Jazdi, N.: Cyber physical systems in the context of Industry 4.0. In: 2014 IEEE International Conference on Automation, Quality and Testing, Robotics, pp. 1–4 (2014)
5. Lin, Z., Pearson, S., et al.: An inside look at industrial Ethernet communication protocols. White Paper Texas Instruments (2013)
6. The Time-Sensitive Networking Task Group: IEEE 802.1 Time-Sensitive Networking Task Group (2017). http://www.ieee802.org/1/pages/tsn.html. Accessed 18 Sept 2018
7. Ahmed, K., Blech, J.O., Gregory, M.A., Schmidt, H.: Software defined networking for communication and control of cyber-physical systems. In: 2015 IEEE 21st International Conference on Parallel and Distributed Systems (ICPADS), pp. 803–808 (2015)
8. Hanzálek, Z., Burget, P., Sucha, P.: Profinet IO IRT message scheduling with temporal constraints. IEEE Trans. Ind. Inform. **6**(3), 369–380 (2010)
9. Steiner, W.: An evaluation of SMT-based schedule synthesis for time-triggered multi-hop networks. In: 2010 31st IEEE Real-Time Systems Symposium, pp. 375–384 (2010)
10. Nayak, N.G., Dürr, F., Rothermel, K.: Incremental flow scheduling and routing in time-sensitive software-defined networks. IEEE Trans. Ind. Inform. **14**(5), 2066–2075 (2018)
11. Barabási, A.-L., Albert, R.: Emergence of scaling in random networks. Science **286**(5439), 509–512 (1999)

Engineering Micro-intelligence at the Edge of CPCS: Design Guidelines

Roberta Calegari[1]([✉])(ID), Giovanni Ciatto[2](ID), Enrico Denti[1](ID), and Andrea Omicini[2](ID)

[1] Dipartimento di Informatica – Scienza e Ingegneria (DISI),
Alma Mater Studiorum–Università di Bologna, 40136 Bologna, Italy
{roberta.calegari,enrico.denti}@unibo.it
[2] Dipartimento di Informatica – Scienza e Ingegneria (DISI),
Alma Mater Studiorum–Università di Bologna, 47521 Cesena, Italy
{giovanni.ciatto,andrea.omicini}@unibo.it

Abstract. The Intelligent Edge computing paradigm is playing a major role in the design and development of Cyber-Physical and Cloud Systems (CPCS), extending the Cloud and overcoming its limitations so as to better address the issues related with the physical dimension of data—and therefore of the data-aware intelligence (such as context-awareness and real-time responses). Despite the proliferation of research works in this area, a well-founded software engineering approach specifically addressing the distribution of intelligence sources between the Edge and the Cloud is still missing. In this paper we propose some general criteria along with a coherent set of *guidelines* to follow in the *design of distributed intelligence* within CPCS, suitably exploiting Edge and Cloud paradigms to effectively enable data intelligence and accounting for both symbolic and sub-symbolic approaches to reasoning. Then, we exploit the notion of *micro-intelligence* as situated intelligence for Edge computing, promoting the idea of *intelligent environment* embodying rational processes meant to complement the cognitive process of individuals in order to reduce their cognitive workload and augment their cognitive capabilities. In order to demonstrate the general applicability of our guidelines, we propose *Situated Logic Programming* (SLP) as the conceptual framework for delivering micro-intelligence in CPCS, and *Logic Programming as a Service* (LPaaS) as its reference architecture and technological embodiment.

Keywords: Design guidelines · CPCS · Micro-intelligence · LPaaS · Situated Logic Programming · Edge intelligence

1 Introduction

According to the so-called "CPS Revolution", Cyber-Physical Systems (CPS) are radically changing human needs and expectations, ultimately affecting every aspect of human life through application domains such as smart grids, buildings,

© Springer Nature Switzerland AG 2019
R. Montella et al. (Eds.): IDCS 2019, LNCS 11874, pp. 260–270, 2019.
https://doi.org/10.1007/978-3-030-34914-1_25

factories, and so on [18,21,22]. The steady growth of Cloud services pushes the horizon of Edge computing forward as a new paradigm and promising architecture to address the challenges of Cyber-Physical and Cloud Systems (CPCS). In particular, Edge computing makes it possible to manage CPS devices by directly taking into account their situated nature, as well as to match real-time requirements by avoiding communication bottlenecks between CPS and the Cloud. This is why most CPCS applications are designed around Edge computing principles, decentralising computation towards the edge of the network to lessen the pressure on the Cloud, hence improving user experience through task offloading and by acting in-between sensors and actuators and the Cloud.

Fully addressing CPCS issues and challenges mandates for intelligence, so that intelligent capabilities – such as context-awareness and real-time planning – become crucial for Edge devices in order to fill the gap between the CPS and the Cloud ends. In particular, research efforts on Edge computing demonstrate the benefits of distributing intelligence between the Cloud and the Edge [7,17,20]. However, most of the existing research work is basically strict in scope and compartmentalised, so it does not provide for a general software engineering standpoint [1,13,20]. As a consequence, criteria, guidelines, and methodologies on how to design and distribute intelligence in CPCS according to the Edge computing paradigm are mostly missing [8].

This is why in this paper we propose some general guidelines for the design of distributed intelligence in CPCS. The proposed design approach accounts for both symbolic and sub-symbolic approaches to reasoning, fruitfully combined to produce intelligent behaviour—as the synergies between the two sorts of techniques make it possible to deal with the diverse requirements of CPCS. Then, we define *micro-intelligence* as the *situated intelligence* of Edge computing, promoting the idea of intelligent environment embodying rational processes meant to complement the cognitive process of individuals in order to reduce their cognitive workload and augment their cognitive capabilities. In particular, we propose Situated Logic Programming (SLP) as the conceptual framework for delivering micro-intelligence in CPCS, and *Logic Programming as a Service* (LPaaS) [5] as its reference architecture and technological embodiment.

2   Design Guidelines for Distributing Intelligence

Different CPCS come with different requirements in terms of *intelligence*. However, intelligence is often the result of several design choices which effectively fit a given scenario. In this section we motivate and describe a number of guidelines, summarised in Table 1, aimed at steering designers in the complex task of endowing CPCS with intelligence. Columns represent the *design choices* available to software engineers dealing with the issue of spreading intelligence in CPCS, whereas rows represent the *design criteria* they should adopt and assess so as to make informed, well-founded decisions, based on the specific application scenario. Checkboxes represent *suggestions*, reasonable choices—which are by no means intended to be strict.

Table 1. Design choices *(columns)* and design criteria *(rows)* to distribute intelligence in CPCS in a principled way. Checkmarks within parentheses represent weak preferences.

intelligence	which		where		who		
	symbolic	sub-symbolic	Cloud	Edge	individual	environment	e-institution
no requirement	✓		✓				✓
real-time req.		(✓)		✓	✓		
no requirement	✓		✓				✓
fault-tolerance req.				✓	✓		
no requirement	✓		✓				✓
safety critical req.	✓			✓	✓		
big data		✓	✓				✓
small data	✓			✓	✓		
macro scale		✓	✓				✓
micro scale	✓			✓	✓		
commonsense KB	✓		✓		(✓)		
contextual KB				✓		✓	
disembodied	✓		(✓)				✓
embodied				✓	✓		
no requirement	✓		✓				✓
situatedness req.	(✓)			✓	✓		

Designers may obviously incur in some cases where the best decision contrast with our guidelines—as it typically happens for design guidelines in SE: as "guidelines" they are meant to *guide* decision making towards the most probable path to follow, and demanding for thorough reasoning when leaving such a path. In fact, it could even be argued that the most important contribution of Table 1 are the *criteria* after which column and row headings are labelled, rather than the mere checkboxes within: to the best of our knowledge, such a detailed and pragmatically-motivated categorisation is novel in the literature on CPCS software engineering.

The design guidelines presented in this paper concern first of all the distribution of the sources of intelligence along three dimensions, conveniently reported in Table 1 (columns):

- *which* sort of intelligent source should be delivered—i.e., which approaches (symbolic vs. sub-symbolic) are to be used for equipping the (portion of the) CPCS with intelligence
- *where* such approaches and techniques should be deployed (Cloud vs. Edge)
- *who* – that is, which part/component of the CPCS – should be exhibiting the designed intelligent behaviour.

With respect to the *who* feature, intelligence can be displayed by the active *individuals* inhabiting the CPCS and performing their own decision making process based on ascribed goals and rules, and their perceptions of the environment.

There, the *environment* is the basic infrastructure enabling sensing, monitoring, and feedback control, while adding intelligence in the form of, for instance, traffic flow forecast, data analytics, self-healing capabilities (e.g., resolution of traffic congestion). Finally, there is another, possibly less "visible" entity which may exhibit intelligence: the *e-institution* [11], that is, the conceptual place where all the norms, goals, constraints which set the boundaries for the overall system behaviour are defined and, possibly, enforced (e.g. through sanctions and penalties).

A few amongst the design criteria reported in the rows of Table 1 are simply extracted from the peculiar features of CPS as devised out by the existing literature[1]—namely, their *real-time* nature, the need for *fault tolerance*, and the fact that CPS are often *safety-critical* systems. A few others stem from the addition of the Cloud to the picture, which enables CPS to reach unprecedented *scale* and provide them with the ability to gather and process a large amount of *(big) data*, continuously sent to the Cloud by devices. The remaining criteria are rather novel, and stem from two related aspects: the rise of Edge computing, on the one hand, and the need for more powerful software engineering abstractions, on the other.

Let us now discuss the guidelines in detail—that is, all the checkboxes appearing in Table 1 cells.

Real-Time Requirement. Most CPS have strict *real-time* requirements constraining decision making, hence time from analysis of input data down to taking action is typically severely limited. In that case, sub-symbolic approaches to deliver intelligence, deployed at the Edge on individuals and environmental resources, are the most likely to succeed, given that pressing timing constraints make answers from Cloud easily too slow. Moreover, e-institutions are also usually concerned with both enforcing norms governing the space of admissible interactions between system components, and monitoring the long-term evolution of the system so as to guarantee desired properties and detect misbehaviour. Indeed, the Edge computing paradigm is precisely born with the foremost goal of reducing latency of processing and communications. Finally, *application* (*not* training) of a sub-symbolic approach – which may amount at, for instance, traversing a decision tree – is likely to be more performing compared to a symbolic one, which usually implies some form of exhaustive reasoning or joint planning.

Fault-Tolerance Requirement. As depicted in the *which* column of Table 1, *fault-tolerance* has little to do with the sort of approach to intelligence. In fact, fault-tolerance – in the sense of ensuring that system faults or miscommunications have the least possible impact on the outcomes of intelligent behaviour – is greatly enhanced by leveraging *decentralised* approaches enabled by the Edge computing paradigm, where individual devices and environmental resources can replicate storage and functionality to achieve greater availability and reliability of both information processing and services provided. Although the Cloud

---

[1] See http://cyberphysicalsystems.org for a quick and nice overview.

is intrinsically a fault-tolerant computational environment – in the sense that services and storage are usually replicated, and a fail-over mechanism is in place – it is also a communication bottleneck as well as a single point of failure.

Safety-Critical Requirement. At least a portion of any given CPS is usually a *safety-critical* system. This is the reason why whenever that requirement holds, symbolic approaches deployed at the Edge under responsibility of individual actors of the system are to be preferred. By no means, there, failure in, e.g., sensor devices perceptions or communications between a group of collaborating actors (governed by an e-institution) should lead to catastrophic consequences. For the same reason, the *opaque* nature of sub-symbolic approaches cannot guarantee absence of errors under any given circumstance, whereas symbolic approaches can encode strict safety rules to be applied no matter what.

Big Data Available? The next design criterion concerns the nature of the data available for processing with the goal of delivering intelligence: has it *variety*, *velocity*, and *volume*, or, has it not? In the former case, it is desirable to exploit sub-symbolic techniques so as to find relevant patterns buried in data by leveraging the Cloud horsepower. Such data may be well used to perform long-term planning and predictive adaptation at the level of e-institution. Also, it is usually unfeasible to process large amounts of data streams coming into the system at a fast pace at the Edge, and symbolic approaches often suffer from degraded performance as the *knowledge base* increases in size.

Scale of Interest. It is worth emphasising the symmetry with the *scale* of interest for delivering intelligence: as big data best suits the Cloud and e-institutions to power sub-symbolic techniques, so does focussing on the macro scale of CPCS as the target of intelligent behaviour. Indeed, as already mentioned, long-term planning is likely to need lots of data, gathered in a considerable time span from many heterogeneous sources, demanding statistical approaches to make sense of it and find valuable insights. On the contrary, symbolic approaches pervasively deployed at the Edge of the CPCS are much more meaningful for small data analysis, so as to leave individuals and intelligent environmental resources perform local inference with the twofold goal of alleviating the computational burden on the Cloud and deliver intelligence on a shorter time horizon, locally.

Nature of Knowledge. Here, we intend to focus on the kind of information that artificial intelligence techniques exploit for delivering intelligence: is it general knowledge of a problem domain, of the physical world, of the basics semantics behind everyday objects and their relationships, or, is it specific information which has value only in well-defined situations and w.r.t. precise goals? In other words: is it *commonsense* or *contextual knowledge*?

The distinction is of paramount importance, in practice, and is reflected by the checkmarks in Table 1. First, contextual knowledge is usually acquired *dynamically* during the system operation by the sensor devices displaced at the Edge of the CPCS, and is meant to keep the system informed about the ever changing situation that individuals and environment resources should deal with. Commonsense knowledge, instead, has a more static and less "situational" nature, since it is meant to capture the innate knowledge that we, as humans, take for granted—an extremely complex task for machines, though. Depending on how critical such information is, it may be stored and exploited either in the Cloud or at the Edge. Going forward, the *who* column in Table 1 deserves special attention: in fact, contextual knowledge has been attributed to the environment and the institutional dimension, whereas commonsense to individuals and the environment. While the environment is an obvious choice for the former – as gathering and processing contextual knowledge is usually a typical sensors' and actuators' responsibility –, involving the e-institution abstraction may seem odd, at first. Conversely, the environment is not an obvious choice for commonsense knowledge, as individuals instead possibly are.

Embodied Computation? Another design criterion is the notion of *embodiment*— namely, the feature of a computation of being strictly bound to the *physical nature* of its hosting device. Embodied computations are better suited for Edge computing and should be responsibility of individuals and environmental resources. Those are in fact the devices and physical components usually equipped with sensing and actuating capabilities, hence whose computations are inevitably bound to the available equipment. Disembodied computations are instead the typical use case for the abstraction of e-institutions, which are meant to encapsulate all the norms that rule interaction and behaviour of individuals. As such, disembodied computations are typically hosted on the Cloud, but nothing goes strong against executing them also at the Edge—after all, they are just ordinary computations. Finally, since the embodiment of computations has little to do with the technical approach to deliver intelligence, this criterion does not impact the choice of whether to exploit either symbolic or sub-symbolic models.

Situatedness Requirement. Even if no preference is made explicit as regards the "Which" of intelligence, there exist arguments in favour of a stronger prevalence of symbolic approaches when situatedness *is required*. Intended as the property of computations to heavily depend on environmental conditions, situatedness is a key requirement for delivering intelligence in this context. Since, by definition, it may correspond to rare (if not unique) occurrences of events out of the normal system operations, few examples may exist for training a sub-symbolic model to detect and classify them: this is why a symbolic approach may be well suited to explicitly handling such exceptional conditions.

Finally, w.r.t. the last two criteria, we mean to emphasise that embodied vs. disembodied, situated vs. non-situated computations should be viewed and dealt with as complementary facets, to be exploited in synergy so as to better tackle real-world problems with the proper "degree of situatedness" [15].

3   Micro-intelligence in CPCS with LPaaS

In order to demonstrate the feasibility of our guidelines – that is, the actual applicability in the architectural design phase –, in this Section we present the micro-intelligence approach and LPaaS as its reference architecture and technology—which can be used in the detailed design and development stages to implement the guidelines. More precisely, the *micro-intelligence* approach [2] is exploited as a way to reify the guidelines in the LPaaS technology, thus completing the tile of intelligence in CPCS by acting synergically with sub-symbolic techniques.

In a nutshell, micro-intelligence is about scattering small chunks of machine intelligence all over a distributed, situated system, capable of enabling the individual intelligence of any kind of devices [16]: the main idea is that (micro-) intelligence can be encapsulated in devices of any sort, making them both smart and capable to work together in groups, aggregates, societies. Accordingly, the reference scenario assumes that *(i)* knowledge is locally scattered in the distributed environment, hence its situated nature; *(ii)* inference capabilities are admissible and available over this knowledge, with the goal of extending the local knowledge through induction, deduction, abduction, and the like.

Philosophically, micro-intelligence can be interpreted as the *externalised rationality* of cognitive agents (individual), complementing their own in the sense of Clark and Chambers' *active externalism* [9], and under the perspective of Hutchins' *distributed cognition* [12]. In that context, *external* means that it does not strictly belong to individuals—in fact, it is a process independently possibly executed by another entity (for instance the environments, the infrastructure) to whom the individual is (possibly, temporarily) coupled. It is also rational because it is supposed to convey a sound inference process. It complements individuals' own cognitive process because, by embodying situated knowledge about the local environment along with the inference processes admissible therein, augments the cognitive capabilities of agents that can be unaware of the knowledge embodied in the environment.

Moving from the widely-accepted consideration that pervasive and distributed systems have no global state (intended as a single, coherent knowledge base), but are rather composed of local, fragmented knowledge chunks, Situated Logic Programming (SLP) [3] introduces a possible framework for the embodiment of the micro-intelligence vision: there, multiple logical theories, scattered in the environment, can co-exist to represent the local, possibly partial knowledge base (KB). In this perspective, SLP can be seen as an extension of LP where *each logic theory is situated* in space, time, and (possibly) w.r.t. a specific environmental resource. LPaaS [5] can be seen as the natural instantiation of the SLP idea [5], designed according to the architectural style and principles of the Service-Oriented Architecture (SOA) paradigm [10] and, in particular, of the microservice vision [6]. As such, LPaaS constitutes a suitable reference architecture for delivering micro-intelligence to the CPCS edge [4], enabling situated reasoning via the explicit definition of the spatio-temporal structure of the environment where situated entities act and interact: by doing so, it suitably re-interprets the notion of distribution of LP accordingly to the SLP framework.

It is worth noting that its SOA nature further emphasises the role of *situatedness*, already brought along by distribution in itself—developing the idea of LP as a situated service while promoting key features such as encapsulation, statelessness, and locality. Concretely, LPaaS features distributed service instances (servers) scattered in a CPCS environment, each exposing its functionalities concurrently to multiple client agents, via suitable interfaces: its implementation is freely available at [14].

3.1 Symbolic Micro-intelligence at the Edge

In this section we discuss why the micro-intelligence vision and its incarnation in LPaaS and technology can be seen as the reification of the above guidelines for spreading intelligence in compliance with the Edge computing paradigm.

Scale of Interest. LPaaS is conceived for delivering intelligence at the *micro* scale of the system, at the connected (intelligent) things level—as suggested in [19], where the need for different scales of intelligence is highlighted. There, intelligence at the Edge is provided by gathering information and inference processes closer to the devices, by enabling local (symbolic) reasoning to complement global sub-symbolic reasoning (usually in the cloud).

Big Data or Small Data. Micro-intelligence proposes to synergistically exploit symbolic and sub-symbolic approaches, so as to better cope with the different requirements arising when, for instance, dealing with big data or small data analytics. Indeed, reasoning over symbolic knowledge bases allows consistency checking (i.e., detecting contradictions between facts or statements), classification (i.e., generating taxonomies), and other forms of deductive inference (i.e., revealing new, implicit knowledge given a set of facts).

Thus, we envision intelligent CPCS mitigating some of the issues experienced in sub-symbolic approaches by adding symbolic techniques to the picture, ultimately enabling novel forms of distributed and local reasoning. For instance, machine learning algorithms could generate the knowledge to be scattered across the Edge of the network, containing general information about the domain: then, such a knowledge could be refined by local constraints (e.g. specific spatio-temporal data). An LPaaS service can then reason over such knowledge to, e.g., guarantee consistency, or, infer novel information.

Fault-Tolerance Requirement. By isolating the failures of individual microservices, the LPaaS architecture helps achieving fault tolerance: since services can fail at any time, it is of paramount importance both that failures are quickly detected and, mostly, that services are automatically and quickly restored. "Failover" could be provided by the life-cycle management of the service itself, ensuring that a failed inference process is taken over by another LPaaS service.

Safety-Critical Requirement. Delivering the LPaaS services at the Edge delegates the individual system actors to take autonomous decisions, preventing possible failures in communication from leading to catastrophic consequences: hence, it helps supporting safety-critical applications. Although communication problems could arise because of the service architecture, such issues can be limited by embedding the LPaaS service in both individual agents and the environment, as well as by exploiting it as a library.

Nature of Knowledge. Being inherently rooted in the notion of situatedness, micro-intelligence is a natural choice for the design and implementation of contextual knowledge and reasoning: in fact, the LPaaS resolution process is intrinsically bound to the general computational context, both in terms of spatio-temporal context and environmental resources. This is why the LPaaS knowledge base contains (those) specific rules whose validity is bound in space and time (the "context"). Along this line, reasoning is delegated to components embedding the situated knowledge, which are the only capable of timely recognising exceptional situations: the inference capabilities enable the enactment of specific countermeasures, possibly taking real-time requirements into account. New facts and rules can also be acquired during the service lifetime, keeping the system up-to-date about the ever changing situation that individuals and environment resources are supposed to deal with. New rules can be inferred, as well.

Embodied Computation. Micro-intelligence lays its roots in the IoT world and its inner physical nature: accordingly, the LPaaS service comes with an *ad hoc* API for dealing with data collected by sensors and with streams of data (and therefore of solutions). As a result, LPaaS turns out to be an effective choice for capturing the *embodiment* feature of intelligence.

Situatedness Requirement. Stemming directly from the two previous considerations, LPaaS can well be regarded as an effective embodiment of the Situated Logic Programming paradigm. Indeed, the situated nature of the service is twofold: first, the LP inference process is itself situated in the spatio-temporal context, thus affecting solutions in relation to both the place where the service is physical located, and the time of the query; second, extra solve operations are provided for dealing with streams of solutions and with timed requests, while a dedicated API supports the exploration of services in a neighbourhood (the reader is referred to [3] for a thorough discussion).

4   Conclusion

The CPS revolution is characterised by decentralisation – from the Cloud towards the Edge – and by the need of exploiting low-level devices for the decision-making process in order to deal with issues including distributed processing, low latency, fault tolerance, better scalability and situated deliberation. However, there is still no general, well-founded software engineering approach specifically addressing the issues of intelligent Edge computing for CPCS. Along this line, in this paper we define a some general design criteria along with a coherent set of design guidelines for distributing intelligence in CPCS. Such guidelines could lay the foundation for the definition of a full-fledged methodology for intelligent CPCS. To reify the guidelines in concrete architectures and technologies, following the insights from distributed cognition, we introduce the concept of *micro-intelligence* as the way to distribute chunks of symbolic intelligence at the Edge of CPCS. We exploit Situated Logic Programming (SLP) as the reference framework for micro-intelligence, empowering the Edge with knowledge and inference capabilities of computational logic, and show how LPaaS can straightforwardly work as the reference architecture ass well as a potential technological embodiment.

References

1. Ananthanarayanan, G., et al.: Real-time video analytics: the killer app for edge computing. IEEE Comput. **50**(10), 58–67 (2017). http://ieeexplore.ieee.org/document/8057318

2. Calegari, R.: Micro-intelligence for the IoT: logic-based models and technologies. Ph.D. thesis, Alma Mater Studiorum-Università di Bologna, Bologna, Italy (2018). http://amsdottorato.unibo.it/8521

3. Calegari, R., Ciatto, G., Mariani, S., Denti, E., Omicini, A.: Logic programming in space-time: the case of situatedness in LPaaS. In: Cossentino, M., Sabatucci, L., Seidita, V. (eds.) 19th Workshop "From Objects to Agents" (WOA 2018), CEUR Workshop Proceedings, vol. 2215, pp. 63–68. Sun SITE Central Europe, RWTH Aachen University, June 2018. http://ceur-ws.org/Vol-2215/paper%5F11.pdf

4. Calegari, R., Ciatto, G., Mariani, S., Denti, E., Omicini, A.: LPaaS as micro-intelligence: enhancing IoT with symbolic reasoning. Big Data Cogn. Comput. **2**(3) (2018). http://www.mdpi.com/2504-2289/2/3/23

5. Calegari, R., Denti, E., Mariani, S., Omicini, A.: Logic programming as a service. Theor. Pract. Logic Program. **18**(3–4), 1–28 (2018). https://doi.org/10.1017/S1471068418000364

6. Calegari, R., Denti, E., Mariani, S., Omicini, A.: Logic programming as a service in multi-agent systems for the Internet of Things. Int. J. Grid Util. Comput. **10**(4), 344–360 (2019). https://doi.org/10.1504/IJGUC.2019.10022135

7. Chen, M., Li, W., Fortino, G., Hao, Y., Hu, L., Humar, I.: A dynamic service migration mechanism in edge cognitive computing. ACM Trans. Internet Technol. **19**(2) (2019). http://dl.acm.org/citation.cfm?id=3239565

8. Cicirelli, F., Guerrieri, A., Mercuri, A., Spezzano, G., Vinci, A.: ITEMa: a methodological approach for cognitive edge computing IoT ecosystems. Future Gener. Comput. Syst. **92**, 189–197 (2019). http://www.sciencedirect.com/science/article/pii/S0167739X17330224

9. Clark, A., Chalmers, D.J.: The extended mind. Analysis **58**(1), 7–19 (1998). http://www.jstor.org/stable/3328150

10. Erl, T.: Service-Oriented Architecture: Concepts, Technology, and Design. Prentice Hall/Pearson Education International, Upper Saddle River (2005). http://dl.acm.org/citation.cfm?id=1088876

11. Esteva, M., de la Cruz, D.D.L., Rosell, B., Arcos, J.L.A., Rodríguez-Aguilar, J.A., Cuní, G.: Engineering open multi-agent systems as electronic institutions. In: 19th National Conference on Artifical Intelligence (AAAI 2004), pp. 1010–1011. AAAI Press (2004). http://dl.acm.org/citation.cfm?id=1597303

12. Hollan, J., Hutchins, E., Kirsh, D.: Distributed cognition: toward a new foundation for human-computer interaction research. ACM Trans. Comput.-Hum. Interact. **7**(2), 174–196 (2000). http://dl.acm.org/citation.cfm?id=353487

13. Hu, L., Miao, Y., Wu, G., Hassan, M.M., Humar, I.: iRobot-factory: an intelligent robot factory based on cognitive manufacturing and edge computing. Future Gener. Comput. Syst. **90**, 569–577 (2019). http://www.sciencedirect.com/science/article/pii/S0167739X1831183X

14. Logic Programming as a Service (LPaaS) (2018). http://lpaas.apice.unibo.it/

15. Mariani, S., Omicini, A.: TuCSoN on cloud: an event-driven architecture for embodied/disembodied coordination. In: Aversa, R., Kołodziej, J., Zhang, J., Amato, F., Fortino, G. (eds.) ICA3PP 2013. LNCS, vol. 8286, pp. 285–294. Springer, Cham (2013). https://doi.org/10.1007/978-3-319-03889-6_33

16. Omicini, A., Calegari, R.: Injecting (micro)intelligence in the IoT: logic-based approaches for (M)MAS. In: Lin, D., Ishida, T., Zambonelli, F., Noda, I. (eds.) MMAS 2018. LNCS (LNAI), vol. 11422, pp. 21–35. Springer, Cham (2019). https://doi.org/10.1007/978-3-030-20937-7_2

17. Pace, P., Aloi, G., Gravina, R., Caliciuri, G., Fortino, G., Liotta, A.: An edge-based architecture to support efficient applications for healthcare Industry 4.0. IEEE Trans. Ind. Informatics **15**(1), 481–489 (2019). http://ieeexplore.ieee.org/document/8370750/

18. Rauch, E., Linder, C., Dallasega, P.: Anthropocentric perspective of production before and within industry 4.0. Comput. Ind. Eng. (In press). http://www.sciencedirect.com/science/article/pii/S0360835219300233

19. Rosenberg, D., Boehm, B., Wang, B., Qi, K.: Rapid, evolutionary, reliable, scalable system and software development: the resilient agile process. In: 2017 International Conference on Software and System Process (ICSSP 2017), pp. 60–69. ACM (2017). http://dl.acm.org/citation.cfm?id=3084107

20. Tang, B., Chen, Z., Hefferman, G., Pei, S., Wei, T., He, H., Yang, Q.: Incorporating intelligence in fog computing for big data analysis in smart cities. IEEE Trans. Ind. Inf. **13**(5), 2140–2150 (2017). http://ieeexplore.ieee.org/document/7874167/

21. Um, J.-S.: Futurology and future prospect of drone CPS. Drones as Cyber-Physical Systems, pp. 257–274. Springer, Singapore (2019). https://doi.org/10.1007/978-981-13-3741-3_8

22. Waschull, S., Bokhorst, J., Molleman, E., Wortmann, J.: Work design in future industrial production: transforming towards cyber-physical systems. Comput. Ind. Eng. (In press). http://www.sciencedirect.com/science/article/pii/S0360835219300683

NIOECM: A Network I/O Event Control Mechanism to Provide Fairness of Network Performance Among VMs with Same Resource Configuration in Virtualized Environment

Jaehak Lee$^{(\boxtimes)}$ ⓘ, Jihun Kang$^{(\boxtimes)}$ ⓘ, and Heonchang Yu$^{(\boxtimes)}$ ⓘ

Department of Computer Science and Engineering,
Korea University, Seoul, Korea
{smreodmlvl, k2j23h, yuhc}@korea.ac.kr

Abstract. In the virtualization environment, a hypervisor scheduler determines the degree of shared resource occupancy of the virtual machine (VM) according to the degree of CPU processing and it provides a fair CPU processing on virtual machines (VMs). But VMs are experiencing unfair network performance due to the hypervisor scheduler's policy occupying resources based on CPU processing time. In this paper, we present NIOECM which is a network IO event control technique that controls the network-intensive VM's network IO event to guarantee a fairness network performance of VMs which have the same resource configuration. The NIOECM performs a network delay processing on the network-intensive VMs which have a high network I/O event set. As a result, the network-intensive VMs which have a low network I/O event set will have more chance to occupy the network resource. In the result of experiments, our approach provides more fairness of network performance and does not give a performance interference on VM which is performing another task.

Keywords: Cloud · Virtualization · Network I/O · Hypervisor · Bandwidth · Fairness · Mitigation · Workload aware

1 Introduction

With the advent of cloud computing, it is changing from an age of using local computing resources to sharing a centralized high-performance computing resource. These results have made user applications with diverse workloads running on physical servers in the form of VM. Most hypervisor schedulers in a virtualized environment with diverse workloads are implementing VM scheduling policies based on the degree of CPU utilization to provide cloud users with fair resource utilization. However, these scheduling policies provide relatively fair CPU performance for CPU-intensive VMs, but provide unfair network performance for network-intensive VMs [7–9]. This is because, in a virtualized environment, a VM's I/O operations occupy shared hardware resources depending on the degree of VM's CPU occupancy [9, 12]. This problem causes cloud users to experience I/O latency, the unfairness of network performance

© Springer Nature Switzerland AG 2019
R. Montella et al. (Eds.): IDCS 2019, LNCS 11874, pp. 271–283, 2019.
https://doi.org/10.1007/978-3-030-34914-1_26

and degrading QoS of network-intensive VM. Various studies are continuing to improve existing network performance issues.

Rodrigues [7], using link bandwidth rate limit mechanism, presents gatekeeper which gives a powerful network isolation per a VM. But because of the limitation of link bandwidth for each VM, it is difficult to use the spare bandwidth dynamically. Mei [8] presents a method which allocates dynamic network bandwidth to VM with demand and priority based on real-time bandwidth monitoring. However, this method does not consider about the unfairness of network bandwidth among VMs which have the same bandwidth capacity. All of these studies have guaranteed the network bandwidth each VMs, but do not provide a solution for fair network performance among VMs which have the same resource configuration.

We designed a NIOECM based on Xen's credit-scheduler [5, 6, 9, 10, 13]. Our approach provides a fair network performance to VMs which have the same resource configuration without changing the scheduling order of run-queues on VM scheduler and giving no performance interference on VM which is performing another task. The contents of this paper are as follows. In Sect. 2, we will explain the motivation of our approach on the existing virtualization environment. In Sect. 3, we will show the implementation of NIOECM to solve the issue. In Sect. 4, the performance evaluation on NIOECM will be presented. Finally, we will conclude the paper in Sect. 5.

2 Motivation

Xen has adopted a split driver model where DOM0 processes the I/O of all guest VMs for efficiency. When packets come to a specific VM, hypervisor knows the packet and then queues the network I/O request for packet to shared I/O ring buffer through DOM0. Then DOM0 sends a network I/O event for alarm of network I/O request's arrival to a specific VM's event-channel [4, 5, 10, 14]. When a specific VM's virtual CPU (vCPU) occupies the physical CPU (pCPU), it first checks the event-channel about whether a pending event exists. If it exists, the specific VM processes the network I/O request [8–10, 14, 15].

In this section, we explain unfairness in communication between guest VMs which have the same resource configuration and an exterior HOST due to the limited time slice of driver domain (DOM0). Let's suppose that all guest VMs perform the network-intensive task. In Fig. 1, all VMs, including DOM0, have two vCPUs and are assigned to pCPU0 and pCPU1. The green dotted box on the run-queue is the ideal network I/O event processing range of DOM0's vCPU for fair network performance among VMs. The red dotted box at the DOM0's event-queue represents the actual range of network I/O events processed by the vCPU of DOM0 because of DOM0's limited time slice and multi-BOOST problem [9] in credit-scheduler. The VM's vCPU in run-queues will occur network I/O events to DOM0 in the order in which the VMs are scheduled and then all of network I/O events will be inserted in DOM0's event-queue based on FIFO policy [15]. The vCPUs in the DOM0's event-queue can be seen as a network I/O event set that corresponding VM's vCPU has generated. In first DOM0's time slice represented by first red dotted box in the event-queue, the network I/O events of VM1 and VM3 are included in the network I/O event processing range of DOM0 and are

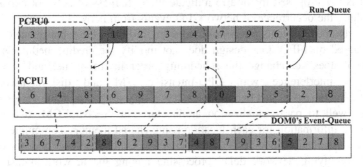

DOM0	VM1	VM2	VM3	VM4
vCPU0	vCPU2	vCPU4	vCPU6	vCPU8
vCPU1	vCPU3	vCPU5	vCPU7	vCPU9

Fig. 1. Limited DOM0's network I/O events processing range (Color figure online)

processed immediately. But network I/O latency occurs in VM4 because vCPU8 of
VM4 didn't enter in the network I/O event processing range of vCPU1 which is one of
DOM0's vCPUs. So, vCPU8's network I/O event set will wait to be processed until
DOM0's vCPU0 occupies the pCPU1, and network I/O latency occurs. An example of
such situation is shown at a yellow box of the event-queue.

In the next time slice of DOM0, vCPU 8 of the VM4 which has unprocessed
network I/O event set and vCPU-6, 2, 9, 3, and 7 in the second red dotted box will be
processed. In this situation, vCPUs of VM2 and VM4 are not included in vCPU0's
network I/O event processing range but rather will be processed at DOM0's next time
slice. This will cause them to have a network I/O latency. The next time slice of DOM0
is represented by the third red dotted box in DOM0's event-queue. The network I/O
events of vCPU-4,8,7,9,3,6 will be processed but VM2 will be processed at next time
slice of DOM0 with the same reason above. If this situation is persisted, VM1 and
VM3 have a high possibility to enter the DOM0's network I/O event processing range
but VM2 and VM4 do not. Also, vCPUs of VM1 and VM3 which are in the range of
network I/O event processing of DOM0 will be located in the head of pCPU's run-
queue more than vCPUs of VM2 and VM4. VM1 and VM3 will have high network I/O
responsiveness than VM2 and VM4, and there will be a performance discrepancy of
network I/O between VM1, VM3 and VM2, VM4. As a result, VM2 and VM4 have
lower network I/O compared to VM1 and VM3.

Let's assume that VMs perform CPU-intensive task and VM1 and VM3 occupy
more pCPU than VM2 and VM4. However, in this case, CREDIT will be exhausted,
and CREDIT of VM1 and VM3 will be less than 0, becoming OVER state. VM2 and
VM4, which consumed less CREDIT, will maintain the UNDER priority which pre-
empts the pCPU with the highest priority than OVER priority. This can provide fair
CPU processing performance. As a result, CPU-intensive guest VMs get fairness of
CPU performance. However, in situations where the percentage of VMs performing
I/O intensive tasks is high, fair I/O performance is not presented due to the mentioned
situation.

3 Design and Implementation

3.1 Design Overview

NIOECM is our proposed method to mitigate the unfairness of network performance by controlling the occurrence of network I/O events from network-intensive VMs. By doing so, network I/O events can be inserted more fairly into the event-queue of DOM0 which is based on FIFO. Our design does not modify the credit-scheduler's policy. Therefore, it does not change the scheduling order in run-queue, and there is no performance interference with CPU-intensive VM and disk-intensive VM. The NIOECM consists of just two modules. It is a very simple, portable design and can be applied well to para-virtualization architecture. In the NIOECM, two modules exchange the information for each location using shared memory communication.

A task classification module (TCM) operates in credit-scheduler and decides candidates for applying network delay processing among the network-intensive VMs which have same resource configuration obtained from event delay module (EDM). EDM classifies the actual network-intensive VM among the VMs on candidate-pool obtained from the TCM. And then, it performs network delay processing for network-intensive VMs that have a relatively high network I/O event set. As a result, it gives the opportunity to network-intensive VM with relatively low network I/O event set to use more network resources. The NIOECM's overall structure is presented in Fig. 2.

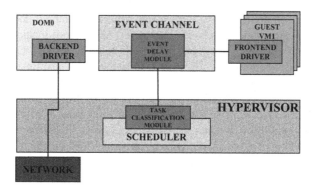

Fig. 2. NIOECM workflow

3.2 Task Classification Module (TCM)

The TCM operates in the scheduler and evaluates the degree of I/O about VMs based on the number of BOOST to judge whether or not it is a candidate for applying the network delay processing. In the event-channel on which the EDM is operating, there is no mechanism to know about the VM's degree of I/O responsiveness. Therefore, TCM sends a list of network delay processing candidates using shared memory communication. The detailed operation of TCM is as follows.

(1) Count the number of BOOSTs generated from network-intensive VM

There are two kinds of the main reason for BOOST generation from event in Xen hypervisor. The first reason is INTER-DOMAIN communication. As described in Sect. 2, when HOST's NIC driver receives a packet from exterior, the hypervisor fetches the packet from the NIC driver and queuing the packet information (in guest VM's standpoint, called as a network I/O request) to the shared I/O ring buffer to forward the packet to the destination VM and then sends a network I/O event to destination VM. When destination VM's vCPU which is in an idle state wakes up, it checks the event-channel first. If there is a pending event, vCPU's priority changes into BOOST priority and then vCPU is placed at the head of pCPU's run-queue. The second reason is INTRA-DOMAIN communication. A specific VM which is performing a disk I/O sends a disk I/O event to DOM0 for notifying the disk I/O request. And DOM0 sends a disk I/O event to notify the arrival of disk I/O response to a specific VM. In both cases, the result of the I/O request delivery to the destination VM is a BOOST generation of the destination VM. The more number of BOOSTs on VM is, the more I/O requests are occurred at VM. So we can say the more number of BOOSTs on VM, the more likely the VM will be a high I/O intensive with a high I/O responsiveness. We will use this BOOST mechanism [5, 9, 11, 14] to evaluate the degree of I/O intensive VMs. TCM counts the number of BOOSTs occurred from network-intensive VM which is in the list obtained from EDM. Regarding the classification method of network-intensive VM and disk-intensive VM, we will discuss in Sect. 3.3.

(2) Select the network delay processing candidate

TCM selects the network delay processing candidate with BOOST ratio on all of network-intensive VMs which are classified by EDM. VM's are classified into two types as below.

(a) **NONCANDIDATE-VM:** A network-intensive VM that BOOST ratio is under *the average BOOST × 0.3*. These VMs generate relatively low BOOST and are not included in the candidate-pool. We consider that the VM has a low I/O intensive workload or CPU-intensive VM.

(b) **CANDIDATE-VM:** A VM that BOOST ratio is over *the average BOOST × 0.3*. These VMs are included in a candidate pool and generate a relatively large amount of BOOST. In other words, they have high I/O intensive workload.

After selecting candidates of network delay processing, a list of CANDIDATE-VMs in the candidate-pool is sent to the EDM via shared memory communication.

3.3 Event Delay Module (EDM)

EDM actually performs network I/O event control to give a fairness network performance among network-intensive VMs. Figure 3 presents the workflow of EDM that VMs send network I/O events to the DOM0's event-queue wherein DOM's event-channel to handle the network I/O request. EDM's main purpose is to give a network delay processing to guest VMs which have a relatively high ratio of network I/O request (VM1, 3 in Fig. 3) wherein candidate-pool. As a result, VMs which have a

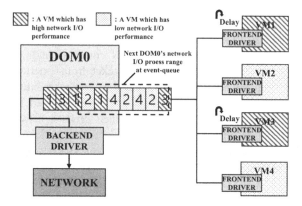

Fig. 3. EDM workflow

relatively low network I/O request ratio can take a chance to occupy the NIC driver. By doing so, the network I/O events can be inserted more fairly in the DOM0's event-queue. EDM's operation is as follows.

(1) **Classify network-intensive VM**

The main reasons for BOOST occurrence in the credit-scheduler can be divided into two as described in Sect. 3.2, disk I/O and network I/O. In credit-scheduler, we can't know the reason for BOOST occurrence. To know the degree of network I/O responsiveness, we need to know if a boost has occurred from a network-intensive VM, or if a boost has occurred from a disk-intensive VM. Thanks to the event-channel mechanism, the reason for BOOST occurrence can be classified using an INTER-DOMAIN event (In NIOECM, known as a network I/O event) and an INTRA-DOMAIN event (In NIOECM, known as a disk I/O event) [4]. The destination VM of the I/O event of the disk-intensive VM is itself. So, this case will generate an INTRA-DOMAIN event. For a network-intensive VM, the INTER-DOMAIN event will be generated because the destination of the I/O event is not itself. With the above information, we define the VM which generates the INTER-DOMAIN event between VMs in the candidate-pool as a network-intensive VM. At last, the EDM sends a list of network-intensive VMs which are performing the network I/O to the TCM through shared memory communication. The reason is that list is to monitor the BOOST which is occurred from network-intensive VMs in the credit-scheduler.

(2) **Count the number of network I/O event generated from network-intensive VM**

EDM counts the number of network I/O events generated from each of VM obtained from the TCM for *30* ms × *number of running VMs*, which is the same as EDM's operation period. The reason for 30 ms is because it is a default time slice of credit-scheduler. And the reason for multiplying *the number of running VMs* is to measure the number of network I/O events from all running VMs under hypervisor.

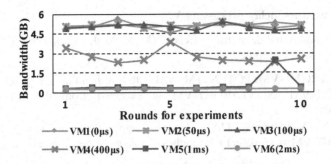

Fig. 4. Network bandwidth per different static delay time

(3) Calculate the delay time per POTENTIAL-VM

EDM calculates the delay time of network I/O event of each network-intensive VM by difference based on network-intensive VM which has the lowest number of network I/O events. Network I/O event delay time is calculated as follows. For all of network-intensive VMs, EDM obtains *the average amount of network I/O events*. If the VM has more than *the average amount of network I/O events × 0.3*, it is classified as a POTENTIAL-VM to ignore the network-intensive VM which has a high degree of BOOST caused by disk I/O. The value of *0.3* is the constant value that determines the degree of selection of POTENTIAL-VM among network-intensive VMs. Then the POTENTIAL-VM with the lowest number of network I/O events is designated as a LOWEST-VM. EDM obtains the difference between the number of events for each POTENTIAL-VM and the number of LOWEST-VM's events and calculates the average of difference about all of POTENTIAL-VMs which we got except LOWEST-VM. For each difference of POTENTIAL-VM, EDM multiplies *400* μs which is the fixed delay value and then divides with the average of difference. In Fig. 4, we make a small experiment on network delay processing. In the experiments, all of VMs continuously send a packet which window-size is 86 KB to DOM0 during 1 min with 15 times. We apply the network delay processing with a different delay time to each of 6 VMs. As a result of the experiments, the VM's throughput started to decrease from about *200* μs.

Through this experiments, we set the fixed delay value of *400* μs. The reason for the fixed delay value of *400* μs is because it is the best value that affects network-intensive VMs with relatively large number of events without affecting the overall network bandwidth of the HOST through this experiment. The difference between the number of POTENTIAL-VM's events and the number of LOWEST-VM's events is the relative value that determines the degree of network delay processing time for each POTENTIAL-VM based on LOWEST-VM. The following Eq. (1) is as below.

$$Delay\ time(\mu s) = \frac{PVMEC - LVMEC}{Average\ of\ difference} 400\ \mu s \qquad (1)$$

PVMEC: Number of POTENTIAL-VM's events
LVMEC: Number of LOWEST-VM's events.

(4) **Define network delay processing VM**

After calculating the delay time of each VM, EDM defines the VM which should apply the network delay processing.

(a) **NONTARGET-VM:** POTENTIAL-VM with less than the average difference and LOWEST-VM. NONTARGET-VM is excepted from the network delay processing.
(b) **TARGET-VM:** POTENTIAL-VM with upper than the average difference. TARGET-VM is an object that applies the network delay processing.

(5) **Perform three stages for network delay processing**

EDM applies network delay processing to VMs in three steps. The first and second network delay processing operations are performed with the delay time which is calculated during one monitoring cycle. Assume that the occurrence of network I/O events of VM1, 3 is relatively higher than that of VM2, 4. In the first round, the VM1 and VM3 are selected to TARGET-VM and are network delay processing is applied. And the VM2 and VM4 are selected to the NONTARGET-VM and are network delay processing is not applied. In the round second, VM2 and VM4 will have more events than VM1 and VM3 which have network delay processing adopted.VM2 and VM4, to which delay processing is not applied, have a larger probability that the number of event occurrences is higher than that in VM1 and VM3 to which delay processing is applied. So, VM2 and VM4 will have a high probability to be TARGET-VM. In the last three rounds, network delay processing is performed on the average number of network I/O events of each VM in the first, second and third monitoring cycle to make the each of VM's event occurrence evenly.

4   Performance Evaluation

4.1   Experimental Setup

In this section, we present the evaluation of the NIOECM prototype. Our experimental environment consists of two HOSTs that connected via a gigabit switch. Table 1 shows the configuration of two HOSTs. Based on the Iperf [2] which is a powerful network streaming generator, we evaluated the NIOECM's fair network performance among VMs which have the same resource configuration. Additionally, we evaluated the

Table 1. HOST configuration

	HOST1	HOST2
CPU	Intel core i5-4690 CPU @ 3.50 GHZ × 4	Intel core i5-4590T @ 2.00 GHZ × 4
RAM	DDR3 20 GB	DDR3 8 GB
Network	Qualcomm E220x Gigabit	Intel I217-LM Gigabit
OS	Ubuntu 14.04 for all VMs, including DOM0	Ubuntu 16.04
Hypervisor	Xen-4.4.1	N/A
Guest VM	2 vCPUs, 2048 MB	N/A
DOM0	2 vCPUs, 2048 MB	N/A

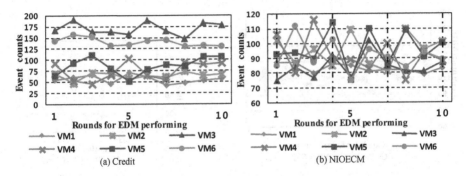

Fig. 5. Network I/O event counts of credit-scheduler and NIOECM per rounds

NIOECM's interference with CPU-intensive VMs, disk-intensive VMs and VM with intermittent network tasks. We conducted comparison of the credit-scheduler with the NIOECM applied credit-scheduler (referred to as NIOECM) in all of the experiments.

4.2 NIOECM Effects on Network I/O Event

In the experiments, we specify 6 VMs as clients and DOM0 as a server. Each VM concurrently transmits 86 KB packets to DOM0 for one minute. And during performing the NIOECM and credit-scheduler, we measured the number of occurrences of network I/O events before the EDM's network delay processing in a specific section. The experimental results are as follows. In Fig. 5(a), VM3 and VM6 have the high number of network I/O events. We can see this situation that VM3 and VM6 are always included in network I/O event processing range of DOM0 very well, and the other VM didn't. In Fig. 5(b), network I/O events of all of VMs occurs evenly very well than that in Fig. 5(a). The dotted line of in Fig. 5(b) represents the 3rd network I/O delay processing on three stage network delay processing from EDM. For the number of network I/O events in first round of experiment, VM3 is lower than that of VM4. After 3rd network I/O processing of EDM (second round of experiment), the number of network I/O events of VM3 and VM4 cross each other. And then, the number of network I/O events of VM3 exceeds that of VM4 (fourth round of experiment). It can be seen that 3 stage network delay processing of EDM is applied very well. For a VM1, the number of network I/O events of VM1 is about 80. So this experiment shows that VM1 does not affect network delay processing. As an overall result, we can see that NIOECM can take control of network I/O event of each VM as well through these experiments.

4.3 NIOECM Effects on Network-Intensive VMs

In this experiment, based on the Iperf benchmark results, NIOECM is compared to the credit-scheduler to see if it provides fair network performance. HOST1 acts as a client and HOST2 as a server every 3 min for 1 min in each number of 6 VMs. from HOST1 to HOST2 on the credit-scheduler and NIOECM, we take TCP/IP test 100 times respectively. The packet window size is 256 KB. The red circle is a NIOECM's degree

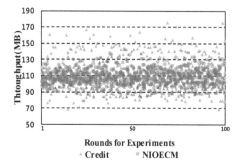

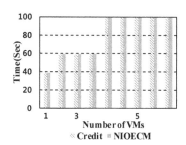

Fig. 6. Iperf throughput distribution

Fig. 7. Sysbench execution time by number of CPU-intensive VMs with running network-intensive VMs

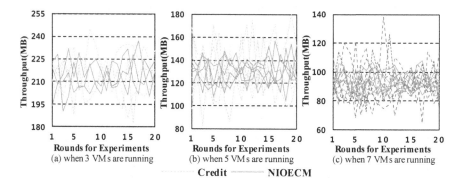

Fig. 8. Iperf throughput by number of network-intensive VMs with running CPU-intensive VMs

of distribution of the network throughput and the blue triangle is credit-scheduler's. In Fig. 6, NIOECM is generally more concentrated in the middle than credit-scheduler and the total average throughput is 662.8 MB on NIOECM and 658.8 MB on credit-scheduler, respectively, which is not much different. This experiment shows that NIOECM gives a fair network performance than a credit-scheduler and does not degrade the total bandwidth on HOST machine.

4.4   NIOECM Impacts on CPU-Intensive VM

NIOECM does not affect the scheduling order for the run-queues of pCPU. The TCM of NIOECM just counts the number of BOOSTs which are generated from network-intensive VMs in the credit-scheduler, and then picks up the list of network delay processing candidates and delivers the list to the EDM running on the event-channel through shared memory communication. Because NIOECM performs network delay processing in a separate area from the scheduler, CPU intensive VMs and network intensive VMs do not interfere with each other. To measure the performance of CPU-intensive VM under NIOECM, we leverage the Sysbench [1] which is generating CPU task that finds a prime number between 1 and predefined numbers in this experiment. For a network-intensive VM, we leverage the Iperf with configuration that specific number of VMs on HOST1 send packets which window size is 256 KB to HOST2 concurrently. The experiment is divided into two types. The first experiment measures the impact of NIOECM on CPU intensive VMs and the other measures the impact of CPU-intensive VMs on the performance of NIOECM. Both experiments proceed in comparison to the credit-scheduler. In the first experiment, 8 VMs perform a Sysbench that is configured to find prime numbers between 1 and 50,000. And we gradually increased the number of network-intensive VMs. The second experiment is performed by the reverse of the procedure of the first experiment, 8 VMs are run Iperf that is performed 20 times for 1 min. And we gradually increase the CPU-intensive VM. The experimental results are shown in first experiment of Fig. 7 and second experiment of Fig. 8. Figure 7 shows that NIOECM has no difference of results with the CPU performance of the credit-scheduler when increasing the network-intensive. This is because NIOECM's network delay processing is performed in a separate area from the scheduler, and it does not affect the scheduling order of the scheduler. There experiments show that NIOECM does not change the policy of the credit-scheduler and does not make an overhead on any VMs that are performing CPU-intensive tasks.

In the assessment of second experiment, we use the Eq. (2) which calculates the throughput average distribution (TAD) for all rounds of experiment. According to (2), in Fig. 8(a), the NIOECM's TAD is 20.9085 MB and the credit-scheduler's TAD is 27.4286 MB. As a result, three network-intensive VMs are enough to belong to network I/O event processing range of DOM0. The results of TAD on NIOECM and credit-scheduler are much slightly different. However, In Fig. 8(b), TAD of credit-scheduler is 50.8238 MB and that of NIOECM is 28.2905 MB. Finally, Fig. 8(c) shows that the credit-scheduler's TAD is 38.9 MB and that of NIOECM is 13.7 MB. For an all of rounds of experiment, we compare the highest throughput VM (HVM) and the lowest throughput VM (LVM). In Fig. 8(b), HVM and LVM of NIOECM are 157 MB and 108 MB respectively, and that of credit-scheduler are 180 MB and 82.5 MB. In Fig. 8(c), HVM and LVM of NIOECM are 108 MB and 79 MB, and that of credit-scheduler are 138 MB and 64 MB. According to the two experimental results, it shows that NIOECM does not degrade the performance of CPU-intensive VMs and performs fair network I/O operations among the network-intensive VMs rather than the credit-scheduler.

$$TAD\,(MB) = \frac{\sum_{i=1}^{r} HVM_i - LVM_i}{r} \tag{2}$$

HVM: VM which throughput is highest
LVM: VM which throughput is lowest
r: Rounds for experiments.

4.5   NIOECM Impacts on Disk-Intensive VMs

To evaluate the impact of NIOECM on the performance of disk-intensive VM, we leverage the 'dd' command-line [3] in Linux, whose purpose is to convert and copy files. There are 8 VMs, a half of them running the disk-intensive workload and the others running a network-intensive workload. We configure the 'dd' to read/write 512 times with block size of 2048 Bytes. In Fig. 9, the result shows that NIOECM has no negative impact on the disk-intensive VMs, because EDM of NIOECM performs the network delay processing only on a network-intensive VM.

4.6   NIOECM Impacts on Intermittent-Network VMs

In this experiment, we evaluate whether the NIOECM impacts on VMs that have an intermittent network workload. 8 VMs on HOST1 perform Iperf at HOST2. The half of them continually send a packet where the window size is 256 KB to HOST2 and the others periodically send a packet where the window size is 32 KB to HOST2 15 times for 4 s. The result shows that NIOECM does not perform a network delay processing on intermittent-network VMs, as shown in Fig. 10.

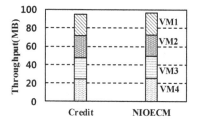

Fig. 9. dd throughput of 4 disk-intensive VMs with 4 network-intensive VMs

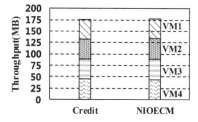

Fig. 10. Iperf throughput of 4 intermittent network-intensive VMs with 4 network-intensive VMs

5   Conclusion

In this paper, we presented a network I/O event controller, called NIOECM, to mitigate the unfairness of network performance among VMs which have the same resource configuration. In NIOECM, there are two modules, TCM, which measures the degree of network-intensive of the VM, and EDM, which is responsible for the actual network delay processing. Our experimental results showed that NIOECM provides more fair network performance than in existing Xen environments, and does not give a negative impact on VMs running other workload types.

Acknowledgement. This work was supported by IITP (Institute for Information & communications Technology Promotion) grant funded by the Korea government (MSIT, Ministry of Science and ICT) (No. 2018-0-00480, Developing the edge cloud platform for the real time services based on the mobility of connected cars) and the MSIT, Korea, under the ITRC (Information Technology Research Center) support program (IITP-2018-0-01405) supervised by the IITP.

References

1. Sysbench. https://launchpad.net/sysbench
2. Iperf. https://iperf.fr/
3. dd. http://man7.org/linux/man-pages/man1/dd.1p.html
4. Event-channel. https://wiki.Xen.org/wiki/Event_Channel_Internals
5. Credit-scheduler. https://wiki.Xen.org/wiki/Credit_Scheduler
6. Barham, P., et al.: Xen and the art of virtualization. In: Proceedings of the ACM Symposium on Operating Systems Principles (SOSP 2003), pp. 164–177 (2003)
7. Rodrigues, H., Santos, J.R., Turner, Y., Soares, P., Guedes, D.: Gatekeeper: supporting bandwidth guarantees for multi-tenant datacenter networks. In: Proceedings of the 3rd Conference on I/O Virtualization. WIOV 2011, p. 6 (2011)
8. Mei, L., Lv, X.: Optimization of network bandwidth allocation in Xen. In: 2015 IEEE 17th International Conference on High Performance Computing and Communications (HPCC), pp. 1558–1566 (2015)
9. Ongaro, D., Cox, A.L., Rixner, S.: Scheduling I/O in virtual machine monitors. In: Proceedings of the Fourth ACM SIGPLAN/SIGOPS International Conference on Virtual Execution Environments (VEE) (2008)
10. Asyabi, E., et al.: TerrierTail: mitigating tail latency of cloud virtual machines. IEEE Trans. Parallel Distrib. Syst. **29**, 2346–2359 (2018)
11. Zeng, L., et al.: Raccoon: a novel network I/O allocation framework for workload-aware VM scheduling in virtual environments. IEEE Trans. Parallel Distrib. Syst. **28**, 2651–2662 (2017)
12. Jiang, C., et al.: Interdomain I/O optimization in virtualized sensor networks. Sensors (Basel) **18**, 4395 (2018)
13. Li, J., et al.: Accurate CPU proportional share and predicable I/O responsiveness for virtual machine monitor: a case study in Xen. IEEE Trans. Cloud Comput. **5**, 604–616 (2015)
14. Qu, H., Liu, X., Xu, H.: A workload-aware resources scheduling method for virtual machine. Int. J. Grid Distrib. Comput. **8**, 247–258 (2015)
15. Xi, S. et al: Prioritizing local inter-domain communication in Xen. In: 2013 IEEE/ACM 21st International Symposium on Quality of Service (IWQoS), pp. 1–10 (2013)

Learning and Prediction of E-Car Charging Requirements for Flexible Loads Shifting

Salvatore Venticinque and Stefania Nacchia[(✉)]

Department of Engineering, University of Campania "Luigi Vanvitelli",
Via Roma 9, Aversa, Italy
{salvatore.venticinque,stefania.nacchia}@unicampania.it

Abstract. The availability of distributed renewable energy sources (RES), such as photo-voltaic panels, allows to locally consume or accumulate energy, avoiding power peaks and loss along the power network. However, as the number of utilities in a household or a building increases, and the energy must be equally and intelligently shared among the utilities and devices, demand side management systems must exploit new solution for allowing such energy usage optimisation. The current trends of demand side management systems highly exploit loads shifting, as a concrete solution to align consumption to the fluctuating produced power, and to maximise the energy utilisation avoiding its wastage. Moreover the introduction, in the latest years, of e-cars has given a boost to smart charging, as it can increase the flexibility that is necessary for maximising the self-consumption. However we strongly believe that a performing demand side management system must be able to learn and predict user's habits and energy requirements of her e-car, to better schedule the loads shifting and reduce energy wastage. This paper focuses on the e-car utilisation, investigating the exploitation of machine learning techniques to extract and use such knowledge from the power measures at charging plug.

Keywords: Smart energy · Energy management system · Clustering · Machine learning

1 Introduction

In recent years, the technology shift of power grid reached the users' household, where IoT devices make people aware of the energy resource they can manage and how to take part to a common overall strategy for smart grids [18]. Wise scheduling of smart appliances, that can be shifted in time (shiftable loads) [7], is a valuable solution to provide high scheduling flexibility for *demand side management (DSM)* [14]. Moreover the degree of flexibility can be increased by the exploitation of *battery electric vehicles (BEV), plug-in hybrids (PHEV)* or *hydrogen fuel cell electric vehicles (FCEV)*. Above all, the new concept of

© Springer Nature Switzerland AG 2019
R. Montella et al. (Eds.): IDCS 2019, LNCS 11874, pp. 284–293, 2019.
https://doi.org/10.1007/978-3-030-34914-1_27

Vehicle to Grid (V2G) energy exchange [10], has recently arisen. It allows the bi-directional energy exchange between EV and the power grid, which can provide additional resource to the power grid for preventing grid overloading, levelling peak load, reducing energy loss and providing backup power. The predictive smart scheduling of shiftable loads has been investigated in the CoSSmic project [5] to optimise the utilisation of green energy production from photo-voltaic panels. The CoSSmic approach was based on the possibility to predict the energy production and to learn the load profiles of appliances. However, the users had to plan in advance the usage of their appliance in order to let the scheduler know about the future energy requirements. In this context, our contribution aims at investigating the possibility to learn the energy consumption of an e-car in order to predict the future usage for supporting an autonomic smart scheduling of loads. The remainder of the paper is organised as follows. In the following section we highlight the work that has been done up till now in the context of load characterisation, forecasting and its application on DSM strategies. In Sect. 3 we further explain our objectives and how we model a charging load. In Sect. 4 we describe the various steps of our methodology for load characterisation and forecasting, focusing on the formulation of the learning problems and the used algorithms. Finally in Sect. 6 we discuss the evaluation results of the implemented learning and forecasting methods.

2 Related Work

Predicting and modelling energy demand profiles is a well studied field, many research activities have been pursued and brought up significant results. In [9] power consumption signatures are used to describe the behaviours of home appliances, which include information such as time of use, on-and-off duration and patterns, power demands, etc; the authors in [12] propose an agent based model with the possibility of flattening of the daily electricity load curve, shifting the demand from one time period to other time periods in response to hourly prices. Due to the expected large quantity of PHEVs that will be integrated into the power grid in the near future, the impact of substantial PHEVs charging on the power grid needs to be investigated [8]. Due to their ability to deal with non-linearities of the input data, artificial neural networks (ANNs) and fuzzy logic (FL) models are commonly used techniques for modelling and forecasting load demand [6].

Many approaches base their forecasting model on statistic modelling: the paper [1] provides a stochastic model useful to simulate and predict the electricity demand resulting from a general arrival and charging pattern for EVs/PHEVs. In [2] authors develop a complete stochastic model for the load, by modelling arrivals of charge requests as a Poisson process and using queuing theory to derive the statistics of the load. About machine-learning based approaches, the paper [11] proposes a charging strategy to determine when to charge by making real-time charging decisions based on various auxiliary data, including driving, environment, pricing, and demand time series, in order to minimise the overall vehicle energy cost. While in [19] the authors focus more on users' driving behaviours and propose a data-driven method introduced to model the EV user behaviour based on EV user charging records collected in public charging facilities over 4 years. An approach which combines K-Means clustering and multilayer-perceptron is developed and tested. To the best of our knowledge the works that obtained the best results with a similar approach and algorithm to the one we used are [16], where the expected demand from a PHEV is modelled by assigning certain probability distributions to the PHEV's required charging time and the starting time of charge follows the real world practice, and then support vector machines are employed in order to find the best model to fit the data; the other one is [15] where the use of such algorithms has been proposed for short-term load forecasting.

3   Problem Definition

Load scheduling can be modelled as a constrained multi-criteria optimisation problem. On one hand the load shift can be used to lowering the power peaks or to maximise the usage of green energy. On the other hand, it needs to take into account preferences and constraints set by the users. In particular, regarding the schedule of ev-charging, other relevant objectives are the minimisation of waiting time of the user or the maximum utilisation of charging spots. Here we focus on the capability to predict the energy requirement of an EV as it would allow to take decisions about the charge scheduling in a charging station or it could be used by an household as well as by an energy management system that aims at maximising the utilisation of PV energy for money saving. In this context the objective is to learn:

- when the EV is usually charged: time of the day or day of the week
- where it is charged
- how long it is charged
- how much energy is charged
- when the EV will leave

Training the model on historical data, we will try to forecast: *when* the next charge could be scheduled and for *how long* it will charge.

3.1   Problem Formulation and Selection of Features

Practically, we focus on forecasting three main parameters, namely *Time of arrival* t_a, which can be seen as the next time when a charge is due, the energy charged e_c, and the time of leaving t_l. The objective is to train a learning model exploiting some relevant information measured when the EV arrives and leaves the charging station. The relevant parameters are:

- $TimeOfArrival: t_a$, which represents the arrival time at the charging station
- $SoC(t_a)$, the state of the battery at the time the user arrives at the charging station

- $Pos(t_a)$, the user's position coordinates when it charges.
- $TimeOfLeaving : t_l$, the time the user unplugs the EV
- $SoC(t_l)$, which the state of the battery when the user leaves the charging station.

In order to simplify the problem, we will assume that:

- The EV will charge always at the same charging point.
- We only measure and predict the charged energy: $e_c = SoC(t_l) - SoC(t_a)$
- The EV leaves, or at least is unplugged, when the the battery is fully charged or the target energy level is reached. It means that the charging duration $d_c = t_l - t_a$

The introduced measures have been further processed to build a data-set composed of a sequence of records whose fields are:

- *Event type (et $\in E = \{P, U\}$)*: this feature helps identifying when an EV starts charging or stop charging. P stands for *Plug* and U for *Unplug*.
- *Day hour (h is an integer $\in H = [0, 23]$)*: this is relevant because we suppose that the user behaves according to certain habits depending on the week day, or even a specific time of day
- *Week of day (d is an integer $\in D = [0, 7]$)*:
- *Weekend (w is a Boolean value)*: the weekend information is also valuable, for possibly the weekend days could influence the user behaviour.
- *Charging duration (ct is an integer $\in N$)*: represents how long the user charges and is derived from the *event type* feature.
- *Charging power (pp $\in N$)*: this value shows the power (KW) capability of the charging station
- *Charged Energy (ce $\in N$)*: this value represents the energy charged (number of Wh) from the plug and the unplug events.
- *Time next plug ($t_{np} \in N$)*: this another basic feature and it represents the time (in seconds) between two charges and it defines when the next charge is due.

The prediction problem is formulated according to two points of view. In fact the forecasting of the time the next charge is due is formulated as a non linear regression problem, that allows us to forecast the next continuous value of the target variable ($t_{np}(i + 1)$).

Prediction of energy requirements for the next charge is, instead, formulated as a clustering problem, as we observed, that the amounts of charged energy accumulates according to few different values mostly according to the week day or time of the day.

4   Data Processing and Model Training

The designed methodology is based on a series of recursive phases that aim at developing a reliable forecasting model the Fig. 1 shows every step of the methodology workflow.

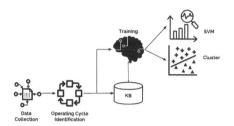

Fig. 1. Methodology phases

- *Data Collection*: the data is collected and stored and the *Knowledge Base*, and it constitutes the baseline of the forecasting procedure.
- *Operating Cycle Identification*: once the data is collected we extract meaningful features from it and identify the operating cycle of an EV.
- *Training*: the data is used for training the forecasting model.
- *Forecasting*: we use our trained model to forecast the observed features.

The assumption made in the previous section allow us to exploit a set of data collected in a private household by a smart-meter that measured energy used for charging one EV for more than one year. Data are collected every three minutes and are provided as a time-series of cumulative energy values (Wh), the finale data set comprises 52.000 samples.

4.1   Operating Cycle Identification

An operating cycle, in simple terms, has been identified from a plug event and an unplug event, which, under our simplification, corresponds the act of charging an EV or unplugging it from the charging station. Nevertheless since the data is usually full of noise and odds energy peaks, it is not so easy to identify an operating cycle, and the data must be subjected to various stage of data modelling and cleaning. We have defined a *data-cleaning pipeline* that comprises a series of actions performed on the data set in order to obtain better and more significant data as input of the learning process.

Event Categorization: as of now, we are interested in identifying and characterise the plug/unplug event, for these are fundamental to understand how and when the appliance is used during the day, if there are usage peaks in specific days or hours. We have based the event identification on two hypothesis, both based on the fact that the usage follows a square wave progressing:

- **Plug Event:** let's consider a time series $t_1, t_2, ...t_n$, if at a time point t_i the corresponding value of power is $p(t_i) == 0$ and $p(t_{i+1}) > power\_threshold$ then that peak is identified as a *plug event*
- **Unplug Event:** considering a time series $t_1, t_2, ...t_n$, if at a time point t_i the corresponding value of power is $p(t_i) > power\_threshold$ and $p(t_{i+1}) == 0$ then that peak is identified as an *unplug event*

Outliers Drop: an outlier is an observation that significantly differs from other observations of the same feature. If a time series is plotted, outliers are usually the unexpected spikes or dips of observations at given points in time. The presence of the outliers in the collected data could be caused by different reasons: measurement errors, transmission or memorisation error, timing error. The outliers are removed by identifying if the *time_delta* between an *unplug* and the subsequent *plug* event is less than *outlier_time*, a dynamic threshold statistically calculated.

Remove False Unplug: the next step of the raw data cleaning process is due to the presence of *"false unplug"* in the time series. As the time series unfolds itself we have identified a series of subsequent plug/unplug event; as the procedure for the categorisation is quite naive many *"false positive"* event are identified, and among them it is possible to find a plug/unplug event where the power value has a peak fall that lasts much less than an actual event, so the *remove false unplug procedure* revolves around the *time_delta* between the various plugs/unplugs event.

4.2   Model Training

To start the actual learning process, first we need to frame our problem and choose the model that could best fit our purpose:

- The *Time Next Plug* forecasting is undoubtedly a supervised learning problem as we start from training data and produce an inferred function, which can be used for mapping new examples.
- As our target feature is a numeric value our problem can be framed as *Multivariate Regression problem*, and we would try to approximate a mapping function f from a vector of input variables X, our features, to a continuous output variable y, that is *Time next plug*. The chosen model for forecasting this feature is *SVM regression model* with a *radial basis function* kernel; this model permits for construction of a non-linear model without changing the explanatory variables.
- The *Charging Time* clustering will be addressed as a unsupervised learning problem, thus we will apply a clustering algorithm for identifying common charging values. i.e *K-Means*, in order to evaluate effectively:

  - When usually, during the day, the users plug into a charging station
  - After how long the user usually schedule another charge
  - Is it possible that the charging duration or the capacity stored influence the time of the next charge?

5   Experimental Results

5.1   Time Next Charge Prediction

A first experiment aims at evaluating the results the regression algorithm, namely the *SVM* regression algorithm to predict the *time to next plug*.

In particular we provide the following measures:

- *Mean Absolute Error (MAE)*: measures the average absolute deviation of forecasted values from original ones.
- *Root Mean Squared Error (RMSE)*: represents the sample standard deviation of the differences between predicted values and observed values (called residuals).
- *Coefficient of Determination (R^2)*: is a statistical measure of how close the data are to the fitted regression function [13].

5.2   SVM Regression

The whole data set has been divided into *training set* and *test set*, with the widely accept 70% - 30% ratio. Since the data set is series of time related values, we don't want to lose the consequentiality of the events, considering that most certainly, one or more previous values influence the next ones, in this ratio we have maintained the ordered sequence, without shuffling the values. The hyper-parameter optimisation is implemented using the grid search algorithm [3]. It is an exhaustive searching through a manually specified subset of the hyper-parameter space of a model. The grid search has evaluated the various parameters combinations, and the one resulting in the best performance is:

- C: 1000
- γ: 0.001
- R^2 score obtained is 0.691
- *MAE* 0.124
- *RMSE* 0.158

Figure 2 shows, for every instance of the test set, the corresponding value of *Observed Time Next Plug*(blue line). This observed value is the actual one in the test set, the magenta line instead shows the *Predicted Time Next Plug* values forecasted using the trained SVM regression model. The observed and predicted values are in minutes, but for the sake of clarity the showed scale is in hour. It is worth noticing that the predicted values are an approximation of the observed values with an error that is approximately 10%.

It means that, respect to a value of *Time Next Plug* equal to 20 h, a scheduler should shift other loads approximately 1 h before the predicted arrival of the e-car, or 1 h after plus the forecasted duration of next charge.

5.3   Charging Time Prediction

A second experiment aims at evaluating the prediction error on the next energy charged (that is the estimated time to charge if the charging power is) by clustering and classification. To determine the cluster analysis goodness we use the *Silhouette score* [17]. The features used in the clustering phase are a subset of the entire data set, specifically we focus the analysis on: *Day Week, Day Hour, Charging Time, Time Next Plug*. Le it be k the best number of clusters, the correct choice of k, clusters number, is often ambiguous, with interpretations

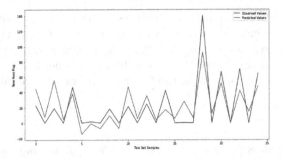

Fig. 2. SVM regression (C: 10, γ: 0.01) (Color figure online)

depending on the shape and scale of the distribution of points in a data set and the desired clustering resolution. For this reason we have opted for the elbow method. It is an iterative algorithm that tries to fit the data using a K-Means model while reducing the *squared euclidean distance* among the samples of the same cluster. We observed that $k = 6$ can classify very well the different duration of charging for the analysed data-set.

Figure 3 shows the six clusters projected along two of four dimensions, which are the *charging time* feature against the hour of the day.

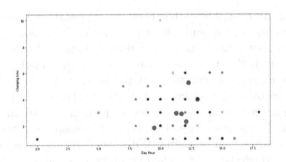

Fig. 3. Charging Time vs Day Hour Clustering

Seeing the figure the clusters seems to overlap in many points, but is just a visual thing because in our experiments we have reached a *Silhouette score* of approximately 0.7, which is a very good results, the main reason behind the visual overlap is the fact that the times of the day in which the user usually is more active are very close, in fact the majority of samples fall in the range between 10:00 a.m and 15:00 pm. The second step after the identification of the clusters is to use a classification algorithm in order to classify the future instances that are collected. We have opted for a *k-nearest neighbours algorithm*, [4]. We have carried out two experiments: one with the clustered that set and the measured features values, and the other with the predicted *time next plug*.

For both of them we have used as goodness metrics, the *precision score* which tells ability of the classifier not to label as positive a sample that is negative and the *recall score*, which shows ability of the classifier to find all the positive samples, i.e. to classify correctly. For our first experiment, the classification is based on the effective value of all the features, and we have obtained:

- Precision: 0.504
- Recall: 0.466

While the other classification experiment the 30% of the *time next plug* values are predicted using the regressor presented in Sect. 5.1. In this experiment the obtained classifier score are:

- Precision: 0.47
- Recall: 0.45

It is possible to see that the results are almost the same, considering the error that can be introduced by the predicted values, the overall classification is not very good but it is due to the reduced data set size, with the collection of more data it will be possible to improve the classification performance.

6   Conclusion

The objective of this contribution has been the exploitation of machine learning to provide the extract the required knowledge that allow smart applications for the supporting an autonomous smart scheduling of energy loads that could well fit in the DSM strategies We investigated and set up a methodology to learn users' every day energy consumption, related to an e-car usage. We started by presenting the problem of learning and predicting the e-car charging requirements, identifying the relevant features for a suited model. We implemented the model assuming that none of these features can be easily monitored except the power measured at the charging plug. With this premises we selected the most relevant features to effective learn when and how long the next charge is due or how much energy is charged. We investigate the two sub-problem with different techniques. A regression model has been used to forecast the time when the next charge is due, while a clustering/classification algorithm has been evaluated to identify and predict the energy/time requirements.

References

1. Alizadeh, M., Scaglione, A., Davies, J., Kurani, K.S.: A scalable stochastic model for the electricity demand of electric and plug-in hybrid vehicles. IEEE Trans. Smart Grid **5**(2), 848–860 (2014)
2. Alizadeh, M., Scaglione, A., Wang, Z.: On the impact of smartgrid metering infrastructure on load forecasting. In: 2010 48th Annual Allerton Conference on Communication, Control, and Computing (Allerton), pp. 1628–1636. IEEE (2010)

3. Bergstra, J., Bengio, Y.: Random search for hyper-parameter optimization. J. Mach. Learn. Res. **13**(Feb), 281–305 (2012)
4. Cover, T., Hart, P.: Nearest neighbor pattern classification. IEEE Trans. Inf. Theory **13**(1), 21–27 (1967)
5. Jiang, S., Venticinque, S., Horn, G., Hallsteinsen, S., Noebels, M.: A distributed agent-based system for coordinating smart solar-powered microgrids, pp. 71–79 (2016). https://doi.org/10.1109/SAI.2016.7555964
6. Khan, A.R., Mahmood, A., Safdar, A., Khan, Z.A., Khan, N.A.: Load forecasting, dynamic pricing and dsm in smart grid: a review. Renew. Sustain. Energy Rev. **54**, 1311–1322 (2016)
7. Khodaei, A., Shahidehpour, M., Choi, J.: Optimal hourly scheduling of community-aggregated electricity consumption. J. Electr. Eng. Technol. **8**(6), 1251–1260 (2013)
8. Li, G., Zhang, X.P.: Modeling of plug-in hybrid electric vehicle charging demand in probabilistic power flow calculations. IEEE Trans. Smart Grid **3**(1), 492–499 (2012)
9. Liang, J., Ng, S.K., Kendall, G., Cheng, J.W.: Load signature study—part I: basic concept, structure, and methodology. IEEE Trans. Power Deliv. **25**(2), 551–560 (2010)
10. Liu, C., Chau, K., Wu, D., Gao, S.: Opportunities and challenges of vehicle-to-home, vehicle-to-vehicle, and vehicle-to-grid technologies. Proc. IEEE **101**(11), 2409–2427 (2013)
11. López, K.L., Gagné, C., Gardner, M.A.: Demand-side management using deep learning for smart charging of electric vehicles. IEEE Trans. Smart Grid **10**, 2683–2691 (2018)
12. López, M., De La Torre, S., Martín, S., Aguado, J.: Demand-side management in smart grid operation considering electric vehicles load shifting and vehicle-to-grid support. Int. J. Electr. Power Energy Syst. **64**, 689–698 (2015)
13. Nagelkerke, N.J., et al.: A note on a general definition of the coefficient of determination. Biometrika **78**(3), 691–692 (1991)
14. Palensky, P., Dietrich, D.: Demand side management: demand response, intelligent energy systems, and smart loads. IEEE Trans. Industr. Inf. **7**(3), 381–388 (2011)
15. Pellegrini, M.: Short-term load demand forecasting in smart grids using support vector regression. In: 2015 IEEE 1st International Forum on Research and Technologies for Society and Industry Leveraging a better tomorrow (RTSI), pp. 264–268. IEEE (2015)
16. Pellegrini, M., Rassaei, F.: Modeling daily electrical demand in presence of PHEVs in smart grids with supervised learning. In: 2016 IEEE 2nd International Forum on Research and Technologies for Society and Industry Leveraging a Better Tomorrow (RTSI), pp. 1–6. IEEE (2016)
17. Rousseeuw, P.J.: Silhouettes: a graphical aid to the interpretation and validation of cluster analysis. J. Comput. Appl. Math. **20**, 53–65 (1987)
18. Sanseverino, E.R., Di Silvestre, M., Zizzo, G., Graditi, G.: Energy efficient operation in smart grids: optimal management of shiftable loads and storage systems. In: 2012 International Symposium on Power Electronics, Electrical Drives, Automation and Motion (SPEEDAM), pp. 978–982. IEEE (2012)
19. Xiong, Y., Wang, B., Chu, C.C., Gadh, R.: Electric vehicle driver clustering using statistical model and machine learning. arXiv preprint arXiv:1802.04193 (2018)

Making IoT Services Accountable: A Solution Based on Blockchain and Physically Unclonable Functions

Carmelo Felicetti$^{(\boxtimes)}$ ⓘ, Angelo Furfaro$^{(\boxtimes)}$ ⓘ, Domenico Saccà ⓘ,
Massimo Vatalaro, Marco Lanuzza ⓘ, and Felice Crupi ⓘ

DIMES - University of Calabria, 87036 Rende, CS, Italy
{carmelo.felicetti, a.furfaro, sacca, massimo.vatalaro,
marco.lanuzza, felice.crupi}@unical.it

Abstract. Nowadays, an important issue in the IoT landscape consists of enabling the dynamic instauration of interactions among two or more objects, operating autonomously in a distributed and heterogeneous environment, which participate in the enactment of accountable cross-organization business processes. In order to achieve the above goal, a decentralized and reliable approach is needed. Here, we propose a solution based on physical unclonable function (PUF) and blockchain technologies that represent the building blocks of the devised IT infrastructure. The core of the authentication process is based on a purposely designed circuit for the PUF bitcell, implemented in a 65 nm CMOS technology. One of the most important aspects of this work is represented by the concept of accountability node, an element inspired to a blockchain 3.0 masternode. This is the key element of the proposed architecture, acting as the main interface for cooperating services and IoT objects which relieve the users/objects from the burden of having to directly interact with the blockchain.

Keywords: Accountability services · Blockchain · PUFs · IoT

1 Introduction

The exponential growth of the IoT devices market is acting as primary driver regarding the development of new software services [1], and the improvement of performance in terms of connectivity concerning the options currently available.

Those intelligent objects need to operate quickly, safely and reliably, and to act autonomously when they are involved in processes that also concern particular entities [2], such as contracts or transactions, where who is carrying out the action is in charge of what is going on. In order to attribute these strong responsibilities, you need to trace every single operation and guarantee the identity of every single actor who takes part in the process itself [3].

At the basis of the proper operation of information technology (IT) services involving multiple actors belonging to independent organizations working in completely different domains, there is this assumption of responsibility regarding the interactions that take place within a specific process, in which these actors are required

© Springer Nature Switzerland AG 2019
R. Montella et al. (Eds.): IDCS 2019, LNCS 11874, pp. 294–305, 2019.
https://doi.org/10.1007/978-3-030-34914-1_28

to collaborate each other. However, two different types of actions can be carried out: the former only involving operations within an individual organization, and the latter that regards several organizations that interact each other. Normally an intra-organization operation is managed by an internal authority which keeps track of the identity and manages the responsibilities of the organization's employees. Therefore, it is possible to consider any intra-organization operation as already accountable. In an opposite way when an operation occurs between different organizations where the concept of actor's identity is not clearly and globally defined, it would be more difficult to know who is responsible for the execution of a such operation, which is the reason why would be at risk. Only a trustable platform able to deliver an accountability service would provide the needed support for several parties involved in an inter-organization operation.

The easiest and secure working solution in that context would be a centralized coordination service, that may be deployed in short-term. A centralized service requires, however, that cooperating entities trust in a strong way the third-part, that takes in charge all the responsibilities. Anyway, even if it could be considered an easy solution, it is obviously the weakest in terms of reliability, because the only entity in which the others need to have trustiness represents also a single point of failure. Regardless of the defense measures adopted by the organization that should guarantee the correct execution of the operations, if the organization's systems were compromised, the sensitive data would be at risk, therefore, to the need to trust an external actor is added to the one related to the IT security of the actor himself, and this is the reason why it is necessary to move to a higher level, where security and trust requirements can be obtained without relying on reputation systems or direct relationships. A choice that allows the improvement of the interaction and cooperation among several parties involves the use of a decentralized system. However, whilst decentralization has the advantage of not requiring the presence of a central authority, it is sometimes more complicated to reach a global consensus to approve a transaction. For many years the problem of consensus has meant a problem of difficult resolution, but fortunately in recent times the introduction of blockchain technology [4] has allowed this limitation, through the introduction of a peer-to-peer network whose nodes efficiently manage the difficulties related to the achievement of consensus, while the transactions are recorded transparently on a distributed ledger. The blockchain technology, thanks to the use of cryptography, is nowadays considered as one of the most reliable and safe methods, since the transactions cannot be altered in any way, but in the same way they can be verified by anyone, with the maximum of transparency [5]. In this way the requirements of trust and security are largely satisfied, however it remains very difficult to identify uniquely and authoritatively the parties involved in the process, which is why a system for assigning responsibilities through an accountability system is required [6].

Nowadays there is no correlation between the digital identity on the blockchain and the user in the real world, and the problem becomes even more serious when operations need accountability of an IoT device. So, our idea is to use blockchain technology combined with PUFs physical unclonable function (PUF) in order to guarantee security and trustiness, but also to uniquely identify the actors, specifically the IoT smart objects, which require cooperation services, and therefore must be also considered accountable. Through the use of PUFs it is possible to create something similar to a digital identity of an IoT device, since this technology that exploits the process variations of integrated circuits is based on the extraction of some parameters that can be considered as a fingerprint or the DNA of the chip itself. In the past, solutions have already been presented which are based on the joint use of blockchain technology and public digital identity systems (e.g. SPID [7]), but they concern natural persons, with the big difference that this work focuses on the use of IoT devices [8]. The approach proposed in this work takes into account numerous factors, including the use of a modified version of Ethereum [9] which implements an agent very similar to the concept of the master node introduced in the blockchain technology starting from version 3.0 [10]. This node, whose name is Accountability Node (AN) acts as a bridge between the identification system based on the use of the PUFs and the distributed ledger related to the blockchain, acting as the main interface of the cooperation services. In this way it is possible to operate without the need for the IoT device to interact directly with the blockchain.

From this perspective, the various processes and services that characterize the infrastructure are implemented through appropriate smart contracts, which represent the main elements of the Ethereum platform. When one or more IoT devices have to cooperate in the same process [11], they must first authenticate themselves through the use of a PUF, and then proceed to request the accountability service. At this stage the authenticated smart objects that have already requested the accountability service are authorized to exchange any information relating to the operation they are carrying out, with the supervision of the blockchain that keeps track of the transaction through the relative memorization in the public ledger. The operation inside the ledger, even if traced, stores inside it only the final result of the job accomplished, without the need to make the blockchain active in all the intermediate steps, thus enhancing performance and issue cost saving.

The remainder of the paper is the following. In the Sect. 2 we describe how key technologies at the basis of our infrastructure work. Then Sect. 3 provides a detailed explanation of the infrastructure, including main actors that interact with it and its key components. Finally, Sect. 4 present our conclusions and food for thought related to further works.

2 Key Technologies

2.1 Blockchain

One of the most difficult challenges in the field of service accountability is the difficulty of reaching the consensus of all the actors that are part of a decentralized system. This problem has very distant roots, but in recent years a particularly effective solution has been found thanks to the development of blockchain technology. Created to support the development of cryptocurrencies, in particular the bitcoin, the blockchain technology essentially consist of a peer-to-peer network, which does not include any central authority, but rather a distributed ledger and a database of all the resources that is always shared in the network. All the participants have an identical copy of the ledger and collaborate in order to obtain the ledger itself updated to an identical version for all through a certified and reliable mechanism, in which the transactions are always signed by the various authors and in addition to being verified and validated, they are also public. In order to understand how the mechanism works, it is important know that each actor is characterized by a public key used to sign on the blockchain each transaction in with he is involved. This happens without any need to link this virtual entity with the physical identity in the real world. In a short time, the rising interest generated by the blockchain, due to the potential expressed by the technology itself, have encouraged a constant and rapid evolution represented by the introduction of a new entity, so called smart contract, a very useful item that can be used in order to programming on the blockchain, through customization actions and development of applications.

In this context, Ethereum appears to be the most famous example of programmable blockchain. However, in recent time, a new element has been added to the basic components of the blockchain technology, which is in charge of providing resource intensive services, behaving like a server running on a peer-to-peer network. Due to the importance of the role that play it is considered the main element that leads to the evolution of the technology, gaining the title of Master Node (MN), main characteristic of the version 3.0 referring to blockchain technology (Table 1). The activation of a MN is subordinated to a very conspicuous initial investment, the gain is instead represented by the interests coming from the work done by the node itself.

Table 1. Main features related to Blockchain version.

	Distributed ledger technology	Smart contracts	Decentralized application
Blockchain 1.0	V	X	X
Blockchain 2.0	V	V	X
Blockchain 3.0	V	V	V

The purpose of investing very large initial amounts is essentially due to the fact that the fear of losing the investment leads users to keep the network in good condition, watch over it, and prevent malicious users from trying to damage it. Whenever an illegal action is detected by one of the main nodes, its owner loses forever the initial investment guarantee.

2.2 Physical Unclonable Functions

With the technological scaling and the entry of sub nanometric technologies, it is more difficult to have the exact control on the manufacturing process of the devices.

These intrinsic process variations lead to fluctuation in the physical and geometric transistor parameters (e.g. channel length, oxide thickness and doping levels), which translate into different electrical characteristics. PUF are a promising innovative primitive that are used for authentication that exploit these inherent process variations to generate a unique key for each hardware device as a kind of DNA. The main PUF figures of merit [12] are:

- **Uniqueness**, for which same PUF implemented on different chips in the same technology generates different response at the same challenge;
- **Unpredictability**, due to the fact that these process variations cannot be replicated through mathematical algorithms;
- **Randomness**, which ensures the balance between 0 and 1 in the PUFs response, to make information deduction more difficult;
- **Physical Unclonability**, which ensures the impossibility to create another PUF instance with same challenge response pair.

The device identification and authentication process are based on a challenge-response mechanism [13], in which the authenticator must verify the device identity before granting it the required access. The authenticator stimulates the device with an input challenge and the untrusted device generates a corresponding response using its internal PUF. The authenticator stores all possible challenge-response pairs in a database, so that during authentication phase, the authenticator compares the current device's response with all those stored to verify if the device is genuine or not. The database may be subject to attacks, for this reason every time a challenge-response pair (CRP) is used, it is definitively deleted. Once all the stored CRPs are used, a refresh phase is performed to generate new CRPs.

Generally, the PUF architecture is composed by a transformation block which transforms a challenge in a measurable quantity (voltage, current or delay) and by a conversion block which produces a binary response.

In this paper, we propose a bistable silicon-based PUF based on a voltage divider, implemented by two identical series-connected circuits. The intrinsic advantages of this solution are a perfect balance between the two logic states, and a strong robustness against temperature variations, voltage variations, inter-die variability and aging.

As shown in (Fig. 1) a previously proposed solution [14], which consists of a two transistors (2T) voltage divider implemented by the series of two identical nMOSFETs operating in the deep subthreshold region; a new proposed PUF bitcell circuit, which consists of a four transistors (4T) voltage divider operating in the deep subthreshold region.

The 2T and 4T voltage dividers have been implemented by using low-voltage threshold nMOS transistors in 65-nm TSMC technology.

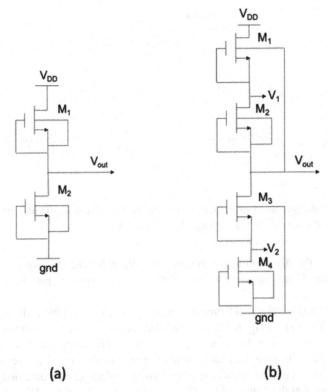

Fig. 1. Previous PUF bitcell circuit based on 2T voltage divider (a) and new proposed PUF bitcell circuit based on 4T voltage divider (b).

As reported in [14], the output voltage of the 2T divider is strongly dependent on the mismatch between M1 and M2, caused by process variations. The key property of the 2T voltage divider is the amplification effect, due to drain-induced barrier lowering (DIBL) effect, of the threshold voltage mismatch between the two transistors.

We propose a 4T solution, where the body terminal of the top transistor of each block is connected to the source terminal of the bottom transistor. The aim of this body connection consists of introducing a positive feedback. This means that for the less conductive block, where the voltage drop is higher, the body effect is higher, thus further reducing the block conductance. The amount of positive feedback depends on the transistor size, with the constraint $M_1 = M_3$ and $M_2 = M_4$. The maximum positive feedback is obtained by using a short channel bottom transistor and a long channel top transistor. In a range included between 60 and 200 nm, the optimum was found by selecting a channel length of 80 nm for the bottom transistor and a channel length of 200 nm for the top transistor. The distributions of the proposed solutions are shown in (Fig. 2).

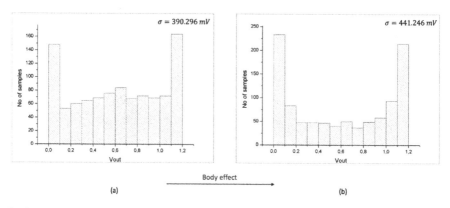

Fig. 2. Statistical distribution of the output voltage for the 2T voltage divider (a) and the 4T voltage divider (b) at nominal bias voltage ($V_{DD} = 1.2$ V).

To analyze the distributions of the output voltage for the two solutions, we performed Monte Carlo simulation on 1000 samples, considering only transistor mismatch.

As shown in (Fig. 2), the 4T circuit exhibits a higher bistability with respect to the 2T circuit. It is worth noting that the desired distribution should be completely bistable with all the values close to 0 or V_{DD}. The ideal bistability guarantees a strong robustness against interferences and a smaller number of required conversion stages. The distribution of (Fig. 3) shows the output voltage of the circuit obtained by adding one inverter stage at the output of the 2T voltage divider (a) and the 4T voltage divider (b). It is evident that one inverter stage is enough to reach an almost ideal bistability, especially in the case of the 4T voltage divider.

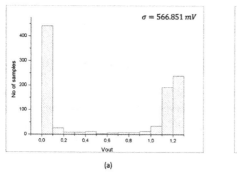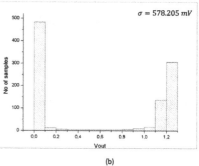

Fig. 3. Statistical distribution of the output voltage of the circuit obtained by adding one inverter stage at the output of the 2T voltage divider (a) and the 4T voltage divider (b) at nominal bias voltage ($V_{DD} = 1.2$ V).

3 Accountability Service Infrastructure

The accountability service originates from the two key components that build the infrastructure, represented by the authentication system based on the use of PUFs and the blockchain. Each of the components meets certain basic criteria for the service accountability implementation. The goal of the blockchain is to decentralize the service, and provide maximum transparency on the operations carried out, keeping track of them, without the risk that they may be altered. In this way all operations are made public and anyone can verify them, in order to guarantee the reliability of the actors involved in the process.

Purpose of the PUF-based authentication mechanism is to take in charge the responsibility attribution, as it serves to manage the digital identities impersonated by the IoT devices, in order to be uniquely recognized during the entire process. Consequently, a device that needs to access to a service where accountability is required, first of all it needs to authenticate itself through its PUF, subsequently every single operation is transferred to the blockchain which has the task of storing the information ensuring maximum transparency.

The entities that interact with the infrastructure are two, i.e. users and managers. Users are those who carry out the cooperation process, therefore they must be considered accountable for their actions. The managers instead coordinate the management services and have the task of assigning the permits to the users, in order to limit their power to act to the only operations necessary to carry out the cooperation process. Both, before accessing the accountability service, need to be authenticate by the identity PUF provider that uniquely identifies each device that must take responsibility for their actions.

Thus, the operational of the infrastructure requires that when the object attempts to access for the first time it must register its digital identity and the name of the organization on behalf the device will operate. Following this phase, the object is assigned to a specific accountability node. The services provided by the infrastructure, on the other hand, operate by using smart contract, this means that when a user needs a specific service provided by the infrastructure, a smart contract is activated, which involves a blockchain transaction. The various transactions are therefore not performed directly by the users, but rather by the associated accountability node, which signs and executes transactions and pays the fee in the name and on behalf of the user assigned to the IoT related device.

Each user belonging to a specific organization that takes part in a process is assigned a specific role, that means it is involved in a limited number of operations. This underlies the fact that by default the entity is not authorized to perform any operation unless it has first obtained a specific permission. As previously stated, the manager lead permission by the activation of smart contract, therefore both grant and cancellation of permits are subordinated to the execution of smart contracts that generate transactions on the blockchain, leaving track on the ledger. Similarly, the service request by any IoT device activates a smart contract. Users and managers operate within the infrastructure through specific web services. In the following section, architecture and key infrastructure components will be analyzed in detail.

3.1   Architecture

The (Fig. 4) shows the architecture of the system and focus on the most important components that make up the infrastructure.

The choice regarding the implementation of the blockchain for the realized architecture fell on the Ethereum platform, which in the past has been already target of cyber-attacks that were successfully handled by the development team. It represents a very stable, extremely flexible and easily extensible solution and as we have already said also secure. A high number of useful complementary services are also integrated in thus platform, although for the specific purpose, some changes were made as this was created to meet the needs of the blockchain 2.0, while the infrastructure implemented uses technologies specific to blockchain 3.0, and therefore not directly supported.

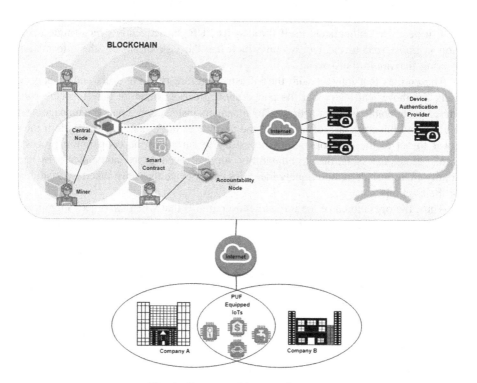

Fig. 4. System architecture diagram.

As already discussed in [15], in the proposed architecture two new types of nodes have been introduced: Accountability Node, already mentioned above, and Central Node, which has not yet been introduced. The former in addition to maintaining the network in good state of health, also provides the accountability service, while the Central Node, invisible to the user, has instead a central role within the infrastructure as it has the role of managing the various Accountability Node. It also acts to verify the registration process and affiliation to the relative Accountability Node and is liable for rewarding the work done by each Accountability Node. Finally, not considering the accountability process there is another kind of node, a node miner, whose target is essentially to create new blocks.

Another fundamental element of the architecture is represented by the authentication service provider as regards the devices that must take part in the cooperation process. In this case the service is offered by an independent third-part represented by the PUF vendor that certifies the unique and unambiguous identity of the IoT object that will carry out the operations.

Lastly it is important to emphasize that the implementation of the used blockchain does not include additional software levels, which normally also introduce a greater grade of complexity and vulnerability to attacks. A focus will be given below on the key components that have been introduced, i.e. the AN and the CN.

Accountability Node. Designed by taking inspiration from the master node that represent one of the fundamental characteristic of the blockchain 3.0 technology, the Accountability Node can be generated starting from a miner that has raised enough money to cover the cost of the investment to be supported to start the process of registration in order to be accredited as Accountability Node. The money amount is needed as deposit to encourage the Accountability Node to maintain a correct behavior within the blockchain network, because of the role of responsibility that it covers, acting as intermediary between the user and the same blockchain. Each accountability node keeps track of the relative list of IoT objects assigned to it during the registration phase, on whose behalf it acts as a delegate within the blockchain, thus lightening the task of the users themselves, who are also exonerate from the burden of having to manage a wallet. The service provided by the accountability nodes requires that the smart objects furnish their certified digital identity, through the recognition by the provider of the authentication services that query the PUF present in each device (typically this role is performed by the manufacturer). Each accountability node must therefore be federated with different identity providers, as the various producers do not share their information externally and are the only ones able to validate the authentication process. Accountability nodes have enough money to perform many transactions. In fact, they are rewarded by the central node with a grant proportional to the work provided in the cooperation process. Each time a new block is created the reward is divided between the miner and the central node, then the latter distributes the relative gain to the various nodes of accountability that have taken part to the process. In this context the equilibrium is guaranteed by the fact that every action considered illegal is detected and punished by the system that disables the accountability node and confiscates the security deposit provided as guarantee. Furthermore, the digital identity of the malicious accountability node owner is included in a blacklist that does not allow him to generate other accountability nodes.

Central Node. The central node essentially operates a role of lifecycle management and remuneration of accountability nodes based on the work they perform. It communicates exclusively with the accountability nodes and smart contracts that implement processes and services. The central node manages also the deposit paid by the accountability nodes and certify the transaction, mandatory to the registration of accountability nodes because of the specific role. It also implements and manages many smart contracts that execute processes and services offered by the blockchain. Analyzing the data coming from the accountability nodes, it acts by deciding which nodes must be rewarded or eventually banned from the blockchain. The central node is periodically elected through a distributed voting algorithm. The role of the central node can be covered only by an accountability node, and its "variable" nature makes it so that it cannot be considered a single point of failure.

4   Conclusion

This work was created with the aim of presenting an infrastructure to offer decentralized accountability services for IoT devices participating in cooperation processes that involve different organizations. The main goal was to relate two key technologies such as the blockchain and PUF-based authentication mechanism.

To maintain the level of reliability and security of these technologies, no software substrate has been added. In opposite we exploit ad-hoc smart contract and some particular elements such as accountability node, in order to monitor the behavior and the health status of the blockchain. Finally, after having succeeded in creating an infrastructure capable of authenticating and certifying the smart object action, the next objective could be to enable human-IoT device collaboration [16] within an accountable service [17] process.

References

1. Ryan, P.J., Watson, R.B.: Research challenges for the internet of things: what role can or play? Systems 5(1), 24 (2017)
2. Zhu, X., Badr, Y.: Identity management systems for the internet of things: a survey towards blockchain solutions. Sensors **18**, 4215 (2018)
3. Lou, W., Ren, K.: Security, privacy, and accountability in wireless access networks. IEEE Wirel. Commun. **16**(4), 80–87 (2009)
4. Nakamoto, S.: Bitcoin: a peer-to-peer electronic cash system. White Paper (2008). https://bitcoin.org/bitcoin.pdf
5. Fortino, G., Messina, F., Rosaci, D., Sarne, G.M.L.: Using blockchain in a reputation-based model for grouping agents in the internet of things. IEEE Trans. Eng. Manage., 1–13 (2019, in press). https://doi.org/10.1109/TEM.2019.2918162
6. Weber, R.H.: Accountability in the internet of things. Comput. Law Secur. Rev. **27**(2), 133–138 (2011)
7. AgID - Agenzia per l'Italia Digitale: Spid – regole tecniche (2017). https://media.readthedocs.org/pdf/spid-regole-tecniche/latest/spid-regole-tecniche.pdf
8. Frustaci, M., Pace, P., Aloi, G., Fortino, G.: Evaluating critical security issues of the IoT world: present and future challenges. IEEE Internet Things J. **5**(4), 2483–2495 (2018)
9. Jani, S.: An overview of ethereum & its comparison with bitcoin (2018)
10. Ackermann, J., Meier, M.: Blockchain 3.0 - the next generation of blockchain systems (2018)
11. Di Martino, B., Esposito, A., Nacchia, S., Maisto, S.A.: Towards an integrated internet of things: current approaches and challenges. In: Di Martino, B., Li, K.-C., Yang, L.T., Esposito, A. (eds.) Internet of Everything. IT, pp. 13–33. Springer, Singapore (2018). https://doi.org/10.1007/978-981-10-5861-5_2

12. Halak, B.: Physically Unclonable Functions From Basic Design Principles to Advanced Hardware Security Applications. Springer, Southampton (2018). https://doi.org/10.1007/978-3-319-76804-5
13. Herder, C., Yu, M., Koushanfar, F., Devadas, S.: Physical unclonable functions and applications: a tutorial. Proc. IEEE **102**, 1126–1141 (2014)
14. De Rose, R.: A physical unclonable function based on a 2-transistor subthreshold voltage divider. Int. J. Circ. Theory Appl. **45**, 260–273 (2017)
15. Furfaro, A., Argento, L., Saccà, D., Angiulli, F., Fassetti, F.: An infrastructure for service accountability based on digital identity and blockchain 3.0. In: CRYBLOCK 2019: INFOCOM Workshop - 2nd Workshop on Cryptocurrencies and Blockchains for Distributed Systems, Paris (2019)
16. Kum, S.W., Kang, M., Park, J.I.: IoT delegate: smart home framework for heterogeneous IoT service collaboration. KSII Trans. Internet Inform. Syst. **10**, 3958–3971 (2016)
17. Wohlgemuth, S., Umezawa, K., Mishina, Y., Takaragi, K.: Competitive compliance with blockchain. In: IEEE International Conference on Pervasive Computing and Communications Workshops (PerCom Workshops), Kyoto, Japan, pp. 967–972 (2019)

Generation of Network Traffic Using WGAN-GP and a DFT Filter for Resolving Data Imbalance

WooHo Lee[1(✉)], BongNam Noh[1], YeonSu Kim[1],
and KiMoon Jeong[2(✉)]

[1] Chonnam National University, Gwangju Campus, Gwangju,
Republic of Korea
leeouho@naver.com
[2] HPC Cloud Team in Korea Institute of Science
and Technology Information, Daejeon, South Korea
kmjeong@kisti.re.kr

Abstract. The intrinsic features of Internet networks lead to imbalanced class distributions when datasets are conformed, phenomena called Class Imbalance and that is attaching an increasing attention in many research fields. In spite of performance losses due to Class Imbalance, this issue has not been thoroughly studied in Network Traffic Classification and some previous works are limited to few solutions and/or assumed misleading methodological approaches. In this study, we propose a method for generating network attack traffic to address data imbalance problems in training datasets. For this purpose, traffic data was analyzed based on deep packet inspection and features were extracted based on common traffic characteristics. Similar malicious traffic was generated for classes with low data counts using Wasserstein generative adversarial networks (WGAN) with a gradient penalty algorithm. The experiment demonstrated that the accuracy of each dataset was improved by approximately 5% and the false detection rate was reduced by approximately 8%. This study has demonstrated that enhanced learning and classification can be achieved by solving the problem of degraded performance caused by data imbalance in datasets used in deep learning based intrusion detection systems.

Keywords: Deep learning · Intrusion detection · Security · Generative adversarial network

1 Introduction

Machine learning and data mining techniques have fascinated researchers worldwide owing to superior performance results in various application domains. In the field of intrusion detection systems (IDS), these techniques demonstrate promising results by predicting future attack patterns using learning paradigms [1]. Learning is the process of constructing a predictive model using a dataset. It is comprised of several categories including supervised, unsupervised, and reinforced learning.

© Springer Nature Switzerland AG 2019
R. Montella et al. (Eds.): IDCS 2019, LNCS 11874, pp. 306–317, 2019.
https://doi.org/10.1007/978-3-030-34914-1_29

In particular, supervised learning uses classified (labeled) training data to create a model that would then be applied to future unknown data. Furthermore, the objective of supervised learning systems is to obtain a high classification accuracy and to reduce the false positive rate [2, 3].

However, if IDSs are applied to real world environments, there are problems that reduce accuracy and increase false detection rate. The purpose of this study was to analyze the performance degradation caused by data imbalances in learning data.

A data imbalance problem occurs when the number of observations explored for the purpose of classification differs significantly by class. For example, if there are 10,000 samples in the X1 category, but only 20 samples in the X2 category, then X2 is considered relatively small when compared to X1. The data imbalance issue is a factor that degrades the classification performance by treating the minor class instance as a major class instance to minimize the error rate. Data imbalance in learning data is a problem of algorithm degradation that is addressed in a variety of studies including those on intrusion detection systems. Initially, Zhu et al. [4] proposed a way to improve classification accuracy by using a generative adversarial network (GAN) to categorize data objectively. Douzas and Bacao's [5] work suggested ways to improve classification performance by modifying the synthetic minority oversampling technique (SMOTE) algorithm through data combination by creating a sample of minority classes using GAN. Finally, Mariani [6] proposed a study that uses GAN to improve classification of datasets using landscape photographs. The common factor in all the above studies was GAN, one of the generative models of deep learning that was used to solve the data imbalance problem caused by small amounts of data in a class.

The GAN algorithm is an algorithm that produces data that is so sophisticated that the difference between real data and peak data is not known. Therefore, it is a suitable model for solving performance degradation problems caused by smaller classes [7]. In this study, similar network traffic was generated for classes with low data counts using the proposed Wasserstein GAN with gradient penalty (WGAN-GP). A Fourier transform based filter was used to make assumptions regarding the classification accuracy and improvement in performance for IDSs. To evaluate the proposed method, a classification experiment was conducted on each data set using a convolutional neural network (CNN). In the above experiment, we have improved the performance of the depth-based intrusion system by reducing the data imbalance of the dataset used for network traffic classification.

In Sect. 2, related work on intrusion detection using deep learning is described. Section 3 provides details of how similar traffic will be generated using the proposed GAN. Section 4 discusses the experimental results and Sect. 5 outlines the conclusions of the study.

2 Related Work

2.1 Deep Learning Based Intrusion Detection

Research on intrusion detection using deep learning was conducted to improve the accuracy of intrusion detection by extracting the attack data characteristics using the undersampling and few-shot methods [8, 9]. Most studies on intrusion detection use the undersampling method to increase the layers of the neural network because it is effective for detecting certain classes [10]. However, the undersampling method exhibits a low accuracy in a real-world environment although its accuracy in an experimental environment is high [26]. In a real-world environment, the data imbalance problem becomes worse than it is in the experimental environment and the detection rate decreases [11]. Therefore, in this study, to apply the oversampling method as a solution to the data imbalance problem, a similar traffic generation method that will increase the attack class traffic training data using a GAN is proposed, as shown in Fig. 1.

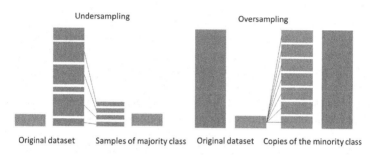

Fig. 1. Learning method using oversampling method

2.2   GAN Learning Based Intrusion Detection

Research on malware detection using a GAN has been conducted. Initially, Chintala [12], Gulrajani et al. [13], Kim, Bu and Cho [14] described the detection of malicious software using a GAN that used an autoencoder to improve performance through learning and transferring weights. They verified the accuracy of this method to be 96.3%. Sun et al. [15] proposed solutions to classify distributed DoS (DDoS) attacks with flash crowds (FC) using a least-squares GAN. A method to distinguish legitimate traffic from attackers is to analyze traffic behavior and statistics for users of DDoS and FC.

Yin et al. [16] focused on increasing the botnet detection model, eliminating the use of network payload information, and improving the performance of GAN. Li et al. [17] proposed a GAN anomaly detection method. Several sensors were time series modeled and an anomaly detection method was proposed that utilized actual data sample differences. In research by Lin et al. [18], the IDSGAN (Generative Adversarial Networks for Attack Generation against Intrusion Detection) extracted session data used by a botnet to generate and classify similar traffic and utilized the NSL-KDD dataset to generate traffic and increase the classification model. The generated data contributed to the improved learning performance of the RF and principal component analysis models.

As mentioned earlier, research using the GAN is advancing rapidly. GAN was used to improve classification performance. However, the data imbalance problem for the network traffic classifier has not yet been resolved.

2.3   Dataset Analysis

The datasets generally used in intrusion detection studies using deep learning were analyzed. The NSL–KDD and UNSW-NB15 datasets have insufficient attack traffic when compared to normal traffic. Furthermore, the DDoS attack traffic accounts for more than 50% of all attack traffic, causing the imbalanced data problem. Dainotti, Pescape, and Claffy [19] suggested that the uniformity of shared trace datasets for test data is the primary obstacle to traffic classification method progress. Many studies of abnormal traffic classification use traffic from self-collection tools or security companies, which are unreliable.

Because the classical machine learning approach focuses on function selection techniques, many current public traffic datasets are flow function datasets, not raw traffic datasets. For example, the famous KDD Cup 1999 and NSL-KDD datasets provide 41 predefined functions in the dataset and there are several similar datasets [20].

UNSW-NB15 [21] is a dataset composed of nine attack traffic and general traffic packets created by the IXIA PerfectStorm tool at the Cyber Range Lab at the Australian Centre for Cybersecurity (ACCS). The problem of data imbalance was analyzed for these two data sets to determine the accuracy of classification of the minority class data.

3   Proposed Method Network Feature Extraction

3.1   Network Feature Extraction

Deep Packet Inspection (DPI) was conducted for the attack packets in the dataset. In this study, 15 dataset characteristics, such as duration, header length, IP version, protocol, flag, and session, were extracted and correlated to detect malware. Through correlation analysis, six features; duration, transmission control protocol header, port, session data, and flag were selected and applied to the GAN algorithm. To adjust the size of the data, the hash value was applied and quantified. This allowed images of the same size to be created.

Mode-specific normalization for numerical variables was used. Numerical variables in tabular datasets sometimes follow a multimodal distribution. A Gaussian kernel density estimation to estimate the number of modes of a continuous variable was used.

In the three datasets we used in this study, we found 22 out of 27 continuous variables in the NSL- KDD dataset that had multiple modes. Simply normalizing numerical features to $[-1, 1]$ and using tanh activation to generate these features did not work well. For example, when there is a mode close to -1 or 1, the gradient will saturate when back-propagating through tanh.

To effectively sample values from a multimodal distribution, we cluster values of the numerical variables using a Gaussian Mixture model (GMM). GMM for classification using input data X is performed as outlined in Fig. 2.

Input : *a ginven data* $X = \{x_1, x_2, \ldots, x_n\}$

$$\pi = \{\pi_1, \pi_1, \ldots \pi_k\},$$

$$\mu = \{\mu_1, \mu_2, \ldots, \mu_k\},$$

$$\Sigma = \{\Sigma_1 \Sigma_2, \ldots, \Sigma_k\}$$

output : *class labes* y $\{y_1, y_2, \ldots, y_n\}$ *for* X

$$\gamma(z_{nk}) = p(z_{nk} = 1 | X_n)$$

for n = 1: T do

$$y_n = \underset{k}{\operatorname{argmax}} \gamma(z_{nk})$$

end

Fig. 2. GMM classification algorithm

Smoothing for categorical variables was used. In generating categorical variables, the model faces a similar challenge to the one it faces in natural language generation: how to make the model differentiable. In natural language generation, people use reinforcement learning [22] or Gumbel Softmax [23] to deal with this issue. We are facing a similar challenge; however, the number of categories is much smaller than the size of vocabulary in the natural language. Therefore, we can generate the probability distribution directly using Gumbel Softmax. However, we find it necessary to convert categorical variables to one-hot encoding representation and add noise to binary variables. In this study, we filter by word for Sequecncial data (Payload, URL etc.). After that, we converted to vector processing method using tokenizer.

3.2   Image Generation

Network traffic consists of .pcap files, and it was generated by the portable network graphic file structure outlined in Fig. 3. The session data was extracted from the .pcap file and the byte size was used to create the image with the correct proportions.

For WGAN-GP, the conversion was made because it generates analogue traffic based on the image. The images created were stored for each class and used as training data.

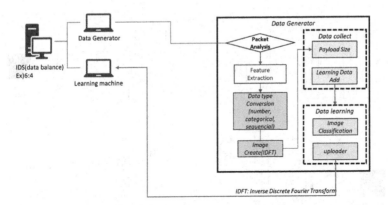

Fig. 3. Illustration of similar traffic created based on a GAN

3.3   Training

The generator and critic architecture of the WGAN-GP model used for training is illustrated in Fig. 4 [24] and is one of the algorithms validated by Gullajani [11]. The critic generator training iteration ratio was maintained at 5:1, for every five training iterations of the critic, the generator was updated once. A default value of $\lambda = 10$, as suggested in [13], was used as the gradient penalty hyperparameter in the WGAN-GP loss function. Adam [25] optimization algorithm was used for training the network with a learning rate of 0.0001, 1 = 0, and 2 = 0.9. The model was trained for approximately a day across 45,000 generated iterations with final negative critic losses (averaged across mini-batches of an epoch) of 0.4262 on the training set and 1.365 on the validation set. Figure 4 details the training cost (across each iteration) and the validation cost (for every 100 iterations) of the critic on a minibatch of 64 images. This demonstrated a stable training run without any overfitting. The Wasserstein distance estimate converged close to zero consistently across training and validation. Figure 4 shows a sample of 64 synthetic images generated by the trained generator network G.

Similar traffic was generated for each class using the WGAN-GP algorithm. The criteria for generating similar traffic was updated in the traffic data by a class with a generator loss function of 0.98 or higher and a discriminator loss function of 0–1 or higher. In addition, a Fourier transform was applied to each characteristic of the packet to convert the time domain into a value in the frequency domain to allow learning. The value of the frequency domain with Fourier transforms decreased the computation of classifying network traffic, improving performance. Finally, Fourier transforms can be high-frequency filtered images generated by WGAN to validate data with code transformations. In addition, images created using .pcap data were filtered through Fourier transforms. The advantage of using Fourier transformation is they have the ability to highlight the features of images in the encoding process. Additionally, loss value is minimized when decoding a generated image.

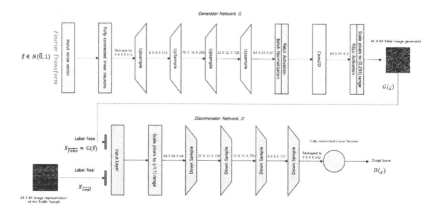

Fig. 4. Architecture of the generator and the critic networks of the WGAN-GP model

The following Fig. 5 describes the creation of a similar image using WGAN-GP and Discrete Fourier Transform (DFT). DFT can filter images to maximize the characteristics of the data to enhance learning performance. Similar traffic creation criteria were used to generate analogous traffic for a class when the amount of all attack traffic data in the class was less than 40%. The data generated by GAN algorithm was used only for training data, because over-fitting problems can occur when using validation data for testing. Therefore, only the original data was used for testing.

4 Performance Analysis

This study investigated a method to improve detection accuracy by creating similar traffic to GAN and increasing the ratio of attack traffic. The method presented in this paper solves the problem of performance degradation due to data imbalance in datasets using GAN. Existing datasets have a data imbalance problem that impedes the detection of attacks or improved learning. As a solution to this problem, we added learning data to similar traffic generated by GAN algorithm and improved attack detection accuracy in experiments. Initially, the performance comparison of GAN algorithm by generating similar traffic was completed. Performance was compared using DC-GAN and WGAN-GP. WGAN-GP exhibited increased precision and reduced learning time when compared to DC-GAN. Based on this result, performance comparison of the datasets by generating data using WGAN-GP was conducted.

It was observed that accuracy was improved and false positivity rates declined. The time required for data generation was also reduced when WGAN-GP used DC-GAN. Mode collapse is a phenomenon that produces similar images for one class. This phenomenon will continue to produce images for specific classes, and it can be used

```
#define calc(A,B) (A*B /100)

D_A = Dataset(Attack Traffic Image)

D_s[n] = Similar Traffic Class

D_c = DFT filter using Similar Traf-
fic Create Image

g = Generate loss

d = Discriminator loss

function-GAN(D_A)
FOR counter i = 0 to Ds length DO

    IF (D_A * 40 /100) > (D_A
*D_s[counter i] / 100) THEN

        FOR counter B = 0 to file
length DO

            IF d>0.98 && d < 1 THEN

            IF g >0 && g<0.1 THEN

                D_T = D_A+D_c

            ENDIF

        ENDIF

        ENDFOR

    ENDIF

ENDFOR

RETURN with D_T
```

Fig. 5. GAN image creation algorithm

only to identify a particular class. In the case of network traffic, the difference in the amount of data between classes is large and similar data is repeatedly generated.

If the loss function does not properly represent the distance between the actual and the generated data distribution, eventually the gradient fails to properly update the parameters, making convergence difficult. There are various ways to measure the distance between the two distributions p_r and p_θ. For WGAN-GP, we used the Wasserstein resistance distance function. The Wasserstein resistance is as follows [11]:

$$W_p\left(P_r,P_\theta\right) \; = \; \inf_{\gamma \in \Gamma} \; E_{(x,y) \sim \gamma(x,y)}\left(|x - y|^p\right) \tag{1}$$

Wasserstein resistance is the process of moving masses to change one distribution to another to match two marginal probability distributions. Thus, because of the probability of simultaneous occurrence, it is called the Wasserstein resistance when each distance is minimal. In the case of network traffic, the manifold is concentrated in a small space and classes have many characteristics. Thus, the performance was improved when the Wasserstein resistance was used because of the variety of ambient probability distributions.

Table 1 lists the performance comparison of the DC-GAN and WGAN-GP detection ratio and duration. While using the DC-GAN, the false detection rate was reduced by 0.02 and the detection time was also reduced.

Table 1. Online anomaly detection results on GAN intrusion detection

	TP rate	FP rate	Time (sec)
WGAN-GP	0.9583 ± 0.0223	0.0426 ± 0.0054	≈1.0e−1
DCGAN	0.9335 ± 0.0327	0.0665 ± 0.0188	<1.0e−4

Based on the above experiment, the study time and the amount of learning were increased when normal traffic, by dataset category and generated using WGAN-GP, was added to the training dataset. The learning speed was analyzed when traffic was doubled on each set of data with the exception of the DDoS data. The accuracy of epochs 1–5000 was measured by increasing the total data generated by GAN by 30% for non-normal traffic other than DDoS. Figures 6 and 7 show a graph of the accuracy of each set of data.

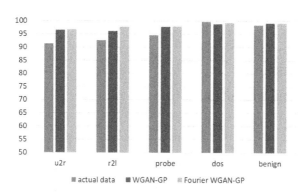

Fig. 6. NSL-KDD dataset precision analysis

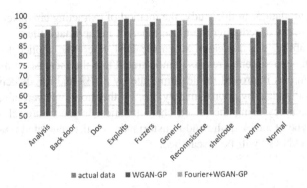

Fig. 7. UNSW-NB15 dataset precision analysis

From Figs. 6 and 7 it was observed that the validation test at epoch 3500–4000 was measured with an accuracy of approximately 81–87%, which is an improvement of approximately 8–12% compared to when the model produced similar traffic. In addition, the learning accuracy for test data also increased by 6–7%. This confirmed that the greater the number of studies, the greater the accuracy. It was also observed that detection performance improved by removing the dataset's data imbalance profile due to classes with less data from the WGAN-GP algorithm.

Table 2 contains the experimental results of the attack traffic classification for the KDD-NSL and UNSW NB15 datasets using a CNN and by adding data generated using WGAN-GP to the existing dataset. The accuracy of the overall dataset validation for categorizing dataset attack traffic was improved by 16% and the test data accuracy was improved by 14%. This demonstrated that by using GAN to continuously increase the amount of attack traffic, the amount of malicious traffic can be used as an effective detection method to increase accuracy in a research environment where there is minimal attack traffic.

Table 2. Comparisons of attack traffic classification experiments using CNN

Dataset	Before	Accuracy	Precision	Recall	F1
NSL-KDD	83–87%	93–99%	98.64%	98.21%	98.42%
UNSW-NB15	76–81%	93–96%	97.65%	98.53%	98.08%

5 Conclusion

In this study, WGAN-GP was used to analyze datasets used in training the intrusion detection system and to resolve the problem of data imbalance. The existing datasets UNSW-NB15 and KDD-NSL were analyzed for minority classes. Based on the analysis results, 50% to 200% of the data for minority classes were generated. The generator that produced similar traffic used only values with a loss value of 0.98 to 1. .pcap files were created as images. These files contain a large amount of noise, causing performance degradation. In this study, the method of extracting characteristics using a DFT filter was applied, reducing the noise inherent in the image files. As a result, the discrimination ability was increased when the DFT filter was applied to the existing WGAN-GP. The experimental results demonstrated that the increase in the creation of similar traffic images improved the learning rate by 3–7% and the detection accuracy for the attack traffic data by approximately 8%. Furthermore, we were able to improve classification accuracy using the attack characteristics. In the future, classification to determine the type of attack traffic and transformation of the generated images into text form using WGAN-GP will be researched.

References

1. Tama, B.A., Rhee, K.H.: Performance analysis of multiple classifier system in DoS attack detection. In: Kim, H.-W., Choi, D. (eds.) WISA 2015. LNCS, vol. 9503, pp. 339–347. Springer, Cham (2016). https://doi.org/10.1007/978-3-319-31875-2_28
2. Tama, B.A., Rhee, K.H.: A combination of PSO-based feature selection and tree-based classifiers ensemble for intrusion detection systems. In: Park, D.S., Chao, H.C., Jeong, Y.S., Park, J. (eds.) Advances in Computer Science and Ubiquitous Computing. LNEE, vol. 373, pp. 489–495. Springer, Singapore (2015). https://doi.org/10.1007/978-981-10-0281-6_71
3. Tama, B.A., Rhee, K.H.: Data mining techniques in DoS/DDoS attack detection: a literature review. Information 18(8), 3739–3747 (2015)
4. Zhu, X., Liu, Y., Li, J., Wan, T., Qin, Z.: Emotion classification with data augmentation using generative adversarial networks. In: Phung, D., Tseng, V.S., Webb, G.I., Ho, B., Ganji, M., Rashidi, L. (eds.) PAKDD 2018. LNCS (LNAI), vol. 10939, pp. 349–360. Springer, Cham (2018). https://doi.org/10.1007/978-3-319-93040-4_28
5. Douzas, G., Bacao, F.: Effective data generation for imbalanced learning using conditional generative adversarial networks. Expert Syst. Appl. 91, 464–471 (2018)
6. Mariani, G., et al.: BAGAN: data augmentation with balancing GAN. arXiv, preprint arXiv: 1803.09655 (2018)
7. He, H., Garcia, E.A.: Learning from imbalanced data. IEEE Trans. Knowl. Data Eng. 21(9), 1263–1284 (2009)
8. Yao, H.P., Liu, Y.Q., Fang, C.: An abnormal network traffic detection algorithm based on big data analysis. Int. J. Comput. Commun. Control 11(4), 567–579 (2016)
9. Li, Y., Ma, R., Jiao, R.: A hybrid malicious code detection method based on deep learning. Methods 9(5), 205–2016 (2015)
10. Tavallaee, M., et al.: A detailed analysis of the KDD CUP 99 data set. In: IEEE Computational Intelligence for Security and Defense Applications, CISDA. IEEE Symposium (2009)
11. Hariharan, B., Girshick, R.B.: Low-shot visual recognition by shrinking and hallucinating features. In: ICCV (2017)
12. Arjovsky, M., Chintala, S., Bottou, L.: Wasserstein GAN. arXiv, preprint arXiv:1701.07875 (2017)
13. Gulrajani, I., et al.: Improved training of Wasserstein GANs. In: Advances in Neural Information Processing Systems (2017)

14. Kim, J.Y., Bu, S.J., Cho, S.B.: Malware detection using deep transferred generative adversarial networks. In: Liu, D., Xie, S., Li, Y., Zhao, D., El-Alfy, E.S. (eds.) International Conference on Neural Information Processing. LNCS, vol. 10634, pp. 556–564. Springer, Cham (2017). https://doi.org/10.1007/978-3-319-70087-8_58

15. Sun, D., et al.: A new mimicking attack by LSGAN. Tools with artificial intelligence (ICTAI). In: IEEE 29th International Conference on IEEE (2017)

16. Yin, C., et al.: An enhancing framework for botnet detection using generative adversarial networks. In: 2018 International Conference on Artificial Intelligence and Big Data (ICAIBD). IEEE (2018)

17. Li, D. et al.: Anomaly detection with generative adversarial networks for multivariate time series. arXiv, preprint arXiv:1809.04758 (2018)

18. Lin, Z., Shi, Y., Xue, Z.: IDSGAN: generative adversarial networks for attack generation against intrusion detection. arXiv, preprint arXiv:1809.02077 (2018)

19. Dainotti, A., Pescape, A., Claffy, K.: Issues and future directions in traffic classification. Netw. IEEE 26(1), 35–40 (2012)

20. Creech, G., Hu, J.: Generation of a new IDS test dataset: time to retire the KDD collection. In: IEEE Wireless Communications and Networking Conference (WCNC), pp. 4487–4492 (2013)

21. Moustafa, N., Slay, J.: UNSW-NB15: a comprehensive data set for network intrusion detection systems (UNSW-NB15 network data set). In: 2015 Military Communications and Information Systems Conference (MilCIS). IEEE (2015)

22. Yu, L., Zhang, W., Wang, J., Yu, Y.: SeqGAN: sequence generative adversarial nets with policy gradient. In: AAAI, pp. 2852–2858 (2017)

23. Kusner, M.J., Hernández-Lobato, J.M.: GANs for sequences of discrete elements with the gumbel-softmax distribution. arXiv preprint arXiv:1611.04051 (2016)

24. Bhaskara, V.S., et al.: Emulating malware authors for proactive protection using GANs over a distributed image visualization of dynamic file behavior. arXiv, preprint arXiv:1807.07525 (2018)

25. Kingma, D.P., Ba, J.: Adam: a method for stochastic optimization. In: International Conference on Learning Representations (ICLR) (2015)

26. Gómez, S.E., et al.: Exploratory study on class imbalance and solutions for network traffic classification. Neurocomputing 343, 100–119 (2019)

Secure Cross-Border Exchange of Health Related Data: The KONFIDO Approach

Sotiris Diamantopoulos[1]([⊠]), Dimitris Karamitros[1], Luigi Romano[1,2],
Luigi Coppolino[2], Vassilis Koutkias[3], Kostas Votis[3], Oana Stan[4],
Paolo Campegiani[5], David Mari Martinez[6], Marco Nalin[7],
Ilaria Baroni[7], Fabrizio Clemente[8], Giuliana Faiella[8],
Charis Mesaritakis[9], Evangelos Grivas[9], Janne Rasmussen[10],
Jan Petersen[10], Isaac Cano[11], Elisa Puigdomenech[12], Erol Gelenbe[13],
Jos Dumortier[14], and Maja Voss-KnudeVoronkov[15]

[1] EXUS Software LTD., London, UK
{s.diamantopoulos,d.karamitros}@exus.co.uk
[2] Consorzio Interuniversitario Nazionale Per L'Informatica, Florence, Italy
{luigi.romano,luigi.coppolino}@uniparthenope.it
[3] Centre for Research and Technology Hellas, Thermi, Greece
{vkoutkias,kvotis}@certh.gr
[4] Commissariat a l'Energie Atomique et Aux Energies Alternatives,
Paris, France
oana.stan@cea.fr
[5] Bit4id s.r.l., Naples, Italy
pca@bit4id.gr
[6] Fundacio Eurecat, Barcelona, Spain
david.mari@eurecat.org
[7] TELBIOS s.r.l., Milan, Italy
{marco.nalin,ilaria.baroni}@telbios.com
[8] Fondazione Santobono Pausilipon onlus, Naples, Italy
fabrizio.clemente@ibb.cnr.it,
giuliana.faiella@gmail.com
[9] Eulambia Advanced Technologies LTD., Agia Paraskevi, Greece
{charis.mesaritak,evangelos.grivas}@eulambia.com
[10] MedCom, Odense, Denmark
{jar,jap}@medcom.dk
[11] Consorci Institut D'Investigacions Biomediques August Pi I Sunyer,
Barcelona, Spain
iscano@clinic.ub.es
[12] Agencia de Qualitat i Avaluacio Sanitaries de Catalunya, Barcelona, Spain
epuigdomenech@gencat.cat
[13] Imperial College of Science Technology and Medicine, London, UK
e.gelenbe@imperial.ac.uk
[14] Time Lex CVBA, Brussels, Belgium
jos.dumortier@timelex.eu
[15] Sundhed.dk IS, Copenhagen, Denmark
mvk@sundhed.dk

© Springer Nature Switzerland AG 2019
R. Montella et al. (Eds.): IDCS 2019, LNCS 11874, pp. 318–327, 2019.
https://doi.org/10.1007/978-3-030-34914-1_30

Abstract. This paper sets up the scene of the KONFIDO project in a clear way. In particular, it: (i) defines KONFIDO objectives and draws KONFIDO boundaries; (ii) identifies KONFIDO users and beneficiaries; (iii) describes the environment where KONFIDO is embedded; (iv) provides a bird's eye view of the KONFIDO technologies and how they will be deployed in the pilot studies of the project; and (v) presents the approach that the KONFIDO consortium will take to prove that the proposed solutions work. KONFIDO addresses one of the top three priorities of the European Commission regarding the digital transformation of health and care in the Digital Single Market, i.e. citizens' secure access to their health data, also across borders. To make sure that KONFIDO has a high-impact, its results are exposed to the wide public by developing three substantial pilots in three distinct European countries (namely Denmark, Italy, and Spain).

Keywords: eHealth · OpenNCP · Trusted computing

1   Introduction, Rationale, and Motivation

One of the top three priorities of the European Commission regarding the digital transformation of health and care in the Digital Single Market constitutes citizens' secure access to their health data, also across borders - enabling citizens to access their health data across the European Union [1]. Up to now, the core effort in the EU for enabling cross-border health data exchange has been resolving interoperability aspects, with projects such as epSOS and OpenNCP (the software implementation of epSOS) providing the foundations for that. However, limited focus has been given on cybersecurity aspects that are entailed in this data exchange, despite the sensitive nature of health data. KONFIDO is an H2020 project aiming to address this issue through a holistic paradigm at the systemic level by gathering a number of state-of-the-art technologies in its toolset, such as blockchain [2], photonic Physical Unclonable Functions [3], homomorphic encryption [4], and trusted execution [5] based on Intel SGX [11].

In a nutshell, KONFIDO is about improving the security of cross-border exchange of eHealth data using OpenNCP. Since KONFIDO's objective is to improve the security of OpenNCP (and not to extend OpenNCP functions), there is a clean-cut separation in KONFIDO between Functional and Non-Functional requirements, and specifically:

- Functional requirements (particularly, interoperability) must be satisfied by OpenNCP.
- Non-functional requirements (particularly, security) must be satisfied by KONFIDO.

Nevertheless, it is worth noting that even if KONFIDO does not implement new functional requirements for OpenNCP, this does not mean that KONFIDO does not have functional requirements at all. In fact, the addition of security features to OpenNCP results in the need to implement new functions (e.g. for strong authentication of users), and the requirements of these functions collectively represent functional requirements for KONFIDO.

A high-level view of how KONFIDO can be deployed to improve the security of OpenNCP is given in Fig. 1.

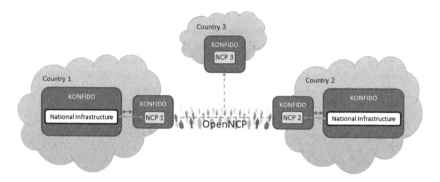

Fig. 1. How KONFIDO can be deployed to improve the security of OpenNCP

It is worth emphasizing that the implementation of secure National Infrastructures is beyond the scope of KONFIDO. Nevertheless, National Infrastructures play an important role in KONFIDO, since they enable the delivery of KONFIDO services to KONFIDO users and beneficiaries. In particular, National Infrastructures are in charge of implementing delegation mechanisms, e.g. enabling a legitimate user of the IT systems of the national eHealth infrastructures of individual Member States that are authorized to access Patient Summaries and ePrescriptions to do so (e.g. a doctor at a hospital emergency service of European country A who has been authorized by a patient of European country B to access his/her data cross-border). Some KONFIDO technologies are dependent on OpenNCP, and are thus only applicable where OpenNCP is available. Several KONFIDO technologies are instead – to a large extent – technically re-usable also outside OpenNCP. These technologies are potentially exploitable within other platforms, including National Infrastructures.

2   KONFIDO Users and Beneficiaries

Since KONFIDO implements secure cross-border data exchange on top of OpenNCP, the only users who interact directly with KONFIDO are the Certified Health Professionals (CHPs) of the National Contact Points (NCPs), NCP system administrators and personnel of the IT staff, and, in general, roles who have direct access to NCP services. We call these users "First Level Users". First Level Users might also – depending on factors such as implementation decisions, deployment options, and policies – include additional stakeholders (e.g. doctors of eHealth institutions in individual Member States). They can also include non-human users (e.g. hardware/software entities).

KONFIDO has also a number of "Second Level Users", i.e. users that do not access KONFIDO directly, but rather delegate First Level Users to do so. These include several categories of stakeholders, virtually all legitimate users of the IT systems of the national eHealth infrastructures of individual Member States that are authorized to access Patient Summaries and ePrescriptions (e.g. a doctor at a hospital emergency service of European country A who has been authorized by a patient of European country B to access his/her data cross-border).

Citizens are not KONFIDO users, as they do not access KONFIDO services directly or by delegating First Level Users to do so. Nevertheless, they benefit from the availability of OpenNCP services (as improved – with regards to security – by KONFIDO). Thus, we call them KONFIDO "Beneficiaries". A bird's eye view of how KONFIDO users and beneficiaries interact with the system and among them is given in Fig. 2.

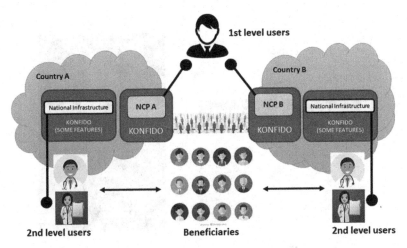

Fig. 2. How KONFIDO users and beneficiaries interact with the system and among them

As already mentioned, some KONFIDO solutions are dependent on OpenNCP, and are thus only applicable where OpenNCP is available, i.e. in the IT infrastructure connecting the NCPs. Nevertheless, although the implementation of secure National Infrastructures is beyond the scope of KONFIDO, some of the KONFIDO solutions that are technically re-usable outside OpenNCP will also be deployed in the National Infrastructures.

Finally, it is worth emphasizing that delegation mechanisms may range from very simple schemes (e.g. a 1-to-1 mapping of a 2nd level user to the corresponding 1st level user) to quite complex ones (e.g. a N-to-1 mapping of multiple 2nd level users to a specific 1st level user). Delegation mechanisms are particularly complex when delegation happens across borders, i.e. a beneficiary from country A delegates a Second Level User of Country B (e.g. an Italian citizen needs treatment at a Spanish Hospital). These mechanisms are being thoroughly analysed in KONFIDO, also based on the requirements set out by the GPDR [7].

3   KONFIDO Design Principles and System Boundaries

KONFIDO takes a user centric approach that it is driven by the real needs of its users and – above all – beneficiaries [6]. It relies on a federated architecture with multiple (2+) levels of hierarchy and on a clean-cut separation between Functional and Non-Functional requirements. More specifically, functional requirements (particularly, interoperability) are satisfied by OpenNCP, while non-functional requirements (specifically, security) must be satisfied by KONFIDO. It is aligned to the eHealth Digital Service Infrastructure (eHDSI or eHealth DSI), the initial deployment and operation of services for cross-border health data exchange under the Connecting Europe Facility (CEF), which is illustrated in Fig. 3.

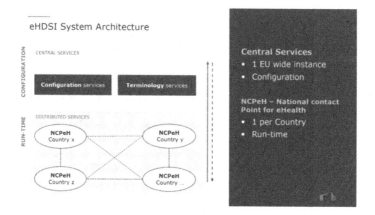

Fig. 3. eHDSI conceptual architecture

To set up KONFIDO validation and demonstration infrastructure, a number of software stubs will have to be developed. By "software stubs" we mean prototype software artefacts – as opposed to commercial grade applications – that implement the "glue code" for exposing OpenNCP functions (as secured by KONFIDO) to pilot users. These stubs are essential to "feed" KONFIDO with inputs and to "consume" KON-FIDO outputs. Importantly, these stubs will enable effective demonstration of the KONFIDO results also to Second Level Users and Beneficiaries, to ultimately maxi-mize KONFIDO impact.

4   National Infrastructures of KONFIDO Pilots

4.1   The Italian National Infrastructure

The Italian Healthcare System is a federated system, meaning that each Region is free to implement its own local policies, reimbursement models, structure, etc. For this reason, a real Italian Electronic Health Record does not exist as a unique National

Infrastructure. The reference for the its development is the "Fascicolo Sanitario Elettronico" (FSE), a set of functions that must be implemented by each Region for eHealth data exchange in Italy. Every Region will have to implement its own (vendor-specific) version of the FSE and make sure it properly exchanges data with the FSEs of the other Regions through the National Interoperability Infrastructure (INI – Infrastruttura Nazionale per l'Interoperabilità).

Currently, the FSE is only partially implemented and adopted in the different Regions. Data available at the time of the writing of this document are updated at 2018 Q2, and they present a picture where there are 17 (out of 21) active Regions trying to implement the FSE, with 11 of them already adhering properly to the INI. Yet, the actual usage from healthcare professionals and patients is still quite low. Therefore, a unified Italian National Infrastructure is considered as not available, at least not for a research project to be tested out. The identified infrastructure used for the Italian NI is composed by:

- A node representing the Italian NCP equipped with OpenNCP and a gateway to forward the request to the specific Italian regional node;
- Two regional nodes, one for PAUSIL and one for TELBIOS, that use the TELBIOS code.

The two regional nodes can exchange any clinical documents at National level, based on the FSE definition, including tele-monitoring data. However, they will exchange ONLY Patient Summary and ePrescription data at European level.

Since the FSE and the epSOS information included in the documents to be exchanged are the same and the reference format is HL7 CDA v2 [10], the epSOS format for these two documents will also be used in the Italian NI.

Since the actual access to the INI for the exchange of FSE data is not accessible for research purposes, software stubs will be developed for the currently available implementations of the FSE (EHR), whenever possible, for data exchanges between healthcare institutions participating in the construction of KONFIDO input data and/or the consumption of KONFIDO output data.

4.2 The Spanish National Infrastructure

In Catalonia (Spain), the provision of healthcare is done by multiple contracted providers having different ownership: public organizations – the Catalan Health Institute (ICS) is the biggest one –, consortia, municipal foundations and private foundations. The provision of healthcare is organized into four main levels: primary care; specialized or hospital care; socio-sanitary care; and mental health. Primary care is the gatekeeper and responsible for coordinating the patients' care along the care continuum. Since the primary healthcare reform (in 1985), primary care has evolved from a predominantly curative care model (upon demand from the user population and the work of individual healthcare professionals) to a model that focuses simultaneously on preventive healthcare, curative healthcare, rehabilitative care and the promotion of community health. This transformation was structurally achieved through the creation of basic health areas and the gradual introduction of primary care teams. Nowadays, there are 369 primary care centres, with around 77% of them being managed by the public provider ICS.

Specialized or hospital care acts as a consultant of primary care and is responsible for more complex care. There is a public network of hospitals distributed over the territory following the schemes of population distribution. The model of hospital has changed in recent years, progressing from a traditional model of a more closed centre that provides conventional inpatient care, emergencies and an outpatient department, to a centre with a greater outpatient focus, with significant roles for ambulatory major and minor surgery, day hospital and home hospitalization. Nowadays, there are 69 hospitals (the ICS manages 8 of those). Around 79% of the specialized care is managed by non-public providers.

The current development of the Spanish National Contact Point is provided under the framework of the European call "Connecting Europe Facility (CEF) 2017"[1].

The OpenNCP project in Spain consists of funding national regions executing and preparing their local IT infrastructures to be able to connect to the Spanish NCP. The goal of the project is to deploy the Patient Summary interchange for 2019 and ePrescription capabilities for 2020.

To align the implementation of KONFIDO with the results of the CEF project, the following infrastructure will be considered:

- A patient management platform with Adaptive Case Management and Self-Management Services as the main emulator;
- An OpenNCP node to be integrated with the emulator platform, enhanced by the KONFIDO cybersecurity toolkit.

4.3   The Danish National Infrastructure

The Danish infrastructure builds on a national Health Data Network for secure exchange of all health-related information between all actors in health and social care provision and the National Service Platform (NSP) for the instant and on-demand access to all national registries and services. The NSP is the central national infrastructure for access to and sharing of health information. Through this platform, all relevant partners in the Danish health care services are able to access and share health data using common standardized interfaces and exchange formats. A part of the health data are based on HL7 CDA standards made accessible through an IHE framework. The platform also facilitates uniform access control and common security components.

Denmark also has a national eHealth portal 'sundhed.dk', where not only citizens can access their own medical information, but also authenticated health care professionals have access to the same information.

During the epSOS project, Denmark established an NCP and OpenNCP node to test ePrescriptions across borders. Since, the node has become inactive and, at present time, it seems very unlikely that Denmark is going to use OpenNCP anytime soon. To provide tangible evidence of the advantages that could be brought to Danish citizens, as

---

[1] https://ec.europa.eu/inea/en/connecting-europe-facility/cef-telecom/apply-funding/2017-cef-telecom-call-ehealth-cef-tc-2017-2.

well as to European citizens visiting Denmark, KONFIDO will stick to its commitment (as per the DoA) of setting up a Danish pilot based on an OpenNCP instance created specifically for KONFIDO. A detailed plan will be issued in the related KONFIDO deliverables.

5   Integration, Validation, and Demonstration in KONFIDO

It is important to clearly distinguish between integration, validation, and demonstration. In KONFIDO, system integration is the process of bringing together individual sub-systems into one system. The system is an aggregation of subsystems cooperating so that it is able to deliver its overarching functionality. Sub-systems include computing systems, software applications, and physical devices. Validation is the process of demonstrating that the proposed solutions are valid, meaning that they solve the problems they were designed for. Demonstration includes all the activities needed to expose the proposed solutions to potential stakeholders (i.e. KONFIDO 2nd level users) and/or to the public in general (i.e. KONFIDO beneficiaries).

Figure 4 provides a high-level view of the approach taken by KONFIDO for integration and validation.

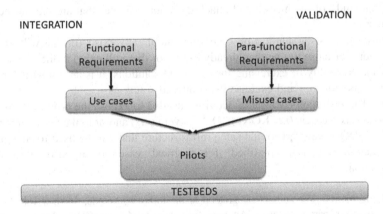

Fig. 4. KONFIDO approach to integration and validation

A use case is an example of correct – proper and, in particular, non-malicious – use of a system. Since KONFIDO is "added" to OpenNCP, integration in KONFIDO means providing evidence that OpenNCP still works properly after KONFIDO has been applied. As such, use cases are the right tool for demonstrating that the integration of KONFIDO (in OpenNCP and in the surrounding context) has been successful.

A misuse case is an example of malicious use of a system. Since KONFIDO's goal is to "add" security to OpenNCP, validating KONFIDO, i.e. providing evidence that it does what it is supposed to do, means collecting tangible evidence that KONFIDO effectively protects OpenNCP from major risks, such as putting the infrastructure out of service; stealing confidential data from eHealth documents; modifying sensitive fields of clinical documents; enabling a malicious user to impersonate a legitimate user. Thus, misuse cases are the right tool for validating KONFIDO para-functional requirements, since they test the ability of KONFIDO to protect OpenNCP from attempts of violating the security of the data that is exchanged and/or of the infrastructure that enables data exchange.

To counter a misuse, monitoring and control actions can be taken within the system, both at the request (A) level, and at the receiver (B) level. In fact, for each attempted use of the system, we can imagine that such controls will be carried out by both parties, and that further controls may also take place at a higher system level where reports from the bilateral lower levels can also be monitored. At the same time, we may consider that an attempted misuse, when detected and rejected, may come back, either in a similar or disguised form, so that such detections and rejections will not be "final" but may lead to repeated attempts under different guises. In addition to the effect of the misuse itself, even with a perfect detection and rejection system, the whole security detection and control scheme creates additional workload and possible congestion for the system which will need to be evaluated and quantified, and for which resources have to be provisioned during normal system operations [8, 9].

In addition, detection schemes are not perfect and will be subject to false alarms. Thus, the analysis should also provide estimates of the additional delays, costs and user frustration that is introduced by such false alarms. This analysis can lead to a cost/benefit study of the misuse and attack detection schemes that are introduced into the system.

A pilot is a realistic application – i.e. one that already exists (or that will exist) in the real world or close to one that already exists (or that will exist) in the real world – that has the capability of exercising the proposed solutions. It is an infrastructure that allows the pilots to run and exercise the proposed solutions.

Since demonstration consists of activities needed to expose the proposed solutions to potential stakeholders (i.e. KONFIDO 2nd level users) and/or to the public in general (i.e. KONFIDO beneficiaries), the same infrastructure that will be used for integration and validation (possibly simplified[2] for practical reasons) will also be used for demonstration.

Acknowledgements. The authors are grateful to the following people, for their valuable contributions to this paper: Salvatore D'Antonio and Giovanni Mazzeo (CINI), Pantelis Natsiavas (CERTH), Jesper Soederberg Knudsen (MEDCOM).

The research leading to these results has received funding from the European Union's Horizon 2020 research and innovation programme under grant agreement No 727528 (KONFIDO - Secure and Trusted Paradigm for Interoperable eHealth Services). This paper reflects only the authors' views and the Commission is not liable for any use that may be made of the information contained therein.

---

[2] As an example, for demonstration purposed it might be irrelevant if the pilots run on an infrastructure that spans multiple countries or if they are deployed on a more compact – yet fully fledged – distributed setup.

References

1. European Commission: Communication to the European Parliament, the Council, the European Economic and Social Committee and the Committee of the Regions on enabling the digital transformation of health and care in the Digital Single Market; empowering citizens and building a healthier society, Brussels, 25.4.2018 COM (2018) 233 final. http://ec.europa.eu/newsroom/dae/document.cfm?doc_id=51628

2. Theodouli, A., Arakliotis, S., Moschou, K., Votis, K., Tzovaras, D.: On the design of a Blockchain-based system to facilitate healthcare data sharing. In: Proceedings of the 17th IEEE International Conference on Trust, Security and Privacy in Computing and Communications/12th IEEE International Conference on Big Data Science and Engineering (TrustCom/BigDataSE), pp. 1374–1379 (2018)

3. Mesaritakis, C., et al.: Physical unclonable function based on a multi-mode optical waveguide. Sci. Rep. 8(1), 9653 (2018). https://doi.org/10.1038/s41598-018-28008-6

4. Carpov, S., Tortech, T.: Secure top most significant genome variants search: iDASH 2017 competition. BMC Med. Genomics 11(Suppl 4), 82 (2018). https://doi.org/10.1186/s12920-018-0399-x

5. Coppolino, L., D'Antonio, S., Mazzeo, G., Romano, L., Sgaglione, L.: Exploiting new CPU extensions for secure exchange of eHealth data at the EU level. In: 14th European Dependable Computing Conference (EDCC2018) (2018). https://doi.org/10.1109/EDCC.2018.00015

6. Natsiavas, P., et al.: Comprehensive user requirements engineering methodology for secure and interoperable health data exchange. BMC Med. Inform. Decis. Mak. 18(1), 85 (2018). https://doi.org/10.1186/s12911-018-0664-0

7. Regulation (EU) 2016/679 of the European Parliament and of the Council of 27 April 2016 on the protection of natural persons with regard to the processing of personal data and on the free movement of such data, and repealing Directive 95/46/EC (General Data Protection Regulation) (Text with EEA relevance) ELI. http://data.europa.eu/eli/reg/2016/679/2016-05-04

8. Staffa, M., et al.: An OpenNCP-based solution for secure ehealth data exchange. J. Netw. Comput. Appl. 116, 65–85 (2018). https://doi.org/10.1016/j.jnca.2018.05.012. ISSN 1084-8045

9. Gelenbe, E., et al.: Security in Computer and Information Sciences. First International ISCIS Security Workshop 2018, Euro-CYBERSEC 2018, London, UK, February 26–27, 2018, Revised Selected Papers. Lecture Notes, Vol. CCIS 821, Springer, Berlin (2018). https://link.springer.com/content/pdf/10.1007%2F978-3-319-95189-8.pdf

10. http://www.hl7.org/implement/standards/product_brief.cfm?product_id=185

11. Coppolino, L., D'Antonio, S., Mazzeo, G., Romano, L.: A comparative analysis of emerging approaches for securing java software with Intel SGX. Future Gener. Comput. Syst. 97, 620–633 (2019). https://doi.org/10.1016/j.future.2019.03.018. ISSN 0167-739X

Safety Management in Smart Ships

Massimo Cossentino[(⊠)], Luca Sabatucci, and Flavia Zaffora

National Research Council,
Istituto di Calcolo e Reti ad Alte Prestazioni (ICAR-CNR), Palermo, Italy
{massimo.cossentino,luca.sabatucci,flavia.zaffora}@icar.cnr.it

Abstract. Smart Ships represent the next-generation of ships and they use ICT to connect all the devices on board to support integrated monitoring and safe management. In such cyber-physical systems, software has the responsibility of bridging the physical components and creating smart functions. Safety is a critical concern in such kind of systems whose malfunctioning may result in damage to equipment and injury to people. In this paper, we deal with this aspect, by identifying two interconnected sub-systems: shipboard power system and emergency management. The proposed architecture is developed through the H-entity multi-paradigm approach, in which heterogeneous technologies are interconnected. We propose to extend the MOISE+ organisational model to deal with systems of H-entities.

Keywords: Safety · Multi-paradigm · System of systems

1 Introduction

Smart Ships are new generation of vessels using ICT to connect all the systems and devices on board, aiming at supporting integrated monitoring and control but also safety, energy-efficient operations and management. They can be defined as a system of systems, their main requirements include smartness and safety. Safety-critical systems are those in which a system failure could harm human life, other living things, physical structures, or the environment. Safety in a smart ship may be defined as the avoidance of hazards to people and ship components due to the operation of a device under normal or single fault condition (including mechanical, electrical and software failures). Several European Projects (e.g. Decision Support System for Ships in Degraded Condition, DSS-DC[1],) have been developed in the direction of shipboard safety, deepening the field of Integrated safety and emergency management systems (ISEMS) [16]. Our approach, in line with Cyber-Physical Systems [19], is to integrate heterogeneous components, namely in this case: the Shipboard Power System (SPS) and the emergency procedure management system. The challenge is to combine different parts, both physical and software, to achieve a smart ship solution pursuing

---

[1] https://trimis.ec.europa.eu/project/decision-support-system-ships-degraded-condition.

© Springer Nature Switzerland AG 2019
R. Montella et al. (Eds.): IDCS 2019, LNCS 11874, pp. 328–337, 2019.
https://doi.org/10.1007/978-3-030-34914-1_31

the overall goal of safety. We propose a multi-paradigm approach, that combines multi-agent systems and actor models, and adopts existing organizational models (MOISE+ [10]) to create a system of systems. The paper is structured as follows: a first part introducing the concept of safety in smart ships and the emergency procedures especially related to the SPS, a second part presenting the proposed architecture and a third one describing the multi-paradigm approach, with a special focus on the organizational side.

2 Safety in the Smart Ship

In the last decade, we are witnessing an advancement of the marine sector, due to the integration of smart technology and automation, aimed at making ships more and more autonomous. In this context, crew and passengers safety is a paramount civil responsibility. In practice, onboard safety depends on: (1) assuring the correct functioning of the equipment necessary for addressing the current mission, and (2) adopting specific emergency procedures to contain or recover failure conditions.

The **Shipboard Power System (SPS)** is the component responsible for granting energy to navigation, communication, and operational systems [2]. It consists of various electric and electronic equipments, such as generators, cables, switchboards, circuit breakers, fuses, buses, and many kinds of loads. In order to grant continuity of services, the electrical circuit is designed for being robust to failures. Loads often are distributed in zones and fed power from the main electric buses. It is usual to classify loads according to their importance into vital and non-vital categories [15], where vital loads are non-sheddable loads that directly affect the survivability of the ship, while the non-vital ones may be shed in order to prevent a total loss of ship's electrical power, or for protection purposes. Moreover, the circuit is instrumented with sensors and actuators for enabling reconfiguration procedures and maintaining safety during operations. The classification of loads into vital and non-vital (sometimes the semi-vital category is considered as well) is not static but it rather depends on the current operational profile and status of the ship. The strategy that enables restoration of the electrical power system is called *SPS Reconfiguration*. Recently, reconfiguration techniques are based on close integration between hardware and software, enabling smart and timely reconfiguration of the electrical layer due to a fault (typically multiple/cascade faults).

The **Emergency Management** is a wide field of studies involving many different disciplines and stakeholders. Its definition is connected to Preparedness and, consequently, to Safety, respectively referring to the ability to respond to an emergency and the need to avoid damages and disasters in a broad sense. Its applications spread from plans at regional/citizen scale to solutions for confined spaces, such as ships and vessels. The issue concerning confined spaces has a precise literature because it leads to very peculiar risks and dangerous situations [6]. The management of emergency has a direct impact on the safety of ship crew and passengers. The onboard procedures established with the emergency plans should handle at least the following emergencies [12] or combinations of them: fire; damage to ship; pollution; unlawful acts threatening the safety of the ship and the security of people; personnel accidents; cargo-related accidents; emergency assistance to other ships. The hardware basis of the emergency management provides all the information collected via devices arranged in different parts of the ship. Sensing is used for the acquisition of physical events and data, also including various types of physical quantities (for example, fire source, temperature, humidity etc). The software basis is the enactment of emergency procedures. It should be in charge to provide all the possible plans related to the current emergency (or concurrent emergencies) and be the smart and safe support for human decisions.

3   The Proposed Architecture

When smartness comes from the union between cyber and physical components, it is the case of framing the product as a Cyber-Physical System (CPS). A CPS integrates the dynamics of the physical processes with those of the digital systems [19] intending to extend the capabilities of the physical layer. Adding the word "smart" to CPS means to define it with a specific quality of *intelligence* that the CPS does not necessarily require. Nevertheless, the smartness of a CPS lies in the property of the reasoning, and in the ability of communicating and sharing knowledge among dissimilar components to take run-time decisions. Developing a smart cyber-physical system is an open challenge due to (1) the inherent complexity of integrating the physical layer with the software layer and (2) the fact that the cyber part must encompass adaptivity, environment programming, open, distributed and scalable functionalities, with an intensive participation of humans. By surveying the state of the art, two main paths emerge for facing this complexity: actors and agents. The choice of a suitable paradigm is not trivial.

The problem of *SPS reconfiguration* has been recently faced off in [17]. The proposed solution has been obtained by adopting MUSA, a Middleware for User-driven Service Adaptation. This middleware, in its last version[2], is implemented as a hierarchy of Akka actors. The advantage of adopting a middleware for self-adaptation in this context consists in achieving the capability to adapt the repair strategy to the operative context, including the external environment and the current mission the ship is undertaking. In practice, different goals derive from different missions, and therefore, the various components of the ship (loads) assume a different priority. Reconfiguration plans are a verticalization in this domain of the approach proposed by [18]. The actor model enables implementing an autonomous monitor-analyse-plan-execute model. In the literature, *Emergency Management* is often faced off by integrating Multi-Agent Systems and Internet of Things [13,20]. The IoT is supposed to provide functionalities for the overall perception of information, reliable transmission of information and intelligent processing of information which can achieve the object of intelligent control

---

[2] MUSA is available online at https://github.com/icar-aose/musa_2_scala.

and management, especially useful for emergency cases [21]. An integrated safety and emergency management system applied to ships can be defined as computer-based support to maintain all safety functions onboard [16]. It should coordinate all the involved entities, by integrating the captain's decision, crew's operations, passengers' movements and navigation main functions to pursue safety during an emergency.

The proposed architecture[3] is obtained as the integration of the Multi-Agent System for the enactment of emergency procedures, as discussed in [13], with the actor model for the SPS reconfiguration [17]. However, the problem of integrating these two subsystems is not trivial because of the mutual dependencies that may exist. The objective of the following sections is providing a framework for multi-paradigm development.

4   The H-entity Multi-paradigm Approach

The proposed aim here is to develop a smart cyber-physical system respecting some requirements especially involving the information exchange among hetero-geneous systems, an ability we can refer to as "interoperability". Therefore, inter-operability could determine a sort of "translation" among elements, languages, frameworks originally independent, acting on the communication-side of a CPS. A "smart" CPS uses specific frameworks involving some reasoning, and the need for communication has to include a social aspect along with an aptitude to adaptation. These elements explicitly belong to agent-oriented languages, while the necessity of enacting feedback loops and scaling system's functionalities sug-gest to adopt an actor-based language. Dealing with the above-mentioned Smart Ship architecture, under the constraint of using different available technologies (the CPS challenge), lead to the adoption of a multi-paradigm approach. Unlike Multi-Paradigm Modeling [11], that refers to a domain dealing with a complex heterogeneity of models, the problem here exposed is to use different program-ming paradigms with different underlying programming languages: multi-agent systems and actor models. In the specific, JADE [3], Jason [5] and Akka [9] have been taken into account, highlighting their common points and their pecu-liarities [7]. Although they are all Java-based, their differences are several, and they descend from the concepts behind their main entity, the *agent* for JADE and Jason, the *actor* for Akka. Moreover, Jason's agents are based on a BDI model, whereas the JADE platform is compliant with FIPA standards [1]. In the following, their strengths will be summarized.

– *Jason* is based on a BDI (belief-desire-intention) model, thus the agent shows a decision-making ability [5]. Human-like, this ability is realised by a sequence of tasks composing a plan that is enacted to pursue a goal.

---

[3] Further details about the proposed Shipboard Power System reconfiguration system and its architecture are available at http://ecos.pa.icar.cnr.it/research-topic/.

- *JADE* [3] exploits the object-oriented paradigm and a cooperative task scheduling to implement autonomous agents. The main features are protocols-oriented communications, strong support to ontologies and full support for FIPA specifications.
- *Akka* is the Scala implementation of the actor model whose peculiar structure lies in the father-children hierarchy [9]. It is greatly useful when developing a reactive system in terms of parallel, asynchronously communicating processing.

For the above-mentioned aim, none of them can be substituted without losing something, so instead of settle with just one, the adopted strategy was creating an *H-entity* in order to choose all of them, basically adopting each entity strength points. A briefly introduction of the H-entity is provided in the following section.

4.1   The H-entity Metamodel

The so-defined H-entity, where 'H' stands for *heterogeneous*, holds the entire philosophy here proposed. It can be considered as a polyhedral organism characterized by autonomous entities and explicable only by reference to the interconnection of these parts. We distinguish an internal and an external view of an H-entity.

The **Internal view**: an H-entity is a (closed world) organization of heterogeneous but collaborating autonomous entities (typically agents and actors). The whole H-entity is characterized by its own design goal, and by a complex behavior. Each member is devoted to one or more tasks for addressing the collective goal. Members have different responsibilities. The *Manager* is responsible for reasoning and decision making (it is typically a Jason agent). The *Worker* is responsible for providing core functionalities and services. It is typically an Akka actor (more than one are usually employed in the solution). The *Diplomat* maintains external relations with other H-entities. It is typically a JADE agent. In the context of a CPS, an H-entity is a cohesive team aimed at solving a specific macro-functionality. However, the overall system is generally constituted by several H-entities. Designing the smart ship, we identify an H-entity for the SPS reconfiguration subsystem and 1..n H-entities for each emergency procedure (fire, flooding, sanitary, evacuation and so on).

The **External view**: the interaction of many H-entities leads to the concept of system of systems, where the open world hypothesis holds. H-entities are not pre-defined and may appear/disappear at run-time; the overall behaviour emerges contextually. For instance, the SPS H-entity must consider active emergency H-entities, when it modifies the configuration of powered components. To allow unknown entities to profitably interact, communications must be done on formal basis, establishing a common language, semantics and protocols. This paper focuses on the external view (only a few details will refer to the internal one). Figure 1 details the external view of the H-entity meta-model.

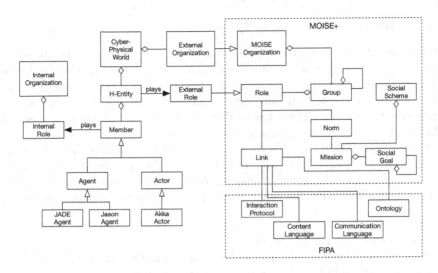

Fig. 1. A portion of the meta-model of the H-entity highlighting the External View.

4.2   The External Organization

A system of systems is defined as a large-scale concurrent and distributed system, the components of which are complex systems themselves. This paradigm grants the operational independence of the individual systems [14]. H-entities are complex systems because they are made of many heterogeneous entities. They are designed to address some functional requirement, but also to live in an open world. Therefore, the idea is that an overall behaviour emerges by the interaction among H-entities. It is necessary to adopt an instrument to formalize the formation of organizations of H-entities to realize a "system of systems". An example of such instrument is MOISE+ [10], a framework for specifying the organization of a multi-agent system by defining the structure as well as functional and deontic aspects. In MOISE+, the functional aspect describes organization goals, the structural aspect defines groups and roles and the deontic aspect describes the relation between goals and roles via permissions and obligations. Roles are an excellent instrument to decompose and distribute goals without specifying agent responsibilities. Indeed agents may dynamically play roles. This dynamicity is necessary when designing open systems whose participants are not assigned apriori. The choice of MOISE+ is supported by the fact that it has already integrated with Jason agents (in the Jacamo framework [4]). We propose to extend the current version of MOISE+ in order to explicitly deal with some of the problems of the open-world systems. Indeed, the ability of agents to interoperate in open and dynamic environments would be facilitated by the use of public and standard specifications. To this aim, the Foundation for Intelligent Physical Agents [1] (FIPA) provides the specifications for open distributed computing environment integrating unknown agents through the use of technologies such as interaction protocols, agent communication languages, and ontology.

4.3   MOISE+ for Systems of Systems

Integrating MOISE+ with the grounding principles of FIPA would create a language to specify organizations operating as open and interoperable systems of systems. In MOISE+, the Organisational Specification (OS) is defined by its three dimensions: structural, functional, and normative [10]. We focus on the Structural Specification (SS) that is defined by: 1. a set of roles, 2. a set of inheritance relations among roles, 3. the root group.

Groups represent the shared context for agents playing roles in it. A Group is composed by Roles, Links and Role Compatibility Relations. The original definition of Link is "the relation between roles that directly constrains the agents in their interaction with the other agents playing the corresponding roles". A Link is defined by:

- source and target roles of the link;
- the type of the link (e.g. acquaintance, communication, or authority);
- the scope of the link (e.g. inter-group or intra-group).

In order to support the open-world hypothesis, we add four constraints into the definition of Link:

- the Interaction Protocol, i.e., the specification of the pre-agreed sequence of messages to be exchanged to communicate effectively;
- the Communication Language (typically grounding on the speech-act theory) that defines the set of performatives and their meaning; examples are FIPA-ACL [1] and KQML [8] (Knowledge Query and Manipulation Language);
- the Ontology, i.e., the concepts, predicates and actions to be used to formalize the semantics of messages content.
- the Content Language, i.e., the language used to serialize and deserialize the content of a message; examples are SL, KIF and RDF.

The following source code shows an example of structural specification with the new definition of Link. At lines 19–22, protocol, language and ontology are specified. These additional elements represent the formal aspects that are expected to be used for implementing a communication among H-entities. A Link prescribes interaction protocol, communication language and an ontology for the interaction be effective.

```
 1  <structural-specification>
 2    <role-definitions>
 3      <role id="SPS"></role>
 4      <role id="emergency"></role>
 5      <role id="fire"><extends role="emergency" /></role>
 6      <role id="evacuation"><extends role="emergency" /></
           role>
 7      ...
 8    </role-definitions>
 9
```

```
10    <group-specification id="smart_ship_safety">
11      <roles>
12        <role id="SPS" min="1" max="1" />
13        <role id="emergency" min="1" max="10" />
14      </roles>
15      <links>
16        <link
17          from="SPS_diplomat" to="emergency_diplomat"
18          type="communication"
19          protocol="IteratedValidation"
20          acl="FIPAACL"
21          language="SLO"
22          ontology="onboard_components"
23          scope="intra-group" bi-dir="false"/>
24      </links>
25    </group-specification>
26  </structural-specification>
```

4.4   The Diplomat Role

To let the internal view and the external view be integrated, one (or more) specific member(s) of the H-entity will play the role of *Diplomat*, being responsible for the communications with other H-entities.

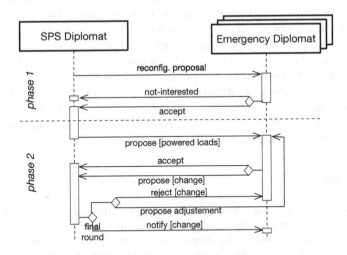

Fig. 2. The IteratedValidation, i.e. an Iterated Contract Net adapted for the SPS/Emergency interaction.

The *Diplomat* is an expert in using standard languages and protocols, also referring to a formalized conceptualization of the domain (ontologies). The presence of the Diplomat ensures the ability of the H-entity to act in an open world where entities developed by different providers could live, interact, and cooperate. We suggest JADE agents act as diplomats because they can exploit FIPA-compliant semantic communications organized through interaction protocols.

In Fig. 2, we provide an example of the IteratedValidation protocol used to allow an orchestrated validation of the SPS reconfiguration plan with the help of the interested emergency H-entities. It is a variant of the Iterated Contract Net [1], modified to allow the SPS manager to refine the electrical reconfiguration taking into account conflicts with the active emergency management H-entities. Indeed, when the generators do not produce enough energy for powering the whole ship components, the reconfiguration strategy often provides power to only a subset of the loads, and therefore it shades some physical components, according to the mission priorities. However, it may happen an emergency plan requires a specific load to be switched on (for instance a corridor for evacuation purposes). The protocol has a first phase in which emergency diplomats who are involved in enacting emergency procedures respond to the call. The second part is multi-step interaction in which the SPS diplomat and the active Emergency diplomats negotiate about which components of the ship may be switched off. The use of this protocol allows applying market strategies to let a better allocation of the physical resources.

5   Conclusion

Safety is a paramount requirement in a smart ship, in which the automation of most of the functions is critical for the crew and the passengers. A possible solution for integrating many independent safety sub-systems is to adopt a multi-paradigm approach: agents and actors live together in abstract structures called H-entities. This paper proposes to use agents' organization to glue together H-entities, but the open-world hypothesis mandates the use of an additional layer based on interaction protocols, languages and ontologies that is realised by extending MOISE with link constraints. An example of a specific interaction protocol (Iterated Validation) is presented as a solution for coordinating the actions of the SPS and Emergency H-entities.

References

1. Foundation for Intelligent Physical Agents (FIPA): FIPA Specification Repository (2005). http://www.fipa.org/repository/index.html
2. Agnello, L., Cossentino, M., De Simone, G., Sabatucci, L.: Shipboard power systems reconfiguration: a compared analysis of state-of-the-art approaches. In: Smart Ships Technology 2017, Royal Institution of Naval Architects (RINA), pp. 1–9 (2017)
3. Bellifemine, F., Poggi, A., Rimassa, G.: JADE: a FIPA2000 compliant agent development environment. In: Proceedings of the Fifth International Conference on Autonomous Agents, pp. 216–217. ACM (2001)
4. Boissier, O., Bordini, R.H., Hübner, J.F., Ricci, A., Santi, A.: Multi-agent oriented programming with JaCaMo. Sci. Comput. Program. **78**(6), 747–761 (2013)

5. Bordini, R., Hübner, J., Wooldridge, M.: Programming Multi-agent Systems in AgentSpeak using Jason, vol. 8. Wiley, Hoboken (2007)
6. Botti, L., Duraccio, V., Gnoni, M.G., Mora, C.: A framework for preventing and managing risks in confined spaces through IoT technologies. In: Safety and Reliability of Complex Engineered Systems-Proceedings of the 25th European Safety and Reliability Conference, ESREL, pp. 3209–3217 (2015)
7. Cossentino, M., Lopes, S., Nuzzo, A., Renda, G., Sabatucci, L.: A comparison of the basic principles and behavioural aspects of Akka, JaCaMo and Jade development frameworks. In: 19th Workshop From Objects to Agents (WOA 2018), Palermo, 28–29 June 2018
8. Finin, T., Fritzson, R., McKay, D., McEntire, R.: KQML as an agent communication language. In: Proceedings of the Third International Conference on Information and Knowledge Management, pp. 456–463. ACM (1994)
9. Gupta, M.: Akka Essentials. Packt Publishing, Birmingham (2012)
10. Hannoun, M., Boissier, O., Sichman, J.S., Sayettat, C.: MOISE: an organizational model for multi-agent systems. In: Monard, M.C., Sichman, J.S. (eds.) IBERAMIA/SBIA -2000. LNCS (LNAI), vol. 1952, pp. 156–165. Springer, Heidelberg (2000). https://doi.org/10.1007/3-540-44399-1_17
11. Hardebolle, C., Boulanger, F.: Exploring multi-paradigm modeling techniques. Simulation **85**(11–12), 688–708 (2009)
12. House, D.J.: Seamanship Techniques: Shipboard and Marine Operations. Routledge, Abingdon (2013)
13. Katayama, K., Takahashi, H., Yokoyama, S., Gäfvert, K., Kinoshita, T.: Evacuation guidance support using cooperative agent-based IoT devices. In: 2017 IEEE 6th Global Conference on Consumer Electronics (GCCE), pp. 1–2. IEEE (2017)
14. Olivier, J.P., Balestrini-Robinson, S., Briceño, S.: Approach to capability-based system-of-systems framework in support of naval ship design. In: 2014 IEEE International Systems Conference Proceedings, pp. 388–395. IEEE (2014)
15. Padamati, K.R., Schulz, N.N., Srivastava, A.K.: Application of genetic algorithm for reconfiguration of shipboard power system. In: 2007 39th North American Power Symposium, pp. 159–163. IEEE (2007)
16. Rødseth, Ø.J., et al.: Passenger ship safety and emergency management control. In: Lloyds register and Fairplay conference Cruise and Ferry (2005)
17. Sabatucci, L., Cossentino, M., Simone, G.D., Lopes, S.: Self-reconfiguration of shipboard power systems. In: Proceedings of the 3rd eCAS Workshop on Engineering Collective Adaptive Systems (2018)
18. Sabatucci L., Cossentino M.: Supporting dynamic workflows with automatic extraction of goals from BPMN. ACM Trans. Auton. Adapt. Syst. (TAAS). (in printing)
19. Shi, J., Wan, J., Yan, H., Suo, H.: A survey of cyber-physical systems. In: 2011 International Conference on Wireless Communications and Signal Processing (WCSP), pp. 1–6. IEEE (2011)
20. Turoff, M., Hiltz, S.R., Bañuls, V.A., Van Den Eede, G.: Multiple perspectives on planning for emergencies: an introduction to the special issue on planning and foresight for emergency preparedness and management. Technol. Forecast. Soc. Change **80**(9), 1647–1656 (2013). https://doi.org/10.1016/j.techfore.2013.07.014
21. Yang, L., Yang, S.H., Plotnick, L.: How the Internet of Things technology enhances emergency response operations. Technol. Forecast. Soc. Chang. **80**(9), 1854–1867 (2013)

Managing Privacy in a Social Broker Internet of Thing

V. Carchiolo[1] , A. Longheu[2]([✉]) , M. Malgeri[2] , and G. Mangioni[2]

[1] Dip. Matematica e Informatica, Università degli Studi di Catania, Catania, Italy
vincenza.carchiolo@unict.it
[2] Dip. Ingegneria Elettrica, Elettronica e Informatica, Università degli Studi di Catania, Catania, Italy
{alessandro.longheu,michele.malgeri,giuseppe.mangioni}@dieei.unict.it

Abstract. Smart homes, smart cities, smart everything and the Internet of Things (IoT) have incredible impact in our life. Typically, IoT devices are though vulnerable to attacks and the strategy to manage IoT security is influenced by the IoT model and the application field. Social Internet of Things (SIoT) can be viewed as the evolution of IoT in the same way social networks can be considered an evolution of the Internet. In this paper, we discuss about security issues on social IoT approach based on a social broker paradigm. In particular, we present a solution to manage information privacy in a SIoT environment built on a social broker.

Keywords: Social networks · IoT · Information broker · Publish-subscribe model · Trust network · Security and privacy

1 Introduction

IoT represents an approach that is changing the world from both users' and developers' point of view. IoT is creating a giant network where all the devices are connected to each other with interactive capabilities. IoT has a big impact on both communication technologies and overlay networks that aims to manage logical devices. It is driving the automation to the next level where devices will communicate each other and make decisions on their own without any human intervention.

Among the variety of facets of IoT, the *Social* IoT emerged from embedding the social networks paradigma into IoT; within SIoT, four scenarios can be considered: Thing-to-Thing Social IoT (TTS-IoT) [14,20], Thing-to-Human Social IoT (THS-IoT) [18], Application-to-Application Social IoT (AAS-IoT) [27] and Broker-to-Broker Social IoT (BBS-IoT) [11]. Briefly, TTS-IoT is one of the oldest SIoT paradigms where wireless sensor nodes build temporary social relationships, THS-IoT paradigm is the most natural and it is based on semantic

This work has been partially supported by the Università degli Studi di Catania - Piano della Ricerca 2016–2018 Linea di intervento 2.

© Springer Nature Switzerland AG 2019
R. Montella et al. (Eds.): IDCS 2019, LNCS 11874, pp. 338–348, 2019.
https://doi.org/10.1007/978-3-030-34914-1_32

technologies, AAS-IoT is a new social approach that promotes data exchange and reuse among IoT applications, so they can use mutual social relationships to leverage their services; finally BBS-IoT is a distributed multi-broker overlay based on social inspired algorithm to query forwarding and answering [5].

In this last approach each application realm lives only inside its ecosystem and the communication links are static and often manually configured, therefore it can be difficult to easily share information among different ecosystems. The architecture proposed in [5] aims to overcome this limitation by creating a *social network* between brokers to foster information exchange among such ecosystems.

The social approach increases the chances to share information and data allowing the global system to react more promptly, to calculate environment parameters more accurately, leading to better decisions. Unfortunately, like any other social network, security and privacy management are a huge problem to deal with. Although security and privacy are correlated, in this paper we propose a mechanism to tackle the latter issue. We propose to use the well-known and accepted concept of *k-anonymity* to limit the access to full information only to a subset of brokers and to push only anonymized information to all subscribers.

The state of the art on security in IoT context is discussed in Sect. 2 focusing on the concepts useful in the context of SIoT. Section 3 presents the BBS-IoT and the querying/answering algorithm based on Prosa [6]. In Sect. 4, we consider privacy and propose a solution to improve the privacy of the overall systems, discussing concluding remarks in Sect. 5.

2   Security Issues in Internet of Things

The question of security plays a remarkable role in the Internet of Things paradigm. Security in IoT had a lot of attention by the research community and it can be addressed at different levels. A lot of surveys show the limitation of security issue in relation with the key characteristic of IoT devices (e.g. battery lifetime) [42], other evaluate the available middleware approaches and show how security is handled by each approach [44]. In [19,34], authors addressed the security and privacy issues in IoT at each layer of a 3-layer architecture. Low-level IoT security issues are addressed by many studies arguing solutions and implications. The impact of security at physical and link layer are discussed with respect to disruption as well as denial-of-service [23,41], network disruption [10,12,39,40] privacy violation [9,13,24] and energy consumption [3].

Other authors discuss the implication at the intermediate level. The 6LoW-PAN adaptation layer and network layer security issue are discussed with respect to disruption and denial-of-service [18], blocking of reassembly buffer [15] whereas some authors discussed solution about IP Spoofing [25], denial-of-service [36,38], privacy violation, spamming, byzantine faults, unreliable broadcast [1] in the network layer. Finally, some studies address the security issue at High level in terms of network bottleneck, denial-of-service, and privacy violation [43]. A different approach to classify security matters is proposed in [30], where entities involved are exploited for classification purposes: things, users or applications and technological ecosystems; authors propose to model security issues as relations between these entities.

Privacy comes from the need for protecting data related to humans. Recently, data has become a major concern in many processes and it led to concrete actions such as the General Data Protection Regulation (GDPR) within EU countries. Even if privacy in IoT seems a contradictory aspect (IoT indeed fosters information sharing) it is though essential to fulfill privacy requirements due to the risk of technology mishandling by legitimate and/or illegitimate users. This contradiction must be resolved e.g. by adopting specific IoT applications that may require different levels of data privacy. For example, health applications are normally required with a high degree of protection that might not be necessary in another context.

In smart environments, to make the right assessment is necessary to trust the involved device(s) to evaluate their report and/or actions. Indeed, establishing and managing trust for a huge number of objects in heterogeneous and large-scale environments is a considerable challenge for researchers and manufacturers. Trust management definition and operations (establishing, updating, and revoking credentials, keys, and certificates) have to be addressed as a key security issue in IoT.

Another aspect to investigate is how to control access and identify both devices and other players, that is how to manage identifiers, make them unique and how to easily retrieve the profile associated with a given identifier. Identification affects many aspects of the global IoT system, including conception, architecture, access rules, etc. [21].

Reliability and safety are essential in many applications where the effective use of intelligent objects must be assessed; to the best of our knowledge, research efforts in IoT reliability are still limited. Moreover, the software embedded into autonomous objects may sometimes cause random or unpredictable behavior, so it has to be carefully checked to avoid catastrophic consequences for the whole system and the physical environment.

Finally, [2] surveys the security of the main IoT frameworks comparing security architectures and authors show that several IoT frameworks are based on the same standards for securing communications, whereas different methodologies followed to provide other security properties. In a SIoT context, the security issue can be redefined based on the social relation introduced by the adopted social model; indeed, also security matters may be modeled by taking inspiration from social behaviors.

Considering security on social behavior in IoT, it can have a different meaning that reflects the different visions of a Social IoT paradigm. It can be assumed that only some security issues are affected by social model and most of the solutions proposed for secure IoT can be used for a secure SIoT mainly low and intermediate level security matters. In summary, the preeminent issues are:

- Auto-immunity in Thing-to-Thing Social IoT (TTS-IoT);
- Social Identification/access control in Thing-to-Human Social IoT (THS-IoT);

- Reliability in Application-to-Application Social IoT (AAS-IoT).
- Trust and privacy matters in Broker-to-Broker Social IoT (BBS-IoT).

One of the first studies on privacy issue in the context of social approach in IoT can be found in [26], where authors introduce an attacker model that can be applied to both centralized and distributed IoT architectures and in [37] that deeply discussed the implication of privacy in IoT. Authors of [17] introduce a novel privacy-preserving technique based on homomorphic encryption scheme working via an aggregation mechanism.

In SIoT we often discuss trust-based services as services that perform better than non-trust-based services. There exist a plethora of solutions which considered trust in all different forms but with the same goal. Most of trust-based solutions aim at balancing the connectivity between the service seekers and the service providers, which is a remarkable issue for maintaining user control while defining the trust rules [10,33]. An important survey on this topic can be found in [32] that analyses several approaches and proposes some solutions to maintain trust by identifying malicious nodes in the network [22,31].

3 Social Broker Network

This SIoT paradigm is an extension of IoT system following the *publish-subscribe* pattern. This pattern introduces a Broker entity which acts as a mediator between publisher and subscriber objects that can be either machines or humans. An object advises the broker about its information and it will take care of the delivery to those other objects who are interested in. This pattern allows implementing an effective Machine-to-Machine (M2M) asynchronous communication, thus inspiring several protocols over these last years as CoAP, MQTT, AMQP, and many others [16,35]. Most of them use topics for modeling classes of interest that clients can subscribe to.

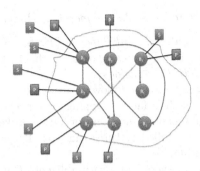

Fig. 1. The brokers network (Color figure online)

In [5] and [8] we proposed a solution based on social behavior. The idea proposed in [5] is to create a *social network* among brokers to foster information exchange among such a group of *friends broker*. This solution allows a broker to answer a request from a subscriber either with the information collected by its clients or asking other brokers that may be part of a different ecosystem.

We model the connection between two brokers with three different kinds of direct link (Fig. 1):

- *acquaintances link (AL)*, meaning that the two brokers are just acquaintances (red link);
- *temporary semantic link (TSL)*, that models a weak friendship (yellow link);
- *full semantic link (TSL)*, modeling a true friendship (green link);

Usually, human beings classify people into three categories: trusted friends, friends, and acquaintances according to his/her direct experience with them. Whenever He/she needs information, the steps are first to ask trusted friends, moving then to *basic* friends in case of unsatisfactory results and finally asking acquaintances as last option. The strategy used by a broker to share information resembles human strategy: the broker asks FSL, TSL, and AL to share information.

As in real life, in the proposed network of brokers relationships change over time. It may happen for instance that new acquaintances are acquired, or acquaintances become friends and they become true friends; to avoid that an incoming broker remains isolated forever, it is linked with AL to some random brokers.

The information exchange in this network between Publisher and Subscriber is indexed according to *Topics*; each publisher sends information tagged by several topics to a broker which in turn sends it to all the subscribers that have previously registered to some of those topics.

In the Social Broker Network, each broker B stores the topics inside a *BrokersList* that traces all existing links ($Link_i$). Therefore each $Link_i$ is the triple

$$Link_i = \{Address_i, LinkType_i, LocalListTopic_i\} \qquad (1)$$

where $Address_i$ is B_i's address, $LinkType_i \in \{FSL, TSL, AL\}$ is the type of link between B and B_i and $LocalListTopic_i$ is the List of topics of B_i and $BrokersList = \{Link_i \forall (B, B_i) \in Edges\}$.

For a sake of clarity, we use the following use case to explain the algorithm (formally presented in [8]). In a large shopping center, every shop has its smart management system that can include one or more brokers depending on the shops' size, among the controlled features there are humidity and temperature that is used to conditioning.

The broker B_i manages the set of local publishers $Pub_{B_i} = \{p_{i1}, p_{i2}, ..., p_{in}\}$ and the set of local subscribers $Sub_{B_i} = \{s_{i1}, s_{i2}, ..., s_{im}\}$, each publisher send information about a specific topic (e.g. humidity, temperature, etc.) and each subscriber receive information according with the topics it subscribed.

At the very beginning, brokers are not connected to each other, so they cannot access any information but local. To startup the social network, any broker B_i

that wants to join selects some others randomly (or according to some strategy depending on shops' owners) adding them as AL sending them its *BrokersList*.

Let'us suppose that the smart system of a shoe shop want to know external temperature, but its Broker B_i has not its sensor, hence it first tries to contact Brokers in its FSL; supposing that is empty, brokers moves to TSL and (being empty too) finally it contacts someone in its AL that contains almost an element. If B_i receives a response from B_j, it promotes B_j into TSL. Then, if B_j continues to answer it is raised to FSL. After enough time the FSL, TSL and AL sets of all brokers will contain someone and the network will be able to cover all the shopping center. Indeed, a broker is contacted according to a *similarity function* that takes into account both the tag and the localization, e.g. if the shoe store asks humidity nearby is the main door the broker will select all links that concern humidity, but also moisture, damp, dryness, and whose location is not so far from the main door.

Of course, if B_i does not receive responses for a while or the quality of information is not satisfactory, it downgrades a link from FSL to TSL and from TSL to AL.

4 Managing Privacy in a Social Broker Network

The basic algorithm doesn't take into account privacy and security, and this represents a big challenge in the social approach. In this section, we propose a solution aiming at (partially) addressing the privacy matter while demanding the security matters to the underlying communication network.

Indeed, human beings usually classify information he/she owns according to their sensibility and he/she shares some of them only with trusted people. Of course, the attitude to share information is a personal characteristic since some people are private persons while others are tattletales. Since the goal of the proposed approach is to share information, we must avoid that *strong* private nodes prevent the evolution of the broker networks simply by not sharing anything.

We then introduce two levels of privacy management: the former is based on a policy that resembles the natural attitude to classify information while the latter attempts to anonymize (or pseudo-anonymize) some of the sensitive information.

4.1 Introducing Policies

To tackle sharing policy, we globally define a sensitiveness scale and let publishers use it to inform their own broker to manage the propagation of the information. Then, a topic is defined as follows:

$$t_i = \{location_i, value_i, policyId_i\} \tag{2}$$

The broker selects the diffusion algorithm according to the policy chosen by the publisher:

1. *public information*: broker uses basic algorithms as discussed in the previous section;
2. *slightly reserved*: broker uses the basic algorithm but it sends the complete information only along the FSLs if exist otherwise it sends anonymized information to ALs.
3. *moderately reserved*: in this case, the broker sends information only to FSL and TSL always anonymized;
4. *secretive*: information is not shared, i.e. it is only available to local subscribers. Note that this policy, although possible, does not allow the social network to evolve.

The dynamic of the Broker Network is *moderately reserved* with respect to the algorithm presented in [8]. Indeed, the AL is upgraded to TSL with the same strategy i.e. when the broker behaves as a "virtual publisher" for it. To guarantee privacy, the upgrade of a TSL to FSL is limited to brokers that are trusted. The trust of a broker is managed by a trust network, whose functionality is currently out of the scope of the present paper.

4.2 Anonymization

The nature of the social network implies that some information about the publisher must be sent to some other people that can use the information to violate privacy. While the policy can reduce the amount of the information published outside the local realm, it can avoid that some of them must be transmitted to allows the network to properly evolves. Therefore, we propose to anonymize both the localization and the corresponding value according to the well-known technique called *k-anonymity*. The concept of k-anonymity [28,29] addresses the problem: *"Given person-specific field-structured data produce a release of the data with scientific guarantees that the individuals who are the subjects of the data cannot be re-identified while the data remain practically useful."*. Information has the *k-anonymity property* if the information for each element contained in the release cannot be distinguished from at least $k - 1$ individuals. The anonymization will be performed both in the local and global realm. The former anonymizes the data provided by the local publisher while the latter uses the data shared by all brokers directly connected with an FSL.

Management in the local realm is quite easy since it uses the canonical approaches, i.e. suppression and generalization, managed by standard brokers. Both suppression and generalization can modify localization and/or associated values (or measures) For instance, when the broker receives multiple information dealing with same topics from different publishers it creates a new *virtual publisher* that emits a topic with correct value but a localization that is calculated (generalized) using the real localizations, or it can randomly suppress some records. The broker could create new records by shuffling localizations with respect to values, ensuring that the aggregate value is correct (e.g. the final average value is the same as the original set of topics).

The anonymization in the global realm is quite more complex because it involves the exchange of information among the nodes connected by FSLs. For a sake of clarity, we describe the proposal using the same example (shopping center) presented in the previous section, hence the steps to follow are:

1. each broker receives the topic from all publishers inside the shop it controls;
2. the broker performs the local anonymization, this implies that all brokers could share the topic humidity. Of course, an attacker is able to know the shop that is the source of information.
3. the broker performs global anonymization asking nearby brokers, connected by FSL, the availability to share humidity token;
4. all brokers that agree to share the topic exchange the topics (temporary broker group = TBG) and each one applies the same generalization/suppression algorithm used in the local realm to hide shop localization.

Therefore, all brokers belonging to TBG can localize the source of information, all other brokers still receive information but cannot localize the real source. Finally, all subscribers receive the information and can use it to assess the average humidity inside all the shopping center but none can know the real status of any shop.

5   Conclusions and Future Works

In this paper, privacy issues about Social Broker Network based on self-organising algorithm are discussed. The algorithm emulates the way social relationships among people naturally arise and evolve. The problem of trust of the shared Topic is under investigation; Social-based reputation approach [4] can be taken into account and the solution can still be inspired by PROSA [7]. The solution presented in this article is currently being tested within an IoT network for managing a smart office and on smart health solution. The test will be used to evaluate the different security levels requested by different SIoT application.

References

1. Abu-Elkheir, M., Hayajneh, M., Ali, N.A.: Data management for the Internet of Things: design primitives and solution. Sensors **13**(11), 15582–15612 (2013). https://doi.org/10.3390/s131115582. https://www.mdpi.com/1424-8220/13/11/15582
2. Ammar, M., Russello, G., Crispo, B.: Internet of Things: a survey on the security of IoT frameworks. J. Inf. Secur. Appl. **38**, 8–27 (2018). https://doi.org/10.1016/j.jisa.2017.11.002
3. Butun, I., Morgera, S.D., Sankar, R.: A survey of intrusion detection systems in wireless sensor networks. IEEE Commun. Surv. Tutor. **16**(1), 266–282, First 2014. https://doi.org/10.1109/SURV.2013.050113.00191
4. Buzzanca, M., Carchiolo, V., Longheu, A., Malgeri, M., Mangioni, G.: Direct trust assignment using social reputation and aging. J. Ambient Intell. Hum. Comput. **8**(2), 167–175 (2017). https://doi.org/10.1007/s12652-016-0413-0

5. Carchiolo, V., Longheu, A., Malgeri, M., Mangioni, G.: A social inspired broker for M2M protocols. In: Proceedings of COMPLEXIS 2019, pp. 101–105 (2019). https://doi.org/10.5220/0007765101010105. ISBN 978-989-758-366-7

6. Carchiolo, V., Malgeri, M., Mangioni, G., Nicosia, V.: PROSA: P2P resource organisation by social acquaintances. In: Joseph, S., Despotovic, Z., Moro, G., Bergamaschi, S. (eds.) AP2PC 2006. LNCS (LNAI), vol. 4461, pp. 135–142. Springer, Heidelberg (2008). https://doi.org/10.1007/978-3-540-79705-0_12

7. Carchiolo, V., Longheu, A., Malgeri, M., Mangioni, G.: The cost of trust in the dynamics of best attachment. Comput. Inf. **34**, 167–184 (2015)

8. Carchiolo, V., Longheu, A., Malgeri, M., Mangioni, G.: Smart topic sharing in IoT platform based on a social inspired broker: a case study. In: Kotenko, I., Badica, C., Desnitsky, V., El Baz, D., Ivanovic, M. (eds.) Accepted for Publication in Proceedings of IDC 2019 Conference, vol. 868, pp. 48–55. Springer, Heidelberg (2019)

9. Chae, S.H., Choi, W., Lee, J.H., Quek, T.Q.S.: Enhanced secrecy in stochastic wireless networks: artificial noise with secrecy protected zone. IEEE Trans. Inf. Forensics Secur. **9**(10), 1617–1628 (2014). https://doi.org/10.1109/TIFS.2014.2341453

10. Chen, Y., Trappe, W., Martin, R.P.: Detecting and localizing wireless spoofing attacks. In: 2007 4th Annual IEEE Communications Society Conference on Sensor, Mesh and Ad Hoc Communications and Networks, pp. 193–202, June 2007. https://doi.org/10.1109/SAHCN.2007.4292831

11. D'Elia, A., Viola, F., Roffia, L., Cinotti, T.S.: A multi-broker platform for the Internet of Things. In: Balandin, S., Andreev, S., Koucheryavy, Y. (eds.) ruSMART 2015. LNCS, vol. 9247, pp. 34–46. Springer, Cham (2015). https://doi.org/10.1007/978-3-319-23126-6_4

12. Demirbas, M., Song, Y.: An RSSI-based scheme for sybil attack detection in wireless sensor networks. In: Proceedings of the 2006 International Symposium on on World of Wireless, Mobile and Multimedia Networks, WOWMOM 2006, pp. 564–570. IEEE Computer Society, Washington, DC, USA (2006). https://doi.org/10.1109/WOWMOM.2006.27. http://dx.doi.org/10.1109/WOWMOM.2006.27

13. Foundation, O.: OWASP foundation, Accessed 2019. https://www.owasp.org

14. Holmquist, L.E., Mattern, F., Schiele, B., Alahuhta, P., Beigl, M., Gellersen, H.-W.: Smart-its friends: a technique for users to easily establish connections between smart artefacts. In: Abowd, G.D., Brumitt, B., Shafer, S. (eds.) UbiComp 2001. LNCS, vol. 2201, pp. 116–122. Springer, Heidelberg (2001). https://doi.org/10.1007/3-540-45427-6_10

15. Hummen, R., Hiller, J., Wirtz, H., Henze, M., Shafagh, H., Wehrle, K.: 6LoWPAN fragmentation attacks and mitigation mechanisms. In: Proceedings of the Sixth ACM Conference on Security and Privacy in Wireless and Mobile Networks, WiSec 2013, pp. 55–66. ACM, New York, NY, USA (2013). https://doi.org/10.1145/2462096.2462107. http://doi.acm.org/10.1145/2462096.2462107

16. Hunkeler, U., Truong, H.L., Stanford-Clark, A.: MQTT-S - a publish/subscribe protocol for wireless sensor networks. In: 2008 3rd International Conference on Communication Systems Software and Middleware and Workshops (COMSWARE'08), pp. 791–798, January 2008. https://doi.org/10.1109/COMSWA.2008.4554519

17. Jayaraman, P.P., Yang, X., Yavari, A., Georgakopoulos, D., Yi, X.: Privacy preserving Internet of Things: from privacy techniques to a blue print architecture and efficient implementation. Future Gener. Comput. Syst. **76**, 540–549 (2017). Kindly provide complete details for Ref. [19]

18. Kim, H.: Protection against packet fragmentation attacks at 6LoWPAN adaptation layer. In: 2008 International Conference on Convergence and Hybrid Information Technology, pp. 796–801, August 2008. https://doi.org/10.1109/ICHIT.2008.261
19. Kumar, J.S., Patel, D.R.: A survey on Internet of Things: security and privacy issues (2014)
20. Mendes, P., Mendes, P.A.: Social-driven internet of connected objects (2011)
21. Miettinen, M., Marchal, S., Hafeez, I., Asokan, N., Sadeghi, A., Tarkoma, S.: IoT sentinel: automated device-type identification for security enforcement in IoT. In: 2017 IEEE 37th International Conference on Distributed Computing Systems (ICDCS), pp. 2177–2184, June 2017. https://doi.org/10.1109/ICDCS.2017.283
22. Nitti, M., Girau, R., Atzori, L.: Trustworthiness management in the social Internet of Things. IEEE Trans. Knowl. Data Eng. **26**(5), 1253–1266 (2013)
23. Noubir, G., Lin, G.: Low-power DoS attacks in data wireless LANs and counter-measures. SIGMOBILE Mob. Comput. Commun. Rev. **7**(3), 29–30 (2003). https://doi.org/10.1145/961268.961277. http://doi.acm.org/10.1145/961268.961277
24. Pecorella, T., Brilli, L., Mucchi, L.: The role of physical layer security in IoT: a novel perspective. Information **7**(3) (2016). https://doi.org/10.3390/info7030049, https://www.mdpi.com/2078-2489/7/3/49
25. Riaz, R., Kim, K., Ahmed, H.F.: Security analysis survey and framework design for IP connected LoWPANs. In: 2009 International Symposium on Autonomous Decentralized Systems, pp. 1–6, March 2009. https://doi.org/10.1109/ISADS.2009.5207373
26. Roman, R., Zhou, J., Lopez, J.: On the features and challenges of security and privacy in distributed Internet of Things. Comput. Netw. **57**(10), 2266–2279 (2013). https://doi.org/10.1016/j.comnet.2012.12.018. http://dx.doi.org/10.1016/j.comnet.2012.12.018
27. Saleem, Y., Crespi, N., Pace, P.: SCDIoT: social cross-domain IoT enabling application-to-application communications. In: 2018 IEEE International Conference on Cloud Engineering (IC2E), pp. 346–350, April 2018. https://doi.org/10.1109/IC2E.2018.00068
28. Samarati, P.: Protecting respondents identities in microdata release. IEEE Trans. Knowl. Data Eng. **13**(6), 1010–1027 (2001)
29. Samarati, P., Sweeney, L.: Protecting privacy when disclosing information: k-anonymity and its enforcement through generalization and suppression. Technical report, SRI International (1998)
30. Sfar, A.R., Natalizio, E., Challal, Y., Chtourou, Z.: A roadmap for security challenges in the Internet of Things. Digit. Commun. Netw. **4**(2), 118–137 (2018). https://doi.org/10.1016/j.dcan.2017.04.003. http://www.sciencedirect.com/science/article/pii/S2352864817300214
31. Sharma, V., You, I., Jayakody, D.N.K., Atiquzzaman, M.: Cooperative trust relaying and privacy preservation via edge-crowdsourcing in social Internet of Things. Future Gener. Comput. Syst. **92**, 758–776 (2019). https://doi.org/10.1016/j.future.2017.12.039. http://www.sciencedirect.com/science/article/pii/S0167739X17312748
32. Sicari, S., Rizzardi, A., Grieco, L., Coen-Porisini, A.: Security, privacy and trust in Internet of Things: the road ahead. Comput. Netw. **76**, 146–164 (2015). https://doi.org/10.1016/j.comnet.2014.11.008. http://www.sciencedirect.com/science/article/pii/S1389128614003971
33. Truong, N.B., Um, T.W., Lee, G.M.: A reputation and knowledge based trust service platform for trustworthy social Internet of Things. Innovations in clouds, Internet and networks (ICIN) (2016)

34. Vikas, B.: Internet of Things (IoT): a survey on privacy issues and security. Int. J. Sci. Res. Sci. Eng. Technol. IJSRSET **1**, 168–173 (2015)

35. Vinoski, S.: Advanced message queuing protocol. IEEE Internet Comput. **10**(6), 87–89 (2006). https://doi.org/10.1109/MIC.2006.116

36. Wazid, M., Das, A.K., Kumari, S., Khan, M.K.: Design of sinkhole node detection mechanism for hierarchical wireless sensor networks. Secur. Commun. Netw. **9**(17), 4596–4614 (2016). https://doi.org/10.1002/sec.1652. https://doi.org/10.1002/sec.1652

37. Weber, R.H.: Internet of Things ? New security and privacy challenges. Comput. Law Secur. Rev. **26**(1), 23–30 (2010). https://doi.org/10.1016/j.clsr.2009.11.008. http://www.sciencedirect.com/science/article/pii/S0267364909001939

38. Weekly, K., Pister, K.: Evaluating sinkhole defense techniques in RPL networks. In: 2012 20th IEEE International Conference on Network Protocols (ICNP), pp. 1–6, October 2012. https://doi.org/10.1109/ICNP.2012.6459948

39. Xiao, L., Greenstein, L., Mandayam, N., Trappe, W.: Fingerprints in the ether: using the physical layer for wireless authentication. In: 2007 IEEE International Conference on Communications, pp. 4646–4651, June 2007. https://doi.org/10.1109/ICC.2007.767

40. Xiao, L., Greenstein, L.J., Mandayam, N.B., Trappe, W.: Channel-based detection of sybil attacks in wireless networks. IEEE Trans. Inf. Forensics Secur. **4**(3), 492–503 (2009). https://doi.org/10.1109/TIFS.2009.2026454

41. Xu, W., Trappe, W., Zhang, Y., Wood, T.: The feasibility of launching and detecting jamming attacks in wireless networks. In: Proceedings of the 6th ACM International Symposium on Mobile Ad Hoc Networking and Computing, MobiHoc '05, pp. 46–57. ACM, New York (2005). https://doi.org/10.1145/1062689.1062697. http://doi.acm.org/10.1145/1062689.1062697

42. Yang, Y., Wu, L., Yin, G., Li, L., Zhao, H.: A survey on security and privacy issues in Internet-of-Things. IEEE Internet Things J. **4**(5), 1250–1258 (2017). https://doi.org/10.1109/JIOT.2017.2694844

43. Yu, S.: Big privacy: challenges and opportunities of privacy study in the age of big data. IEEE Access **4**, 2751–2763 (2016). https://doi.org/10.1109/ACCESS.2016.2577036

44. Zhang, Z., Cho, M.C.Y., Wang, C., Hsu, C., Chen, C., Shieh, S.: IoT security: ongoing challenges and research opportunities. In: 2014 IEEE 7th International Conference on Service-Oriented Computing and Applications, pp. 230–234, November 2014. https://doi.org/10.1109/SOCA.2014.58

A PageRank Inspired Approach to Measure Network Cohesiveness

V. Carchiolo[1], M. Grassia[2], A. Longheu[2], M. Malgeri[2], and G. Mangioni[2(✉)]

[1] Dip. di Matematica e Informatica, Università degli Studi di Catania, Catania, Italy
vincenza.carchiolo@unict.it
[2] Dip. Ingegneria Elettrica Elettronica Informatica,
Università degli Studi di Catania, Catania, Italy

Abstract. Basics of PageRank algorithm have been widely adopted in its variations, tailored for specific scenarios. In this work, we consider the Black Hole metric, an extension of the original PageRank that leverages a (bogus) black hole node to reduce the arc weights normalization effect. We further extend this approach by introducing several black holes to investigate on the cohesiveness of the network, a measure of the strength among nodes belonging to the network. First experiments on real networks show the effectiveness of the proposed approach.

1 Introduction

The role of ranking as a tool to order information according to their importance has been consolidated in the last decades. To fulfill this goal to the best extent possible, several evolution of the original well known PageRank algorithm [1–3] were developed over the years, e.g. [4–7]; this allowed its basics to be applied in a plethora of contexts, ranging from recommendation networks to E-learning, classical web search and the newest social networks [8–13].

Each context usually requires the original PageRank to be modified, extended and/or adapted to the specific needs. Sometimes the purpose is to improve its features, as in [14] where a PageRank extension is designed to be used as an h-index, or in [7] where authors introduce a personalized PageRank within the Twitter's *"Who To Follow"* architecture. In other scenarios the motivation is to cope with some limitations, e.g. the "zero-one gap problem", with a possible solution proposed in [15], or the computational issues that lead to optimized [16] and distributed version [17] of the original PageRank.

In this work we start from the solution of normalization problem presented in [18]. In particular, authors introduce a new metric named *Black Hole* aiming at mitigating the arc weights normalization effect introduced by PageRank by inserting a new bogus node (the black hole) and by performing a weights transformation that guarantees that the modified adjacency matrix of the original network is still stochastic.

Here, we move one step forward by introducing several black holes nodes; in addition to the original idea of overcoming the PageRank normalization problem,

© Springer Nature Switzerland AG 2019
R. Montella et al. (Eds.): IDCS 2019, LNCS 11874, pp. 349–356, 2019.
https://doi.org/10.1007/978-3-030-34914-1_33

our proposal allows to study the *cohesiveness* of the network, that is a measure of the level of strength among nodes belonging to the network. We apply this idea to analyze a couple of toy examples, moving towards real networks; results show the effectiveness of this approach in capturing the global distribution of nodes relationships.

The paper is organized as follows: in Sect. 2 we summarize the Black Hole metric, whereas in Sect. 3 we describe our multi Black Hole proposal. In Sect. 4 we illustrate and discuss some experiments we performed to assess the proposal and finally in Sect. 5 conclusions and open questions are presented.

2   The Black Hole Metric

As introduced in the previous section, the Black Hole metric addresses the PageRank's normalization effect. Indeed, weights normalization has a twofold negative effect: (1) it is not able to preserve the absolute arc weights, modifying the weight distribution asymmetry and (2) it shadows the social implications of assigning low weights to all of a node's neighbours (that would be a clear indication of bad social relationships). For a more in depth discussion of the Black Hole metric advantages, we refer to [18], where the authors present a toy example that clearly illustrates the drawbacks of PageRank and the benefits of using the Black Hole metric.

In a few words, the Black Hole metric consists in an arc weights scaling procedure and in the introduction of a new special node named *Black Hole*. The arc weights transformation only requires the knowledge of the maximum and the minimum value each weight can assume. This range may be global (each node has the same scale) or local (each node has its own weight scale). The transformations applied on the original weights (as detailed below) doesn't preserve the out-strength s_i of each node i. Then, the authors introduce a new node, the black hole, and node i is connected to it with the strength of $1 - s_i$. In other words, the Black Hole absorbs the missing weight amount to reach 1 as the total i's out-strength. This transformation is applied to all nodes in the network.

More formally, let i be a generic node in the network. Let the interval $[l_i, h_i]$ be the *local* scale of node i. Let r_{ij} be the weight that node i assigns to the arc pointing towards node j. Let out_i be the number of neighbours of node i. Given that $l_i \leq r_{ij} \leq h_i$, the modified weight $\bar{a}_{ij}$ of the arc that goes from i to j is defined as:

$$\bar{a}_{ij} = \frac{r_{ij} - l_i}{out_i(h_i - l_i)} \tag{1}$$

which is significantly different from the normalized arc weight required by PageRank:

$$a_{ij} = \frac{r_{ij}}{\sum_{k=1}^{out_i} r_{ik}} \tag{2}$$

The contribute of the arc from node i to the black hole is given by:

$$b_i = \sum_{j=1}^{out_i} \frac{h_i - r_{ij}}{out_i(h_i - l_i)} \tag{3}$$

After the application of the above described transformations, the PageRank computed on the transformed network takes into account the absolute strength of each arc, thus it overcomes some of the mentioned limitations of the original PageRank algorithm.

3   Our Proposal

As cited in the introduction, while in [18] the authors introduce one Black Hole node for the entire network in order to make it consistent with the PageRank dynamics, in this work we extend this approach by introducing several Black Hole nodes, in order to use their PageRank to measure the node's cohesiveness, as detailed in this section.

Generally speaking, arc weights measure the *strength* of each link; in virtual social network, for instance, they can be easily associated to the *trust* [19,20] a person assigns to his/her acquaintances (assuming nodes as people and links as their relationships). Similarly, in peer-to-peer network they could represent the number of exchanged files among peers, or in power grid the amount of energy transmitted and so on; in the following, we continue considering the social network scenario (using the word *trust* to indicate the arc weight) without affecting the generality of our proposal.

A first point to consider is to investigate the meaning of Black Hole's PageRank. Since each black hole node is pointed by weighted arcs whose values depend on how much the pointing nodes trust their respective neighbours, the PageRank of the Black Hole can assume higher values only if the pointing nodes poorly trust each other, whilst a low value of the PageRank of the black hole is a clear symptom that the pointing nodes are trusting each other a lot; this comes from Eqs. 1 and 1, showing that black hole nodes gather the residual "amount of trust" not assigned to neighbours.

For these reasons, we define the *cohesiveness* of a network as:

$$C = 1 - PR_b \tag{4}$$

Where the term PR_b is the PageRank value of the Black Hole node. C ranges from 0 to 1. It assumes a value of 0 in the extreme case of a fully un-trusted network, i.e. a network where each node assigns the (lowest) l_i value of trust to its neighbours. Conversely, $C = 1$ means that the network is fully trusted, i.e. each node assign an h_i value to its neighbours; therefore, C is an indicator of the level of trustworthiness among the nodes of the network.

The cohesiveness coefficient can be further extended and generalized to the case of a network partitioned in several groups. Let us consider a directed weighted network $G = (V, E)$, where V is the set of nodes, and E is the set of weighted arcs among nodes. Let P be a partition of the network in g disjoint groups of nodes, $P = (G_1, G_2, ..., G_g)$. In this general case, we can introduce g black hole nodes to measure the groups internal cohesion and $g(g-1)$ black hole nodes to measure the mutual cohesion between groups. Formally, the cohesiveness between group p and group q is defined as:

$$C_{pq} = 1 - PR_{b^{pq}} \quad where \; p, q = 1...g \tag{5}$$

The term $PR_{b^{pq}}$ indicates the PageRank value of the black hole node between group G_p and G_q; it is pointed by those nodes of the group G_p trusting nodes of the group G_q with a weight given by:

$$b_i^{pq} = \sum_{\substack{j = 1 \\ j \in G_q}}^{out_i} \frac{h_i - r_{ij}}{out_i(h_i - l_i)} \quad \forall i \in G_p \tag{6}$$

Figure 1 shows a simple example of a network with two groups of nodes. The network consists of 9 nodes: 4 in the group G_1 and 5 in the group G_2. As discussed above, we transform the network by introducing 4 black holes: b^{11} and b^{22} to measure the internal cohesion of respectively G_1 and G_2, and b^{12} and b^{21} to asses the mutual cohesion between groups G_1 and G_2.

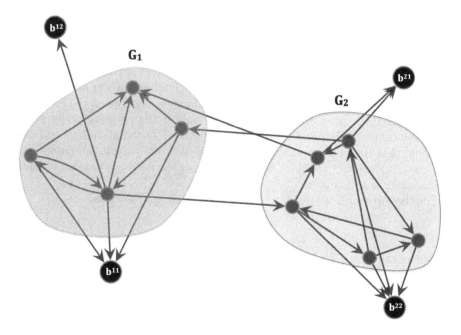

Fig. 1. An example of a network modified in order to measure groups cohesion.

4   Experiments

In this section we present some experiments to better investigate the behaviour of proposed measure of the *cohesiveness* and also its application to a real-world network.

As a first step, we craft a toy example network to show how the PageRank of the black hole nodes changes as the weights of the links in the network change. In particular, we build two clusters as directed cliques with 50 nodes each and intra-cluster link weight equal to 1 and connect them using 10 inter-cluster links with weight 1. The resulting network is shown in Fig. 2a. Then, we compute the PageRank of the black hole nodes while we scale the intra-group weights from 1 to 0 (that we assume as maximum and minimum value respectively). While all

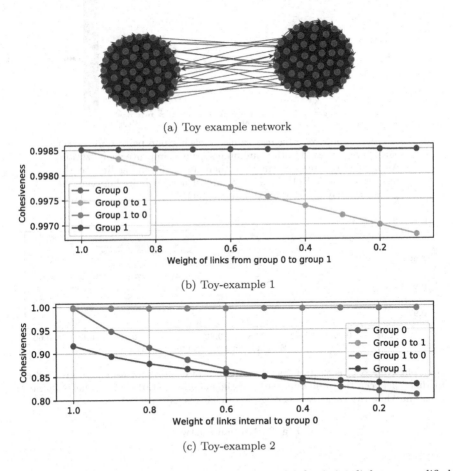

(a) Toy example network

(b) Toy-example 1

(c) Toy-example 2

Fig. 2. Inter/intra-group cohesiveness as the strength of existing links are modified between the minimum (0.1) and the maximum (1.0) in our synthetic toy-examples. Specifically, we change the intra-group links in (c) and the intergroup links in (b).

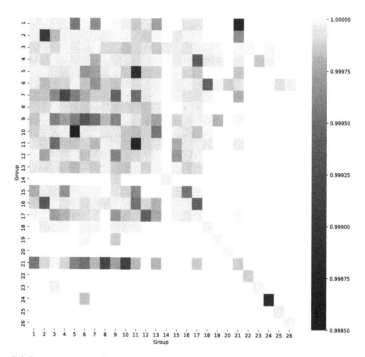

(a) Inter-group *cohesiveness* values of each group pair (x, y). Lower values are increased to the minimum shown to improve visualization. Also, missing values mean that there is no incoming link to the respective Black Hole (i.e., there are either no links between the groups or they all have maximum weight).

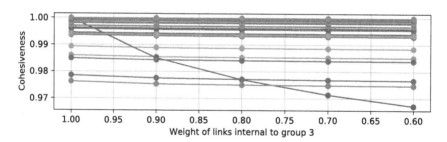

(b) Cohesiveness of each group as the strength of existing intra-links of group 3 are modified between the minimum (0.6) and the maximum (1.0). Every value is (almost) constant while the *cohesiveness* of group 3 changes as expected.

Fig. 3. Advogato network

other PageRank values are constant as seen in Fig. 2b, the one of the black hole associated to the inter-group links (originating from the nodes in the first group and targeting the ones in the second) grows linearly as the weights decrease.

In a similar way, we built a second toy example setting all the intra-group weights of the second group to 0.5 and scaling the weights of the first group. As reported in Fig. 2c, the *cohesiveness* of the second group changes as well. This is expected as the PageRank values are normalized to 1, but also highlights how our proposed *cohesiveness* measure depends on the whole network and on its partitioning instead of being a local group property.

It should be noted that in both examples, the constant values due to the fact that black hole nodes do not have any incoming link while the respective inter/intra-group links have maximum weight.

As a second step, we apply proposed *cohesiveness* measure to a real-world network. Specifically, we find 26 communities in the *advogato* network [21,22] using the Louvain algorithm implemented in Pajek [23], and compute the *cohesiveness* between those groups. As shown in Fig. 3a, the various communities have very different *cohesiveness* values. For instance, some have very high intra-group cohesiveness values, while other groups tend to be way less cohere (e.g., group 2). A similar consideration can be made for the inter-group cohesiveness.

We also repeat our first experiment on this far more complex network by changing the intra-group link weights of the largest community found, namely group 3. As shown in Fig. 3b, the *cohesiveness* still captures the decreasing internal trust and the group eventually becomes the less cohere in the network.

5 Conclusions

In this paper, we extended the Black Hole metric present in literature by introducing several black hole nodes instead of a single one. The purpose is to leverage their presence to measure the cohesiveness of a network, based on the PageRank values of black holes. Proposed experiments, from toy examples to real networks, show the effectiveness of this approach in capturing the global network partitioning.

As future works we plan to exploit the cohesiveness measure to discover the most cohesive groups in a network, by using some optimization algorithm.

Acknowledgements. This work was supported in part by the Piano per la Ricerca 2016/2018 DIEEI Universitá degli Studi di Catania.

References

1. Brin, S., Page, L.: The anatomy of a large-scale hypertextual web search engine. In: Seventh International World-Wide Web Conference (WWW 1998) (1998)
2. Bianchini, M., Gori, M., Scarselli, F.: Inside pagerank. ACM Trans. Internet Technol. **5**(1), 92–128 (2005)
3. Langville, A.N., Meyer, C.D.: Deeper inside pagerank. Internet Math. **1**, 335–380 (2004)
4. Lee, H.C., Borodin, A.: Perturbation of the hyper-linked environment. In: Warnow, T., Zhu, B. (eds.) COCOON 2003. LNCS, vol. 2697, pp. 272–283. Springer, Heidelberg (2003). https://doi.org/10.1007/3-540-45071-8_29

5. Richardson, M., Domingos, P.: The intelligent surfer: probabilistic combination of link and content information in PageRank. In: Advances in Neural Information Processing Systems 14. MIT Press (2002)
6. Zhirov, A.O., Zhirov, O.V., Shepelyansky, D.L.: Two-dimensional ranking of Wikipedia articles. CoRR abs/1006.4270 (2010)
7. Gupta, P., Goel, A., Lin, J., Sharma, A., Wang, D., Zadeh, R.: WTF: the who to follow service at Twitter. In: Proceedings of the 22nd International Conference on World Wide Web, WWW '13, Republic and Canton of Geneva, Switzerland, International World Wide Web Conferences Steering Committee, pp. 505–514 (2013)
8. Chen, L., Chen, G., Wang, F.: Recommender systems based on user reviews: the state of the art. User Model. User-Adap. Interact. **25**(2), 99–154 (2015)
9. Carchiolo, V., Longheu, A., Malgeri, M., Mangioni, G.: Searching for experts in a context-aware recommendation network. Comput. Hum. Behav. **51**, 1086–1091 (2015). Computing for Human Learning, Behaviour and Collaboration in the Social and Mobile Networks Era
10. Kim, Y.A., Phalak, R.: A trust prediction framework in rating-based experience sharing social networks without a web of trust. Inf. Sci. **191**, 128–145 (2012)
11. Carchiolo, V., Longheu, A., Malgeri, M.: Reliable peers and useful resources: searching for the best personalised learning path in a trust- and recommendation-aware environment. Inf. Sci. **180**(10), 1893–1907 (2010). Special Issue on Intelligent Distributed Information Systems
12. Serrano-Guerrero, J., Romero, F., Olivas, J.: Hiperion: a fuzzy approach for recommending educational activities based on the acquisition of competences. Inf. Sci. **248**, 114–129 (2013)
13. Roa-Valverde, A.J., Sicilia, M.A.: A survey of approaches for ranking on the web of data. Inf. Retr. **17**(4), 295–325 (2014)
14. Senanayake, U., Piraveenan, M., Zomaya, A.: The PageRank-index: going beyond citation counts in quantifying scientific impact of researchers. PLoS ONE **10**(8), e0134794 (2015)
15. Wang, X., Tao, T., Sun, J.T., Shakery, A., Zhai, C.: DirichletRank: solving the zero-one gap problem of pagerank. ACM Trans. Inf. Syst. **26**(2), 1–29 (2008)
16. Bahmani, B., Chowdhury, A., Goel, A.: Fast incremental and personalized PageRank. Proc. VLDB Endow. **4**(3), 173–184 (2010)
17. Zhu, Y., Li, X.: Distributed PageRank computation based on iterative aggregation-disaggregation methods. In: Proceedings of the 14th ACM International Conference on Information and Knowledge Management, pp. 578–585 (2005)
18. Buzzanca, M., Carchiolo, V., Longheu, A., Malgeri, M., Mangioni, G.: Black hole metric: overcoming the PageRank normalization problem. Inf. Sci. **438**, 58–72 (2018)
19. Buzzanca, M., Carchiolo, V., Longheu, A., Malgeri, M., Mangioni, G.: Direct trust assignment using social reputation and aging. J. Ambient Intell. Hum. Comput. **8**(2), 167–175 (2017)
20. Carchiolo, V., Longheu, A., Malgeri, M., Mangioni, G.: Trusting evaluation by social reputation. In: Badica, C., Mangioni, G., Carchiolo, V., Burdescu, D.D. (eds.) Intelligent Distributed Computing, Systems and Applications, pp. 75–84. Springer, Heidelberg (2008). https://doi.org/10.1007/978-3-540-85257-5_8
21. Advogato network dataset - KONECT, April 2017
22. Massa, P., Salvetti, M., Tomasoni, D.: Bowling alone and trust decline in social network sites. In: Proceedings of the International Conference Dependable, Autonomic and Secure Computing, pp. 658–663 (2009)
23. Batagelj, V., Mrvar, A.: Pajek - program for large network analysis. Connections **21**(2), 47–57 (1998)

TaRad: A Thing-Centric Sensing System for Detecting Activities of Daily Living

Haiming Chen[1(✉)], Xiwen Liu[1], Ze Zhao[2], Giuseppe Aceto[3], and Antonio Pescapè[3]

[1] FEECS, Ningbo University, Ningbo 315211, Zhejiang, China
chenhaiming@nbu.edu.cn
[2] Institute of Computing Technology, CAS, Beijing 100190, China
zhaoze@ict.ac.cn
[3] University of Napoli Federico II, 80125 Napoli, Italy
{giuseppe.aceto,pescape}@unina.it

Abstract. Activities of Daily Living Scale (ADLs) is widely used to evaluate living abilities of the patients and the elderly. Most of the currently proposed approaches for tracking indicators of ADLs are human-centric. Considering the privacy concerns of the human-centric approaches, a new thing-centric sensing system, named TaRad, for detecting some indicators of ADLs (i.e. using fridge, making a phone call), through identifying vibration of objects when a person interacts with objects. It consists of action transceivers (named ViNode), smart phones and a server. By taking into account the limited computation resource of the action transceiver, and the drift and accuracy issues of the cheap sensor, a method of extracting features from the vibration signal, named ViFE, along with a light-weight activity recognition method, named ViAR, have been implemented in ViNode. Besides, an operator recognition method, named ViOR, has been proposed to recognize the acting person who generates vibration of action transceiver, when two or more people exist simultaneously within an area. Experimental results verify the performance of TaRad with different persons, in terms of the sensitivity to correctly detect the activities, and probability to successfully recognize the operators of the activities.

Keywords: Activities of Daily Living · Thing-centric sensing · Action transceiver · Activity detection · Operator recognition

1 Introduction

Aging population has become one of the main concerns in both developed countries and developing countries, according to a report from World Health Organization (WHO) [1]. People may suffer with a higher probability from many kinds of diseases when getting older. Activities of Daily Living Scale (ADLs) [2] is widely used to evaluate living abilities of the patients and the elderly, especially for those who need to be under medical control. There are many indicators of

© Springer Nature Switzerland AG 2019
R. Montella et al. (Eds.): IDCS 2019, LNCS 11874, pp. 357–368, 2019.
https://doi.org/10.1007/978-3-030-34914-1_34

ADLs, such as leaving house, using toilet, taking a shower, going to bed, preparing dinner, using fridge, making a phone call, getting drink and so on.

Traditionally, these indicators were usually evaluated by professional institutions via asking the involved people to fill questionnaire periodically, or requiring them to record their own activities manually and then collecting the recorded data into electronic forms. This method is not only inaccurate, but also obtrusive to the elderly or the patient's living. With rapid development of sensing technology, both wearable sensors (e.g. Radio frequency identification (RFID) sensors [3], body sensor networks [4,5], accelerometer in smart watch [6] and wrist-worn sensors [7]) and fixed sensing infrastructure (e.g. Passive InfraRed (PIR) sensors [8], camera [9], radio tomography networks [10], WiFi network [11–13], light sensing [14,15]) have been exploited to track indicators of ADLs. Although these approaches make the ADLs assessment more objective and mitigate obtrusiveness for the assessed people, they are based on rich information about people's lives and biometrics (i.e. *human-centric* [16]), which raise some severe privacy concerns [17].

Considering the privacy concerns, some researchers proposed to take contact switches [18], binary sensors [19], RFID [20] to detect object usage, and infer human activities using such kind of environmental information on things. In [21], the authors record electricity consumed by room lights and various appliances and then translate it into the probability of a particular ADL. We call them *thing-centric* activity recognition. Because vibration is a commonly occurring phenomenon when a person poses an activity on an object, some researchers have exploring activity recognition through vibration sensors [22]. However, there are still two main problems existing to be addressed. (i) Resource limitation problem, which means how to design activity recognition algorithm, so that it can perform high recognition accuracy, against the limited computation resource of the action transceiver, and the drift and accuracy issues of the cheap sensor. (ii) Multiple-people interference problem, which means how to recognize the acting person who generates vibration of action transceiver, when there are two or more people exist simultaneously within an area.

In this paper, we propose a new thing-centric sensing system, named TaRad, which consists of action transceivers, smart phones and a server, for detecting some indicators of ADLs, through identifying vibration of objects when a person interacts with objects. Through solving these two problems, we make the following contributions:

(i) A method of extracting features from the vibration signal, named ViFE, along with a light-weight activity recognition method, named ViAR, have been implemented in resource limited action transceivers, named ViNode, in TaRad. Considering the limited computation resource of the sensor nodes, we only need to detect whether the object is moved or not through processing vibration signal, but not to analyze different vibration patterns of different actions posed on the objects, such as tap and swipe on object surface [23].

(ii) An operator recognition method, named ViOR, has been proposed to solve the multiple-people interference problem, by exploiting the potentially

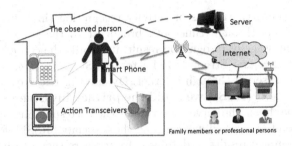

Fig. 1. System architecture of TaRad.

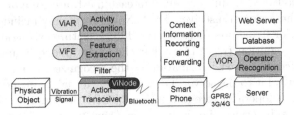

Fig. 2. Hardware and software modules comprising the TaRad system.

different RSSI values between the action transceiver and the smart phone when different persons conduct a same activity. To the best of our knowledge, the multiple-people interference problem has not been solved in the existing thing-centric sensing systems.

(iii) The system has been implemented to detect two kinds of activities, which are making a phone call and using fridge, and evaluated with real experimental tests. Results verify the performance of TaRad with different persons, in terms of the sensitivity to correctly detect the activities, and probability to successfully recognize the operators of the activities.

The rest of the paper is organized as follows. Section 2 gives an overview of our proposed thing-centric sensing system for tracking indictors of ADLs. Section 3 elaborates the algorithms and implementation of ViNode, ViFE, ViAR and ViOR. Section 4 presents the evaluation experiments and results. Section 5 makes a conclusion.

2   System Design

The system architecture of TaRad, which is a thing-centric sensing approach for detecting activities of daily living, is shown in Fig. 1. It mainly consists of three key components, including action transceiver, smart phone and server. The action transceiver is an embedded device, which is attached on a certain home facility like phone and fridge, for sensing the vibration of the attached object, and recognizing the activity exerted on the object.

The action transceiver is composed of a motion sensor and a micro processor, for collecting vibration data and doing data processing on the site for activity recognition. It sends the results of activity recognition (including the identity of the used object) through Bluetooth broadcast to the smart phone. When this receives a message of recognition result, it records the context information, e.g. the Received Signal Strength Indicator (RSSI), and then forwards these information to the server through Internet. **By having the smart phone just measuring context (RSSI) we avoid the privacy invasiveness of human-centric approaches.** The server determines the corresponding operator of the activity based on the received message and the associated RSSI information, and stores the determined results in database, from where they can be retrieved by enabled caregivers and professionals.

The main software modules running in each hardware component are shown in Fig. 2. For the action transceiver (i.e. ViNode), it mainly includes three modules, which are for signal preprocessing (i.e. filter), feature extraction (i.e. ViFE), and activity recognition (i.e. ViAR). For the smart phone, it mainly includes a module to record context information of the recognized activity as described above, and forward it to the server. For the server, it mainly includes three modules, which are for operator recognition (i.e. ViOR), data storage (i.e. database) and providing web service (i.e. web server). Due to space limitation, we will present the implementation of the most challenging hardware component and software modules in TaRad, which are the ViNode, ViFE, ViAR, and ViOR, in the following sections.

3   System Implementation

3.1   Action Transceiver (ViNode)

To make a feasible thing-centric passive sensing system for detecting activities of daily living, the action transceiver has to be small in dimension and low in cost, while maintaining a long battery life. We have chosen the chipset CC2540 and the accelerometer LIS3DH to compose the action transceiver (ViNode) for their suitable characteristics. As shown in Fig. 6, the ViNode size (40 mm by 40 mm) makes it small enough to be fixed on the surface of physical objects, as a fridge door and a telephone handset.

The chipset CC2540 integrates a *low power Bluetooth* (IEEE 802.15.1) compliant radio transceiver and an 8KB SRAM. The CC2540 chip is set in the **broadcast mode**, i.e. no long-lasting connection is required between pairs of devices. This allows multiple action transceivers to advertise their information to listening smart phones in a limited area in a scalable way. Because CC2540 SRAM and computational capability are limited, it is required that the algorithms running on it should be light-weight. These algorithms, particularly ViFE and ViAR, are elaborated as follows.

3.2   Feature Extraction (ViFE)

As shown in Fig. 2, when the physical objects are moved by the observed person, the accelerometer in the action transceiver will generate some signals. The

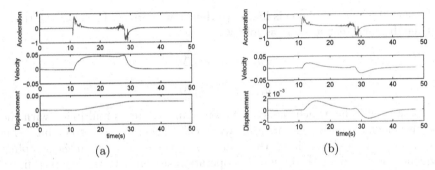

Fig. 3. Comparison of the results of integral of the acceleration (a) before using ViFE and (b) after using ViFE.

original acceleration signals include (i) acceleration signal caused by motion of the object, (ii) acceleration signal of gravity, (iii) noise generated by jitter, (iv) random drift signal caused by accelerometer. Because the signal components (ii) and (iii) both have a lower frequency, they can be removed by a high-pass filter. Because the high-pass filter is widely used in the signal processing, we save some space by omitting the detail of the filter. Here, we elaborate more on the feature extraction module.

Compared with other features in frequency domain, *vibration* and *movement distance* are easier to be recognized (leading to a lower-complexity algorithm), therefore they are chosen as classification features for detecting some indicators of ADLs (i.e. using fridge, making a phone call). The acceleration signal generated by the accelerometer of ViNode can be directly taken as the feature of vibration. As for the feature of movement distance, it can be calculated by using a secondary integral of the acceleration data. In particular, denoting the acceleration at time t as a_t, velocity at time t as v_t, we have the velocity $v_{t'}$, where $t' = t + \Delta t$:

$$v_{t'} = v_t + a_t \Delta t. \tag{1}$$

Accordingly, denoting the displacement at time t as d_t, we can get the displacement at time t':

$$d_{t'} = d_t + v_t \Delta t. \tag{2}$$

We refer to these two equations as velocity formula and displacement formula respectively. Using the data of making a phone call as an example, the calculated velocity and distance result is showed in Fig. 3(a). From the figure, we can see that the acceleration data has a positive pulse at 11 s, when the velocity and the displacement start increasing. After 2 to 3 s, the handset of the telephone is lifted, therefore the acceleration decreases to zero, while the velocity remains unchanged. However, as the velocity is larger than 0 after 14 s, the displacement keeps increasing. The result is against common sense, because the displacement should be unchanged rather than increasing after the handset is lifted. The reason why the displacement keeps increasing is that the acceleration data also reflects the rotation of the handset. Furthermore, as the displacement does not go back to 0 when the phone is hung up. Hence, we correct the velocity formula and the displacement formula as follows.

$$v_{t'} = kv_t + a_t \Delta t \tag{3}$$

$$d_{t'} = kd_t + v_t \Delta t \tag{4}$$

k is a coefficient, which ranges between 0 and 1, and is multiplied with the current velocity v_t or displacement d_t when calculating the corresponding value at time t' ($t' = t + \Delta t$). It is worth noting that k is correlated with the sampling frequency, as it realizes the integration operation similar with the low-pass filter.

The calculation of velocity and displacement formulated by Eqs. (3) and (4) comprises the significant step of feature extraction, which is called ViFE. The calculated velocity and displacement after using ViFE is shown in Fig. 3(b). From the figure, we can see that when the handset is lifted or putted down, the velocity and displacement signal both rise to a certain level and then resume to 0 after a time period of about 20 s. This result demonstrates the possibility of detecting the activity (i.e. making a phone call) by setting a threshold on the displacement calculated with ViFE. It can also be applied in calculating the dragging distance of a fridge door and be effective in detecting the activity of using fridge. Next, we will describe the algorithm of detecting activity based on the result of ViFE.

3.3   Activity Recognition (ViAR)

Considering the limited computational capacity of the action transceiver (ViNode), as presented in Sect. 3.1, we design an activity recognition algorithm based on decision tree, which is called ViAR. A decision tree has a flowchart-like structure, in which each non-leaf node represents a "test" on an attribute while each branch represents the outcome of the test and each leaf node represents a class label. The paths from root to leaves represent classification rules.

The main process of ViAR is depicted by Fig. 4, which roots from the acceleration and has a branch in displacement. The results of decision tree are represented by the two class labels at the leaves, which are "object is used" and "object is not used". The challenge of constructing the decision tree is how to properly set the two thresholds, namely T_{acc} and T_{dis}. We firstly set initial values, $T_{acc} = t_a$ and $T_{dis} = t_d$, for these two thresholds, and then adjust them by a training process. The training data is expressed as a triad $(acc, dis, stat)$, where acc means the acceleration, dis means the displacement, and $stat$ means the labeled class of object usage. For each triad in the training set, when the classified status s equals to $stat$, the thresholds don't need to be adjusted. Otherwise, the thresholds need to be adjusted as formulated by the following equations.

$$T_{acc} = acc + (acc - T_{acc}/2) \tag{5}$$

$$T_{dis} = dis + (dis - T_{dis}/2) \tag{6}$$

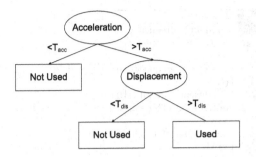

Fig. 4. The decision tree of ViAR.

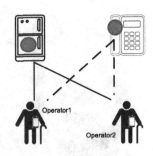

Fig. 5. Illustration of a scenario causing the multiple-people interference problem.

3.4 Operator Recognition (ViOR)

Since it is highly probable that there are more than one observed persons coexist in the same area, a broadcast of the recognized activity by an action transceiver will be received by multiple smart phones carried by them. As illustrated in Fig. 5, two operators live in the same room, where the operator1 makes a phone call while the operator2 uses the fridge. However, both of the smart phones carried by the operators will forward the received results of action detection to the server, which will cause mixed decision of who is generating the activity. Therefore, we design an operator recognition method, named ViOR, in TaRad.

As mentioned in Sect. 2, when the smart phone receives a message of recognition result, it forwards the message along with the RSSI recorded when it receives the message. Firstly, we build models for each person operating on an object. For example, $M(opr, obj)$ denotes the model of operator opr on object obj. Considering the instability of Bluetooth signal, to ensure the integrity of the RSSI data, the ARQ (Automatic Retransmission Request) mechanism and a time window strategy are used to preprocess the data before building the model. The size of time window n can be calculated by using the equation $P = 1 - (1 - \text{PRR})^n$, if we know the packet reception ratio (PRR) of the link between the action transceiver and the smart phone, and specify the probability (P) of successfully receiving at least one RSSI message in the time window.

We denote the RSSI data for model training as $T = \{D_i\}, i \in [0, t]$, $D_i = \{d_i^j\}, j \in [0, v]$, d_i^j represents every valid RSSI value in the ith time window, and v is the number of valid data in the ith time window, t is the number of time windows for training. The model established based on the training data is expressed as $M(opr, obj) = \{m_i\}, i \in [0, t]$, where

$$m_i = \frac{\Sigma_{j=0}^{v} d_i^j}{v}. \tag{7}$$

Then, when the server receives a set of messages about a recognized activity, denoted as (opr, obj, R), where $R = \{r_i\}$, r_i is the carried RSSI value with each message, it uses interpolation method to do curve fitting based on $M(opr, obj)$ to

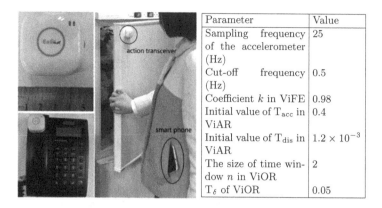

Parameter	Value
Sampling frequency of the accelerometer (Hz)	25
Cut-off frequency (Hz)	0.5
Coefficient k in ViFE	0.98
Initial value of T_{acc} in ViAR	0.4
Initial value of T_{dis} in ViAR	1.2×10^{-3}
The size of time window n in ViOR	2
T_δ of ViOR	0.05

Fig. 6. Demonstration of the experimental scenarios and the parameter settings.

judge whether opr is the operator of the object obj. In particular, ViOR computes the similarity between M and R based on the Euclidean distance equation, as shown in Eq. (8). If $\delta(M, R)$ is less than a threshold T_δ, opr is judged as the operator of the object obj.

$$\delta(M, R) = \sqrt{\sum_{i=0}^{t}(m_i - r_i)^2} \qquad (8)$$

4   Experimental Evaluation

4.1   System Setups

The system has been implemented to detect two kinds of activities, which are making a phone call and using fridge. We have done some experiments on the system. The experimental scenario is shown in Fig. 6, from which we can see that ViNode is fixed on the handset of a telephone or the door of a fridge, and a smart phone is carried by each observed person. The parameter settings of the experiments are shown in Fig. 6.

4.2   Evaluation Metrics

The metrics, namely true positive (TP), true negative (TN), false positive (FP) and false negative (FN), are commonly used in a classification problem. In our experiments, positive instance means an activity is carried out, while negative instance means no activity is carried out. We take positive instances as the ground truth, and adopt the two metrics defined in Eq. (9) to evaluate the performance of TaRad. The metric named recall rate (R) is adopted to evaluate the sensitivity to correctly detect the indicators of ADLs (i.e. using fridge,

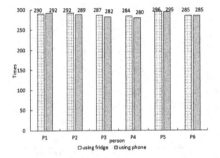

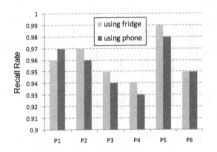

Fig. 7. True positive (TP) times of recognizing two activities for the 6 persons in our experiments, where each person take 300 times of each activity.

Fig. 8. Recall rate of recognizing two activities for the 6 persons in our experiments, where each person take 300 times of each activity.

making a phone call). The metric named accuracy (Acc) is adopted to evaluate the probability to successfully recognize the operators of the activities.

$$R = \frac{TP}{TP+FN}, Acc = \frac{TP+TN}{TP+TN+FP+FN}. \tag{9}$$

4.3 Evaluation Results of ViFE and ViAR

We recruited 6 persons as volunteers of our experiments. For each person, we asked him to intermittently conduct the activities, namely making a phone call and using fridge, for 300 times respectively. Figure 7 shows the true positive (TP) times of recognizing the activity for each person in our experiments.

The recall rate of recognizing these two activities with ViFE and ViAR is shown in Fig. 8. We can see that the recall rates of recognizing the activity of using fridge for the 6 persons vary from 94% to 99%, which is 96% on average. For the activity of using phone, the recall rates vary from 93% to 98%, which is 95% on average.

From Fig. 8, we can also find that the recall rates of recognizing the activity of using phone for the 6 persons are little lower than those of recognizing the activity of using fridge, which is mainly caused by unintended touch of the handset of telephone during the experiments. In other words, the handset of telephone may be moved without making phone calls, which may cause the ViNode to make a mistaken judgement of the activity, so that it leads to a time of false positive classification.

4.4 Evaluation Results of ViOR

To evaluate the performance of ViOR in recognizing the operator, we firstly asked each of the volunteers to conduct the activity of using fridge for 40 times solely. The RSSI data in the messages sent from the ViNode on the surface of the fridge to the smartphone carried by each operator were collected in these

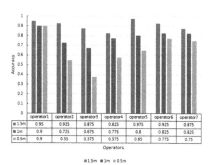

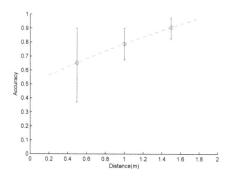

Fig. 9. Recognition accuracy of ViOR with different distances between the operator and the interferer.

Fig. 10. The averages and different variation ranges of accuracy for different distances between the operator and the interferer.

experiments for training the model $M(opr, obj)$, as presented in Sect. 3.4. Then, we collected RSSI data in situations with two persons as a group. When one person conducted the activity, the other person was asked to walk around him as an interferer. In this part, we added one person to take part in the experiments, so totally 7 volunteers were recruited. We test the performance of ViOR in cases with different distances between the operator and the interferer, which are 1.5 m, 1 m, and 0.5 m. In each case, the operator conducted the activity of using fridge for 40 times. The recognition accuracy of ViOR with different distances between the operator and the interferer is shown in Fig. 9. The results listed at the bottom of Fig. 9 show that when the distance between the operator and the interferer gets smaller, the accuracy of recognizing the operator gets lower. Figure 10 shows the average accuracy of recognizing operator over the 7 persons in the three situations with different distances between the operator and the interferer. Generally speaking, ViOR can get an accuracy of 90.7% on average at a distance of 1.5 m, an average accuracy of 78.9% at a distance of 1 m and an average accuracy of 65.3% at a distance of 0.5 m. From Fig. 9, we can also see that in the situation that the distance is 1.5 m, the accuracy of recognizing the operator for different persons varies from 0.825 to 0.975. However, in the situation that the distance is 0.5 m, the accuracy varies from 0.375 to 0.9. Figure 10 also shows the different variation ranges of accuracy for different distances between the operator and the interferer through the error bars.

The reduced performance of ViOR when the distance between the operator and the interferer gets smaller is mainly due to the following reason. It is probable that the operator and the interferer have a similar habit when they use the fridge, like keeping a similar distance from the fridge, which would build a similar model $M(opr, obj)$ for them. When the operator and the interferer keep a distance about 1.5 m, the RSSI values are indistinguishable enough to make the similar models still work. However, when they get close, the RSSI values are indistinguishable, so that the models constructed by ViOR are unserviceable.

5 Conclusion

In this paper, a thing-centric human activity sensing system named TaRad has been proposed for passively tracking some indicators of ADLs. It consists of action transceivers (ViNode), smart phones and a server. By taking into account the limited computation resource of the action transceiver, and the drift and accuracy issues of the cheap sensor, a method of extracting features from the vibration signal, named ViFE, along with a light-weight activity recognition method, named ViAR, have been implemented in ViNode. Besides, an operator recognition method, named ViOR, has been proposed to recognize the acting person who generates vibration of action transceiver, when there are two or more people exist simultaneously within an area. Experimental results show the recall rates of recognizing the activities of using fridge and making phone call for 6 persons are up to 96% and 95% respectively on average. The accuracy of recognizing the right operator ranges from 90.7% to 65.3% on average when the operator and the interferer are apart from 1.5 m to 0.5 m. ViOR is not so efficient in recognizing operators in situations where coexisting persons have similar habits when conducting the same activity. We will improve the accuracy of ViOR by seeking a better method to construct more precise models for distinguishing operators in our future work.

Acknowledgment. The authors would like to thank Jun Xie, Lihua Dong, Zhenghong Peng, Wenzhen Du, Wenqing Liu, Meng Li and Wenwen Gao, from the Wireless Sensor Networks Laboratory at the Institute of Computing Technology Chinese Academy of Sciences for participating in the experimental evaluation of the system. This work was supported in part by the Zhejiang Provincial Natural Science Foundation of China under Grant LY18F020011 and Ningbo Natural Science Foundation under Grant 2018A610154.

References

1. World Health Organization: Global Health and Aging. National Institutes of Health, Bethesda (2011)
2. Debes, C., Merentitis, A., et al.: Monitoring activities of daily living in smart homes. IEEE Signal Process. Mag. **33**(2), 81–94 (2016)
3. Fujinami, T., Miura, M., Takatsuka, R., Sugihara, T.: A study of long term tendencies in residents' activities of daily living at a group home for people with dementia using RFID slippers. In: Abdulrazak, B., Giroux, S., Bouchard, B., Pigot, H., Mokhtari, M. (eds.) ICOST 2011. LNCS, vol. 6719, pp. 303–307. Springer, Heidelberg (2011). https://doi.org/10.1007/978-3-642-21535-3_46
4. Keally, M., Zhou, G., et al.: PBN: towards practical activity recognition using smartphone-based body sensor networks. In: Proceedings ACM SenSys, pp. 246–259 (2011)
5. Fortino, G., Gravina, R., Li, W., Ma, C.: Using cloud-assisted body area networks to track people physical activity in mobility. In: EAI BodyNets, pp. 85–91 (2015)
6. Lee, S., Kim, Y., Ahn, D., et al.: Non-obstructive room-level locating system in home environments using activity fingerprints from smartwatch. In: Proceedings ACM UBICOMP, pp. 939–950 (2015)

7. Galluzzi, V., Herman, T., Polgreen, P.: Hand hygiene duration and technique recognition using wrist-worn sensors. In: Proceedings PSN, pp. 106–117 (2015)
8. Erickson, V.L., Carreira-Perpinan, M.A., Cerpa, A.E.: OBSERVE: occupancy-based system for efficient reduction of HVAC energy. In: Proceedings of the ACM IPSN, pp. 258–269 (2011)
9. Lao, W., Han, J., de With, P.H.N.: Automative video-based human motion analysis for consumer surveillance system. IEEE Trans. Consum. Electron. **55**(2), 591–598 (2009)
10. Wilson, J., Patwari, N.: See-through walls: motion tracking using variance based radio tomography networks. IEEE Trans. Mob. Comput. **10**(5), 612–621 (2011)
11. Wu, C.S., Yang, Z., Zhou, Z., et al.: Non-invasive detection of moving and stationary human with Wi-Fi. IEEE J. Sel. Areas Commun. **33**(11), 2329–2342 (2015)
12. Karrer, R.P., Matyasovszki, I., Botta, A., Pescapé, A.: Experimental evaluation and characterization of the magnets wireless backbone. In: Proceedings of ACM WiNTECH, pp. 26–33 (2006)
13. Karrer, R.P., Matyasovszki, I., Botta, A., Pescapé, A.: Magnets-experiences from deploying a joint research-operational next-generation wireless access network testbed. In: Proceedings of IEEE TridentCom 2007, pp. 1–10 (2007)
14. Yang, Y., Hao, J., Luo, J., Pan, S.J.: CeilingSee: device-free occupancy inference through lighting infrastructure based led sensing. In: Proceedings IEEE Percom (2016)
15. Nguyen, V., Ibrahim, M., Rupavatharam, S., et al.: EyeLight: light-based occupancy estimation and activity recognition from shadows on the floor. In: Proceedings IEEE INFOCOM (2018)
16. Srivastava, M., et al.: Human-centric sensing. Philos. Trans. Roy. Soc. **370**(1958), 176–97 (2012)
17. Caine, K., Fisk, A., Rogers, W.: Benefits and privacy concerns of a home equipped with a visual sensing system: a perspective from older adults. In: Proceedings of the Human Factors and Ergonomics Society Annual Meeting (2006)
18. Dickerson, R.F., Gorlin, E.I., Stankovic, J.A.: Empath: a continuous remote emotional health monitoring system for depressive illness. In: Proceedings ACM Conference on Wireless Health, pp. 5–14 (2011)
19. Ordnez, F.J., Toledo, P., Sanchis, A.: Activity recognition using hybrid generative/discriminative models on home environments using binary sensors. Sensors **13**(5), 5460–5477 (2013)
20. Yang, J., Lee, J., Choi, J.: Activity recognition based on RFID object usage for smart mobile devices. J. Comput. Sci. Technol. **26**(2), 239–246 (2011)
21. Franco, G.C., Gallay, F., Berenguer, M., et al.: Noninvasive monitoring of the activities of daily living of elderly people at home - a pilot study of the usage of domestic appliances. J. Telemed. Telecare **14**(5), 231–235 (2008)
22. Zigel, Y., Litvak, D., Gannot, I.: A method for automatic fall detection of elderly people using floor vibrations and sound - proof of concept on human mimicking doll falls. IEEE Trans. Biomed. Eng. **56**(12), 2858–2867 (2009)
23. Pan, S., Ramirez, C.G., Mirshekari, M., et al.: SurfaceVibe: vibration-based tap & swipe tracking on ubiquitous surfaces. In: Proceedings of ACM IPSN, pp. 197–208 (2017)

Distributed Genomic Compression in MapReduce Paradigm

Pasquale De Luca[1](✉)[ID], Stefano Fiscale[2][ID], Luca Landolfi[2][ID],
and Annabella Di Mauro[3][ID]

[1] Department of Computer Science, University of Salerno, 84084 Fisciano, Italy
p.deluca16@studenti.unisa.it
[2] Science and Technologies Department, University of Naples "Parthenope",
80143 Naples, Italy
{stefano.fiscale001,luca.landolfi}@studenti.uniparthenope.it
[3] Department of Pathology, Istituto Nazionale Tumori,
IRCCS-Fondazione "G. Pascale", 80131 Naples, Italy
annabella.dimauro@istitutotumori.na.it

Abstract. In recent years the biological data, represented for computational analysis, has increased in size terms. Despite the representation of the latter is demanded to specific file format, the analysis and managing overcame always more difficult due to high dimension of data. For these reasons, in recent years, a new computational framework, called Hadoop for manage and compute this data have been introduced. Hadoop is based on MapReduce paradigm to manage data in distributed systems. Despite the gain of performance obtained from this framework, our aim is to introduce a new compression method DSRC by decreasing the size of output file and make easy its processing from ad-hoc software. Performance analysis will show the reliability and efficiency achieved by our implementation.

Keywords: Hadoop · Distributed computing · Genomic compression data

1 Introduction

Nowaday computational genomic is strongly growing in research field. During its computation the dataset of genomic sequence are computed, sometime the size of dataset reach very large size over Petabytes dimension. This problem regards several research fields such as astrophysics, geographics and economy. From previous problem borns Big Data notion. Thanks to Moore's Law there is a performance growing of computational power of supercomputers which gave birth to news algorithms [1–3] and in particular stands up the genomic curve but with growing of the latter the related storage and computation problem are increased. Cloud computing services are able to make easy and convenient the scalability of both dataset and computations, i.e. is possible make in fast time virtual machine [4] by building, in cloud environment, distributed supercomputers [5,6]. In recent years a new framework for distributed cloud computing called

© Springer Nature Switzerland AG 2019
R. Montella et al. (Eds.): IDCS 2019, LNCS 11874, pp. 369–378, 2019.
https://doi.org/10.1007/978-3-030-34914-1_35

Hadoop [7] by Apache has been widely used. Hadoop is the most important and commonly used cluster computing framework for Big Data analytics, thanks to its architecture based on MapReduce paradigm that in next section will be presented. In order to obtain a compressed output for computing a large operation, in this work we present a new Hadoop module which implements a codec based on DSRC genomic compression algorithm [8]. The paper is organized as follows: in Sect. 2 the compression genomic procedure is shown; Sect. 3 deals with the description of our approach for involving new codec in Hadoop environment; in Sect. 4 we provide tests in order to confirm our contribution by showing results during execution of example software; finally, in Sect. 5, we draw conclusions.

2   Genomic Compression

Genomic compression is a technique for facilitating the translation of genomic information due to this reason we propose the introduction of an ad-hoc genomic compression in Hadoop Environment.

2.1   FASTQ Format

FASTQ format is a text-based format for storing biological sequence. The sequence letters and related quality score are encoded with a single ASCII character for brevity.

A FASTQ format is based mainly on four lines per sequence:

- Line 1 starts with a '@' character and is followed by a sequence identifier
- Line 2 contains the raw sequence letters
- Line 3 begins with a '+' character and is optionally followed by the same sequence identifier (and any description) again
- Line 4 encodes the quality values for the sequence in Line 2, and must contain the same number of symbols as letters in the sequence

The following Fig. 1 shows a FASTQ file structure:

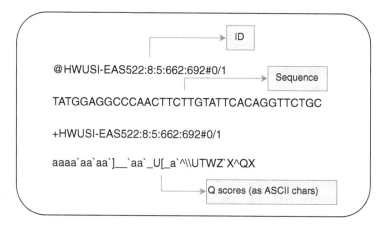

Fig. 1. FASTQ file structure

In order to encode the sequence letters (q) an encoding function has been used.

$$c = f(q)$$

One of the most used encoding function is based on the following structure:

$$c = ASCII(min(q, 93) + 33)$$

Where the integer values 93 and 33 are constants. In particular following steps are necessary to obtain c:

1. if q> 93 then q $= 93$.
2. the 33 value is added to q.
3. the integer obtained in the previous point is converted to ASCII.

2.2 DSRC Compression Algorithm

Overtime the genomic data amounts has constantly grown. This phenomenon make several problem to compute and store data on hard disk. Moreover the effective computation and managing of these data has became necessary. One of the most technique to manage data is the compression. Gzip is the most used compression algorithm but it is not a perfect solution in terms of performance. Recently several FASTQ ad-hoc compression algorithm have been proposed. The latter are good method to compress genomic data but present bad performance in terms of time.

In this work, we deal to involve DSRC (DNA Sequence Reads Compression) algorithm in Hadoop environment which is able to obtain an acceptable and better compression ratio than current solutions, moreover it is fast and flexible.

DSRC is multithread-based tool written in C which uses Boost [17] libraries. Its computation is made by several steps. In first step one thread reads a set blocks of data, split from input file, and puts each block in input queue. Moreover in the second step, in order to exploit a good parallelism of overall work a pool of threads compress previous blocks by storing them in an output queue. In third step a single threads writes in an output file the compressed blocks. The decompression process has made in similar way [10].

3   Hadoop Environment

Hadoop is a framework created in order to develop applications able processing huge amounts of data based on MapReduce paradigm which works following Divide et Impera algorithm, dividing input dataset into small chunks in fixed size. Each chunk is assigned to a node of the cluster, known as DataNode, and processed by the latter. Input dataset are processed by nodes, then each result will be sent to main node, the NameNode. It performs single result by merging previous computing. Our Hadoop environment is based on eight slave machines and one additional machine by running master. One for controlling the NameNode where Hadoop Distributed File System, from now on HDFS, is collocated. Other slave node used for resource management. In order to understand the architecture of HDFS an ad-hoc figure is showed following (Fig. 2):

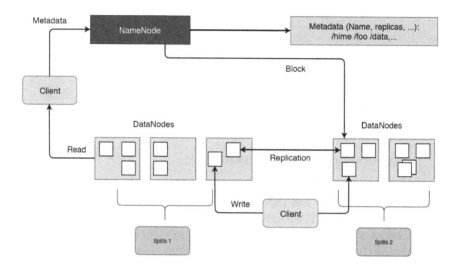

Fig. 2. HDFS architecture

3.1 Involving DSRC in Hadoop

Our motivation to involve this codec in Hadoop environment is due to facilitate the managing and computation of biological data in MapReduce paradigm. So, a gain of performance should be obtained if the input data have a strong compressed structure, in other words is possible give in input the same data capacity but in compression mode in order to manage more data from original. Hadoop jobs are data-intensive due to compression data can speed up the IO operations. Compressed data can save storage space and speed up data transfers by using the network. Despite the high CPU utilization and processing due to computing of huge dataset, the reduced IO obtained by compression can bring significant performance improvements. DSRC compression algorithm [10] in C++ programming language has been written. To perform a lite implementation in order to have good results, a porting by using JNI [12] interface framework in Hadoop environment has been done. JNI is able to us interface large native programming language in Java runtime executions. Each JNI call wraps related C++ function in original code. Moreover, default Hadoop codecs are located in specifics packages, i.e. `org.apache.hadoop.io.compress` where during compilation phase will be loaded by using an ad-hoc compilation flag. *CompressionCodec* interface is important kernel that contains the instruction for compress input sequences. A simple code for compressing and decompressing FASTQ file has been wrote following DefaultCodec template of Hadoop. We perform two methods of this object related to Map and Reduce phase of process.

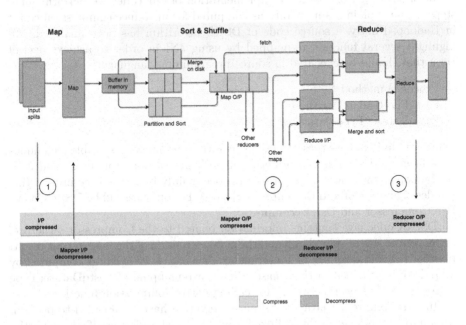

Fig. 3. MapReduce compression/decompression scheme

Figure 3 shows several steps for compute all steps to complete the compression/decompression processes. We can chose two options for compress or decompress input data:

1. During the *Sort & Shuffle* phase, in other words in Map phase after the splitting operation of input data each Map jobs compute the compression or decompression. In order to send the compress chunk to Reduce jobs, previous chuck will be saved on HDFS.
2. Assuming a Genomic Assembly algorithm is running, during the assembling phase the split chunks arrive in Reduce jobs in FASTQ format. So, in this phase each DataNode, in order to save compressed/decompressed output on HDFS runs the compression/decompression on each split.

In order to perform a good configuration of codec *Hive* [13] and *Oozie* [14] frameworks have been used. Hive is able to us facilitate reading, writing, and managing large datasets residing in HDFS storage using SQL. Oozie is a workflow

scheduler system to manage Apache Hadoop jobs. Oozie integrated with the rest
of the Hadoop stack supporting several types of Hadoop jobs out of the box as
well as system specific jobs. Previous framework only for optimizing execution
have been used.

In order to perform a good implementation of our codec we perform some
steps whose explain main operations computed for introduce compression codec
in Hadoop. Firstly, a source code of DSRC algorithm has been analysed. We
highlight several function re-mapped by using JNI in order to achieve overall
work that should be executed in source programming language:

- Process() method
- FastqFileReader() method
- FastqDatasetType datatype.

In order to link and use these functions in Java environment a suitable techniques
have been used such as the powerful of both *extern* operator, in C, and JNI.
In Hadoop environment a compression codec mainly by 3 files is composed (i.e.
{Codec, Compressor and Decompressor}.java). For our case will be DSRCCodec,
DsrcCompressor and DsrcDecompressor.

DSRCCodec.java contains information related to the Compressor structure,
moreover the size of split chunk and the suffix extension of the final output result.
In order to avoid deadlock or IO problems a format check of chunk computed by
Map Task is provided in this phase. Hence, a remapping of FastqDatasetType
by using JNI has been necessary for calling native compression function.

In DsrcCompressor.java several native function have been called to perform
the compression on each chunk linked from Map Task to Reduce Task, in particular every chunk will be compressed via multithread implementation of DSRC
native codec. A strong gain in time execution terms has been obtained by using
previous technique.

In DsrcDecompressor the native decompression functions due to obtain
started dataset have been called, in particular the reverse process of compression is done. *Process()* method is involved in compression and decompression
object which runs two different processes by using an ad-hoc parameter *op* that
can assume `CompressMode` or `DecompressMode` value. Hence, FastqDatasetType
datatype is necessary in order to read input split files on HDFS, to perform
compress/decompress operation FastqFileReader() method has been converted
by using JNI.

In order to use correctly our new codec in Hadoop environment a new compil-
ing of Hadoop source code with DSRCCodec's files have been done with *maven*,
in particular by inserting codec's file in hadoop-common subproject related folder
and running maven compilation the final jar files contain also new codec. The
latter is callable from Hadoop by editing ad-hoc configuration of relate xml files.

Following pseudo-code shows main simply operations computed in DSRC-
Codec.java file:

Algorithm 1. DSRCCodec Map Phase - Compression

1: check chunk mapped % *check exetension of input split*
2: if check **then**
3:    set CompressionMode for native interface
4:    start compression of each chunk
5:    send to Reduce jobs compressed chunk
6: **else**
7:    ExtensionException()
8:    exit from job
9: **end if**

Each compressed chuck will be transferred in Reduce phase by *dsrc* extension in order to save on HDFS each part by using this extension.

The same operations for decompression process has been executed in similar way. According to Algorithm 1 in Reduce phase we set output suffix with *dsrc*. After, we perform final configuration steps by editing configuration Hadoop file such as *core-site.xml* which informs Hadoop daemon where NameNode runs in the cluster by sending configurations chosen.

Listing 1.1. core-site.xml configuration

```
<property>
   <name>io.compression.codecs</name>
   <value>org.apache.hadoop.io.compress.DSRCCodec</value>
   <final>true</final>
</property>
```

In order to add our compression codec to Hadoop deamon, it is need append *io.compress.DSRCCodec* to the io.compression.codecs property. Moreover to use our custom codec set in core-site.xml file, the second step configuration provides to add the properties on mapred-site.xml file. Following the Listing 1.1, we edit mapred-site.xml by setting true value, for:

- mapreduce.map.output.compress.codec
- mapreduce.output.fileoutputformat.compress.codec

Previous configuration is able to us to execute the compression during MapReduce jobs. We perform a restart of all Hadoop related services in particular YARN service for the DSRCCodec configurations to be distributed.

4   Tests

This section shows several useful information to confirm the good performance of DSRC codec in Hadoop by using large FASTQ dataset.

4.1   Our Cluster Configuration

According to Hadoop architecture, a cluster by Amazon Web Service has been built by following configuration in order to 1 node runs as NameNode and 8 node run as slave (Datanode) which execute each local computation. Every node is a *t2.2xlarge* AMI instance which own technical specifications are:

- 8 Virtual CPUs
- 32 GB RAM
- 1 TB HDD Storage.

According to Cloud Computing environment, the nodes are connected by using *ssh* protocol. More precisely, unlike of classic cluster built in LAN, our cluster runs on the Cloud Services. In order to respect Cloud computing paradigm, an ad-hoc framework for interconnect nodes **zerotier** [11] has been used.

4.2   Reliability Analysis

In order to highlight our contribution in this section a comparison with multi-thread owner execution will be showed.

Firstly the original source code of DSRC Algorithm [8] has been compiled on the cluster. Then, Hadoop source code has been recompiled by involving DSRC compression codec. In order to compile in correct way we use the flag -Dnative which is able to us write native code that can be used in MapReduce jobs. Hence, several large dataset have been used as inputs of original software's executions. Same dataset have been used by running a suitable Hadoop-based software for Genomic Assembly, *contrail* by OmicX [15], with DSRC Codec imported in Hadoop. Next a comparison among previous execution will be showed by high-lighting both compression rate and execution times.

During each computing a confirmation message has been noticed for confirm-ing the good loading of our custom codec in runtime MapReduce jobs. For Map jobs following message has been showed:

```
INFO [main] org.apache.hadoop.io.compress.DSRCCodec: Got brand-new compressor
```

while for Reduce jobs following message:

```
INFO [fetcher\#2] org.apache.hadoop.io.compress.DSRCCodec: Got brand-new decompressor
```

Previous messages confirms us the correct loading of DSRC Codec during the execution of the jobs on each datanode. In order to use this codec during the job execution it is necessary that the programmer uses explicitly in source code.

4.3   Experimental Test

In this subsection we perform our experimental test to confirm the good results in performance terms obtained.

For our experimental tests, four large genomic sequence dataset [16] have been used.

Table 1. Execution time

Name	Size	Compression rate	DSRC time execution (s)	
			Multithread	Hadoop
SRR074262	1.17 GB	80.42%	13.7	2.43
SRR2980545	1.44 GB	78.96%	24.4	3.75
ERR2778144	9.93 GB	85.90%	97.2	14.25
SRR9655291	28.80 GB	69.10%	Crash	23.80

The Table 1 shows the time executions of original Dsrc software and Hadoop execution. As we can see the compression is the same for both execution. In particular we achieved good results in resources managements thanks to Hadoop architecture where a strong IO throughput is used. Moreover a gain of performance has been obtained by using the powerful of distributed computing mixed in Hadoop mixed with multithread technique used in C source code. Hence The correctness of Hadoop version of DSRC is confirmed by a decompression execution performed original version of DSRC. We highlight our main contribution due to gain of performance in time terms obtained in Hadoop environment. As we see gain of performance achieved in particular we note the last experimental test on the largest dataset, a crash of software is detected. The latter is due to large size of input data which make owner software is not able to split initial dataset. Our proposed implementation in Hadoop environment allows us to solve previous problem due to large dataset.

5   Conclusions and Future Works

In this work a new compression codec, based on DSRC algorithm, in Hadoop Environment has been proposed. The main contribution has been achieved and confirmed by experimental results and tests that highlight the gain of performance. A future work could to be employ an implementation of this compression codec in Spark environment. Spark works in-memory. It has a different architecture than Hadoop, provides to developers some API in Java through which is possible to implement our codec using the Java Native Interface. For previous reason its performance guarantees its possible use in future developments.

References

1. Cuomo, S., De Michele, P., Galletti, A., Marcellino, L.: A GPU parallel implementation of the local principal component analysis overcomplete method for DW image denoising. In: IEEE Symposium on Computers and Communication (ISCC), Messina 2016, pp. 26–31 (2016). https://doi.org/10.1109/ISCC.2016.7543709
2. Cuomo, S., Galletti, A., Marcellino, L.: A GPU algorithm in a distributed computing system for 3D MRI denoising. In: 2015 10th International Conference on P2P, Parallel, Grid, Cloud and Internet Computing (3PGCIC), Krakow, 2015, pp. 557–562 (2015). https://doi.org/10.1109/3PGCIC.2015.77

3. De Luca, P., Galletti, A., Giunta G., Marcellino, L., Raei, M.: Performance analysis of a multicore implementation for solving a two-dimensional inverse anomalous diffusion problem. In: Proceedings of the 3rd International Conference and Summer School, NUMTA2019. LNCS (2019)

4. Montella, R., et al.: Accelerating Linux and Android applications on low-power devices through remote GPGPU offloading. Concurr. Comput. Pract. Exp. **29**(24), e4286 (2017)

5. Marcellino, L., et al.: Using GPGPU accelerated interpolation algorithms for Marine Bathymetry processing with on-premises and cloud based computational resources. In: Wyrzykowski, R., Dongarra, J., Deelman, E., Karczewski, K. (eds.) PPAM 2017. LNCS, vol. 10778, pp. 14–24. Springer, Cham (2018). https://doi.org/10.1007/978-3-319-78054-2_2

6. Montella, R., Di Luccio, D., Kosta, S., Giunta, G., Foster, I.: Performance, resilience, and security in moving data from the fog to the cloud: the DYNAMO transfer framework approach. In: Xiang, Y., Sun, J., Fortino, G., Guerrieri, A., Jung, J.J. (eds.) IDCS 2018. LNCS, vol. 11226, pp. 197–208. Springer, Cham (2018). https://doi.org/10.1007/978-3-030-02738-4_17

7. https://hadoop.apache.org

8. Roguski, L., Deorowicz, S.: DSRC 2-industry-oriented compression of FASTQ files. Bioinformatics **30**(15), 2213–2215 (2014)

9. Oliveira Jr., W., Justino, E., Oliveira, L.S.: Comparing compression models for authorship attribution. Forensic Sci. Int. **228**(1–3), 100–104 (2013)

10. Deorowicz, S., Grabowski, S.: Compression of genomic sequences in FASTQ format. Bioinformatics **27**(6), 860–862 (2011)

11. https://www.zerotier.com

12. https://docs.oracle.com/javase/7/docs/technotes/guides/jni/spec/functions.html

13. https://hive.apache.org

14. http://oozie.apache.org

15. https://sourceforge.net/p/contrail-bio/code/ci/master/tree/

16. https://www.ebi.ac.uk/ena

17. https://www.boost.org

Distributed ACO Based Reputation Management in Crowdsourcing

Safina Showkat Ara[✉], Subhasis Thakur, and John G. Breslin

Insight Centre for Data Analytics, NUI Galway, Galway, Ireland
{safina.ara,subhasis.thakur,john.breslin}@insight-centre.org

Abstract. Crowdsourcing is an economical and efficient tool that hires human labour to execute tasks which are difficult to solve otherwise. Verification of the quality of the workers is a major problem in Crowd sourcing. We need to judge the performance of the workers based on their history of service and it is difficult to do so without hiring other workers. In this paper, we propose an Ant Colony Optimization (ACO) based reputation management system that can differentiate between good and bad workers. Using experimental evaluation, we show that, the algorithm works fine on the real scenario and efficiently differentiate workers with higher reputations.

Keywords: Crowdsourcing · Reputation · Ant Colony Optimization · Decentralised social network

1 Introduction

Crowdsourcing is an economical and scalable tool that allows one to hire workers to perform certain tasks which are difficult to perform with a computer program. Workers of a crowdsourcing platform have different levels of expertise. Due to the unknown level of expertise of the workers, it is difficult to ensure quality control on crowdsourced tasks. The difficulty of verification of the quality of workers of crowdsourcing originates as it is an example of the principle agent problem [10]. The only way to verify the performance of the workers is to employ other workers to perform the same task.

Selecting a resourceful an efficient worker is a very crucial challenge in crowdsourcing. For any types of crowdsourcing, the reputation of a worker is very helpful to analyse the performance of the worker and for selecting appropriate worker [5]. In this paper, borrowing the idea of Ant Colony Optimizations, we propose a reputation management algorithm for generating the reputation of the workers in the crowd. Ant-Colony Optimization (ACO) is a heuristic design proposed by Dorigo [7]. In ant colony optimization Ants deploy pheromone trail as they walk; this trail guides other ants to choose the path that has the higher pheromone. We create a reputation management algorithm based on the fundamental idea of ACO to find some resources in crowdsourcing. Alike the ACO's random walk, to initiate the search process each worker will have a random walk

© Springer Nature Switzerland AG 2019
R. Montella et al. (Eds.): IDCS 2019, LNCS 11874, pp. 379–390, 2019.
https://doi.org/10.1007/978-3-030-34914-1_36

in their neighbourhood and explore the first resourceful neighbour and afterwards, other workers will follow the trail of the search. The contribution of our work lies in two points: first, design and implement the algorithm. The second is to evaluate the performance of the algorithm. Here we have used [1] dataset and arranged it as a decentralised social network, and on this social network, we executed the search for the workers with higher reputation.

The rest of the paper has been organized as below. Section 2 states the problem definition, including the search approach. In Sect. 3, we Develop our algorithm for the reputation management and we are showing an experimental evolution of the algorithm in Sect. 4. In Sect. 5, we have discussed the related work that has done on reputation management for crowdsourcing and in Sect. 6 we conclude our work.

2   Problem Statement

Each crowd-sourcing job is executed in the following sequence. Let there be k tasks $(t_1, t_2, t_3, \ldots t_n)$. Tasks are executed in the sequence of their subscripts. Let there be n workers $w = (w_1, \ldots, w_n)$. $w^g \subset w$ and $w^b \subset w$ will indicate the sets of good and the bad workers such that $w^g \cup w^b = w$ and $w^g \cap w^b = \emptyset$. We assume that, a good worker performs each task correctly and a bad worker randomly chooses an answer. For each task $\alpha \geq 1$ workers are chosen from w uniformly at random. We denote the set of chosen workers for task i as $w(i) \subset W$. In each task, every worker gets $\beta \geq 1$ options to choose from as the solution. From the above mentioned execution of k crowd-sourcing tasks we form a network among the workers as follows:

1. We create a graph G with n vertices $v = (v_1, \ldots, v_n)$. Next, we add the edges as follows.
2. For each task say t_i, for each worker $w_x \in w(i)$ we do the following:
   (a) We add an edge (w_x, w_y) for each $w_y \in w(i)$ (if the edge is not added previously).
   (b) If the answer of w_x matches the answer of w_y then we increase the weight of the edge by 1 (initially weights of all edges is 0). Otherwise we decrease the edge weight by 1.
3. After the construction of the graph G, we create G^P (the positive graph) and G^N (the negative graph) as follows:
   (a) G^P and G^N has the same vertex set as G.
   (b) If the weight of an edge is positive the it is added to G^P and if it is negative then it is added to G^N.

We will illustrate the above mentioned graph construction process with a small simulation. Let there are 100 workers and among them only 10 are good workers. We construct the positive and the negative graph after 50 tasks using the above mentioned procedure. The graphs are shown in Fig. 1. Note that, we have used two parameters α and β. They control the graph formation process as follows:

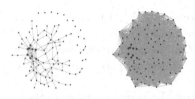

Fig. 1. The positive graph is shown in the left-hand side and the negative graph is shown in the right-hand side. The set of good workers are shown as the green colored vertices. (Color figure online)

Fig. 2. The induced sub graph (with the vertices representing the good workers) on the positive graph is shown on the left-hand side and the induced sub graph (with the vertices representing the good workers) on the negative graph is shown on the right-hand side.

1. By increasing α (number of workers performing the same task) we can construct the graph quickly. But α depends on the budget for executing the tasks. In a low budget task, we may not be able to employ many workers.
2. β is the number of candidate solutions for each task. If the value of β is increased then, it is more likely that the answers of the bad workers with any other worker will not match. Hence the negative graph will get dense (also the total weight of its edges will increase). The growth of the positive graph will become slow with higher values of β.

Our objective is to identify the vertices belonging to the good workers from the above constructed graphs. We can do so by identifying certain characteristics of the vertices owned by good workers. Let $v^g \subset v$ be the vertices belonging to the good workers. The induced sub graph by v^g on G^P is a connected graph (after certain number of tasks). This is because, the good workers always provide correct answer. Thus their answer matches and the weight of the edges among them increases. The induced sub graph by v^g on G^N is always an empty graph. This is because the good workers do not contradict each other. We consider these as the basic characteristics of these vertices.

The above mentioned characteristics of the vertices belonging to the good workers is shown in Fig. 2. The graphs G^P and G^N changes as more and more tasks are executed. The characteristics of the vertices owned by the good workers is as follows:

1. We consider two parameters, (a) the weight of the edges in the sub graph induced by v^g on the positive (negative) graph and (b) the total weight of edges from vertices $v - v^g$ to v^g. The first parameter indicates the cohesiveness of the answers provided by the good workers. The second parameter indicates the 'difficulty' to separate a good worker from a bad worker. A Higher value for the second parameter means that answers of the good and the bad workers have matched and hence it is difficult to distinguish among them.

2. We evaluate the simulation results of 100 workers (with 10 good workers) with the interval of 30 tasks. The observations are as follows:

- The weight of the sub graph induced by v^g on the positive graph increases as more and more tasks are executed. This is because good workers agree with each other's answer.
- Weight of the edges from $v - v^g$ to v^g on the positive graph initially increase and then after the execution of certain number of tasks they decrease. This is because, as the number of times a bad worker participates in the same task with a good worker increases it gets less likely that their answers will match at every instance.
- The weight of the edges from $v - v^g$ to v^g on the negative graph decreases.

Based on the above mentioned characteristics of the graphs we define the problem of identification of the good workers as follows:

- Partition the vertices v into groups as $\pi = (\pi_1, \ldots, \pi_z)$, such that $\pi_1 \cup \pi_2 \cup \cdots \cup \pi_z = v$, $\pi_i \cap \pi_j = \emptyset$ for all $\pi_i, \pi_j \in \pi$ and there is no $\pi_i \in \pi$ such that $\pi_i = \emptyset$. Each π_i induces a connected graph in G^P and induces an empty graph in G^N. The total weight of induced sub graphs on G^P is the maximum.

3 Algorithm

Algorithm 1 Ant colony algorithm for partitioning

$G^P = (V, E^P)$ and $G^N = (V, E^N)$ be the positive and the negative graph respectively.
A partition over V's of G^P $Ant_i \leftarrow$ be the ant at v_i
Each round Each ant Ant_i $Walk_i \subset V$ be the set of vertices generated by a walk.
$P \leftarrow v_i$, $Q \leftarrow \emptyset$
Each $v_x \in Walk_i$ $G_1 \leftarrow Induced - Subgraph(G^N, \{v_x, P\})$
$G_2 \leftarrow Induced - Subgraph(G^N, \{v_x, Q\})$
$|E(G_1)| > 0$ Add v_x to Q
$|E(G_2)| > 0$ Add v_x to P

% Increase pheromones on edges among P %
Each edge e_i in $Induced - Subgraph(G^P, P)$ $e_i\$Ph \leftarrow (1 - \alpha)e_i\$Ph + \alpha\beta(1 - exp^{-e_i\$weight})$ % Decrease pheromones on edges between P and Q %
Each edge e_i in edges between P and Q in G^P $e_i\$Ph \leftarrow (1 - \alpha)e_i\$Ph$

% After every R rounds%
Delete the edges with an amount of pheromone less than the average pheromone on all edges.

We use an ant colony algorithm to find the partition. The algorithm is as follows:

1. We create an ant for each vertex. The objective of each ant is to construct a neighborhood surrounding its vertex so that it contains vertices that induce a connected maximum weighted sub graph in G^P and that induce an empty graph in G^N.
2. The number of vertices of G^P can be very high and hence we restrict the exploration of each ant within a limited surroundings around its vertex. δ (positive integer) will be used for such restriction.
3. At each round, each ant makes an random walk of length δ starting from its vertex. The random walk is as follows: Each vertex is added to the random walk as follows:
   (a) Generate a random number between $(0, 1)$ uniformly at random and if it is less than .5 then choose a neighbor (in G^P) of the last vertex in the walk uniformly at random.
   (b) Else, order the neighbors of the last vertex(v_x) in the random walk with decreasing weight, calculated as follows:

$$\textbf{Pheromone} - \textbf{level} * (\textbf{edge} - \textbf{weight})^x$$

   where x is ≥ 1.
4. After constructing a random walk for each ant, we partition the vertices of the walk into two sets P and Q. P contains the vertices which can induce a connected graph in G^P and empty graph in G^N. Other vertices in the random walk are added to Q.
5. We increase the pheromone level among the edges in P with the following formula:

$$e_i(\textbf{Ph}) \leftarrow (1 - \alpha)e_i(\textbf{Ph}) + \alpha\beta(1 - \textbf{exp}^{-e_i\$\textbf{weight}})$$

6. We decrease the pheromone level on the edges among P and Q with the following formula:

$$e_i(\textbf{Ph}) \leftarrow (1 - \alpha)e_i(\textbf{Ph})$$

7. After every R rounds, we delete edges whose pheromone level is less than the average pheromone level in G^P.

4   Experimental Evaluation

In this section, we present the experimental evaluation of our proposed crowd-sourcing algorithm on both synthetic and real datasets. We implemented algorithms where in each iteration we reduced the social graph with number of bad worker with the lowest score and recomputed the score for the remaining workers. We conducted this evaluation with three significant datasets. Firstly, We prepared a synthetic training dataset for checking the accuracy confirmation of the algorithms. Secondly, we used a synthetic test dataset for the experiment with 100 and 500 workers, where good and bad workers are unknown. Finally, we prepared the dataset with the text of 10% of questions and answers from the Stack Overflow programming Q&A website and Stack Overflow website datasets, to evaluate the performance of our reputation management algorithms on real data.

Algorithm 2 Random walk algorithm

$G^P = (V, E^P)$ and $G^N = (V, E^N)$ be the positive and the negative graph respectively, v_i be the start location and δ be the length of the walk. A random walk of length δ from v_i. $Walk_i \leftarrow \emptyset$

$Next \leftarrow v_i$

Each i in $[1 : \delta]$ $Random(1) > .5$ $N(Next)$ be the neighbors of $Next$ in G^P which are not in $Walk_i$

Wt be a matrix with 1 row and $|N(Next)|$ columns

$x \in [1 : |N(Next)|]$ e_x be the edge between x and $Next$ in V^P

$wt[x] < -e_x \$Ph * (e_x \$Weight)^\gamma$

$v_y \in N(Next)$ be the neighbor with maximum wt

Add v_y to $Walk_i$ and $Next \leftarrow v_y$

v_x be a neighbor of $Next$ and $\notin Walk_i$

Add v_x to $Walk_i$ and $Next \leftarrow v_x$

Return $Walk_i$

4.1   Modeling and Simulation

We generate a graph for the simulation, considering the users/workers as node and their weight as the score for the calculation of reputation. Users/workers are connected to other users/workers following the relation that exists in the stack overflow i.e. users create an edge with other user who answered a question or commented on the question. We model the dynamic crowd-sourcing platform as follows:

Growth rate: At every step ρ (positive integer) new workers are registered and available for work. Let $\alpha\rho$ and $(1 - \alpha)\rho$ be the sets of good and bad new workers.

Decay rate: ω is the decay rate. At every round ω workers becomes inert, i.e., do not participate in crowd sourcing anymore. We assume that the probability that a worker becomes inert depends on the number of jobs it has completed. For example at step t, if x is the total number of jobs executed by all active workers and y is the number of jobs executed by the worker w_i then the probability that w_i becomes inert at step $t + 1$ is y/x.

Crossing time/steps: Using following equations we are calculating the crossing time t, along with the expectation of edges with a good worker E and expected increase of weight W. n_1 be the number of good workers. The probability that a good worker is chosen in a job is $\frac{\alpha}{n}$. In the same job the probability that $k \leq \alpha - 1$ good workers are also chosen is: $(\frac{n_1-1}{n-1})^k$.

Expectation of edges with good workers is shown in the Eq. 1:

$$E = \frac{\alpha}{n}(1\frac{n_1 - 1}{n - 1} + 2(\frac{n_1 - 1}{n - 1})^2 + \cdots + k(\frac{n_1 - 1}{n - 1})^k) \quad = \frac{\alpha}{n}(\frac{a}{1 - r} + \frac{rd}{(1 - r)^2})$$

$$= \frac{\alpha}{n}(\frac{1}{1 - (\frac{n_1-1}{n-1})} + \frac{1(\frac{n_1-1}{n-1})}{(1 - (\frac{n_1-1}{n-1}))^2})$$

$$= \frac{\alpha}{n}(\frac{n - 1}{n - n_1} + \frac{(n_1 - 1)(n - 1)}{(n - n_1)^2})$$

$$= \frac{\alpha}{n}(\frac{(n - 1)(n - n_1 + n_1 - 1)}{(n - n_1)^2})$$

$$= \frac{\alpha}{n}(\frac{(n - 1)(n - 1)}{(n - n_1)^2}) \qquad\qquad = \frac{\alpha}{n}(\frac{(n - 1)^2}{(n - n_1)^2})$$

$$(1)$$

Expected weight of the graph induced by good workers after t steps is: $tn_1\frac{\alpha}{n}(\frac{(n-1)^2}{(n-n_1)^2}) = tZ$, Where $Z = n_1\frac{\alpha}{n}(\frac{(n-1)^2}{(n-n_1)^2})$. The probability that a good worker will meet k bad workers in a job is: $(\frac{\alpha}{n}(\frac{n-n_1}{n})^k)$. The expected increase of weight is:

$$W1 = \frac{\alpha}{n}(1(\frac{n - n_1}{\beta n})^1 + 2(\frac{n - n_1}{\beta n})^2 + \cdots + k(\frac{n - n_1}{\beta n})^k) \qquad (2)$$

$$= \frac{\alpha}{n}(\frac{a}{1 - r} + \frac{rd}{(1 - r)^2}) \qquad (3)$$

$$= \frac{\alpha}{n}(\frac{1}{1 - \frac{n-n_1}{\beta n}} + \frac{\frac{n-n_1}{\beta n}}{(1 - \frac{n-n_1}{\beta n})^2}) \qquad (4)$$

$$= \frac{\alpha}{n}(\frac{\beta n}{\beta n - n + n_1} + \frac{\beta n(n - n_1)}{(\beta n - n + n_1)^2}) \qquad (5)$$

$$= (\frac{\alpha\beta^2 n}{(\beta n - n + n_1)^2}) \qquad (6)$$

At step t the total expected increase in weight is: $((t)(n_1)(\frac{\alpha\beta^2 n}{(\beta n-n+n_1)^2}))$. $w_x \in W^G$ and $w_y \in W^B$: w_x has met w_y before and their answer does not match. Step is t. Probability of choosing both w_x and w_y in one step is: $(\frac{\alpha}{n})^2$. Hence the probability that they met before at least once in the last $t - 1$ steps is: $((t - 1)(\frac{\alpha}{n})^2)$. The probability that their answers do not match is $(\frac{\beta-1}{\beta})$. Thus the probability that they have met before and their answers do not match is $((t - 1)(\frac{\alpha}{n})^2\frac{\beta-1}{\beta})$. Now the expected loss of weight due to one good worker is:$((n - n_1)(t - 1)(\frac{\alpha}{n})^2\frac{\beta-1}{\beta})$, and the expected loss from all good workers is : $((n_1)(n - n_1)(t - 1)(\frac{\alpha}{n})^2\frac{\beta-1}{\beta})$. Thus the weight W_1 after t steps is:

$$= tX - (t - 1)Y \qquad (7)$$

where $(X = n_1(\frac{\alpha\beta^2 n}{(\beta n - n + n_1)^2}))$ and $(Y = (n_1)(n - n_1)(\frac{\alpha}{n})^2\frac{\beta-1}{\beta})$. At a certain time t, the following holds:

$$t > Y/(Z - X + Y)$$
$$t > 1/(Z/Y - X/Y + 1) \tag{8}$$

$$Hence, t > 1/(\frac{\beta}{\alpha(\beta - 1)} - \frac{\beta^3}{\alpha(\beta - 1)^3} + 1) \tag{9}$$
$$> (\alpha(\beta - 1)^3)/(\beta(\beta - 1)^2 - \beta^3 + \alpha(\beta - 1)^3) \tag{10}$$

4.2   Experiments

Synthetic Datasets: We simulate a social network with 500 workers to generate the negative and positive sub graph. We assume that 10% of workers have a with high reputation score. We analysed the performance of our reputation management algorithm on random partitioned graph, After collecting a list of each worker's resourceful neighbors from random search, the algorithm partitions the graph into a negative and positive sub graphs. In this scenario, the worker-reputation graph forms inevitably after the update of worker performance scores.

Real Datasets: We evaluate our algorithm on some standard datasets. We combine [1] and [2] datasets. It is observed that the best accuracy achieved when up to 500 workers are filtered using our reputation management algorithms. The dataset contain questions and answers of the user with their score. In our setup we simulate the scenario in a distributed manner such that when a question triggers in the system the reputation management algorithm floods the question to users with higher score as good workers. In this way after each question and answer the system will update the score of the users. Figure 3 describe the comparison of negative and positive graph and show they way we are accumulating good workers. Figures 4 and 5 shows the outcome of the reputation management algorithm executed with synthetic data. Moreover, We execute the simulation with the identified good and bad users in Stack-Overflow dataset. Figures 7 and 9 shows the outcome for the execution of 100 task with 100150 Users of Stack-Overflow, and the algorithm allocate reputation to 90% and 80% of the good worker respectively. Figures 6, 8 and 9 shows the reputation of 500 workers after the execution of 100 tasks with both dataset. The algorithm allocate 50% and 80% of the good workers respectively with 1% and 2% of the bad workers reputation which are greater than the average reputation of all workers.

It clearly shows that the difference between the reputation of good and bad workers is much higher than the difference between the score of the good and the bad worker. Hence, using our algorithm of reputation management it is easy to distinguish between a good and a bad workers.

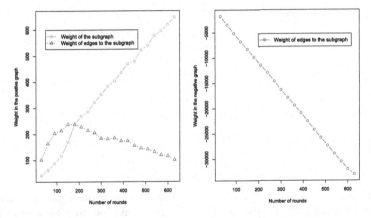

Fig. 3. Graph on the left-hand side: The green points indicates the weight of the induced sub graph on the positive graph by the vertices representing the good workers. The red points indicates the weight of the edges from any vertex (not good workers) to the good workers. Graph on the right-hand side: The red points indicates the weight of the edges from any vertex (not good workers) to the good workers. (Color figure online)

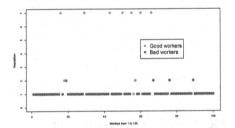

Fig. 4. Shows the reputation of the workers after the execution of 120 tasks. The algorithm allocate high reputation to 70% of the good workers.

Fig. 5. Shows the reputation of the workers after the execution of 150 tasks. The algorithm allocate high reputation to 80% of the good workers.

5   Related Work

In search for a good optimization algorithm in crowdsourcing we explore the concept and method used for optimisation. [21] solves an optimization problem that includes various factors as interest of different stakeholders in the CS and trade-off between the quality and the quantity of the CS. [13,19] proposed a trust evaluation model to differentiate honest workers and dishonest workers. Classification of trust on the workers based on various contexts, i.e., type of task and task reward amount. [8] designs matrices to calculate trust which includes various parameters regarding software development process. [11,20] present a model for deriving the correct answers along with difficulty levels of questions and ability levels of participants in multiple problem domains. They are also claiming that the joint inference of correct answers is the key attribute a high

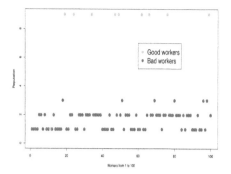

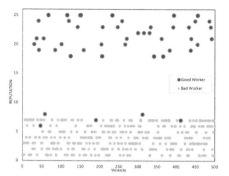

Fig. 6. Shows the algorithm allocate high reputation to 90% of the good workers in synthetic data.

Fig. 7. Shows the algorithm allocate high reputation to 90% of the good workers in real data.

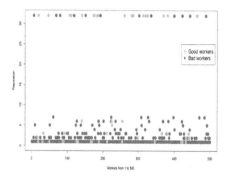

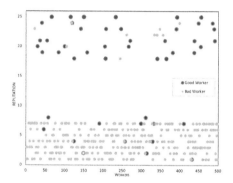

Fig. 8. Shows the algorithm allocate 50% of the good workers and 1% of the bad workers more reputation than the average reputation of all workers.

Fig. 9. Shows the algorithm allocate 80% of the good workers and 2% of the bad workers more reputation than the average reputation of all workers in real data.

level of accuracy. [17] designed a method for real-time, automatic prediction of the quality of submissions to a knowledge base, their model immediately verifies the accuracy of submission. [3,12] develop a fair incentive mechanism for crowdsourcing that enhances the operation of crowd sourcing for both task authors and contributors. [4] develop an algorithm to search expertise in decentralised social network and provide incentives for them. It is a general problem in crowd sourcing to map the set of users and a set of binary choice questions with the truthful answer. [6] generalized setting of the problem where the user–question graph can be arbitrary. [14] presented a mechanism to induce truthful report for crowd sourced consensus tasks. They devised a scoring system that infer honest reporting of customer reviews and the evaluated honest review found to be a Nash equilibrium. [15] Provided a solution for multi objective Optimization

Problem using a distributed ACO (Ant Colony Optimization) algorithm based on a crowd sourcing model. [7] solves Ant Colonies and the Mesh-Partitioning Problem. Ant-Colony Optimization (ACO) is a heuristic design to optimize the search highly motivated by the nature of real ant's walking and food collection. [16] conducted an in-depth analysis of the reputation system, studying the historical data they presented a method to predict the influential long-term contributors. [18] detected local communities around a trusted node for the defence of Sybil attack. [9] presented a model for worker's decision that whether the worker will compute the task.

6   Conclusions

In this paper, we have developed reputation management algorithm using the ant colony optimization concept. In our experimental evaluation we have shown how the algorithm is giving us separated sets of good workers and bad workers. This is very helpful to identify the reputation of workers in crowd sourcing. Moreover, our customised real dataset for this experimental evaluation is a unique one, using this we can extend our work for the comparison of centralised and decentralised Stack Overflow's reputation management. For future work, we are implementing other optimization algorithms to analyse competitive characteristics of our algorithms.

Acknowledgement. This publication has emanated from research supported in part by a research grant from Science Foundation Ireland (SFI) under Grant Number SFI/12/RC/ 2289-P2(Insight) and by a research grant from SFI and the Department of Agriculture, Food and the Marine on behalf of the Government of Ireland under Grant Number SFI/12/RC/3835(VistaMilk), co-funded by the European Regional Development Fund.

References

1. https://stackoverflow.com/
2. https://www.kaggle.com/stackoverflow/stacksample
3. von Ahn, L., Dabbish, L.: Labeling images with a computer game. In: Proceedings of the SIGCHI Conference on Human Factors in Computing Systems (2004)
4. Ara, S.S., Thakur, S., Breslin, J.G.: Expertise discovery in decentralised online social networks. In: ASONAM 2017 (2017)
5. Awwad, T.: Context-aware worker selection for efficient quality control in crowdsourcing (2018)
6. Dalvi, N., Dasgupta, A., Kumar, R., Rastogi, V.: Aggregating crowdsourced binary ratings. In: WWW 2013 (2013)
7. Dorigo, S.: Ant Colonies and the Mesh-Partitioning Problem, pp. 203–208. MIT Press, Cambridge (2004)
8. Dwarakanath, A., Shrikanth, N.C., Abhinav, K., Kass, A.: Trustworthiness in enterprise crowdsourcing: a taxonomy and evidence from data. In: ICSE 2016 (2016)

9. Anta, A.F., Georgiou, C., Mosteiro, M.A., Pareja, D.: Algorithmic mechanisms for reliable crowdsourcing computation under collusion. PLoS One **10**, e0116520 (2015)
10. Ho, C.J., Slivkins, A., Vaughan, J.W.: Adaptive Contract Design for Crowdsourcing Markets: Bandit Algorithms for Repeated Principal-Agent Problems (2014)
11. Jagabathula, S., Subramanian, L., Venkataraman, A.: Reputation-based worker filtering in crowdsourcing. In: Advances in Neural Information Processing Systems 27 (2014)
12. Kamar, E., Horvitz, E.: Incentives for truthful reporting in crowdsourcing. In: AAMAS 2012 (2012)
13. Liu, N., Yang, H., Hu, X.: Adversarial detection with model interpretation. In: KDD 2018 (2018)
14. Liu, S., Miao, C., Liu, Y., Yu, H., Zhang, J., Leung, C.: An incentive mechanism to elicit truthful opinions for crowdsourced multiple choice consensus tasks. In: WI-IAT (2015)
15. Lu, J., Pan, L., Liu, S., Liu, X.: Distributed ACO based on a crowdsourcing model for multiobjective problem. In: CSCWD (2017)
16. Movshovitz-Attias, D., Movshovitz-Attias, Y., Steenkiste, P., Faloutsos, C.: Analysis of the reputation system and user contributions on a question answering website: stackoverflow. In: ASONAM 2013 (2013)
17. Tan, C.H., Agichtein, E., Ipeirotis, P., Gabrilovich, E.: Trust, but verify: predicting contribution quality for knowledge base construction and curation. In: WSDM 2014 (2014)
18. Viswanath, B., Post, A., Gummadi, K.P., Mislove, A.: An analysis of social network-based sybil defenses. SIGCOMM Comput. Commun. Rev. **41**, 363–374 (2011)
19. Ye, B., Wang, Y., Liu, L.: Crowd trust: a context-aware trust model for worker selection in crowdsourcing environments. In: ICWS (2015)
20. Bachrach, Y., Graepel, T., Minka, T., Guiver, J.: How to grade a test without knowing the answers - a Bayesian graphical model for adaptive crowdsourcing and aptitude testing. In: ICML 2012 (2012)
21. Yu, H., Shen, Z., Leung, C.: Bringing reputation-awareness into crowdsourcing. In: ICICS 2013 (2013)

Osmotic Flow Deployment Leveraging FaaS Capabilities

Alina Buzachis[1]($\boxtimes$), Maria Fazio[1]($\boxtimes$), Antonio Celesti[1,2]($\boxtimes$),
and Massimo Villari[1]($\boxtimes$)

[1] MIFT Department, University of Messina, Messina, Italy
{abuzachis,mfazio,acelesti,mvillari}@unime.it
[2] On behalf of Gruppo Nazionale Per il Calcolo Scientifico (GNCS) - INdAM,
Rome, Italy

Abstract. Nowadays, the rapid development of emerging Cloud, Fog, Edge, and Internet of Things (IoT) technologies has accelerated the advancement trends forcing applications and information systems (IS) to evolve. In this hybrid and distributed ecosystem, the management of service heterogeneity is complex, as well as, the service provisioning based on the classification and allocation of suitable computational resources remains a challenge. Osmotic Computing (OC), a new promising paradigm that allows the service migrations ensuring beneficial resource utilization within Cloud, Edge, and Fog Computing environments, was introduced as a potential solution to these issues. Driven by the needs of complex management mitigation, greater agility, flexibility and scalability, this paper aims to propose an innovative OC ecosystem leveraging Functions-as-a-Service (FaaS); there is also introduced the concept of hybrid architectural style combining both microservices and serverless architectures. Furthermore, to support the FaaS-based OC ecosystem, an osmotic flow model for video surveillance in smart cities is presented. To validate the functionality and assess the performance and to further improve the understanding of the usability of the OC flow in real-world applications, several experiments have been carried out.

Keywords: Osmotic Computing · MELs · Serverless · FaaS · Microservice architecture · IoT · Video surveillance

1 Introduction

In the era of globalization and information technology, the rapid development of Cloud Computing, Fog Computing, Edge Computing (i.e., CC, FC, EC) and Internet of Things (IoT) technologies has accelerated the advancement trends forcing applications and Information Systems (IS) for smart environments to evolve. In this hybrid ecosystem, the management of service heterogeneity is complex, as well as, the service provisioning based on the classification and allocation of appropriate computational resources remains a challenge.

© Springer Nature Switzerland AG 2019
R. Montella et al. (Eds.): IDCS 2019, LNCS 11874, pp. 391–401, 2019.
https://doi.org/10.1007/978-3-030-34914-1_37

Osmotic Computing (OC) [10] is a new promising paradigm that has been introduced to address such issues. It can manage heterogeneous computing infrastructures and processing devices transparently, orchestrating the deployment of MicroElements (MELs) among Cloud, Edge and IoT nodes according to the specific requirements of IoT applications and physical/virtual resources availability. Usually, OC relies on the microservice-oriented architectures, which structures each application as a collection of loosely coupled fine-grained MicroElements (e.g., microservices and microdata). This approach is not always suitable for deploying applications in a complex osmotic ecosystem that must extend between Cloud, Fog, Edge, and IoT because it requires an enormous effort for careful planning and management. Recently, a serverless and lightweight technology, also known as Functions-as-a-Service (FaaS), has appeared as a disruptive alternative that organizes applications as a set of stateless functions, and delegates the management of the execution environment to the infrastructure provider, thus simplifying the development, management and execution of such functions.

IoT applications and related services can be complex systems that require statefully interconnected and cooperating MELs. Thus, the FaaS approach can not always be used due to its stateless nature; hence, microservice-based solutions are needed. FaaS can introduce significant overhead management and complexity, as well. Besides, according to different application and developer requirements, in an OC ecosystem, a hybrid architectural approach that combines microservices and serverless FaaS technologies must be adopted.

In this paper, we study the deployment of an OC flow over heterogeneous systems using FaaS. In particular, we modelled a video processing application, that can be usually adopted in video surveillance scenarios, as an osmotic flow of MELs. The flow management benefits from mainstream Edge, private and public Cloud Computing infrastructures and MELs rely on a set of FaaS implemented leveraging OpenFaaS. OpenFaaS is a framework for building serverless functions executed within Docker containers, and their orchestration is performed through Docker Swarm from the Edge up to private and public clouds. The proposed approach is capable of efficiently distributing and allocating MELs by following the principles of OC. The experiments carried out helps us to analyze the execution times for different implemented FaaS according to different deployment strategies across heterogeneous Edge and Cloud systems.

The remainder of the paper is organized as follows. Section 2 analyzes the current state of the art. In Sect. 3 we discuss our motivations behind the integration of FaaS in OC. The osmotic flow design is presented in Sect. 4. Experimental analysis is discussed in Sect. 5. Finally, our conclusions and the highlight for future work are discussed in Sect. 6.

2   Related Works

OC has attracted considerable interest from researchers; there have been qualitative works that have highlighted the significance of using this new computing paradigm. In [7], the authors focused on the efficient distribution and allocation of services in an osmotic ecosystem according to a fitness-based function. [8] proposes a pervasive trust management framework capable of generating high trust value between the users with a lower cost of monitoring using Flexible Mixture Model (FMM) to develop the system and leveraging the concept of OC to perform computational offloading using 3 different solutions: (i) fitness-based movement, (ii) probabilistic movement, and (iii) threshold-based movement. In [5], the authors propose an osmotic flow model to manage microservice-based MELs across Cloud and Edge datacenters. In [6], a Message Oriented Middleware (MOM) to facilitate device-to-device communication in IoT environments and also to integrate complex Edge Computing applications that rely on message brokers, such as distributed real-time data analytics applications is proposed. In [3], the authors investigate the feasibility of applying OC in healthcare by designing a closed-loop flow model for a gamified cognitive rehabilitation use case. Moreover, the use case introduces the development of a customized virtual reality system based on a serious game executed by a microservice-based MEL to allow patients to carry out physical and cognitive rehabilitation.

The above-mentioned research works make use of microservice architecture to implement MELs in OC, but, in some cases, microservice-based MELs can overload edge nodes and therefore degrade the overall performances [9]. For example, smart IoT applications usually require the use of various streaming sensor data and need significant processing capacity for different AI algorithms. Thus, different aspects need to be taken into account such as the dynamic nature of IoT devices (e.g., whether they are moving or static), type of Big Data problems (e.g., velocity, veracity, variety, volume), the computational complexity of data analytics, and similar. Moreover, the workload can significantly change depending on various events in the runtime environment [2]. This requires new elasticity mechanisms to be used at the Edge of the network. To this aim, serverless architectures, also known as Functions-as-a-Service (FaaS), introduce an additional granularity level allowing to further decompose microservices into lightweight and specialized functions that makes the entire process of developing and testing software programs agile in a highly dynamic and evolving environment [4].

We differentiate our work from the ones in the literature because we investigate an event-driven OC where osmotic flows leverage FaaS capabilities. This paper also introduces an OC ecosystem that uses a hybrid architectural approach that combines microservice and serverless FaaS to deploy and manage MELs.

3   Motivation

OC is derived from the term "osmosis" which refers to the equalization of a solution concentration by allowing the solvent to move through a semipermeable membrane [10]. A similar analogy can be applied to modern computing infrastructures, separating the services to acquire processors to balance the load and use of resources without redundancy.

The microservice architecture is a variant of the traditional Service-Oriented Architecture (SOA) that structures an application as a collection of loosely coupled fine-grained services (i.e., microservices) based on lightweight protocols. Microservices deployed in an osmotic system represent a graph of MELs [10] where a MEL: (i) implements specific functionalities and can be deployed and migrated across different infrastructures (MicroServices or MicroFunction), or (ii) represents a piece of information flowing from and to IoT sensor or actuator devices, edge or cloud nodes (MicroData). The benefit of decomposing an application into different smaller services is that it improves modularity, making applications more resilient and expansible. In OC, a microservice-based solution allows deploying MELs over different computation nodes, thus optimizing the usage of available resources. Virtualization technologies, such as containerization, increase the flexibility in using heterogeneous devices and infrastructures even characterized by different constraints, such as in the case of IoT, edge, and cloud nodes. Nevertheless, splitting an application into independent microservices is a complex task that requires careful planning, massive programming effort, and skills. Due to this distributed approach in managing MELs, one of the major issues in microservice-based OC is represented by the configuration of the network among MELs cooperating for the same application. To address this issue [7], network softwarization approaches can be used to enable the creation of virtual overlay networks that meet the application requirements. However, this introduces much more complexity and overhead for developers. Another limitation of microservice architecture is that often, some microservices overload edge nodes and therefore degrade the performances.

Recently, serverless architectures, also known as Functions-as-a-Service (FaaS), appeared as a disruptive alternative typically referring to a software architecture where an application is decomposed into "triggers" and "actions" (or functions), that delegates the management of the execution environment (in the form of stateless functions) to the infrastructure provider [4]. Functionalities offered by FaaS are more general-purpose in nature because they aim to implement separate serverless functions on demand. As a consequence, a FaaS platform provides seamless hosting and execution of functions using provider-managed containers which execute functions (MS), without pre-allocating computing capability or dealing with scalability and load-balancing burden. Functions are more granular than microservice architecture. However, serverless functions can also act as scheduled jobs, event handlers, etc., and not just as application-oriented services.

An OC platform must orchestrate and deploy over IoT, Cloud and Edge infrastructures different MELs; some of them are strictly related to the specific purpose of the application; others are necessary for the management of the OC ecosystem (e.g., network monitoring and management, security management, and so forth). Since these MELs can be highly interdependent, a FaaS approach to implementing them is not always feasible. For this reason, we aim to investigate a hybrid architectural approach for OC that combines microservices and FaaS. Where boot time counts, where many users access even indirectly, where applications are complex, where flexibility is needed, and where cost is mounting, their microservices can replace those spots to increase performance and decrease costs. As well as, where event-driven is required, where need a speed of development, automatic scaling and significantly lowered runtime costs the serverless architecture should be adopted [1]. Summarizing, the integration of FaaS in OC brings the following advantages:

- *Elasticity and scalability:* rather than scaling the entire service, MELs can be automatically and independently scaled with usage; it is managed entirely by the service provider and potentially optimized, reducing the execution time, and then the costs.
- *Built in availability and fault tolerance*; the system must be able to manage failures to avoid the service downtimes.
- *Productivity and ease of deployment:* the code is "packaged" and loaded, ready to be executed.
- *Provisioning:* decrease in the application complexity; fewer infrastructure components (e.g., servers, load balancers) to manage
- *Reusability:* possibility to reuse components for different applications;
- *Costs:* the user will pay only for the resources he has used; as well as reduced operational costs;
- *Decreased Time To Market*: Create new apps in hours and days instead of weeks and months.

Even if the primary goal of OC is to bridge the gap between edge cloud and public cloud, it can also be demonstrated by adopting the private cloud. The latter is mainly grounded to provide a "cloudlet" closed to the users that requires an efficient way to decide the procedures for the execution of the service. Moreover, private cloud/"cloudlet" enhances resource-constrained edge nodes (e.g., in terms of computation offloading and data staging or to provide an execution environment for cloud-centric IoT applications.

4 Design of the Osmotic Flow Model

Let us consider a contemporary smart IoT application scenario composed by different private/public cloud and edge nodes, where several IoT devices are disseminated all over the urban environment as shown in Fig. 1. To manage such IoT devices, several public/private cloud, edge and IoT MELs are distributed on each node. In such a heterogeneous and highly distributed scenario, each IoT device must be managed independently; this is due to the multitude and diversity of such devices (e.g., sensors and gateways) that require different hardware and software capabilities. As well as, according to the OC principles, the management must be done following different QoS policies as explained in Sect. 3. Therefore, MELs can be migrated from the public cloud to the private cloud, and up to the edge nodes and vice-versa according to different QoS, where each policy is managed through a pipeline. Given the complexity of the OC ecosystem, a very challenging task is, therefore, the management of the pipeline.

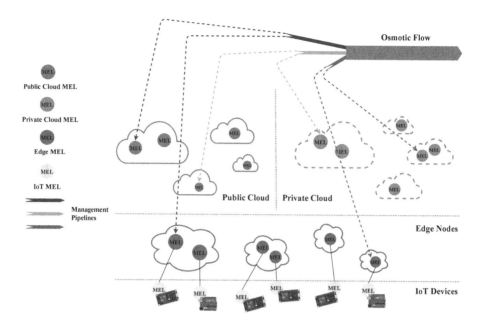

Fig. 1. Reference Osmotic Computing Scenario

To this aim, we present an innovative osmotic flow model able to holistically manage deployment, execution, and migration of MELs according to different pipelines (e.g., violet, grey, orange). Thus, each osmotic flow will be independent by each other, scalable and flexible. To efficiently implement the osmotic flow, we leverage FaaS capabilities. In detail, the osmotic flow is implemented using functions acting as triggers, while pipelines are implemented using functions acting as event handlers. MELs are just functions acting as generic IoT services.

5   Experimentation and Evaluation

To validate the functionality, assess the performance, and improve the understanding of the usability of the OC flow in real-world applications, several experiments have been carried out.

5.1   Use Case Definition: Face Recognition in a Video Surveillance Application

Over the past decades, Digital Video Surveillance (DVS) in smart cities has attracted more and more researchers due to its enormous application prospects. Even though the development of complex DVS schemes constitutes a great challenge, the importance along with the necessity of preserving the safeness of society have played a decisive role as one of the main incentives for researchers and developers to work on the integration of some technologies, such as data management and computer vision, to produce systems that are reliable and effective to serve as solution for tasks like cities surveillance, video analytics and efficient video management to support city officials and/or security employees.

Contemporary smart cities are in prompt need of means for intelligent decision-making, where a crucial role belongs to smart DVS systems necessary to monitor and detect early events in indoor and outdoor scenes of airports, train stations, highways, parking lots, stores, to avoid disasters such as fire, terrorist attacks, traffic congestion. Therefore, there is a need for the development of smart DVS systems which will be able to detect potentially dangerous situations automatically. Furthermore, DVS may be performed using different VIoT characterized by heterogeneous constrained visual sensor nodes, with lower cost, smaller size, limited processing power, average quality cameras, and smartphone cameras.

Let us consider a contemporary smart city scenario, where multi VIoT (Video Internet of Things) Connected Surveillance Cameras (CCTV) are disseminated all over the urban environment. Moreover, CCTVs can be HD and none, as well as the video frame acquisition, can be variable, e.g., 30, 60 FPS. A challenging task is, therefore, realizing such complex video surveillance architecture satisfying different requirements. To this aim, an osmotic flow must be adopted. For example, by considering an HD CCTV and a frame rate of 60 FPS, an edge node could not be able to manage the acquisition from an HD CCTV due to its hardware constraints; so, the acquisition will be managed by a private cloud node more powerful and able also to minimize latency - crucial for video surveillance. Hence, the FaaS which manages the video frames acquisition will be deployed on the private cloud node, which will also be connected to the CCTV camera.

5.2   Environment

Experiments were carried out in three different scenarios: (i) Public Cloud-to-Edge, (ii) Private Cloud-to-Edge and (iii) Hybrid Cloud (Private and Public). For each scenario, the cloud node is deployed on a public cloud platform provided by GARR (an Italian no-profit organization) having the following hardware and software characteristics: 4 VCPUs @3.2 GHz, RAM 18 GB, OS Ubuntu 18.04 LTS. The private cloud node is deployed on a locally hosted server having 2 VCPUs @2.4 GHz, RAM 4 GB, OS Ubuntu 18.04 LTS. The edge node is hosted by a Raspberry PI 3 Model B+ having a quad-core CPU @1.4 GHz and RAM 1 GB, OS Raspbian Jessie. Each node has installed Docker version 18.09.1 with Docker Swarm and OpenFaaS version 0.8.9.

For each scenario, we connected a 5 MP video camera on the private cloud/edge node according to the configuration scenario to capture frames. Since the OpenFaaS functions follow the stateless principle, they do not provide data saving during execution; they are also distributed on the cluster, so they do not see precisely the locally hosted data. To overcome this limitation, we used MongoDB to firstly save the video frames; then, each frame is accessed by the

OpenFaaS functions. Hence, our osmotic flow is composed by three different functions: $FaaS_1$, $FaaS_2$ and $FaaS_3$ respectively.

Workflow: As previously explained, the experimentation objective is to validate the functionality and assess the performance of our OC flow based on FaaS in a smart city video surveillance scenario, detecting and recognizing objects/faces in a video stream coming from a video camera.

To achieve this, we created the $FaaS_1$ - a Python function that acquires the frames from the video camera and sends them, one by one, to a $FaaS_2$ - which saves frames into MongoDB, and then read from and elaborated by $FaaS_3$ - a Python function which uses OpenCV, an Open Source Computer Vision library, to process them and return the name of the recognized object/face.

We have chosen to use the MongoDB because, for example, in scenario (i) the video camera is connected to the edge node on which we deployed $FaaS_1$ and on the cloud one we deployed $FaaS_2$ and $FaaS_3$, the latter, given the stateless nature of OpenFaaS functions, will not be able to access the frames produced by the $FaaS_1$ because hosted by the edge node. As well as, passing directly the image acquired from the video camera to the OpenFaaS function is not simple, because it is needed to convert it into the required format, which is limited from this point of view; in fact, the OpenFaaS functions read the input from the STDIN channel coming from terminals. To overcome this limitation, we introduced the $FaaS_2$, which saves the frames acquired from the video camera into MongoDB, and then $FaaS_3$ will do the processing reading directly them from the database. We also have evaluated the $FaaS_3$'s container creation time on the edge, private, and public cloud nodes.

To verify the feasibility of applying this workflow in real-world applications, we collected the execution time of each proposed FaaS. To have accurate results, for each proposed scenario, we collected 30 subsequent experiments and calculated the average times and confidence interval of 95% for all proposed FaaS.

5.3   Results

Here, we illustrate the results obtained in the three proposed scenarios.

Scenario #1: Public Cloud-to-Edge. Here, $FaaS_2$ and $FaaS_3$ execution is forwarded to the public cloud, while $FaaS_1$ is deployed on the edge. As well as, the video camera is connected to the latter one. Hence, we capture frames and invoke the $FaaS_3$ from the edge node. This scenario exemplifies a situation where the requested $FaaS_3$ is hardware intensive, therefore taking much time to execute on edge. Due to the high processing power of the cloud node, it is beneficial to forward the execution request to the public cloud. Figure 2a shows the collected execution times for all three FaaS in this scenario. We notice that $FaaS_1$ requires in average 0.96 s, $FaaS_2$ 0.69 s and $FaaS_3$ 5.05 s respectively.

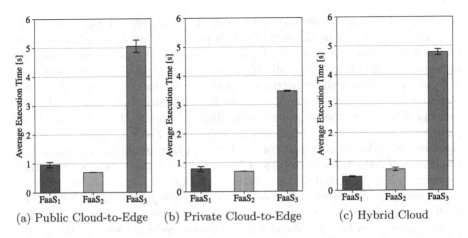

(a) Public Cloud-to-Edge   (b) Private Cloud-to-Edge   (c) Hybrid Cloud

Fig. 2. Average Execution Time [s]

Scenario #2: Private Cloud-to-Edge. This scenario is similar to the previous one, but with the difference that $FaaS_2$ and $FaaS_3$ are deployed on the private cloud; also, in this case, $FaaS_3$ is invoked from the edge node. In detail, this scenario describes a situation where the requested $FaaS_3$ is latency-sensitive as well as it requires computational capabilities that cannot be fulfilled by the edge node. Figure 2b illustrates the execution times gathered in this scenario. Comparing the results with those obtained in Scenario #1 we notice that $FaaS_3$ has lower execution time. This trend is because the private cloud node is closer to the edge node respect to the public cloud one, hence, the latency is reduced. The remaining $FaaS_1$ and $FaaS_2$ require almost the same execution times.

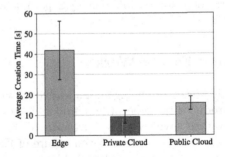

Fig. 3. $FaaS_3$'s Container Creation Time [s] (Color figure online)

Scenario #3: Hybrid Cloud. Here, $FaaS_2$ and $FaaS_3$ are deployed on the public cloud, while $FaaS_1$ is deployed on the private cloud. This scenario exemplifies a situation where $FaaS_1$ captures frames coming from a high-resolution video camera. This FaaS should be executed on a private cloud node instead of an edge one because the latter does not fulfil the hardware requirements. Moreover, the processing done through $FaaS_3$ is hardware intensive and is executed on the public cloud endowed with higher computational capabilities. MongoDB is hosted on the cloud, given the high dimension of the captured frames, as well. Figure 2c shows the collected executions times for all three FaaS in this scenario. As we expected, $FaaS_1$ requires less execution time because the private cloud has more computational capabilities respect to the edge node; thus, being able to manage the frame acquisition better. $FaaS_2$ requires in average the same execution time as that collected in both Scenario #1 and Scenario #2. Conversely, $FaaS_3$ takes in average 4.78 s. As we expected, the execution time required by $FaaS_3$ is slightly lower than that obtained in Scenario #1. Even if in Scenario #1, $FaaS_3$ execution is forwarded to the public cloud, the communication latency between the public and private clouds is lower respect to that registered between the public cloud and the edge node. As well as, the $FaaS_3$ execution time is higher than that obtained in Scenario #2; even if $FaaS_3$ execution is forwarded to the public cloud node endowed with higher computational capabilities, thus, faster to process, the communication latency of the hybrid cloud is greater and clearly affects the average execution time.

We have also evaluated the $FaaS_3$'s container creation time on edge, private, and public cloud nodes. Figure 3 illustrates the trend obtained. As we expected, the $FaaS_3$'s container creation time on the edge is slower respect to those obtained on the private cloud and edge; as well as, the $FaaS_3$ creation time on the private cloud is slower than that obtained on the public cloud. This behaviour is due to the hardware constraints of the edge node respect to a private and public cloud.

To conclude, we notice that in all three scenarios the obtained execution times are acceptable for video surveillance real-world applications; almost in average 0.7 s for $FaaS_1$, 0.55 s for $FaaS_2$ and 4.4 s for $FaaS_3$ respectively. Moreover, the choice of each scenario depends on different QoS parameters, as explained in Sect. 4.

6   Conclusion and Future Work

The focus of this article was on providing an innovative OC ecosystem leveraging FaaS; there is also introduced the concept of hybrid architecture combining both microservice and serverless architectures. Furthermore, to support the FaaS-based OC ecosystem, by using the event-driven nature of FaaS as well as given that serverless functions can also act as scheduled jobs, event handlers, etc., and not just as services, an osmotic flow model for video surveillance in smart cities is presented. This one allows to simplify the management complexity due to the highly distributed and heterogeneous nature of the OC ecosystem and to ensure a high level of scalability, elasticity, and flexibility. To validate the functionality and assess the performance of our OC flow based on FaaS, several experiments have been done. These experiments furthermore improve the understanding of the usability of the OC flow in real-world applications.

In our on-going work, we plan to investigate the feasibility of the osmotic flow in more real use cases; we also plan to implement and test the OC ecosystem using hybrid architectures based on microservices and FaaS respectively.

References

1. Serverless or microservices - which is better? https://www.quora.com/Serverless-or-microservices-which-is-better
2. Alam, K.M., Saini, M.K., El-Saddik, A.: Workload model based dynamic adaptation of social internet of vehicles. Sensors **15**, 23262–23285 (2015)
3. Buzachis, A., Bernava, G.M., Busa, M., Pioggia, G., Villari, M.: Towards the basic principles of osmotic computing: a closed-loop gamified cognitive rehabilitation flow model. In: 2018 IEEE 4th International Conference on Collaboration and Internet Computing (CIC), pp. 446–452, October 2018. https://doi.org/10.1109/CIC.2018.00067
4. Fox, G., Ishakian, V., Muthusamy, V., Slominski, A.: Status of serverless computing and function-as-a-service (FaaS) in industry and research, August 2017. https://doi.org/10.13140/RG.2.2.15007.87206
5. Nardelli, M., Nastic, S., Dustdar, S., Villari, M., Ranjan, R.: Osmotic flow: osmotic computing + IoT workflow. IEEE Cloud Comput. **4**(2), 68–75 (2017)
6. Rausch, T., Dustdar, S., Ranjan, R.: Osmotic message-oriented middleware for the internet of things. IEEE Cloud Comput. **5**, 17–25 (2018)
7. Sharma, V., Srinivasan, K., Jayakody, D.N.K., Rana, O., Kumar, R.: Managing service-heterogeneity using osmotic computing. ArXiv e-prints, April 2017
8. Sharma, V., You, I., Kumar, R., Kim, P.: Computational offloading for efficient trust management in pervasive online social networks using osmotic computing. IEEE Access (2017). https://doi.org/10.1109/ACCESS.2017.2683159
9. Taherizadeh, S., Stankovski, V., Grobelnik, M.: A capillary computing architecture for dynamic internet of things: orchestration of microservices from edge devices to fog and cloud providers. Sensors **18**, 2938 (2018)
10. Villari, M., Fazio, M., Dustdar, S., Rana, O., Ranjan, R.: Osmotic computing: a new paradigm for edge/cloud integration. IEEE Cloud Comput. **3**(6), 76–83 (2016). https://doi.org/10.1109/mcc.2016.124

Secure and Distributed Crowd-Sourcing Task Coordination Using the Blockchain Mechanism

Safina Showkat Ara[✉], Subhasis Thakur, and John G. Breslin

Insight Centre for Data Analytics, NUI Galway, Galway, Ireland
{safina.ara,subhasis.thakur,john.breslin}@insight-centre.org

Abstract. A complex crowd-sourcing problem such as open source software development has multiple sub-tasks, dependencies among the sub-tasks and requires multiple workers working on these sub-tasks to coordinate their work. Current solutions of this problem employ a centralized coordinator. Such a coordinator decides on the sub-task execution sequence and as a centralized coordinator faces problems related to cost, fairness and security. In this paper, we present a futuristic model of crowd-sourcing for complex tasks to mitigate the above problems. We replace the centralized coordinator by a blockchain and automate the decision-making process of the coordinator. We show that the proposed solution is secure, efficient and the computational overhead due to employing a blockchain is low.

Keywords: Crowd-sourcing · Task coordination · Blockchain · Trust

1 Introduction

In this paper, we study complex Crowd-Sourcing (CS) task which has multiple sub-tasks, constraints among these sub-tasks. It will require multiple workers to coordinate their effort to solve such a complex task. Coordination among the workers is recognized as an important aspect for future CS platforms [6,16]. For example in open source software development [11], a developer works on a specific part of the software and it must coordinate with other developers working on other parts of the software. Another example of such CS task may be a multi-player version of the protein folding game [3]. The challenges with executing such complex CS tasks are as follows:

Cost of Coordination: We may assign the CS sub-tasks to the workers and the workers must coordinate their efforts to comply with the constraints among the sub-tasks. Coordinated execution of these sub-tasks is a sequence of sub-task executions where a worker must consider previous solutions while solving its task. The most efficient coordinator would minimize the length of such a sub-task execution sequence. Apart from deciding on the sub-task execution sequence, the coordinator must also evaluate compatibility among solutions of the sub-tasks.

© Springer Nature Switzerland AG 2019
R. Montella et al. (Eds.): IDCS 2019, LNCS 11874, pp. 402–413, 2019.
https://doi.org/10.1007/978-3-030-34914-1_38

It may hire additional workers to perform such evaluations and hence the cost to execute the task will increase.

Fairness: Workers may need to execute the sub-tasks multiple times to comply with constraints among the sub-tasks. We need a method to ensure fairness in this process, i.e., the coordinator must follow certain rules to ensure fairness as it asks a certain worker to solve its sub-task again.

Trust on the Coordinator: Either the CS platform or the workers may act as the coordinator. The problem with the first option is that it is a centralized solution and the workers must trust the centralized coordinator for correct evaluations of coordination decisions. The problem with the second option is that a worker may be malicious and may manipulate the coordination decisions. Note that a worker may need to execute its task multiple times to comply with constraints among the sub-tasks. If the solutions of two workers are in conflict then one of them should backtrack and solve its task again. If the coordinator is malicious then it may favor certain workers and they may not execute their task again. Such activities will reduce the cost of task execution of malicious workers but it will reduce the quality of the overall solution.

The existing solutions [12,14,16] for CS task coordination do not mitigate these challenges. In this paper, we propose a BlockChain (BC) based distributed coordinator for CS where any worker may act as the coordinator and the BC mechanism ensures that such a worker remains honest while acting as the coordinator. Hence the proposed solution erases the requirement that the workers must evaluate their trust on the coordinator. Using the BC mechanism, we may securely store transaction records among peers of a peer to peer network. We use the BC mechanism to develop the CS platform as follows:

- Every worker acts as a miner and each worker keeps the entire record of the solutions produced by the workers.
- We propose a distributed coordination mechanism where each worker may act as a coordinator. The BC mechanism ensures that a worker behaves honestly while acting as a coordinator. Hence, this BC-based distributed coordination mechanism erases the requirement that a worker must evaluate its trust on the coordinator.
- We keep solutions in a BC, it becomes impossible to overwrite the records of the solutions.

In this paper we present the following results:

Security: We present a BC maintained CS platform where CS data (such as task, worker selection, solutions) is securely stored and it is infeasible to overwrite it. Also, blockchain ensures that the workers behave honestly while acting as the coordinator.

Fairness: We develop rules to ensure fairness in sub-task re-execution. These rules are part of the blockchain's data structure and consensus protocol to ensure enforcement of such rules.

Convergence: We show that the distributed coordination mechanism converges quickly.

Computational Overload: We show that the proposed coordination mechanism has negligible computational overload due to participating in a blockchain.

Efficiency: We show that the proposed distributed coordination mechanism is efficient. An efficient coordinator minimizes the number of times each worker executes its subtask.

The paper is organized as follows: In Sect. 2 we describe the task coordination problem. In Sect. 3 we present a brief description of the BC mechanism. In Sect. 4 we present the BC-based distributed coordination mechanism. In Sect. 5 we present an experimental evaluation of the proposed coordination mechanism. In Sect. 6 we mention relevant literature and we conclude the paper in Sect. 7.

2   Problem Statement

In this section, we describe a CS task which requires coordination among multiple workers. There are n workers $W = (w_1, \ldots, w_n)$. A task $T = (t_1, \ldots, t_n)$ has n subtasks. Each subtask is assigned to one worker. $W(t_i) \in W$ indicates the worker of the subtask t_i. subtasks require coordination among workers to satisfy constraints among them. There are k constraints $\theta = (\theta_1, \ldots, \theta_k)$. A constraint θ_i requires coordination of workers corresponding to tasks $\theta_i(T) \subset T$. In centralized coordination, workers will report solutions of their respective subtasks to the coordinator who decides the execution of next set of subtasks, i.e., based on the present solutions who should again execute their tasks to satisfy constraints among the subtasks.

We represent the task, subtask allocation to workers and constraints among subtasks using a task graph. A task graph is an undirected graph $G = (W, E)$ whose vertices are the workers and there is an edge $(w_i, w_j) \in E$ if there is a constraint θ_x such that $t_a, t_b \in \theta_x(T)$ and $W(t_a) = w_i$ and $W(t_b) = w_j$. For example consider a sudoku puzzle, cells with label 0 are empty cells and we have to assign a value between 1 to 9 to the empty cells. A subtask is to assign a value to an empty cell. A worker w_i (with subtask t_i) is neighbour of another worker w_j (with subtask t_j) if t_i and t_j are on the same row (or column) of the sudoku puzzle.

In this paper, we will use sudoku puzzle as a complex task to be solved by multiple workers in a CS platform. The challenges for a distributed coordinator are as follows:

- **Secure records:** As the workers act as coordinator they can access the data on task execution by the workers. They can modify this data. Hence we need a security mechanism for safe storage and access to these data.
- **Task generation:** A worker executes its task with the information about solutions to subtasks solved by its neighbours to produce a solution which does not violate any constraints or maximally complies with the constraints. It incurs a certain cost every time it executes its subtask. We need a mechanism

that can correctly identify the worker who should adjust its solution, i.e., execute its subtask again based on the solutions produced by other workers. It may happen that a malicious worker would deny to execute its task again and ask its neighbours to adjust their respective solutions.

3   The Blockchain Mechanism (BC)

BC allows peers of a peer to peer network to transfer tokens among them using transactions. We will provide a detailed description of the transaction data structure. If a peer P_1 wants to send x tokens to P_2 then it creates the transaction T_1 and announces it to its neighbours in the BC peer to peer network. Once such a neighbour P_3 receives the transaction T_1, P_3 attempts to verify it. If it can verify T_1 as a valid transaction it forwards T_1 to its neighbours. BC mechanism stores consistent replicas of transaction history among the peers of a peer to peer network on multiple peers. Valid transactions are grouped into a block and blocks are stored as BC where each block has only one parent block. A new block can be added to the BC as the child of the most recent block. Any peer can verify transactions and add a new block to the BC provided it satisfies the conditions of the distributed consensus protocol. Distributed consensus protocol ensures that all peers have the same replica of the BC, i.e., they have the same history of transactions.

4   BC Based Task Coordination

We use blockchain as a coordinator for complex CS task is as follows:

- Workers form the blockchain peer to peer network. Two workers are neighbours in this network if their corresponding sub-tasks have at least one constraint.
- Each worker solves its sub-task and the solution is converted as a blockchain transaction by attaching the solution file (i.e., a textfile, a media file, etc.) to a blockchain transaction.
- After solving the sub-task, the worker announces its solution by creating the above transaction whose recipient is one of its neighbours in the blockchain peer to peer network. For example, as shown in Fig. 1, worker w_1 and w_2 send the solutions of their sub-tasks t_1 and t_2 to the worker w_3 as transactions τ_1 and τ_2.
- A worker (a peer) regularly compares the solutions it has received from its neighbours. The worker follows a set of rules to evaluate the solutions.
- The solutions a worker has to compare and evaluate is represented by its unspent transactions. For example in Fig. 1, w_3 has to compare solutions in τ_1 and τ_2. For each such unspent transaction, it first checks if there is any other unspent transaction such that there are constraints among the corresponding sub-tasks. Thus w_3 checks if the sub-tasks whose solutions are mentioned in τ_1 and τ_2 have any constraints. In this example, we assume that there are such constraints $(\theta_1, \theta_2, \theta_3)$.

– After the evaluation of solutions mentioned in its unspent transactions, each
  worker performs the following steps:
   • Let w_3 evaluated that solution mentioned in τ_1 is valid compared with
     the solution mentioned in τ_2.
   • w_3 will create two new transactions. In the transaction τ'_1 it will copy the
     content of τ_1 and send it to a neighbour w_4. In the transaction τ'_2 it will
     copy the content (the solution to the sub-task) of τ_2 and send it to w_2
     who is the creator of the content of τ_2.
– If a worker receives a transaction such that it had created the content then
  it must solve its sub-task again.
– The above-mentioned procedure continues until a time limit as solutions to
  each sub-tasks are evaluated against other sub-tasks and invalid sub-tasks are
  solved again.

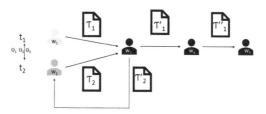

Fig. 1. Sub-tasks t_1 and t_2 with a set of constraints among them are assigned to w_1
and w_2. They solve t_1 and t_2 and create τ_1 and τ_2 with w_3 as the recipient. w_3 evaluate
these solutions and decides that the solution of t_1 is valid. It sends the solution to t_1
to another neighbour for further evaluation and sends the solution of t_2 back to its
creator w_2. w_2 solves its sub-task again.

In the above approach we observe the following:

– A solution of a sub-task is evaluated against solutions to other sub-tasks (with
  which it has certain constraints). Thus the number of times a solution to a
  sub-task is compared with solutions for related sub-tasks is an indicator of
  its validity compared with valid solutions for all sub-tasks.
– We need additional data fields in the transaction data structure to indicate
  who and when the solution to a sub-task was found.

Now we present a detailed description of the above mentioned distributed
coordination mechanism.

4.1   Peer to Peer Network

We construct a BC peer to peer network from a task $T = (t_1, \ldots, t_n)$, $\theta = (\theta_1, \ldots, \theta_k)$ constraints over the subtasks and a set of workers $W = (w_1, \ldots, w_n)$.
We assign task t_i to worker w_i. The peer to peer network is an undirected graph
$G = (W, E)$ where E is the set of edges. Two workers w_i and w_j are neighbours
if there is a constraint θ_x such that $t_i, t_j \in \theta_x$.

4.2   Transactions

We augment the transaction data structure as follows:

Content: A transaction contains a file describing the solution to a sub-task. This file may be a text file or a media file but must be in a predefined file format. It replaces the 'amount' information of a BC transaction.

Checksum: It will contain checksum value of the file to ensure the integrity of the file and hence the solution.

Origin: It will contain the identity of the peer who created the content file. It will store such peer's public key.

Origin Time: It will record the time when the content file was created.

Trail Number: It will record the number of times the solution corresponding to a transaction is compared with solutions corresponding other transactions and this solution was verified as a valid solution (does not violate any constraint) at every instance of such comparison.

UTXO: Unspent transaction output (UTXO) ensures that only unspent transactions are used as input to new transactions. We use the following procedure to enforce the UTXO requirement.

– Transaction for solution generation: A worker w_i should create a new solution for its subtask if either of the following holds:
  (1) It has received a transaction τ_x whose origin is w_i and trail number is 0. τ_x indicates that the previous solution of w_i for its subtask is rejected by other workers and hence it must execute its subtask again. w_i will execute its task again and such a solution will be included in a new transaction τ_y whose Content is the new solution, 'checksum' is the checksum of the new solution and it uses τ_x as the input to τ_y.
  (2) Each worker is endowed with an empty transaction τ^0 and it is used as the input to the first transaction that the worker creates whose content is its solution to its subtask.
– Transaction forwarding: A worker w_i forwards its unspent transactions τ whose *Origin* is not w_i by following this procedure:
  (1) For each transaction $\tau_x \in \tau$, if there is no other transaction in τ with which τ_x shares at least one constraint then w_i forwards τ_x to a neighbouring worker by creating a new transaction $\tau_{x'}$ whose input is τ_x. Content, Origin, Origin time and trail number of $\tau_{x'}$ remains same as τ_x. Note that trail number indicates the number times a transaction (hence a solution to a subtask) is evaluated as a valid transaction against other relevant transactions (corresponding subtasks share constraints). As there are no other relevant transactions we do not increase the trail number.
  (2) For each transaction $\tau_x \in \tau$, if there are other transaction in $\tau' \subseteq \tau$ with which τ_x shares at least one constraint then (a) if trail number of τ_x is more than any other transaction in τ' and Origin time of τ_x is less than

the same of any other transaction $\tau_y \in \tau'$ whose trail number of τ_y is same as τ_x then w_i forwards τ_x to a neighbouring worker by creating a new transaction $\tau_{x'}$ whose input is τ_x. Content, Origin and Origin time of $\tau_{x'}$ remain the same as τ_x. But we increase trail number of $\tau_{x'}$ as 1 more than the same for τ_x. (b) If τ_x does not satisfy the previous criteria then w_i forwards τ_x to $Origin(\tau_x)$ by creating a new transaction $\tau_{x'}$ whose input is τ_x and content, origin remains same as τ_x. But $\tau_{x'}$'s trail number becomes 0. Hence if a new solution is in conflict with an old solution then the new solution is regarded as a valid solution if its trail number is same as the trail number of the old solution.

Figure 2 shows an example of the above transaction data structure. w_1 and w_2 solved their respective sub-tasks (with a constraint among them) and sent the solution as transactions τ_1 and τ_2 to w_3. $Origin$ field of τ_1 is marked with the public key of w_1 (we just use w_1) and its trail number is 1. w_2 evaluates that solution in τ_1 is valid compared with the solution in τ_2. Hence it forwards the solution in τ_1 to w_4 for further evaluation by creating a new transaction τ_1' with $origin$ as w_1 and trail number as 1 more than the trail number of τ_1. It also rejects the solution mentioned in τ_2 as it creates a new transaction τ_2' with trail number 0 and $Origin$ as w_2. Hence the solution is τ_1 is further evaluated with solutions from other sub-tasks and w_2 generates a new solution for its sub-task.

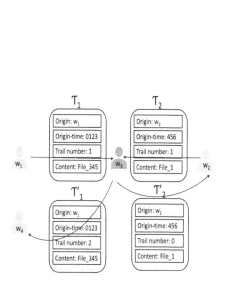

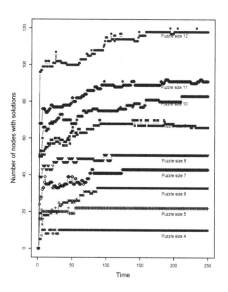

Fig. 2. It shows how data fields of transaction are changed. For a valid transaction trail number will be increased by 1 and for an invalid transaction it will be zero.

Fig. 3. Convergence time for distributed coordination mechanism.

We will use proof of work as the distributed consensus protocol. We summarize the fairness rules for sub-task re-execution such as Any worker must re-execute its sub-task if it is not maximally compatible with other related sub-tasks. If two related sub-tasks are in conflict then the sub-task which is least tested for compatibility with solutions for related sub-tasks will be executed again. If two related sub-tasks are in conflict and the number of times these sub-tasks are tested for compatibility with solutions for related sub-tasks are equal then, the sub-task which was solved earlier will be executed again.

5   Experimental Evaluation

In this section present an experimental evaluation of the proposed BC based distributed coordination mechanism. We simulate a BC using agent based modelling and asynchronous event simulation in Python. Peers (workers for a CS task) are modelled as autonomous agents. There are two types of workers (a) good quality workers and (b) bad quality workers. A good quality worker quickly finishes its subtask and a bad quality worker takes more time. In the following experiments, a bad quality worker, takes 5 times more time to finish its subtask compared with any good quality worker. We implement each worker's workflow as two processes. The first process is concerned with solving its subtask and the second process is concerned with forwarding transactions according to the transaction forwarding rules described in Sect. 4. Execution time for the first process depends on the worker's quality. We simulate these processes using SIMPY package of Python which simulates asynchronous events. For a bad quality worker we suspend its subtask solving process for next 5 time instances and the same is suspended for 1 time instant for good quality workers. q_i will denote the 'Timeout' (the time duration for which this process will sleep) amount for this process. We assume that verifying whether a solution for a subtask is correct or not is an easy problem and hence we do not impose any 'Timeout' for transaction forwarding process. There is no standard benchmark dataset for task coordination in CS [12,14]. We propose to use sudoku puzzles as benchmark dataset. Each empty cell of a sudoku puzzle is a subtask and one subtask is assigned to one worker. We use puzzles of size 4 to 14. By increasing the puzzle size we can increase the number of subtasks, the complexity of constraints and number of constraints.

Algorithm 1 describes the workflow for each worker. It executes two processes. The first process (line 5 to line 9) solves the subtask and the second process (line 10 to 27) forwards transactions. The first process checks if the worker w_i received a transaction with origin w_i and trail number 0. Such a transaction indicates the solution proposed by w_i is discarded by other workers as it is in conflict with solutions for other subtasks. If there is such a transaction then w_i finds a new solution for its subtask and creates a new transaction. The second process checks if it has received any transaction whose origin is not w_i. For each of such transaction τ_x, it checks if trail number and origin time of τ_x is more and at most the same of any other transaction $\tau_{x'}$. If τ_x satisfies these conditions then it forwards τ_x to a neighbour by increasing the trail number. Additionally, it

---

Algorithm 1. Simulation

Data: A task $T = (t_1, \ldots, t_n)$, Task graph $G = (W, E)$ and set of constraints
$\theta = \{\theta_i \in 2^T\}$

Result: Solution to T

1 **begin**

2   **for** *Every iteration* **do**

3   **for** *Every worker w_i* **do**

4           $\tau \leftarrow$ unspent transactions of w_i

5   **if** $\tau_x \in \tau : Origin(\tau_x)$ *is w_i and* $Trail(\tau_x) = 0$ **then**

6   Solve subtask t_i while complying with $\{\theta_x\}$ and other solutions with trail number 0 (*subtask is the CS subtask for example developing part of a software*)

7   Create new transaction τ' with the new solution

8   Send the new transaction to a random neighbour

9   Sleep(q_i)

10           $\tau \leftarrow$ unspent transactions of W_i whose $Origin$ is not w_i

11   **if** $\tau \neq \emptyset$ **then**

12   **for** *Each transaction $\tau_x \in \tau$* **do**

13                 $\tau' = \tau \backslash \tau_x$

14                 $\tau'' \subseteq \tau'$ such that for any $\tau_y \in \tau''$ there is a constraint θ_i where $\tau_y, \tau_x \in \theta_i$

15   **if** $\tau'' = \emptyset$ **then**

16   Create transaction $\tau_{x'}$ with input τ_x

17   set $Trail(\tau_{x'}) = Trail(\tau_x)$

18   Forward $\tau_{x'}$ to a neighbour w_k

19   **else**

20   **if** $Trail(\tau_x) > Trail(\tau_{x'})$ *and* $T^0(\tau_x) \leq T^0(\tau_{x'})$ **then**

21   Create transaction $\tau_{x'}$ with input τ_x

22   set $Trail(\tau_{x'}) = Trail(\tau_x) + 1$

23   Forward $\tau_{x'}$ to a neighbour w_k

24   **else**

25   Create transaction $\tau_{x'}$ with input τ_x

26   set $Trail(\tau_{x'}) = 0$

27   Forward $\tau_{x'}$ to a peer w_k whose public key is $Origin(\tau_x)$

28        $\beta \leftarrow$ create new block

29   Solve BC puzzle and augment BC and announce β

30        $\beta' \leftarrow$ received new block

31   If β' is valid then Augment BC & announce β'

---

executes proof of work protocol with two more processes. The first process (line 28–29) creates and new block, solves the puzzle and announces puzzle solution and new block to the network. The second process (line 30–31) receives a new block from its neighbour. If the peer can verify that the block and associated puzzle solution is correct then it augments its BC according to the rules described in Sect. 3 and it forwards the block to its neighbours. The second process may interrupt the block creation process if a new received block contains transactions which are included in the new block under construction of the former process. If the block creation process is interrupted then the peer restarts it.

First, we analyze convergence time of the distributed coordination mechanism. We measure convergence time as the minimum number of iteration required by the above simulation to find a valid solution for each subtasks. Note that 'time' is measured as the number of iteration. We may calculate the minimum convergence time for a centralized coordinator as follows: It will allow subtasks with no constraints among them to run in parallel and other tasks will be executed serially. There are at most x^2 subtasks for a puzzle with puzzle size x. As a subtask has common constraint with at most $2x$ other subtasks, in every iteration $x^2/2x = x/2$ subtasks can be executed in parallel. Hence the minimum convergence time is $x^2/(x/2) = 2x$. We use 9 datasets as sudoku puzzles with size from 4 to 12. The number of subtasks (and workers) for each dataset is at most x^2, each worker has 2 constraints and number of variables in each constraint is at most x where x is the puzzle size. Figure 3 shows the convergence time for these datasets. It shows the number of workers with valid solutions for their respective subtasks w.r.t time. We observe that convergence time increases as we increase the puzzle size. We conclude that distributed coordination mechanism has finite and short convergence time.

Next, we measure the efficiency of the distributed coordination mechanism in terms of the number of times each worker solves its subtask. The most efficient coordination mechanism requires each worker to execute its subtask only once. Although this problem can be classified as distributed constraint satisfaction problem and the complexity of such problems is [15] NP-complete. Hence it is unlikely that there exists the most efficient algorithm. We evaluate the efficiency of the proposed distributed coordination mechanism with datasets consisting of sudoku puzzles with puzzle size 4, 6, 8, 10, 12 and 14. Figure 4 shows the efficiency results as we plot the number of times each worker execute its subtask. We found that on average each worker executes its subtask twice.

Finally, we measure the computational overhead of the proposed distributed coordination mechanism. We measure it as the number of times each worker needs to execute their subtasks and input size of each transaction forwarding instances. In Fig. 5 we plot the average number of transactions per transaction forwarding instances. We found that the input size remains approximately 2 while we increase puzzle size from 4 to 14. Also as shown in Fig. 4 workers need to execute subtasks approximately twice while we increase puzzle size from 4 to 14. Hence it shows that both these parameters do not increase as the puzzle size is increased. Hence we claim that computational overhead of the proposed distributed coordination mechanism is negligible.

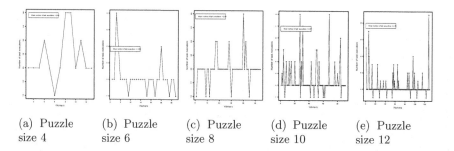

(a) Puzzle   (b) Puzzle   (c) Puzzle   (d) Puzzle   (e) Puzzle
size 4   size 6   size 8   size 10   size 12

Fig. 4. Efficiency of the distributed coordination mechanism

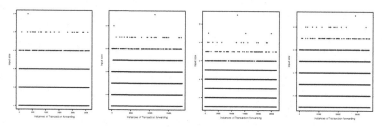

(a) Puzzle size 4 (b) Puzzle size 10 (c) Puzzle size 12 (d) Puzzle size 14

Fig. 5. Computational overhead of the distributed coordination mechanism

6   Related Literature

It is difficult to verify the solution produced by the workers. As mention by [5] low quality workers and spammers are big threats to CS. Workers may also collude in data labelling tasks [7]. [1] develop an algorithm to search expertise in decentralised social network and provide incentives for them. Various mechanisms are developed to address the problem of low quality work in CS. In [13] trust and reputation are used to identify honest workers. In another approach, mechanism design is used to encourage the workers to remain honest. These mechanisms [2,8,9] developed rules for paying the workers in such a way that honest workers receive better payment than dishonest workers. It should be noted that these CS tools can be used in CS tasks which require coordination among workers. Algorithms developed for distributed constraint satisfaction [15] may be used to coordinate the workers. [12] proposed task coordination for CS but these algorithms do not guarantee the security of CS platform and workers may collude to overwrite transactions which recorded their work history. The first BC mechanism [10] uses proof of work as the distributed consensus protocol. Peercoin (https://peercoin.net/) introduced the proof of stake protocol which uses stake as the voting power instead of computing resource [4].

7   Conclusion

In this paper, we have proposed a BC-based solution for CS complex task which requires coordination among the workers. The BC provides a secure CS environment which does not need a trusted coordinator.

Acknowledgement. This publication has emanated from research supported in part by a researchgrant from Science Foundation Ireland (SFI) under Grant Number $SFI/12/RC/$ 2289-P2(Insight) and by a research grant from SFI and the Department of Agriculture, Food and the Marine on behalf of the Government of Ireland under-Grant Number SFI/12/RC/3835 (VistaMilk), co-funded by the European Regional Development Fund.

References

1. Ara, S.S., Thakur, S., Breslin, J.G.: Expertise discovery in decentralised online social networks. In: ASONAM 2017 (2017)
2. Kamar, E.: Incentives for truthful reporting in crowdsourcing. In: AAMAS 2012 (2012)
3. Khatib, F., Cooper, S., Tyka, M.D., Xu, K.: Algorithm discovery by protein folding game players. Proc. Natl. Acad. Sci. **108**, 18949–18953 (2011)
4. King, S., Nadal, S.: PPCoin: peer-to-peer crypto-currency with proof-ofstake (2012). http://www.peercoin.net/assets/paper/peercoin-paper.pdf
5. Kittur, A., Chi, E.H., Suh, B.: Crowdsourcing user studies with mechanical turk. In: CHI 2008 (2008)
6. Kittur, A., Nickerson, J.V., Bernstein, M., Gerber, E., Shaw, A.: The future of crowd work. In: CSCW 2013 (2013)
7. Lee, K., Tamilarasan, P., Caverlee, J.: Crowdturfers, campaigns, and social media: tracking and revealing crowdsourced manipulation of social media. In: ICWSM 2013 (2013)
8. Liu, S., Miao, C., Liu, Y., Yu, H., Zhang, J., Leung, C.: An incentive mechanism to elicit truthful opinions for crowdsourced multiple choice consensus tasks. In: WI-IAT (2015)
9. Miller, N., Resnick, P., Zeckhauser, R.: Eliciting informative feedback: the peer-prediction method (2009)
10. Nakamoto, S.: Bitcoin: a peer-to-peer electronic cash system (2009). http://www.bitcoin.org/bitcoin.pdf
11. Olson, D.L., Rosacker, K.: Crowdsourcing and open source software participation. Serv. Bus. **7**, 499–511 (2013)
12. Rahman, H., Roy, S.B., Thirumuruganathan, S., Amer-Yahia, S., Das, G.: "The whole is greater than the sum of its parts": optimization in collaborative crowdsourcing. CoRR (2015)
13. Ren, J., Zhang, Y., Zhang, K., Shen, X.: SACRM: social aware crowdsourcing with reputation management in mobile sensing. CoRR (2014)
14. Tavakoli, A., Nalbandian, H., Ayanian, N.: Crowdsourced coordination through online games. In: HRI 2016 (2016)
15. Yokoo, M., Durfee, E.H., Ishida, T., Kuwabara, K.: The distributed constraint satisfaction problem: formalization and algorithms. IEEE Trans. Knowl. Data Eng. **10**, 673–685 (1998)
16. Zhang, H., Law, E., Miller, R., Gajos, K.: Human computation tasks with global constraints. In: CHI 2012 (2012)

CUDA Virtualization and Remoting for GPGPU Based Acceleration Offloading at the Edge

Antonio Mentone[1](✉) ⓘ, Diana Di Luccio[1](✉) ⓘ, Luca Landolfi[1] ⓘ,
Sokol Kosta[2] ⓘ, and Raffaele Montella[1] ⓘ

[1] Science and Technologies Department, University of Naples "Parthenope",
Napoli, Italy
{antonio.mentone001,luca.landolfi}@studenti.uniparthenope.it,
{diana.diluccio,raffaele.montella}@uniparthenope.it
[2] Department of Electronic Systems, Aalborg University Copenhagen,
Copenhagen, Denmark
sok@cmi.aau.dk

Abstract. In the last decade, GPGPU virtualization and remoting have
been among the most important research topics in the field of computer
science and engineering due to the rising of cloud computing technologies. Public, private, and hybrid infrastructures need such virtualization
tools in order to multiplex and better organize the computing resources.
With the advent of novel technologies and paradigms, such as edge computing, code offloading in mobile clouds, deep learning techniques, etc.,
the need for computing power, especially of specialized hardware such as
GPUs, has skyrocketed. Although many GPGPU virtualization tools are
available nowadays, in this paper we focus on improving GVirtuS, our
solution for GPU virtualization. The contributions in this work focus on
the CUDA plug-in, in order to provide updated performance enabling the
next generation of GPGPU code offloading applications. Moreover, we
present a new GVirtuS implementation characterized by a highly modular approach with a full multithread support. We evaluate and discuss the
benchmarks of the new implementation comparing and contrasting the
results with the pure CUDA and with the previous version of GVirtuS.
The new GVirtuS yielded better results when compared with its previous implementation, closing the gap with the pure CUDA performance
and trailblazing the path for the next future improvements.

Keywords: HPC · GPGPU · Cloud computing · Virtualization

1 Introduction

In a grid environment, computing power is offered on-demand to perform large
numerical simulations on a network of machines, potentially extended all over
the world [5]. Virtualization techniques represent a good solution to the problem

© Springer Nature Switzerland AG 2019
R. Montella et al. (Eds.): IDCS 2019, LNCS 11874, pp. 414–423, 2019.
https://doi.org/10.1007/978-3-030-34914-1_39

of executing generic complex high performance scientific software on a grid, and have inspired a novel computing paradigm in which virtualized resources are spread in a cloud of real high performance hardware infrastructures [6].

This model, well known as Cloud Computing, is *an internet-based model providing a convenient on demand access to a shared pool of configurable computing resources which can be rapidly assigned and released with a minimal management effort or service provider interaction* [9].

Latest-generation supercomputers take advantage of GPUs (Graphics Processing Units) processing power in order to speed up calculations. GPUs are parallel microprocessors attached to a graphics card. They are extremely flexible, completely programmable and able to achieve extremely high performance during the parallel processing of large sets of data. GPUs' high performance can also be used for general purpose scientific computing and starting from this definition the GPGPU technology is born [2]. GPGPU is exploited by using parallel programming environment such as **OpenCL** and **CUDA** [12].

In this paper, we consider the case of GVirtuS (GPU Virtualization Service) [10], one of the state-of-the-art solutions that allows sharing the power of a GPGPU among different applications running concurrently on a single machine. GVirtuS uses a virtualization approach: the virtualized service is transparent to the users running a GPGPU application, and there is little overhead compared to bare metal GPGPU setup. The fields of application are many, including Internet of Things, mobile code offloading, and others [11,13].

In this work, we present the evolution of GVirtuS[1], featuring a redesigned architecture and a general *code refactoring*. In order to modernize the framework and improve its performance, we have adopted and integrated new technologies and multi-threading techniques. We have also improved and restructured the build process, in order to improve software portability and simplify the management of external libraries.

The rest of the paper is organized as follows: Sect. 2 describes related work, Sect. 3 contains a description of the software architecture and the main design choices; Sect. 4 presents the new implementation of the GPU virtualization; Sect. 5 describes the performance tests and the obtained results; and finally, Sect. 6 draws conclusions and discusses some of the future planned developments.

2   Related Work

A comprehensive survey about GPGPU virtualization and remoting techniques is discussed in [7]. GPU virtualization solutions such as GVirtuS have been implemented by other research projects such as rCUDA [4,15,17] and Distributed-Shared CUDA (DS-CUDA) [14]. They use an approach similar to GVirtuS, providing CUDA API wrappers on the front-end application in the guest OS while the back-end in the host OS accesses the CUDA devices. We now discuss some of the differences between these solutions.

---

[1] https://github.com/gvirtus/GVirtuS.

CUDA Toolkit Supported Version: All GPGPU computing solutions mentioned above implement their functionalities using the CUDA Runtime API. None of them supports rendering specific graphic APIs, such as OpenGL[2] and Direct3D[3].

Communicator: The component that connects guest and host systems. GVirtuS supports several communicator protocols: TCP/IP sockets, WebSocket, Unix Sockets, VMSocket (for KVM based virtualization), and VMCI (for VMWare based virtualization). By default, rCUDA and DS-CUDA use InfiniBand Verbs and TCP/IP sockets as fallback.

Plug-in Architecture: GVirtuS supports CUDA and OpenCL, while rCUDA and DS-CUDA only support NVIDIA CUDA.

Transparency: Using GVirtus and rCUDA, CUDA enabled software is able to run on the remote GPUs without further changes to the source code. In order to enable DS-CUDA support, an application must include DS-CUDA specific extensions and it must be compiled using DS-CUDA specific tool-chain.

License: GVirtuS and DS-CUDA are both open source projects: the former is licensed under the Apache 2.0, while the latter is licensed under the GPLv3. rCUDA is proprietary software, but it is distributed for free under specified terms and conditions of use.

ARM Support: GVirtuS supports x86_64 and ARM hardware platforms. It supports all combinations of ARM and x86_64 on the front-end and the back-end (e.g. it is possible to run code from ARM front-end on a x86_64 back-end, and vice-versa). rCUDA also supports ARM and x86_64 platforms in a manner similar to GVirtuS [1], while DS-CUDA supports ARM front-ends but only x86_64 back-ends [8].

3   System Architecture and Design

GVirtuS is a generic virtualization framework for virtualization solutions. GVirtuS offers virtualization support for generic libraries such as accelerator libraries (CUDA, OpenCL), with the advantage of independence from all the involved technologies: hypervisor, communicator, and target virtualization. This feature is possible thanks to the plug-in design of the framework, enabling the choice of different communicators or different stub-libraries which mock the virtualization targets. GVirtuS is transparent for developers: no changes in the software source code are required to virtualize and execute applications, and there is no need to recompile an already compiled executable.

---

[2] https://www.opengl.org/.

[3] https://docs.microsoft.com/en-gb/windows/win32/direct3d.

3.1   Architecture

The virtualization system of GVirtuS is based on a *split driver approach* with two main components, **front-end** and **back-end**. The front-end component is deployed on the lightweight machines that don't have a GPU, while the back-end component is hosted on the real machine that accesses directly the GPU device. A hypervisor concurrently deploys the applications requiring access to the GPU accelerators as VM appliances. The device is under control of the hypervisor. An access to the GPU is routed via the front-end/back-end layers under control of a management component, and data are moved from GPU to guest VM application, and vice-versa. The front-end and the back-end layers implement the decoupling between the hypervisor and the communication layer. A key property of the proposed system is its ability to execute CUDA kernels and OpenCL with an overall performance similar to that obtained by real machines with direct access to the accelerators. This has been achieved by developing a component that provides a high performance communication between virtual machines and their hosts. The choice of the hypervisor deeply affects the efficiency of the communication between the guest and host machines and then between the GPU virtualization front-end and back-end. GVirtuS provides efficient communication for VMware[4] and KVM/Qemu[5] hypervisors (Fig. 1).

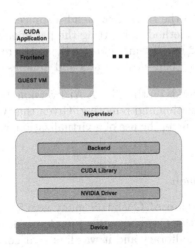

Fig. 1. Block diagram of the GVirtuS architecture.

3.2   Design

The front-end/back-end communication is abstracted by the *Communication* interface concretely implemented by each communicator component. The methods implemented by concrete communicator classes support request preparation,

---

[4] https://www.vmware.com/.

[5] https://www.linux-kvm.org.

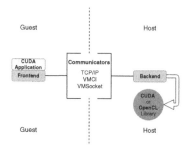

Fig. 2. The GVirtuS components.

input parameters management, request execution, error checking, and output data recovery. The back-end is executed on the host machine: it is a server program that runs as a user with enough privileges to interact with the CUDA driver (Fig. 2).

The back-end accepts new connections and spawns a new process to serve the front-end requests. The CUDA enabled application running on the virtual or remote machine requests GPGPU resources to the virtualized device using the stub-library. Each function in the stub-library follows these steps:

1. Obtains a reference to the single `Frontend` instance;
2. Uses `Frontend` class methods for setting the parameters;
3. Invokes the `Frontend` handler method specifying the remote procedure name;
4. Checks the remote procedure call results and handles output data.

GVirtuS strictly depends on the CUDA API version, because of the nature of the transparent virtualization and remoting. Given that CUDA is a proprietary solution and not open source, the use of a virtualization/remoting layer becomes inherently non trivial.

3.3   A Novel Approach

With the **third generation of GVirtuS** many new features have been added. The loading process of the *Communicator* has changed. Before, the *Communicator* was part of a static library and it was linked at compile time. In the new version, it is loaded at run time using a dynamic loading technique, the same used with the plug-in libraries. Moreover, the back-end can now use several `Communicator` objects: in this way the server can listen on multiple endpoints, each of them using a different communication protocol.

When the server is started, it launches a new process for each type of communicator indicated in the configuration file. When a process receives a request, it creates a new thread that serves it, and then it keeps listening for new requests from the clients. Thanks to this new thread model, each module and dynamic library is now loaded at startup and it is not unloaded after a request is served, whereas the old version loaded and unloaded modules for each different request.

As a result, the overall overhead is reduced for subsequent requests, as we show in Sect. 5.2.

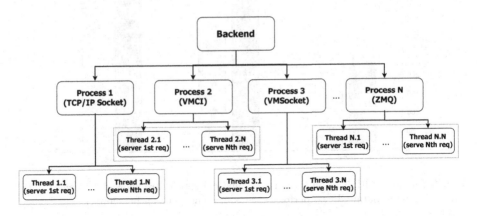

Fig. 3. The new back-end design.

There are several other features that have been added, such as JSON configuration file, signal state handlers, exceptions hierarchy, and much more. In order to support these changes, the overall architecture of the framework has undergone a substantial re-design (Fig. 3).

4   Implementation Details

Several new technologies have been used in the new version of GVirtuS.

Web-Sockets have been added to the Communicator suite, facilitating real-time data transfers from and to the server. **GTest** and **GMock**, powered by Google, have made possible to write test units quickly and easily. An important effort has been made to update the framework to the latest standards, such as the new **C++1z** standard[6], and many tools like **JSON** (JavaScript Object Notation), **TLS** (Transport Layer Security), and **zlib**[7] (DEFLATE data compression algorithm). Finally, an initial effort to introduce *asynchronous I/O* has been made, using the **libuv** library[8] (Node.js engine written in C). However, this feature is not fully tested and is not meant to be used in production yet.

5   Performance Evaluation

5.1   Workstation Setup

The workstation used for testing is equipped with a double Intel®Xeon®E5-**2609** v3 @ 1.90 GHz, a six-core hyper-threaded CPU with **15 MB** cache, and

---

[6] https://isocpp.org/std/status.

[7] https://www.zlib.net/.

[8] https://github.com/libuv/libuv.

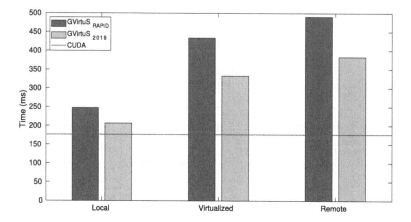

Fig. 4. Matrix multiplication test. Three physical setups are showed for each framework. The bare-metal CUDA performance is also showed as a benchmark line.

32 GB of DDR4 RAM. The GPU sub-system is composed of two NVIDIA GeForce GTX TITAN X GM200[9]. They are equipped with 3072 CUDA cores and **12 GB** of GDDR5 memory. The CUDA cores run at 1000 MHz, and the graphic memory runs at 1753 MHz. The testing system has been built on top of the CentOS 7 Linux operating system, the NVIDIA CUDA/OpenCL driver, and the SDK/Toolkit version 9.0.

5.2 Benchmarks

In this section, we show the benchmarks executed to test the performance of the latest version of GVirtuS, namely GVirtuS$_{2019}$ in the rest of the paper, against the bare CUDA and against the previous implementation of the framework, namely GVirtuS$_{RAPID}$. The performance has been measured using a program that computes **matrix multiplication**, a classic but highly relevant problem in scientific computing. The size of the real valued matrices (using 32 bit floating point arithmetic) used for testing are 320×320 and 320×640. First, we perform the matrix multiplication on the bare-metal CUDA setup, which is used as a benchmark for the other results achieved in the other physical setups, which are the following:

Local. The front-end and back-end is running on the same machine.
Virtualized. The front-end is running inside a virtual machine.
Remote. The front-end is running on a remote host and communicates with the back-end using TCP/IP sockets.

Figure 4 presents the results of the experiments, where the execution times using three physical setups for each framework are shown. Each column presents

---

[9] https://www.geforce.com/hardware/desktop-gpus/geforce-gtx-titan-x/specificat ions.

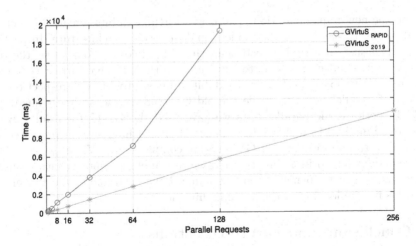

Fig. 5. Average times of parallel requests to the old and new version of GVirtuS.

the average execution time of 1000 runs of the matrix multiplication program using the matrices described above. Notice that in the presented experiments the matrices remain the same during all the executions. However, randomizing the values of the matrices still yields the same results. As it can be seen from the figure, the new release of GVirtuS has improved significantly from its previous version, performing 20% better in the *Local* setup and 25% better in the *Virtualized* and the *Remote* setups.

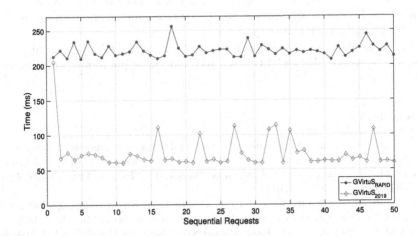

Fig. 6. After the first request is served, response times are reduced in GVirtuS2019.

Figure 5 shows the average response time for an increasing number of parallel requests to the GVirtuS back-end, and compares the performance between the old and the new implementation. The new GVirtuS exhibits remarkably better overall performance due to the modern multi-threaded architecture. In particular, it can sustain a higher load than the old version. In our tests, the old framework was indeed not able to sustain more than 128 concurrent requests. Moreover, GVirtuS$_{2019}$ performance exhibits a linear growth with respect to the number of parallel requests, while the old GVirtuS degrades almost quadratically. To perform the parallel tests we have used the **GNU Parallel power tool** [18]. Finally, Fig. 6 shows the impact of the caching system presented in Sect. 3.3 on the performance of GVirtuS$_{2019}$ compared to GVirtuS$_{RAPID}$. The first request is served in a time comparable to the old version, but each subsequent request greatly benefits from the reduced overhead due to the now eliminated loading/unloading of the dynamic libraries.

6   Conclusions and Future Directions

In this paper, we presented the third generation of the GVirtuS framework, a GPU virtualization and sharing service. The main aim of this upgrade was to improve the performance of the framework and to make it compliant with the latest technological standards. We have reported the results of an extensive testing process. We compared the performance of GVirtuS$_{2019}$ against the previous version, GVirtuS$_{RAPID}$. The results clearly show the performance boost achieved by GVirtuS$_{2019}$ compared to its predecessor. Moreover, considering benchmarks available in literature [3] and experiments performed with rCUDA, which we could not present in this paper due to its license restrictions[10], rCUDA performs slightly better than GVirtuS$_{2019}$. On the other hand, GVirtuS still offers advantages compared to a proprietary solution like rCUDA: it has an open source license, it supports a vast series of communication protocols, and provides OpenCL back-end support.

As future work, we will explore the performance of GVirtuS on high performance networks like 10G Ethernet and add the support for the Infiniband protocol [16].

References

1. Castelló, A., et al.: On the use of remote GPUs and low-power processors for the acceleration of scientific applications. In: The Fourth International Conference on Smart Grids, Green Communications and IT Energy-Aware Technologies (ENERGY), pp. 57–62 (2014)
2. Di Lauro, R., Giannone, F., Ambrosio, L., Montella, R.: Virtualizing general purpose GPUs for high performance cloud computing: an application to a fluid simulator. In: 2012 IEEE 10th International Symposium on Parallel and Distributed Processing with Applications, pp. 863–864. IEEE (2012)
3. Duato, J., Pena, A.J., Silla, F., Fernandez, J.C., Mayo, R., Quintana-Orti, E.S.: Enabling CUDA acceleration within virtual machines using rCUDA. In: 2011 18th International Conference on High Performance Computing, pp. 1–10. IEEE (2011)

---

[10] http://www.rcuda.net/pub/rCUDA_TOS.pdf.

4. Duato, J., Pena, A.J., Silla, F., Mayo, R., Quintana-Ortí, E.S.: rCUDA: reducing the number of GPU-based accelerators in high performance clusters. In: 2010 International Conference on High Performance Computing & Simulation, pp. 224–231. IEEE (2010)

5. Foster, I., Zhao, Y., Raicu, I., Lu, S.: Cloud computing and grid computing 360-degree compared. arXiv preprint arXiv:0901.0131 (2008)

6. Giunta, G., Montella, R., Agrillo, G., Coviello, G.: A GPGPU transparent virtualization component for high performance computing clouds. In: D'Ambra, P., Guarracino, M., Talia, D. (eds.) Euro-Par 2010. LNCS, vol. 6271, pp. 379–391. Springer, Heidelberg (2010). https://doi.org/10.1007/978-3-642-15277-1_37

7. Hong, C.H., Spence, I., Nikolopoulos, D.S.: Gpu virtualization and scheduling methods: a comprehensive survey. ACM Comput. Surv. (CSUR) 50(3), 35 (2017)

8. Martinez-Noriega, E.J., Kawai, A., Yoshikawa, K., Yasuoka, K., Narumi, T.: CUDA enabled for android tablets through DS-CUDA (2013)

9. Mell, P.: The NIST definition of cloud computing v15. http://csrc.nist.gov/groups/SNS/cloud-computing/ (2009)

10. Montella, R., Coviello, G., Giunta, G., Laccetti, G., Isaila, F., Blas, J.G.: A general-purpose virtualization service for HPC on cloud computing: an application to GPUs. In: Wyrzykowski, R., Dongarra, J., Karczewski, K., Waśniewski, J. (eds.) PPAM 2011. LNCS, vol. 7203, pp. 740–749. Springer, Heidelberg (2012). https://doi.org/10.1007/978-3-642-31464-3_75

11. Montella, R., Ferraro, C., Kosta, S., Pelliccia, V., Giunta, G.: Enabling Android-based devices to high-end GPGPUs. In: Carretero, J., Garcia-Blas, J., Ko, R.K.L., Mueller, P., Nakano, K. (eds.) ICA3PP 2016. LNCS, vol. 10048, pp. 118–125. Springer, Cham (2016). https://doi.org/10.1007/978-3-319-49583-5_9

12. Montella, R., et al.: On the virtualization of CUDA based GPU remoting on arm and X86 machines in the GVirtuS framework. Int. J. Parallel Prog. 45(5), 1142–1163 (2017)

13. Montella, R., et al.: Accelerating Linux and Android applications on low-power devices through remote GPGPU offloading. Concurr. Comput.: Pract. Exp. 29(24), e4286 (2017). https://doi.org/10.1002/cpe.4286. https://onlinelibrary.wiley.com/doi/abs/10.1002/cpe.4286, e4286 cpe.4286

14. Oikawa, M., Kawai, A., Nomura, K., Yasuoka, K., Yoshikawa, K., Narumi, T.: DS-CUDA: a middleware to use many GPUs in the cloud environment, pp. 1207–1214 (2012)

15. Reaño, C., Silla, F.: A performance comparison of CUDA remote GPU virtualization frameworks. In: 2015 IEEE International Conference on Cluster Computing, pp. 488–489. IEEE (2015)

16. Reaño, C., Silla, F.: Reducing the performance gap of remote GPU virtualization with InfiniBand Connect-IB. In: 2016 IEEE Symposium on Computers and Communication (ISCC), pp. 920–925. IEEE (2016)

17. Reaño, C., Silla, F., Shainer, G., Schultz, S.: Local and remote GPUs perform similar with EDR 100G InfiniBand. In: Proceedings of the Industrial Track of the 16th International Middleware Conference, p. 4. ACM (2015)

18. Tange, O., et al.: GNU parallel-the command-line power tool. USENIX Mag. 36(1), 42–47 (2011)

Design of Self-organizing Protocol for LoWPAN Networks

Matteo Buffa[✉], Fabrizio Messina[✉], Corrado Santoro[✉], and Federico Fausto Santoro[✉]

Department of Mathematics and Computer Science, University of Catania, Viale Andrea Doria, 6, 95123 Catania, Italy
{buffa,messina,santoro}@dmi.unict.it, federico.santoro@unict.it

Abstract. IoT technology is widely employed to solve the problem of large-scale monitoring, e.g. in the context of smart cities or smart industries. Nevertheless, several issues have to be addressed in this context. The number of nodes can be very large and, sometimes, nodes can be not be easily reachable for humans interventions. Other important issues are battery life and node failure, two aspects that can affect the quality of service provided by the IoT system as well as related costs. To deal with the aspects above we propose a LoWPAN (Low power Wire-less Personal Area Network) network protocol that supports an automatic network construction without any human intervention. The resulting network is a tree structure featuring a main node which, in turn, is linked with the wireless gateway and a number of middle nodes (the first layer of the tree), while the leafs are called End nodes. The network structure and the underlying protocol described in this paper are designed to face the problem of configuration and to balance inter-node communication to ensure a fair power consumption. The proposed approach also features self-repair capabilities, as it is able to perform automatic recovery after a node failure. A case study is briefly discussed to show a potential application of the described approach.

Keywords: Internet of Things · Wireless networks · Edge computing · Low power

1 Introduction

In the last few years, we witnessed an impressive growth of the *Internet-of-Things* technology [2,10], with the consequent widespread of IoT devices that, used in any kind of large-scale applications, are employed to form very big networks and manage very large quantities of data.

Among IoT applications, the theme of *Smart Cities* [19] is becoming increasingly popular: in such a context, IoT devices are used to exchange information about public transportation, traffic, air quality (pollution), etc., and, in the near future, it is expected that also traffic lights will be automated according to the historical data collected over time. Such devices can send these information to

© Springer Nature Switzerland AG 2019
R. Montella et al. (Eds.): IDCS 2019, LNCS 11874, pp. 424–433, 2019.
https://doi.org/10.1007/978-3-030-34914-1_40

our cars, allowing drivers (or even cars themselves) to choose the best route, in terms of efficiency (time navigation) and air quality [19]. Devices can be also installed directly in sensitive parts of city buildings, collecting information through appropriate sensors (like accelerometers) with the objective of making the system able to try to predict stability problems or identify events due to natural forces, such as earthquakes.

Also in the context of *smart industries*, IoT technology is giving a great support: indeed, in production chains, not only a timely monitoring of the operating machines is essential but, above all, the just-in-time prediction of failures is very important [7].

However, even if the IoT technology promises to solve the problem of large-scale monitoring, it poses a series of important issues that, in many cases, represent a big limitation. In IoT applications, the size of the system, in terms of number of nodes, is very large, ranging from hundreds to thousand of devices, thus posing a serious problem in terms of configuration, initialization and maintenance of the network, operations that cannot surely be done using a manual intervention device-per-device. From this point of view, there is not a common or standardized or even state-of-the-art approach, but each specific application follows its own rules and guidelines.

Another critical issue is battery life: basically IoT devices consume a lot of energy when communicating with the access point (that often acts also as a gateway), therefore power consumption must be optimized and balanced otherwise the switching-off of a devices–if frequent–would cause network structure's changes and the consequent waste of energy, thus reducing the whole network's lifetime.

Battery depletion, as well as other kind of node failures, causes the disappearance of that node from the network, with consequences that, in some cases, could be quite harmful (think, for example, to the case in which the failed node acts as a gateway). While human intervention could surely solve the problem, the ability of self-repairing is surely a desirable feature.

Given the premises above, this paper presents a LoWPAN (Low power Wireless Personal Area Network) network protocol aimed at facing the cited issues. Basically, it supports an automatic network construction (without human intervention) by creating a layered tree structure featuring one *Lead node*, linked with the wireless gateway, some *Middle nodes*, acting as normal nodes and as links between their child nodes and the rest of the network, forwarding packets; finally the *End nodes* (at the leaves of the tree) with the role of sending and receiving data from them to the rest of the network. Such a network structure, as well as the underlying protocol, not only faces the problem of configuration but is also able to balance communication among nodes in order to ensure a fair power consumption. In addition, the protocol features self-repair capabilities since it is able to identify node failures and perform automatic recovery and re-configuration of the network, if needed.

The paper is organized as follows. Section 2 discusses the related work. Section 3 present the details of the proposed protocol. Section 4 discusses a relevant case study in the field, in order to show the advantages of the proposed approach. Finally, Sect. 5 reports our conclusions.

2   Related Works

The advent of low-cost, low-powers smart devices has encouraged the development of novel technologies aimed at supporting low-power communications for low-cost devices.

Contiki [6] is an open source, lightweight operating system designed to support dynamic loading and replacement of IoT programs and services. The Contiki kernel is event-driven and provides optional preemptive multi-threading; it provides feasibility for resource constrained environment, as it allows the developer to keep the base system lightweight and compact. Contiki supports IPv4 and IPv6, as well as several low-power wireless standard, as 6lowpan [15], RPL [1] and CoAP [3]. It provides interesting capabilities as ContikiMAC [5] and sleepy routers [12] to support battery-operated routers.

OpenThread [11,13] was released by Google as an open-source implementation of the IoT standard named Thread [9]. Google released OpenThread to support networking into its own products known as Google Nest (smart devices for home), and to allow developers to easily develop applications. The focus of OpenThread is portability which is achieved by a platform abstraction layer and a small memory footprint. It supports both system-on-chip (SoC) [16] and network co-processor (NCP) designs [8].

LoRaWAN [4,17] (Long Range Wide Area Network Protocol for Internet of Things) is a data-link layer with long range, low power, and low bit rate specifically designed for the IoT. The LoRaWAN architecture define a "star of stars" topology, where the physical layer, LoRa, enables the long range link. The protocol has positive effects on the node battery lifetime, the network capacity, QoS and security.

As we discuss in the next section, the protocol described in this paper relies on the 802.15.4 protocol [14].

3   The Proposed Protocol

The proposed protocol is built on top of 802.15.4 protocol [14] which allows IoT devices to connect to each other under a single LoWPAN in a large physical area. In the following of this section, we will describe the various elements of the protocol.

Network Topology. The protocol is designed to construct the network as a tree of variable depth. In the tree, every node can act as a repeater and can have several down links and a single up link. The protocol provides an upper limit for the down links of each node.

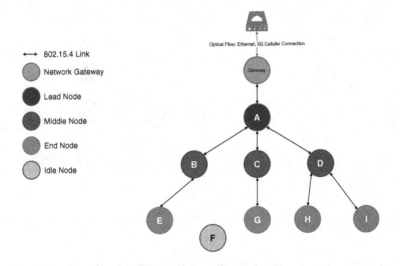

Fig. 1. A network protocol topology and node types.

As Fig. 1 shows, the network is a multi-hop network on which the "lead node" (i.e. the root of the tree) is linked to the gateway. The Lead node is the top node in the network (the root of the tree) and is connected to the Gateway. Only one Lead node can exists in a network and can have only one up link with the Gateway. The Gateway (or hub) is a device with which the IoT devices (so the other nodes) can communicate thought the internet. Typically, this device is connected to the Internet via cable connection (Optical Fiber, Ethernet) or mobile connection (LTE/4G, 5G). The protocol also specifies an upper bound for the number of layers (depth of the tree). The remaining nodes of the tree are labeled End nodes, Middle nodes and Idle nodes. An End node is a leaf of the tree, it will send packets to its own neighbours towards the gateway. A Middle node has a single uplink to its parent and a number of downlinks to its own child nodes. Any node can send packets to any other node through its own neighbours. An Idle node is a node that has to join the network and, therefore, it will attempt to form an up link with a middle node.

Presentation Frame. Every node is able to make a downlink transmitting, periodically, a special packet that is a presentation frame. The presentation frame allows the node itself to send its own identity to the other nodes: the protocol uses the device information as well as metadata related to the role of node (lead, middle, end, idle), current layer, maximum number of allowed layers in the network, current number of downlinks (children number) and the maximum number of allowed down links. Other important data are also available such as the uptime of each node and the mean RSSI (Received Signal Strength Indicator); these values are used to quantify the reliability of the node itself. We will discuss in detail this aspect later.

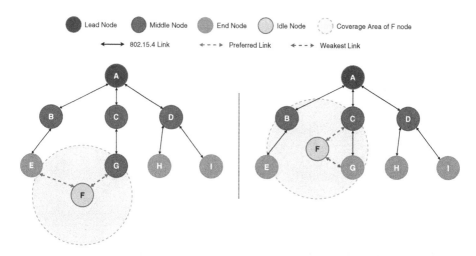

Fig. 2. Left: the idle node prefer the node with stronger RSSI. Right: the idle node prefer the node with higher layer level.

An Idle node listens for these special packets in order to collect a list of nodes which can potentially become its own parent. When an Idle node receives a presentation frame it saves the RSSI. In particular, in order to prevent the creation of weak uplinks, the protocol specifies a threshold for the RSSI: the sender of the presentation frame is added to the list of candidates only in the case the frame RSSI is above the threshold. When an Idle node has more than one candidates, it will look at the (i) layer to which the node belongs to, then the (ii) number of down links, (iii) the RSSI and (iv) finally the node uptime. The Idle node will select the candidate having the lowest layer number (i.e. the candidate that resides in the layer nearest to the Lead node). If there is only one node satisfying this criteria, it will be the new parent, otherwise it has to look at the number of downlink of the several candidates. In this case the node having the lowest number of downlink (i.e. with the lowest number of child nodes) is selected (this choice allows the protocol to balance the communication load of the network). If there are several nodes with the same (lowest) number of child nodes, the Idle node will look at the RSSI value (the highest is preferred) and, finally the value of uptime. An example of this process is depicted in Fig. 2.

Routing. The routing process is very simple. Each node maintains its own routing table containing the MAC (Medium Access Protocol) addresses of all the nodes belonging to the node's sub-network, while the lead node holds the global routing table of the network. As a consequence, any node, having to send a message to another node, can have or not the destination address in its own routing table. In the first case, the node forwards the data packet to the destination MAC address contained in the sub-network owned by the node itself. In the latter case, the node will send the packet to its parent node. The routing mechanism prevents loop back during the middle node selection, excluding nodes that are already present in the selecting middle node's routing table, thus preventing that a node connects to any node within its sub-network.

Lead Node Selection. This process is based on a voting mechanism, involving all the nodes in the network. Each node will broadcast its own RSSI and its own MAC address to each other. In a second phase the nodes will send a broadcast message containing the couple {MAC address, RSSI} with the highest RSSI among those received from all the other nodes, as well as its own couple {RSSI,MAC}. This message is, in fact, a vote for the candidate represented by the first couple {RSSI, MAC} of the message. This process is repeated until the nodes reach a convergence on the best node in terms of RSSI. There may be the case that two or more nodes have the same (highest) RSSI and the same number of votes to become a lead node; in this case the decision mechanism is mainly based on the candidate's nodes uptime, while the RSSI is no more a discrimination value.

Network Node Connection. In a real environment, devices do not power-on synchronously, therefore the network will be built according to the power-on order of devices. For this reason, in the proposed protocol, the following set of rules holds:

1. When an idle node has to join the network, it must evaluate which role it will cover. In case a Lead node already exists, even if the Idle node has a stronger RSSI with Gateway than the Lead node, it will not start an election to become lead node, to prevent the energy waste during the process; it will join the network minimizing the network's structure changes. Therefore the node will join the network as Idle node and it will connect to the best middle node selected among the received presentation frames, as discussed before.

2. When a node connects to the network (to create an up link to its own parent) it may become a new potential middle node for some other nodes. This is possible with a periodically transmission of presentation frame allowing to check the availability of a highest (in terms of height in the tree) middle node. In this way, the network can automatically rectify itself to guarantee that each link has a high connection quality and the number of layers in the network is minimized.

Node Failure. In the event of a node failure, the protocol holds different strategies, depending on the role of the failing node, which can be (A) the Lead Node (B) a Middle Node or an (C) End Node.

(A) When the Lead Node fails (Fig. 3), the new Lead nodes will be chosen by only the nodes of the second layer of the network. The voting mechanism is the same used at network construction time. Once elected, the new Lead node will connect to the gateway, and the nodes residing in the second

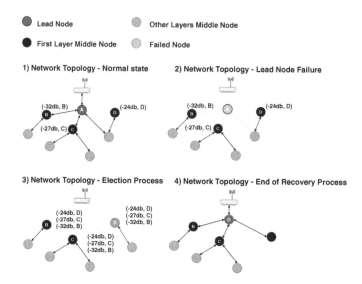

Fig. 3. Lead Node failure: the recovery process involves only nodes residing in the first layer and thus the only ones with the strongest RSSI to the gateway.

layer will link to it. The strategy to limit the election of the Lead node to the nodes residing in the first layer is aimed at minimizing the energy consumption. Moreover, given the construction rules of the network, which are based on the evaluation of node with strong RSSI, it is generally not very useful to involve nodes with an RSSI lower than the first layer's nodes.

(B) When a Middle node fails (Fig. 4), all the nodes previously connected to them become idle for a certain amount of time, waiting that the same node returns available. After a given timeout, it is assumed that the middle node is in failing state, then the idle nodes will look for the first available node to connect to. The choice is based on the mechanism discussed before for the connection of a new node. It may also arise a scenario where there is no any eligible node (i.e. RSSI under the threshold) to replace the failed Middle node. In this case the orphan nodes will create a link with one of the node residing in their current layer. This will result in the addition of a new layer in the tree. If the maximum number of layers is already reached, then a new layer cannot be added. In this case the system will modify the RSSI threshold in order to allow the orphans to select a new Middle node from the same layer of the failed Middle node.

(C) When an End Node fails, the only task to perform is represented by the deletion of the corresponding entry in the routing table of any node previously attached to it.

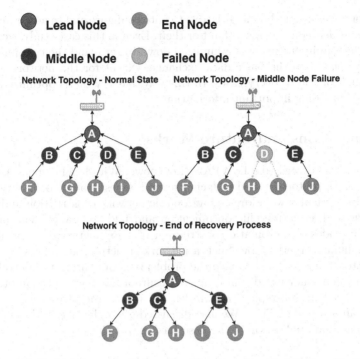

Fig. 4. Middle Node failure: the Recovery process involves End Nodes directly linked to the failed Middle Node.

4   Case Study

The approach described in this paper can be adopted to monitor the production status of hives in beekeeping [18]. Sensors of the LoWPAN network can be placed into every beehive to monitor the internal temperature of the hives and even the sound made by bees, which is an health indicator for them.

Moreover, it is desirable that the LoWPAN network can act as anti theft because beehives are often stolen. To this end, the protocol must be able to adapt and distinguish a fault from a theft; in the last case, a theft can be perceived as an abnormal change in the typical behaviour of one or more node: the gyroscope of the device will record an unusual movement (that excludes a fall from the original position), and start also evaluating the latency of communication. The latency measure is useful to understand how many other hives are being stolen and allows them to form a subnet that lasts as much as possible. Only one node a time is selected to use GPS (Global Positioning System) until it exhaust the battery. All other nodes will follow the same behaviour until all of them will consume their own battery. This represents an optimization to maximize network duration. More in general, every hive is seen as a single node; each node has a precise role inside of the network, and is responsible of its own communication and to forward other node's communication. It has a routing table with a MAC address of the associated node. It is able to auto configure and to adapt and make autonomous decisions in case of fault or theft. Even in this case study, we remark that the human intervention is minimized down to zero, and the communication is strictly related to the basic data exchange, except for the network building process and for the recovery cases. In this way, battery life is optimized to last more without losing important information.

5   Conclusions and Future Works

In this paper we described a LoWPAN (Low power Wire-less Personal Area Network) network protocol aimed at facing several issues related to the Internet of Things. In particular we addressed automatic network construction and configuration as well as battery life optimization and fault tolerance. The proposed solution provides an automatic construction of a IoT network which does not need any human intervention. Such a network structure, as well as the underlying protocol are designed to face the problem of configuration and to balance communication among nodes in order to ensure a fair power consumption. We have described its self-repair capabilities, as well as the process of automatic recovery after a node failure. We also discussed a simple case study in order to show a potential application of the described approach.

References

1. Accettura, N., Grieco, L.A., Boggia, G., Camarda, P.: Performance analysis of the RPL routing protocol. In: 2011 IEEE International Conference on Mechatronics, pp. 767–772. IEEE (2011)
2. Atzori, L., Iera, A., Morabito, G.: The Internet of Things: a survey. Comput. Netw. **54**(15), 2787–2805 (2010)
3. Bormann, C., Castellani, A.P., Shelby, Z.: CoAP: an application protocol for billions of tiny internet nodes. IEEE Internet Comput. **2**, 62–67 (2012)
4. de Carvalho Silva, J., Rodrigues, J.J., Alberti, A.M., Solic, P., Aquino, A.L.: LoRAWAN–a low power wan protocol for Internet of Things: a review and opportunities. In: 2017 2nd International Multidisciplinary Conference on Computer and Energy Science (SpliTech), pp. 1–6. IEEE (2017)
5. Dunkels, A.: The ContikiMAC radio duty cycling protocol (2011)
6. Dunkels, A., Gronvall, B., Voigt, T.: Contiki-a lightweight and flexible operating system for tiny networked sensors. In: 29th Annual IEEE International Conference on Local Computer Networks, pp. 455–462. IEEE (2004)
7. Gaur, A., Scotney, B., Parr, G., McClean, S.: Smart city architecture and its applications based on IoT. Procedia Comput. Sci. **52**, 1089–1094 (2015)
8. Giladi, R.: Network Processors: Architecture, Programming, and Implementation. Morgan Kaufmann, Burlington (2008)
9. Group T.T.: Thread (2019). https://www.threadgroup.org/
10. Gubbi, J., Buyya, R., Marusic, S., Palaniswami, M.: Internet of Things (IoT): a vision, architectural elements, and future directions. Future Gener. Comput. Syst. **29**(7), 1645–1660 (2013)
11. Openthread Inc., G: Openthread (2019). https://openthread.io/

12. Kalyoncu, S.: Wireless solutions and authentication mechanisms for Contiki based Internet of Things networks (2013)
13. Kim, H.S., Kumar, S., Culler, D.E.: Thread/openthread: a compromise in low-power wireless multihop network architecture for the Internet of Things. IEEE Commun. Mag. **57**, 55–61 (2019)
14. Kushalnagar, N., Montenegro, G.: Transmission of IPv6 packets over IEEE 802.15. 4 networks (2007)
15. Mulligan, G.: The 6LoWPAN architecture. In: Proceedings of the 4th Workshop on Embedded Networked Sensors, pp. 78–82. ACM (2007)
16. Rajsuman, R.: System-on-a-Chip: Design and Test. Artech House Inc., Norwood (2000)
17. Sornin, N., Luis, M., Eirich, T., Kramp, T., Hersent, O.: Lorawan Specification. LoRa Alliance, London (2015)
18. Zacepins, A., Kviesis, A., Ahrendt, P., Richter, U., Tekin, S., Durgun, M.: Bee-keeping in the future—smart apiary management. In: 2016 17th International Carpathian Control Conference (ICCC), pp. 808–812. IEEE (2016)
19. Zanella, A., Bui, N., Castellani, A., Vangelista, L., Zorzi, M.: Internet of Things for smart cities. IEEE Internet Things J. **1**(1), 22–32 (2014)

Rough–Fuzzy Entropy in Neighbourhood Characterization

Antonio Maratea and Alessio Ferone$^{(\boxtimes)}$

Department of Science and Technologies, University of Naples "Parthenope",
80143 Naples, Italy
{antonio.maratea,alessio.ferone}@uniparthenope.it

Abstract. The Entropy has been used to characterize the neighbourhood of a sample on the base of its k Nearest Neighbour when data are imbalanced and many measures of Entropy have been proposed in the literature to better cope with vagueness, exploiting fuzzy logic, rough set theory and their derivatives. In this paper, a rough extension of Entropy is proposed to measure uncertainty and ambiguity in the neighbourhood of a sample, using the lower and upper approximations from rough–fuzzy set theory in order to compute the Entropy of the set of the k Nearest Neighbours of a sample. The proposed measure shows better robustness to noise and allows a more flexible modeling of vagueness with respect to the Fuzzy Entropy.

Keywords: Rough–fuzzy Entropy · Fuzzy classification · Imbalanced classification

1 Introduction

While probability in all of its interpretations is the undisputed queen of the measures of uncertainty, there is no general agreement on who is the king when it comes to measure ambiguity, imprecision and vagueness. Fuzzy logic is certainly one pillar on top of which subsequent theories of vagueness have been founded, but many hybridizations of fuzzy logic with other theories of vagueness (even with probability, see for example [3]) have been proposed in the literature over the years.

When the neighborhood of a sample should be characterized with respect to a classification problem, such characterization can be based on the clustering structure of the data, on the data density in a given neighborhood of each instance x_i or on its k Nearest Neighbours. The underlying idea in all these cases is first to evaluate *locally* the class distribution and then to use this information in order to scale the importance of x_i during learning, reducing the weight for the most ambiguous (or uncertain) instances. Among local methods, fuzzy classifiers have been proposed to handle overlapping and ambiguous classes, in a variety of ways, but most of them use the Shannon Entropy to derive memberships. Intuitively, the more the neighborhood of an instance is uncertain, the more

© Springer Nature Switzerland AG 2019
R. Montella et al. (Eds.): IDCS 2019, LNCS 11874, pp. 434–443, 2019.
https://doi.org/10.1007/978-3-030-34914-1_41

balanced should be its membership to the various classes and the less important should be its influence on the learning process (see for example [1,2,4,6,9,10]).

In the following, a new rough–fuzzy measure of Entropy will be introduced to characterize the neighborhood of an instance, showing that it is more robust to noise and more flexible with respect to the fuzzy Entropy when evaluating the influence of that instance on the learning process.

The paper is organized as follows: in Sect. 2, the theory underlying different rough and fuzzy hybridizations is presented; in Sect. 3, the classical Shannon Entropy measure, along with the fuzzy and the proposed rough–fuzzy extensions, are analyzed in detail; in Sect. 4, preliminary results are reported; in Sect. 5, final considerations are drawn and future developments pinpointed.

2 Rough and Fuzzy Hybridizations

Rough Sets can be framed into classic set algebra, where the subsets of the Universe U are the bricks that build the lower and the upper approximation of a set: for a given set, the collection of subsets of the Universe representing its lower approximation, or *core*, are the elements that certainly belong to the set, while the collection of subsets representing its upper approximation are the elements that possibly belong to the set; finally, the set difference between the upper and the lower approximation is called *boundary*. This representation allows to explicitly model the lack of information and to account for vagueness, even if all involved sets are crisp.

Alternatively, Rough Sets can be framed into fuzzy set algebra, where the subsets of the Universe building the upper and lower approximations of a set are identified through a fuzzy equivalence relation, with separate membership functions for the lower an the upper approximation. In this case, the rough membership functions can be thought as a special type of fuzzy memberships, simply derivable by cardinality of sets. A probability function on the Universe can actually be used to define rough membership functions [15].

From a fuzzy perspective, lower and upper approximations can be defined with respect to a fuzzy set X as follows:

$$\underline{X} = \{x | \mu_X(x) = 1\} \tag{1}$$

$$\overline{X} = \{x | \mu_X(x) > 0\} \tag{2}$$

where $\underline{X}$ and $\overline{X}$ are the core and the support of the fuzzy set X and μ_X is its membership function, respectively.

Rough and fuzzy set theories model different facets of vagueness and it comes as no surprise that many efforts have been done in the scientific literature to combine them and exploit the advantages of both [7,8].

Much of the hybridization efforts between fuzzy and rough set theory is logically based, backing on their origins, however three combinations of rough set theory and fuzzy set theory have become dominant and have led to distinct generalizations of classical set theory:

- given a crisp equivalence relation on the universe of discourse, a fuzzy set
  can be approximated with a lower and upper approximation of the fuzzy set,
  obtaining a *rough–fuzzy set*;
- given a fuzzy equivalence relation on the universe of discourse, a crisp set can
  be approximated with a fuzzy lower and upper approximation of the crisp
  set, obtaining a *fuzzy rough set* [5];
- given a fuzzy equivalence relation on the universe of discourse, a fuzzy set can
  be approximated with a fuzzy lower and upper approximation of the fuzzy
  set, obtaining a *fuzzy rough–fuzzy set*.

Hence the approximation of a fuzzy set in a crisp approximation space is called
a rough-fuzzy set and the approximation of a crisp set in a fuzzy approximation
space is called a fuzzy–rough set. The approximation of a fuzzy set in a fuzzy
approximation space is considered to be a more general model, unifying the two
theories. The different combinations are listed in Table 1 (please see [12]). By
consequence, the expressions for the lower ($\underline{R}X$) and upper ($\overline{R}X$) approximations of a set X depend on the nature of relation R (crisp or fuzzy) and set X
(crisp or fuzzy).

Table 1. Different combinations of rough and fuzzy sets.

X	R	$\langle \underline{R}X, \overline{R}X \rangle$	U/R
Crisp	Crisp equivalence relation	Rough set of X	Crisp approximation space
Fuzzy	Crisp equivalence relation	Rough–fuzzy set of X	Crisp approximation space
Crisp	Fuzzy equivalence relation	Fuzzy–rough set of X	Fuzzy approximation space
Fuzzy	Fuzzy equivalence relation	Fuzzy–rough–fuzzy set of X	Fuzzy approximation space

The general formulae including all the above cases follow:

$$\underline{R}X = \{(x, \underline{\mu}(x)) | x \in U\} \tag{3}$$
$$\overline{R}X = \{(x, \overline{\mu}(x)) | x \in U\} \tag{4}$$

where

$$\underline{\mu}(x) = \sum_{Y \in U/R} \mu_Y(x) \times \inf_{\varphi \in U} \max(1 - \mu_Y(\varphi), \mu_X(\varphi)) \tag{5}$$

$$\overline{\mu}(x) = \sum_{Y \in U/R} \mu_Y(x) \times \sup_{\varphi \in U} \min(\mu_Y(\varphi), \mu_X(\varphi)). \tag{6}$$

$\underline{\mu}(x)$ is the degree of membership of element x to the lower approximation $\underline{R}X$
and $\overline{\mu}(x)$ is the degree of membership of element x to the upper approximation
$\overline{R}X$; the membership function μ_Y represents the degree of belonging of each
element $x \in U$ to a granule $Y \in U/R$ and takes values in $[0, 1]$, and μ_X is the

membership function associated with X that takes values in $[0, 1]$. When X is a crisp set, μ_X would take values only from the set $\{0, 1\}$. Similarly, when R is a crisp equivalence relation, μ_Y would take values only from the set $\{0, 1\}$.

The operators for fuzzy union and intersection are chosen based on their suitability to the considered application. The pair of sets $\langle \underline{R}X, \overline{R}X \rangle$ and the approximation space U/R are referred to differently, depending on whether X is a crisp or a fuzzy set and the relation R is a crisp or a fuzzy equivalence relation.

Another hybridization possibility is reported in [14], where the negative, boundary and positive regions of a rough set are expressed by means of a fuzzy membership function: all objects in the positive region have membership 1, all objects in the boundary have membership 0.5, while all objects in the negative region have membership 0 (do not belong at all to the rough set). After suitable modifications of the rough union and intersection operators, this model allows to express a rough set as a fuzzy set.

3   Entropy Measures

Many generalizations of the classic Shannon Entropy have been proposed in the literature, exploiting the different theories that handle vagueness. In the following, the k Nearest Neighbours of an instance x_i will be considered to evaluate the local ambiguity in the neighbourhood of x_i so to cope with vagueness and noise. A two-class problem will be assumed.

3.1   Shannon Entropy

The Shannon Entropy H_i is computed considering x_i's k Nearest Neighbors:

$$H_i = -p_{+i} ln(p_{+i}) - p_{-i} ln(p_{-i}) \tag{7}$$

where

$$p_{+i} = \frac{num_{+i}}{k}, \; p_{-i} = \frac{num_{-i}}{k} \tag{8}$$

num_{+i} and num_{-i} are the number of instances belonging to positive and negative class, respectively.

When H is maximum, classes in the neighbourhood of x_i are equally likely and there is the maximum ambiguity. H has been used in [6] to compute fuzzy memberships as:

$$f(x_i) = 1 - H_i \tag{9}$$

3.2   Fuzzy Entropy

The Fuzzy Entropy FH_i is computed considering x_i's k Nearest Neighbors:

$$FH_i = -\mu_{+i} p_{+i} ln(p_{+i}) - \mu_{-i} p_{-i} ln(p_{-i}) \tag{10}$$

where

$$\mu_{+i} = \frac{\sum_{j=1}^{k} u_{+i}(1/ \parallel x_i - x_j \parallel^{2/(m-1)})}{\sum_{j=1}^{k}(1/ \parallel x_i - x_j \parallel^{2/(m-1)})} \tag{11}$$

$$\mu_{-i} = \frac{\sum_{j=1}^{k} u_{-i}(1/ \parallel x_i - x_j \parallel^{2/(m-1)})}{\sum_{j=1}^{k}(1/ \parallel x_i - x_j \parallel^{2/(m-1)})} \tag{12}$$

and $u_{+i} = 1$ if x_i belongs to positive class and 0 otherwise; $u_{-i} = 1$ if x_i belongs to negative class and 0 otherwise.

FH has been used in [11], it considers also the distance among the k neighbours and hence it has proven to be more powerful in evaluating actual ambiguity with respect to H. The *Fuzzy Entropy*-based fuzzy membership is:

$$f(x_i) = 1 - FH_i \tag{13}$$

3.3 Rough–Fuzzy Entropy

According to [14], objects in the lower approximation of a set are unambiguous, clearly discernible, hence they should have an unambiguous assignation and an higher influence on the Entropy; while objects in the boundary are ambiguous, indiscernible, hence they should have a non-zero membership to more than one set and a lower influence on the Entropy. Translated into fuzzy terms, this means that objects in the lower approximations of different sets should have membership 1 in their sets and 0 in the other sets; while object in the boundary region should have a non zero membership in at least two sets.

In this paper the set of the k Nearest Neighbors is modelled as a rough–fuzzy set, where objects belonging to the lower approximation and those belonging to the boundary contribute differently to the Entropy of each object x_i. Specifically, all objects (among the k) belonging to the lower approximation are unambiguous and less affected by noise and hence contribute more to the membership, while objects in the boundary are ambiguous, more sensitive to the noise, and contribute with a lower weight to the membership.

The lower approximation of a set of k Nearest Neighbors is defined as:

$$\underline{R}X_i = \{x_j| \parallel x_i - x_j \parallel^{2/(m-1)} < \epsilon\} \tag{14}$$

$$\overline{R}X_i = \{(x_j| \parallel x_i - x_j \parallel^{2/(m-1)} \geq \epsilon\} \tag{15}$$

from which, the rough–fuzzy Entropy RFH_i is computed considering the k Nearest Neighbors of x_i:

$$RFH_i = -\mu_{+i}p_{+i}ln(p_{+i}) - \mu_{-i}p_{-i}ln(p_{-i}) \tag{16}$$

where

$$\mu_{+i} = \frac{\sum_{j=1}^{k} u_{+i}(1/ \parallel x_i - x_j \parallel^{2/(m-1)})}{\sum_{j=1}^{k}(1/ \parallel x_i - x_j \parallel^{2/(m-1)})} \tag{17}$$

$$\mu_{-i} = \frac{\sum_{j=1}^{k} u_{-i}(1/ \parallel x_i - x_j \parallel^{2/(m-1)})}{\sum_{j=1}^{k}(1/ \parallel x_i - x_j \parallel^{2/(m-1)})} \tag{18}$$

and $u_{+i} = 1$ if x_i belongs to positive class and $x_i \in \underline{R}X_i$, $u_{+i} = \alpha$ if x_i belongs to positive class and $x_i \in \overline{R}X_i$ and 0 otherwise. Similarly, $u_{+i} = 1$ if x_i belongs to negative class and $x_i \in \underline{R}X_i$, $u_{+i} = \alpha$ if x_i belongs to negative class and $x_i \in \overline{R}X_i$ and 0 otherwise.

The final Fuzzy Entropy-based fuzzy membership is computed as follows:

$$f(x_i) = 1 - RFH_i \tag{19}$$

4   Experiments

In this section some preliminary tests are reported showing that the memberships computed using rough–fuzzy Entropy better handle noise with respect to the pure fuzzy memberships, keeping the same level of expressiveness. A two classes dataset $D1$ has been generated by drawing 1000 2-D points (350 points from class 1 and 650 from class 2) from two bi-variate Gaussian distributions with co-variance matrix $\Sigma = \begin{bmatrix} 0.01 & 0.001 \\ 0.001 & 0.01 \end{bmatrix}$ and means $\mu_1 = [0.4, 0.5]$ for class 1 and $\mu_2 = [0.6, 0.5]$ for class 2.

Another dataset $D2$ has been generated adding Gaussian noise to $D1$, with $\mu = 0$ and $\sigma = 0.1$. For each dataset the following plots have been generated:

- histogram of memberships based on fuzzy Entropy;
- histogram of memberships based on rough–fuzzy Entropy;
- histogram of memberships difference;
- boxplot of fuzzy entropies;
- boxplot of rough–fuzzy entropies;
- boxplot of memberships difference.

In the following: $k = 10$; the parameter ϵ used to define the lower and upper approximation is set so that $1/3$ of the k points belong to the lower approximation and $2/3$ belong to the boundary; $\alpha = 0.5$.

Figure 1 shows how rough–fuzzy memberships are slightly higher than fuzzy memberships. Moreover the rough–fuzzy memberships span a broader range of values, meaning a slightly better capability in handling uncertainty. The same consideration stands for the noisy dataset $D2$ (Fig. 2).

More interesting is the ability to handle noisy samples when using the rough–fuzzy approach. In order to highlight the difference, the histogram of the differences between the memberships computed with and without noise are presented for both approaches in Fig. 3.

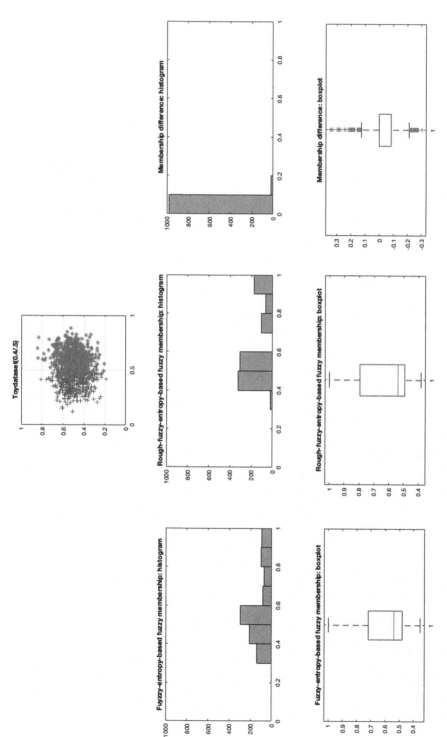

Fig. 1. Plots of dataset D1 (without noise). Left: histogram and boxplot of fuzzy memberships; Center: histogram and boxplot of rough–fuzzy memberships; Right: histogram and boxplot of the difference between rough–fuzzy and fuzzy memberships.

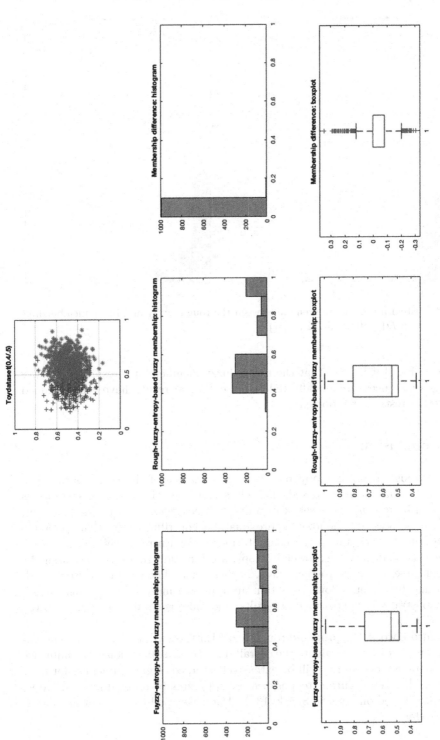

Fig. 2. Plots of dataset *D2* (with added noise). Left: histogram and boxplot of fuzzy memberships; Center: histogram and boxplot of rough–fuzzy memberships; Right: histogram and boxplot of difference between rough–fuzzy and fuzzy memberships.

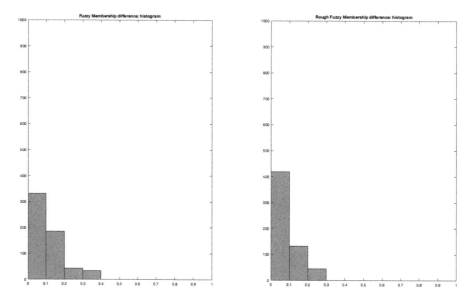

Fig. 3. Histogram of the differences between the rough–fuzzy and fuzzy memberships computed on $D1$ (left) and $D2$ (right).

From Fig. 3 it is clear that the rough–fuzzy memberships, resulting in lower average differences, are less affected by noise. Similar results have been obtained with other tests (not reported).

5   Conclusion

A novel rough–fuzzy Entropy–based characterization of the neighbourhood of an instance has been proposed. The class certainty of a training instance is evaluated by modeling the set of its k–Nearest Neighbors as a rough–fuzzy set, in which instances in the lower approximations contribute more than instances in the boundary region to the computation of the Entropy: the samples with higher class certainty, i.e., lower Entropy, are less ambiguous and are assigned an higher memberships to their class, or vice versa. The combined use of both rough and fuzzy sets allows to obtain an approach more robust against noise, as demonstrated by experimental results, and more general with respect to the fuzzy Entropy.

In future work, the proposed rough fuzzy Entropy will be tested in a classification task in order to evaluate the overall robustness against noise; the influence of the parameters ϵ and m will be extensively studied to give guidelines for their choice and a new solution to perform an approximate rough–fuzzy k-Nearest Neighbors based on Apache Spark [13] will be developed to cope with challenging real data.

References

1. Batuwita, R., Palade, V.: FSVM-CIL: fuzzy support vector machines for class imbalance learning. IEEE Trans. Fuzzy Syst. **18**(3), 558–571 (2010)
2. Boonchuay, K., Sinapiromsaran, K., Lursinsap, C.: Decision tree induction based on minority entropy for the class imbalance problem. Pattern Anal. Appl. **20**(3), 769–782 (2017)
3. Buckley, J.J.: Fuzzy Probability and Statistics. Springer, Heidelberg (2006). https://doi.org/10.1007/3-540-33190-5
4. Chen, Y., Wu, K., Chen, X., Tang, C., Zhu, Q.: An entropy-based uncertainty measurement approach in neighborhood systems. Inf. Sci. **279**, 239–250 (2014)
5. Dubois, D., Prade, H.: Rough fuzzy sets and fuzzy rough sets*. Int. J. Gen Syst **17**(2–3), 191–209 (1990)
6. Fan, Q., Wang, Z., Li, D., Gao, D., Zha, H.: Entropy-based fuzzy support vector machine for imbalanced datasets. Knowl.-Based Syst. **115**, 87–99 (2017)
7. Ferone, A., Galletti, A., Maratea, A.: Variable width rough-fuzzy c-means. In: 2017 13th International Conference on Signal-Image Technology Internet-Based Systems (SITIS), pp. 458–464, December 2017
8. Ferone, A., Maratea, A.: Integrating rough set principles in the graded possibilistic clustering. Inf. Sci. **477**, 148–160 (2019)
9. Kaleli, C.: An entropy-based neighbor selection approach for collaborative filtering. Knowl.-Based Syst. **56**, 273–280 (2014)
10. Lin, C.F., Wang, S.D.: Fuzzy support vector machines. IEEE Trans. Neural Netw. **13**(2), 464–471 (2002)
11. Maratea, A., Ferone, A.: Fuzzy entropy in imbalanced fuzzy classification. In: Esposito, A., et al. (ed.): Proceedings of Wirn, 2019. Springer, Heidelberg (2019, in press)
12. Sen, D., Pal, S.K.: Generalized rough sets, entropy, and image ambiguity measures. IEEE Trans. Syst. Man Cybern. Part B (Cybern.) **39**(1), 117–128 (2009)
13. Song, G., Rochas, J., Huet, F., Magoulés, F.: Solutions for processing k nearest neighbor joins for massive data on mapreduce. In: 2015 23rd Euromicro International Conference on Parallel, Distributed, and Network-Based Processing, March 2015, pp. 279–287 (2015)
14. Wygralak, M.: Rough sets and fuzzy sets-some remarks on interrelations. Fuzzy Sets Syst. **29**(2), 241–243 (1989)
15. Ziarko, W.: Probabilistic rough sets. In: Ślezak, D., Wang, G., Szczuka, M., Düntsch, I., Yao, Y. (eds.) RSFDGrC 2005. LNCS, vol. 3641, pp. 283–293. Springer, Heidelberg (2005). https://doi.org/10.1007/11548669_30

StormSeeker: A Machine-Learning-Based Mediterranean Storm Tracer

Raffaele Montella[1]($\boxtimes$) , Diana Di Luccio[1] , Angelo Ciaramella[1] ,
and Ian Foster[2,3]

[1] Science and Technologies Department, University of Naples "Parthenope",
Naples, Italy
{raffaele.montella,diana.diluccio,angelo.ciaramella}@uniparthenope.it
[2] Computer Science Department, University of Chicago, Chicago, USA
[3] Data Science and Learning Division, Argonne National Laboratory, Argonne, USA

Abstract. The Mediterranean area is subject to a range of destructive
weather events, including middle-latitudes storms, Mediterranean sub-
tropical hurricane-like storms ("medicanes"), and small-scale but violent
local storms. Although predicting large-scale atmosphere disturbances is
a common activity in numerical weather prediction, the tasks of recognizing, identifying, and tracing trajectories of such extreme weather events
within weather model outputs remains challenging. We present here a
new approach to this problem, called StormSeeker, that uses machine
learning techniques to recognize, classify, and trace the trajectories of
severe storms in atmospheric model data. We report encouraging results
detecting weather hazards in a heavy middle-latitude storm that struck
the Ligurian coast in October 2018, causing disastrous damages to public
infrastructure and private property.

Keywords: Machine learning · Distributed computing ·
Computational environmental data science · Extreme weather forecast

1 Introduction

The Mediterranean Sea is subject to destructive storms at multiple scales, including (i) middle-latitudes storms, originating in the Atlantic Ocean, Iceland cyclo-
genetic region [2]; (ii) sub-tropical Mediterranean hurricanes, termed "medicanes" [16]; and (iii) localized, highly violent small-scale atmospheric events [18],
due to steep environmental parameter gradients [6].

We are particularly concerned here with medicanes, which are expected to
become more violent over time due to climate change [19], raising risks for human
activities, particularly in the main Mediterranean islands (Corsica, Sardinia and
Sicily), the small islands of the southern central Mediterranean Sea (Pantelleria,
Lampedusa and Malta), Crete and the Aegean islands [30]. Medicanes typically
arise within the Balearic and Sardinian seas, west Sicily channel, or south Ionian
Sea in the September/December period. These peculiar extreme weather events

© Springer Nature Switzerland AG 2019
R. Montella et al. (Eds.): IDCS 2019, LNCS 11874, pp. 444–456, 2019.
https://doi.org/10.1007/978-3-030-34914-1_42

are smaller and shorter-lived than hurricanes, spanning a few hundred kilometers at most, and lasting only a few days to a week [11]. They present characteristics similar to tropical cyclones, but often lack a well-defined center of rotation.

Forecasting the emergence and evolution of medicanes via analysis of numerical weather and marine prediction model outputs is technically possible and indeed has been used in production scenarios for several decades [1]. However, their unique characteristics mean that early detection, tracking, and landfall risk evaluation remain open issues [17].

In this paper, we propose StormSeeker, an approach to the recognition, classification, and tracking of Mediterranean storms based on the application of machine learning techniques to data produced by numerical weather prediction models. StormSeeker uses a two-stage approach to this problem, with (1) unsupervised learning used to identify data points with similar characteristics, via an autoencoder that produces a reduced dimensionality representation of weather model output, to which clustering is applied to group similar data points; and (2) supervised learning, in the form of a neural network trained on expert-labeled data, used to identify clusters that represent storms. We have applied this method to data from a severe Mediterranean storm that hit the Italian Tyrrhenian coast from October 27–31, 2018, with encouraging results.

The rest of this paper is as follows. Section 2 reviews methodologies for meteorological event identification and Sect. 3 describes the Pathenope weather forecasting system that StormSeeker extends. Then, Sect. 4 describes the overall system and the StormSeeker approach, Sect. 5 presents experimental results, and Sect. 6 concludes.

2   Related Work

We review previous approaches to the problem of detecting and tracking storms in numerical weather prediction model data.

Bosler et al. [4] present a storm detection algorithm, Stride Search, that can be applied to atmospheric data produced by numerical weather prediction models. This algorithm first performs a spatial search to identify possible storm centers, applying an array of criteria (multi-criteria approach) on each time step. Then, it looks for temporal correlations between the selected storm centers, considering the storm center translation speed. The final result is polished to remove all events shorter than a given number of days. As we describe in Sect. 4.1, we use a modified version of Stride Search in StormSeeker.

Lionello et al. [25] suggest two distinct approaches to the study of storm activity in the Mediterranean area: storm tracking algorithms and analysis of synoptic variability. The goal of a storm tracking algorithm is to detect the regions of storm development (*cyclogenesis*) and decay (*cyclolysis*), as well as the specific paths of individual storms [24,28]. Different models have been implemented for accurate storm prediction, identification, and tracking, and most of these models has been tested on hurricane phenomena [12,13,32,35]. The identification of synoptic variability using a band-pass filter retaining the mainly variability of the sea level pressure or the geopotential height at 500 hPa/850 hPa on the 2–8 day period has been used to quantify the synoptic activity associated with high and low North Atlantic Oscillation (NAO) indices [22].

Trigo et al. [34] developed an objective cyclone detection and tracking methodology for the Mediterranean basin based on the use of a k-means clustering procedure to summarize trajectory information obtained from the 18-year climatology. They demonstrated that cyclones developed in different regions within the Mediterranean area have quite different characteristics. This is a crucial point in terms of defining identification criteria and detection thresholds. The choice of one detection method (e.g., sea-level pressure threshold) instead of another (e.g., a wind speed threshold) introduces arbitrary thresholds, which can produce differences in the obtained results. For example, not all low sea-level pressures can be retained as cyclones [25].

Racah et al. [29] applied an auto-encoder method similar to that used here for semi-supervized learning of extreme weather events. Kim et al. [21] use a convolutional long-short-term-memory (LSTM) NN [36], trained on large collections of labeled hurricane data, to identify and label hurricane tracks in global climate model datasets. Autoencoders have also been applied to satellite imagery to identify cloud classes [23]. In contrast, we focus on smaller-scale severe weather events in a limited region, for which few labeled data are available.

3   The Parthenope Weather Forecasting System

We integrate StormSeeker within a weather forecasting workflow run on a regular basis by the Center for Marine and Atmosphere Monitoring and Modelling at the Department of Science and Technologies of the University of Naples "Parthenope" (http://meteo.uniparthenope.it). This system is depicted in the left-hand size of Fig. 2.

This workflow generates weather forecasts and simulations by using the WRF weather research and forecast community model initialized with NCEP Global Forecast System model results. The data pre-processing, simulation, post-processing, and inter-comparison dataflow is implemented by the DagOnStar workflow engine [26], which here is used to orchestrate diverse and different distributed computing resources, both on-premise HPC and on cloud.

The first workflow component is the atmospheric model, WRF-ARW, which computes the 10 m wind fields and other atmospheric parameters. This model in turn yields the initial storm trace reconstruction. In order to produce the numerical simulations presented in this paper, we configured the WRF model, initialized with the Global Forecast System (GFS) produced by the National Center for Environmental Prediction (NCEP), with three nested computational domains: a coarse domain (d01) covering the whole of Europe at 25 km spatial resolution; an intermediate domain (d02) covering the Italian peninsula and related surrounding seas at 5 km spatial resolution; and a fine domain (d03) covering the eastern sectors of the Central and Southern Tyrrhenian Sea and related coastal areas at 1 km spatial resolution. Data are permanently stored on local facilities in NetCDF format in both model history and processed/projected format, and are distributed via an OPeNDAP Server and a RESTful API.

The **Weather Labelling Web Application** enables field experts (meteorologist) to select date and time, retrieve WRF reanalysis or daily forecast data and perform the labelling drawing polygons on weather phenomena. The user interface automatically adjusts the selected domain to the current zoom level and map center. An expert can thus leverage detail available where model resolution is higher. The output of the Weather Labelling Web Application is a collection of date/time labelled polygons saved as GeoJSON in the **Weather Labels Storage** MongoDB database. In this paper we use the web application to label the clusters produced by the unsupervised step described in Sect. 4.1 in order to train the supervised algorithm detailed in Sect. 4.2.

4   The StormSeeker Approach

The StormSeeker system (Fig. 2, right) analyzes weather model prediction data, such as that produced by the Parthenope forecasting system, and produces information about potential storm trajectories within those data.

StormSeeker proceeds in two stage. First, it uses an unsupervised machine learning method, comprising an autoencoder followed by clustering, to create a set of clusters of the data comprising each weather model time step. The second, supervised step then uses a set of clusters hand labeled with the Weather Labelling Web Application as "storm" or "not storm" to train a neural network that can subsequently be applied to clusters to identify storm trajectories.

4.1   Unsupervised Step: Identify Clusters

We train the StormSeeker autocoder on a large quantity of weather model output. New weather model output can then be processed by first applying the trained autoencoder to generate a reduced dimensionality latent space representation and then applying NEC clustering to that latent space representation. Let the weather prediction model output data be a matrix $\mathbf{X}$ with dimensions $N \times m$, where N is the number of observations and m is the number of features (wind, atmospheric pressure, ...). We note that, for each hour, we observe a $q \times r$ matrix, where each cell is a vector of m features. Stacking all vector information, we obtain a $N \times m$ matrix $\mathbf{X}$, where $N = q\hat{r}$. We apply the autoencoder to $\mathbf{X}$ to generate as a latent space representation a matrix $\mathbf{Y}$ with dimensions $N \times d$, where $d < m$, $\mathbf{Y}^T = \mathbf{D}\mathbf{X}^T$ and $\mathbf{D}$ is $d \times m$. We then apply NEC clustering to assign a cluster label to each point in $\mathbf{Y}$.

An autoencoder is an unsupervised neural network (NN) that learns a nonlinear representation (encoding) of a set of data [20]. Our autoencoder serves as a non-linear Principal Component Analysis technique [31]. We use a sparse autoencoder network (as shown in Fig. 1), which consists of an encoder and a decoder. The encoder maps the input to a hidden representation. The decoder attempts to map this representation back to the original input. In our experiments, the encoder has 17 inputs and 4 outputs (neural network hidden nodes), with saturating linear transfer functions. The decoder has 4 inputs and 17 outputs, with linear transfer functions on the output neurons. Training determines values for the weights that minimize a loss function defined in terms of the distance between the input and output of the autoencoder network. The loss function to use for training corresponds to the mean squared error function, adjusted for training a sparse autoencoder [20].

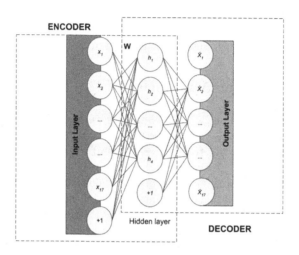

Fig. 1. Autoencoder architecture.

We then apply NEgentropy based hierarchical Clustering (NEC) to the latent space representation to generate a set of clusters. NEC is a hierarchical clustering method developed by Ciaramella et al. [9]. In general, a K-means clustering algorithm aims to groups the elements of a dataset into non-overlapping sets, such that all elements belonging to the same set are as similar as possible [10]. In detail, given N data points $S = \{\mathbf{x}_1, \mathbf{x}_2, \ldots, \mathbf{x}_N\}$, with $\mathbf{x}_i \in \mathbb{R}^D$, for $i = 1, 2, \ldots, N$, the algorithm seeks to find K clusters $C = \{C_1, C_2, \ldots, C_K\}$ such that each $\mathbf{x}_i$ is assigned to a cluster C_k with centroid $\mathbf{v}_k$ and the assignments minimize the objective function

$$J = \sum_{i=1}^{K} \sum_{j=1}^{N} u_{ij}^m d(\mathbf{v}_i, \mathbf{x}_j)^2,$$

where $\mathbf{v}_i \in \mathbb{R}^D$ is the centroid of the i-th cluster, $d(v, x)$ is a distance measure (e.g., Euclidean distance), and the partition matrix $U = [u_{ij}]$ is used to store the results of clustering (partitioning) the points into clusters, with $u_{ij}=1$ if $\mathbf{x}_j$ is in cluster i, and 0 otherwise. The partition matrix must satisfy requirements that ensure nonempty clusters.

Computing this K-means clustering precisely is expensive. A cheaper agglomerative clustering heuristic first creates N clusters, one per data point, and then repeatedly combines the two closest clusters until K clusters remain. The NEC algorithm is a variation of this approach, in which a Probabilistic Principal Surfaces (i.e., a density-based modelling) or Winner Take All approach [33] is first used to find an initial rough clustering (with a large number of clusters); agglomeration then proceeds on the basis of a specific non-Euclidean metric defined in terms of Fisher's and Negentropy information. This technique has been efficiently applied to large datasets and in particular to microarray data [7].

4.2 Supervised Step: Training and Applying a Storm Tracker

We need labeled data to train the NN that will subsequently be used for predicting new phenomena. We use a **Weather Labeling Web Application** (see Fig. 2) to allow experts to mark and label the found clusters by polygons in weather model output that correspond to severe weather events.

Successively, we use these labeled data to train a MultiLayer Perceptron (MLP), a class of feed-forward artificial NN [3] consisting of at least three layers of nodes having universal approximation properties, with nonlinear activation functions for the hidden nodes. MLP uses a supervised learning technique called backpropagation for training and is used for classification and regression (e.g., prediction). We train, using a cros-validation methodology, a MLP with a single hidden layer on the labeled data $\mathbf{Y}$ to obtain a predictive model, $\mathbf{M}$. The model $\mathbf{M}$ has d inputs and it is applied to new projected observations $\mathbf{Y}_t$ at time t with $t = 0, 1, 2, \ldots, 23$, where $\mathbf{Y}_t^T = \mathbf{W}_t \mathbf{X}_t^T$ is the projection of the source observation $\mathbf{X}_t$ at time t and $\mathbf{W}_t$ is the autoencoder-estimated matrix of the weather model's execution to classify these severe phenomena. That is, at each step t and for the i-th observation $y_t^i \in \mathbf{Y}_t$, we compute $\mathbf{M}(y_t^i)$ to determine what label to apply to it (i.e., "storm" or "no storm").

Although Stride Search performs well in hurricane applications, we consider the need for an algorithm that behaves correctly with Mediterranean storms. The clustering algorithm described in this paper is intended to be used in a customized version of the Stride Search as machine learning based criteria in a production workflow for weather and marine forecasts and simulations.

In order to implement an algorithm for Mediterranean storm detection, recognition and tracking we have to take into account atmospheric parameters (Table 1) as suggested in [25,34]. The table shows the parameters we considered for unsupervised clustering as described in this paper and the parameters we will use in the planned supervised approach.

In the context of a full production operational workflow, StormSeeker will then generate a semi-automatic weather alert.

5   Experimental Results

We present the results of a first experiment involving the reconstruction and prediction of a Mediterranean storm.

Table 1. Features used for supervised machine learning ("S") and unsupervised clustering ("U").

Name	Description	Unit	S	U
T2C	Temperature at 2 m	°C	✓	✓
SLP	Sea level pressure	hPa	✓	✓
WSPD10	Wind speed at 10 m	ms^{-1}	✓	✓
WDIR10	Wind direction at 10 m	°	✓	✓
HR2	Relative humidity at 2 m	%	✓	✓
UH	Updraft helicity	$\text{m}^{-2}/\text{s}^{-2}$	✓	✓
MCAPE	Max. convective available potential energy	JKg^{-1}		✓
TC500	Temperature at 500 hPa	°C		✓
TC850	Temperature at 850 hPa	°C		✓
GPH500	Geopotential height at 500 hPa	m		✓
GPH850	Geopotential height at 850 hPa	m		✓
CLOUD	Cloud fraction	%	✓	✓
U10M	Wind at 10 m (u-component)	ms^{-1}		✓
V10M	Wind at 10 m (v-component)	ms^{-1}		✓
$WSPD10_\Delta$	Wind speed change from previous time step	ms^{-1}		✓
$WDIR10_\Delta$	Wind direction change from previous time step	°N		✓
RAIN	Hourly cumulative rain	mm	✓	✓

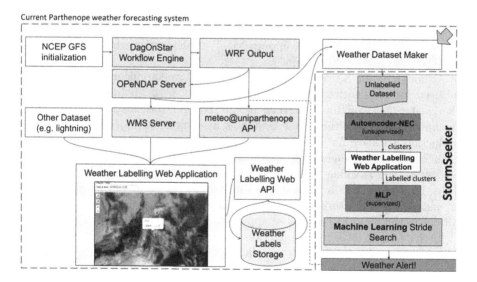

Fig. 2. StormSeeker is part of a larger workflow devoted to the production of operational weather forecasts. In this paper we describe the components in the green boxes. (Color figure online)

5.1   The Example Storm Event

We focus on a storm event that, during the period October 27–31, 2018, that first struck the eastern sectors of the Central and Southern Tyrrhenian Seas and then caused significant damage on the Ligurian Sea coasts [5], such as the collapse of the breakwater of the Marina at Rapallo in Liguria.

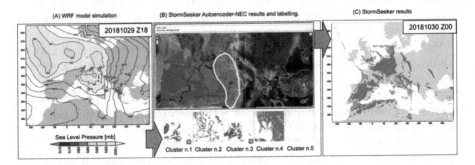

Fig. 3. An example of StormSeeker: (A) The WRF output is reduced in its dimensions using the Autoencoder-NEC; (B) the clusters 1 and 3 are overlayed on the WRF output in order to assist the field expert in severe weather events labelling; (C) Final result.

We used the weather forecasting model described in Sect. 3 to reconstruct the spatial and temporal evolution of this storm event, initializing the WRF model with NCEP GFS.

5.2   Cluster Identification with StormSeeker

We applied the clustering algorithm to the data just described, experimenting with different numbers of features (m), latent space dimensions (d) in the autoencoder, and number of clusters (K) in the NEC clustering. We first tuned the parameters by using a "grid-search" strategy [3] and we adopt $m = 17$ (see Table 1), $d = 4$, and $K = 5$.

Successively, the five clusters, obtained by unsupervised part of StormeSeeker (Autoconder and NEC), are labeled as "storm" or "no storm" by Weather Labelling Web Application for the whole period October 28–31, 2018. The dataset **X**, obtained using the stacking approach described in the previous Section, after the projection by the Autoencoder, is adopted for training a MLP, **M**, for classification. Experimentally, we found that the best configuration is a NN with $d = 4$ inputs, a single hidden layer with 10 nodes and sigmoidal activation functions. The output neurons compute a linear activation function. We also consider a cross-validation methodology considering 70% of data for training, 15% for validation, and 15% for testing of dataset **X**. The classification accuracy (confusion matrices) is around 97% for training, validation and test sets, respectively (as shown in Fig. 4).

5.3   Discussion

In Figure 3 the results of the unsupervised processing during October 29–30, 2018 are shown. We highlight that StormSeeker permits to obtain selective clusters (e.g., the cluster 4 of sub-figures c, g, and m) that could be associated with the core storm activity. In detail, for this example, the cluster reveals a particularly strong activity in Italy. This process can help the expert in the phase of labelling by **Weather Labeling Web Application**. We also stress that Storm-Seeker reveals these clusters for almost the entire October 28–29, 2018, period allowing us to track the storm's main activities.

Moreover, in Fig. 4 we show the confusion matrices obtained by model **M** on training, validation and test sets, respectively. A confusion matrix is a specific table layout that allows visualization of the performance of an unsupervised algorithm. Each row of the matrix represents the instances in a predicted class by model **M**, while each column represents the instances in an actual class. All correct predictions are located in the diagonal of the table (highlighted in green) and visually inspecting the table we found the prediction errors, as they will be represented by values in red cells outside the diagonal. The gray cell summarize the overall diagonal classification accuracy. In particular, True Positive (TP) is the number of correct predictions that an example is positive which means positive class correctly identified as positive, False Negative (FN) is the number of incorrect predictions that an example is negative which means positive class incorrectly identified as negative, False positive (FP) is the number of incorrect predictions that an example is positive which means negative class incorrectly identified as positive and True Negative (TN) is the number of correct predictions that an example is negative which means negative class correctly identified as negative. Moreover, we can describe some advanced classification metrics based on confusion matrix:

- Sensitivity - also referred as True Positive Rate or Recall and it measures the positive examples labeled as positive by classifier

$$\frac{TP}{TP + FN} \tag{1}$$

- Specificity - also know as True Negative Rate, it measures the negative examples labeled as negative by classifier

$$\frac{TN}{TN + FP} \tag{2}$$

- Precision - ratio of total number of correctly classified positive examples and the total number of predicted positive examples

$$\frac{TP}{TP + FP} \tag{3}$$

- Negative Predictive Value - it measures the negative examples labeled as negative by classifier

$$\frac{TN}{TN + FN} \tag{4}$$

– Accuracy - is the proportion of the total number of predictions that are correct.

$$\frac{TP + TN}{TP + TN + FP + FN} \tag{5}$$

These preliminary results suggests that the learned model **M** can be used for the automatic identification and tracking of storms given new observations.

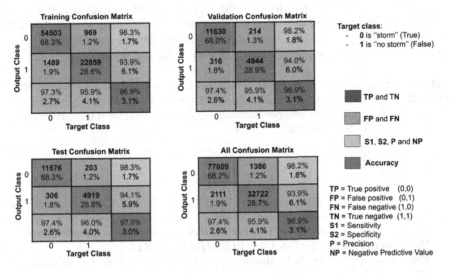

Fig. 4. MLP classification performance: confusion matrices w.r.t. training, validation, test and overall sets. Each row of the matrix represents the instances in a predicted class by **M** while each column represents the instances in an actual class. All correct predictions are located in the diagonal of the table highlighted in green. The gray cells summarize the whole percentage of correct prediction. (Color figure online)

6   Conclusion and Future Directions

We have introduced StormSeeker, a methodology for recognizing, classifying, and tracing the trajectories of severe storms in the Mediterranean area. This methodology uses unsupervised and supervised machine learning techniques. We have applied StormSeeker to data corresponding to an extreme weather event observed in the Mediterranean area from October 27–31, 2018. This preliminary result indicates that the StormSeeker approach can be used for automatic detection, tracking, and prediction of storms.

We aim next to collect further data and adopt different and more robust machine learning techniques (e.g., deep NNs, such as CNN and LSTM [20], compressive sensing, and adaptive dictionary learning [8]). We plan to leverage supervised learning to continue our research effort on those issues. We also intend to integrate StormSeeker in the Parthenope forecasting workflow.

We also plan to investigate how machine learning can be used to predict the emergence of small-scale storms in the relatively low-resolution output produced by typical numerical weather prediction models. To this end, we will extend the methodology proposed in this paper to use a supervized approach in which we train the machine learning model with high resolution labelled data and then perform storm recognition on lower resolution model output.

These early results suggest that the proposed techniques may have value in a range of contexts characterized by different temporal and spatial scales, for example to enhance the safety at sea [14], preserve archaeological sites menaced by coastal vulnerability [15], and improve human health conditions in areas where mussel farming has environmental, economic, and social impacts [27].

Acknowledgments. This research was supported by project PAUN (ex RIPA PON03PE_00164) and DOE Contract DE-AC02-06CH11357. We are grateful to the University of Napoli "Parthenope" forecast service (http://meteo.uniparthenope.it) for know-how and HPC facilities.

References

1. Ascione, I., Giunta, G., Mariani, P., Montella, R., Riccio, A.: A grid computing based virtual laboratory for environmental simulations. In: Nagel, W.E., Walter, W.V., Lehner, W. (eds.) Euro-Par 2006. LNCS, vol. 4128, pp. 1085–1094. Springer, Heidelberg (2006). https://doi.org/10.1007/11823285_114
2. Bengtsson, L., Hodges, K.I., Roeckner, E.: Storm tracks and climate change. J. Clim. **19**(15), 3518–3543 (2006)
3. Bishop, C.M.: Pattern Recognition and Machine Learning. Springer, Heidelberg (2006)
4. Bosler, P., Roesler, E., Taylor, M., Mundt, M.: Stride search: a general algorithm for storm detection in high resolution climate data. Geosci. Model Dev. Discuss. **9**, 1383–1398 (2016)
5. Brandini, C., Perna, M., Taddei, S., Boninsegni, G., Cipriana, L.E.: Monitoring, risk forecasting and coastal planning in the region of Tuscany. In: Abstract Booklet, Convegno Gestione e Difesa delle Coste. Accademia Nazionale dei Lincei (2019). http://bit.ly/2NJiJ3e
6. Cassola, F., Ferrari, F., Mazzino, A.: Numerical simulations of Mediterranean heavy precipitation events with the WRF model: a verification exercise using different approaches. Atmos. Res. **164**, 210–225 (2015)
7. Ciaramella, A., et al.: Interactive data analysis and clustering of genomic data. Neural Netw. **21**(2–3), 368–378 (2008)
8. Ciaramella, A., Gianfico, M., Giunta, G.: Compressive sampling and adaptive dictionary learning for the packet loss recovery in audio multimedia streaming. Multimed. Tools Appl. **75**(24), 17375–17392 (2016)
9. Ciaramella, A., Longo, G., Staiano, A., Tagliaferri, R.: NEC: a hierarchical agglomerative clustering based on fisher and negentropy information. In: Apolloni, B., Marinaro, M., Nicosia, G., Tagliaferri, R. (eds.) NAIS/WIRN -2005. LNCS, vol. 3931, pp. 49–56. Springer, Heidelberg (2006). https://doi.org/10.1007/11731177_8
10. Ciaramella, A., Staiano, A.: On the role of clustering and visualization techniques in gene microarray data. Algorithms **12**(6), 123 (2019)

11. Claud, C., Alhammoud, B., Funatsu, B.M., Chaboureau, J.P.: Mediterranean hurricanes: large-scale environment and convective and precipitating areas from satellite microwave observations. Natural Hazards Earth Syst. Sci. **10**(10), 2199 (2010)
12. Demaria, M., Aberson, S.D., Ooyama, K.V., Lord, S.J.: A nested spectral model for hurricane track forecasting. Mon. Weather Rev. **120**(8), 1628–1643 (1992)
13. Demaria, M., Jones, R.W.: Optimization of a hurricane track forecast model with the adjoint model equations. Mon. Weather Rev. **121**(6), 1730–1745 (1993)
14. Di Luccio, D., Benassai, G., Budillon, G., Mucerino, L., Montella, R., Pugliese Carratelli, E.: Wave run-up prediction and observation in a micro-tidal beach. Natural Hazards Earth Syst. Sci. **18**(11), 2841–2857 (2018)
15. Di Luccio, D., et al.: Monitoring and modelling coastal vulnerability and mitigation proposal for an archaeological site (Kaulonia, Southern Italy). Sustainability **10**(6), 2017 (2018)
16. Emanuel, K.: Genesis and maintenance of Mediterranean hurricanes. Adv. Geosci. **2**, 217–220 (2005)
17. Gaertner, M.Á., et al.: Simulation of medicanes over the Mediterranean Sea in a regional climate model ensemble: impact of ocean-atmosphere coupling and increased resolution. Clim. Dyn. **51**(3), 1041–1057 (2018)
18. Gascón, E., Laviola, S., Merino, A., Miglietta, M.: Analysis of a localized flash-flood event over the central Mediterranean. Atmos. Res. **182**, 256–268 (2016)
19. Giorgi, F., Lionello, P.: Climate change projections for the Mediterranean region. Global Planet. Change **63**(2–3), 90–104 (2008)
20. Goodfellow, I., Bengio, Y., Courville, A.: Deep Learning. MIT Press, Cambridge (2016). http://www.deeplearningbook.org
21. Kim, S., Kim, H., Lee, J., Yoon, S., Kahou, S.E., Kashinath, K., Prabhat: deep-hurricane-tracker: tracking and forecasting extreme climate events. In: IEEE Winter Conference on Applications of Computer Vision, pp. 1761–1769. IEEE (2019)
22. Krichak, S., Alpert, P.: Signatures of the NAO in the atmospheric circulation during wet winter months over the Mediterranean region. Theoret. Appl. Climatol. **82**(1–2), 27–39 (2005)
23. Kurihana, T., et al.: Cloud characterization with deep learning. In: 9th International Workshop on Climate Informatics (2019)
24. Lionello, P., Dalan, F., Elvini, E.: Cyclones in the Mediterranean region: the present and the doubled CO2 climate scenarios. Clim. Res. **22**(2), 147–159 (2002)
25. Lionello, P., et al.: Cyclones in the Mediterranean region: climatology and effects on the environment. In: Developments in Earth and Environmental Sciences, vol. 4, pp. 325–372. Elsevier (2006)
26. Montella, R., Di Luccio, D., Kosta, S.: DagOn*: executing direct acyclic graphs as parallel jobs on anything. In: IEEE/ACM Workshop on Workflows in Support of Large-Scale Science, pp. 64–73. IEEE (2018)
27. Montella, R., Di Luccio, D., Troiano, P., Riccio, A., Brizius, A., Foster, I.: WaComM: a parallel water quality community model for pollutant transport and dispersion operational predictions. In: 12th International Conference on Signal-Image Technology and Internet-Based Systems (SITIS), pp. 717–724. IEEE (2016)
28. Murray, R.J., Simmonds, I.: A numerical scheme for tracking cyclone centres from digital data. Part II: application to January and July general circulation model simulations. Aust. Meteorol. Mag. **39**(3), 167–180 (1991)
29. Racah, E., Beckham, C., Maharaj, T., Kahou, S.E., Prabhat, Pal, C.: ExtremeWeather: a large-scale climate dataset for semi-supervised detection, localization, and understanding of extreme weather events. In: Advances in Neural Information Processing Systems, pp. 3402–3413 (2017)

30. Romero, R., Emanuel, K.: Medicane risk in a changing climate. J. Geophys. Res.: Atmos. **118**(12), 5992–6001 (2013)
31. Scholz, M., Fraunholz, M., Selbig, J.: Nonlinear principal component analysis: neural network models and applications. In: Gorban, A.N., Kégl, B., Wunsch, D.C., Zinovyev, A.Y. (eds.) Principal manifolds for data visualization and dimension reduction, vol. 58, pp. 44–67. Springer, Heidelberg (2008). https://doi.org/10.1007/978-3-540-73750-6_2
32. Shen, B.W., et al.: Hurricane forecasts with a global mesoscale-resolving model: preliminary results with Hurricane Katrina (2005). Geophys. Res. Lett. **33**(13), (2006)
33. Staiano, A., et al.: Probabilistic principal surfaces for yeast gene microarray data mining. In: 4th IEEE International Conference on Data Mining, pp. 202–208 (2004)
34. Trigo, I.F., Davies, T.D., Bigg, G.R.: Objective climatology of cyclones in the Mediterranean region. J. Clim. **12**(6), 1685–1696 (1999)
35. Xie, L., Bao, S., Pietrafesa, L.J., Foley, K., Fuentes, M.: A real-time hurricane surface wind forecasting model: formulation and verification. Mon. Weather Rev. **134**(5), 1355–1370 (2006)
36. Xingjian, S., Chen, Z., Wang, H., Yeung, D.Y., Wong, W.K., Woo, W.C.: Convolutional LSTM network: a machine learning approach for precipitation nowcasting. In: Advances in Neural Information Processing Systems, pp. 802–810 (2015)

Smart Cities and Open WiFis: When Android OS Permissions Cease to Protect Privacy

Gabriella Verga, Salvatore Calcagno, Andrea Fornaia,
and Emiliano Tramontana[⊠]

Dipartimento di Matematica e Informatica, University of Catania, Catania, Italy
gabriella.verga@unict.it, {fornaia,tramontana}@dmi.unict.it

Abstract. The wide-spread availability of open WiFi networks on smart cities can be considered an advanced service for citizens. However, a device connecting to WiFi network access points gives away its location. On the one hand, the access point provider could collect and analyse the ids of connecting devices, and people choose whether to connect depending on the degree of trust to the provider. On the other hand, an app running on the device could sense the presence of nearby WiFi networks, and this could have some consequences on user privacy. Based on permission levels and mechanisms proper of Android OS, this paper proposes an approach whereby an app attempting to connect to WiFi networks could reveal to a third part the presence of some known networks, thus a surrogate for the geographical location of the user, while she is unaware of it. This is achieved without resorting to GPS readings, hence without needing dangerous-level permissions. We propose a way to counteract such a weakness in order to protect user privacy.

Keywords: Android OS · Privacy · Permission levels · WiFi networks · Big data

1 Introduction

Android libraries provide several APIs to determine the device position (i.e. *geolocation*) [13]. The most obvious one is `android.location.LocationManager` class, which gives an app the current GPS coordinates, along with the ability to receive a notification when reaching a chosen area (e.g. the destination of a travel route). However, the device position could also be determined using other signal information, such as the cellular GSM/LTE state. The collaborative initiative of *OpenCellID* dataset[1] provides the GPS positions of over 36 million unique GSM Cell IDs. By knowing the list of the cell towers sensed on the device, which is given by `android.telephony.TelephonyManager` class, it is possible to geolocate the user device with a fair level of precision. This can be preferred

---

[1] http://wiki.opencellid.org.

© Springer Nature Switzerland AG 2019
R. Montella et al. (Eds.): IDCS 2019, LNCS 11874, pp. 457–467, 2019.
https://doi.org/10.1007/978-3-030-34914-1_43

to GPS for coverage improvement (i.e. inside buildings), or to reduce the energy consumption, avoiding the activation of the GPS receiver.

Information on WiFi networks available can be used in a very similar way. *Wigle*[2] dataset has over 565 million geolocated WiFi network service set identifiers (SSIDs) around the globe. By scanning the WiFi networks and obtaining the ids of the visible ones, by means of `android.net.wifi.WifiManager` class, the device position can be disclosed, again without using the GPS sensor [22].

Android OS has two main levels of permissions (normal and dangerous) and apps have to declare a proper permission before using the related APIs, e.g. for using internet connectivity, normal permission INTERNET has to declared in AndroidManifest.xml [11,13]. Normal-level permissions are automatically accepted by the user upon installation of the app, whereas dangerous-level permissions are asked to the user at runtime [21]. By considering the privacy implication of the above described use of cell and WiFi ids, the recent versions of Android OS and APIs require an app to declare dangerous-level permissions `ACCESS_FINE_LOCATION` or `ACCESS_COARSE_LOCATION`, for using the APIs revealing the list of nearby WiFi networks or to get the cell id, and the user will be asked to grant permissions at runtime. For the WiFi scan this was only added in Android APIs version 28[3], which is the last Android release at the date of writing. However, according to the official *Android Distribution Dashboard*[4], currently the number of Android devices using the latest Android version is less than 11% of all Android devices in use (July 2019).

The enforcement of the said dangerous-level permissions restricts WiFi network scanning capabilities when looking for surrounding *possibly unknown* SSIDs. However, it is possible for an app to attempt a connection to a known WiFi network access point without needing dangerous-level permissions, hence without asking the user to grant permission at runtime. By using such a feature and by leveraging the OpenData about free WiFi networks, the proposed approach presents a misuse case for determining the device position with a fair level of precision. More specifically, a malicious app can be implemented to force the Android device to systematically try to connect, and suddenly disconnect, to a list of known open (i.e. with no password required), and even some password-protected, geolocated WiFi networks, in the quest for locating the user.

Open data initiatives taken by several government institutions, such as for the City of Rome[5] and New York City[6], give access to datasets about geolocated open WiFi SSIDs, e.g. to help tourists finding a free network access near monumental buildings or historical sites. Moreover, other *WiFi Finder* apps like *WiFi Map*[7], used to spot nearby free WiFi networks while sharing newly discovered

---

[2] https://wigle.net.

[3] https://developer.android.com/guide/topics/connectivity/wifi-scan.

[4] https://developer.android.com/about/dashboards.

[5] http://www.datiopen.it/it/opendata/Provincia_di_Roma_WiFi.

[6] https://data.cityofnewyork.us/City-Government/NYC-Wi-Fi-Hotspot-Locations/yjub-udmw.

[7] https://www.wifimap.io.

ones, often provide commercial plans for developers needing API access to the whole geolocated dataset.

2 Related Work

Previous works on smartphone security can be organised in two sections: the first concerning the problems related to the management of permissions [11], and the second concerning the WiFi networks with multiple examples on possible passive attacks using WiFi connections [1].

ANDROID SECURITY: due to its popularity and open architecture, in the literature we find various descriptions of attacks on Android mobile devices [10], along with several malware detection techniques [4,7,20], and data leak prevention approaches [2,3]. One of the problems is related to the risk of private data flowing from the device to an unknown remote actor. In this context, while the user could be aware that an app is reading his contacts (or GPS coordinates) and has allowed the app to access them, she is unaware that her data are transmitted remotely. The previous literature has proposed to analyse apps in order to check whether sensitive data sources are connected to unwanted sinks [2,3]. Some weaknesses have been observed on Android OS permission design and mechanisms. By systematically analysing the Android APIs code, a previous research study has shown the APIs that are unprotected by any permission, and using them allows an app to discover sensitive data, such as device id, setting data, power modes, etc., as well as perform actions such as set volume, change alarm tones, etc. [15]; Even when APIs are protected by permissions, some unexpected app behaviour cannot be averted. E.g. an app could turn on the microphone, having previously obtained the needed permission, when the user is checking the list of messages or when the app runs in background, this leads to risks for users [21]. Moreover, apps often gain more privileges than strictly needed, and the several resources used can be combined in a way to breach privacy [12,19]. In such a context, the most discussed permissions are the *dangerous-level permissions* followed by their companions *normal-level permissions*. In several studies, the use of normal-level permissions has been linked to possible attacks and loss of sensitive data [1,21]. A framework has been proposed to further protect users by allowing them to define policies when accessing APIs, and such a framework will introduce needed checks into apps [14].

WIFI NETWORKS: WiFis are at the centre of many attacks on the privacy of users, who rely on devices such as smartphone or tablet [6,9]. Among various methodologies, attacks based on the enabled phone's WiFi connectivity options stand out, so that the device can be connected to fake WiFi without an explicit user operation; exploiting so-called Man-in-the-middle attack [5,17]. E.g., in [8] the WiFi connection enabled option is used to connect the device to fake access points, or in [16] a detection mechanism is created to find an evil twin Access Point attack which steals sensitive data. Such attacks are effective when an access point acts as a malicious agent, and sends user requests to a fake server. The effects can be very vicious.

Our work presents a new attack to Android mobile devices that can determine geographical location by attempting WiFi connections, which users are unaware of. Unlike previous studies, the attack comes from a misleading app, installed on the device, that forces WiFi to be enabled. Our approach is compatible with all Android OS versions, despite the security policies of the latest version, and does not require dangerous-level permissions.

3   Misuse Case Based on Sensing WiFi Networks

The goal of a malicious agent is that of using an app to track the position of the device without giving any warning to the user. This is possible thanks to an appealing application, or an App Twin (e.g. an app letting the user log into two different accounts of the same service at the same time) of a well-known app; and a WiFi dataset containing SSIDs and GPS coordinates. First of all, Sect. 3.1 presents how to carry out the attack on an Android device and the needed permissions. Then, Sect. 3.2 shows how to find, for WiFi networks, SSID and GPS coordinates thanks to the use of open data.

```
1  public void WiFiSearch() {
2      boolean inactiveWifi = false;
3      if (!isWifiEnabled()) {
4          inactiveWifi = true;
5          enableWifi();
6      }
7      List<WifiEntity> wifiEntities = database.wifiDao().getAll();
8      for (WifiEntity entity : wifiEntities) {
9          wifiConf.SSID = String.format("\"%s\"", entity.getSsid());
10         setCryptography(entity.getCryptographyType(), entity.getKey());
11         int netId = wifiManager.addNetwork(wifiConf);
12         if (tryToConnect(netId, entity.getSsid())) break;
13     }
14     if (inactiveWifi) disableWifi();
15 }
16 private boolean tryToConnect(int netId, String ssid) {
17     wifiManager.disconnect();
18     if (!wifiManager.enableNetwork(netId, true)) return false;
19     sendInfoToServer(deviceid, ssid);
20     return true;
21 }
```

Fig. 1. Code trying to connecting to known WiFi networks.

3.1   Hostile App Activities

To carry out the attack, it is first necessary to induce the user to download the app. This can be done by creating an appealing app or an app twin or an app similar to a well-known one. Once the app has been downloaded and installed, it works in the background performing the following activities: (i) turn WiFi on, (ii) use a provided list of known networks (see Sect. 3.2) and try to connect to each one. Then, as soon as a connection has been successful, (iii) it sends a feedback to the server (with device ID and SSID of the found WiFi network). Finally, (iv) it disconnects the device and disables the WiFi (if it has been enabled by the app). Data arriving at the server suffice to identify the user's position, since the GPS coordinates for the SSID are looked up on a known dataset.

Figure 1 shows the detail of the attack. Lines 3 to 6 turn WiFi on if needed. Line 7 reads WiFi networks data from a database. On the for loop (lines 8–13), each network is configured and, *tryToConnect()* method (lines 16–21) attempts to connect to the configured network, then if successful a server is notified (line 19). Finally, if needed, the WiFi is turned off (line 14). Once the app has successfully connected to a WiFi, for performing subsequent connections attempts, a newer WiFi list will be used (updated by the server), which has given the highest priority to the nearest WiFi networks according to their geographical location.

The permission-level required for the above set of steps is normal, therefore no warning will be shown to the user at runtime and the app will run undetected. Needed permissions are: CHANGE_WIFI_STATE, to perform operations on the WiFi (class WiFiManager), i.e. to enable, disable and connect to a WiFi network; and INTERNET to send information to a server.

3.2   WiFi Network IDs Dataset

In order to carry on a misuse case, an app needs a set of public and private WiFi network ids. The attacker determines, a priori, the type of attack to carry on. E.g. the attacker chooses whether he wishes to monitor the overall movements of the victim, or whether to keep track of the victim on a given area. In the first case, to reveal her position the device has to be hooked to many WiFi networks, hence it needs the list of a wide number of free WiFi networks ids. In the second case, a few WiFi networks (on the selected area) suffices, therefore the attacker can take advantage of knowing some private WiFi networks.

For each public WiFi network, the SSID and the geographical location are needed. Public WiFi network lists can be found on several websites that offer open data (see e.g. Table 1). E.g., *DatiOpen*[8] is one of the major Italian Open Data databases, and it offers a list of WiFi networks in Rome area, hence the data needed by our proposed scenario. In this case, the dataset has over 1600 WiFi networks and tells whether the WiFi is public or private. For each private WiFi network, it is necessary to know the password and the type of encryption (such data are read by means of line 7 of *WiFiSearch()* method, in Fig. 1). Private WiFi networks can be chosen individually by the attacker who provides the app with data of some controlled WiFi networks, because the password (in general not public) is a fundamental element for connecting to the network.

Figure 2 shows geo-localised free WiFi networks in New York City. Such data are available from Open Data initiatives for many cities around the globe.

---

[8] http://www.datiopen.it.

Fig. 2. Dataset *data.cityofnewyork.us* has 3345 SSIDs for New York City.

4   Distributed Interactions for the Misuse Case

This section details the interactions of a malicious app running on an Android device, detecting the presence of a WiFi network, and a server side.

The *malicious app* will periodically contact the *server side*, providing its device id and (implicitly with the http request) the IP address assigned by the *Internet Service Provider* (ISP). There are several IP geolocalisation APIs and datasets the server side can use as an *ip2gps* service (see Table 2). Even though IP geolocalisation is not always reliable [18], this can be used as a coarse indication of the device position, and as a starting point to filter from a large amount of SSIDs for the entire globe. Hence, knowing the IP address allows the server (at least) to exclude all the public SSIDs belonging to different countries or cities. Therefore, the more widespread the servers of an ISP the more accurate the inferred position.

Table 1. Dataset examples of geolocalised free WiFi SSIDs

Location	Free WiFi SSIDs	Reference
Open data initiatives		
Rome	1,566	datiopen.it
New York City	3,345	data.cityofnewyork.us
Austin	1,575	data.austintexas.gov
Commercial initiatives		
North America	667,275	www.wifimap.io
South America	550,733	www.wifimap.io
Europe	1,278,081	www.wifimap.io
Asia Pacific	252,070	www.wifimap.io
Middle East	1,103,220	www.wifimap.io
Africa	626,381	www.wifimap.io
Worldwide	100.000.000+	www.wifi-map.it.aptoide.com
Worldwide	600.000	www.wiffinity.com

The geolocalised IP information, *resolved* by the *ip2gps* service, is then used to *update* the *position cache* saved on the server side. This collects the history of all position data gathered from the device, and in turn let the server determine a list of likely nearby *public SSIDs* to be used on the Android device by the app for the WiFi networks scanning.

Figure 3 shows the steps aiming at disclosing the device location. With the *getScanList()* the server side asks for the first most probable *public SSIDs* the device should be close to, according to the available information inside the *position cache*, prioritising the recurrent locations for the user (on the time of the day), then previous frequented locations, then nearby networks, and finally the networks located in more popular areas (e.g. city centre, shopping malls, etc.).

Table 2. Dataset examples of geolocalised IP addresses

Dataset	IPs	Scope	Reference
ip2c.org	4,272,142,696	country	about.ip2c.org
GeoLite2	3,226,865 (blocks)	city	dev.maxmind.com
IP2Location lite	2,959,842	latitude/longitude	lite.ip2location.com

This reduced SSIDs list, say *[netA, netB, netC]* is then sent to the device as a response to its periodic request. Then, for each SSID, the device attempts a *password-less* connection, hence performing a WiFi scan, yet without requiring the dangerous-level permission (not needed when using the network details for an attempted connection). In case none of the connection attempts succeeded, a new list will be requested (the next most probable ones). In case a connection attempt succeeded (e.g. *netY* in Fig. 3), this information will be sent to the server side, which will use the *ssid2gps* dataset to get the GPS coordinates for the device, and then update its *position cache*. Next requests for a scan list will be answered giving the SSIDs close to the last one the device had connected to, in an attempt to constantly track the device position. For a user who has been located before, one or very few attempts for connections would suffice when is near a recurrent visited location. This would not be costly for battery. For first time attempts to locate a user, more attempts are needed and how many depends on several factors, how much spread are the servers of his ISP, how close he is to the clues that can be used, e.g. a shopping mall, a public service, etc.

5   Countermeasures for the Misuse Case

After having shown the hostile activities that an app on an Android device performs, and its interactions with a server side, we show a way to block the app from carry on such activities, hence protecting the user privacy.

As mentioned above, the attack involves attempting the connection to certain WiFi networks and sending the user device ID to a server, in order to identify

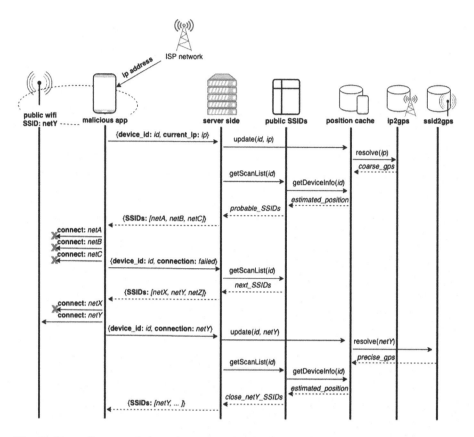

Fig. 3. Flow diagram of the misuse case for disclosing a device location. An app on the device sends network ids to a server, and the server uses geolocalisation datasets *ssid2gps* and *ip2gps* to translate sensed ids into GPS coordinates.

```
1   @Aspect public class BlockNetAspect {
2       private static final String PCUT =
3           "call (* android.net.wifi.WifiManager.addNetwork(..))";
4
5       @Pointcut(PCUT) public void blockedNetID() {}
6
7       @Around("blockedNetID()")
8       public Object blockNet(ProceedingJoinPoint jp) throws Throwable {
9           if (inWhiteList(jp)) return jp.proceed();
10          return -1;
11      }
12  }
```

Fig. 4. Aspect intercepting calls to *addNetwork()* of WifiManager and executing instead *blockNet()* method. The call on line 9 checks whether the net id is on the white list and if so lets the call go through, otherwise a connection failure value is returned.

the victim and map the location. There are two moments when our defence mechanism can act. Both drastically reduce the data provided to the attacker. The first moment is when the app reads the device ids, the second is when the app attempts a network connection. Inspired by the method in [21], for bypassing or blocking calls to Android APIs that need further protection, the defence mechanism consists of hardening an app modifying its code, by using Aspects Oriented Programming (AOP), to intercept a specific call and then masking the device id, and the WiFi connection details.

Assuming that the user sets up a white list, the aspect will let an app access only the WiFi networks in it. The white list, managed by a proper control panel the user can access, contains just the WiFi networks the user trusts and is confident that have not been tampered with, such as e.g. the ones at home, work. By trapping calls to *addNetwork()* (lines 3 and 5 in Fig. 4), the additional code checks whether the call to connect has an SSID contained in the white list, then connection is attempted, otherwise will return -1, not having attempted connection. A further protection aspect can be deployed which checks whether the device ID is read by an app. Reading the device ID can be trapped by guarding calls to methods of *android.provider.Settings.Secure* class. By checking every time the device ID is read, it is possible to mask the id, giving instead a fake one that changes at each call.

By employing the first protection aspect, when a malicious app works as described above, no network ids will be found, except the ones on the white list, then the app will send sparse data or no data to the remote attacker. Moreover, by using the second protection aspect, the remote attacker will receive fake device ids, which change over time, hiding the real id of the smartphone. In both cases, the attack cannot be carried on: the attacker cannot identify the user and consequently cannot monitor his movements, or identify the exact number of people who hook onto a WiFi network, and the users crossing a specific area.

6   Conclusions

This paper has presented a misuse case consisting of the steps a malicious app could perform in order to reveal the user position. The app would try to connect to known WiFi networks and when successful send this occurrence to a server. For attempting WiFi connections to known networks, an app needs to declare just normal-level permissions, hence no alert is given to users. The server receiving network ids, when connections have been successful, can associate them with GPS locations, e.g. by using freely available datasets. We have proposed a way to protect the user from such an attack by means of a general mechanism which could be enforced on any app, without specific knowledge on it, by simply weaving the app with a provided aspect.

Acknowledgement. This work has been supported by project CREAMS—Codes Recognising and Eluding Attacks and Meddling on Systems—funded by Università degli Studi di Catania, Piano della Ricerca 2016/2018 Linea di intervento 2.

References

1. Achara, J.P., Cunche, M., Roca, V., Francillon, A.: Short paper: WifiLeaks: under-estimated privacy implications of the access_wifi_state android permission. In: Proceedings of ACM Conference on Security and Privacy in Wireless and Mobile Networks (2014)
2. Arzt, S., et al.: Flowdroid: precise context, flow, field, object-sensitive and lifecycle-aware taint analysis for android apps. ACM Sigplan Not. **49**(6), 259–269 (2014)
3. Ascia, G., et al.: Making android apps data-leak-safe by data flow analysis and code injection. In: Proceedings of IEEE International Conference on Enabling Technologies: Infrastructure for Collaborative Enterprises (WETICE), pp. 205–210 (2016)
4. Burguera, I., Zurutuza, U., Nadjm-Tehrani, S.: Crowdroid: behavior-based malware detection system for android. In: Proceedings of ACM Workshop on Security and Privacy in Smartphones and Mobile Devices, pp. 15–26 (2011)
5. Conti, M., Dragoni, N., Lesyk, V.: A survey of man in the middle attacks. IEEE Commun. Surv. Tutor. **18**(3), 2027–2051 (2016)
6. Demir, L.: Wi-fi tracking: what about privacy. Master thesis, Grenoble (2013)
7. Di Stefano, A., Fornaia, A., Tramontana, E., Verga, G.: Detecting android malware according to observations on user activities. In: Proceedings of IEEE International Conference on Enabling Technologies: Infrastructure for Collaborative Enterprises (WETICE) (2018)
8. Dondyk, E., Zou, C.C.: Denial of convenience attack to smartphones using a fake Wi-Fi access point. In: Proceedings of IEEE Consumer Communications and Networking Conference (CCNC), pp. 164–170 (2013)
9. Fahl, S., Harbach, M., Muders, T., Baumgärtner, L., Freisleben, B., Smith, M.: Why eve and mallory love android: an analysis of android SSL (in) security. In: Proceedings of ACM Conference on Computer and Communications Security (2012)
10. Faruki, P., et al.: Android security: a survey of issues, malware penetration, and defenses. IEEE Commun. Surv. Tutor. **17**(2), 998–1022 (2014)
11. Felt, A.P., Chin, E., Hanna, S., Song, D., Wagner, D.: Android permissions demystified. In: Proceedings of ACM Conference on Computer and Communications Security (2011)
12. Fernandes, E., Jung, J., Prakash, A.: Security analysis of emerging smart home applications. In: Proceedings of IEEE Symposium on Security and Privacy (SP) (2016)
13. Google: Android. developer.android.com/topic/libraries/support-library (2019)
14. Krupp, B., Sridhar, N., Zhao, W.: SPE: security and privacy enhancement framework for mobile devices. IEEE Trans. Dependable Secure Comput. **14**(4), 433–446 (2015)
15. Kywe, S.M., Li, Y., Petal, K., Grace, M.: Attacking android smartphone systems without permissions. In: Proceedings of IEEE Conference on Privacy, Security and Trust (PST), pp. 147–156 (2016)
16. Mustafa, H., Xu, W.: CETAD: detecting evil twin access point attacks in wireless hotspots. In: Proceedings of IEEE Conference on Communication and Network Security (2014)
17. Park, M.W., Choi, Y.H., Eom, J.H., Chung, T.M.: Dangerous Wi-Fi access point: attacks to benign smartphone applications. Pers. Ubiquit. Comput. **18**(6), 1373–1386 (2014)
18. Poese, I., Uhlig, S., Kaafar, M.A., Donnet, B., Gueye, B.: Ip geolocation databases: unreliable? ACM SIGCOMM Comput. Comm. Review **41**(2), 53–56 (2011)

19. Sarma, B.P., Li, N., Gates, C., Potharaju, R., Nita-Rotaru, C., Molloy, I.: Android permissions: a perspective combining risks and benefits. In: Proceedings of ACM Symposium on Access Control Models and Technologies, pp. 13–22 (2012)

20. Shabtai, A., Kanonov, U., Elovici, Y., Glezer, C., Weiss, Y.: "Andromaly": a behavioral malware detection framework for android devices. J. Intell. Inform. Syst. **38**(1), 161–190 (2012)

21. Tramontana, E., Verga, G.: Mitigating privacy-related risks for android users. In: Proceedings of IEEE International Conference on Enabling Technologies: Infrastructure for Collaborative Enterprises (WETICE) (2019)

22. Verga, G., Fornaia, A., Calcagno, S., Tramontana, E.: Yet another way to unknowingly gather people coordinates and its countermeasures. In: Montella, R., et al. (eds.) Proceedings of International Conference on Internet and Distributed Computing Systems (IDCS). LNCS, vol. 11874. Springer (2019)

Multidimensional Neuroimaging Processing in ReCaS Datacenter

Angela Lombardi[1][(✉)], Eufemia Lella[1,2], Nicola Amoroso[2], Domenico Diacono[1], Alfonso Monaco[1], Roberto Bellotti[1,2], and Sabina Tangaro[1]

[1] Istituto Nazionale di Fisica Nucleare, Sezione di Bari,
via E. Orabona 4, 70125 Bari, Italy
angela.lombardi@ba.infn.it

[2] Dipartimento Interateneo di Fisica "M. Merlin", Universitá degli Studi di Bari,
via E. Orabona 4, 70125 Bari, Italy

Abstract. In the last decade, a large amount of neuroimaging datasets became publicly available on different archives, so there is an increasing need to manage heterogeneous data, aggregate and process them by means of large-scale computational resources. ReCaS datacenter offers the most important features to manage big datasets, process them, store results in efficient manner and make all the pipeline steps available for reproducible data analysis. Here, we present a scientific computing environment in ReCaS datacenter to deal with common problems of large-scale neuroimaging processing. We show the general architecture of the datacenter and the main steps to perform multidimensional neuroimaging processing.

Keywords: Neuroimaging · Pipeline · Datacenter · Parallel computing · Big data

1 Introduction

Recent advances in neuroimaging analysis have been also supported by the high-throughput analysis of large amounts of data [7,17,19]. In this field standard approaches for data acquisition and analysis are required to increase global collaboration and promote replicability and reliability of brain imaging findings. Big data open sharing brain imaging repositories have improved these goals: Alzheimer's Disease Neuroimaging Initiative (ADNI) [10], Autism Brain Imaging Data Exchange (ABIDE) [5] are two examples of international collaboration of cross-sectional imaging sites that have aggregated neuroimaging data openly shared to improve the understanding of physiological phenomena in some brain diseases.

Huge computational resources such as gpu hardware, grid infrastructure and network bandwidth are required to support parallelization and distribution of efficient computational and communication resources [6]. If on one hand these

© Springer Nature Switzerland AG 2019
R. Montella et al. (Eds.): IDCS 2019, LNCS 11874, pp. 468–477, 2019.
https://doi.org/10.1007/978-3-030-34914-1_44

resources facilitate the processing of large amounts of data and allow a more efficient analysis of the resulting imaging datasets, on the other hand they introduce a considerable complexity of resource management and demand of experienced users. In order to facilitate interoperability between interdisciplinary figures in the computational neuroscience field, it is appropriate to build pipelines that formalize the main steps to be taken to achieve high-quality results [20]. In addition, different analysis pipelines can produce significantly different results, raising questions about the replicability and reliability of scientific findings. Hence, it is important to integrate more strategies to explore the impact of particular processing decisions by allowing users to run multiple analysis pipelines, with a different set of preprocessing options.

Here, we present a scientific computing environment in ReCaS datacenter [1] to deal with common problems of large-scale neuroimaging processing. We show the general architecture of the datacenter and the main steps to perform multidimensional neuroimaging processing. In particular, some examples of studies in which the scientific computing structure has been used for multimodal processing of structural and functional images, massive computation of features relevant to the classification of subjects with Alzheimer's disease and schizophrenia will be shown.

2   ReCaS Infrastructure

2.1   General Architecture

The general architecture of ReCaS is shown in Fig. 1. The ReCaS-Bari computing farm has been built by the ReCaS project[1], funded by the Italian Research Ministry of Education, University and Research to the University of Bari and INFN (National Institute for Nuclear Physics), whose goal is to enpower preexisting computing infrastructures located in Catania, Cosenza, Napoli and Bari. In particular the data center offers 128 servers, 64 cores per server, for a total amount of 8192 new cores, reaching 12000 cores with the old computing farm. Each new server hosts 256 GB RAM, 4 GB RAM per core per server. Additionally, it offers about 3.5 PB of disk space and 2.5 PB of tape space, together with a 20 Gbps link to/from WAN. The mentioned resources are far enough to fulfil the needs of the project. So the data center is one of the biggest italian supercomputers built with public funds. It is well integrated into national and international infrastructures like WLCG (World LHC Computing Grid), EGI (European Grid Infrastructure), EGI Federated Cloud. The ReCaS Farm supports several life science communities and projects (Medical Phisycs, Elixir project, LifeWatch), etc. In particular the lifescience community uses up 6% of the farm resources. The centre offers:

- the possibility to require specific services on virtual machines;
- the possibility to execute parallel jobs based on MPI library;

---

[1] http://www.pon-recas.it.

– facilities to manage the execution of a bunches of independent jobs (automatic grid scheduling) also by means of WebServices;
– "Cloud Storage" services based on WebDav and ownCloud.

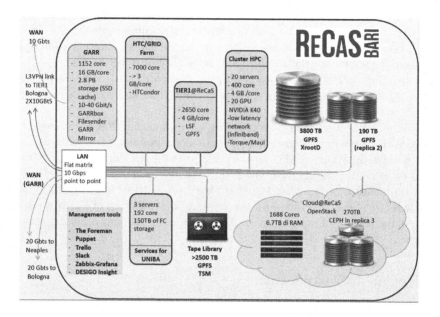

Fig. 1. The general architecture of ReCaS.

2.2   Access to Services

High-Throughput Computing. The farm batch has approximately 9000 job slots each with 4 GB of RAM available. Each calculation server, which contains up to 64 slots, can access, at a speed of 10 Gbps, all the disk space of ReCaS-Bari equal to 3800 TB in a single replication plus 180 Tb in two replication (for the most valuable data). The distributed GPFS file system is used for storage management. The operating system used is CentOS 7, and queues are managed by the HTCondor batch system, which can perform mono- and multi-core jobs. The choice of the queue system operator (Batch System) finally fell on HTCondor for a number of reasons:

– it is an open source product;
– it is oriented to High Throughput Computing and therefore suitable to manage the applications that will be run in ReCaS data center;
– it is able to operate with heterogeneous hardware, assembling together servers with different technical characteristics;
– it has proved to be stable and able to manage the expected load volume for a data center of the size of ReCaS;
– it has proven to scale easily in the event that resources increase in the future.

High Performance Computing. The cluster has up to 400 physical cores (800 considering hyperthreading) each with 4 GB of RAM. It consists of 20 servers connected to each other with low-latency connections (Infiniband), each equipped with an NVIDIA K40 graphics accelerator card. Each computing server can access, at a speed of 10 Gbps, the entire disk space of ReCaS-Bari (3800 TB in a single replication plus 180 TB in two replication) managed through the distributed GPFS file system.

The operating system used is CentOS 7 while Torque/MAUI (PBS) is used for queue management.

Cloud Computing. The INFN Bari Cloud infrastructure is an open source software platform providing a federated IaaS/PaaS cloud computing solution developed by the PRISMA project[2].

The cloud INFN respects all the paradigms at the base of the definition of cloud computing: on- demand self-service resources that are pooled, can be accessed via a network, and can be elastically adjusted by the user. The pooling of resources across a large user base enables economies of scale, while the ability to easily provision and elastically expand the resources provides flexible capabilities. The INFN Cloud is OpenStack based. OpenStack is an Open Source cloud software stack that is able to control large pools of computing, storage, and networking resources throughout a datacenter, all managed through a dashboard that gives administrators control while empowering their users to provision resources through a web interface. OpenStack is designed to provide flexibility in the design of the cloud, with no proprietary hardware or software requirements and the ability to integrate with legacy systems and third party technologies. It is designed to manage and automate pools of compute resources and can work with widely available virtualization technologies, as well as bare metal and high-performance computing (HPC) configurations.

3 Multidimensional Processing

In ReCaS datacenter it is possible to create a custom pipeline for preprocessing and analysis of structural and functional neuroimaging data by efficiently combining different tools or by running open-source already published software pipelines such us C-PAC (for fMRI data) [4] or MRtrix (for DTI imaging) [18]. The most useful pre-installed tools are:

- AFNI [3] is an environment for processing and displaying functional MRI data. The basic unit of data storage is the "3D dataset", which consists of one or more 3D arrays of voxel values (bytes, shorts, floats, or complex numbers), plus some control information stored in a header file.
- FSL [11] is a comprehensive library of analysis tools for fMRI, MRI and DTI brain imaging data. The most popular tools for MRI processing are: BET to

---

[2] http://www.ponsmartcities-prisma.it.

segment brain from non-brain in structural and functional data, and models skull and scalp surfaces; FLIRT to linear inter- and intra-modal registration; TBSS is a tool for voxelwise analysis of multi-subject diffusion data.
- FreeSurfer [8] provides a full processing stream for structural MRI data, including skull stripping, B1 bias field correction; gray-white matter segmentation and reconstruction of cortical surface models.
- The SPM software package [16] has been designed for the analysis of brain imaging data sequences. The sequences can be a series of images from different cohorts, or time-series from the same subject. The current release is designed for the analysis of fMRI, PET, SPECT, EEG and MEG.

In addition, existing pipelines can be integrated with new tools, thus resulting in a highly scalable and flexible system.

The following steps describe the framework to run a processing neuroimaging pipeline in ReCaS datacenter. They are also reported in Fig. 2.

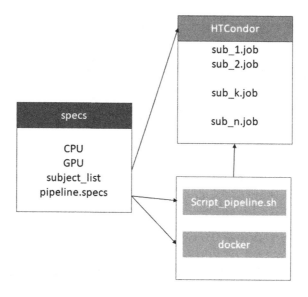

Fig. 2. Framework to generate neuroimaging pipelines.

First of all, downloaded data are re-organized according to BIDS standard [9]. The specification is based on simple file formats and folder structures to reflect current lab practices and largely adopted by scientists coming from different backgrounds.

A specification file for the selected (or customized) pipeline is required in order to facilitate the submission and execution of jobs in this computing environment by using batch-queuing systems such as HTCondor[3]. In particular, users

---
[3] https://research.cs.wisc.edu/htcondor/.

define computational resources such as CPU, GPU, memory requirements, number of processors, etc., pipeline specifications by means of a *pipeline.specs* file and a list of subjects whose data need to be processed. The resulting configuration file (*specs.json*) is then used to generate:

1. external scripts for customized pipelines;
2. docker images of available published pipelines.

Both external scripts and docker images can be executed by a final htcondor submission file which allows the pipeline to be run with parallel jobs for the different subjects specified in the list. Indeed, pipelines nodes can be run in parallel if they have no inter-dependencies. As example, data from different participants or sessions do not have inter-dependencies. Data from different series collected on same participant and session have some inter-dependencies but are mostly independent.

The computing environment enables multiple pipelines to be run for the same subject by specifying a simple option in *specs.json* and the list of pipelines. In addition to the final images processed, the other outputs of each pipeline include: log files, crash files and quantitative metrics of imaging quality that can be used to compare the effectiveness of different processing techniques and parameters set in the pipelines. It is also possible to generate docker files for the pipelines, thus making the customized pipelines reproducible.

4   Example Studies

4.1   Diffusion Weighted Imaging

In [13] and [12] we performed two different pipelines to compute probabilistic tractography and construct connectivity matrix of each subject of two normal and pathological cohorts from the ADNI database.

In [13] we analysed DWI images of 122 subjects, both male and female. In accordance with diagnosis, the subjects were grouped into 52 HCs, 40 AD patients and 30 MCI converter subjects. We employed the diffusion toolkit FDT of FSL to define a processing pipeline.

- First, eddy current correction was performed to mitigate artefacts, such as enhanced background, image intensity loss and image blurring, caused by eddy currents and head motion.
- Brain Extraction Tool (BET) was used in order to delete non-brain tissues from each subject scan.
- An affine registration of all scans was employed in order to spatially normalize the whole data set to the MNI152 standard space.
- Then, a single diffusion tensor was fitted at each voxel in every image by using DTIfit. From the diffusion tensor, FA and MD can be calculated accordingly.
- Finally, probabilistic tractography was performed using ProbTrackX [2] in order to obtain the connectivity matrix of each subject.

We defined these specifications in a configuration files to build the external scripts for each subject. Then the pipeline was run with parallel jobs for all the subjects specified in a subject list. We also used parallel computing to perform the machine learning classification framework to study the most important connectivity metrics for the HC/AD and HC/AD/MCI classification. To this end, a 50-times repeated 10-fold cross-validation was performed. Moreover, we repeated the 10-fold cross-validation 50 times for permutation testing for computing the reference null model and assessing statistical significance of the classification results.

In [12], after the preprocessing and co-registration steps, instead a structural connectome generation pipeline was performed. We run the docker images of the MRtrix pipeline by specifying the parameters in a input file for each subject.

4.2   Functional Magnetic Resonance Imaging

In [14] fMRI data of 49 participants and 42 patients with schizophrenia performing 2-back and 0-back experiments were used to define task-evoked networks. We performed standard fMRI preprocessing steps using SPM12:

- The images were realigned to correct for motion artifacts. Movement parameters were extracted to exclude data affected by excessive head motion;
- Realigned images were resliced to a 3.75 mm isotropic voxel size, co-registered to high-resolution T1-weighted structural images, spatially normalized into a standard space (Montreal Neurological Institute), smoothed with a 10 mm full-width at half-maximum isotropic kernel and temporal band-pass filtered.
- Additionally, nuisance signal correction was done on the data by regressing out (1) linear trends in the time series; (2) mean time-series from the white matter (WM) and the cerebrospinal fluid (CSF); (3) 24 motion parameters obtained by motion correction (as specified in the Friston24 model; and (4) signals extracted using the CompCor algorithm.
- To extract mean time-series from the WM, gray matter, and CSF the anatomical MR data were automatically segmented.

After parallel preprocessing running on all the subjects with the defined pipeline, we applied a framework to define 17 connectivity matrices for each subject, each matrix describing a dynamic synchronization behaviour among the fMRI time series. This framework was also executed on all subjects. Then, we applied a graph-based analysis to extract a matrix of features used to classify controls/schizophrenic patients with repeated cross-validation scheme. In this work we also performed 5000 permutations for comparison of the classification performance to the chance level. The computational scheme of the running jobs is reported in Fig. 3.

4.3   Structural Magnetic Resonance Imaging

In [15] a novel strategy for fully automated hippocampal segmentation in MRI is presented. In this work two datasets are employed, both obtained from the

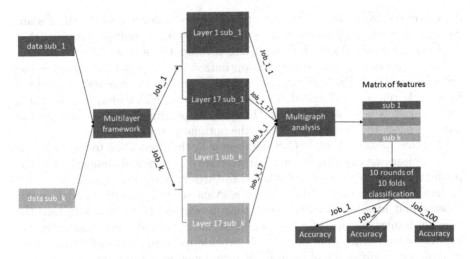

Fig. 3. Example of computing framework for the analysis published in [14]

ADNI database, consisting of MR images and their corresponding expert manual labels produced with a standard harmonized protocol. The first data set,
DB1, was used for training the algorithms and estimating evaluation metrics
via cross validation. The second data set, DB2, was employed for an assessment
of the performance of the fully trained classifiers. Preprocessing involved a first
registration through a six-parameter affine transformation to the Montreal Neurological Institute MNI152 template. Then a gross peri-hippocampal volume was
extracted for left and right hippocampi for each scan and for the template; these
regions underwent a further affine registration using the template hippocampal boxes as reference images. In this way, two Volumes of Interest (VOIs) of
dimension $50 \times 60 \times 60$ were obtained. The two registrations and box extraction were fully automated. The 3D segmentation was performed using for each
voxel a vector of 315 elements representing information about position, intensity,
neighboring texture, and local filters. Parallel computing was used to perform
multiple rounds of CV using different partitions of the training set consisting of
$180000\times$ the number of training (test) images $\times$ the number of components.

5   Discussion and Conclusion

In this work, we have shown the general architecture of a scientific computing environment in ReCaS datacenter for neuroimaging processing In the last
decade, a large amount of neuroimaging data became publicly available on different archives, with different structure, so there is an increasing need to manage
heterogeneous data, aggregate and process them by means of large-scale computational resources. ReCaS environment offers the most important features for
manage big datasets, process them, store results in efficient manner and make
all the pipeline steps available for reproducible data analysis. In particular, the

data retrieved from different servers are aggregated according to the BIDS standard and the resulting images can be processed by using multiple pipelines that are easily customized and integrated into a computational workflow. The neuroimaging processing environment is optimized for large datasets since it has been designed to reliably preprocess and analyize data for hundreds of subjects in a single run, on a distributed environment using HTCondor. The resulting environment is scalable and make the analysis pipelines easier to compare in order to select the best strategy with the optimal parameters.

Another advantage of ReCaS datacenter is the possibility to run multiple machine learning algorithms for a multivariate experimental comparison of the predictive power of neuroimaging-based features for clinical purposes. As shown in Sect. 4, it has been used to produce relevant scientific results in Alzheimer's Disease and in schizophrenia. For future developments we will integrate the different frameworks used for the analysis of the examined diseases in the implemented pipelines. In addition, we will provide more tools in order to support extensive multidimensional analysis of neuroimaging datasets for deep leaning modeling.

References

1. Amoroso, N., et al.: Medical physics applications in Bari ReCaS farm. In: High Performance Scientific Computing Using Distributed Infrastructures: Results and Scientific Applications Derived from the Italian PON ReCaS Project, pp. 271–278. World Scientific (2017)
2. Behrens, T.E., Berg, H.J., Jbabdi, S., Rushworth, M.F., Woolrich, M.W.: Probabilistic diffusion tractography with multiple fibre orientations: what can we gain? Neuroimage **34**(1), 144–155 (2007)
3. Cox, R.W.: AFNI: software for analysis and visualization of functional magnetic resonance neuroimages. Comput. Biomed. Res. **29**(3), 162–173 (1996)
4. Craddock, C., et al.: Towards automated analysis of connectomes: the configurable pipeline for the analysis of connectomes (C-PAC). Front Neuroinform. **42** (2013)
5. Di Martino, A., et al.: The autism brain imaging data exchange: towards a large-scale evaluation of the intrinsic brain architecture in autism. Mol. Psychiatry **19**(6), 659 (2014)
6. Dinov, I., et al.: Efficient, distributed and interactive neuroimaging data analysis using the LONI pipeline. Front. Neuroinform. **3**, 22 (2009)
7. Dinov, I.D., et al.: High-throughput neuroimaging-genetics computational infrastructure. Front. Neuroinform. **8**, 41 (2014)
8. Fischl, B.: Freesurfer. Neuroimage **62**(2), 774–781 (2012)
9. Gorgolewski, K.J., et al.: The brain imaging data structure, a format for organizing and describing outputs of neuroimaging experiments. Sci. Data **3**, 160044 (2016)
10. Jack Jr., C.R., et al.: The Alzheimer's disease neuroimaging initiative (ADNI): MRI methods. J. Magn. Reson. Imaging: Off. J. Int. Soc. Magn. Reson. Med. **27**(4), 685–691 (2008)
11. Jenkinson, M., Beckmann, C.F., Behrens, T.E., Woolrich, M.W., Smith, S.M.: FSL. Neuroimage **62**(2), 782–790 (2012)
12. Lella, E., et al.: Communicability characterization of structural DWI subcortical networks in Alzheimer's disease. Entropy **21**(5), 475 (2019)

13. Lella, E., et al.: Communicability disruption in Alzheimer's diseaseconnectivity networks. J. Complex Netw. **7**(1), 83–100 (2018)
14. Lombardi, A., et al.: Modelling cognitive loads in schizophrenia by means of new functional dynamic indexes. NeuroImage **195**, 150–164 (2019)
15. Maglietta, R., et al.: Automated hippocampal segmentation in 3D MRI using random undersampling with boosting algorithm. Pattern Anal. Appl. **19**(2), 579–591 (2016)
16. Penny, W.D., Friston, K.J., Ashburner, J.T., Kiebel, S.J., Nichols, T.E.: Statistical Parametric Mapping: The Analysis of Functional Brain Images. Elsevier, Amsterdam (2011)
17. Poldrack, R.A., Gorgolewski, K.J.: Making big data open: data sharing in neuroimaging. Nat. Neurosci. **17**(11), 1510 (2014)
18. Tournier, J.D., Calamante, F., Connelly, A.: MRtrix: diffusion tractography in crossing fiber regions. Int. J. Imaging Syst. Technol. **22**(1), 53–66 (2012)
19. Van Horn, J.D., Toga, A.W.: Human neuroimaging as a "big data" science. Brain Imaging Behav. **8**(2), 323–331 (2014)
20. Zuo, X.N., et al.: An open science resource for establishing reliability and reproducibility in functional connectomics. Sci. Data **1**, 140049 (2014)

A Data Preparation Approach for Cloud Storage Based on Containerized Parallel Patterns

Diana Carrizales[1], Dante D. Sánchez-Gallegos[1(✉)], Hugo Reyes[1],
J. L. Gonzalez-Compean[1], Miguel Morales-Sandoval[1], Jesus Carretero[2],
and Alejandro Galaviz-Mosqueda[3]

[1] Cinvestav Tamaulipas, Ciudad Victoria, Mexico
{dcarrizales,dsanchez,hreyes,jgonzalez,mmorales}@tamps.cinvestav.mx
[2] Universidad Carlos III de Madrid, Madrid, Spain
jesus.carretero@uc3m.es
[3] CICESE, Ensenada, Mexico
agalaviz@cicese.edu.mx

Abstract. In this paper, we present the design, implementation, and evaluation of an efficient data preparation and retrieval approach for cloud storage. The approach includes a deduplication subsystem that indexes the hash of each content to identify duplicated data. As a consequence, avoiding duplicated content reduces reprocessing time during uploads and other costs related to outsource data management tasks. Our proposed data preparation scheme enables organizations to add properties such as security, reliability, and cost-efficiency to their contents before sending them to the cloud. It also creates recovery schemes for organizations to share preprocessed contents with partners and end-users. The approach also includes an engine that encapsulates preprocessing applications into virtual containers (VCs) to create parallel patterns that improve the efficiency of data preparation retrieval process. In a study case, real repositories of satellite images, and organizational files were prepared to be migrated to the cloud by using processes such as compression, encryption, encoding for fault tolerance, and access control. The experimental evaluation revealed the feasibility of using a data preparation approach for organizations to mitigate risks that still could arise in the cloud. It also revealed the efficiency of the deduplication process to reduce data preparation tasks and the efficacy of parallel patterns to improve the end-user service experience.

Keywords: Deduplication systems · Virtual containers · Parallel patterns · Content delivery · Cloud storage

This research was supported by "Fondo Sectorial de Investigación para la Educación", SEP-CONACyT Mexico, through projects 281565 and 285276.

© Springer Nature Switzerland AG 2019
R. Montella et al. (Eds.): IDCS 2019, LNCS 11874, pp. 478–490, 2019.
https://doi.org/10.1007/978-3-030-34914-1_45

1   Introduction

The volume of data managed by the organizations has been incremented dramatically over the past years [3]. This trend has been mainly produced because the end-users associated with organizations produce and store data in a consistent manner, which produces a data accumulation effect [15].

The outsourcing of data management tasks with cloud providers has become a popular solution for organizations to manage large volumes of data in a cost-efficient manner [13]. Nevertheless, outsourcing data management commonly also means a lack of controls over outsourced data [18]. This could result in critical incidents such as outages, violations of confidentiality, and unauthorized access [1]. Currently, end-to-end and in-house solutions have been proposed for adding properties such as security [11,20], reliability [5,6], and integrity [19] to the contents. This type of solution mitigates and, in some cases, eliminates the effects produced by a given incident that could arise in the cloud.

However, applying these techniques to the data in real scenarios represents a challenge for the organizations as this process is expensive in terms of operations sent to the outsourcing service and, depending on the data volume, it could be a time-consuming task.

The accumulation of data could increase the inefficiency and costs issues associated with preprocessing solutions. For instance, the existence of duplicated data produced by lousy management of documents versions, or accumulated backups performed by the end-users could result in unnecessary processing time associated to cloud operations of such duplicated data.

Data preparation is a technique mainly used in big data scenarios to preprocess and transform data for improving its quality. We propose to apply this technique to the preprocessing tools used by organizations to prevent suffering side-effects from the lack of control of the outsourced data previously described.

In this paper, we present the design, implementation, and evaluation of an efficient data preparation approach. This approach has been designed to achieve two goals: *(i)* to reduce the number of contents or amount of data to be preprocessed, which also reduce the data sent to the cloud and also reduces the costs of the outsource data management tasks; and *(ii)* to execute the preprocessing operations in parallel to improve the efficiency of the data preparation process.

To achieve the first goal, our approach includes a deduplication system that calculates the hash of each file and indexes them to identify data already prepared. It is expected that this system reduces the amount of data to be preprocessed in the data preparation process. Whereas to achieve the second goal, the approach also includes a preprocessing scheme based on parallel patterns encapsulated into VCs [16,17] that improve the efficiency of the application executed in the data reparation process.

A prototype of this approach was developed and included as an intermediary between the users' folders and a cloud storage service. In a study case, real repositories of satellite images and organizational files were prepared to be migrated to the cloud by using data preparation and retrieval schemes built by using our approach.

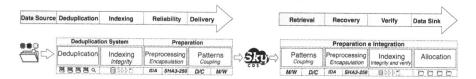

Fig. 1. Conceptual representation of schemes for *data preparation and delivery in cloud* as well as *data decoding and retrieval from cloud*

The data preparation schemes considered in the prototype included applications performing tasks such as compression, encryption, encoding for fault tolerance, and access control. The implementation of these schemes provided to organizations with storage cost-efficiency, security, reliability, and attribute-based access control. The retrieval scheme enables organizations to share prepared data with partners and end-users.

The experimental evaluation revealed the feasibility of using a data preparation approach for organizations for mitigating risks that could arise in the cloud. Retrieval schemes also were evaluated for end-users to share data with other end-users. It also revealed the efficiency of the deduplication process to reduce data preparation and retrieval tasks. It also revealed the efficacy of parallel patterns to improve the end-user service experience.

The paper is organized as follows: Sect. 2 presents the design strategies of a virtual container-based service for cost-efficient data preparation. Section 3 presents the implementation details of a prototype based on the proposed approach. Section 4 describes the experimentation methodology. Section 5 presents the results of the experimentation. Section 6 describes the related work. Finally, Sect. 7 gives conclusion remarks.

2   A Data Preparation Approach Based on Containerized Parallel Patterns

In this section, we describe the design principles of the two components considered in the data preparation approach proposed in this paper. The first one is a deduplication system, and the second one is an engine for the data preparation and retrieval schemes.

Figure 1 shows the conceptual representation of a Client application that *Uploads* contents to the cloud by using data preparation scheme (left). Figure 1 also shows how this client *Downloads* shared contents by using a retrieval scheme (right). As it can be seen, the preparation scheme includes stages such as deduplication and indexing, as well as reliability and delivery. The distribution of the files to the cloud and/or to the end-users is managed by using a content delivery service, called SkyCDS [4], which compresses and encrypts data in-house before transporting them to a multi-cloud storage environment. The retrieval scheme includes stages such as retrieval of prepared data by using SkyCDS, the recovery from codification performed in the data preparation scheme, the verification of the recovered data integrity, and the allocation of these data in the storage locations of the end-users and partners. Figure 1 will be used to describe each component of the preparation and retrieval schemes.

2.1 A Deduplication System for Cloud Storage

The deduplication service for cloud storage is based on a hash algorithm h (SHA-3-256 [2]), which is used to generate the contents fingerprint $h(C)$ and used to detect duplicates: if $C_1 = C_2$ then $h(C_1) = h(C_2)$. So, h allows identifying replicated contents before sending them to the data preparation scheme. In this system, the hash of each dataset is calculated and compared to the hashes previously discovered by the system (See deduplication system in Fig. 1).

The hashes constitute metadata and the delivery of associated content to the cloud is rejected as these hashes already have been preprocessed in the past. In turn, the hashes that are not found by the deduplication system (*unique data*) are indexed in a hashing metadata database (implemented in MongoDB), and these files are sent to the data preparation system (See indexing in Fig. 1).

In this system, two types of granularity can be used to detect replicated files. The fine-grained control is used by the system to identify, file-by-file, the replicated data. In this type of control, a simple query determines whether a data is replicated or not. In turn, coarse-grained control is used to detect sets of data that are replicated (directories or partitions). In this case, the system implements Merkle trees [12] (also based on hashing) to determine whether a directory already has been preprocessed or not.

In the prototype for preparation data, as showed in Fig. 1 the deduplication system is executed when uploading data in the cloud, whereas the integrity ensuring method is applied to the downloads of contents in information sharing operations for end-users and partners to discover and register alterations in retrieved contents.

2.2 Building Data Preparation and Retrieval Schemes

The second component of our approach is an engine that creates data preparation and retrieval schemes, which are used to preprocessing contents not filtered by the deduplication system. The basic idea of this engine is encapsulating all the components of the schemes created by the approach (including deduplication system, indexing system, and preprocessing applications) into VCs.

The VCs provide the preparation/retrieval schemes with portability property. This enables the schemes to be deployed on different platforms. This means all the software components of each data preparation and retrieval scheme are encapsulated into the VCs with its dependencies such as libraries, packages, OS, and environment variables.

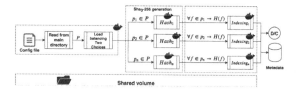

Fig. 2. Deduplication pattern based on VCs.

The VCs are managed in the form of Building Blocks (BBs) that can be coupled by using I/O interfaces such as memory, network, and file system to create a directed graph [16].

In a directed graph, the nodes represent BBs, whereas the edges represent the I/O interfaces used to connect two BBs. A dataflow for either preprocessing or retrieving data is created, when a preparation/retrieval procedure starts by using a directed graph as a guide.

2.3   Parallel Patterns for Data Preparation and Retrieval Schemes

The directed graphs used in this approach enable the approach to build parallel patterns for facing up efficiency issues that arise when preparing and retrieving a large amount of data. In this paper, parallel patterns such as a Manager/worker, Divide&Conquer and fork-join are considered.

Manager/Worker. In this pattern, the *Manager* processes data in phases such as cloning, task definition/distribution, and task execution supervision. In the cloning phase, the Manager creates VC instances of a given stage image included in either preparation or recovery schemes. These clones are used as *worker* instances. In the task definition/distribution phase, the Manager reads, in a recursive fashion, the contents stored in a data source directory DS. In this phase, the manager also creates a list of paths $\mathbf{P} = \{Path_1, Path_2, \cdots, Path_n\}$ and distributes each path to each worker in a load-balanced manner by using the two choices algorithm [10]. In the supervision phase, the *Manager* verifies that all workers are delivering results for the tasks previously assigned to them.

Figure 2 depicts the conceptual representation of the deduplication service as a parallel pattern deployed over VCs. Each worker includes a pipeline that performs the hashing and indexing stages over a sub-list $p_i \in P$ of content paths delivered to the worker by the *Manager*.

The *workers* performs the calculation of the hash $h(\cdot)$ of each content in p_i ($\forall f \in p_i \rightarrow h(f)$) using SHA-3 technique. The hashes calculated are immediately send to a indexing container, called *metadata*. The indexing service finds all the unique hash from the list, saving them in a table ($\mathbf{T}[f_u]$) as $<h(f_u), [f_1, f_2, f_3, \ldots, f_n]>$, where $H(f_u)$ represents the hash of a unique file, and $[f_1, f_2, f_3, \ldots, f_n]$ is a list of paths to the files with the same hash ($h(f_1) == h(f_2) == h(f_3) == h(f_n)$). In order to keep consistency between the

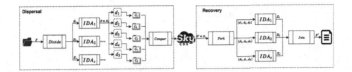

Fig. 3. Reliability and recovery processes by using $D\&C$ pattern.

replicated files through the *clients*, the table of hashes is sent to the *metadata* database, where each hash is registered in.

Divide & Conquer. In this pattern ($D\&C$), a software instance called *divide* splits each incoming data into s segments, which are sent to s number of workers previously cloned and launched in configuration time. A software instance called *Conquer* receives the results produced by the workers and consolidates the results to send them to either a next stage in a scheme or to the cloud.

The reliability and recovery stages of the preparation and retrieval schemes are based on the well-known information dispersal algorithm (IDA) [14]. This algorithm splits files into n segments (called dispersal files). In the preparation scheme, the basic idea of using IDA is to add redundancy to each dispersal and to distribute them to n different storage locations. In the retrieval scheme, the idea is recovering the original file by downloading any m segments from n ones created initially and sent them to the cloud (whenever $m < n$). As a result, a file is not sent to the cloud, but its dispersal and the schemes can withstand the failure/unavailability of $n - m$ dispersal files.

In the data preparation scheme, IDA was implemented by using the $D\&C$ pattern. Figure 3 shows an example of this pattern. As it can be seen, *divide* instance splits each data (per processed processed data (d_j)) into c chucks, which are send to c workers. Each worker ($W \in \{IDA_1, \cdots, IDA_n\} \in D\&C$) executes the IDA algorithm to process one segment and produces five dispersal files ($n = 5$); as a result, the pattern produces ($c * n$) redundant portions, which are allocated in shared memory. These portions are retrieved by the *Conquer* from the shared memory and allocates five consolidated dispersal files in each of the five storage locations. In this IDA configuration, the system can withstand the failure/unavailability of two storage locations ($n - m$), which means the retrieval of three dispersal files is sufficient to reconstruct d_j. The redundancy produced by this algorithm is $R = (L/M) * (n - M)$. This pattern produces data parallelism that is quite effective when processing large files (e.g., satellite and health images as well as multimedia and backups).

The recovery stage of the retrieval scheme was implemented as a fork-join pattern. This means a manager retrieves ($m = 3$) three dispersal files from the CDS per each data (d_j) and sends these files to a worker, which reconstructs the original data (d_j). At this point, the patterns deliver d_j to the next stage in the retrieval scheme (e.g., allocation) for end-user can use either store it in a local storage path or send it forward to another CDN or other end-user.

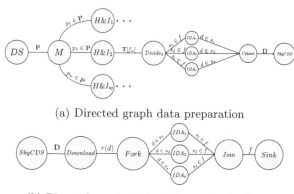

(a) Directed graph data preparation

(b) Directed graph of the data retrieval scheme

Fig. 4. Parallel data preparation and retrieval schemes based on directed graphs.

2.4 Data Preparation and Retrieval Schemes as Directed Graphs

In order to show the interconnection and combination of patterns, we describe the directed graphs of the data preparation and retrieval schemes. Figure 4 shows the data preparation and retrieval scheme represented as a directed graph.

As can be seen, the data are prepared through a set of stages, creating dataflows in pipelines. Bifurcations, producing parallelism, are created when parallel patterns are used in a given stage (see the *Manager/Worker* at deduplication stage and *D&C* at reliability stage in the directed graph of the data preparation scheme).

3 Prototype Implementation Details

The components such as deduplication system, the IDA component, and the hash algorithm h (SHA-3-256) were implemented mainly in C programming. The client implementing the data preparation and retrieval schemes also were developed in C programming.

The integrity verification metadata service has been developed as a web service and a database *Mongo* database deployed in the cloud.

The BBs and the parallel patterns were created by using a framework based on a construction model called Kulla [16]. The content delivery was implemented as a client and multi-cloud storage service instances provided by SkyCDS [4] (which is developed by using web services). An LZ4 compression programmed in C and a cryptosystem based on AES and CP-ABE that were programmed in java and incorporated to SkyCDS catalogs.

All the components of the preparation and reliability schemes were encapsulated into VCs created by using the Docker platform.

Table 1. Repositories and IT infrastructure features

	IT features	Set of files			Size (GB)			Duplicated percent	
		Total	Unique	Duplicated	Total	Unique	Duplicated	Files	Capacity
Compute 7	6cores; 24ram	219	130	89	58.29	34.18	24.10	40.63%	41.35%
Compute 8	16cores; 64ram	317465	148147	169318	302.16	146.20	155.96	53.33%	51.61%
Compute 9	12cores; 64ram	126115	43360	82755	300.15	82.54	217.61	65.61%	72.49%
Compute 8	16cores; 64ram	13537	6350	7187	11.63	9.32	2.31	53.09%	11.90%

4   Experimental Evaluation Methodology

The evaluation methodology based on a study case was conducted to evaluate
the performance of the prototype of the data preparation and retrieval schemes
created by the approach proposed in this paper. The study case was based on
real repositories of satellite images and organizational files, which were prepared
to be migrated to the cloud by using processes such as compression, encryption,
encoding for fault tolerance and access control.

4.1   Metrics

The metrics chosen to evaluate the performance of the prototype were the
response time and throughput. The response time represents the time observed
by end-users when uploading/downloading contents in the cloud. This time
includes the elapsed time spent by a preparation/retrieval scheme to preprocess data (service time) plus the transportation time spent by content delivery
network tool. Whereas, the throughput metric represents the number of contents
prepared/retrieved per unit time.

4.2   Repositories and Infrastructure

Table 1 shows the features of four servers, which stores the contents of four repositories. The preparation/retrieval schemes were installed in these four servers to
preprocess contents of a given directory. SkyCDS was configured to cipher and
compress the preprocessed data and then to upload/download them in the cloud.
The first repository (allocated in *Compute 7*) includes 219 files (58.31 GBs).
The 95.45% of the files are satellite imagery of *Landsat5*, 277 MB in mean (see
data distribution of this repository in Fig. 5a). The second repository (stored in
Compute 8) includes 317, 465 files (302.16 GB). Figure 5c depicts the distribution
of the size of the files of this repository. As it can be observed, the 99.96% of
the files of this repository is less than 250 MB. The third repository (stored in
Compute 9) includes 126, 115 files (300.15 GB). In this repository, the 99.85% of
the files have a size of less than 250 MB. This repository was constructed only
for experimental purposes, collecting and duplicating files from different data
sources.

4.3 Experiments

The data preparation and retrieval schemes were evaluated in two phases. In the first one, was evaluated the costs of the deduplication and integrity verification. The experiments of this phase were performed by varying number of workers in patterns deployed on the stages. In the second phase, reliability and recovery schemes were evaluated, including also deduplication and integrity verification as well as including parallel patterns. The results of these experiments were compared with a system including only the reliability and recovery schemes by using the data form Compute7 repository.

5 Results

In this section, the results of the performed experiments in the two evaluation phased previously described are presented and analyzed.

5.1 Analyzing the Costs of the Deduplication and Integrity Verification

Figure 5b and d show, in the left vertical axis, the response time in hours for the stage of deduplication, including analysis and hashing of the files in the data set of *compute 8* and *compute 9*, respectively by using parallelism patterns including a different number of workers (horizontal axis). The right-vertical axis, in both Figures, shows the throughput measured in gigabytes per hour (GB/H).

As it can be seen, the task parallelism pattern based on VCs significantly reduces the response time of this stage of the deduplication and integrity indexing, which also reduces the response time of the *Upload/Download operations* performed by the client of cloud storage. This increases the files processed per hour. For instance, the preparation scheme executed in *Compute 7* processed 58.31 GB in 0.71 h (42.72 min) with only one worker. Whereas with six workers completed the very same task in 0.35 h (21.34 min), which means that the parallel pattern with six workers has an improvement of 50.05% with an acceleration of $2x$ in comparison with running only one worker (see Fig. 5b). We also observed that the improvement of the throughput stops when the $NumOfVCs > RealCores$ (number of VCs running in parallel and the number of real processors in a computer) For instance, in Fig. 5b, the response time increase when the pattern was launching 12 workers, improving the performance of the solution by up 44.46% in comparison with running only one worker.

In *Compute 8*, the schemes spent 22.2 h for preprocessing 285 GB by launching only one worker. This produced a throughput of 12.76 GB/H, whereas the M/W with 28 workers completed the same task in 2.2 h. This means an improvement of 89.70% with an acceleration of $9x$ with the 28 workers in contrast with the version of one worker (see Fig. 5d).

As expected, the task-based parallel patterns based on VCs reduced the response time, increasing the throughput of data preparation and retrieval processes. We observed that this improvement depends on the number of physical cores used by the patterns.

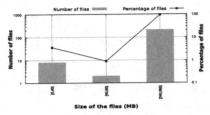

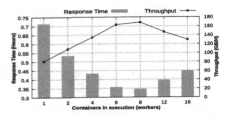

(a) Data distribution of the data set on *Compute 7*.

(b) Response time with a different number of VCs.

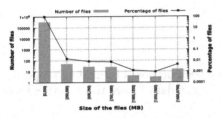

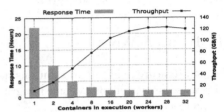

(c) Data distribution of the data set on *Compute 8*.

(d) Response time with a different number of VCs.

Fig. 5. Data distribution of the datasets on *Compute 7* and *Compute 8*, and their the response time to process them

The results of replicated contents discovered and indexed in the integrity verification database are shown in Table 1.

5.2 Analyzing the Impact of Deduplication and Integrity Verification on Reliability and Recovery Stages

The results of the second evaluation phase are described in this section. In this phase we studied the following configurations: *(i) RegularIDA*: This configuration represents the implementation of sequential IDA algorithm; *(ii) Dedup*: This configuration represents the implementation of IDA but including deduplication system; and *(iii) Dedup-IDA-Patterns*: This configuration represents a data preparation scheme (including deduplication and IDA by using D&C pattern).

Figure 6a shows, in the vertical axis, the response time of data reliability preparation and, in the horizontal-axis, the evaluated configurations. The recovery process is shown in Fig. 6b.

As expected, *Dedup-IDA-Patterns* produce the best performance both in preparation and recovery schemes. The response time produced by *RegularIDA* when coding all files (including duplicates) was 79.51 min, the response time produced for *Dedup* configurations was 64.23 min, whereas *Dedup-IDA-Patterns* (by using four workers) was 27.82 min. This means an improvement of 65% for an acceleration of 2.8x.

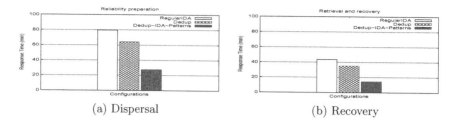

Fig. 6. Response time of the reliability schema for the generation of the dispersals stage (a) and the recovery stage (b).

6 Related Work

In the literature, end-to-end solutions have been proposed for adding properties such as security, reliability, and integrity to the data before transporting them to the cloud.

Morales-Sandoval et al. [11] proposed AES4SEC an end-to-end multi-security service for hybrid clouds, which adds security properties to data by using attribute-based encryption (ABE) and short signatures (SSign). Gonzalez-Compean et al. [5] proposed Sacbe, a BB approach for constructing efficient and flexible end-to-end cloud storage to add reliability property to data.

To provide integrity to data, Xiong et al. [19] proposed CloudSeal, a scheme for securely sharing and distributing data via cloud-based data storage, where the data is encrypted before end-users sharing them with other users. It ensures the confidentiality of contents stored in the cloud. Nevertheless, the major drawbacks of applying these techniques in real scenarios are that organizations have to spend time and resources to manage the operations sent to the outsourcing service, and depending on the volume of the data, this could be cause efficiency problems.

Deduplication techniques to find replicated data have been proposed [7]. StorReduce [9] and Dedupv1 [8] are few examples of this type of solution. There is still an opportunity area to add efficiency property to this type of solutions, which is required for these solutions processing large volumes of data. Moreover, these solutions are commonly developed for a specific platform (OS). This reduces the portability of this type of solution, which is not the case of the approach proposed in this paper.

7 Conclusions and Future Directions

In this paper, we presented the design, implementation and evaluation of an efficient data preparation approach for cloud storage. The approach includes a deduplication system and integration verification method to reduce the number of contents to be preprocessed, which reduce the data sent to the cloud and also reduces the costs of the outsource data management tasks. It also enables end-users to discover alterations of downloaded files. The approach also includes a preprocessing scheme based on parallel patterns encapsulated into

VCs that improve the efficiency of the application executed in the data preparation process. The experimental evaluation revealed the feasibility of using a data preparation approach for organizations to mitigate risks that still could arise in the cloud. It also revealed the efficiency of the deduplication process to reduce data preparation tasks and the efficacy of parallel patterns to improve the end-user service experience. As future work we are working in the evaluation of our approach with other study cases, such as medical imagery and organizational environments.

References

1. Chow, R., et al.: Controlling data in the cloud: outsourcing computation without outsourcing control. In: CCSW 2009, pp. 85–90. ACM (2009)
2. Dworkin, M.J.: SHA-3 standard: permutation-based hash and extendable-output functions (2015)
3. Gantz, J., Reinsel, D.: The digital universe in 2020: big data, bigger digital shadows, and biggest growth in the far east. IDC iView **2007**(2012), 1–16 (2012)
4. Gonzalez, J.L., Perez, J.C., Sosa-Sosa, V.J., Sanchez, L.M., Bergua, B.: SkyCDS: a resilient content delivery service based on diversified cloud storage. Simul. Model. Pract. Theory **54**, 64–85 (2015)
5. Gonzalez, J.L., Sosa, V., Diaz, A., Carretero, J., Yanez, J.: Sacbe: a building block approach for constructing efficient and flexible end-to-end cloud storage. J. Syst. Softw. **135**, 143–156 (2018)
6. Mao, B., Wu, S., Jiang, H.: Improving storage availability in cloud-of-clouds with hybrid redundant data distribution. In: IPDPS 2015m, pp. 633–642. IEEE (2015)
7. Meister, D., Brinkmann, A.: Multi-level comparison of data deduplication in a backup scenario. In: Proceedings of SYSTOR 2009, p. 8. ACM (2009)
8. Meister, D., Brinkmann, A.: dedupv1: improving deduplication throughput using solid state drives (SSD). In: MSST 2010, pp. 1–6. IEEE (2010)
9. Miller, K.: Cloud deduplication, on-demand: storreduce, an apn technology partner: Amazon web services, March 2018. https://aws.amazon.com/blogs/apn/cloud-deduplication-on-demand-storreduce-an-apn-technology-partner/
10. Mitzenmacher, M.: The power of two choices in randomized load balancing. IEEE TPDS **12**(10), 1094–1104 (2001)
11. Morales, M., Gonzalez, J.L., Diaz, A., Sosa, V.J.: A pairing-based cryptographic approach for data security in the cloud. IJISP **17**(4), 441–461 (2018)
12. Ng, W., Wen, Y., Zhu, H.: Private data deduplication protocols in cloud storage. In: Proceedings of the SAC 2012, pp. 441–446. ACM (2012)
13. Plummer, D.C., Bittman, T.J., Austin, T., Cearley, D.W., Smith, D.M.: Cloud computing: defining and describing an emerging phenomenon. Gartner, 17 June 2008
14. Rabin, M.O.: Efficient dispersal of information for security, load balancing, and fault tolerance. JACM **36**(2), 335–348 (1989)
15. Reinsel, D., Gantz, J., Rydning, J.: The digitization of the world: from edge to core. International Data Corporation, Framingham (2018)
16. Reyes, H., Gonzalez, J., Morales, M., Carretero, J.: A data integrity verification service for cloud storage based on building blocks. In: 2018 8th CSIT, pp. 201–206. IEEE (2018)

17. Sánchez, D., Gonzalez, J., Alvarado, S., Sosa, V., Tuxpan, J., Carretero, J.: A containerized service for clustering and categorization of weather records in the cloud. In: CSIT, pp. 26–31. IEEE (2018)
18. Singh, A., Chatterjee, K.: Cloud security issues and challenges: a survey. J. Netw. Comput. Appl. **79**, 88–115 (2017)
19. Xiong, H., Zhang, X., Zhu, W., Yao, D.: CloudSeal: end-to-end content protection in cloud-based storage and delivery services. In: Rajarajan, M., Piper, F., Wang, H., Kesidis, G. (eds.) SecureComm 2011. LNICST, vol. 96, pp. 491–500. Springer, Heidelberg (2012). https://doi.org/10.1007/978-3-642-31909-9_30
20. Zhang, J., Zhang, Z.: Secure and efficient data-sharing in clouds. CCPE **27**(8), 2125–2143 (2015)

Distributed Training of 3DPyranet over Intel AI DevCloud Platform

Emanuel Di Nardo[2(✉)] 🆔 and Fabio Narducci[1(✉)] 🆔

[1] University of Naples Parthenope, 80143 Naples, Italy
fabio.narducci@uniparthenope.it
[2] University of Milan, 20122 Milan, Italy
emanuel.dinardo@unimi.it

Abstract. Neural network architectures have demonstrated to achieve impressive results across a wide range of different domains. The availability of very large datasets makes possible to overcome the limitation of the training stage thus achieving significant level of performance. On the other hand, even though the advancements in GPU hardware, training a complex neural network model still represents a challenge. Long time is required when the computation is demanded to a single machine. In this work, a distributed training approach for 3DPyraNet model built for a specific domain, that is the emotion recognition from videos, is discussed. The proposed work aims at distributing the training procedures over the nodes of the Intel DevCloud Platform and demonstrating how the training performance are affected in terms of both computational demand and achieved accuracy compared to the use of a single machine. The results obtained in an experimental design suggests the feasibility of the approach for challenging computer vision tasks even in presence of limited computing power based on exclusive use of CPUs.

Keywords: Deep learning · Distributed computing · Distributed training · Parallel computation · 3DPyranet

1 Introduction

Nowadays, with the increasing popularity of Artificial Intelligence (AI), more and more computing power is required. In the AI field, and more specifically in the deep learning context, a large amount of data is required to be used by complex mathematical models that in turn require an enormous amount of operations to achieve the expected results. In this scenario, Emotion Recognition, a branch of the wider field of research called *Affective Computing*, is one of the most sensitive topic. The aim is to recognise emotions through facial expressions, an intriguing task but also a significantly difficult computer vision challenge. Computer vision in general has kept big advantages from GPU-based hardware, which makes easier to get a parallelism of computer vision tasks. On the other hand, highly performing GPUs can be very expensive and quite often unavailable. The following study intends to make a comparison of the computational resources needed

© Springer Nature Switzerland AG 2019
R. Montella et al. (Eds.): IDCS 2019, LNCS 11874, pp. 491–497, 2019.
https://doi.org/10.1007/978-3-030-34914-1_46

to be able to deal with the problem of distributed training of complex neural network models. With this objective in mind, it was compared the *de-facto* standard architectures, i.e. training on GPUs, with the less frequently explored one consisting in distributed computation over multiple CPUs and computational nodes, in order to make an analysis of the performance of both. To this end, a known technique in literature for emotion recognition has been used. It is called 3DPyraNet [9] and more specifically its implementation called EmoP3D [4]. It is a deep methodology, strongly inspired by biological neurons, which aims to provide a lighter model with a fewer parameters number compared to similar approaches, like the convolutional neural network (CNN). Moreover, a drastic reduction in the depth of the deep neural network has assured still maintaining the highest possible accuracy. EmoP3D implements a classical pyramidal network model in a monolithic fashion and in this work its paralleled version is proposed. The aim of this work is to explore the benefits deriving from distributing a pyramidal neural network model in a distributed architecture to keep advantage from the availability of CPUs. Moreover, the objective is to investigate how significantly the distributed nature of the training affects the learning performance of the deep neural network.

The paper is organised as follows: Sect. 2 presents the basis of distributed training of deep neural networks providing the common approaches and the state-of-the-art in the field; Sects. 3 and 4 discuss the pyramidal network considered in this study for the problem of emotion recognition and the proposed distributed approach for the training of the network; Sect. 5 discusses the experimental results while Sect. 6 draws the conclusion of this study.

2   Related Work

Data parallelism and Model Parallelism are two common approaches in the literature to deal with the problem of distributing training of neural networks [2]. The former consists in equally dividing the datasets among the nodes of the distributed system while the second approach consists in distributing the network model among the nodes. In this paper, the data parallelism approach has been chosen. All nodes have a local copy of the network model and update local weights. The weights are then shared to compute the global weights to spread to the nodes themselves. If working with batches, a common practice in neural network training, the nodes can synchronise their tasks so that they update the weights with the global ones after processing a batch and before passing to the next one. Asynchronous distributed training, on the other hand, can even introduce a greater level of parallelism with the side effect of being inferior in accuracy compared to the synchronous setting. To this purpose, the recent trend is working with the batch sizes in a synchronous setting in order to fill the gap with the asynchronous approaches. It has been in fact experimentally demonstrated that decreasing the learning rate produces similar results to those obtained by increasing the size of the batch [8]. It also introduces another important benefit because a large batch size requires a fewer number of iteration and therefore a reduced number of overall weight updates a model has to perform. This reasonably implies to faster training time. However, increasing the batch size when the training is performed on a single machine is not particularly effective. The distributed setting can overcome this limitation. By using the distributed synchronous Stochastic Gradient Descent (SGD), the popular ImageNet [3] has been trained in 1 h [5]. Another similar technique known as Layer-wise Adaptive Rate Scaling (LARS) has been proposed to adaptive increase the size of the batches according to the training performance, again demonstrating how increasing the batch size is beneficial.

3   3DPyranet for Emotion Recognition

The biological neuron has a pyramidal structure that shares information with intra-level neurons and, at the end of the computation, it sends a signal to higher layers in the pyramid. 3DPyranet is a deep neural network that has been inspired by the neurons in lower cortical layers, using a pyramidal architecture [1]. It is based on the extraction of spatial and temporal features since it does not work on 2D image space only, but also on a sequence of successive frames to work on the 3rd dimension, which is the time in a video clip in our case. 3DPyranet has been studied in [7] as an alternative to convolutional neural networks. The main component is the 3D Weighted Sum operation (WS3D), defined as:

$$y^l_{u,v,z} = f_l\Big(\sum_{i \in R^l_{u,v,z}} \sum_{j \in R^l_{u,v,z}} \sum_{k \in R^l_{u,v,z}} [W^l_{i,j,k} \circ x^{l-1}_{i,j,k}] + b^l_{u,v,z} \Big) \qquad (1)$$

where l is the current layer $N^l_{u,v,z}$ is a neuron associated with a receptive kernel area $R^l_{u,v,z}$. It uses a modified cross-correlation strategy, where each operation is not performed using the same kernel in a single layer, but using a partially shared kernel. The semi-shared nature is given by the fact that weights in 2D space are different for each point in the input space, instead, weights in the 3D space are the same across the whole region. Using this strategy, each resulting neuron's activation achieves more relevance. Giving importance to each computational unit gives the advantage of using a fewer number of hidden layers, thus strictly reducing the depth of the architecture while preserving the same number of features maps on each layer. Though this strategy increases the number of parameters per layer, it helps to reduce the total number of trainable values allowing an efficient reduction of the network architecture. 3DPyranet uses also another kind of layer that is a 3D Max-Pooling, which aim is the same of the max-pooling commonly used in literature. However, it differs from the common max-pooling due to modifications with a twofold benefit: (i) helping the regularisation of the WS3D output and (ii) reducing the problems on the translation invariance that is a logical consequence of the non-sharing policy of the network. It implies a non-linear dense transformation on the temporal pooling in order to find the highest responsive neurons as shown in the following equation:

$$y^l_{u,v,z} = f_l\Big(W^l_{u,v,z} \times \max_{i,j,k \in R^l_{u,v,z}} y^{l-1}_{i,j,k} + b^l_{u,v,z} \Big) \qquad (2)$$

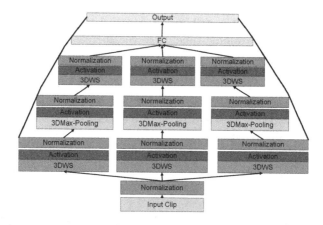

Fig. 1. 3DPyranet model for features extraction and classification

For each layer, a normalisation term is applied to remove the data variance from a layer to another. In order to achieve it a zero mean, unit variance policy is applied to the output of each layer.

The described architecture can be effectively used in an end-to-end fashion, training the model only on the regions that identify the face in a frame without pre-processing them but leaving the network to do all the work needed to extract the most relevant features. Face extraction phase is done using a state-of-the-art algorithm, based on multi-task convolutional neural networks called MTCNN [10]. It is composed of three networks defined as:

- "Proposal Network" (PNet), that finds many bounding boxes in an image that are candidates to be faces of part of a face.
- "Refinement Network" (RNet), which tries to reduce the total number of bounding boxes to the most relevant candidates.
- "Output Network" (ONet), that gives a single bounding box that represents the face in the image.

Faces from consecutive frames are packed together to give the right frame sequences. The methodology uses an overlap of 8 frames for each sequence with a total length of 16 frames on time dimension.

4   Distributed EmoP3D

Deep neural networks are known to be computationally heavy particularly in the training phase. Unfortunately resources are very expensive and it is not simple to build an environment with multiple nodes to provide distributed computation ability. In our work to face this situation a cloud, free and optimised architecture is used. It is the Intel DevCloud environment that provides a multi-node capability each of them with a Intel Xeon Scalable Processors that has 24 cores with 2-way hyper-threading and 187 GB of RAM. To take advantage of this cluster EmoP3D is serialised and distributed using Spark on YARN with the *data parallelism* approach. Spark uses three kind of components: master, worker and executor. Spark master distributes the task on each worker that is responsible of a single node. Workers start many executors to run the deep network with a subset of the data. At the end of the training step results are collected on the master node that performs the averaging of the weights. Such weights are then shared across all nodes in the distributed architecture as a way of updating the weights of the neural model.

5   Experimental Results

The experimental tests have been performed on YouTube dataset [6], containing videos of people from different age and gender in various topics. It is a multimodal opinion mining dataset because there are samples of video, text transcription and speech that all together express emotion in a different manner. Furthermore there is not a "controlled" environment because an emotion recognition system should be able to work in heterogeneous contexts. As name suggests, data was acquired from Youtube website using the following keywords: opinion, review, product review, best perfume, toothpaste, war, job, business, cosmetics review, camera review, baby product review, I hate, I like. There are 20 female subjects and 27 male subjects with age in the range 14–60. Figure 2 is an example of the kind of videos in the dataset. Independently from the ethnicity, all sample subjects are English speakers.

Fig. 2. Three sample subjects from Youtube dataset.

To test the capabilities of our architecture we compared what happens varying the number of workers and the number of parallel executors. At the end, we also compare the best performance of the training over a distributed multi-node environment in comparison with a training over a single GPU. Varying the number of workers also varies the data split over the nodes. Our tests are conducted using 4 workers and 2 workers. In the first case we obtain a data split of 882 samples per node, in the last we get a split of 1780 samples per node.

From Table 1 we can observe that the best performance are obtained with a parallelism of 8 executors, instead using too much executors or fewer of them is not helpful.

Similar results are observable from Table 2. In both cases, the best results are achieved with a parallelism of 8 executors. Not surprisingly, the level of parallelism should be chosen according to the machine capacity as well as on the data, how them fit in memory and on the task type.

Last comparison in Table 3 is between multi-node CPU and a single GPU. GPU uses a large amount of CUDA cores as computational units. Each CPU node uses 2 PPN (Processor Per Node) with all cores available for the afore-mentioned CPU model. It is very helpful to check that although a single GPU unit (NVIDIA Titan X) has a better performance we are able to achieve similar performance using a free cloud distributed environment.

Table 1. Results using 4 nodes/workers by varying the number of executors

Workers	Executors	Time per Epoch (s)	Total time (s)
4	2	73	3692
4	4	69	3450
4	**8**	**55**	**2750**
4	12	72	6350
4	24	70	3800

Table 2. Results using 2 nodes/workers by varying the number of executors

Workers	Executors	Time per Epoch (s)	Total time (s)
2	2	138	6900
2	4	140	7000
2	**8**	**107**	**5350**
2	12	137	6850
2	24	108	5400

Table 3. Comparison between CPU/GPU

Device	# Devices	# Units	Time per Epoch (s)	Speedup
GPU	1	3072 CUDA Cores	46	~19%
Multi-Node CPU	4	2 PPN x 24 Cores	55	-

6   Conclusions

Distributed training of complex neural network models can represent a signifi-cant and viable solution to overcome the limitations of the reduced availability of high computing monolithic architectures. When training in a distributed fashion, however, new challenges arise. In particular the problem of sharing the weights during the training steps can be crucial according to the type of synchronisation used. In this paper a distributed training approach for a pyramidal network model is proposed. It explores the use of Intel DevCloud architecture, a free and distributed cloud architecture for heavy computational demand, for the distributed training of 3DPyraNet model for facial emotion recognition from videos. Considering the nature of the pyramidal model explored in this study, the experimental results show that it is feasible, besides being effective, the arrangement of the training stage of a monolithic neural model in a distributed fashion while keeping the advantages of traditional training on single and expensive architectures.

References

1. Cantoni, V., Petrosino, A.: Neural recognition in a pyramidal structure. IEEE Trans. Neural Netw. **13**(2), 472–480 (2002)
2. Chahal, K., Grover, M.S., Dey, K.: A hitchhiker's guide on distributed training of deep neural networks. arXiv preprint arXiv:1810.11787 (2018)
3. Deng, J., Dong, W., Socher, R., Li, L.-J., Li, K., Fei-Fei, L.: ImageNet: a large-scale hierarchical image database. In: 2009 IEEE Conference on Computer Vision and Pattern Recognition, pp. 248–255. IEEE (2009)
4. Di Nardo, E., Petrosino, A., Ullah, I.: EmoP3D: a brain like pyramidal deep neural network for emotion recognition. In: Proceedings of the European Conference on Computer Vision (ECCV) (2018)
5. Goyal, P., et al.: Accurate, large minibatch SGD: training imagenet in 1 h. arXiv preprint arXiv:1706.02677 (2017)
6. Morency, L.-P., Mihalcea, R., Doshi, P.: Towards multimodal sentiment analysis: harvesting opinions from the web. In: Proceedings of the 13th International Conference On Multimodal Interfaces, pp. 169–176. ACM (2011)
7. Phung, S.L., Bouzerdoum, A.: A pyramidal neural network for visual pattern recognition. IEEE Trans. Neural Netw. **18**(2), 329–343 (2007)
8. Smith, S.L., Kindermans, P.-J., Ying, C., Le, Q.V.: Don't decay the learning rate, increase the batch size. arXiv preprint arXiv:1711.00489 (2017)
9. Ullah, I., Petrosino, A.: A strict pyramidal deep neural network for action recognition. In: Murino, V., Puppo, E. (eds.) ICIAP 2015. LNCS, vol. 9279, pp. 236–245. Springer, Cham (2015). https://doi.org/10.1007/978-3-319-23231-7_22
10. Zhang, K., Zhang, Z., Li, Z., Qiao, Y.: Joint face detection and alignment using multitask cascaded convolutional networks. IEEE Sig. Process. Lett. **23**(10), 1499–1503 (2016)

Parallel and Distributed Computing Methodologies in Bioinformatics

Giuseppe Agapito[(⊠)] [ID]

Department of Medical and Surgical Sciences, Magna Graecia University,
88100 Catanzaro, IT, Italy
agapito@unicz.it

Abstract. The significant advantage of using experimental techniques such as microarray, mass spectrometry (MS), and next generation sequencing (NGS), is that they produce an overwhelming amount of experimental omics data. All of these technologies come with the challenges of determining how the raw omics data should be efficiently processed or normalized and, subsequently, how can the data adequately be summarised or integrated, in order to be stored and shared, as well as to enable machine learning and/or statistical analysis. Omics data analysis involves the execution of several steps, each one implemented through different algorithms, that demand for a lot of computation power. The main problem is the automation of the overall analysis process, to increase the throughput and to reduce manual intervention (e.g., users have to manually supervise some steps of the analysis process). In this scenario, parallel and distributed computing technologies (i.e., Message Passing Interface (MPI), GPU computing, and Hadoop Map-Reduce), are essential to speed up and automatize the whole workflow of omics data analysis. Parallel and distributed computing enable the development of bioinformatics pipeline able to achieve scalable, efficient and reliable computing performance on clusters as well as on cloud computing.

Keywords: Bioinformatics · High performance computing · Cloud computing · Distributed computing · Parallel computing

1 Introduction

The strong advances in experimental technologies such as microarray, mass spectrometry (MS), and next generation sequencing (NGS) continue to support the exponential growth of the available genomic data, interactomics data, and proteomics data. Thus, the integration and interpretation of these vast volumes of data could increase in terms of magnitude the enhancements in health and clinical outcomes, representing an opportunity to move genomic, proteomics, interactomics research in the clinical activities [23]. Data obtained by the experimental assays contains bias and noise. Indeed, it is mandatory to clean and uniform the input data to be used in the knowledge extraction phase. Data cleaning is known

© Springer Nature Switzerland AG 2019
R. Montella et al. (Eds.): IDCS 2019, LNCS 11874, pp. 498–507, 2019.
https://doi.org/10.1007/978-3-030-34914-1_47

as pre-processing, it is an iterative methodology that has to be performed many times demanding a lot of computational power. A significant advantage of the pre-processing phase is that some steps can be easily parallelized which drastically reduces computation times exploiting the huge computational power that is available on various parallel computers. However, different types of data require different kinds of analysis and each one has different computing requirements, as described in [22]. The pre-processing of microarray data is a CPU-Bound process and it requires vast quantities of RAM in order to perform each single step of the pre-processing such as filter out the existing noise, eliminate artifacts due to the surface chemistry etc. Differently, MS has led to very large data sets producing several GB of data per day. It's elaboration requires a lot of computational power, precluding the analysis on a standalone personal computer and requiring the development of scalable databases able to store this massive amount of data based on the NoSQL model, that allows to manage, store, and query analysis results systematically and efficiently. In the NGS the sequences alignment is the computing bottleneck requiring vast quantities of RAM. Thus, sequence alignment algorithms can be implemented using the principle of parallel computation in order to exploit the power of a multicore environment as well as distributed computing environment to speed up and improve, in terms of magnitude, the alignment algorithms performance. To support the massive data and computational demands of the experimental assays analysis algorithms, a solution could be to employ high performance computing (HPC) techniques to speed-up the analysis. The applications can be built to exploit the modern hybrid computing systems equipped with multi-core CPUs and graphics processing units (GPUs). Because GPUs provide local memories and extensive multi-processing capabilities, which typically exceed those of CPUs, GPUs are perfect for performing massive parallel data analysis. However, to benefit from the increased computational capability of multi-core CPU and GPU, it is mandatory to implement algorithms able to take advantage of the high-performance hardware. The message passing interface (MPI) and openMP are pioneer application programming interfaces (APIs) for parallel computing. MPI is widely used as a traditional parallel programming model based on message passing, openMP consists of a set of compiler directives, library routines, and environment variables that are interpreted at run-time by the compiler. On the other hand, to easily take advantage of multi-cores CPU it is possible to use the built-in Java multithreading library, as well as, Apache Hadoop for developing distributed application. Hadoop is based on the MapReduce, aiming to implement reliable, scalable and distributed computing. In [17,18] are presented distributed application for distributed data mining applications. Some of those challenges can be overcome by employing customized computational techniques. But still computational power and efficiency remain the major bottleneck that limits the execution of such analysis. Although the cost of hardware has reduced considerably in the past years, extensive investments are necessary to establish and manage scientific computing infrastructure. For small labs which don't have access to significant funds, acquiring, configuring and continuing to work on the computing infrastructure is an obstacle and even a limit to the advancement of the research. In addition to the previous costs, software able to exploit parallel computation is necessary and a team must be employed to develop and maintain the software on the computing infrastructure. An alternative for buying and maintaining the computing infrastructure could be to use Cloud computing. In the last years, cloud computing has risen as an option to quickly and easily obtain the computational resources needed for the analysis of big omics data sets [10]. Cloud computing provides network access to the computational resources in the form of a virtual machine (i.e., a complete working machine) that a user has individual and full control on. As a result, cloud computing has the potential to allow simple configure and access to a variety of different types of machines, eliminating the necessity to build and maintain the given infrastructure. Recent studies are showing that cloud computing is playing a decisive role in the improvement of healthcare services and biomedical research. Despite the many benefits that correlate cloud computing to healthcare, several new problems have to be addressed, such as management, technology, and security issues. For example, the collecting of personal health information into a remote data center raises serious problems related to patient privacy. The possibility that the patient's data could be lost, misused, or fall into the wrong hands, could affect the rapid spread of cloud computing. The remainder of this paper is structured as follows: Sect. 2 describes the principal omics data formats. Section 3 presents some biological databases, while, Sect. 4 describes parallel and distributed data analysis pipelines for analyzing omics data. Finally, Sect. 5 outlines possible future research opportunities on using parallel distributed computing in bioinformatics.

2   Omics Data

Omics data are obtained through the high-throughput experimental assays (e.g., microarray, mass spectrometry, next generation sequencing) that produce huge amount of data per single experiment.

2.1   Microarray Data

A typical microarray experiment requires a large quantity of cDNA (complementaryDNA) or oligonucleotide DNA sequences (spots) that are attached to a glass, nylon, or quartz plate. The microarray is then reacted with two series of mRNA (messenger-RNA) probes (cases and controls) that are labeled with two different colors of fluorescent probes. At the end of probes hybridization phase, the microarray is washed; thus, only the hybridized probes will remain attached into the spots on the slide. After washing, the microarray is scanned using a laser beam that generates an image of all the spots' intensity. The intensity of the fluorescent signal in each place is a measure of the mRNA level associated with the specific hybridized sequence on that spot. The image of all spots, is analyzed using special proprietary software to convert the intensity value in numerical information for gene expression microarray or in SNP through genotype translation. Gene expression microarray allows the study of the expression level of the messenger RNA (mRNA) associated to several genes in a single experiment, along with the study of the micro-RNA (miRNA) molecules of RNA composed of about 22 nucleotides. Also, miRNA plays a role in various biological functions, especially in the regulation of gene expression. Gene expression data are arranged in a tabular form where each row indicates a specific gene, a column denotes a specific sample, the element (k, l) indicates the expression level of gene k for the sample l. SNP microarray allows the study of genetic alteration among the DNA's bases. DNA is made up of four bases called Adenine, Cytosine, Guanine, and Thymine {A, C, G, T}. Each individual has a unique sequence of DNA that determines his/hers characteristics. The differences among sequences are measured in terms of substitutions of bases in the same position. The substitution of a single base is called single nucleotide polymorphism only if it occurs in the human genome about one in every 300 nucleotide base. For example a SNP might change the DNA sequence AAGG to AGGG, then the SNP is denoted with the symbol A/G. SNP data are encoded as strings and are arranged as a table. In the SNP table each row indicates a gene or a specific chromosomal region, each column indicates a sample, a cell (i, j) contains the detected SNP on the gene i and sample j.

2.2 MassSpectrometry Data

Proteomics concerns the large-scale study of the proteins expressed in an organism or a cell [27]. Computational proteomics is about the algorithms, databases and methods used to manage, store, and analyze proteomics data [11]. Mass spectrometry (MS) is the main experimental platform for proteomics, it uses the mass spectrometer to investigate the proteins contained in a sample [2]. Straightforwardly, MS measures the mass (in Dalton) of the molecules contained in a sample. The output of an MS study is called a spectrum, a long sequence of numbers pairs (i, m_Z), where, m_Z is the ratio mass-to-charge of a molecule and i is the intensity or concentration of that molecule. Manual inspection of spectra is unfeasible, so various algorithms to manage and analyze them are available. An important role is played by pre-processing algorithms regarding how the spectra are cleaned, pre-processed, organized and stored efficiently. MS output are stored in a XML like document designed to contain all the information for a single MS run, including metadata about the spectra. All the spectra themselves and the (i, m_Z) couples are stored in binary format.

2.3 Next Generation Sequencing Data

Next-generation sequencing allows to define the sequence of nucleotides in a section of DNA [14]. Understanding the DNA sequence could elucidate the structure and function of proteins as well as RNA, leading to the understanding of the underlying causes of disease. NGS is a robust and powerful platform that made sequencing of thousands of DNA molecules concurrently possible. This powerful tool is revolutionizing disciplines such as personalized medicine, genetic diseases and clinical diagnostics by providing a high throughput option with the ability to sequence many individuals at the same time. The raw NGS data is a collection of DNA sequences called NGS reads, usually reported in the universally accepted FASTQ format. An NGS output file is a text-based format containing the sequence of each read along with the confidence score of each base. An typical output has a size of several gigabytes and may contain about 200 million reads or more.

3   Omics Database

In this section some of the main databases containing omics data are presented, with special focus on protein sequences databases and proteomics databases.

3.1   Sequence Database

Sequences databases contain information about the primary structure of proteins, the amino acids sequence and related annotations.

The EMBL Nucleotide Sequence Database. The European Molecular Biology Laboratory (EMBL) Nucleotide Sequence Database[1] [9] stores nucleotide sequences and it has been obtained from an international cooperation between DNA Data Bank of Japan (DDBJ) and GenBank (USA). The database contains information about the coding DNA sequence (CDS), that is the coding region of genes and other information. In the current version it contains more than 3.6 Gigabases of nucleotides and millions of sequences. Data are made available as text, XML, or FASTA. FASTA is a standard format to represent nucleotide or peptide sequences. For sequence similarity searching a variety of tools (e.g., BLITZ, FASTA, BLAST) are available which allow external users to compare their own sequences against the most currently available data in the EMBL Nucleotide Sequence Database.

Uniprot database[2] is the most comprehensive publicly accessible non-redundant protein sequence collection available. Uniprot is the result of the fusion between the Swiss-Prot [7], Tr-EMBL [9] and the PSD-PIR [8] databases. The UniProt databases consist of three database layers: (i) The UniProt Archive (UniParc) provides a stable, non-redundant sequence collection by storing the complete body of publicly available protein sequence data. (ii) The UniProt Knowledgebase (UniProt) provides the access point for information about protein function, classification and cross-references. (iii) The UniProt NREF databases (UniRef) provide non-redundant data collections based on the unique UniParc identifier.

dbSNP database[3]. Single Nucleotide Polymorphism database [28] is a database of genetic polymorphisms. SNPdb includes single nucleotide polymorphisms - SNPs, deletion insertion polymorphisms or DIPs and short tandem repeats or STRs, multinucleotide polymorphisms (MNPs), heterozygous sequences and

---

[1] https://www.ebi.ac.uk/ena.

[2] https://www.uniprot.org.

[3] https://www.ncbi.nlm.nih.gov/projects/SNP/.

named variants. dbSNP is freely available and in the current version contains millions distinct genetic variations within and across different species including Homo Sapiens.

3.2   Proteomics Databases

Mass spectrometry databases include a vast number of MS spectra covering a wide range of chemical types-pharmaceuticals, peptides, with which to perform various screening, identification and annotation activities.

Advanced Mass Spectral Database[4] is a curated database of high-resolution tandem mass spectra [19] acquired at various collision energies. mzCloud uses the spectra-tree data structure to store data. Each database record contains the compound name with synonyms, the chemical structure, computationally and manually annotated fragments (peaks), mass resolution and other identifiers. mzCloud is a fully queryable and allows spectra searches, structure and substructure searches, peak searches, name searches.

Peptide Atlas[5] [15] is a database that stores mass spectra and data about peptides and proteins. PeptideAtlas uses spectra as principal information allowing the identification of peptides, genome annotation using peptide data and storage of such genomics and proteomics data. Users can query PeptideAtlas using a web interface or can download the database.

4   Parallel and Distributed Analysis of Omics Data

In the last years high-throughput methodologies have become fundamental in omics research due to the considerable amount of data produced per single experiment. Moreover, the number of applications where microarray, NGS and MS data are involved, are increasing faster than the development of proper data analysis models and tools, generating an increasing demand for adequate statistical and data mining tools. On the other hand, the need to provide researchers with scalable and efficient software tools arises as well.

4.1   Parallel and Distributed Analysis Tools for Microarray Data

Microarray can concurrently analyze thousands of genes in parallel to identify new biomarkers, monitor the adverse reaction of a drug, shed light on the mechanisms involved in the progress of disease as explained in [16]. Thus, the development of parallel analysis tools able to exploit the computational power of multicore CPUs and GPU can significantly improve data processing and analysis performance.

coreSNP [20] is a tool implemented using Java language for parallel preprocessing and statistical analysis of SNP data set. The scalable implementation based on multi-threading allows coreSNP to manage huge volumes of SNP

---

[4] https://www.mzcloud.org/Features.

[5] www.peptideatlas.org.

data. The automatic association analysis among the variations of the patient genomes and the clinical conditions of patients is obtained by using the well known Fisher's test, e.g., the different response to drugs.

Cloud4SNP [3] is a novel Cloud-based bioinformatics tool for the parallel pre-processing and statistical analysis of pharmacogenomics SNP microarray data. It is a Cloud-based version of *DMET-Analyzer* [21], that has been implemented on the Cloud using the Data Mining Cloud Framework [1], a software environment for the design and execution of knowledge discovery workflows on the Cloud [24]. Cloud4SNP allows to statistically test the significance of the presence of SNPs in two classes of samples, it employs an optimization technique aiming to avoid the execution of useless Fisher tests through the filtering of probes with similar SNPs distributions.

PARES (Parallel Association Rules Extractor from SNPs) [5] is a multi-thread software tool implemented in Java for the parallel extraction of association rules that correlate the presence of a series of allelic variants with the clinical condition of patients, for example, the combination of alleles typical of a class responsible for the different response to drugs. PARES is a multi-thread version of DMET-Miner [4] algorithm. PARES incorporates a customized SNPs datasets pre-processing approach based on a Fisher's Test Filter to discard the trivial transactions, decreasing the search space from which to build many independent FP-Trees. In this section have been described some distributed and parallel algorithms for the analysis of omics data, developed at the Bioinformatics Laboratory of the University of Catanzaro. The developed algorithms, delineating how parallelism and high performance techniques have been employed to efficiently support the preprocessing and analysis of omics data, making possible to use omics data in clinical activity [6].

4.2   Parallel and Distributed Analysis Tools for NGS Data

Many NGS data analysis steps can be parallelized increasing significantly the execution speed. Although millions of reads are generated from a single NGS run, mapping these reads to a reference genome is a process embarrassingly parallelizable as each read is mapped independently from the others.

CloudBLAST [25] uses the MapReduce paradigm to parallelize tools and manage their execution, machine virtualization to encapsulate their execution and network virtualization to connect resources behind firewalls/NATs while preserving the necessary performance and the communication environment. Cloud-BLAST splits query sequences among the available nodes while copying a complete sequence database to each node. Query splitting achieves efficient performance for large sequences databases.

CloudBurst [26] is a parallel read-mapping algorithm optimized for mapping next-generation sequence data to the human genome and other reference genomes. CloudBurst employs Hadoop to parallelize execution, whereas the short read-mapping algorithm is based on the short read-mapping program (RMAP) [29]. CloudBurst maps short reads against a reference genome, running time scales linearly as the number of reads increases.

4.3   Parallel and Distributed Analysis Tools for Mass Spectrometry Data

MS has revolutionized proteomics allowing the identification with high accuracy of proteins in an organism. The identification, quantification and characterization of all proteins of the cell are essential to understanding the molecular processes. Below, the description of some well known MS data analysis applications is reported.

ProteoCloud [30] is a freely available cloud-based platform used to perform computationally intensive peptide identification algorithms. ProteoCloud is entirely open source and is built around an easy to use cross-platform software client with a rich graphical user interface. The client has full control over the number of cloud instances used to initiate and over the spectra assigned for identification. It also enables the user to visualize, export and interpret the results in detail.

BioDCV [12] is a grid-based distributed software for the analysis of both proteomics and genomics data for biomarker discovery. BioDCV solves the selection bias problem that is the discovery of the correct discriminating features (employing support vector machines algorithm) and allowing to setup complex predictive biomarker discovery experiments on proteomics data.

MS-Analyzer is a distributed platform to classify mass spectrometry proteomics data on the grid [13]. It uses ontologies to support the composition of spectra pre-processing workflows, implementing data mining algorithms as services.

5   Conclusion

High-throughput analysis methodologies have greatly influenced the transformation of the omic sciences into data-driven sciences. The speed, the high density and the accuracy of the results obtained through the use of microarrays, MS and NGS, made possible the study of complex phenomena, due to an intrigued network of interactions between multiple biological elements, e.g., genes, miR-NAs and proteins. On the other hand, the availability of such vast amounts of data poses many challenges from the computational point of view, that is, to transform these enormous amounts of data into biological understanding. Consequently, it is necessary to resort to the use of parallel computing architectures known as HPC. Although the computing power of HPC devices is continuously increasing, it is essential to develop highly scalable parallel software tools as the size of the data to analyze increases. Then, such software will be able to make the most of HPC resources, which translates into continuous improvement in performance as the number of CPUs and computational cores increase. Finally, parallel computing has become an indispensable tool in all areas of science because it enables the development of applications that can benefit from the improvements in high-performance computing in order to overcome computational limitations they have by definition. Those applications will be developed to allow the investigation of problems infeasible up to now, such as to decode multi-level brain's complexity, as well as to provide a positive impact on several real applications in medicine fields, e.g., the development of personalized therapies reducing the insurgence of adverse drug reactions.

References

1. Marozzo, F., Talia, D., Trunfio, P.: A cloud framework for big data analytics workflows on azure. In: Big Data. IOS Press (2013)
2. Aebersold, R., Mann, M.: Mass spectrometry-based proteomics. Nature **422**(6928), 198 (2003)
3. Agapito, G., Cannataro, M., Guzzi, P.H., Marozzo, F., Talia, D., Trunfio, P.: Cloud4SNP: distributed analysis of SNP microarray data on the cloud. In: Proceedings of the International Conference on Bioinformatics, Computational Biology and Biomedical Informatics (2013)
4. Agapito, G., Guzzi, P.H., Cannataro, M.: DMET-miner: efficient discovery of association rules from pharmacogenomic data. J. Biomed. Inf. **56**, 273–283 (2015). https://doi.org/10.1016/j.jbi.2015.06.005. http://www.sciencedirect.com/science/article/pii/S153204641500115X
5. Agapito, G., Guzzi, P.H., Cannataro, M.: Parallel extraction of association rules from genomics data. Appl. Math. Comput. **350**, 434–446 (2017)
6. Arbitrio, M., et al.: Polymorphic variants in NR 1I3 and UGT 2B7 predict taxane neurotoxicity and have prognostic relevance in patients with breast cancer: a case-control study. Clin. Pharmacol. Ther. **106**, 422–431 (2019)
7. Bairoch, A., Boeckmann, B.: The SWISS-PROT protein sequence data bank. Nucleic Acids Res. **19**(Suppl.), 2247 (1991)
8. Barker, W.C., et al.: The PIR-international protein sequence database. Nucleic Acids Res. **26**(1), 27–32 (1998)
9. Boeckmann, B., et al.: The SWISS-PROT protein knowledgebase and its supplement TrEMBL in 2003. Nucleic Acids Res. **31**(1), 365–370 (2003)
10. Calabrese, B., Cannataro, M.: Cloud computing in bioinformatics: current solutions and challenges. Technical report, PeerJ Preprints (2016)
11. Cannataro, M.: Computational proteomics: management and analysis of proteomics data (2008)
12. Cannataro, M., et al.: A grid environment for high-throughput proteomics. IEEE Trans. Nanobiosci. **6**(2), 117–123 (2007)
13. Cannataro, M., Veltri, P.: MS-analyzer: preprocessing and data mining services for proteomics applications on the grid. Concurrency Comput. Pract. Experience **19**(15), 2047–2066 (2007)
14. Daugelaite, J., O'Driscoll, A., Sleator, R.D.: An overview of multiple sequence alignments and cloud computing in bioinformatics. ISRN Biomathematics **2013** (2013)
15. Desiere, F., et al.: The peptideAtlas project. Nucleic Acids Res. **34**(Suppl. 1), D655–D658 (2006)
16. Deyholos, M.K., Galbraith, D.W.: High-density microarrays for gene expression analysis. Cytometry **43**(4), 229–238 (2001)
17. Di Fatta, G., Blasa, F., Cafiero, S., Fortino, G.: Fault tolerant decentralised k-means clustering for asynchronous large-scale networks. J. Parallel Distrib. Comput. **73**(3), 317–329 (2013)

18. Di Fatta, G., Fortino, G.: A customizable multi-agent system for distributed data mining. In: Proceedings of the 2007 ACM Symposium on Applied Computing, pp. 42–47. ACM (2007)
19. Gardinassi, L.G., Xia, J., Safo, S.E., Li, S.: Bioinformatics tools for the interpretation of metabolomics data. Curr. Pharmacol. Rep. **3**(6), 374–383 (2017). https://doi.org/10.1007/s40495-017-0107-0
20. Guzzi, P.H., Agapito, G., Cannataro, M.: CoreSNP: parallel processing of microarray data. IEEE Trans. Comput. **63**(12), 2961–2974 (2014). https://doi.org/10.1109/TC.2013.176
21. Guzzi, P.H., Agapito, G., Di Martino, M.T., Arbitrio, M.M., Tagliaferri, P., Cannataro, M.: DMET-analyzer: automatic analysis of affymetrix DMET data. BMC Bioinf. **13**(258) (2012)
22. Huda, S., Yearwood, J., Jelinek, H.F., Hassan, M.M., Fortino, G., Buckland, M.: A hybrid feature selection with ensemble classification for imbalanced healthcare data: a case study for brain tumor diagnosis. IEEE Access **4**, 9145–9154 (2016)
23. Kanehisa, M., Goto, S., Sato, Y., Furumichi, M., Tanabe, M.: KEGG for integration and interpretation of large-scale molecular data sets. Nucleic Acids Res. **40**(D1), D109–D114 (2011)
24. Marozzo, F., Talia, D., Trunfio, P.: Using clouds for scalable knowledge discovery applications. In: Caragiannis, I., et al. (eds.) Euro-Par 2012. LNCS, vol. 7640, pp. 220–227. Springer, Heidelberg (2013). https://doi.org/10.1007/978-3-642-36949-0_25
25. Matsunaga, A., Tsugawa, M., Fortes, J.: CloudBLAST: combining MapReduce and virtualization on distributed resources for bioinformatics applications. In: 2008 IEEE Fourth International Conference on eScience, pp. 222–229, December 2008. https://doi.org/10.1109/eScience.2008.62
26. Schatz, M.C.: CloudBurst: highly sensitive read mapping with MapReduce. Bioinformatics **25**(11), 1363–1369 (2009). https://doi.org/10.1093/bioinformatics/btp236
27. Schmidt, A., Forne, I., Imhof, A.: Bioinformatic analysis of proteomics data. BMC Syst. Biol. **8**(2), S3 (2014)
28. Sherry, S.T., Ward, M.H., Kholodov, M., Baker, J., Phan, L., Smigielski, E.M., Sirotkin, K.: dbSNP: the NCBI database of genetic variation. Nucleic Acids Res. **29**(1), 308–311 (2001). https://doi.org/10.1093/nar/29.1.308
29. Smith, A.D., et al.: Updates to the rmap short-read mapping software. Bioinformatics **25**(21), 2841–2842 (2009)
30. Specht, M., Kuhlgert, S., Fufezan, C., Hippler, M.: Proteomics to go: proteomatic enables the user-friendly creation of versatile MS/MS data evaluation workflows. Bioinformatics **27**(8), 1183–1184 (2011). https://doi.org/10.1093/bioinformatics/btr081

Author Index